REVISION CHECKLIST

Considering Your Whole Essay–Chapter 4

Using the FACT acronym, ask yourself these questions:

❏ Does my essay FIT together, presenting a central point for a specific audience? Does my thesis statement accurately reflect the content of my essay, or have I included material that has no bearing on the main point?

❏ Have I included all the material my reader will need to grasp my meaning, or do I need to ADD information or examples?

❏ Have I included material that fits the thesis but needs to be CUT because it is uninteresting, uninformative, or repetitious?

❏ Does a TEST of my organization show that the writing flows smoothly, with clear transitions between the various ideas?

Strengthening Paragraph Structure and Development–Chapter 15

❏ Does each paragraph have only one central idea?
❏ Is the idea stated in a topic sentence or clearly implied?
❏ Does the topic sentence help to develop the thesis statement?
❏ Does each paragraph contain enough supporting detail?
❏ Is each paragraph appropriately organized?
❏ Is the relationship between successive sentences clear?
❏ Is each paragraph clearly and smoothly related to those that precede and follow it?
❏ Does the introduction arouse interest and set the appropriate tone?
❏ Does the conclusion reflect the content of the essay and provide a sense of completeness?

Sharpening Sentences and Words–Chapters 16 and 17

❏ Are my sentences clearly and effectively constructed?
❏ Have I varied the pattern and length of my sentences?
❏ Do I know the meanings of the words I use?
❏ Do I explain meanings my reader may not know?
❏ Have I used the appropriate tone and level of diction?
❏ Does/would figurative language enhance my style?
❏ Have I avoided wordiness, euphemisms, clichés, mixed metaphors, and sexist language?

Editing the Draft–Handbook

❏ Have I inspected my writing for the types of errors listed in the editing symbols on the last page of the book?

SEVENTH EDITION

STRATEGIES FOR SUCCESSFUL WRITING

A Rhetoric, Research Guide, Reader, and Handbook

James A. Reinking
Robert von der Osten

Both of Ferris State University

PEARSON

Prentice Hall

Upper Saddle River, New Jersey 07458

Library of Congress Cataloging-in-Publication Data

Reinking, James A.
    Strategies for successful writing : a rhetoric, research guide, reader, and
handbook / James A. Reinking, Robert von der Osten.– 7th ed.
        p. cm.
    Includes index.
    ISBN 0-13-189195-2
1. English language--Rhetoric--Handbooks, manuals, etc. 2. English language--
Grammar--Handbooks, manuals, etc. 3. Report writing--Handbooks, manuals, etc. 4.
College readers. I. Von der Osten, Robert. II. Title.

PE1408.R426 2004
808'.0427--dc22   2004000861

Editor-in-Chief: *Leah Jewell*
Senior Acquisitions Editor: *Corey Good*
Assistant Editor: *Karen Schultz*
Editorial Assistant: *Steve Kyritz*
Media Project Manager: *Christy Schaack*
VP/Director of Production and Manufacturing: *Barbara Kittle*
Production Liaison: *Maureen Benicasa*
Production Assistant: *Marlene Gassler*
Copyeditor: *Joan Flaherty*
Director of Marketing: *Beth Mejia*
Executive Marketing Manager: *Brandy Dawson*
Marketing Assistant: *Allison Peck*
Permissions Coordinator: *Ron Fox*
Prepress and Manufacturing Manager: *Nick Sklitis*
Prepress and Manufacturing Assistant Manager: *Mary Ann Gloriande*

Creative Design Director: *Leslie Osher*
Designer: *Carmen DiBartolomeo*
Interior Design: *Carmen DiBartolomeo*
Cover Design: *Carmen DiBartolomeo*
Director, Image Resource Center: *Melinda Reo*
Manager, Rights and Permissions: *Zina Arabia*
Interior Image Specialist: *Beth Boyd-Brenzel*
Image Permission Coordinator: *Carolyn Gauntt*
Photo Researcher: *Melinda Alexander*
Composition: *Laserwords*
Full-Service Project Management: *Beth Fuller, nSight, Inc.*
Printer/Binder: *Quebecor World Book Services, Taunton*
Cover: *The Lehigh Press*

Credits and acknowledgments borrowed from other sources and reproduced, with permission, in this textbook appear on appropriate page within text (or on page 603).

Microsoft® and Windows® are registered trademarks of Microsoft Corporation in the U.S.A. and other countries. Screen shots and icons reprinted with permission from the Microsoft Corporation. This book is not sponsored or endorsed by or affiliated with Microsoft Corporation.

ISBN 0-13-189195-2 (student text with Handbook)
ISBN 0-13-178784-5 (student text without Handbook)

PEARSON EDUCATION LTD., *London*
PEARSON EDUCATION AUSTRALIA PTY, LIMITED
PEARSON EDUCATION SINGAPORE, PTE. LTD
PEARSON EDUCATION NORTH ASIA LTD
PEARSON EDUCATION, CANADA, LTD
PEARSON EDUCACIÓN DE MEXICO, S.A. DE C.V.
PEARSON EDUCATION–*Japan*
PEARSON EDUCATION MALAYSIA, PTE. LTD
PEARSON EDUCATION, *Upper Saddle River, New Jersey*

10 9 8 7 6 5 4 3

CONTENTS

v

Contents **vii**

Thematic Table of Contents

Contemporary Issues

WOMEN'S ISSUES

DIVERSITY IN OUR LIVES

SECURITY AND LIBERTY

LANGUAGE USE AND ABUSE

STRUGGLING WITH ETHICAL ISSUES

HANDBOOK   603

PREFACE

The seventh edition of *Strategies for Successful Writing: A Rhetoric, Research Guide, Reader, and Handbook* is a comprehensive textbook that offers ample material for a full-year composition course. Instructors teaching a one-term course can make selections from Chapters 1–17, from whatever types of specialized writing suit the needs of their students, and from appropriate essays in the Reader.

Because we strongly believe that an effective composition textbook should address the student directly, we have aimed for a style that is conversational yet clear and concise. We believe that our style invites students into the book, lessens their apprehensions about writing, and provides a model for their own prose. This style complements our strong student-based approach to writing, and together they help create a text that genuinely meets student needs.

Changes in the Seventh Edition

The enthusiastic response to the six previous editions both by teachers and students has been most gratifying. The seventh edition retains the many popular features of the previous ones and incorporates a number of improvements suggested by users and reviewers, that should considerably enhance the utility of the text. Among these changes the following are noteworthy.

- There is a new chapter on strategies for successful reading to help students master college reading. The chapter includes pointers on writing summaries and critiques.

- The argument chapter has been updated and expanded to include new information on exploratory arguments and more suggestions on organizing arguments.

- The chapter on effective sentences has been revised to stress the basic strategies students can use to write more powerful sentences.

- The chapter on the research paper includes more information on using online catalogs and databases, material on using visuals in reports, and a very handy checklist that can be used for students writing research papers. The text features the most recent versions of APA (2001) and MLA (2003) guidelines.

- Two new sample student essays provide a more contemporary flavor.

- Eleven of the essays in the Reader, one-fourth of the total, are new. These additions increase its coverage of contemporary subjects and expand its discussion potential.

- The Sentence Elements section of the handbook has been revised to make it clearer. The individual-sentence exercises in the section are also new.

- Assorted updates and additions throughout the text, too numerous to mention individually, should help make the text even more effective.

The Rhetoric

In addition to these improvements, the text offers many other noteworthy features. The Rhetoric consists of nineteen chapters, grouped into four parts. The first part includes three chapters. Chapter 1 introduces students to the purposes of writing; the need for audience awareness, which includes a discussion of discourse communities; and the qualities of good writing. Chapter 2 offers suggestions for effective reading. Chapter 3 looks at the planning and drafting stages. Chapter 4 takes students through the various revision stages, starting with a systematic procedure for revising the whole essay and then moving to pointers for revising its component parts. Sets of checklists pose key questions for students to consider. Chapters 3 and 4 are unified by an unfolding case history that includes the first draft of a student paper, the initial revision marked with changes, and the final version. Notes in the margin highlight key features of the finished paper. Students can relate the sequence of events to their own projects as they work through the various stages. Both chapters offer suggestions for using word-processing programs, and Chapter 4 explains peer evaluation of drafts, collaborative writing, and maintaining and reviewing a portfolio.

The ten chapters in the second part (Chapters 5–14) feature the various strategies, or modes, used to develop papers. These strategies, which follow a general progression from less to more complex, are presented as natural ways of thinking, as problem-solving strategies, and therefore as effective ways of organizing writing. One chapter is devoted to each strategy. This part concludes with a chapter on mixing the writing strategies, which explains and shows that writers frequently use these patterns in assorted combinations for various purposes. Planning and writing guidelines are presented for problem/solution and evaluation reports, two common types that rely on a combination of strategies.

Except for Chapter 14, the discussion in each chapter follows a similar approach, first explaining the key elements of the strategy; next pointing out typical classroom and on-the-job applications to show students its practicality; and then providing specific planning, drafting, and revising guidelines. Practical heuristic questions are also posed. A complete student essay, accompanied by questions, follows the discussion section. These essays represent realistic, achievable goals and spur student confidence, while the questions reinforce the general principles of good writing and underscore the points we make in our discussions. Twenty carefully chosen writing suggestions follow the questions in most chapters. All chapters conclude with a section entitled "Critical Edge." These sections, intended for above-average students, explain and illustrate how they can advance their writing purpose by synthesizing material from various sources. Synthesis, of course, helps students develop and hone their critical reading and thinking skills. Furthermore, the *Annotated Instructor's Edition* includes suggestions for using the Reader essays and writing strategies to build assignments around themes.

In the third part, we shift from full-length essays to the elements that make them up. Chapter 15 first discusses paragraph unity; it then takes up the topic sentence, adequate development, organization, coherence, and finally introductory, transitional, and concluding paragraphs. Throughout this chapter, as elsewhere, carefully selected examples and exercises form an integral part of the instruction.

Chapter 16 focuses on various strategies for creating effective sentences. Such strategies as coordinating and subordinating ideas and using parallelism help students to increase the versatility of their writing. The concluding section offers practical advice on crafting and arranging sentences so that they work together harmoniously. Some instructors may wish to discuss the chapters on paragraphs and sentences in connection with revision.

Chapter 17, designed to help students improve their writing style, deals with words and their effects. We distinguish between abstract and concrete words as well as between specific and general terms, and we also discuss the dictionary and thesaurus. Levels of diction—formal, informal, and technical—and how to use them are explained, as are tone, various types of figurative language, and irony. The chapter concludes by pointing out how to recognize and avoid wordiness, euphemisms, clichés, mixed metaphors, and sexist language.

The fourth and final part of the Rhetoric concentrates on three specialized types of college and on-the-job writing. Chapter 18 offers practical advice on studying for exams, assessing test questions, and writing essay answers. To facilitate student comprehension, we analyze both good and poor answers to the same exam question and provide an exercise that requires students to perform similar analyses.

Chapter 19 uses Stephen Crane's "The Bride Comes to Yellow Sky" as a springboard for its discussion. The chapter focuses on plot, point of view, character, setting, symbols, irony, and theme—the elements students will most likely be asked to write about. For each element, we first present basic features and then offer writing guidelines. Diverse examples illustrate these elements. The chapter ends with sections that detail the development of a student paper and explain how to include the views of others when writing about literature.

Like other parts of the text, Chapter 20 speaks to a practical reality by reminding students that the value of writing extends beyond the English classroom. Sample letters address a variety of practical situations—for example, applying for a summer job.

The Research Guide

The Research Guide consists of three chapters. Chapter 21 is a thorough and practical guide to writing library research papers. A sample pacing schedule not only encourages students to plan their work and meet their deadlines but also enables them to track their progress. As in Chapters 2 and 3, a progressive case history gradually evolves into an annotated student paper, which includes the results of a personal interview, thus demonstrating that primary research can reinforce secondary research.

Chapter 22 details and illustrates the correct formats for bibliographical references and in-text citations for both the MLA and APA systems of documentation. Guidelines are based on the 2001 edition of the *Publication Manual of the American Psychological Association* and current online updates as well as the 2003 edition of *The MLA Style Manual*. The chapter also explains how to handle the various types of quotations and how to avoid plagiarism. Our detailed treatment in Chapters 20 and 21 should make supplemental handouts or a separate research-paper guide unnecessary.

Chapter 23 offers an in-depth discussion of interview, questionnaire, and direct-observation reports. After pointing out the nature, usefulness, and requirements of primary research, we explain how to plan and write each report, concluding with an annotated student model that illustrates the guidelines.

The Reader

The Reader, sequenced to follow the order of the strategies presented in the Rhetoric, expands the utility of the text by providing a collection of forty-four carefully selected professional models that illustrate the various writing strategies and display a wide variety of style, tone, and subject matter. These essays, together with the nine student models that accompany the various strategy chapters, should make a separate reader unnecessary.

Supplementing the chapter on reading strategies, the Reader comes with reading suggestions for each strategy that detail how to read the essays of a given type, how to read essays critically, and how to read the essays as a writer.

Each essay clearly illustrates the designated pattern, each has been thoroughly class tested for student interest, and each provides a springboard for a stimulating discussion. In making our selections we have aimed for balance and variety:

1. Some are popular classics by acknowledged prose masters; some, anthologized for the first time, are by fresh, new writers.

2. Some are straightforward and simple, some challenging and complex.

3. Some adopt a humorous, lighthearted approach, some a serious, thoughtful one.

4. Some take a liberal stance, some a conservative one; and some address ethnic, gender, and cultural diversity.

5. A few are rather lengthy; most are relatively brief.

The first essay in each strategy section is annotated in the margin to show which features of the strategy are included. These annotations not only facilitate student understanding but also help link the Rhetoric and Reader into an organic whole. A brief biographical note about the author and a photograph, when available, precede each selection, and stimulating questions designed to enhance student understanding of structure and strategy follow it. In addition, a segment entitled "Toward Key Insights" poses one or more broad-based questions prompted by the essay's content. Answering these questions, either in discussion or writing, should help students gain a deeper understanding of important issues. Finally, we include a writing assignment suggested by the essay's topic.

The Handbook

The comprehensive Handbook, which features tab indexing on each page for easy access to all material, consists of five parts: "Sentence Elements," "Editing to Correct Sentence Errors," "Editing to Correct Faulty Punctuation and Mechanics," "Spelling," and "Glossary of Word Usage." Explanations skirt unneeded grammatical terminology and are reinforced by sets of sentence exercises in the first three sections. The section on "Sentence Elements" explains how students can use these elements to improve their writing skills. We also include connected-discourse exercises—unfolding narratives that engage and retain student interest and therefore facilitate learning—in the "Sentence Errors" and "Punctuation and Mechanics" sections. Extra sets of twenty-item exercises that parallel those in the Handbook are available upon request to instructors who adopt the book. The "Spelling" unit presents four useful spelling rules and an extensive list of commonly misspelled words. The "Glossary of Word Usage" offers similarly comprehensive coverage of troublesome usages. Instructors can use the Handbook either as a reference guide or as a basis for class discussion.

Supplementary Material for Instructors and Students

The *Annotated Instructor's Edition* (0-13-189532-X) consists of the entire student edition as well as strong instructional support. The material in the margins of the text consists of background information on particular aspects of writing; key insights into how students view writing projects and why they experience difficulties; case studies that raise ethical issues for student discussion; answers to all discussion questions and to appropriate exercises in the text; supplementary exercises; teaching strategies and classroom activities that instructors may want to consider; and Reader/Theme strategies that show how to use the Reader to build writing assignments based on themes.

The *Teaching Composition with Strategies for Successful Writing*, Seventh Edition (0-13-041731-9), supplement offers various suggestions for teaching first-year composition, a sample syllabus for a sequence of two fifteen-week semesters, numerous guidelines for responding to student writing, and a detailed set of grading standards. In addition, it contains an extra set of twenty-item exercises that parallel those in the Handbook section of *Strategies*. The exercises can be used either in the classroom or as assignments.

The Companion Website™ for *Strategies for Successful Writing*, Seventh Edition, can be accessed at www.prenhall.com/reinking. The site includes lecture notes, self-check quizzes, additional writing models, bulletin board/chat topics, critical thinking questions, and essay questions. WEB CT and Blackboard courses for *Strategies* are complete online courses that include all of the content from the Web site as well as additional material for students and instructors. These courses are available at a discounted price for instructors who adopt *Strategies*.

The online service www.turnitin.com allows teachers to check if students are copying their assignments from the Internet and is now free to professors using *Strategies for Successful Writing*, Seventh Edition. In addition to helping teachers easily identify instances of Web-based student plagiarism, Turnitin.com offers a digital archiving system and an online peer review service. Professors set up a "drop box" at the Turnitin.com Web site where their students submit papers. This online service then cross-references each submission with millions of possible online sources. Within 24 hours, teachers receive a customized color-coded "Originality Report," complete with live links to suspect Internet locations, for each submitted paper. Professors can access the Turnitin.com site free through the faculty resources section of the Reinking Web site at www.prenhall.com/reinking.

The following supplements are free when instructors order any Prentice-Hall English textbook. Contact your local representative for details.

■ *The New American Webster Handy College Dictionary*, Third Edition

This dictionary provides more than 115,000 definitions. It includes phrases, slang, scientific terms, advice on usage and grammar, notes on etymology, foreign words and phrases, and a word gazetteer. ISBN: 0-13-032870-7

■ *English on the Internet 2001: Evaluating Online Sources*

This site explains how to access online sources, indicates the most useful English sites, notes popular search engines, and includes a glossary of terms and the latest MLA documentation guidelines for electronic sources. ISBN: 0-13-022073-6

■ *Guide to Research and Documentation: Prentice-Hall Resources for Writing* by Kirk G. Rasmussen

This useful paperback booklet provides students with research and documentation guidelines and is designed for ease of use and portability. It features the most recent information on MLA, APA, CBE, and CM formats and also covers the research process. ISBN: 0-13-081627-2

■ *Model Student Essays* by Mark Gallaher

This anthology features twenty-five student essays collected from around the country, which are organized into three broad writing categories: writing to explore a personal experience, writing to explain or inform, and writing to argue a position. ISBN: 0-13-645516-6

■ *The Writer's Guide Series* (new)

This series provides students and instructors with in-depth coverage of relevant topics, which allows instructors to convey information based on their course structure and students' needs.

Writer's Guide to Document & Web Design ISBN: 0-13-018929-4
Writer's Guide to WAC & Oral Presentations ISBN: 0-13-018931-6
Writer's Guide to Writing About Literature ISBN: 0-13-018932-4

Acknowledgments

Like all textbook writers, we are indebted to many people. Our colleagues at Ferris State University and elsewhere, too numerous to mention, have assisted us in several ways: critiquing the manuscript; testing approaches, essays, and exercises in their classrooms; and suggesting writing models for the text. In addition, we thank our reviewers, whose many suggestions have greatly improved our text: Elizabeth S. Bruton, Catawba Valley Community College; Judith A. Burnham, Tulsa Community College; Annie Lou Burns, Meridian Community College; Dallie B. Clark, Eastfield College; Donna Thomsen, Johnson & Wales University; and Stephen Wilhoit, University of Dayton.

Special thanks are also due to the outstanding team at Prentice Hall, whose editorial expertise, genial guidance, and promotional efforts have been vital to this project: Phil Miller, former President of Humanities and Social Sciences Division, who first saw the potential in our approach, proposed the Annotated Instructor's Edition, and suggested and supported many other improvements; Leah Jewell, Editor in Chief for English, and Corey Good, Senior Acquisitions Editor, whose efficiency, knowledge, and understanding of authors' concerns have enhanced our pleasure in preparing this edition; Maureen Benicasa and Beth Fuller, our Production Editors; Joan Flaherty, who did a superb job of copyediting; and Brandy Dawson, whose marketing expertise will help our book find its way.

Finally, we thank Brian Franke for his valuable contribution to the section on the Internet.

J.A.R.
R.v.d.O

To Andrew Hart, one of the founding authors of this text, go special thanks for his immeasurable contributions to the first six editions. We wish him well in his retirement.

No matter what career you choose, your ability to communicate clearly and effectively will directly affect your success. In the classroom, your instructor will often evaluate your mastery of a subject in part by the papers and examinations you write. Prospective employers will make judgments about your qualifications and decide whether to offer you an interview on the basis of your job application letter and résumé. On the job, you will be expected to write clear, accurate reports, memorandums, and letters.

There is nothing mysterious about successful writing. It does not require a special talent, nor does it depend on inspiration. It is simply a skill, and like any other skill, it involves procedures that can be learned. Once you understand them and the more you practice, the easier the writing becomes.

Strategies for Successful Writing will help you become a successful writer. And after you graduate it can serve as a useful on-the-job reference if writing problems occur. The first, third, and fourth chapters explore the fundamentals of writing and the general steps in planning, drafting, and revising papers. The next ten explain the basic writing strategies as well as papers that mix them. The following three chapters zero in on paragraphs, sentences, and writing style, and the final six turn to specialized writing—essay examinations, papers about literature, business correspondence, library research papers, and papers based on your own original research results. The book concludes with a Reader and, if you are using the complete version of the text, a Handbook.

From time to time you have probably had the unpleasant experience of using textbooks that seemed to be written for instructors rather than students. In preparing this book, we have tried never to forget that *you* are buying, reading, and using it. As a result, we have written the text with your needs in mind. The book uses simple, everyday language and presents directions in an easy-to-follow format. The chapters on writing strategies provide examples of student essays that supplement the professional essays in the Reader. These student examples represent realistic, achievable goals. When you compare them to the professional examples, you'll see that students can indeed do excellent work. We are confident that by learning to apply the principles in this text, you will write well too.

Here's wishing you success!

RHETORIC

WRITING: A FIRST LOOK

Why write? Hasn't the tempest of technology swept all of us into a brave new electronic world? Aren't e-mail, voice mail, cellular phones—all the magical devices of our new electronic estate—fast dooming ordinary writing? Not long ago, some people thought and said so, but events haven't supported those predictions. Although electronic devices have made some writing unnecessary, the written word flourishes both on campus and in the world of work. Furthermore, there's every evidence that writing will become even more important.

Writing offers very real advantages to both writers and readers:

1. It gives writers time to reflect on and research what they want to communicate and then lets them shape and reshape the material to their satisfaction.
2. It makes communication more precise and effective.
3. It provides a permanent record of thoughts, actions, and decisions.
4. It saves the reader's time; we absorb information more swiftly when we read it than when we hear it.

Many people will expect you to write for them. College instructors ask you to write reports, research papers, and essay exams. Job hunting usually requires you to write application letters. And once you're hired, writing will probably figure in your duties. You might be asked to discuss the capabilities of new computer equipment, report on a conference you attended, or explain the advantages of new safety procedures to supervisors or staff. Perhaps you'll propose that your organization install a new security system, conduct a market survey, or develop an alternative traffic flow pattern. The ability to write will help you earn better grades, land the job you want, and advance in your career.

Furthermore, writing ability yields personal benefits. You might need to defend a medical reimbursement claim that you filed with your health insurer, request clarification of an inadequate or ambiguous set of directions, or document a demand for replacement of a faulty product. Skill in writing will help you handle these matters.

As you can see, we usually write in response to a situation. This situation often determines the purpose and audience of our paper as well as its content, style, and organization. We don't, then, write in isolation but rather to communicate with others who have an interest in our message. To do an effective job, you will need to understand the different situations that can prompt a piece of writing and respond accordingly.

The Purposes of Writing

Whenever you write, some clear purpose should guide your efforts. If you don't know why you're writing, neither will your reader. Fulfilling an assignment doesn't qualify as a real writing purpose, although it may well be what sends you to your desk. Faced with a close deadline for a research paper or report, you may tell yourself, "I'm doing this because I have to." An authentic purpose, however, requires you to answer this question: What do I want this piece of writing to do for both my reader and me?

Purpose, as you might expect, grows out of the writing situation. You explore the consequences of the greenhouse effect in a report for your science instructor. You write an editorial for the college newspaper to air your frustration over inadequate campus parking. You propose that your organization replace an outdated piece of equipment with a state-of-the-art model. Clearly, your purpose stems from the writing situation.

Here are four common *general writing purposes,* two or more of which often join forces in a single piece:

To Inform   Presenting information is one of the most common writing purposes. The boating enthusiast who tells landlubber classmates how to handle a skiff plays the role of teacher, as does the researcher who summarizes the results of an investigation for co-workers. Some professional writers carve careers out of writing articles and books that fill gaps in the public's knowledge of timely topics. Instructors often ask you to write exams and papers so that they can gauge how well you have mastered the course material.

To Persuade   You probably have strong views on many issues, and these feelings may sometimes impel you to try swaying your reader. In a letter to the editor, you might attack a proposal to establish a nearby chemical waste dump. Or, alarmed by a sharp jump in state unemployment, you might write to your state senator and argue for a new job-training program.

To Express Yourself   Creative writing includes personal essays, fiction, plays, and poetry, as well as journals and diaries. But self-expression has a place in other kinds of writing too. Almost everything you write offers you a chance to display your mastery of words and to enliven your prose with vivid images and fresh turns of phrase.

To Entertain   Some writing merely entertains; some writing couples entertainment with a more serious purpose. A lighthearted approach can help your reader absorb dull or difficult material. Satire lets you expose the shortcomings of individuals, ideas, and institutions by poking fun at them. An intention to entertain can add savor to many kinds of writing.

Besides having one or more *general purposes,* each writing project has its own *specific purpose.* Consider the difference in the papers you could write about solar homes. You might explain how readers could build one, argue that readers should buy one, express the advantages of solar homes to urge Congress to enact a tax credit for them, or satirize the solar home craze so that readers might re-evaluate their plans to buy one.

Having a specific purpose assists you at every stage of the writing process. It helps you define your audience; select the details, language, and approach that best suit their needs; and avoid going off in directions that won't interest them. The following example from the newspaper *USA Today* has a clear and specific purpose.

We'll Trash *USA Today,* Too

J. Winston Porter

1   What will you do with *USA Today* after you finish reading it? If you're like most of us, you'll put the paper out with the garbage and it'll end up buried in a landfill. Over 80% of all household and commercial garbage ends up this way, and this is a problem.

2   The USA is relentlessly producing more and more trash, and we are rapidly running out of landfill space. At the same time, new landfills and incinerators are encountering local opposition. Before we are truly wallowing in waste, we need to declare a war on garbage.

3   The first battle we need to win is for public acceptance of a strategy that includes reducing the amount of waste generated and increasing the amount recycled. EPA is pushing a national goal of recycling 25% of all garbage within the next four years. But waste reduction and recycling aren't enough to stem the tide of trash that threatens to engulf us. We will continue to need safe landfilling of some garbage and incineration, preferably with energy recovery, as another option. EPA and the states are working to strengthen environmental controls on these facilities. The appropriate mix of waste reduction and recycling, landfilling and incineration should be "custom designed" by states and localities.

4   How can we all do our part? To begin with, we must recognize that we all contribute to the garbage problem. Next, we should cooperate in efforts to reduce the amount of trash requiring disposal. Finally, we must adopt new attitudes about disposal, because there will always be trash to be handled. This means that instead of simply opposing any new disposal facilities, citizens should assist in choosing the best options.

5   Recycling is the cornerstone of a sound waste-management strategy. We all have special responsibilities to make recycling work. Individuals must be willing to participate in local programs. Local governments should plan programs and operate required facilities. States should do statewide planning and enforce their own laws and regulations. Industry should step up its recycling efforts. The federal government should provide national leadership, research and information-sharing as well as develop certain underlying regulations.

6   No one segment of society can, alone, lead us to victory in the war on
       garbage. Instead, we need a coordinated national effort to confront the solid-waste
       issue head-on.

From USA Today

Porter hints at his purpose in the first paragraph by noting that the disposal of garbage in landfills poses a problem. The last sentence of paragraph 2 states the purpose clearly. The remaining paragraphs name the strategies that he recommends to wage war on garbage and explain how individuals, government, and industry can all contribute. Everything Porter has written relates to his purpose.

Now examine the next paragraph, which does *not* have a firmly fixed specific purpose:

> Community is a sea in which people swim unconsciously, like fish. We fail to recognize our neighbors as fellow humans, and they show the same lack of fellow feeling for us. A complete lack of concern for one another is evident in today's complex society. What is community? Is it a plant? A building? A place? A state of being? Knowing what it is, we can see if such a place exists. To know community, one must realize who he or she is. Identity of a person is the first step in establishing a community.

This student writer can't decide what aspect of community to tackle. The opening sentence attempts a definition, but the next two veer onto the shortcomings of the modern community. Notice how aimlessly the thoughts drift. The vague leadoff sentence asserts "Community is a sea . . .," but the later question "What is community?" contradicts this opening. Also, if community is a plant, a building, or a place, why must we realize who we are in order to know it? This contradictory and illogical paragraph reveals a writer groping for a purpose.

The paragraph, however, isn't a wasted effort. These musings offer several possibilities. By developing the first sentence, the writer might show some interesting similarities between community and a sea so that instead of taking community for granted, readers can see it in a new light. By pursuing the idea in the second and third sentences, the writer might show the callous nature of modern society to encourage readers to act more humanely. The last two sentences might lead to a statement on the relationship between individual and community in order to overcome the common view that the two are in conflict. A specific purpose can sometimes emerge from preliminary jottings.

The Audience for Your Writing

Everything you write is aimed at some audience—a person or group you want to reach. The ultimate purpose of all writing is to have an effect on a reader (even if that reader is you), and therefore purpose and audience are closely linked. Our discussion on pages 4–5 makes this point clear by noting that your purpose can be to inform *someone* of something, to persuade *someone* to believe or do something, to express feelings or insights to *someone*, or to entertain *someone*.

Any of these objectives requires that you *be able to define* that someone, the audience for your writing.

Writing operates on a delayed-action fuse, detonating its ideas in the readers' minds at a later time and place. Sometimes problems follow. In face-to-face conversations, you can observe your listeners' reactions, and whenever you note signs of hostility, boredom, or puzzlement, you can alter your tone, offer some examples, or ask a question. You can also use gestures and facial expressions to emphasize what you're saying. When you write, however, the words on the page carry your message. Once written work has left your hands, it's on its own. You can't call it back to clear up a misunderstanding or satisfy a disgruntled reader.

Establishing rapport with your audience is easy when you're writing for your friends or someone else you know a great deal about. You can then judge the likely response to what you say. Often, though, you'll be writing for people you know only casually or not at all: employers, customers, fellow townsfolk, and the like. In such situations, you'll need to assess your audience before starting to write and/or later in the writing process.

A good way to size up your readers is to develop an audience profile. This profile will emerge gradually as you answer the following questions:

1. What are the educational level, age, social class, and economic status of the audience I want to reach?
2. Why will this audience read my writing? To gain information? Learn my views on a controversial issue? Enjoy my creative flair? Be entertained?
3. What attitudes, needs, and expectations do they have?
4. How are they likely to respond to what I say? Can I expect them to be neutral? Opposed? Friendly?
5. How much do they know about my topic? (Your answer here will help you gauge whether you're saying too little or too much.)
6. What kind of language will communicate with them most effectively? (See "Level of Diction" in Chapter 17.)

College writing assignments sometimes ask you to envision a reader who is intelligent but lacking specialized knowledge, receptive but unwilling to put up with boring or trite material. Or perhaps you'll be assigned, or choose, to write for a certain age group or one with particular interests. At other times, you'll be asked to write for a specialized audience—one with some expertise in your topic. This difference will affect what you say to each audience and how you say it.

The Effect of Audience on Your Writing

Let's see how audience can shape a paper. Suppose you are explaining how to take a certain type of X-ray. If your audience is a group of lay readers who have never had an X-ray, you might note at the outset that taking one is much like taking an ordinary photograph. Then you might explain the basic process, including the positioning of the patient and the equipment, comment on the safety and reliability of the procedure, and note how much time it takes. You probably would use few technical terms. If, however, you were writing for radiology students, you might emphasize exposure factors, film size, and required views. This audience would understand technical terms and want a detailed explanation of the procedure. You could speak to these readers as colleagues who appreciate precise information.

Audience shapes all types of writing in similar fashion, even your personal writing. Assume you've recently become engaged, and to share your news you write two letters: one to your minister, the other to your best friend back home. You can imagine the differences in details, language, and general tone of each letter. Further, think how inappropriate it would be if you accidentally sent the letter intended for one to the other. Without doubt, different readers call for different approaches.

Discourse Communities

Professionals often write as members of specific communities. For example, biologists with similar interests often exchange information about their research. The members of a community share goals, values, concerns, background information, and expectations, and this fact in turn affects how they write. Because such writing is closely tied to the interests of the community, professional articles often start with a section linking their content to previous research projects and articles. Often, too, custom dictates what information must be included, the pattern of organization, and the style the paper should follow. Throughout college, you will discover that part of learning to write is becoming familiar with the values and customs of different discourse communities. To do this, you'll need to read carefully in your major field, acquainting yourself with its current issues and concerns and learning how to write about them. As you start reading in any professional area, ask yourself these questions:

1. What are the major concerns and questions in this field?
2. What seems to be common knowledge?
3. To what works do writers regularly refer?
4. How do those in the field go about answering questions?
5. What methods do they follow?
6. Which kinds of knowledge are acceptable? Which are not?
7. What values seem to guide the field?
8. What kinds of information must writers include in papers?
9. How are different writing projects organized?
10. What conventions do writers follow?

We all, of course, belong to many different communities. Furthermore, a community can involve competing groups, conflicting values, differing kinds of writing projects, and varying approaches to writing. But as part of your growth as a writer and professional, you'll need to understand the goals and rules of any community you enter.

 EXERCISE   *The following three excerpts deal with the same subject—antigens— but each explanation is geared to a different audience. Read the passages carefully; then answer the following questions:*

1. What audience does each author address? How do you know?

2. Identify ways in which each author appeals to a specific audience.

1. The human body is quick to recognize foreign chemicals that enter it. "Foes" must be attacked or otherwise got rid of. The most common of these foes are chemical materials from viruses, bacteria, and other microscopic organisms. Such chemicals, when recognized by the body, are called *antigens*. To combat them, the body produces its own chemicals, protein molecules called *antibodies*. Each kind of antigen causes the production of a specific kind of antibody. Antibodies appear in the body fluids such as blood and lymph and in the body's cells.

    L. D. Hamilton, "Antibodies and Antigens," *The New Book of Knowledge*

2. [An] *antigen* [is a] foreign substance that, when introduced into the body, is capable of inducing the formation of antibodies and of reacting specifically in a detectable manner with the induced antibodies. For each antigen there is a specific antibody, the physical and chemical structure of which is produced in response to the physical and chemical structure of the antigen. Antigens comprise virtually all proteins that are foreign to the host, including those contained in bacteria, viruses, protozoa, helminths, foods, snake venoms, egg white, serum components, red blood cells, and other cells and tissues of various species, including man. Polysaccharides and lipids may also act as antigens when coupled to proteins.

    "Antigen," *Encyclopaedia Britannica*

3. The substance which stimulates the body to produce antibodies is designated antigen (antibody stimulator). . . .

    Most complete antigens are protein molecules containing aromatic amino acids, and are large in molecular weight and size. However, it has been demonstrated that other macromolecules, such as pure polysaccharides, polynucleotides, and lipids, may serve as complete antigens.

    However, certain other materials, incapable of stimulating antibody formation by themselves can, in association with a protein or other carrier, stimulate antibody formation and are the antigenic determinants. These determinants are referred to as *incomplete antigens* or *haptens* and they are able to react with antibodies which were produced by the determinant–protein complex.

    However, before an antigen can stimulate the production of antibodies, it must be soluble in the body fluids, must reach certain tissues in an unaltered form, and must be, in general, foreign to the body tissues. Protein taken by mouth loses its specific foreign-protein characteristics when digested in the alimentary tract. It reaches the tissues of the body as amino acids or other altered digested products of protein. Consequently, it no longer meets the requirements for antigenic behavior.

    Orville Wyss and Curtis Eklund, *Microorganisms and Man*

Just as you would not dial a telephone number at random and then expect to carry on a meaningful conversation, so you should not expect to communicate effectively without a specific audience in mind.

One other note: As you shape your paper, it is important that the writing please you as well as your audience—that it satisfy your sense of what good writing is and what the writing task requires. You are, after all, your own first reader.

The Qualities of Good Writing

Three qualities—fresh thinking; a sense of style including the use of correct grammar and punctuations; and effective organization—help to ensure that a piece of prose will meet your reader's expectations.

Fresh Thinking   You don't have to astound your readers with something never before discussed in print. Genuinely unique ideas and information are scarce commodities. You can, however, freshen your writing by exploring personal insights and perceptions. Using your own special slant, you might show a connection between seemingly unrelated items, as does a writer who likens office "paper pushers" to different kinds of animals. Keep the expression of your ideas credible, however; farfetched notions spawn skepticism.

Sense of Style   Readers don't expect you to display the stylistic flair of Maya Angelou or E. B. White. Indeed, such writing would impair the neutral tone needed in certain kinds of writing, such as technical reports and legal documents. Readers do, however, expect you to write in a clear style. And if you strengthen it with vivid, forceful words, readers will absorb your points with even greater interest. Readers also expect you to use standard grammar, spelling, and punctuation. The chapters ahead show you how to use language in ways that project your views and personality. Chapters 16 and 17, in particular, will help you develop a sense of style, as will the many readings throughout the book and the Handbook.

Effective Organization   A paper should have a beginning, a middle, and an end, that is, an introduction, a body, and a conclusion. The introduction sparks interest and acquaints the reader with what is to come. The body delivers the main message and exhibits a clear connection between ideas so that the reader can easily follow your thoughts. The conclusion ends the discussion so the reader feels satisfied rather than suddenly cut off. Overall, your paper should follow a pattern that is suited to its content. Organizational patterns, or strategies of development, are the subject of Chapters 5–14. Pages 222–227 discuss introductions and conclusions.

Freshness, style, and organization are weighted differently in different kinds of writing. A writer who drafts a proposal to pave a city's streets will probably attach less importance to fresh thinking than to clear writing and careful organization. On the other hand, fresh thinking can be very important in a description of an autumn forest scene. You will learn more about these qualities throughout this book.

Writing and Ethics

Think for a minute about how you would react to the following situation. You decide to vacation at a resort after reading a brochure that stressed its white-sand beach, scenic trails, fine dining, and peaceful atmosphere. When you arrive, you find the beach overgrown with weeds, the trails littered and the view unappealing, and the restaurant a greasy-spoon cafeteria. Worse, whenever you go outside, swarms of vicious black flies attack you. Wouldn't you feel cheated? Closer to home, think how you'd react if you decided to attend a college because of its distinguished faculty members only to discover upon arrival that they rarely teach on campus. The college counts on their reputations to attract students even though they are usually unavailable. Hasn't the college done something unethical?

As these examples show, good writing is also ethical writing. Like you, readers expect that what they read will be dependable information. Few if any would bother with a piece of writing that they realized was intended to deceive. A good test of the ethics of your writing is whether you would read your own work and act on the basis of it. Would you feel comfortable with it, or would you feel cheated, manipulated, deceived, or harmed in some way? By learning and practicing the principles of ethical writing, you will help ensure that your writing meets the standards your readers expect.

The Principles of Ethical Writing

- Writing perceived as truthful should *be* truthful. Granted, a writer may use humorous exaggeration to make us laugh, and some sales pitches may stretch the truth a bit in order to entice buyers. ("Try Nu-Glo toothpaste and add sparkle to your life.") But most readers recognize and discount such embellishments which, unlike major distortions, harm nobody. Deliberate, serious falsehoods, however, may harm not only the reader but sometimes the writer as well. Angered by the misrepresentations in the vacation brochure, you would certainly warn your friends against the resort and might even take some legal action against it.

- Writing meant to be perceived as truthful should tell the whole truth, omitting nothing the reader needs to know in order to make informed decisions. The text should not be deliberately incomplete so as to mislead. Suppose that a university's recruitment brochures stress that 97 percent of its students get jobs upon graduation. What the brochures don't say is that only 55 percent of the jobs are in the graduates' chosen fields despite strong employer demand for graduates in those areas. Clearly these brochures are deceptive, perhaps attracting students who would otherwise choose schools with better placement records.

- Writing should not be presented as something different from what it is. It would be unethical for a drug company's advertising department or agency to prepare, in the form of an article, an advertisement for a hair-loss treatment (their own, of course) and pass off the article as an impartial news story.

- Writing should be clear to the reader. All of us know the frustration of trying to read a crucial regulation that is impossible to comprehend. A person who writes instructions so unclear that they result in harmful mistakes is partially responsible for the consequences. Readers have a right to expect understandable, accurate information. Thus, it would be deceptive for a group of state legislators to call a proposed bill the

Public Education Enhancement Act when it would in fact bar teachers from belonging to unions.

■ Writing should not be intended to harm the reader. Certainly it is fair to point out the advantages of a product or service that readers might not need. Most people understand the nature of this type of advertising. But think how unethical it would be for a writer to encourage readers to follow a diet that the writer knew was not only ineffective but harmful. Think of the harm a writer might cause by attempting, deliberately, to persuade readers to try crack cocaine.

STRATEGIES FOR SUCCESSFUL READING

Effective reading is not the passive process that many people imagine. On the contrary, it requires the ongoing interaction of your mind and the printed page; bringing your knowledge and experience to bear on a piece of writing can help you assess its events, ideas, and conclusions. For example, an understanding of marriage, love, and conflict, as well as experience with divorce, can help readers comprehend an essay that explores divorce. As you read, you must also understand each point that's made, consider how the various parts fit together, and try to anticipate the direction the writing will take. Successful reading requires work. Fortunately, you can follow specific strategies to help yourself read better.

Orienting Your Reading

Different purposes require different approaches to reading. When reading for pleasure, you can relax and proceed at your own pace, slowing down to savor a section you especially enjoy, speeding up when you encounter less interesting material, and breaking off when you wish. Reading for information, for solid understanding, or to critique the writing calls for a more methodical approach. Even so there are some questions you should ask:

- **Why am I reading this material?** Is it for long-term use, as a reference for a project, as a building block to understanding more material?

- **How well do I need to know the material in the article?** Can you look back to the article as a reference? Is there only one main point you need to know? Are you going to be tested on much of the material in depth?

■ **Is some material in the article more important to me than other material?** Sometimes in doing research you may be looking for a specific bit of information that is only a paragraph in a long article. If so, you can skim for the information. In most things you read, some sections are more important than others. Often you can read to get the main points of the article and not focus on all the details. Sometimes, of course, you need to know the material in depth.

■ **What will I need to do with the material from the article?** If you are looking for ideas for your own writing, you might read quickly. If you will be responsible for writing a critique of the article, you will need to read carefully and critically.

■ **What kind of reading does the material suggest?** The significance, the difficulty, and the nature of the writing all can influence how you read. An easy humorous narrative can be read in a more leisurely fashion. A careful argument on an important issue merits careful attention to the main points and the evidence and may even require you to outline the argument.

◖EXERCISE

Reading Activity

> *Look briefly at "The Appeal of the Androgynous Man" on page 20. Identify three purposes you could have for reading this essay. Identify how these purposes would affect how you would read the essay and what you would look for in the essay.* ◖

⋮ A First Reading

You don't just jump in your car and take off. Usually you take a few minutes to think about where you want to go. Sometimes you even have to check your route. The same is true of effective reading. Because of the challenging nature of most college-level reading assignments, you should plan on more than one reading. A good first reading should orient you to the material.

Orient Yourself to the Background of the Essay Before you begin, scan any accompanying biographical sketch and try to determine the writer's expertise and views on the topic. Alexander Petrunkevitch's background as a college professor and an author of internationally acclaimed books on spiders lends authority to his discussion of the survival process of the pepsis wasp in the essay "The Spider and the Wasp" (pages 459–461). Sometimes there is material by the author or the editor on the writing of the essay. Professional essays often start with an abstract that provides a brief summary of the article. At this point you may want to judge the credibility of the source, a topic discussed in depth on page 169–173.

Use the Title As a Clue   Most titles identify the topic and often the viewpoint as well. Thus "The Sweet Smell of Success Isn't All That Sweet" (pages 532–534) suggests that the author isn't overly impressed with the conventional attitudes toward success. Some titles signal the writer's primary strategy, whether it is a comparison, definition, or argument.

Skim to Get the Gist of the Article   Sometimes you can just read the introductory and concluding paragraphs and the topic sentences (often the first or last sentences of paragraphs). Other times you will need to read the whole essay quickly. Try to gain an idea of the essay's main thrust, the key ideas that support it, and the ways that they are organized. In your first reading, you can skim the more difficult sections without trying to understand them fully.

Make Connections with What You Have Read   When you've finished skimming the essay, and before you reread the essay, think about what you've learned and then, either by saying it to yourself or jotting it down, express it *in your own words.* You can hardly be said to understand what you've read, and you will be less likely to remember it, until you can state its essence in your own words. Go back and underline the thesis statement or, if one is not included, try to formulate one in your own words. Try to identify the strategy used by the writer. Also stop and identify what you already know about the topic and your connection to the issue. You will read more effectively if you can connect what you read to your own knowledge and interests. Jot down questions that the first reading has raised in your mind.

⟨EXERCISE

Reading Activities

1. Identify what you can about the background of the article "The Appeal of the Androgynous Man" (page 20) from the statement about the author.
2. Write what you expect based on the title.
3. Skim the essay and then write down what you identify as the main points of the essay. Identify the essay's thesis. Jot down at least two questions you have.

Additional Readings

If the material was difficult or you need to know it well, a second or even third reading may be necessary. On the second reading, which will take more time than the first, you carefully absorb the writer's ideas.

Read Carefully and Actively   Read at a pace suitable to the material. Underline significant topic sentences as well as other key sentences and ideas or facts that you find important, but keep in mind that underlining in itself doesn't ensure comprehension. Restating the ideas in your own words is more effective. Depending on your purposes, you may want to write down the main points in your own words or jot down the ideas in the margins. As you proceed, examine the supporting sentences to see how well they back up the main idea. Keep an eye out for how the essay fits together.

Consider Reading As a Kind of Conversation with the Text   Develop the habit of asking questions about facts, reasons, ideas—practically anything in the essay. Jot your queries and their answers in the margins. (On page 24 you can see how a student interacted with the first page of Amy Gross's essay "The Appeal of the Androgynous Man.") Good writers anticipate your questions and answer them; and because you have posed the questions yourself, you are more likely to see the connections in the text. If the author hasn't answered your questions, there may be problems with the work.

Master Unfamiliar Words   At times, unfamiliar words can hinder your grasp of the material. Whenever you encounter a new word, circle it, use context to help gauge its meaning, check the dictionary for the exact meaning, and then record it in the margins or some other convenient place. If the writing is peppered with words you don't know, you may have to read the whole piece to figure out its general drift, then look up key words, and finally reread the material.

Take Conscious Steps to Understand Difficult Material   When the ideas of a single section prove difficult, restate the points of those sections you do understand. Then experiment by stating in your own words different interpretations of the problem section and see which one best fits the writing as a whole.

Sometimes large sections or entire texts are extremely difficult. There are several strategies you can use to help yourself.

- State the ideas that are easier for you to understand and use them as keys to unlock meanings that are difficult but not unintelligible. Save the most difficult sections until last. Don't think you have to understand everything completely. Some works take a lifetime to fully understand.
- Discuss a difficult essay with others who are reading it.
- Read simpler material on the topic.
- Go to your teacher for help. He or she may help you find background material that will make the selection easier.

Pull the Entire Essay Together   Whenever you finish a major section of a lengthy essay, express your sense of what it means. Speak it out loud or write it down. If you have trouble seeing the connections between ideas, try visually representing them. You might make an outline that states the main points followed by subpoints (see page 354 for how to outline). For a comparison, you might create a table with the main points of the comparison side by side. You can make a drawing connecting the main ideas in a network, list the steps in an instruction, or write out the main facts.

To strengthen your grasp of material you'll need to remember for some time, try restating its main points a couple of days after the second reading. Sometimes it is helpful to explain the material to a sympathetic listener. If anything has become hazy or slipped your mind, reread the appropriate section(s). If you really must know the material, try making up your own test and giving it to yourself.

Mastering Reading Problems

Master the Problems That Interfere with Reading   Lots of factors are important to effective reading. If your environment is too noisy, you are too tired, or you have something on your mind, you can have trouble reading. Do your reading at the time of day when you are most alert. Be sure you are in an environment that lets you concentrate and that is well lit. Try to be rested and comfortable. If you get tired, take a break for a specific time period; perhaps go for a short walk. If something else is bothering you, try to resolve the distraction or put it out of your mind. If you find the material uninteresting, try to find a connection between the topic and your interests and goals; read more actively.

If you have extensive problems reading for college, you can get help. Most colleges have courses in reading and tutors. College often requires a lot of reading, so take the steps necessary to be the most effective reader possible.

EXERCISE

Reading Activities

1. Read "The Appeal of the Androgynous Man" a second time, continuing to write your own questions and notes in the margin.
2. Create a table with two columns comparing the all-man and the androgynous man.
3. Identify three words that you might find relatively new and find their definitions from the context and a dictionary.
4. Try explaining the article to a friend or your roommate.

Reading to Critique

In college you usually read not only to understand but also to evaluate what you read. Your instructors will want to know what you think about what you've read. Often you'll be asked whether you agree or disagree with a piece of writing. Sometimes you will be asked to write an explicit critique of what you read.

Merely because information and ideas are in print does not mean that they are true or acceptable. An essay, for example, might include faulty logic, unreasonable ideas, suspect facts, or unreliable authorities. Don't hesitate to dispute the writer's information.

- Does it match your experience?
- Do the pieces of evidence support the claim?
- Do the ideas appear reasonable?
- Are there other pieces of evidence or other works that contradict these claims?
- Do the ideas connect in a logical way?

Knowledge of the principles of argumentation and various reasoning fallacies can help you critique a piece of writing. These issues are discussed in the chapter on argumentation, pages 168–198.

EXERCISE

Reading Activities

Prepare your critique of "The Appeal of the Androgynous Man" by doing the following:

1. Identify where and how the claims don't match your experience.
2. Indicate where the evidence does not support the claims.
3. Indicate at least a few places where the ideas do not appear reasonable.
4. Identify any evidence that seems to contradict the author's claims.
5. Evaluate whether the ideas connect in a logical way.

Reading As a Writer

All of us who write can use reading as a springboard for improving our writing. You can do several things to make your reading especially useful.

As you read, the views of others, the experiences they relate, and the information they present often deepen your understanding of yourself, your relationships, and your surroundings. In turn, this broadened perspective can supply you with writing ideas. When possibilities surface, be sure to record them. Some writers keep a reading journal in which they summarize what they've read and jot down writing ideas that come to mind. In addition, you can take down specific ideas, facts, and perhaps even a few particularly telling quotations that you discover. You may want to incorporate this material into your writing at a later time. Carefully record the source so that you can document it properly in order to avoid plagiarism (see pages 404–406).

When you read various sources that explore the same topic or related topics, you may notice connections among their ideas. Since these connections can be fertile ground for a paper of your own, don't neglect to record them. Once you have jotted down these ideas, circle and label related thoughts. You can also draw a line linking the different thoughts to one another and to the main point that relates them. Express as a thesis statement your view of how these ideas fit together. Interacting with various sources and using their ideas to advance the purpose of your writing is a form of synthesis (see pages 82–83). When you proceed in this fashion, as in writing any paper, review your information, determine the points you want to make, and experiment until you find the order that works best. As you write, use the material from your sources as you would any support; be careful, however, to credit the authors properly in order to avoid plagiarism.

Let's see how you might use synthesis in writing an actual essay. Suppose, for example, you've read Amy Gross's "The Appeal of the Androgynous Man" (pages 20–22), Martin Gottfried's "Rambos of the Road" (pages 474–476), and Ellen Goodman's "The Company Man" (pages 482–483). You've noticed several connections among these essays. Gross describes "all-man" men who are insensitive in their treatment of women; Gottfried shows how some men need to assert their masculinity by driving aggressively; and Goodman characterizes a man who works himself to death. You might start your essay with Gross's definition of the "all-man" male and then cite some of her examples along with some of your own that identify how such a man would act. Next, you could stress that this particular concept of masculinity includes aggressiveness, then develop this point by using some illustrations from Gottfried's essay and from your own experience. Finally, you might conclude that being enslaved by such a narrow masculine role can have serious consequences and then support your view with material from Goodman's essay and your own observations. All of these ideas and examples could help you build an essay that points out how men can sometimes become desensitized or trapped, even victimized, by living according to stereotypes of masculinity. If you will be writing a paper that synthesizes material from various sources, review pages 381–395 and 396–401 on how to document your sources properly.

Because writers solve problems, you'll want to pay attention to the techniques and strategies that other writers use. If you find an introduction, an organizational pattern, a transition, a certain description or comparison unusually engaging, study the writer's technique. Perhaps you can use it yourself. Similarly, observe when a piece of writing fails and try to determine why.

EXERCISE

Reading Activities:

1. Identify at least two strategies that the author used that you would find useful.
2. Identify at least two phrases that you found effective.
3. Identify at least two ideas that could spark your own writing.

AMY GROSS

both male and female in one

The Appeal of the Androgynous Man

Amy Gross, a native of Brooklyn, New York, earned a sociology degree at Connecticut College. Upon graduation, she entered the world of fashion publishing and has held writing or editorial positions at various magazines, including Talk, Mademoiselle, Good Housekeeping, Elle, *and* Mirabella. *She is the newly appointed editor-in-chief of* O, *the Oprah* Magazine. *In our selection, which first appeared in* Mademoiselle, *Gross compares androgynous men favorably to macho "all-men."*

Does she favor androgynous men? What kind of appeal?

She will give a woman's perspective. She writes for and edits women's magazines.

Seems like she is going to talk about the advantages of androgynous men as compared to other men. Sees them as better.

Attempt to counter stereotype? Can't androgynous men also be effeminate?

Suggests "All-men" men reject behaviors and interests they consider feminine, but isn't she stereotyping? Are all these men like this? She seems to be exaggerating.

1   James Dean was my first androgynous man.[1] I figured I could talk to him. He was anguished and I was 12, so we had a lot in common. With only a few exceptions, all the men I have liked or loved have been a certain kind of man: a kind who doesn't play football or watch the games on Sunday, who doesn't tell dirty jokes featuring broads or chicks, who is not contemptuous of conversations that are philosophically speculative, introspective, or otherwise foolish according to the other kind of man. He is more self-amused, less inflated, more quirky, vulnerable and responsive than the other sort (the other sort, I'm visualizing as the guys on TV who advertise deodorant in the locker room). He is more like me than the other sort. He is what social scientists and feminists would call androgynous: having the characteristics of both male and female.

2   Now the first thing I want you to know about the androgynous man is that he is neither effeminate nor hermaphroditic. All his primary and secondary sexual characteristics are in order and I would say he's all-man, but that is just what he is not. He is more than all-man.

both male and female sex organs

3   The merely all-man man, for one thing, never walks to the grocery store unless the little woman is away visiting her mother with the kids, or is in the hospital having a kid, or there is no little woman. All-men men don't know how to shop in a grocery store unless it is to buy a 6-pack and some pretzels. Their ideas of nutrition expand beyond a 6-pack and pretzels only to take in steak, potatoes, scotch or rye whiskey, and maybe a wad of cake or apple pie. All-men men have absolutely no taste in food, art, books, movies, theatre, dance, how to live, what are good questions, what is funny, or anything else I care about. It's not exactly that the all-man's man is an uncouth illiterate. He may be educated, well-mannered, and on a first-name basis with fine wines. One all-man man I knew was a handsome individual

[1]James Dean (1931–1955) was a 1950s film star who gained fame for his portrayals of restless, defiant young men.

who gave the impression of being gentle, affectionate, and sensitive. He sat and ate dinner one night while I was doing something endearingly feminine at the sink. At one point, he mutely held up his glass to indicate in a primitive, even ape-like, way his need for a refill. This was in 1967, before Women's Liberation. Even so, I was disturbed. Not enough to break the glass over his handsome head, not even enough to mutely indicate the whereabouts of the refrigerator, but enough to re-member that moment in all its revelatory clarity. No androgynous man would ever brutishly expect to be waited on without even a "please." (With a "please," maybe.)

4   The brute happened to be a doctor—not a hard hat—and, to all appearances, couth. But he had bought the whole superman package, complete with that fragile beast, the male ego. The androgynous man arrives with a male ego too, but his is not as imperialistic. It doesn't invade every area of his life and person. Most activities and thoughts have nothing to do with masculinity or femininity. The androgynous man knows this. The all-man man doesn't. He must keep a constant guard against anything even vaguely feminine (i.e., "sissy") rising up in him. It must be a terrible strain.

5   Male chauvinism is an irritation, but the real problem I have with the all-man man is that it's hard for me to talk to him. He's alien to me, and for this I'm at least half to blame. As his interests have not carried him into the sissy, mine have never taken me very far into the typically masculine terrains of sports, business and fi-nance, politics, cars, boats and machines. But blame or no blame, the reality is that it is almost as difficult for me to connect with him as it would be to link up with an Arab shepherd or Bolivian sandalmaker. There's a similar culture gap.

6   It seems to me that the most masculine men usually end up with the most fem-inine women. Maybe they like extreme polarity. I like polarity myself, but the poles have to be within earshot. As I've implied, I'm very big on talking. I fall in love for at least three hours with anyone who engages me in a real conversation. I'd rather a man point out a paragraph in a book—wanting to share it with me—than bring me flowers. I'd rather a man ask what I think than tell me I look pretty. (Women who are very pretty and accustomed to hearing that they are pretty may feel differ-ently.) My experience is that all-men men read books I don't want to see paragraphs of, and don't really give a damn what I or any woman would think about most issues so long as she looks pretty. They have a very limited use for women. I suspect they don't really like us. The androgynous man likes women as much or as little as he likes anyone.

7   Another difference between the all-man man and the androgynous man is that the first is not a star in the creativity department. If your image of the creative male ac-cessorizes him with a beret, smock and artist's palette, you will not believe the all-man man has been seriously short-changed. But if you allow as how creativity is a talent for freedom, associated with imagination, wit, empathy, unpredictability, and receptivity to new impressions and connections, then you will certainly pity the dull, thick-skinned, rigid fellow in whom creativity sets no fires.

8   Nor is the all-man man so hot when it comes to sensitivity. He may be true-blue in the trenches, but if you are troubled, you'd be wasting your time trying to milk comfort from the all-man man.

9   This is not blind prejudice. It is enlightened prejudice. My biases were con-firmed recently by a psychologist named Sandra Lipsetz Bem, a professor at Stan-ford University. She brought to attention the fact that high masculinity in males (and high femininity in females) has been "consistently correlated with lower over-all intelligence and lower creativity." Another psychologist, Donald W. MacKinnon, director of the Institute of Personality Assessment and Research at the University of

California in Berkeley, found that "creative males give more expression to the feminine side of their nature than do less creative men. . . . [They] score relatively high on femininity, and this despite the fact that, as a group, they do not present an effeminate appearance or give evidence of increased homosexual interests or experiences. Their elevated scores on femininity indicate rather an openness to their feelings and emotions, a sensitive intellect and understanding self-awareness and wide-ranging interests including many which in the American culture are thought of as more feminine. . . ."

10   Dr. Bem ran a series of experiments on college students who had been categorized as masculine, feminine, or androgynous. In three tests of the degree of nurturance—warmth and caring—the masculine men scored painfully low (painfully for anyone stuck with a masculine man, that is). In one of those experiments, all the students were asked to listen to a "troubled talker"—a person who was not neurotic but simply lonely, supposedly new in town and feeling like an outsider. The masculine men were the least supportive, responsive or humane. "They lacked the ability to express warmth, playfulness and concern," Bem concluded. (She's giving them the benefit of the doubt. It's possible the masculine men didn't express those qualities because they didn't possess them.)

11   The androgynous man, on the other hand, having been run through the same carnival of tests, "performs spectacularly. He shuns no behavior just because our culture happens to label it as female and his competence crosses both the instrumental [getting the job done, the problem solved] and the expressive [showing a concern for the welfare of others, the harmony of the group] domains. Thus, he stands firm in his opinion, he cuddles kittens and bounces babies and he has a sympathetic ear for someone in distress."

12   Well, a great mind, a sensitive and warm personality are fine in their place, but you are perhaps skeptical of the gut appeal of the androgynous man. As a friend, maybe, you'd like an androgynous man. For a sexual partner, though, you'd prefer a jock. There's no arguing chemistry, but consider the jock for a moment. He competes on the field, whatever his field is, and bed is just one more field to him: another opportunity to perform, another fray. Sensuality is for him candy to be doled out as lure. It is a ration whose flow is cut off at the exact point when it has served its purpose—namely, to elicit your willingness to work out on the field with him.

13   Highly masculine men need to believe their sexual appetite is far greater than a woman's (than a nice woman's). To them, females must be seduced: Seduction is a euphemism for a power play, a con job. It pits man against woman (or woman against man). The jock believes he must win you over, incite your body to rebel against your better judgment: in other words—conquer you.

14   The androgynous man is not your opponent but your teammate. He does not seduce: he invites. Sensuality is a pleasure for him. He's not quite so goal-oriented. And to conclude, I think I need only remind you here of his greater imagination, his wit and empathy, his unpredictability, and his receptivity to new impressions and connections.

Writing About What You Read

Often in college you will be asked to write about what you read. This culminates in the Research Paper, which is discussed in Chapters 21 and 22. However, sometimes you will have to write shorter summaries and critiques.

Writing a Summary

A summary states the main points of an essay in *your own words*. A good summary lets someone who hasn't read the essay understand what it says. A summary can be one or more paragraphs. It should

- provide a context for the essay,
- introduce the author of the essay,
- and state the thesis, (these first three elements often form the introduction of a multiparagraph summary)
- then state the main points of the essay (sometimes but not always based on the topic sentences),
- and conclude by pulling the essay together.

To prepare to write a summary, follow the steps in effective reading. A brief outline of the main points will make it easy to write a summary. Be careful to avoid using the author's exact wording without using quotation marks. You may want to review the section on plagiarism on page 404. Also, don't interject your views. A summary should reflect only the author's words.

A Sample Single Paragraph Summary of "The Appeal of the Androgynous Man"

What kind of man should appeal to women? According to Amy Gross, the editor-in-chief of *O* magazine, in "The Appeal of the Androgynous Man," her ideal is and the ideal of women should be the "androgynous man," a man who shares the personality characteristics of both male and female. To make her point, Amy Gross contrasts the all-man man and the androgynous man. She believes that the all-man man does not share in activities like shopping, has no taste in the arts, is imperialistic, resists anything feminine, and is interested in only exclusively male topics. Worse, she points to studies that show that more masculine men are less creative. Further, she argues that the all-man tends to see women as something to conquer rather than as partners. The androgynous man, by comparison, is very different. He does not resist things that are feminine and so shares in domestic activities, is comfortable with the arts, and can share interests with women. He is shown by studies to be more creative. Further, according to Gross, "The androgynous man is not your opponent but your teammate." As a result, she concludes that the androgynous man has the qualities that women should really look for in a man.

Writing a Critique

Often you will be asked to give your views on an essay, indicating where you agree and disagree with the author's position. Remember you can always agree with part of what a person says and disagree with other parts. A critique combines a summary of the article with your thoughtful reaction. Most critiques consist of several paragraphs. A critique usually includes

- a context for the essay
- an introduction to the author

- a statement of the essay's thesis
- the thesis for your critique
- a summary of the essay
- a statement of the points with which you agree
- a statement with reasons and evidence for your disagreement
- a conclusion

You are well prepared to write a critique if you follow the steps for reading effectively and reading critically.

A Sample Multiparagraph Critique of "The Appeal of the Androgynous Man"

1   What kind of man should appeal to women? According to Amy Gross, the editor-in-chief of O magazine, in "The Appeal of the Androgynous Man," her ideal is and the ideal of women should be the "androgynous man," a man who shares the personality characteristics of both male and female. But matters are not so simple. Amy Gross falsely divides men into two stereotyped categories. In fact, real men are much more complex.

2   To make her point, Amy Gross contrasts the all-man man and the androgynous man. She believes that the all-man man does not share in activities like shopping, has no taste in the arts, is imperialistic, resists anything feminine, and is interested in only exclusively male topics. Worse, she points to studies that show that more masculine men are less creative. Further, she argues that the all-man tends to see women as something to conquer rather than as partners. The androgynous man, by comparison, is very different. He does not resist things that are feminine and so shares in domestic activities, is comfortable with the arts, and can share interests with women. He is shown by studies to be more creative. Further, according to Gross, "The androgynous man is not your opponent but your teammate." As a result, she concludes that the androgynous man has the qualities that women should really look for in a man.

3   She is right that if the all-man male was like she said, he would truly be undesirable. No woman should want a partner who takes her for granted, doesn't share her interests, or treats her simply as someone to conquer. But is that really what men are like? My brother plays football

and loves to watch it on television. He also hunts and fishes. But that isn't all he does. He plays with kittens, loves to cook, plays the guitar and sings, and secretly likes "chick flicks." As far as I can tell, he treats his girlfriend well. He seems genuinely concerned about her, will spend hours shopping with her, goes to events that interests her, and generally seems sensitive to her needs. Is he an "all-man" or an "androgynous man"? Equally a man can write poetry, love Jane Austen, cook gourmet meals, and still take women for granted. From what I have read, Pablo Picasso treated women dreadfully, even if he was a great artist. Was he an "all-man" man or an "androgynous man"?

4   Ms. Gross seems to present evidence from psychological studies that show that more masculine men are less creative than more feminine men. Maybe so, but she doesn't give us the evidence we need to make up our own minds. How did they actually measure masculinity and femininity? How many people were tested? What did they count as creativity? Personally I have my doubts. Writers such as Ernest Hemingway and Norman Mailer where pretty masculine men and yet were still very creative. I know a lot of men who have feminine characteristics who aren't any more creative than the average person.

5   The mistake Ms. Gross makes is that she believes that women should select types of men. They shouldn't. Women date, love, and marry individual men. As a result, a woman should really be concerned about whether the man shares her interests, treats her well, has qualities she can love, and will be faithful. Where the man fits on Ms. Gross's little chart is far less important than the kind of man he is, regardless of whether he is "androgynous."

CHAPTER 3

PLANNING AND DRAFTING YOUR PAPER

Many students believe that good essays are dashed off in a burst of inspiration by born writers. Students themselves often boast that they cranked out their top-notch papers in an hour or so of spare time. Perhaps. But for most of us, writing is a process that takes time and work. Better writers are not born with their gift but learn through informed practice how to incorporate their ideas into a paper.

Although successful writers can often describe how they go about their work, writing is a flexible process. No one order guarantees success, and no one approach works for every writer. Some writers establish their purpose and draft a plan for carrying it out at the start of every project. Others begin with a tentative purpose or plan and discover their final direction as they write. As a project proceeds, the writer is likely to leapfrog backward and forward one or more times rather than to proceed in an orderly, straightforward sequence. Partway through a first draft, for instance, a writer may think of a new point to present, then pause and jot down the details needed to develop it. Similarly, part of the conclusion may come to mind as the writer is gathering the details for supporting a key idea.

Regardless of how it unfolds, the writing process consists of the following stages. Advancing through each stage will guide you if you have no plan or if you've run into snags with your approach. Once you're familiar with these stages, you can combine or rearrange them as needed.

Understanding the assignment

Zeroing in on a topic

Gathering information

Organizing the information

Developing a thesis statement

Writing the first draft

Understanding the Assignment

Instructors differ in making writing assignments. Some specify the topic; some give you several topics to choose from; and still others offer you a free choice. Likewise, some instructors dictate the length and format of the essay, whereas others don't. Whatever the case, be sure you understand the assignment before you go any further.

Think of it this way: If your boss asked you to report on ways of improving the working conditions in your office and you turned in a report on improving worker benefits, would you expect the boss's approval? Following directions is crucial, so if you have any questions about the assignment, ask your instructor to clear them up right then. Don't be timid; it's much better to ask for directions than to receive a low grade for failing to follow them.

Once you understand the assignment, consider the project *yours*. If you are asked to describe a favorite vacation spot for a local newspaper, here is your chance to inform others about a place special to you. By asking yourself what the assignment allows you to accomplish, you can find your purpose.

Zeroing In on a Topic

A subject is a broad discussion area: sports, college life, culture, and the like. A topic is one small segment of a subject, for example, testing athletes for drug use, Nirvana College's academic probation policy, the Web surfing phenomenon. If you choose your own topic, pick one narrow enough so that you can develop it properly within any length limitation. Avoid sprawling, slippery issues that lead to a string of trite generalities.

In addition, choose a familiar topic or one you can learn enough about in the time available. Avoid overworked topics such as arguments about open visitation in dormitories or the legal drinking age, which generally repeat the same old points. Instead, select a topic that lets you draw upon your unique experiences and insights and offer a fresh perspective to your reader.

Strategies for Finding a Topic

Whenever your instructor assigns a general subject, you'll need to stake out a limited topic suitable for your paper. If you're lucky, the right one will come to mind immediately. More often, though, you'll need to resort to some special strategy. Here are six proven strategies that many writers use. Not all of them will work for everyone, so experiment to find those that produce a topic for you.

Tapping Your Personal Resources   Personal experience furnishes a rich storehouse of writing material. Over the years, you've packed your mind with memories of family gatherings, school activities, movies, concerts, plays, parties, jobs, books you've read, TV programs, dates, discussions, arguments, and so on. All these experiences can provide suitable topics. Suppose you've been asked to write about some aspect of education. Recalling the difficulties you had last term at registration, you might argue for better registration procedures. Or if you're a hopeless TV addict who must write on some advertising topic, why not analyze video advertising techniques?

Anything you've read in magazines or journals, newspapers, novels, short stories, or textbooks can also trigger a topic. Dan Greenburg's "Sound and Fury," (pages 430–432) in which a potentially explosive situation is defused, might suggest a paper on some dangerous encounter in your past. An article reviewing the career of a well-known politician might stir thoughts of a friend's experience in running for the student council. Possibilities crowd our lives, waiting for us to recognize and seize them.

 Select five of the subjects listed below. Tapping your personal resources, name one topic suggested by each. For each topic, list three questions that you might answer in a paper.

Life on a city street	Some aspect of nature
A particular field of work	Contemporary forms of dancing
Some branch of the federal bureaucracy	Youth gangs
Concern for some aspect of the environment	Fashions in clothing
Saving money	Trendiness
Home ownership	Human rights
Schools in your town	Public transportation
Leisure activities	Childhood fears
The two-income family	A new scientific discovery
A best-selling book	A religious experience

Keeping a Journal   Many writers, not comfortable relying on their memories, record their experiences in a journal—a private gathering of entries accumulated over time. Journal keeping provides an abundance of possible writing topics as well as valuable writing practice.

The hallmark of the journal entry is the freedom to explore thoughts, feelings, responses, attitudes, and beliefs. In your own private domain you can express your views without reservation, without concern for "doing it right." *You* control the content and length of the entry without being held to a specified topic or number of words. Furthermore, depending on your instructor's preference, you usually don't have to worry about correct spelling or grammar. Journal writing does not represent a finished product but rather an exploration.

A few simple guidelines ensure effective journal entries:

1. Write in any kind of notebook that appeals to you; the content, not the package, is the important thing.
2. Write on a regular basis—at least five times a week if possible. In any event don't write by fits and starts, cramming two weeks' entries into one sitting.
3. Write for ten to twenty minutes, longer if you have more to say. Don't aim for uniform entry length, for example, three paragraphs or a page and a half. Simply explore your reactions to the happenings in your life or to what you have read, heard in class, or seen on television. The length will take care of itself.

Let's examine a typical journal entry by Sam, a first-year composition student.

Last week went back to my hometown for the first time since my family moved away and while there dropped by the street where I spent my first twelve years. Visit left me feeling very depressed. Family home still there, but its paint peeling and front porch sagging. Sign next to the porch said house now occupied by Acme Realtors. While we lived there, front yard lush green and bordered by beds of irises. Now an oil-spattered parking lot. All the other houses on our side of the street gone, replaced by a row of dumpy buildings housing dry cleaner, bowling alley, hamburger joint, shoe repair shop, laundromat. All of them dingy and rundown looking, even though only a few years old.

Other side of the street in no better shape. Directly across from our house a used-car dealership with rows of junky looking cars. No trace left of the Little League park that used to be there. Had lots of fun playing baseball and learned meaning of sportsmanship. To left of the dealership my old grade school, now boarded and abandoned. Wonder about my fifth-grade teacher Mrs. Wynick. Is she still teaching? Still able to make learning a game, not a chore? Other side of dealership the worst sight of all. Grimy looking plant of some sort pouring foul smelling smoke into the air from a discolored stack. Smoke made me cough.

Don't think I'll revisit my old street again.

This journal entry could spawn several essays. Sam might explore the causes of residential deterioration, define sportsmanship, explain how Mrs. Wynick made learning a game, or argue for stricter pollution control laws.

EXERCISE *Write journal entries over the next week or two for some of the following items that interest you. If you have trouble finding a suitable topic for a paper, review the entries for possibilities.*

Pleasant or unpleasant conversations	Cultural or sporting events
Developing relationships	College life: myth vs. reality
Single or married life	Public figures—politicians; movie,
Parents	rock, or sports stars
Financial or occupational considerations	World trouble spots
Ideas gained through reading	Courses you are taking

Sorting Out a Subject   All of us sort things. We do it whenever we tackle the laundry, clear away a sinkful of dishes, or tidy up a basement or garage. Let's see how we might handle a cluttered basement. To start off, we'd probably sort the contents according to type: books in one spot, clothing in a second, toys in a third. That done, chances are we'd do still more sorting, separating children's books from adults' and stuffed animals from games. As we looked over and handled the different items, long-buried, bittersweet memories might start flooding from our subconscious: memories of an uncle, now dead, who sent this old adventure novel . . . of our parents' pride when they saw their child had learned to ride that now battered bicycle . . . of the dance that marked the debut of the evening gown over there.

Sorting out a subject follows a similar scenario. First, we break our broad subject into categories and subcategories, then allow our minds to roam over the different items and see what topics we can turn up. The chart on page 31 shows what one student found when she explored the general topic of public transportation.

As you'll discover for yourself, some subjects yield more topics than others; some, no topics at all.

 EXERCISE   *Select two of the following subjects, then subdivide those two into five topics.*

Advertising	Movies	The space program
Dwellings	Occupations	Sports
Fashions	Popular music	Television programs
Magazines	Social classes	Vacations

Asking Questions   Often, working your way through these basic questions will lead you to a manageable topic:

1. Can I define my subject?
2. Does it break into categories?
3. If so, what comparisons can I make among these categories?
4. If my subject is divided into parts, how do they work together?
5. Does my subject have uses? What are they?
6. What are some examples of my subject?
7. What are the causes or origins of my subject?
8. What impact has my subject had?

Let's convert these general questions into specific questions about telescopes, a broad general subject:

1. What is a telescope?
2. What are the different kinds of telescopes?
3. How are they alike? How do they differ?
4. What are the parts of each kind of telescope, and how do they work together?
5. What are telescopes used for?
6. What are some well-known telescopes?
7. Who invented the telescope?
8. What impact have telescopes had on human life and knowledge?

Each of these questions offers a starting point for a suitably focused essay. Question 3 might launch a paper comparing reflecting and refracting telescopes; question 6 might be answered in a paper about the Hubble Space Telescope and the problems with it.

Results of Sorting Out the Subject Public Transportation

Land			Water		Air	
Buses	Taxis	Trains	Seagoing	Lake, River	Airplanes	Helicopters
County bus services for the handicapped	Rights of passengers	The Orient Express, the Twentieth Century Limited	The Titanic	Barge cruises	Airline deregulation	Air taxis
Bus tours	Preventing crimes against drivers	Monorails	Luxury liners		Overbooking flights	Cargo
Jitney buses		Preventing subway crimes	Theme Cruises		Making air travel safer	
Improving bus terminals		Guardian Angels	Modern sea pirates		Coping with hijacking	
Designing buses to accommodate the handicapped		Amtrak	Traveling by freighter		Causes and prevention of jet lag	
		Japan's high-speed trains	The impact of overseas flights on ship travel		Development of the stealth bomber	
		Deterioration of railroad track beds			Noise pollution around airports	

EXERCISE   *Select two of the following subjects. Create general questions, then convert them into specific questions. Finally, suggest two essay topics for each of your two subjects.*

Astrology	Games	Shopping malls
Books	Microorganisms	Stars
Colleges	Plays	Television
Emotions	Religions	Warships

Freewriting   The freewriting strategy snares thoughts as they race through your mind, yielding a set of sentences that you then look over for writing ideas. To begin, turn your pen loose and write for about five minutes on your general subject. Put down everything that comes into your head, without worrying about grammar, spelling, or punctuation. What you produce is for your eyes alone. If the thought flow becomes blocked, write "I'm stuck, I'm stuck . . ." until you break the mental logjam. When your writing time is up, go through your sentences one by one and extract potential topic material. If you draw a blank, write for another five minutes and look again.

The following example shows the product of one freewriting session. Jim's instructor had assigned a two- or three-page paper on some sports-related topic; and since Jim had been a member of his high school tennis team, his thoughts naturally turned toward this sport.

> Sports. If that's my subject, I'd better do something on tennis. I've played enough of it. But what can I say that would be interesting? It's very popular, lots of people watch it on TV. Maybe I could write about the major tennis tournaments. I'm stuck. I'm stuck. Maybe court surfaces. That sounds dull. I'm stuck. Well, what about tennis equipment, clothing, scoring? Maybe my reader is thinking about taking up the game. What do I like about tennis? The strategy, playing the net, when to use a topspin or a backspin stroke, different serves. I'm stuck. I'm stuck. Maybe I could suggest how to play a better game of singles. I used to be number one. I can still remember Coach harping on those three C's, conditioning, concentration, consistency. I'm stuck. I'm stuck. Then there's the matter of special shots like lobs, volleys, and overheads. But that stuff is for the pros.

This example suggests at least three papers. For the beginning player, Jim could focus on equipment and scoring. For the intermediate player, he might write on conditioning, concentration, and consistency; for the advanced player, on special shots.

Brainstorming   Brainstorming, a close cousin of freewriting, captures fleeting ideas in words, fragments, and sometimes sentences, rather than in a series of sentences. Brainstorming garners ideas faster than the other strategies do. But unless you move immediately to the next stage of writing, you may lose track of what some of your fragmentary jottings mean.

To compare the results of freewriting and brainstorming a topic, we've converted our freewriting example into this list, which typifies the results of brainstorming:

Popularity of tennis	Equipment
Major tournaments	Clothing
Court surfaces	Scoring
Doubles strategy	Conditioning
Singles strategy	Concentration
Playing the net	Consistency
Topspin	Special shots—lobs, drop volleys, overheads
Backspin	
Different serves	

EXERCISE   *Return to the five subjects you selected for the exercise on page 28. Freewrite or brainstorm for five minutes on each one; then choose a topic suitable for a two- or three-page essay. State your topic, intended audience, and purpose.*

Narrowing a familiar subject may yield not only a topic but also the main divisions for a paper on it. Jim's freewriting session uncovered several possible tennis topics as well as a way of approaching each: by focusing on lobs, drop volleys, and overheads when writing about special shots, for example. Ordinarily, though, the main divisions will emerge only after you have gathered material to develop your topic.

Identifying Your Audience and Purpose

You can identify your purpose and audience at several stages in the writing process. Sometimes both are set by the assignment and guide your selection of a topic. For example, you might be asked to write the college president to recommend improvements in the school's registration system. At other times, you may have to write a draft before you can determine either. Usually, though, the selection of audience and purpose goes hand in hand with determining a topic. Think of the different types of information Jim would gather if he wrote for (1) beginning players to offer advice on improving their game, (2) tennis buffs to point out refinements of the game, (3) a physics professor to show the physical forces controlling the behavior of tennis balls in flight.

CASE HISTORY

Now that you're familiar with some narrowing strategies, let's examine the first segment of a case history that shows how one student handles a writing assignment. This segment illustrates the use of a narrowing strategy to find a topic. Later segments focus on the remaining stages of the writing process.

George's writing class has been talking and reading about the importance people attach to their recreation and the many forms it can take. His instructor asks the class to write a three- or four-page paper on some aspect of recreation. To begin, George uses the sorting strategy and comes up with two major categories of topics: those based primarily on reading and those based on personal experience. Under the first category, he includes legalized casino gambling, vacationing in national parks, and collecting baseball cards; under the second he lists his hobby of coin collecting, his interest in playing bridge, and the recreational possibilities of his hometown, Mt. Pleasant. Because he has only marginal interest in the topics in the first category, he rules all of them out. After weighing the possibilities of the items in the second category, he concludes that Mt. Pleasant offers the most potential and elects to pursue that topic for a high school audience.

This case history continues on page 36.

Gathering Information

Once you have a topic, you'll need things to say about it. This supporting material can include facts, ideas, examples, observations, sensory impressions, memories, and the like. Without the proper backup, papers lack force, vividness, and interest and may confuse or mislead readers. The more support you can gather, the easier it will be for you to write a draft. Time spent gathering information is never wasted.

Strategies for Gathering Information

If you are writing on a familiar topic, much of your supporting material may come from your own head. Brainstorming is the best way to retrieve it. With unfamiliar topics, brainstorming won't work. Instead, you'll have to do some background reading. Whatever the topic, familiar or unfamiliar, talking with friends, parents, neighbors, or people knowledgeable about the topic can also produce useful ideas.

Brainstorming   Brainstorming a topic, like brainstorming a subject, yields a set of words, fragments, and occasionally sentences that will furnish ideas for the paper. Assume that Jim, the student who explored the subject of tennis, wants to show how conditioning, concentration, and consistent play can improve one's game. His brainstorming list might look like this:

keeping ball in play	courtside distractions
don't try foolish shots	temper distractions
placing ball so opponent runs	don't continually drive ball with power
staying in good condition	two-on-one drill
yourself	lobbing ball over opponent's head
running	returning a down-the-line passing
jogging	shot

skipping rope	don't try spectacular overheads
keeps you on your toes	chance for opponent to make
keeping your mind only on	mistake
the game	game of percentages
personal distractions	games are lost, not won

You can see how some thoughts have led to others. For example, the first jotting, "keeping ball in play," leads naturally to the next one, "don't try foolish shots." "Placing ball so opponent runs" leads to "staying in good condition yourself," which in turn leads to ways of staying in condition and so forth.

Branching is a helpful and convenient extension of brainstorming that allows you to add details to any item in your list. Here's how you might use this technique to approach "courtside distractions".

Don't worry if your brainstorming notes look chaotic and if some seem irrelevant. Sometimes the most unlikely material turns out to be the freshest and most interesting. As you organize and write your paper, you'll probably combine, modify, and omit some of the notes, as well as add others.

EXERCISE *Prepare a brainstorming sheet of supporting details for one of the topics you developed for the exercise on page 29.* ◄

Reading   When you have to grapple with an unfamiliar topic, look in the library for material to develop it. Before going there, however, turn to Chapter 21, "The Research Paper," and review the guidelines under the headings "Computerized Card Catalog" and "Periodical and Database Indexes." (If your library uses a conventional card catalog, review the guidelines in that part of the chapter.) These sections tell you how to unearth promising references to investigate. Once you have a list of references, start searching for the books or articles. Look through each one you find and jot down information that looks useful, either as direct quotations or in your own words.

Whenever you use a direct quotation or rephrased material in your paper, you must give proper credit to the source. If you don't, you are guilty of plagiarism, a serious offense that can result in a failing grade for the course or even expulsion from college. See "Handling Quotations" and "Avoiding Plagiarism" in Chapter 22.

Talking with Others   You can expand the pool of ideas gained through brainstorming or reading by talking with some of the people around you. Imagine you're writing a paper about a taxpayers' revolt in your state. After checking the leading state newspapers at the library, you find that most of the discontent centers on property taxes. You then decide to supplement what you've read by asking questions about the tax situation in your town.

Your parents and neighbors tell you that property taxes have jumped 50 percent in the last two years. The local tax assessor tells you that assessed valuations have risen sharply and that state law requires property taxes to keep pace. She also notes that this situation is causing some people on fixed incomes to lose their homes. A city council member explains that part of the added revenue is being used to repair city streets, build a new library wing, and buy more fire-fighting equipment. The rest is going to the schools. School officials tell you they're using their extra funds to offer more vocational courses and to expand the program for learning-disabled students. As you can see, asking questions can broaden your perspective and provide information that will help you to write a more worthwhile paper.

CASE HISTORY

(Continued from page 34)

After choosing to write about the recreational possibilities of his hometown, George brainstorms to gather appropriate material. The result is a twenty-item list. After checking it over, George decides that three items—the local chamber-music orchestra, little theater, and barbershop quartet—would hold little interest for his teenage audience, and he drops them. The remaining items are as follows:

End-of-the-World parties	crazy activities of party-goers
crowded streets	Mt. Pleasant Mall
Cold Water Lake	Embers Restaurant
Lake Isabella Dam	Holiday Inn
Island Park activities	Nelson Park Zoo
live bands	Mt. Pleasant Speedway
baseball games	mall parking
small gatherings	Boomer's Nightclub
Mt. Pleasant Meadows	

This case history continues on page 39.

Organizing the Information

If you have ever listened to a rambling speaker spill out ideas in no particular order, you probably found it hard to pay attention to the speech, let alone make sense of it. So, too, with disorganized writing. A garbled listing of ideas serves no one; an orderly presentation highlights your ideas and helps communication succeed.

Your topic determines the approach you take. In narrating a personal experience, such as a mishap-riddled vacation, you'd probably trace the events in the order they occurred. In describing a process, say caulking a bathtub, you'd take the reader step by step through the procedure. To describe a hillside view near your home, you might work from left to right. Or you could first paint a word picture of some striking central feature and then fan out in either direction. Other topics dictate other patterns, such as comparison and contrast, cause and effect, and illustration. Chapters 5–13 describe the basic patterns in detail.

You can best organize long pieces of writing, such as library research papers, by following a formal outline. (See "Organizing and Outlining," in Chapter 21.) For shorter papers, however, a simple, informal system of *flexible notes* will do nicely.

The Flexible Notes System

To create a set of flexible notes, write each of your key points at the top of a separate sheet of paper. If you have a thesis statement (see page 39), refer to it for your key points. Next, list under each heading the supporting details that go with that heading. Drop details that don't fit and expand points that need more support. When your sheets are finished, arrange them in the order you expect to follow in your essay. The notes for the tennis paper might look like this:

<u>Conditioning</u>

staying in good condition yourself	two-on-one drill
running	lobbing ball over opponent's head
jogging	returning a down-the-line passing shot
skipping rope keeps you on your toes	

<u>Concentration</u>

keeping your mind only on the game
overcome distractions: personal, courtside, temper

<u>Consistency</u>

keeping ball in play
don't try foolish shots
placing ball so opponent runs
don't continually drive ball with power
don't try spectacular overheads

      chance for opponent to make mistake
      game of percentages
      games are lost, not won

Since conditioning, concentration, and consistency are simultaneous concerns, this listing arranges them according to their probable importance—starting with the least important.

    Now you're ready to draft a plan showing how many paragraphs you'll have in each part of the essay and what each paragraph will cover. Sometimes the number of details will suggest one paragraph; other times you'll need a paragraph block—two or more paragraphs. Here's a plan for the tennis essay:

Conditioning

staying in good condition yourself
running
jogging   } Off-the-court conditioning
skipping rope keeps you on your toes

two-on-one drill
lobbing ball over opponent's head   } On-the-court conditioning
returning a down-the-line passing shot

Concentration

keeping your mind only on the game
overcome distractions: personal, courtside, temper

Consistency

keeping ball in play
don't try foolish shots
placing ball so opponent runs   } Placing shots
don't continually drive ball with power
don't try spectacular overheads

chance for opponent to make mistake
game of percentages   } Playing percentages
games are lost, not won

These groupings suggest two paragraphs about conditioning, one about concentration, and two about consistency.

 EXERCISE   *Organize into flexible notes the supporting details that you prepared for the exercise on page 35. Arrange your note pages in a logical sequence and draft a plan showing the number and content of the paragraphs in each section.*

CASE HISTORY *(Continued from page 36)*

A careful look at his brainstorming list shows George that its items fall into six categories: parties, swimming, parks, shopping, racing, and dining. After sorting the items into these categories, he draws up the following paragraph-by-paragraph plan:

<u>Parties</u>

End-of-World parties	One paragraph on partying
crowded streets	
crazy antics of party-goers	

<u>Swimming</u>

Cold Water Lake	One paragraph on each
Lake Isabella Dam	swimming spot

<u>Parks</u>

Island Park activities	One paragraph on each park
live bands	
baseball games	
small gatherings	
Nelson Park Zoo	

<u>Shopping</u>

Mt. Pleasant Mall plenty	One paragraph on shopping
of parking	

<u>Racing</u>

Mt. Pleasant Meadows	One paragraph on each racing
Mt. Pleasant Speedway	spot

<u>Dining</u>

Embers Restaurant	One paragraph on each dining
Holiday Inn	spot
Boomer's Nightclub	

This case history continues on page 42.

Developing a Thesis Statement

A thesis statement presents the main idea of a piece of writing, usually in one sentence. The thesis statement points you in a specific direction, helping you to stay on track and out of tempting byways. In addition, it tells your reader what to expect.

Thesis statements can emerge at several points in the writing process. If an instructor assigns a controversial topic on which you hold strong views, the statement may pop into your head right away. At other times it may develop as you narrow a subject to a topic. Occasionally, you even have to write a preliminary draft to determine your main idea. Usually, though, the thesis statement emerges after you've gathered and examined your supporting information.

As you examine your information, search for the central point and the key points that back it up; then use these to develop your thesis statement. Converting the topic to a question may help you to uncover backup ideas and write a thesis statement. For example:

Topic:	The commercial advantages of computerized data storage systems.
Question:	What advantages do computerized data storage systems offer business?
Thesis statement:	Computerized data storage systems offer business enormous storage capacity, cheap, instant data transmission almost anywhere, and significantly increased profits.

The thesis statement stems from the specifics the student unearthed while answering the question.

Requirements of a Good Thesis Statement

Unless intended for a lengthy paper, a thesis statement *focuses on just one central point or issue.* Suppose you prepare the following thesis statement for a two- or three-page paper:

Centerville College should re-examine its policies on open admissions, vocational programs, and aid to students.

This sprawling statement would commit you to grapple with three separate issues. At best, you could make only a few general remarks about each one.

To correct matters, consider each issue carefully in light of how much it interests you and how much you know about it. Then make your choice and draft a narrower statement. The following thesis statement would do nicely for a brief paper. It shows clearly that the writer will focus on *just one issue:*

Because of the rising demand among high school graduates for job-related training, Centerville College should expand its vocational offerings.

A good thesis statement also *tailors the scope of the issue to the length of the paper.* No writer could deal adequately with "Many first-year college students face crucial adjustment problems" in two or three pages. The idea is too broad to yield more than a smattering of poorly supported general statements. Paring it down to "Free time is a responsibility that challenges many first-year college students," however, results in an idea that could probably be developed adequately.

A good thesis statement further provides *an accurate forecast of what's to come.* If you plan to discuss the effects of overeating, don't say, "Overeating stems from deep-seated psychological factors and the easy availability of convenience foods." Such a statement, incorrectly suggesting that the paper will focus on causes, would only mislead and confuse your reader. On the other hand, "Overeating leads to obesity, which can cause or complicate several serious health problems" accurately represents what's to follow.

Finally, a good thesis statement is *precise, often previewing the organization of the paper.* Assertions built on fuzzy, catchall words like *fascinating, bad, meaningful,* and *interesting,* or statements like "My paper is about . . ." tell neither writer nor reader what's going on. To illustrate:

- New York is a fascinating city.
- My paper is about no-fault divorce.

These examples raise a host of questions. Why does the writer find New York fascinating? Because of its skyscrapers? Its night life? Its theaters? Its restaurants? Its museums? Its shops? Its inhabitants? And what about no-fault divorce? Will the writer attack it, defend it, trace its history, suggest ways of improving it? To find out, we must journey through the paper, hoping to find our way without a road-map sentence.

Now look at the rewritten versions of those faulty thesis statements:

- New York's art museums offer visitors an opportunity to view a wide variety of great paintings.
- Compared to traditional divorce, no-fault divorce is less expensive, promotes fairer settlements, and reflects a more realistic view of the causes of marital breakdown.

These statements tell the reader not only what points the writer will make but also the order they will follow.

Omission of Thesis Statement

Not all papers have explicit thesis statements. Narratives and descriptions, for example, often merely support some point that is unstated but nevertheless clear, and professional writers sometimes imply their thesis rather than state it openly. Nonetheless, a core idea underlies and controls all effective writing.

Changing Your Thesis Statement

Unlike diamonds, thesis statements aren't necessarily forever. Before your paper is in final form, you may need to change your thesis statement several times. If you draft the thesis statement during the narrowing stage, you might change it to reflect what you uncovered while gathering information. Or you might amend it after writing the first draft so that it reflects your additions and deletions.

Tentative or final, formulated early or late, the thesis statement serves as a beacon that spotlights your purpose.

CASE HISTORY

(Continued from page 39)

His paragraph-by-paragraph plan completed, George now drafts a thesis statement that names all categories:

> Mt. Pleasant offers parties, great swimming spots, pleasant parks, racetracks, fine dining, and excellent shopping.

After carefully examining this initial effort, he realizes that three of the categories could be lumped together under the umbrella category "recreation spots." He alters the statement to read as follows:

> Mt. Pleasant offers parties, great recreation spots, fine dining, and excellent shopping.

This case history continues on pages 44.

EXERCISES

1. **Write a thesis statement for the flexible notes that you developed for the exercise on page 38.**

2. **Reread "Requirements of a Good Thesis Statement"; then explain why each of the following does or does not qualify as an effective thesis statement for a two- or three-page essay.**

   a. My paper discusses the problem of employee absenteeism in American industry.
   b. Living on a small island offers three advantages: isolation from city problems, the opportunity to know your neighbors, and the chance to go fishing whenever you want.
   c. Although I don't know much about running a college, I know that Acme College is not run well.
   d. Increasing federal outlays for education will help us construct needed school buildings and create a better-trained workforce.
   e. Many people, wanting simpler and slower-paced lives, have abandoned high-paying executive positions for lower-paying, less stressful jobs.
   f. Vacationing in Britain is a nice way to spend a summer.
   g. Extending Middletown's intracity transit system will save consumers money, reduce pollution, and increase city revenues.
   h. Most cable TV companies provide subscribers with several specialized-program channels.

Writing the First Draft

Now on to the first draft of your essay. The writing should go rather quickly. After all, you have a topic you're qualified to write about, a thesis statement that indicates your purpose, enough information to develop it, and a written plan to follow.

But sometimes when you sit down to write, the words won't come; and all you can do is doodle or stare at the blank page. Perhaps the introduction is the problem. Many writers are terrified by the thought of the opening paragraph. They want to get off to a good start but can't figure out how to begin. If this happens to you, additional brainstorming or freewriting can make you more comfortable and may suggest an opening. Keep in mind that any lead-in you write now can be changed later. If these suggestions don't solve your problem, skip the introduction for the time being. Once you have drafted the body of the paper, an effective opening should come more easily.

Here are some general suggestions for writing a first draft:

1. Stack your thesis statement, flexible notes, and written plan in front of you. They will start you thinking.

2. Skip every other line (double-space) and leave wide margins. Then you'll have room to revise later.

3. Write quickly; capture the drift of your thoughts. Concentrate on content and organization. Get your main points and supporting details on paper in the right sequence. Don't spend time correcting grammatical or punctuation errors, improving your language, or making the writing flow smoothly. You might lose your train of thought and end up doodling or staring again.

4. Take breaks at logical dividing points, for example, when you finish discussing a key point. Before you start to write again, scan what you've written.

Now for some specific suggestions that will help you with the actual writing:

1. Rewrite your thesis statement at the top of your first page to break the ice and build momentum.

2. Write your first paragraph, introducing your essay and stating your thesis. If you get stuck here, move on to the rest of the paper.

3. Follow your plan as you write. Begin with your first main point and work on each section in turn.

4. Look over the supporting details listed under the first heading in your flexible notes. Write a topic sentence stating the central idea of the paragraph.

5. Turn the details into sentences; use one or more sentences to explain each one. Add other related details, facts, or examples if they occur to you.

6. When you move from one paragraph to the next, try to provide a transitional word or sentence that connects each paragraph.

7. Write your last paragraph, ending your essay in an appropriate fashion. If you get stuck, set your conclusion aside and return to it later.

Writing a draft isn't always so systematic. If you are inspired, you may want to abandon your plans and simply use your first draft to explore ideas. You can always revise, so don't be overly concerned if you get off track. You might uncover some of your best material during this type of search.

EXERCISE *Using the plan you prepared for the exercise on page 38, write the first draft of an essay.* ◄

CASE HISTORY (Continued from page 42)

George now uses his thesis statement and paragraph-by-paragraph plan to write the following draft. Notice the slight changes in the thesis statement wording and in paragraphing, a common occurrence at this writing stage. Without question, this draft needs extensive revision. We'll return to it early in the next chapter to discuss the necessary changes.

Mt. Pleasant

Welcome to Mt. Pleasant, the home of Central Michigan University and the oil capital of this state. You have chosen the right town to visit because there are so many things for a high school student here. There are parties, great recreation spots, fine places to dine, and even excellent shopping.

I am sure you have all heard of Mt. Pleasant's famous "End-of-the-World Parties," which have been featured in nationwide news stories. These parties are a riot, both literally and figuratively. At the end of the school year, all the CMU students gather on fraternity row to celebrate the start of summer. For blocks and blocks, the streets are filled to overflowing with people pushing their way along with drinks in their hands to yet another bash. It is probably one of the rowdiest parties you could attend. People do all kinds of crazy things including climbing on rooftops and burning couches in the street. There was even one party-goer who stripped naked. That's what I call rowdy.

If you are not into partying, maybe a mellow day on the beach would do you some good. There is a beautiful lake called Cold Water Lake that has crystal clear water and a scenic beach. This beach is the "hit spot" on a sunny day, so you will want to be there.

If you're out for some wet-n-wild swimming fun, then Lake Isabella Dam is the place for you. It is a huge slippery slide about a hundred yards long pitched at a 160-degree angle. One could spend all day there and not get bored of sliding away.

After swimming, you could go to Island Park in the center of town. This park is unique because it is surrounded by a river that flows around it; it is Mt. Pleasant's own Island of Paradise. There are many activities at the park including live bands, small gatherings, and baseball games. This park is the main hangout for teens in Mt. Pleasant. For the children, there is also Nelson Park, which has a small zoo with bear, deer, badger, and many other kinds of North American wildlife.

If you are a person who likes to shop, then you will want to visit the Mt. Pleasant Mall at the edge of town. It has all the convenience stores necessary for a fulfilling day of shopping. There is always plenty of parking.

Mt. Pleasant also has places for those of you who like to gamble. Mt. Pleasant Meadows has fun-filled, action-packed horse races all weekend long. There is also a concession stand and a bar. The Meadows is just waiting for you to bet and win big.

If you like horse racing, then you might also enjoy the car racing at Mt. Pleasant Speedway. On Fridays there is a high-speed stock car race all night long. So come see the fast cars, bright lights, and the excitement of racing waiting for you.

Let's not forget about the fine dining Mt. Pleasant has to offer. There is an elegant restaurant called The Embers that matches all the fine cuisine in the world. There is also a Holiday Inn which hosts a class A restaurant and nightclub. The club is called Boomers and presents well-known comedians to entertain you throughout the night.

Mt. Pleasant has much to offer you: fine dining, excitement, and relaxation. Why not come and see for yourself.

This essay will be revised in the next chapter.

Planning and Drafting with a Word Processor

Using a computer and word-processing software allows you to compose, save what you write, insert new material, delete unwanted material, move sections around, and when you are ready, print copies. If you can use your college's equipment and software, read the manual for your unit to discover its capabilities before you attempt to compose with it. Trying to write a paper while simultaneously learning about a word-processing program is a fast route to frustration.

Many word-processing programs can help you plan and draft an essay as well as revise and edit it. You can brainstorm or freewrite, entering words, phrases, and ideas as they come to mind. Do this for about ten minutes and then print a copy to comb for promising bits and pieces.

If you approach a topic through the set of questions on page 30, convert them into specific questions related to the broad subject area, and then enter them and your answers to them into your document. If you don't find a topic in the answers, brainstorm or freewrite further.

When you draft, experiment with your ideas by trying out new arrangements of material. If your writing stalls, note the spot with an asterisk or other marker so that you can easily find it later with a search command; then continue to write. Always save each draft in a file, if not in hard copy. You may want to use parts of an early draft in a later version.

REVISING AND EDITING YOUR PAPER

All of us at one time or another have said something careless to a friend, date, or mate and then spent the rest of the night regretting our words. In contrast, when we write we can make sure we say exactly what we mean. Good writers don't express themselves perfectly on the first try, but they do work hard at revising their initial efforts.

Just what is revision? Don't confuse it with proofreading or editing, the final stage of the writing process, where you carefully inspect your word choice, spelling, grammar, and punctuation. Revision is much more drastic, often involving an upheaval of your draft as you change its content and organization in order to communicate more effectively.

Most of what you read, including this book, has been considerably altered and improved as the writers progressed through early drafts. This fact shouldn't surprise you. After all, a rough copy is merely a first attempt to jot down some ideas in essay form. No matter how well you gather and organize your material, you can't predict the outcome until you've prepared a draft. Sometimes only touch-up changes are required. More often though, despite your efforts, this version will be incomplete, unclear in places, possibly disorganized. You might even discover an entirely different idea, focus, or approach buried within it. During revision you keep changing things—your focus, approach to the topic, supporting material, and thesis statement—until the results satisfy you.

Inexperienced writers often mistakenly view initial drafts as nearly finished products rather than as experiments to alter, or even scrap, if need be. As a result, they often approach revision with the wrong attitude. To revise successfully, you need to control your ego and your fear and become your own first critical reader. Set aside natural feelings of accomplishment ("After all, I've put a great deal of thought into this") and dread ("Actually, I'm afraid of what I'll find if I look too closely"). Instead, recognize that revision offers an opportunity to upgrade your strong features and strengthen your weak ones.

Preparing to Revise

To distance yourself from your writing and sharpen your critical eye, set your first draft aside for at least a half day, longer if time permits. When you return to it, gear up for revision by jotting down your intended purpose and audience before you read your paper. These notations will help keep your changes on track. In addition, note any further ideas that have occurred to you.

The right attitude is vital to effective revision. Far too many students hastily skim their essays to reassure themselves that "Everything sounds O.K." Avoid such a quick-fix approach. If your draft appears fine on first reading, probe it again with a more critical eye. Try putting yourself in your reader's place. Will your description of a favorite getaway spot be clear to someone who has never seen it? Will your letter home asking for money really convince parents who might think they've already given you too much? Remember: If you aren't critical now, anticipating confusion and objections, your reader certainly will be later.

Read your essay at least three times, once for each of these reasons:

To improve the development of the essay as a whole

To strengthen paragraph structure and development

To sharpen sentences and words

When you finish reading your paper for content, make a final, meticulous sweep to search for errors and problems that mar your writing. Use the Personal Revision Checklist on the inside back cover of this book to note your own special weaknesses, perhaps some problem with punctuation or a failure to provide specific support. Later chapters discuss paragraphs, sentences, and words in detail. Check these chapters for more information about the points introduced here.

Considering the Whole Essay

If you inspect your draft only sentence by sentence, you can easily overlook how its parts work together. A better approach is to step back and view the overall essay rather than its separate parts, asking questions such as "Does the beginning mesh with the end?" "Does the essay wander?" "Has anything been left out?" In this way you can gauge how part relates to part and to the whole. Use the acronym *FACT* to guide this stage of your revision.

F. Ask yourself first whether the whole essay *FITS* together, presenting a central point for a specific audience. Have you delivered what the thesis statement promises? First drafts often include paragraphs, or even large sections, that have little bearing on the main point. Some drafts contain the kernels of several different essays. Furthermore, one section of a draft might be geared to one audience (parents, for example) and another section to an entirely different audience (students, perhaps). As you read each part, verify its connection to your purpose and audience. Don't hesitate to chop out sections that don't fit, redo stray parts so they accord with your central idea, or alter your thesis statement to reflect better your supporting material. Occasionally, you might even expand one small, fertile section of your draft into an entirely new essay.

A. Whenever we write first drafts, we unwittingly leave out essential material. As we revise, we need to identify and fill these gaps. Ask yourself: "Where will the reader need more information or examples to understand my message?" Then *ADD* the appropriate sentences, paragraphs, or even pages.

C. First drafts often contain material that fits the thesis but doesn't contribute to the essay. Writing quickly, we tend to repeat ourselves, include uninteresting or uninformative examples, and crank out whole paragraphs when one clear sentence would suffice. As you revise, *CUT* away this clutter with a free hand. Such paring can be painful, especially if you're left with a skimpy text, but your message will emerge with much greater clarity. As you've probably guessed, revising a draft often requires both adding and cutting.

T. Carefully *TEST* the organization of your essay. The text should flow smoothly from point to point with clear transitions between the various ideas. Test the organization by outlining your major and minor points, then checking the results for logic and completeness. Alternatively, read the draft and note its progression. Look for spots where you can clarify connections between words and thus help your readers.

Chapters 5–13 explain nine different writing strategies, each concluding with revision questions geared specifically to that strategy. Use these questions, together with the *FACT* of revision, to help you revise more effectively.

CASE HISTORY

(Continued from page 45)

Now let's apply the *FACT* approach to the first draft of George's Mt. Pleasant essay, which you read on pages 44–45. As we indicated there, the draft needs extensive work.

FIT. Much of George's draft doesn't fit his high school audience. Most of these students won't care about Mt. Pleasant being the oil capital of Michigan, won't be able to attend "End-of-the-World Parties" (which some will find distasteful), and won't have money for fine dining or nightclubs, even assuming they would be admitted. How then to proceed? George has two choices: target his intended audience more accurately or change it entirely. Either decision requires drastic revisions.

ADD. Assuming George keeps his high school audience, he needs to expand the essay at several points. As things stand, he offers only skimpy details about the water activities and never indicates where the different attractions are located or why the mall is appealing. These shortcomings must be corrected and other attractions introduced and discussed—for example, affordable places for teens to eat. Another audience would of course require different additions.

CUT. With cutting as with adding, audience determines what parts of the essay go and what parts stay. For high schoolers, George should drop any mention of Mt. Pleasant's oil status, "End-of-the-World Parties," and nightclubs. Similarly, fine dining has no place in the essay except perhaps as something reserved for special occasions. For a different audience, some of the sections mentioned under ADD might be deleted.

TEST. The introduction suggests that the essay will first discuss parties, then recreation spots and places to dine, and finally places to shop. However, the body reverses the order of the last two, and the conclusion summarizes these features in a different order. Such false signals only confuse a reader. George also errs in opening with "End-of-the-World Parties," which could cause some readers to react negatively. The essay does flow well from point to point, although too many paragraphs begin with "If you."

Without question, George's essay requires considerable work, whatever audience he chooses. After weighing his choices, he elects to stay with teenagers and zero in on Mt. Pleasant as a summer fun spot.

This case history continues on page 51.

As you read your own essay, note on a separate sheet of paper problems to solve, ideas to add, and changes to try. When you mark the actual essay, make your job easier by using these simple techniques:

1. To delete something, cross it out lightly; you may decide to resurrect it later.
2. To add a section of text, place a letter *(A, B, C, D)* at the appropriate spot and write the new material on a separate sheet, keyed to the letter. Make changes within sections by crossing out what you don't want and writing the replacement above it or nearby.
3. To rearrange the organization, draw arrows showing where you want things to go, or cut up your draft and rearrange the sections by taping them on new sheets of paper. Use whatever method works best for you.

When you finish revising your draft, you might want to team up with one or more classmates and read one another's work critically. The fresh eye you bring to the task can uncover shortcomings that would otherwise go unnoticed. Pages 61–69 discuss peer editing in detail.

 EXERCISE   *List George's other options for revising this draft; then indicate the necessary changes if he had decided to write for readers between the ages of thirty-five and forty-five.*

EXERCISE *Use the FACT acronym to revise the draft you prepared for the exercise on page 44.* ◄

CASE HISTORY   *(Continued from page 50)*

After setting his draft aside for a couple of days, George revises it carefully. The original draft, showing deleted material, some added information, and a series of letters that mark where other new material should go, appears below. The other new material, keyed to the letters on the draft, appears following. Although this draft is not perfect, George's revisions have considerably improved the paper. He does, however, have more to do. (The final, polished version of the essay appears on pages 58–60.)

Mt. Pleasant

Welcome to Mt. Pleasant, the home of Central Michigan University and the oil capital of this state. You have chosen the right town to visit because there are so many things for a high school student here. There are parties, great recreation spots, fine places to dine, and even excellent shopping. Ⓐ

I am sure you have all heard of Mt. Pleasant's famous "End-of-the-World Parties," which have been featured in nationwide news stories. These parties are a riot, both literally and figuratively. At the end of the school year, all the CMU students gather on fraternity row to celebrate the start of summer. For blocks and blocks, the streets are filled to overflowing with people pushing their way along with drinks in their hands to yet another bash. It is probably one of the rowdiest parties you could attend. People do all kinds of crazy things including climbing on rooftops and burning couches in the street. There was even one party-goer who stripped naked. That's what I call rowdy.

If you ~~are not into partying, maybe a mellow day on the beach would do~~ *like to swim or just lie on the beach, just a few miles west* *of Mt. Pleasant, off Beal City Road* ~~you some good.~~ There is a beautiful ~~lake called~~ Cold Water Lake ~~that has~~ *with its* crystal clear water and a scenic beach. *surrounded by hills and woods* This beach is the "hit spot" on a sunny day. *so* ~~you~~ *You can* will want to be there. *always find a volleyball game to join; or you can simply throw around a frisbee, do some boy or girl watching, or just bask in the sun. The swimming, of course, is great.*

If you're out for some wet-n-wild swimming fun, then Lake Isabella *, just down the road from cold water Lake,* Dam is the place for you. ~~It is~~ *The dam forms* a huge slippery slide about a hundred yards long pitched at a 160-degree angle. ~~One could~~ *You can* spend ~~all~~ *a whole* day there and not get bored of sliding away. ◄ ───── Ⓑ

If you want to stay closer to town, can   *off main street*

~~After~~ swimming, you could go to Island Park in the center of town, This
park is unique because it is surrounded by a river that flows around it; it is
Mt. Pleasant's own Island of Paradise. There are many activities at the
park including live bands, small gatherings, and baseball games. This   *so you will always find something*
park is the main hangout for teens in Mt. Pleasant, ~~For the children, there~~
to do. If you want a break, nearby is
~~is~~ also Nelson Park, which has a small zoo with bear, deer, badger, and
many other kinds of North American wildlife.

If you are person who likes to shop, then you will ~~want to~~ visit the
Mt. Pleasant Mall at the ~~edge of town. It has shopping.~~ There is always
plenty of parking.   ©
If you are looking for something different, on Mission Road north of M-20
Mt. Pleasant also has places for ~~these of you who like to gamble.~~
Mt. Pleasant Meadows has fun-filled, action-packed horse races all weekend
For only $2.00, you can enjoy the suspense of cheering your favorite to victory.
long. There is also a concession stand, ~~and a bar. The Meadows is just~~
~~waiting for you to bet and win big.~~

If you like horse racing, then you might also enjoy the car racing at
                                                          are
Mt. Pleasant Speedway. On Fridays there is a high-speed stock car race all
night long. So come see the fast cars, bright lights, and the excitement of
racing waiting for you.   Ⓓ

Let's not forget about the fine dining Mt. Pleasant has to offer. There is
an elegant restaurant called The Embers that matches all the fine cuisine
in the world. There is also a Holiday Inn which hosts a class A restaurant
and nightclub. The club is called Boomers and presents well-known come-Ⓔ
dians to entertain you throughout the night.
                                                     Swimming, hiking, parks, racing. It
Mt. Pleasant has much to offer you: ~~fine dining, excitement, and relax-~~
is a fun alternative to whatever you are doing   this summer.
~~ation.~~ Why not come and see for yourself.

A.   If you get tired of driving out to the same old Lake Michigan beach
this summer, you might think about giving Mt. Pleasant a try for something
different. The Mt. Pleasant area offers swimming, canoeing, and hiking; a
chance to get together with other teens; horse and auto racing; a college
campus to wander around; movies, museums, video games, and shopping
for rainy days; and lots of places to eat. What more can you ask for?

B.   Canoeing can be great fun. Near the Mt. Pleasant area there are a
number of scenic rivers that are a delight to canoe. There is the Chippewa
River, the Cold Water River, the north and south branches of the Salt River,
and further to the west the exciting white-water Pine River. Near or on
each river are places that rent canoes at a reasonable rate and even provide you with transportation from your destination back to your cars.

For those of you who like to hike, Deerfield Park, a few miles west of town on M-20, provides twenty-five miles of nature trails. These secluded trails that meander through a natural forest and gentle, rolling hills can be a great place to take someone special for a quiet stroll. You will be sure to spot a variety of birds as well as squirrels, raccoons, and chipmunks. If you are really lucky, you might even spot a deer or two. Closer to town, on Harris Street, Mission Creek Woodland Park offers sixty acres of forest trails, a creek, and picnicking area.

C.   For those of you who will be going to college in a few years, you might want to take the time to wander around the Central Michigan University campus and try college on for size. Its ivy-covered brick buildings and tree-lined walkways give you the feel of real college life. When summer semester is in session, you might also want to stroll through a few buildings, look around the library, and visit the bookstore. If you stop to watch students bustle to class, you could be watching your own future.

D.   On rainy days, there is still a lot to do in Mt. Pleasant. There are several multiscreen movie theaters that give you a choice of the most recent releases. You can also engage in a little time travel at the Center for Cultural and Natural History in Rowe Hall on the CMU campus. This museum includes lumbering tools, Civil War artifacts, a variety of household items from different historical periods, and an exhibit of wildlife, including the remains of a mastodon. You can play video games at the Royal Oasis Family Amusement Center in the campus mall on Mission Street. Or you can spend some time shopping.

E.   Because Mt. Pleasant is a college town, there are a number of great cheap places to eat. The McDonald's on Mission Street is the wildest place to get a Big Mac you will ever see. With fancy chrome palm trees and glossy plastic cutouts of people having a great time, it is like an Art Deco scene. You have to see it to believe it. There are, of course, all the great fast-food places and pizza shops. If you are interested in taking a date to some place special and don't mind spending a little money in the process, you might try The Embers, a restaurant rated as "one of Michigan's finest." When you are looking for a place to eat in Mt. Pleasant, you have many great choices.

This case history continues on page 58.

Strengthening Paragraph Structure and Development

Once you finish considering the essay as a whole, examine your paragraphs one by one, applying the *FACT* approach that you used for the whole paper. Make sure each paragraph *FITS* the paper's major focus and develops a single central idea. If a paragraph needs more support or examples, *ADD* whatever is necessary. If a paragraph contains ineffective or unhelpful material, *CUT* it. *TEST* the flow of ideas from paragraph to paragraph and clarify connections, both between and within paragraphs, as necessary. Ask the basic questions in the checklist that follows about each paragraph, and make any needed revisions.

REVISION CHECKLIST FOR PARAGRAPHS

- Does the paragraph have one, and only one, central idea?
- Does the central idea help to develop the thesis statement?
- Does each statement within the paragraph help to develop the central idea?
- Does the paragraph need additional explanations, examples, or supporting details?
- Would cutting some material make the paragraph stronger?
- Would reorganization make the ideas easier to follow?
- Can the connections between successive sentences be improved?
- Is each paragraph clearly and smoothly related to those that precede and follow it?

Don't expect to escape making changes; some readjustments will undoubtedly be needed. Certain paragraphs may be stripped down or deleted, others beefed up, still others reorganized or repositioned. Chapter 15 contains more information on writing effective paragraphs.

 Here are three sample student paragraphs. Evaluate each according to the Revision Checklist for Paragraphs and suggest any necessary changes.

1. I can remember so many times when my father had said that he was coming to pick me up for a day or two. I was excited as a young boy could be at the thought of seeing my father. With all the excitement and anticipation raging inside of me, I would wait on the front porch. Minutes would seem like hours as I would wait impatiently.

2. Going to high school for the first time, I couldn't decide if I should try out for the cheerleading team or wait a year. Since I had time and had been on other squads, I decided "why not?" I had nothing to lose but a lot to

gain. Tryouts were not as hard as I thought, but I just knew I had to be on the squad. The tryout consisted of learning the routine they made up, making up your own routine, doing splits, and making a chant. Yet although these things were not that hard, I still was not sure whether I would make the team or not. The time came for the judges to make their decisions on who made the squad. Totaling the votes, they handed the results to the coach. She gave her speech that all coaches give. We were all good, but only a few could be picked for the team. As she started to read the names, I got hot. When she called my name, I was more than happy.

3. For hours we had been waiting under the overhang of an abandoned hut. None of us had thought to bring ponchos on our short hike through the woods. Soon it would be dark. Earlier in the day it had been a perfectly clear day. We all agreed that we didn't want to stand here all night in the dark, so we decided to make a dash for it. ◁

Sharpening Sentences and Words

Next, turn your attention to sentences and words. You can improve your writing considerably by finding and correcting sentences that convey the wrong meaning or are stylistically deficient in some way. Consider, for example, the following sentences:

> Just Mary was picked to write the report.
> Mary was just picked to write the report.
> Mary was picked to write just the report.

The first sentence says that no one except Mary will write the report; the second says that she was recently picked for the job; and the third says that she will write nothing else. Clearly, each of these sentences expresses a different meaning.

Now let's look at a second set of sentences:

> Personally, I am of the opinion that the results of our membership drive will prove to be pleasing to all of us.
> I believe the results of our membership drive will please all of us.

The wordiness of the first sentence slows the reader's pace and makes it harder to grasp the writer's meaning. The second sentence, by contrast, is much easier to grasp.

Like your sentences, your words should convey your thoughts precisely and clearly. Words are, after all, your chief means of communicating with your reader. Examine the first draft and revised version of the following paragraph, which describe the early morning actions of the writer's roommate. The underlined words identify points of revision.

First Draft

Coffee cup in hand, she <u>moves</u> toward the bathroom. The coffee spills <u>noisily</u> on the tile floor as she <u>reaches</u> for the light switch and <u>turns</u> it on. After <u>looking</u> briefly at the face in the mirror, she <u>walks</u> toward the bathtub.

Revised Version

Coffee cup in hand, she <u>stumbles</u> toward the bathroom. The coffee she spills on the tile floor makes a <u>slapping sound</u> as she <u>gropes</u> for the light switch and <u>flips</u> it on. After <u>squinting</u> briefly at the face in the mirror, she <u>shuffles</u> toward the bathtub.

Note that the words in the first draft are general and imprecise. Exactly how does she move? With a limp? With a strut? With a spring in her step? And what does "noisily" mean? A thud? A roar? A sharp crack? The reader has no way of knowing. Recognizing this fact, the student revised her paragraph, substituting vivid, specific words. As a result, the reader can visualize the actions more sharply.

Don't confuse vivid, specific words with "jawbreaker words"—those that are complex and pretentious. (Most likely all of the words in the revised version are in your vocabulary.) Words should promote communication, not block it.

Reading your draft aloud will force you to slow down, and you will often hear yourself stumble over problem sections. You'll be more likely to uncover errors such as missing words, excessive repetition, clumsy sentences, and sentence fragments. Be honest in your evaluation; don't read in virtues that aren't there or that exaggerate the writing quality.

REVISION CHECKLIST FOR SENTENCES

- What sentences are not clearly expressed or logically constructed?
- What sentences seem awkward, excessively convoluted, or lacking in punch?
- What words require explanation or substitution because the reader may not know them?
- Where does my writing become wordy or use vague terms?
- Where have I carelessly omitted words or mistakenly used the wrong word?

Chapters 16 and 17 discuss sentences and words in detail.

 Reread exercise paragraph 1 on page 54 and revise the sentence structure and word choice to create a more effective paragraph.

Proofreading Your Draft

After revising your draft, proofread or edit it to correct errors in grammar, punctuation, and spelling. Since we often overlook our own errors simply because we know what we meant, proofreading can be difficult. Inch through your draft deliberately, moving your finger along slowly under every word. Repeat this procedure several times, looking first for errors in grammar, then for sentence errors and problems in punctuation and mechanics, and finally for mistakes in spelling. Be especially alert for problems that have plagued your writing in the past.

Effective proofreading calls for you to assume a detective role and probe for errors that weaken your writing. If you accept the challenge, you will certainly improve the quality of your finished work.

Writing the Introduction and Conclusion

If you've put off writing your introduction, do it now. Generally, short papers begin with a single paragraph that includes the previously drafted thesis statement, which sometimes needs to be rephrased so that it meshes smoothly with the rest of the paragraph. The introduction acquaints the reader with your topic; it should clearly signal your intention as well as spark the reader's interest. Pages 222–224 discuss and illustrate effective introductions.

The conclusion wraps up your discussion. Generally a single paragraph in short papers, a good ending summarizes or supports the paper's main idea. Pages 225–227 discuss and illustrate effective conclusions.

Selecting a Title

All essays require titles. Unless a good title unexpectedly surfaces while you are writing, wait until you finish the paper before choosing one. Since the reader must see the connection between what the title promises and what the essay delivers, a good title must be both accurate and specific.

Titling the Mt. Pleasant essay "Shopping in Mt. Pleasant" would mislead the reader, as shopping is mentioned only briefly. A specific title suggests the essay's focus rather than just its topic. For example, "Teenage Fun in Mt. Pleasant" is clearer and more precise than simply "Mt. Pleasant." The essay is geared to teenage activities, not a description of the city as a whole.

To engage your reader's interest, you might try your hand at a clever or catchy title, but don't get so carried away with creativity that you forget to relate the title to the paper's content. Here are some examples of common and clever titles:

Common:	"Handling a Hangover"
Clever:	"The Mourning After"
Common:	"Selecting the Proper Neckwear"
Clever:	"How to Ring Your Neck"

Use a clever title only if its wit or humor doesn't clash with the overall purpose and tone of the paper.

CASE HISTORY   *(Concluded)*

After carefully proofreading and fine-tuning the second draft of his
Mt. Pleasant essay, George prepares the final version, which follows. Margin notes highlight key changes. Compare the revised and final versions to
see how these changes have improved the essay.

Teenage Fun in Mt. Pleasant

General title made specific

If you get tired of driving out to the same old Lake Michigan beach
this summer, you might think about trying Mt. Pleasant for something different. The Mt. Pleasant area offers swimming, canoeing, and hiking; a city
park where you can socialize with other teens; a college campus to wander
around; horse and auto racing; movies, a museum, video games, and shopping for a rainy day; and many places to eat. What more can you ask?

Slightly rearranged listing
reflects organization of essay

For swimming or merely lying on the beach, you can't beat Cold Water
Lake, just a few miles west of Mt. Pleasant off Beal City Road. This lake
boasts crystal clear water and a scenic beach surrounded by hills and
woods. Here you can always find a volleyball game to join, throw a frisbee
around, do some boy or girl watching, or bask in the sun. The swimming,
of course, is great.

First sentence rephrased and
divided into two to avoid
repeated "If you" paragraph
openings and lessen
awkwardness

If you prefer some wet-and-wild swimming fun, then Lake Isabella
Dam, a short drive down the road from Cold Water Lake, is the place for
you. The dam forms a slippery slide about a hundred yards long that is
pitched at a 160-degree angle. You can spend a whole day there and not
get bored with sliding.

Last sentence reworded to
lessen awkwardness

Canoeing can be wonderful fun, and the Mt. Pleasant area offers a number of rivers that will delight anyone who likes this activity. If you prefer
calm-water canoeing, you can try the Chippewa River, the Cold Water River,
or the north or south branches of the Salt River. If your taste runs to the exciting white-water variety, you will find the Pine River made to order. Near
or on each river are places that rent canoes at reasonable rates and even
provide you with transportation from your destination back to your car.

Paragraph rewritten to liven
and add variety to phrasing

For anyone who likes to hike, Deerfield Park, a few miles west of town
on M-20, provides twenty-five miles of nature trails. These secluded trails
that meander through a natural forest and gentle, rolling hills can be a
fine place to take someone special for a quiet stroll. You will no doubt see
a variety of birds as well as squirrels, raccoons, and chipmunks. If you're

"fine place" substituted
because "great" overused in
essay. "see" substituted to
avoid using "spot" twice

really lucky, you might spot a deer or two. Closer to town, on Harris Street, Mission Creek Woodland Park offers sixty acres of forest trails, a creek, and a picnicking area.

Island Park, located in the Pine River just off Main Street, offers you a chance to meet other teenagers without going out of town. Here you can listen to live bands, play or watch baseball games, have picnics, or just get together and talk. This park is the main hangout for Mt. Pleasant teens, so you should have no trouble making new friends. Nearby is Nelson Park, which has a small zoo where you can see deer, bear, badger, and many other kinds of wildlife.

Planning to attend college? If you are, then you might want to spend some time wandering around the Central Michigan University campus and giving it a close look. Strolling past ivy-covered buildings and along tree-lined walkways will give you the feel of real college life. When summer semester is in session, you might also want to walk through a few buildings, look around the library, and visit the bookstore. If you stop to watch students bustle to class, you could be watching your own future.

To sample something different, pay a visit to Mt. Pleasant Meadows on Mission Road north of M-20 some weekend and enjoy the fun-filled, action-packed horse races you'll find there. For just two dollars, you can enjoy the thrill of cheering your favorite to victory. The Mt. Pleasant Speedway offers you the chance to sample a second kind of racing. Each Friday the speedway puts on a nightlong program of high-speed stock car races. Fast horses or fast cars—either ensures you an evening of high excitement.

On rainy days, you can still find much to do in Mt. Pleasant. Several multiscreen movie theaters give you a choice of the most recent releases. You can also do a little time traveling at the Center for Cultural and Natural History in Rowe Hall on the college campus. This museum includes lumbering tools, Civil War artifacts, a variety of household items from different historical periods, and an exhibit of wildlife, including the remains of a mastodon. You can play video games at the Royal Oasis Family Amusement Center in the campus mall on Mission Street. Or you can spend some time shopping for clothing, books, CDs, or gifts in the many mall stores.

Mt. Pleasant has a wide range of great eating places. The McDonald's on Mission Street is the most striking place that you will probably ever see to get a Big Mac. With fancy chrome palm trees and glossy plastic cutouts of people having a good time, it resembles an Art Deco movie set. There

---

Margin annotations:

Paragraph rewritten to avoid "If you" opening, liven and tighten phrasing. Opportunity to make friends added.

Opening reworded to eliminate cliché and liven phrasing

First two sentences reworded and combined to avoid "If you" opening and tighten phrasing

Third sentence made smoother

Final sentence replaced to strengthen ending

First two sentences rewritten to liven phrasing

Final sentence: types of shopping added

Word "cheap" omitted; Embers restaurant expensive; "wildest" replaced with "most striking" for more accuracy are, of course, many other fast-food places such as Arby's, Burger King, Taco Bell, KFC, Wendy's, Hot N Now, and Little Caesar's. If you are interested in taking a date to some place special and don't mind spending the money to do it, you might try The Embers, a restaurant rated as "one of Michigan's finest." There you'll find cloth napkins and tablecloths, soft lights, and a menu offering an outstanding selection of meat and seafood. Your date will be sure to like it.

Mt. Pleasant offers enough diversions to satisfy any teenager. Why not come and investigate for yourself?

It is crucial that you view revision not as a hasty touch-up job or as a quick sweep through your draft just prior to handing it in. Instead, revision should be an ongoing process that often involves an upheaval of major sections as you see your draft through your reader's eyes and strive to write as well as you can. Only when you reach that summit have you finished revising.

Other fast-food restaurants named

Details about Embers added

Weak ending sentence replaced with stronger one

Conclusion changed to reiterate audience

Revising with a Computer

Many writers prefer the advantages of revising on a computer. All word-processing programs allow you to write over unwanted sections of your draft, add new information, delete useless material, and move parts of the text around. Learn all the commands of your particular program and experiment to see exactly what your options are. The following practical tips will improve your efficiency:

1. Always keep a backup copy of everything. Accidentally erasing a file or losing your work to an electrical power surge is not uncommon. In addition, save copies of your earlier drafts, either as printouts or on disk; selected parts may prove useful later, and new papers sometimes sprout from old drafts. You can either save each draft under variations of your file name—"COPY A," "COPY B," "COPY C"—or keep deleted sections in specially labeled files.

2. Jot down helpful ideas or comments in your text as you revise. Enclose them with a special symbol, such as < >, and either save them in a separate file or delete them later if they serve no purpose.

3. If you struggle with a section of the text, write two or three versions and then pick your favorite. You might even open a new file, experiment freely, and then use the best version in your draft.

4. Don't allow the program to control how you revise. The easy-to-use, gentle-touch keyboards can lull you into a lapse of judgment and cause you to forget whether your words are worth writing. Pages of worthless material could pile up. Furthermore, don't be tempted to do what the commands make easiest: fiddle endlessly with sentences and words, never develop the essay as a whole, and move blocks of writing around indiscriminately. Avoid being electronically bewitched and make only those additions and changes that improve your writing.

5. Always revise using a printout. If you use just the computer, you are limited to only one screen at a time. A printed page has a different look. In addition, a printout allows you to compare several pages at once: You can see, for example, how the second paragraph might be more effective if repositioned as paragraph 5.

6. When you finish revising, check the coherence of your draft. The writing must flow smoothly at the points where you have added, deleted, or moved sections of text. In addition, altered sentences must be clearly written and logically constructed. You can best check the essay's flow with a printout.

7. Proofreading with a word processor poses certain dangers. For example, a spelling check function can't judge whether you used the wrong word (*form* instead of *from*) or confused identical sounding but differently spelled words (*their, there, they're*). Furthermore, the unit will sometimes flag words that are not misspelled but are simply not in the computer's list. In addition, there are few good programs to check grammar or punctuation. *You* are still the ultimate proofreader.

Peer Evaluation of Drafts

At various points in the writing process, your instructor may ask you and your classmates to read and respond to one another's papers. Peer response often proves useful because even the best writers cannot always predict how their readers will react to their writing. For example, magazine articles designed to reduce the fear of AIDS have, in some cases, increased anxiety about the disease. Furthermore, we often have difficulty seeing the problems with our own drafts because so much hard work has gone into them. What seems clear and effective to us can be confusing or boring to our readers. Comments from our peers can frequently launch a more effective essay.

Just as the responses of others help you, so will your responses help them. You don't have the close, involved relationship with your peers' writing that you do with your own. Therefore, you can gauge their drafts objectively. This type of critical evaluation will eventually heighten your awareness of your own writing strengths and weaknesses. And knowing how to read your own work critically is one of the most important writing skills you can develop.

Responding to Your Peers' Drafts

Responding to someone else's writing is easier than you might imagine. It's not your job to spell out how to make the draft more effective, how to organize it, what to include, and what language to use. The writer must make these decisions. Your job is to *identify* problems, *not solve* them. You can do that best by responding honestly to the draft.

Some responses are more helpful than others. You don't help the writer by casually observing that the draft "looks O.K." Such a response doesn't point to problem areas; rather it suggests that you didn't read the paper carefully and critically. Wouldn't you inform a friend who was wearing clothes that looked terrible *why* they looked terrible? The same attitude should prevail about the writing of others, something that makes a statement just as clothes do. Nor is a vague comment such as "The introduction is uninteresting" helpful. Point out *why* it is uninteresting. For instance, you might note that "The introduction doesn't interest me in the paper because it is very technical, and I get lost. I ask myself why I should read on." Here are two more examples of ineffective responses and their more effective counterparts.

Ineffective

> The paper was confusing.

Effective

> Paragraphs 2, 3, and 4 confused me. You jumped around too much. First you wrote about your experience on the first day of college, then you went on to how much you enjoyed junior high school, and finally you wrote about what you want to do for a career. I don't see how these ideas relate or why they are in the order that they are.

Ineffective

> More examples would help.

Effective

> When you indicate that college is a scary place. I get no real idea of why or how. What are the things that you think make college scary? I would like some examples.

Here are some steps to follow when responding to someone else's draft. First, read the essay from beginning to end without interruption. On a separate sheet of paper, indicate what you consider to be the main idea. The writer can then see whether the intended message has come through. Next, identify the biggest problem and the biggest strength. Writers need both negative and positive comments. Finally, reread the paper and write either specific responses to each paragraph or your responses to general questions such as the ones that follow. In either case, don't comment on spelling or grammar unless it really inhibits your reading.

PEER RESPONSE CHECKLIST

- What is the main point of this essay?
- What is the biggest problem?
- What is the biggest strength?
- What material doesn't seem to fit the main point or the audience?
- What questions has the author not answered?
- Where should more details or examples be added? Why?

- At what point does the paper fail to hold my interest? Why?
- Where is the organization confusing?
- Where is the writing unclear or vague?

As you learn the various strategies for successful writing, new concerns will arise. Questions geared to these concerns appear in the revision section that concludes the discussion of each strategy.

An Example of Peer Response

The following is the first draft of a student essay and a partial peer response to it. The response features three of the nine general questions and also comments on one paragraph. Before you read the response, try evaluating this essay yourself and then compare your reactions to those of the other student.

Captive Breeding in Zoos

1   This paper is about captive breeding. Today, humans hinder nature's species' right to survive. We are making it hard for over one hundred species of animals to continue to exist. But captive breeding in the world's zoos may be just what the doctor ordered. This rescue attempt is a complex and difficult undertaking. Captive breeding of endangered species is complicated by the special social and physical requirements of individual species.

2   There are many social problems that have to be solved for the successful reproduction of endangered species in zoos. Mating is one of the most important of these problems. One propagation "must" for many felines, pandas, and pygmy hippopotamuses is the complete separation of sexes until they're "ready." Leland Stowe says that cheetahs almost never get together unless they can't see or smell each other ahead of time. When females exhibit a certain behavior, they bring on the male.

3   Male-female compatibility is a social problem. Great apes seem to be as particular as people in choosing mates. Stowe tells about an orangutan that turned a cold shoulder on the females in the National Zoo located in Washington, D.C. Then they shipped him to a zoo in Colorado. There, he took up with one of the females. The curator of the zoo, William Zanten, says he's "been siring offspring ever since."

4   Social factors hurt care of infant primates. Sheldon Campbell talks about this in <u>Smithsonian</u> magazine. He writes about the problems of breeding golden marmosets. These are monkeys that live in Brazil. The scientists found that captive-born parents neglected their young. Sometimes they even killed them. The problem was due to the fact that the marmosets

had no experience living in a family situation. They didn't know what to do. Emily Hahn writes about gorillas in <u>The New Yorker</u>. She says that those raised by humans make poor mothers. Those raised by dutiful mothers make good parents.

5   The second important stumbling block to successful captive breeding is physical problems. Ignorance of dietary needs can be bad. Stowe talks about the captive breeding of gorillas and says that when this breeding was first getting started, infants exhibited a very high mortality rate. Then the babies were given iron and meat protein, the latter rich in vitamin B-12. They were sprinkled on bananas, and the bananas were fed to the babies. The survival rate markedly improved.

6   Animals can be bred more easily if they are in an environment that duplicates that animal's natural habitat. Hooved and horned animals are an easy job because of the similarity in terrain and climate of their natural habitats to zoo habitats. Polar bears are a lot tougher. Mothers want to be let alone until their cubs are up and about. Because of this fact, the bears often kill their babies. Stowe says they solved this problem by building replicas of arctic ice caves. The mothers and cubs are left alone until they emerge from the cave. John Perry, Director of the National Zoo, said this:

> The world is our zoo—a zoo that must be well managed, its resources carefully husbanded, for these are the only resources it can ever have. We have appointed ourselves the keepers of this zoo, but we cannot live outside its gates. We are of it. Our lives are inextricably intertwined with the lives of all that live within. Their fate will be ours.

Our endangered species can survive only by nature's implacable test—sustained births by second and third generations. It will take decades to reach such a verdict of success. Thus we can see that captive breeding is beset by many problems.

What is the main point of this essay?

I think this paper is saying that the only chance for endangered species is that they reproduce in zoos but that it is hard to get them to breed in captivity.

What is the biggest problem?

I can't see how the paragraphs connect to the main part of the paper or to each other. They seem discon-nected. What does "Male-female compatibility is a social problem" have to do with the problem of reproduction or with the previous paragraph on mating? Also, there are a number of very unclear statements that leave me with many questions. How are we making it hard for over a hundred species to exist? What do you mean when you say "Almost never get together," "bring on the male," "took up with," and "an easy job?"

What is the biggest strength?

I hadn't thought much about this question, so it was something new for me. I liked the examples about specific animals and the problems that they have in captivity. I especially liked the fact that the writer gave me several problems that occur when animals are bred in captivity. The writer didn't oversimplify.

Response to paragraph 4

Do social factors always hurt the care of infant primates? Your statement seems too general. Shouldn't you combine some of your sentences? The first six sentences seem to abruptly jump from one point to the next; the writing is not smooth. How did you get from marmosets to gorillas? The jump confuses me. Also, were the dutiful mothers humans or gorillas?

Acting on Your Peers' Responses

Sometimes you need strong nerves to act on a peer response. You can easily become defensive or discount your reader's comments as foolish. Remember, however, that as a writer you are trying to communicate with your readers, and that means taking seriously the problems they identify. Of course, you decide which responses are appropriate, but even an inappropriate criticism sometimes sets off a train of thought that leads to good ideas for revision.

Examine the revised version of the captive breeding essay that follows and note how some of the peer responses have been taken into account. Clear transition sentences link paragraphs to the thesis statement and to each other. Vague statements identified in the earlier draft have been clarified. In paragraph 4 the writer connects the discussion of the marmosets to that of the gorillas by changing the order of the two sentences that precede the final one and combining them, thereby identifying poor parenting as the key problem with both kinds of primates. Finally, she indicates what she means by "dutiful mother."

As you read this version, carefully examine the margin notes, which highlight key features of the revision.

Captive Breeding: Difficult but Necessary

1   Today, as in the past, humans encroach upon the basic right of nature's species to survive. Through ignorance, oversight, and technological developments, we are threatening the survival of over one hundred animal species. Until their environments can be safeguarded against harmful human intrusion, the last chance for the threatened species may be captive breeding in zoos. But this rescue attempt is a complex and difficult undertaking. In particular, each species presents social and physical problems that must be solved if breeding is to succeed.

2   Among the social problems that complicate successful reproduction, mating problems loom especially large. For instance, the male and female of many feline species must be kept completely separated until both animals are ready to mate. Leland Stowe, writing in National Wildlife magazine, notes that cheetahs almost never mate unless kept where the one cannot see or smell the other. Once the female shows signs of receptivity, a male is placed in her cage, and mating then occurs. Pandas and pygmy hippopotamuses show the same behavior.

3   A related social problem with certain species is male-female compatibility. Great apes, for instance, seem to be as particular as human beings in choosing mates. Stowe relates an amusing case of a male orangutan that totally spurned the females in the Washington, D.C., National Zoo. Shipped to a zoo in Colorado, he succumbed to the charms of a new face and has, according to curator William Zanten, "been siring offspring ever since."

4   Social factors can also imperil proper care of infant primates. In a Smithsonian magazine article, Sheldon Campbell talks about the problems scientists encountered in trying to breed golden marmosets, a species of Brazilian monkey. Early attempts failed because the captive-born parents neglected and sometimes accidentally killed their babies. Observation showed that the problem occurred because the marmosets had no experience living in a family situation—they simply didn't know how to handle their offspring. Gorillas reared by humans may also make poor mothers, reports Emily Hahn in The New Yorker. On the other hand, those reared by dutiful mothers, whether human or gorilla, are usually good parents themselves.

5   Physical problems rival social problems as stumbling blocks to successful captive breeding. Ignorance of a species' dietary needs, for instance, can have disastrous consequences. Early in the captive breeding of gorillas,

infants exhibited a very high mortality rate, Stowe notes. Then meat protein and iron, the former rich in vitamin B-12, were sprinkled on bananas and fed to the babies. <u>As a result</u>, the survival rate markedly improved.

6　　<u>An environment that duplicates a species' natural habitat favors easy propagation.</u> Hooved and horned animals present few breeding problems because the zoo habitats are similar in terrain and climate to their natural habitats. Polar bears, <u>on the other hand</u>, present difficult problems. Unless the mothers have complete privacy until the cubs can get around, they often kill the babies. To prevent this from happening, Stowe says, zoos now construct replicas of arctic ice caves and leave mothers and cubs completely alone until the new family emerges from the cave.

7　　In his book <u>The World's a Zoo</u>, John Perry, director of the National Zoo, has spoken of the need to save our endangered species:

> The world is our zoo—a zoo that must be well managed, its resources carefully husbanded, for these are the only resources it can ever have. We have appointed ourselves the keepers of this zoo, but we cannot live outside its gates. We are of it. Our lives are inextricably intertwined with the lives of all that live within. Their fate will be ours.

8　　The difficulty, unfortunately, is as great as the urgency of this problem. Only sustained births by second- and third-generation captive animals can ensure the survival of our endangered species. And it will take decades to achieve the necessary success.

Specific details: problems with gorillas	
Linking device	
Topic sentence	

Linking device

Conclusion: quotation plus statement reinforcing idea that captive breeding presents difficulties

Collaborative Writing

In many careers you'll have to work as part of a group to produce a single document. Recognizing this fact, many instructors assign collaborative writing projects. Writing as part of a group offers some advantages and poses some challenges. You can draw on many different perspectives and areas of expertise, split up the work, and enjoy the feedback of a built-in peer group. On the other hand, you must also coordinate several efforts, resolve conflicts over the direction of the project, deal with people who may not do their fair share, and integrate different styles of writing.

Even though you write as part of a group, the final product should read as though it were written by one person. Therefore, take great pains to ensure that the paper doesn't resemble a patchwork quilt. You can help achieve this goal by following the principles of good writing discussed throughout this book. Here are some suggestions for successful collaborative work:

1. Select a leader with strong organizational skills.
2. Make sure each person has every other group member's phone number.

3. Analyze the project and develop a work plan with clearly stated deadlines for each step of the project.

4. Assign tasks on the basis of people's interests and expertise.

5. Schedule regular meetings to gauge each person's progress.

6. Encourage ideas and feedback from all members at each meeting.

7. If each member will develop a part of the paper, submit each one's contribution to the other members of the group for peer evaluation.

8. To ensure that the finished product is written in one style and fits together as a whole, give each member's draft to one person and ask him or her to write a complete draft.

9. Allow plenty of time to review the draft so necessary changes can be made.

Collaborative writing provides an opportunity to learn a great deal from other students. Problems can arise, however, if one or more group members don't do their work or skip meetings entirely. This irresponsibility compromises everyone's grade. The group should insist that all members participate, and the leader should immediately contact anyone who misses a meeting. If a serious problem develops despite these efforts, contact your instructor.

Collaboration Using E-Mail

Increasing numbers of college students are using e-mail to collaborate on writing projects. E-mail allows you to exchange material and comments at every stage of the writing process. To illustrate, you can share

1. brainstorming ideas developed during the search for a writing topic
2. brainstorming ideas developed during the search for supporting information
3. tentative thesis statements or any general statement that will shape the document
4. individual sections of the writing project
5. copies of the entire original draft.

Whenever you use e-mail for collaborative writing, it's a good idea to designate a project leader who will ensure that all members participate and who will receive and distribute all materials. Your instructor may request copies of the e-mail exchanges in order to follow your work.

Maintaining and Reviewing a Portfolio

A portfolio is an organized collection of your writing, usually kept in a three-ring binder or folder. It's a good idea to retain all your work for each class, including the assignment sheet, your prewriting, and all your drafts. Organize this material either in the order the papers were completed or by type of assignment.

Why assemble a portfolio? Not only can a portfolio be a source of ideas for future writing, but it also allows you to review the progress of your current papers. In addition, should any confusion arise about a grade or an assignment, the contents of your portfolio can quickly clarify matters.

Some instructors will require you to maintain a portfolio. They will probably specify both what is to be included and how it is to be organized. They may use the portfolio to help you gain a better understanding of your strengths and weaknesses as measured by the series of papers. Furthermore, portfolios give your instructor a complete picture of your work. Some departments collect student portfolios to assess their writing program; by reviewing student progress, instructors can determine what adjustments will make the program even more effective.

You can review your own portfolio to gain a better understanding of your writing capabilities. Answer these questions as you look over your materials:

1. With what assignments or topics was I most successful? Why?

2. What assignments or topics gave me the most problems? Why?

3. How has my prewriting changed? How can I make it more effective?

4. How has my planning changed? How can I make it more effective?

5. What makes my best writing good? How does this writing differ from my other work?

6. What are the problem areas in my weakest writing? How does this writing differ from my other work?

7. Did I use the checklists in the front of this text to revise my papers? Do I make significant changes on my own, in response to peer evaluation, or in response to my instructor's comments? If not, why not? What kinds of changes do I make? What changes would improve the quality of my work?

8. What organizational patterns have I used? Which ones have been effective? Why? Which ones have given me trouble? Why?

9. What kinds of introductions have I used? What other options do I have?

10. What kinds of grammar or spelling errors mar my writing? (Focus on these errors in future proofreading.)

CHAPTER

5

NARRATION: RELATING EVENTS

Clicking off the evening news and padding toward bed, Heloise suddenly glimpsed, out of the corner of her eye, a shadow stretching across the living room floor from under the drawn curtains.

"Wh—who's there?"

No response.

Edging backward toward the phone, her eyes riveted on the shadow, she stammered, "I—I don't have any money."

Still no answer.

Reaching the phone, she gripped the receiver and started to lift it from its cradle. Just then . . .

Just now you've glimpsed the start of a *narrative*. A narrative relates a series of events. The events may be real—as in histories, biographies, or news stories—or imaginary, as in short stories and novels. The narrative urge stirs in all of us, and like everyone else, you have responded almost from the time you began to talk. As a child, you probably swapped many stories with your friends, recounting an exciting visit to a circus or amusement park or an unusually funny experience with your pet. Today you may tell a friend about the odd happening in your biology laboratory or on the job.

Many classroom and on-the-job writing occasions call for narratives. Your English instructor might want you to trace the development of some literary character. Your history instructor might have you recap the events leading to a major war, your sociology instructor have you relate your unfolding relations with a stepparent or someone else, your psychology instructor ask you to report on society's changing attitudes toward the treatment of insanity. At work, a police officer may record the events leading to an arrest, a scientist recount the development of a research project, a nurse report on a patient's changing attitudes toward surgery, and a department manager prepare a brief history of an employee's work problems.

Purpose

A narrative, like any other kind of writing, makes a point or has a purpose. The point can either be stated or left unstated, but it always shapes the writing.

Some narratives simply tell what happened or establish an interesting or useful fact. The reporter who writes about a heated city council meeting or a lively congressional committee hearing usually wants only to set facts before the public.

Most narratives, however, go beyond merely reciting events. Writers of history and biography delve into the motives underlying the events and lives they portray, while narratives of personal experience offer lessons and insights. In the following conclusion to a narrative about an encounter with a would-be mugger, the writer offers an observation on self-respect.

> I kept my self-respect, even at the cost of dirtying my fists with violence, and I feel that I understand the Irish and the Cypriots, the Israelis and the Palestinians, all those who seem to us to fight senseless wars for senseless reasons, better than before. For what respect does one keep for oneself if one isn't in the last resort ready to fight and say, "You punk!"?
>
> Harry Fairlie, "A Victim Fights Back"

Action

Action plays a central role in any narrative. Other writing often only suggests action, leaving readers to imagine it for themselves:

> A hundred thousand people were killed by the atomic bomb, and these six were among the survivors. They still wonder why they lived when so many others died. Each of them counts many small items of chance or volition—a step taken in time, a decision to go indoors, catching one streetcar instead of the next—that spared him. And now each knows that in the act of survival he lived a dozen lives and saw more death than he ever thought he would see. At the time, none of them knew anything.
>
> John Hersey, *Hiroshima*

This passage suggests a great deal of action—the flash of an exploding bomb, the collapse of buildings, screaming people fleeing the scorching devastation—but *it does not present the action*. Narration, however, re-creates action:

> When I pulled the trigger I did not hear the bang or feel the kick—one never does when a shot goes home—but I heard the devilish roar of glee that went up from the crowd. In that instant, in too short a time, one would have thought, even for the bullet to get there, a mysterious, terrible change had come over the elephant. He neither stirred nor fell, but every line of his body had altered. He

looked suddenly stricken, shrunken, immensely old, as though the frightful impact of the bullet had paralyzed him without knocking him down. At last, after what seemed a long time—it might have been five seconds, I dare say—he sagged flabbily to his knees. His mouth slobbered. An enormous senility seemed to have settled upon him. One could have imagined him thousands of years old. I fired again into the same spot. At the second shot he did not collapse but climbed with desperate slowness to his feet and stood weakly upright, with legs sagging and head drooping. I fired a third time. That was the shot that did for him. You could see the agony of it jolt his whole body and knock the last remnant of strength from his legs. But in falling he seemed for a moment to rise, for as his hind legs collapsed beneath him he seemed to tower upward like a huge rock toppling, his trunk reaching skywards like a tree. He trumpeted, for the first and only time. And then down he came, his belly towards me, with a crash that seemed to shake the ground even where I lay.

George Orwell, "Shooting an Elephant"

Orwell's account offers a stark, vivid replay of the slaying, leaving nothing significant for the reader to infer.

A few words of caution are in order here. Action entails not only exotic events such as the theft of mass-destruction weapons, then the ransom demand, then the recovery of the weapons and the pursuit of the villains. A wide variety of more normal events also qualify as action: a long, patient wait that comes to nothing, an unexpected kiss after some friendly assistance, a disappointing gift that signals a failed relationship. Furthermore, the narrative action must all relate to the main point—not merely chronicle a series of events.

Conflict

The events in our lives and our world are often shaped by conflicts that need to be resolved. It should not be surprising then that conflict and its resolution, if any, are crucial to a narrative since they motivate and often structure the action. Some conflicts pit one individual against another or against a group, such as a union, company, or religious body. In others, the conflict may involve either an individual and nature or two clashing impulses in one person's head. Read the following student paragraph and note how common sense and fear struggle within the writer, who has experienced a sharp, stabbing pain in his side:

Common sense and fear waged war in my mind. The first argued that a pain so intense was nothing to fool with, that it might indicate a serious or even life-threatening condition. Dr. Montz would be able to identify the problem and deal with it before it worsened. But what if it was already serious? What if I needed emergency surgery? I didn't want anyone cutting into me. "Now wait a minute," I said. "It's probably nothing serious. Most aches and pains aren't. I'll see the doctor, maybe get some pills, and the problem will clear up overnight. But what if he finds something major, and I have to spend the night in the hospital getting ready for surgery or recovering from it? I think I'll just ignore the pain."

Luis Rodriguez

Point of View

Narrative writers may adopt either a first-person or third-person point of view. In first-person narratives, one of the participants tells what happened, whereas with third-person narration the storyteller stays completely out of the tale. Narratives you write about yourself use the first person, as do autobiographies. Biographies and histories use the third person, and fiction embraces both points of view.

In first-person narration, pronouns such as *I, me, mine, we,* and *ours* identify the storyteller. With the third person, the narrator remains unmentioned, and the characters are identified by nouns and such pronouns as *he, she, him,* and *her.* These two paragraphs illustrate the difference:

First-Person Narration

We would go to the well and wash in the ice-cold, clear water, grease our legs with equally cold stiff Vaseline, then tiptoe into the house. We wiped the dust from our toes and settled down for schoolwork, cornbread, clabbered milk, prayers and bed, always in that order. Momma was famous for pulling the quilts off after we had fallen asleep to examine our feet. If they weren't clean enough for her, she took the switch . . . and woke up the offender with a few aptly placed burning reminders.

Maya Angelou, "Momma's Encounter"

As this example shows, first-person narrators may refer to other characters in the narrative by using nouns and third-person pronouns:

Third-Person Narration

In the depths of the city walk the assorted human creatures who do not suspect the fate that hangs over them. A young woman sweeps happily from store to store, pushing a baby carriage along. Businessmen stride purposefully into their office buildings. A young black sulks down the sidewalks of his tenement, and an old woman tugs her shopping basket across a busy thoroughfare. The old woman is not happy: she has seen better days. Days of parks and fountains, of roses and grass, still stir in her memory. Reaching the other side, she stops and strains her neck upward, past the doorways, past the rows and rows of mirror glass, until her eyes rest on the brilliant blue sky so far away. She looks intently at the sky for a few minutes, noting every cloud that rolls past. And the jet plane. She follows the plane with her deep-socketed eyes and for some unexplainable reason suspects danger. She brings her gaze back to earth and walks away as the jet releases a large cloud of brownish-yellow gas. The gas hangs ominously in the air for a while, as if wanting to give humankind just a few more seconds. Then the cloud slowly descends to the surface, dissipating as it goes. By the time it reaches the glittering megalopolis, it is a colorless, odorless blanket of death.

Richard Latta

EXERCISE   *Identify the point of view in each of the following excerpts:*

1. The bus screeched to a stop, and Pat stepped out of it and onto the sidewalk. Night enveloped the city, and a slight drizzle fell around her as she made her way to Al's office. Turning the corner, she stepped into the dark entryway. The receptionist had gone home, so she proceeded directly to the office. She knocked on the door and entered. Al, standing behind his desk and looking out the window, turned toward her with a startled look on his face.

Jennifer Webber

2. It had really begun back in the Charlestown Prison, when Bimbi first made me feel envy of his store of knowledge. Bimbi had always taken charge of any conversation he was in, and I had tried to emulate him. But every book I picked up had few sentences which didn't contain anywhere from one to nearly all of the words that might as well have been in Chinese. When I just skipped those words, of course, I really ended up with little idea of what the book said. So I had come to the Norfolk Prison Colony still going through only book-reading motions. Pretty soon, I would have quit even these motions, unless I had received the motivation that I did.

Malcolm X, *The Autobiography of Malcolm X*

Key Events

Any narrative includes many separate events, enough to swamp your narrative boat if you try to pack them all in. Suppose you wish to write about your recent attack of appendicitis in order to make a point about heeding early warnings of an oncoming illness. Your list of events might look like this:

Awakened	Ate breakfast	Entered building
Showered	Opened garage door	Greeted fellow
Experienced acute	Started car	employees
but passing pain	Drove to work	Began morning's work
in abdomen	Parked in employee	Felt nauseated
Dressed	lot	Met with boss

Took coffee break	Returned to work	Underwent diagnostic
Visited bathroom	Began afternoon's	tests
Experienced more	work	Had emergency
prolonged pain in	Collapsed at work	operation
abdomen	station	
Walked to cafeteria	Was rushed to	
Ate lunch	hospital	

A narrative that included all, or even most, of these events would be bloated and ineffective. To avoid this outcome, identify and build your narrative around its key events—those that bear directly on your purpose. Include just enough secondary events to keep the narrative flowing smoothly, but treat them in sketchy fashion. The pain and nausea certainly qualify as key events. Here's how you might present the first attack of pain:

> My first sign of trouble came shortly after I stepped out of the shower. I had just finished toweling when a sharp pain in my lower right side sent me staggering into the bedroom, where I collapsed onto an easy chair in the corner. Biting my lip to hide my groans, I sat twisting in agony as the pain gradually ebbed, leaving me gray faced, sweat drenched, and shaken. What, I asked myself, had been the trouble? Was it ulcers? Was it a gallbladder attack? Did I have stomach cancer?

This passage convinces, not just tells, the reader that an attack has occurred. Its details vividly convey the nature of the attack as well as the reactions of the victim. As in any good narrative, the reader shares the experience of the writer, and the two communicate.

Dialogue

Dialogue, or conversation, animates many narratives, livening the action and helping draw the reader into the story. Written conversation, however, doesn't duplicate real talk. In speaking with friends, we repeat ourselves, throw in irrelevant comments, use slang, lose our train of thought, and overuse expressions like *you know*, *uh*, and *well*. Dialogue that reproduced real talk would weaken any narrative.

Good dialogue resembles real conversation without copying it. It features simple words and short sentences while avoiding the over-repetition of phrases like *she said* and *he replied*. If the conversation unfolds smoothly, the speaker's identity will be clear. To heighten the sense of reality, the writer may use an occasional sentence fragment, slang expression, pause, and the like, as in this passage:

> Mom was waiting for me when I entered the house.
>
> "Your friends. They've been talking to you again. Trying to persuade you to change your mind about not going into baseball. Honey, I wish you'd listen to them. You're a terrific ballplayer. Just look at all

the trophies and awards you've . . ." She paused. "Joe's mother called me this morning and asked if you were playing in the game on Saturday. Davey, I wish you would. You haven't played for two weeks. Please. I want you to. For me. It would be so good for you to go and— and do what you've always . . ."

"O.K., Mom, I'll play," I said. "But remember, it's just for you."

Diane Pickett

Note the mother's use of the slang expression "terrific" and of sentence fragments like "your friends" and "for me" as well as the shift in her train of thought and the repetition of "and." These strategies lend an air of realism to the mother's words.

Besides making your dialogue realistic, be sure that you punctuate it correctly. Here are some key guidelines: Each shift from one speaker to another requires a new paragraph. When an expression like *he said* interrupts a single quoted sentence, set it off with commas. When such an expression comes between two complete quoted sentences, put a period after the expression and capitalize the first word of the second sentence. Position commas and periods that come at the end of direct quotations inside the quotation marks. Our example illustrates most of these guidelines.

Ethical Issues

Think how you'd react to a supervisor who wrote a narrative about the development of a new product which exaggerated his role and minimized your crucial contribution to the result. The report might cost you the opportunity for a promotion. Think of your response if you were surfing the Internet and came across a narrative about your first date that used your actual name and cast you in an unfavorable light. At the very least you would find it embarrassing. As you mull over any narrative you write, you'll want to think about several ethical issues, especially if you're depicting an actual event.

- Have I provided a truthful account that participants will recognize and accept? Deliberate falsification of someone's behavior that tarnishes that person's reputation is libel and could result in legal action.
- Would the narrative expose any participants to possible danger if it became public? Do I need to change any names in order to protect people from potential harm? Say your narrative includes someone who cooperates behind the scenes with authorities to help solve a case of cyber-vandalism. You should probably give that person a fictitious name.
- Does the narrative encourage unethical behavior? For example, extolling the delights of smoking marijuana for a teenage audience is clearly unethical.

These guidelines don't rule out exaggerated, humorous, or painfully truthful narratives. As with any kind of writing, however, narratives can impact the lives of people; as ethical writers we need to consider the possible consequences of our work.

Writing a Narrative

Planning and Drafting the Narrative

Most of the narratives you write for your composition class will relate a personal experience and therefore use the first person. On occasion, though, you may write about someone else and therefore use the third person. In either case make sure the experience you pick illustrates some point. A paper that indicates only how you violated a friend's confidence may meander along to little purpose. But if that paper is shaped by some point you wish to make—for instance, that you gained insight into the obligations of friendship—the topic can be worthwhile. To get started, do some guided brainstorming, asking yourself these questions:

- What experience in my life or that of someone I know would be worth narrating?
- What point does this experience illustrate? (Try to state the point in one or two sentences.)
- What people were involved and what parts did they play?

When you have pinpointed a topic, use further brainstorming to garner supporting material. Here are some helpful questions:

- What background information is necessary to understand the events?
- What action should I include?
- What is the nature of the conflict? Was it resolved? If so, how?
- Which events play key roles, which are secondary, and which should go unmentioned?
- Is any dialogue necessary?

Before you start to write, develop a plot outline showing the significant events in your narrative. For each one, jot down what you saw, heard, or did, and what you thought or felt.

Use the opening of your paper to set the stage for what follows. You might tell when and where the action occurred, provide helpful background information, note the incident that activated the chain of events, or identify the problem from which the action grew. If you state your main point directly, do it here or in the conclusion.

The body of the narrative should move the action forward until a turning point is about to be reached. Build the body around your key events. To avoid stranding your reader, use time signals whenever the development of the action might be unclear. Words, phrases, and clauses like *now, next, finally, after an hour,* and *when I returned* help the reader understand the sequence of events. Don't get carried away, though; a paper loaded with time signals makes the sequence seem more important than the events themselves. Finally, think about how you can best use conflict and dialogue to heighten narrative interest.

The conclusion should tie up any loose ends, settle any unresolved conflicts, and lend an air of completion to the narrative. Effective strategies to think about include introducing a surprise twist, offering a reflective summary of the events, noting your reaction to them, and discussing the aftermath of the affair.

Revising the Narrative

As you revise, follow the guidelines in Chapter 4, and in addition ask yourself these questions:

Have I made the point, stated or unstated, that I intended?

Does all of the action relate to the main point?

Is the conflict handled appropriately?

Have I included all of the key events that relate to my purpose? Given each the right emphasis? Used time indicators where needed?

Is my point of view appropriate?

Does my dialogue ring true?

Have I considered appropriate ethical issues?

◖▮ SAMPLE STUDENT ESSAY OF NARRATION

● ●

The Beach Bum

Gail Bartlett

1   Pete Miller was his name. I met him that summer on the beach of Sanford Lake. I was lying on my extra-large towel, letting the hot sun soak the water droplets off my body, when some clumsy fool flopped by and flipped sand all over me. Jerking up, an angry glare on my face, I was ready to scream at the clod when my mouth opened wide in surprise. This fox was tall with jet-black hair and sky-blue eyes. The summer sun had tanned his body to a golden brown that made me envious as I compared it to my own vague coloring. It was clearly evident that he had spent most of his summer on this beach. Immediately my anger evaporated, and a smile came to my face. In a flirting tone I joked, "Hey, Bud, watch where you're kicking that sand."

2   He grinned back and said, "Come on out in the water, and I'll help you wash it off, unless, of course, you want it left on. I can see you've already discovered it helps for a deep tan. Ha!"

3   I decided I had nothing to lose and hopped off my towel. As we raced to the water, I could sense him glancing at me, and I knew at once that he had intentionally tripped in the sand only to get my attention. This pleased me

but made me even more self-conscious than usual. Not many guys noticed me, and I never was quite sure how to act.

4   For the rest of the afternoon, we swam in the warm water. Never before would I have wasted a good tanning sun like that day's to play in the water, but for some reason I felt this day was different. He must have been all alone, for I didn't meet any of his friends. It was only the two of us, and I was very grateful, for I knew I would not be so much at ease if there were others around. To my amazement, he asked me out for the next night to go to a bonfire he and his buddies were having farther down the beach. I accepted hesitantly, as I had dated only a few times before.

5   With great pains I tried to decide what I should wear. Wanting to impress him, I didn't wear my usual jeans and grubby sweatshirt. Instead I chose my new plaid slacks and halter top, which were not at all comfortable. While nervously waiting for him, I dabbed on a little extra perfume and a few extra swishes of blusher. The doorbell rang, and instantaneously I was on my feet and at the door. The introduction to my parents wasn't exactly what I would describe as smooth, and I certainly was not at ease.

6   We arrived at the fire about 9:00 P.M., and already twenty of his friends had gathered. They were just beginning to pass the beer, and when he handed me one I accepted for fear of disappointing him if I said no. It was not normal for me to drink, and I didn't feel myself at all. I became afraid of what his friends would think of me. They were laughing and telling jokes, but, not wanting to say something that would embarrass him, I sat silent. When asked a question by his closest friend, I could only shake my head in answer. The first hour went by quickly, for my date stayed by my side and tried in vain to include me in the conversation. I could not force myself to act normally. It was as though I were being rated, and I wanted a high score so badly I would not allow my true personality to show through for fear of not fitting in and being rejected. I felt as if I were going to suffocate. It was hard for me to hold back my laughter as the jokes grew increasingly funny. Only a timid giggle would I let escape my lips. My date became discouraged—I now can see why—but at that time the reason puzzled me. He left me to talk to a girl on the other side of the fire who was casually telling a joke. She spoke freely and with the confidence I wished I had. He enjoyed her easy manner, and so did many of the others. I could tell this by the way they were attracted to her side of the fire. Everyone was having a jolly time, and there I

sat, suppressing myself in fear. Finally the guy I had wanted so much to impress returned and asked in a cold tone, "Are you about ready to go?"

7   I answered with disappointment. "I am, if you are."

8   We slowly trudged to the car, making trite comments along the way. On the way home I wanted so badly to tell him that I was not usually so quiet and shy. I wanted to tell him how much fun I really could be and that I had acted as I had only because I was afraid he or his friends would think me odd or different in some way. But instead of saying all this, I only sat in a quiet closet, drawing myself farther into the corner with every mile.

9   As I climbed into bed, I was angry with myself and vowed that I would never be that way again. I would force myself to be natural, no matter what anyone thought. It seemed certain that I would never be given another chance with this fox. Two weeks passed without my seeing or hearing a word from him. Every day I sat and daydreamed of what could have happened that night had I been myself and a little more at ease. Things could have worked out so nicely for me.

10   Two weeks later, after I had given up all hope, I answered the ringing phone one night with a bored hello. Lo and behold, it was the beach bum! My nerves shook and my eyes watered as I told him I would be happy to go to a skating party with him that weekend. Hanging up the phone, I released an exultant scream and ran to my room to think in quiet. This time I was not going to wear anything but my usual jeans, and I would act the way I felt.

11   Through my upstairs bedroom window, I watched him slowly advance to the door, and I could feel that this was going to be the night I wanted so badly. We left the house, and I glanced quickly over at him with a confident smile as we strolled down the sidewalk. The skating rink was crowded, and I recognized most of the people there as his friends whom I had met before. I was surprised at how much friendlier they were to me than at our previous meeting. It was all because I wore a smile and not only listened to them talk but also offered a few quips of my own. When one of the guys skated up beside me and put his arm around me, I didn't look at the floor and shy away as I had done before but returned his warmness by putting my arm around him. My date seemed to enjoy my company and stayed near me the whole evening, glancing at me every now and then in disbelief that I could be the girl he had taken out two weeks before. We laughed and joked the night away, and things went much more smoothly than the last time.

12   While returning to my home he said, "I had a wonderful time tonight and would like to see you again sometime. You're really a lot more fun than I thought you were. Why were you so quiet at the bonfire?"

13   Slyly I answered, "Oh, was I quiet that night?" With a grin and a look from the corner of his eye, he squeezed my hand. To myself I said, "How much better it is to be yourself and act the way you feel rather than to try to please others." It had seemed such a hard ordeal to get the others to like and accept me in the beginning, but now I realized that it hadn't been their fault at all—only mine.

DISCUSSION QUESTIONS

1. Identify the point of view of the narrative.
2. List the words, phrases, and clauses that serve as time signals. What has the writer accomplished by using them?
3. This narrative spans about two weeks. At what points has the writer omitted events? Why?
4. What sentence states the point of the narrative? Why is it positioned where it is?

SUGGESTIONS FOR WRITING

1. Write a personal narrative about an experience that

   a. altered either your opinion of a friend or acquaintance or your views about some important matter;
   b. taught you a lesson or something about human nature;
   c. caused you great sorrow or joy;
   d. exposed you to the danger of serious injury or death;
   e. acquainted you with some previously unrecognized facet of your character or personality; or
   f. brought about a significant change in your way of life.

   Keep in mind all the key narrative elements: purpose, action, conflict, point of view, key events, and dialogue.

2. A *maxim* is a concise statement of a generally recognized truth. Noting the key elements above, write a personal narrative that illustrates one of the following maxims or another that your instructor approves:

   a. A little learning is a dangerous thing.
   b. The more things change, the more they stay the same.
   c. It's an ill wind that blows no good.
   d. Don't judge a book by its cover.
   e. The road to hell is paved with good intentions.
   f. Pride goeth before a fall.

    g. The long way around is the short way home.

    h. Sometimes too much of a good thing can be wonderful.

    i. Sometimes good intentions have unexpected consequences.

    j. You'll catch more flies with honey than with vinegar.

CRITICAL EDGE Sometimes writers create narratives by weaving together information from different sources. When developing a narrative about some childhood experience, you might supplement your own recollections by asking relatives and friends to supply details that you've forgotten or clear up points that have become hazy. A police officer investigating an accident questions witnesses, examines physical evidence, and uses the findings to draft an accurate report. A historian writing a biography draws upon public documents, newspaper accounts, diaries, notes of other investigators, and—depending on when the subject lived—other material such as newsreels, TV clips, and interviews in order to create a balanced portrait.

Integrating material from several sources into a coherent piece of writing is called *synthesis*. When you synthesize, you reflect on ideas you have found in various sources, establish on your own the connections among those ideas, and then determine how the ideas and connections can advance the purpose of your writing. Thus, synthesis features independent thinking in which *you* evaluate, select, and use the material of others—which, of course, must be properly documented—to further your own purpose. Although synthesis can be challenging and does call for judgment on your part, following an effective procedure can help ensure success. Start by jotting down the main points of information from your sources and identifying where those points agree. Sometimes accounts of the same event differ. A friend's memory of your childhood experience may differ markedly from your own. A police officer may find that two witnesses disagree about how an accident happened. A historian may discover that public documents and newspapers offer different motives for an action by a biographical subject. When you encounter this type of contradiction, you'll need to weigh each position carefully in order to determine the most believable account. Then, as in developing any narrative, arrange your material in a pattern that helps make your point.

Let's say, for example, that you're narrating the history of a suburban housing development for low-income families built on land that was formerly owned by a nearby chemical plant and later was found to be contaminated by toxic chemicals. Company officials admit that wastes were buried there but insist that the chemicals were properly contained and posed absolutely no health threat. After stating the company's position, you present the findings of government investigators who analyzed soil samples from the site. These findings revealed that the containers were corroded and leaking and that the wastes included chemicals that attack the nervous system, as well as highly toxic herbicides designed for chemical warfare operations. You conclude that the company is responsible for the serious health problems that now plague the people living in the housing development. Note how the strategy of presenting the company's position early in the narrative lends added force to the point that shapes your writing—company accountability for the health of the housing development's residents.*

SUGGESTIONS FOR WRITING

1. Review a number of articles in your school or local newspaper to develop a sense of journalistic style. Then interview several people about a recent event on campus or at the place you live and write a narrative that reports the event and draws on the interviews.
2. Read "Momma's Encounter" (page 433), "For My Indian Daughter" (page 437), and "Black Men and Public Space" (page 527) and then write a narrative that relates a particular minority experience and incorporates material from any of the three essays.
3. Take notes from several newspaper accounts of an important or controversial event and write an account of the event that includes your notes.

*Because synthesis involves using several sources, including information from published ones, it is important to read the sections on card catalogs and periodical indexes in Chapter 21 and those on handling quotations and avoiding plagiarism in Chapter 22. As always, follow your instructor's guidelines for documenting sources.

CHAPTER 6

DESCRIPTION: PRESENTING IMPRESSIONS

The sound of hot dogs sizzling on a grease-spattered grill gave way to the whirling buzz of a cotton-candy machine. Fascinated, we watched as the white cardboard cone was slowly transformed into a pink, fluffy cloud. Despite their fiberglass appearance, the sticky puffs dissolved on my tongue into a sugar-like sweetness. Soon our faces and hands were gummed with a sticky mess.

You are there. Seeing, hearing, touching, tasting. This is one student writer's *description* of a small segment of a county fair. Effective description creates sharply etched word pictures of objects, persons, scenes, events, or situations. Sensory impressions—reflecting sight, sound, taste, smell, and touch—form the backbone of descriptive writing. Often, they build toward one dominant impression that the writer wants to evoke.

The human mind is not merely a logical thinking machine. Because of our emotional makeup, we react with shock to a photo of a battered victim of child abuse. We feel stirrings of nostalgia upon hearing a song from our past. We smile with satisfaction when quenching our summer thirst with tart sips from a tall, frosted drink. Responses like these, as much as the ability to think rationally, help define the human makeup.

Many occasions call for description. Your chemistry instructor might ask you to characterize the appearance and odor of a series of substances prepared in the laboratory; your art instructor might want you to describe a painting; your hospitality management instructor might have you portray an appealing banquet room. On the job, a realtor might write a glowing advertisement to sell a house, a nurse describe the postoperative status of a surgical incision, and a journalist describe the eruption of a volcano. All are attempts to capture the world through description.

••• Purpose

Sometimes description stands alone; sometimes it enriches other writing. It appears in histories and biographies, fiction and poetry, journalism and advertising, and occasionally even in technical writing. Some descriptions merely create images and mood, as when a writer paints a word picture of a boggy, fog-shrouded moor. But description can also stimulate understanding or lead to action. A historian may juxtapose the splendor of French court life with the wretchedness of a Paris slum to help explain the French Revolution. And everyone knows the persuasive power of advertising's descriptive enticements.

Description will provide effective backup for the writing you do in your composition classes, helping you to drive home your points vividly.

••• Sensory Impressions

Precise sensory impressions begin with close physical or mental observation. If you can re-examine your subject, do it. If not, recall it to mind; then capture its features with appropriate words. When you can't find the right words, try a comparison. Ask yourself what your subject (or part of it) might be likened to. Does it smell like a rotten egg? A ripe cantaloupe? Burning rubber? Does it sound like a high sigh? A soft rustle? To come across, the comparison must be accurate and familiar. If the reader has never smelled a rotten egg, the point is lost.

Here is a passage marked by particularly vivid sight impressions:

> After our meal we went for a stroll across the plateau. The day was already drawing to a close as we sat down upon a ledge of rock near the lip of the western precipice. From where we sat, as though perched high upon a cloud, we looked out into a gigantic void. Far below, the stream we had crossed that afternoon was a pencil-thin trickle of silver barely visible in the gloaming. Across it, on the other side, the red hills rose one upon another in gentle folds, fading into the distance where the purple thumblike mountains of Adua and Yeha stretched against the sky like a twisting serpent. As we sat, the sun sank fast, and the heavens in the western sky began to glow. It was a coppery fire at first, the orange streaked with aquamarine; but rapidly the firmament expanded into an explosion of red and orange that burst across the sky sending tongues of flame through the feathery clouds to the very limits of the heavens. When the flames had reached their zenith, a great quantity of storks came flying from the south. They circled above us once, their slender bodies sleek and black against the orange sky. Then, gathering together, they flew off into the setting sun, leaving us alone in peace to contemplate. One of the monks who sat with us, hushed by the intensity of the moment, muttered a prayer. The sun died beyond the hills; and the fire withdrew.
>
> Robert Dick-Read, *Sanamu: Adventures in Search of African Art*

At first, the western sky glows with "a coppery fire," which then expands into "an explosion of red and orange" that sends "tongues of flame" heavenward and then withdraws as the sun disappears. Comparisons strengthen the visual impression: the "pencil-thin" stream, the "thumblike" mountains stretching across the sky "like a twisting serpent." The familiar pencil, thumb, and serpent help us to visualize the unfamiliar landscape.

Most descriptions blend several sense impressions rather than focusing on just one. In the following excerpt, Mark Twain, reminiscing about his uncle's farm, includes all five. As you read it, note which impressions are most effective.

> As I have said, I spent some part of every year at the farm until I was twelve or thirteen years old. The life which I led there with my cousins was full of charm, and so is the memory of it yet. I can call back the solemn twilight and mystery of the deep woods, the earthy smells, the faint odors of the wild flowers, the sheen of rain-washed foliage, the rattling clatter of drops when the wind shook the trees, the far-off hammering of woodpeckers and the muffled drumming of wood pheasants in the remoteness of the forest, the snapshot glimpses of disturbed wild creatures scurrying through the grass—I can call it all back and make it as real as it ever was, and as blessed. I can call back the prairie, and its loneliness and peace, and a vast hawk hanging motionless in the sky, with his wings spread wide and the blue of the vault showing through the fringe of their end feathers. I can see the woods in their autumn dress, the oaks purple, the hickories washed with gold, the maples and the sumachs luminous with crimson fires, and I can hear the rustle made by the fallen leaves as we plowed through them. I can see the blue clusters of wild grapes hanging among the foliage of the saplings, and I remember the taste of them and the smell. I know how the wild blackberries looked, and how they tasted, and the same with the pawpaws, the hazelnuts, and the persimmons; and I can feel the thumping rain, upon my head, of hickory nuts and walnuts when we were out in the frosty dawn to scramble for them with the pigs, and the gusts of wind loosed them and sent them down. I know the stain of blackberries, and how pretty it is, and I know the stain of walnut hulls, and how little it minds soap and water, also what grudged experience it had of either of them. I know the taste of maple sap, and when to gather it, and how to arrange the troughs and the delivery tubes, and how to boil down the juice, and how to hook the sugar after it is made, also how much better hooked sugar tastes than any that is honestly come by, let bigots say what they will.
>
> Mark Twain, *Autobiography*

EXERCISE   *Spend some time in an environment such as one of the following. Concentrate on one sense at a time. Begin by observing what you see; then jot down the precise impressions you receive. Now do the same for impressions of touch, taste, smell, and sound.*

1. The woods in the early morning
2. A city intersection
3. A restaurant or cafeteria
4. A scenic spot under a full moon
5. A storm
6. A pool or other recreation area
7. A crowded classroom or hallway
8. A construction site
9. A park or playground
10. A holiday gathering

Dominant Impression

Skillful writers select and express sensory perceptions in order to create a *dominant impression*—an overall mood or feeling such as joy, anger, terror, or distaste. This impression may be identified or left unnamed for the reader to deduce. Whatever the choice, a verbal picture of a storm about to strike, for example, might be crafted to evoke feelings of fear by describing sinister masses of slaty clouds, cannon salvos of thunder, blinding lightning flashes, and viciously swirling wind-caught dust.

The following paragraph establishes a sense of security as the dominant impression:

> A marvelous stillness pervaded the world, and the stars together with the serenity of their rays seemed to shed upon the earth the assurance of everlasting security. The young moon recurved, and shining low in the west, was like a slender shaving thrown up from a bar of gold, and the Arabian Sea, smooth and cool to the eye like a sheet of ice, extended its perfect level to the perfect circle of a dark horizon. The propeller turned without a check, as though its beat had been part of the scheme of a safe universe; and on each side of the *Patna* two folds of water, permanent and sombre on the unwrinkled shimmer, enclosed within their straight and diverging ridges a few white swirls of foam bursting in a low hiss, a few wavelets, a few ripples, a few undulations that, left behind, agitated the surface of the sea for an instant after the passage of the ship, subsided splashing gently, calmed down at last into the circular stillness of water and sky with the black speck of the moving hull remaining everlastingly in its centre.
>
> Joseph Conrad, *Lord Jim*

The first sentence directly identifies the impression, "security," to which the "stillness" and the "serenity" contribute. Other details also do their part: the "smooth" sea, the "perfect circle" of the horizon, the "safe universe," the quick calming of the water, and the moving hull "everlastingly" in the center of water and sky.

> **EXERCISE** *Select one of the following topics and write a paragraph that evokes a dominant impression. Omit details that run counter to your aim.*
>
> 1. A multi-alarm fire
> 2. A repair facility (automobile, appliance, and so on)
> 3. A laboratory
> 4. Some aspect of summer in a particular place
> 5. A religious service
> 6. A doctor's or dentist's office
> 7. A dark street
> 8. A parade or other celebration
> 9. Some landmark on your college campus
> 10. A municipal night court or small-claims court

Vantage Point

You may write a description from either a fixed or a moving vantage point. A fixed observer remains in one place and reports only what can be perceived from there. Here is how Marilyn Kluger describes the Thanksgiving morning sounds she remembers hearing from her bed as a child:

> On the last Thursday in November, I could stay in bed only until the night chill left the house, hearing first the clash of the heavy grates in the huge black iron range, with its flowery scrolls and nickled decorations, as Mother shook down the ashes. Then, in their proper sequence, came the sounds of the fire being made—the rustle of newspaper, the snap of kindling, the rush of smoke up the chimney when Mother opened the damper, slid the regulator wide open, and struck a match to the kerosene-soaked corncobs that started a quick hot fire. I listened for the bang of the cast-iron lid dropping back into place and for the tick of the stovepipes as fierce flames sent up their heat, then the sound of the lid being lifted again as Mother fed more dry wood and lumps of coal to the greedy new fire. The duties of the kitchen on Thanksgiving were a thousand-fold, and I could tell that Mother was bustling about with a quicker step than usual.
>
> Marilyn Kluger, "A Time of Plenty"

A moving observer views things from a number of positions, signaling changes in location with phrases such as "moving through the turnstile" and "as I walked around the corner." Below, H. L. Mencken takes us with him as he observes from a moving express train.

> On a Winter day some years ago, coming out of Pittsburgh on one of the expresses of the Pennsylvania Railroad, I rolled eastward for an hour through the coal and steel towns of Westmoreland county. It was familiar ground; boy and man, I had been through it often before. But somehow I had never quite sensed its appalling desolation. Here was the very heart of industrial America, the center of its most lucrative and characteristic activity, the boast and pride of the richest and grandest nation ever seen on earth—and here was a scene so dreadfully hideous, so intolerably bleak and forlorn that it reduced the whole aspiration of man to a macabre and depressing joke. Here was wealth beyond computation, almost beyond imagination—and here were human habitations so abominable that they would have disgraced a race of alley cats.
>
> I am not speaking of mere filth. One expects steel towns to be dirty. What I allude to is the unbroken and agonizing ugliness, the sheer revolting monstrousness, of every house in sight. From East Liberty to Greensburg, a distance of twenty-five miles, there was not one in sight from the train that did not insult and lacerate the eye. Some were so bad, and they were among the most pretentious—churches, stores, warehouses, and the like—that they were downright startling; one blinked before them as one blinks before a man with his face shot away. A few linger in memory, horrible even there: a crazy little church just west of Jeannette, set like a dormer-window on the side of a bare, leprous hill; the headquarters of the Veterans of Foreign Wars at another forlorn town, a steel stadium like a huge rat-trap somewhere further down the line. But most of all I recall the general effect—of hideousness without a break. There was not a single decent house within eye-range from the Pittsburgh suburbs to the Greensburg yards. There was not one that was not misshapen, and there was not one that was not shabby.
>
> H. L. Mencken, "The Libido for the Ugly"

The phrase "on one of the expresses of the Pennsylvania Railroad" signals that Mencken will be a moving observer, and "From East Liberty to Greensburg" pinpoints the extent of his journey. "West of Jeannette," "another forlorn town," and "somewhere further down the line" specify the positions from which he views the church, the headquarters of the veterans' organization, and the stadium.

Whatever your vantage point, fixed or moving, report only what would be apparent to someone on the scene. If you describe how a distant mountain looks from a balcony, don't suddenly leap to a description of a mountain flower; you couldn't see it from your vantage point.

EXERCISES

1. **Writing as a fixed observer, describe in a paragraph your impressions of one of the following. Be sure to indicate your vantage point.**

   a. A post office lobby two weeks before Christmas
   b. The scene following a traffic accident
   c. A classroom when the bell rings
   d. A campus lounge
   e. An office
   f. The entrance to some building

2. **Writing as a moving observer, describe in a paragraph or two your impressions as you do one of the following things. Clearly signal your movements to the reader.**

   a. Walk from one class to another
   b. Shop in a supermarket or clothing store
   c. Walk from your home to the corner
   d. Cross a long bridge
   e. Water-ski
   f. Go through a ticket line and enter a theater, auditorium, or sports arena

Selection of Details

Effective description depends as much on exclusion as on inclusion. Don't try to pack every possible detail into your paper by providing an inventory of, for example, a room's contents or a natural setting's elements. Such an approach shows only that you can see, not write. Instead, select details that deliberately point toward the mood or feeling you intend to create. Read the following student description:

> At night, a restful stillness falls over the suburbs. . . . Everyone has vanished inside the carefully maintained homes that line the winding streets. The children have gone to bed, leaving the occasional motionless wagon or tricycle in the driveway. A light gleams in some bedroom windows. TV sets silently flicker a tranquil blue in a few living rooms. The street lamps curve protectively over the empty streets and sidewalks. The

stillness is only disturbed by the brief, familiar bark of a neighbor's dog, quickly hushed, intensifying in its wake the silence that holds sway with the dark.

Kim Granger

This writer evokes a sense of stillness by noting "the occasional motionless wagon or tricycle," that "TV sets silently flicker a tranquil blue," that "The street lamps curve protectively," that the dog is "quickly hushed." She ignores the car that cruises homeward, stereo booming; the husband and wife screaming at each other; the caterwauling cat fight. Mentioning these things would detract from the desired mood.

Arrangement of Details

Description, like any other writing, must have a clear pattern of organization to guide the reader and help you fulfill your purpose. Often some spatial arrangement works nicely. You might, for example, move systematically from top to bottom, left to right, front to back, nearby to far away, or the reverse of these patterns. To describe Saturday afternoon at the football game, you might start with the crowded parking lot; move into the bustling stadium; and finally zoom in on the sights, sounds, and smells of the playing field. Or if you wanted to highlight the surroundings rather than the central event, the order could be reversed. Going another route, you might start with some striking central feature and then branch out to the things around it. To capture the center of a mall, you might first describe its ornate fountain illuminated with flashing, multicolored lights, shift to the reflection of the lights on the skylight above, and end by portraying the surrounding store fronts.

Sometimes a description follows a time sequence. A writer might, for example, portray the changes in a woodland setting as winter gives way to spring and spring, in turn, yields to summer.

Ethical Issues

Imagine a police description of an auto accident that misstated the length of a car's skid marks or failed to note the icy patches of road at the scene. It might cost a blameless driver a heavy fine and a steep increase in auto insurance premiums. Imagine your disappointment and anger if you booked a weekend at a distant resort only to find it situated on an algae-covered pond instead of the beautiful lake described in the brochure. Imagine your irritation if a going-out-of-business sale described as "fabulous" turned out to offer only 10 percent price reductions. Clearly, inaccurate descriptions can create a wide range of undesirable consequences. Ask and answer these questions about your description.

- Would readers find my writing credible if they were at the scene?
- Are readers given adequate clues so that they will recognize any deliberate exaggeration?
- Will the description deceive readers in a harmful way?

You have an ethical obligation to present a reasonably accurate portrayal of your topic.

Writing a Description

Planning and Drafting the Description

If you're choosing your own topic, always select one that is familiar. Don't describe the inside of a restaurant kitchen or Old Faithful geyser in Yellowstone National Park if you've never seen either one. Instead, opt for some place where you've actually worked or a locale you've recently visited. If you keep a journal, thumb through it for possible leads.

For each potential topic that surfaces, ask yourself the following questions. They will direct your attention to matters you'll need to address.

What do I want to accomplish by writing this description? Create one or more impressions? Help the reader understand something? Persuade the reader to act?

Who is my audience and why would this topic interest them?

What dominant impression will I develop?

To help gather and organize support for your topic, pose these additional questions:

What details should I include?

What sensory impressions are associated with each detail? (Jot down any words that you feel will best convey the impressions.)

How does each detail contribute to the dominant impression?

What sequence should I follow in presenting my impressions? (Map out the sequence, setting up a 1-2-3 listing or possibly a paragraph-by-paragraph plan.)

After brainstorming a list of potential details, you might use branching (see page 92) to start accumulating sensory impressions. Page 92 illustrates how student writer Kim Swiger used branching to obtain and group the sensory impressions for a paragraph describing the sounds of her kitchen at breakfast time. Note that her grouping provided Swiger with the pattern used to organize her paragraph. Thus, the paragraph begins with stove-related sounds, moves to sounds associated with coffee-making and cooking, and ends with the sounds of mixing orange juice.

```
                                              ┌─── hissing sound
                                  stove ──────┼─── gas whoosh
                                              └─── hum of flame

                                              ┌─── gurgling water
                                  coffee ─────┴─── gloop sound

                                              ┌─── crackling butter
   Breakfast                       food ──────┼─── frying egg
                                              ├─── sizzling bacon
                                              └─── bread wrapper sound

                                              ┌─── whir of opener
                                  juice ──────┼─── whiz of blender
                                              └─── fizz of bubbles
```

Begin your paper with an introduction that eases the reader into your topic. You might, for example, provide a historical overview, ask a provocative question, or snare the reader's attention with an arresting statement.

Develop each major feature in one or more paragraphs. Present each feature in the order you've mapped out. To ensure that the reader follows your thoughts, clearly signal any shifts in vantage point or time. As you write, aim for vivid, original language. We've all encountered writers who tell us that raindrops "pitter-patter," clouds are "fleecy white," and the sun is "a ball of fire." Such stale, worn-out language does nothing to sharpen our vision of the rain, the clouds, or the sun. The Swiger paragraph avoids this pitfall.

> Sure signs of a new day are the sounds in the kitchen as breakfast is prepared. The high sigh of the gas just before it whooshes into flame and settles into a whispering hum blends with the gurgling of the water for the morning coffee. Soon the gloop, gloop, gloop of the coffee sets up a perky beat. Then in mingles the crackle of creamy butter on a hot skillet and the shush of an egg added to the pan. Ribbons of bacon start to sizzle in the spitting grease. The soft rustle of plastic as bread is removed from its wrapper contributes to the medley. The can opener whirs, and the orange juice concentrate drops with a splat into the blender, which whizzes together the orange cylinder and splashed-in water. For minutes after the blender stops, bubbles of various sizes fizz.
>
> Kim Burson Swiger

You are there in the kitchen, hearing the carefully selected and freshly described sounds.

A word of caution about making your writing vivid. Some students are tempted to enhance their descriptions by stringing together a chain of adjectives without considering the effect on a reader. Think how you'd react if told that

> A dented, cylindrical, silver-gray, foul-smelling, overloaded trash can sat in the alley.

As you can see, more than the garbage can is overloaded here. Resist the temptation to inject similar sentences into your description. Carefully examine your adjectives and eliminate those that don't advance your purpose.

End your paper by pulling your material together in some way. If you've created an impression or mood, you might offer your reaction to it. If you want your reader to understand something, you might spell your message out. If you wish to persuade, you might urge some action.

Revising the Description

As you revise, apply the guidelines in Chapter 4 and ask the following questions:

Have I written with a clear sense of purpose and audience in mind?

Have I conveyed how my topic looks, sounds, feels, tastes, or smells? Would comparisons or more precise descriptive terms help convey my perceptions?

Have I evoked one dominant impression? Can I strengthen this impression by adding certain selected details? By eliminating details that detract from the impression?

Have I used an appropriate vantage point? If the observer is moving, have I signaled changes in location? Have I included only details that would be visible to the observer?

Have I arranged my details in an order appropriate to the topic?

Have I considered appropriate ethical issues?

SAMPLE STUDENT ESSAY OF DESCRIPTION

The Big One

Rebecca Mutch

1   With a final crack of a bat and a lofting fly ball, baseball ended for the year. The last swirl of water gurgling down the drain of the community pool marked the end of its season. These closings marked the beginning of another event, the county fair. This season I was elected to take my little brother on a ride—"the big one," in his words.

2   Once again I found myself in the familiar grass lot bordering the fairground. The fair itself was completely surrounded by a fence. No one could see what was inside. The only clues were carried in the wind. Muffled echoes of carnies hawking their games, excited squeals of children, and blaring carnival tunes, frequently punctuated by sharp, crackling static, blended with the tantalizing fragrance of popcorn, the spicy aroma of pizza, and the sweet molasses smell of caramel corn.

3   As we entered the main gate and handed our tickets to the men whose baskets already overflowed with torn stubs, my eyes immediately confirmed what my ears and nose had already reported. In one step we

had gone from a semiquiet and relaxed world into an ever-revolving one. Dazzling lights, blinking out of control, seemed to flirt with anyone and everyone. Children, their white T-shirts covered with splotches of chocolate and mustard, dashed ahead of their parents and returned shortly, screaming about the giant bear that waited ahead. The distant, shuffling crowds appeared as moving shadows, their features blurred.

4   The little tug on my sleeve reminded me of that big ride that waited ahead. The path up the midway, packed with a cushion of sawdust, was strewn with empty popcorn boxes, scraps of papers, and crumpled cigarette packages.

5   Game booths and food huts, their pennants whipping and snapping in the wind, dotted the path on both sides and formed two long serpent-like strings of pleasure. BB's clinked against tin objects in the shooting gallery. Hawkers with greased hands and pudgy fingers tried to lure suckers toward their gaudy booths. A backboard thudded and a hoop clanked as still another young man tried to win the enormous purple teddy bear that smiled down mockingly from its perch above. The sound of hot dogs sizzling on a grease-spattered grill gave way to the whirling buzz of a cotton-candy machine. Fascinated, we watched as the white cardboard cone was slowly transformed into a pink, fluffy cloud. Despite their fiberglass appearance, the sticky puffs dissolved on my tongue into a sugar-like sweetness. Soon our faces and hands were gummed with a sticky mess.

6   We scuffled along with the rhythm of the crowd and before long arrived at those metallic contraptions of nuts and bolts—the rides. The sounds of metal clanging and banging filled the air. Sparks shot out from where the metal pieces slapped together. Swirling and whirling, these pieces caught the reflection of the neon lights and, together with the sparks, produced a world of spectrum colors.

7   This was it. The Ferris wheel stood towering before us. As the seat gently swayed, we waited for the ride to begin. The motor belched and then slowly started to turn; goose bumps formed on my brother's bare arms, and his eyes grew larger as the ride picked up speed. The fairground was soon a kaleidoscope of fantastic images and colors. The wind whipped through my hair and snapped it back, stinging my face at times. Both of us were screaming uncontrollably. Suddenly, with no apparent slowdown, the ride was over, and we made our way dizzily to the car.

8   My brother talked about the big one for weeks. For me it brought back many fond memories and let me, just for an evening, be a child again.

DISCUSSION QUESTIONS

1. This description features a moving observer. Where are the writer's movements indicated?
2. Point out details that appeal to each of the five senses.

3. Reread paragraph 7. Identify perceptual observations used to describe the Ferris wheel ride.

4. How is the essay organized? Given its purpose, why is this pattern effective?

SUGGESTIONS FOR WRITING

Choose one of the following topics or another that your instructor approves for a properly focused essay of description. Create a dominant impression by using carefully chosen, well-organized details observed from an appropriate vantage point. Try to write so that the reader actually experiences your description.

1. Holiday shopping
2. A concert of some type
3. An exercise class
4. A crafts class
5. An amusement park, a miniature or full-sized golf course, or some other type of recreational facility
6. A juice bar or coffee shop
7. A pet store or zoo
8. The lobby of a theater
9. A professional wrestling performance
10. A shopping center or minimart
11. A fast-food restaurant
12. Some type of party
13. An outdoor place of special importance to you
14. A Thanksgiving dinner
15. A reunion of some type
16. A NASCAR race
17. A video game arcade
18. An advertisement
19. A scene of environmental damage
20. A historical building or site

CRITICAL EDGE   Most of us know that any two people are likely to see and describe the same object, place, or event differently. A motorist whose car broke down in the desert would note the impossible distances, the barrenness, the absence of human life, the blazing sun. A biologist who was well-supplied with food and water would see a rich ecosystem with a wide variety of plant life and an interesting population of insects and animals. Each would produce a different description that served a different purpose. The motorist would emphasize the grueling heat and desolation to establish the danger of the situation. The biologist would provide a detailed description of the plants, insects, and animals to advance scientific understanding of the area.

As a writer, you may occasionally need to synthesize (see pages 82–83) information supplied by others when creating your own description. Suppose that you're writing a paper about the old growth forests of Oregon. You may read a naturalist's description of the ancient, rare species of trees and how the forest provides a habitat for much unique wildlife. You might also read a lumber industry study indicating that the trees are an important economic resource. You might even uncover an account by an early explorer that captures the emotions aroused by the discovery of the forest.

Armed with these and other descriptions, you could create a composite picture that captures all the different perspectives. You might start by offering the views of the Native American forest dwellers, then detail the towering majesty of the trees and the abundance of game as reported by early explorers. Next, you might turn to the accounts of early farmers, who regarded the forest as an obstacle to be cleared away, and continue by presenting the view of the forest as a lumber resource, perhaps including a description of a depleted lumbering site. To end the paper, you might note how contemporary conservationists view what remains of the forest. Collectively, this information would offer a stark portrayal of the near-total destruction of a splendid natural resource and by implication argue for preserving what is left. While this kind of writing task seems daunting, you can simplify it if you take up one perspective at a time.

Because different people are likely to see and describe the same object, place, or event differently, it's important to look critically at any description you consider for your paper. When you finish reading, ask yourself what features might have been omitted and what another slant on the material might have yielded. To illustrate, in "Once More to the Lake" E. B. White describes early morning fishing as follows: "We went fishing the first morning. I felt the same damp moss covering the worms in the bait can, and saw the dragonfly alight on the tip of my rod as it hovered a few inches from the surface of the water." (See paragraph 5, page 451.) If White had found fishing repugnant, he could just as easily have described the worms squiggling in the can as if they were afraid of the hook, the slimy feel of his hands after baiting the hook, the swarm of mosquitoes around his face, and the tangle in his line. Clearly, description demands choices. Different impressions and varying emphases can be selected. And like any other writer, you should carefully consider the details and slant of any description you write.*

SUGGESTIONS FOR WRITING

1. Select a famous U.S. landmark, such as the Grand Canyon, and read several writers' descriptions of it. After taking notes, write a description that includes their differing perspectives.
2. Rewrite a shortened version of an essay such as "Once More to the Lake" by building on the original details to create a different emphasis.
3. Interview several students to learn their impressions of your campus and weave those impressions into a descriptive essay.

---

*Because this type of paper includes information from published sources, it is important to read the sections on card catalogs and periodical indexes in Chapter 21 and those on handling quotations and avoiding plagiarism in Chapter 22. As always, follow your instructor's guidelines for documenting sources.

PROCESS ANALYSIS: EXPLAINING HOW

"Hey Bill, I'd like you to take a look at Mr. Gorgerise's car. He's really fuming. Says the engine's burning too much oil, running rough, and getting poor mileage. Check it out and see what you can find."

Bill begins by removing the spark plugs, hooking a remote-control starter to the starter in the car, and grounding the ignition to prevent the car's starting accidentally. Next, he fits a compression pressure gauge into the spark plug hole by cylinder number one, starts the engine, and reads and records the pressure; then he does the same for each of the other cylinders. Finally, he compares the readings with one another and the automaker's engine specs. The verdict? An excessively worn engine that needs rebuilding. Bill has carried out a *process*, just one among many that fill his workdays.

As we pursue our affairs, we perform processes almost constantly, ranging from such daily rituals as brewing a pot of coffee and flossing our teeth to taking a picture, burning a compact disc, preparing for a date, or replacing a light switch. Often we share our special technique for doing something—for example, making chicken cacciatore—by passing it on to a friend.

Many popular publications feature process analyses that help readers to sew zippers in garments, build catamarans, live within their means, and improve their wok technique. Process analysis also frequently helps you meet the writing demands of your courses. A political science instructor may ask you to explain how your state's governor won nomination, or a biology instructor may want an explanation of how bees find their way back to the hive. Another instructor may call for directions relating to some process in your field—for example, analyzing a chemical compound, taking fingerprints, or obtaining a blood sample.

On the job, a greenhouse crew leader may provide summer employees with directions for planting various kinds of shrubs and flowers. A technical writer may prepare a list of steps for workers to follow when unloading a particular solvent from a tank car. A sanitation department technician may write a brochure telling city residents how to get paper, glass, and metal trash ready for recycling.

As these examples show, a process can be nontechnical, historical, scientific, natural, or technical.

Kinds of Process Analysis Papers

Process papers fall into two categories: those intended for readers who will perform the process and those intended to explain the process for nonperformers. Papers in either category can range from highly technical and sophisticated to nonspecialized and simple.

Processes for Readers Who Will Perform Them   The audience for these papers may be technical and professional personnel who need the information to carry out a work-related task or individuals who want to perform the process for themselves.

A how-to-do-it paper must include everything the reader needs to know in order to ensure a successful outcome. Its directions take the form of polite commands, often addressing readers directly as "you." This approach helps involve readers in the explanation and emphasizes that the directions must, not merely should, be followed. Here is an illustration:

> To prepare a bacterial smear for staining, first use an inoculating loop to place a drop of distilled water on a clean glass microscope slide. Next, pass the loop and the opening of the tube containing the bacterial culture to be examined through a Bunsen burner flame to sterilize them. From the tube, remove a small bit of culture with the loop, and rub the loop in the drop of water on the slide until the water covers an area one and one-half inches long and approximately the width of the slide. Next, reflame the opening of the culture tube to prevent contamination of the culture, and then plug it shut. Allow the smear to air dry, and then pass the slide, smear side up, through the flame of the burner until it is warm to the touch. The dried smear should have a cloudy, milky-white appearance.
>
> Darryl Williams

Processes for Readers Who Won't Perform Them   These papers may tell how some process is or was performed or how it occurs or occurred. A paper might, for instance, detail the stages of grief, the procedure involved in an operation, the role of speech in the development of children's thinking, or the sequence involved in shutting down a nuclear reactor. These papers serve many purposes— for example, to satisfy popular curiosity; to point out the importance, difficulty, or danger of a process; or to cast a process in a favorable or unfavorable light. Even though the writers of such papers often explain their topic in considerable detail, they do not intend to provide enough information for readers to carry out the process.

Papers of this sort present the needed information without using polite commands. Sometimes a noun, a pronoun like *I, we, he, she,* or *it,* or a noun–pronoun combination identifies the performer(s). At other times, the performer remains unidentified. Three examples follow.

Pronouns Identify Performer

Thus, when I now approach a stack of three two-inch cinder blocks to attempt a breaking feat, I do not set myself to "try hard," or to summon up all my strength. Instead I relax, sinking my awareness into my belly and legs, feeling my connection with the ground. I breathe deeply, mentally directing the breath through my torso, legs, and arms. I imagine a line of force coming up from the ground through my legs, down one arm, and out through the stone slabs, and down again into the ground, penetrating to the center of the earth. I do not focus any attention on the objects to be broken. Although when I am lifting or holding them in a normal state of consciousness the blocks seem tremendously dense, heavy, and hard, in the course of my one- or two-minute preparation their reality seems to change, as indeed the reality of the whole situation changes. . . . When I make my final approach to the bricks, if I regard them at all they seem light, airy, and friendly; they do not have the insistent inner drive in them that I do.

Don Ethan Miller, "A State of Grace: Understanding the Martial Arts"

Noun–Pronoun Combination Identifies Performers

Termites are even more extraordinary in the way they seem to accumulate intelligence as they gather together. Two or three termites in a chamber will begin to pick up pellets and move them from place to place, but nothing comes of it; nothing is built. As more join in, they seem to reach a critical mass, a quorum, and the thinking begins. They place pellets atop pellets, then throw up columns and beautiful, curving, symmetrical arches, and the crystalline architecture of vaulted chambers is created. It is not known how they communicate with each other, how the chains of termites building one column know when to turn toward the crew on the adjacent column, or how, when the time comes, they manage the flawless joining of the arches. The stimuli that set them off at the outset, building collectively instead of shifting things about, may be pheromones released when they reach committee size. They react as if alarmed. They become agitated, excited, and then they begin working, like artists.

Lewis Thomas, "Societies as Organisms"

Performer Unidentified

The analyzer was adjusted so the scale read zero and was connected to the short sampling tube, which had previously been inserted into the smokestack. The sample was taken by depressing the bulb the requisite number of times, and the results were then read and recorded. The procedure was repeated, this time using the long sampling tube and sampling through the fire door.

Charles Finnie

⊂EXERCISES⊃

1. **Examine your favorite newspaper or magazine for examples of process analysis. Bring them to class for group discussion of which kind each represents and the writer's purpose.**

2. **Examine science textbooks and professional journals for more complex examples of process analysis. Bring your examples to class and discuss how they differ from simple instructions.** ◀

Ethical Issues

Unclear, misleading, incomplete, or erroneous instructions written for someone to follow can spawn a wide range of unwanted consequences. Often frustration and lost time are the only results. Sometimes, though, the fallout is more serious, as in the case of a lab explosion. And in extreme cases, the outcome can be catastrophic, as when an accident occurs in a nuclear power plant. As writers, we have an ethical obligation to write clear and complete instructions. To help you do this, ask and answer the following questions when you're writing a process that the reader will perform.

- Have I used clear and unambiguous language so that the reader will not encounter unnecessary frustration and inconvenience?
- Have I clearly indicated any requirements such as time needed or additional supplies that will have to be purchased?
- Have I clearly warned readers about any possible harm they could face?

Writing a Process Analysis

Planning and Drafting the Process Analysis

As always, when the choice is yours, select a familiar topic. If you're not the outdoor type and prefer a Holiday Inn to the north woods, don't try to explain how to plan a camp-out. Muddled, inaccurate, and inadequate information will result. On the other hand, if you've pitched many a tent, you might want to share your technique with your readers.

Finding a suitable topic should be easy. But if you do hit a snag, turn to the strategies on pages 27–33. In any event, answer the following questions for each potential choice:

Will the reader find the process important, interesting, or useful?

Should I provide directions for the reader to follow, explain how the process takes place, or explain how others perform it?

Can I explain the process adequately within the assigned length?

Processes for Readers Who Will Perform Them   If you will develop a process for readers to follow, ponder this second set of questions to help you accumulate the details you'll need:

> What separate actions make up the process? (Be especially careful not to omit any action that is obvious to you but wouldn't be to your reader. Such an oversight can ruin your reader's chances of success.)
>
> What is the reason for each action?
>
> What warnings will the reader need in order to perform the process properly and safely?

When you have your answers, record them in a chart similar to this one:

Action	Reason for Action	Warning
First action	First reason	First warning
Second action	Second reason	Second warning

Sometimes a reason will be so obvious no mention is necessary, and many actions won't require warnings. When you've completed the chart, review it carefully and supply any missing information. If necessary, make a revised chart.

Once you've listed the actions, group related ones to form steps, the major subdivisions of the procedure. The following actions constitute the first step— getting the fire going—of a paper explaining how to grill hamburgers:

remove grill rack	light briquets
stack charcoal briquets	spread out briquets

EXERCISES

1. **Develop a complete list of the actions involved in one of the following processes; then arrange them in an appropriate order.**

   a. Baking bread
   b. Assembling or repairing some common household device
   c. Carrying out a process related to sports
   d. Breaking a bad habit
   e. Building a fire in a fireplace
   f. Accessing the Internet

2. **Examine your favorite newspaper or magazine for examples of process analysis. Bring them to class for group discussion of how they illustrate step-by-step directions.**

Start your paper by identifying the process and arousing your reader's interest. You might, for example, note the importance of the process, its usefulness, or the ease of carrying it out. Include a list of the items needed to do the work, and note any special conditions required for a successful outcome. The paper explaining how to grill hamburgers might begin as follows:

> Grilling hamburgers on an outdoor charcoal grill is a simple process
>
> that almost anyone can master. Before starting, you will need a clean grill,

charcoal briquets, charcoal lighter fluid and matches, hamburger meat, a plate, a spatula, and some water to put out any flames caused by fat drippings. The sizzling, tasty patties you will have when you finish are a treat that almost everyone will enjoy.

DISCUSSION QUESTION

How does the writer try to induce the reader to perform the process?

Use the body of the paper to describe the process in detail, presenting each step in one or more paragraphs so that each is distinct and easily grasped. If you've ever muttered under your breath as you struggled to assemble something that came with fuzzy or inadequate directions, you know the importance of presenting steps clearly, accurately, and fully. Therefore, think carefully and include everything the reader needs to know. Note the reason for every action unless the reason is obvious. Flag with a cautionary warning any difficult or dangerous step or one that will result in undesirable consequences if not carried out. If two steps must be performed simultaneously, tell the reader at the start of the first one. In some places, you may want to tell readers what to expect if they have completed the instructions properly. Feedback lets readers know they are on track or that they need to redo something.

Let's see how the first step of the hamburger-grilling paper might unfold:

> The first step is to get the fire going. Remove the grill rack and stack about twenty charcoal briquets in a pyramid shape in the center of the grill. Stacking allows the briquets to burn off one another and thus produces a hotter fire. Next, squirt charcoal lighter fluid over the briquets. Wait about five minutes so that the fluid has time to soak into the charcoal. Then toss in a lighted match. The flame will burn for a few minutes before it goes out. When this happens, allow the briquets to sit for another fifteen minutes so that the charcoal can start to burn. Once the burning starts, do not squirt on any more lighter fluid. A flame could quickly follow the stream back into the can, causing it to explode. As the briquets begin to turn from pitch black to ash white, spread them out with a stick so that they barely touch one another. Air can then circulate and produce a hot, even fire, the type that makes grilling a success.

DISCUSSION QUESTIONS

1. At what points has the writer provided reasons for doing things?
2. Where has the writer included a warning?

Some processes can unfold in *only one order.* When you shoot a free throw in basketball, for example, you step up to the line and receive the ball before lining up the shot, and you line up the shot before releasing the ball. Other processes can be carried out in an *order of choice.* When you grill hamburgers, you can make the patties either before or after you light the charcoal. If you have an option, use the order that has worked best for you.

End your paper with a few brief remarks that provide some perspective on the process. A summary of the steps often works best for longer, multistep processes. Other popular choices include evaluating the results of the process or discussing its importance. The paper on hamburger grilling notes the results.

> Once the patties are cooked the way you like them, remove them from the grill and place them on buns. Now you are ready to enjoy a mouthwatering treat that you will long remember.
>
>   E. M. Pryzblyo

Processes for Readers Who Won't Perform Them   Like how-to-do-it processes, those intended for nondoers require you to determine the steps, or for natural processes the stages, that are involved and the function of each before you start to write. In addition, since this type of essay will not enable readers to perform the process, think carefully about why you're presenting the information and let that purpose guide your writing. If, for instance, you're trying to persuade readers that the use of rabbits in tests of the effects of cosmetics should be discontinued, the choices you make in developing your steps should reflect that purpose.

To arouse your reader's interest, you might, among other possible options, begin with a historical overview or a brief summary of the whole process, or you could note its importance. The following introduction to an essay on the aging of stars provides a brief historical perspective:

> Peering through their still-crude telescopes, eighteenth-century astronomers discovered a new kind of object in the night sky that appeared neither as the pin-prick of light from a distant star nor as the clearly defined disk of a planet but rather as a mottled, cloudy disk. They christened these objects planetary nebulas, or planetary clouds. . . . Modern astronomers recognize planetary nebulas as the fossil wreckage of dying stars ripped apart by powerful winds. . . .

Because the reader will not perform the process, supply only enough details in the body of the paper to provide an intelligent idea of what the procedure entails. Make sure the reader knows the function of each step or stage and how it fits into the overall process. Present each in one or more paragraphs with clear transitions between the steps or stages. The following excerpt points out the changes that occur as a young star, a red giant, begins the aging process:

> As the bloated star ages, this extended outer atmosphere cools and contracts, then soaks up more energy from the star and again puffs out: with each successive cycle of expansion and contraction the atmosphere puffs out a little farther. Like a massive piston, these pulsations drive the red giant's atmosphere into space in a dense wind that blows with speeds up to 15 miles per second. In as little as 10,000 years some red giants lose an entire sun's worth of matter this way. Eventually this slow wind strips the star down close to its fusion core.

As with processes aimed at performers, end your paper with a few remarks that offer some perspective. You might, for example, evaluate the results of the process, assess its importance, or point out future consequences. The ending of the essay on star aging illustrates the last option:

> The cloud of unanswered questions surrounding planetaries should not obscure the real insight astronomers have recently gained into the extraordinary death of ordinary stars. In a particularly happy marriage of theory and observation, astronomers have discovered our own sun's fate. With the interacting stellar winds model, they can confidently predict the weather about 5 billion years from now; very hot, with *really* strong gusts from the east.
>
> Adam Frank, "Winds of Change"

Revising the Process Analysis

To revise, follow the guidelines in Chapter 4 and pose these questions:

Have I written consistently for someone who will perform the process or someone who will merely understand it?

If my paper is intended for performers, have I included every necessary action? Explained any purpose that is unclear? Warned about any steps that are dangerous or might be performed improperly?

Are my steps presented in an appropriate order? Developed in sufficient detail?

Have I considered appropriate ethical issues?

◖ SAMPLE STUDENT ESSAY OF PROCESS ANALYSIS
· ·

The ABC's of CPR

Kathy Petroski

1   A heart attack, choking, or an electric shock—any of these can stop a person's breathing. The victim, however, need not always die. Many lives that would otherwise be lost can be saved simply by applying the ABC's of CPR—cardiopulmonary resuscitation. Although presence of mind is essential, CPR requires no special equipment. Here's how it is performed. When you are certain that the victim's breathing and pulse have stopped, start CPR immediately. If breathing and circulation aren't restored within five minutes, irreversible brain damage occurs.

2   <u>A</u> stands for opening the airway. Lay the victim in a supine (face up) position on a firm surface. Then tilt the head as far back as possible by gently lifting the chin with one hand. In an unconscious person, the tongue falls to the back of the throat and blocks the air passages. Hyperextending

the head in this fashion pulls the tongue from that position, thus allowing air to pass. At the same time tilt the forehead back with the other hand until the chin points straight upward. The relaxed jaw muscles will then tighten, opening the air passage to the lungs. Remove your hand from the forehead and, using your first two fingers, check the mouth for food, dentures, vomitus, or a foreign object. Remove any obstruction with a sweeping motion. These measures may cause the patient to start breathing spontaneously. If they do not, mouth-to-mouth resuscitation must be started.

3   <u>B</u> stands for breathing. Position one hand on the forehead and pinch the victim's nostrils shut with the index finger and thumb of your other hand. Open your mouth, and place it over the victim's mouth so that a tight seal is formed. Such contact allows air to reach and expand the lungs. If the seal is incomplete, you will hear your own breath escaping. Deliver two quick, full breaths without allowing the victim's lungs to deflate completely between breaths; then remove your mouth and allow him or her to exhale passively. At this point, check the carotid pulse to determine whether the heart is beating. To do so, place the tips of your index and middle fingers laterally into the groove between the trachea (windpipe) and the muscles at the side of the neck. If no pulse is evident, artificial circulation must be started.

4   <u>C</u> means circulation. Locate the lower end of the sternum (breastbone), and move upward approximately the width of two fingers. At this point, firmly apply the heel of one hand, positioning the fingers at right angles to the length of the body and keeping them slanted upward. If the hand is positioned any higher or lower on the sternum, serious internal injuries in the abdomen or chest are possible. Now place the heel of your second hand on top of your first. The fingers may be interlaced or interlocked, but they must not touch the chest, or the force of your compressions may fracture ribs.

5   Keeping your elbows straight and pushing down from the shoulders, apply firm, heavy pressure until the sternum is depressed approximately one and one-half to two inches. Rock forward and backward in a rhythmic fashion, exerting pressure with the weight of your body. This action squeezes the heart against the immobile spine with enough pressure to pump blood from the left ventricle of the heart into general circulation. Compress the chest, and then immediately release the pressure, fifteen times. Do not, at any point in the cycle, remove your hands from the chest wall. Counting the compressions aloud will help develop a systematic cycle, which is essential for success. When the fifteen have been completed, pinch the nose

as described above, seal the victim's mouth with your own, and deliver two quick breaths of air. Then compress the chest an additional fifteen times. Alternate respiration and compression steps, timing yourself so as to deliver approximately eighty compressions per minute.

6   At various intervals, quickly check the effectiveness of your CPR technique. Lift the eyelids and notice if the pupils are constricted—a key sign that the brain is receiving enough oxygen. In addition, if the bluish color of the victim is decreasing and spontaneous breathing and movement are increasing, the victim has responded favorably.

7   To maximize the chances for survival, do not interrupt this technique for more than five or ten seconds. Continue the ABC's of CPR until competent medical help or life support equipment arrives.

DISCUSSION QUESTIONS

1. How does the writer use the letters *A*, *B*, and *C* from the CPR technique in this paper?
2. How does the opening paragraph prepare the reader for what follows?
3. Where does the essay indicate the purposes of actions?
4. What order has the writer used? Explain why this order was a good choice.
5. Is the writer merely explaining how the process is carried out, or does she intend for the reader to follow the directions? Defend your answer.

SUGGESTIONS FOR WRITING

Write a process analysis on one of the topics below or one approved by your instructor. The paper may provide instructions for the reader to follow, tell how a process is performed, or describe how a process develops. Prepare a complete list of steps, arrange them in an appropriate order, and follow them as you write the body of your essay.

1. A natural process, such as erosion, that you observe or research
2. Overcoming some particular phobia
3. The stages in a technical process such as paper production
4. The stages in a student's adjustment to college
5. Dealing with the bite of a poisonous snake
6. Preparing for a romantic picnic in the park, on the beach, or some other place
7. Using a particular computer program
8. Celebrating a special occasion
9. Carrying out a process related to your hobby
10. Placing an order over the Internet
11. Studying for an examination
12. Performing a process required by your job
13. Performing a process required by one of your classes

14. Breaking a bad habit
15. Performing a weight-training program
16. Throwing a successful party
17. The stages in some type of storm
18. The stages in a developing friendship
19. The steps in pledging a fraternity or sorority
20. The stages in becoming independent

CRITICAL EDGE Is there only one way to study effectively, develop a marketing campaign, or cope with a demanding supervisor? No, of course not. As you've already learned, not all processes unfold in a single, predetermined order. The writing process itself illustrates this point.

If you were to think about how you write and talk with other students about their writing processes, you would learn that different writing occasions call for different approaches. When you write a letter to a good friend, you probably spend little or no time on preliminaries but start putting your thoughts on paper as they occur to you. By contrast, other kinds of correspondence, such as inquiry and claim letters, require careful planning, drafting, and perhaps rewriting.

Sometimes the same writing occasion may allow for differing procedures. If you're writing an essay for your English class, you might brainstorm for ideas, develop a detailed outline, rough out a bare-bones draft, and add details as you revise. In talking to other students with the same assignment, you might find that they prefer to write a much longer draft and then whittle it down. Still other students might do very little brainstorming or outlining but a great deal of revising, often making major changes in several drafts. Research papers present a more complex challenge, requiring that the student find and read source material, take notes, and document sources properly. Here again variations are possible: One student might prepare the list of works cited before writing the final draft, while another might perform this task last.

If you decided to synthesize (see pages 82–83) your findings about student writing practices, you would, of course, need to organize your material in some fashion. Perhaps you might focus on the differences that distinguish one writing occasion from another. You could develop each occasion in a separate section by presenting the practices followed by most students while ignoring variations. A second possibility would be to report different practices used for the same writing occasion, first considering the most common practice and then describing the variations. The result might be likened to a cookbook that gives different recipes for the same dish.

Some important processes have been disputed in print, and if you wanted to investigate them you would need to consult written sources rather than talk to others. Informed disagreements exist about how the human species originated, how language developed, and how children mature. Police officers debate the best way to handle drunks, management experts the best way to motivate employees. When you investigate such controversies, determine which view is supported by the best evidence and seems most reasonable. Then, as a writer, you can present the accounts in an appropriate order and perhaps indicate which one you think merits acceptance.*

SUGGESTIONS FOR WRITING

1. Interview several students about the stages they experienced in a developing friendship and write a paper that discusses these stages. Note any discrepancies in the accounts provided by different students.
2. Research the writing process as presented in several first-year composition textbooks; after pointing out how they differ, indicate which process you prefer and why.
3. Research a controversial process, such as the extinction of the dinosaurs. After presenting different theories about the process, explain which one seems most plausible and why.

*If you'll rely on information obtained through interviews, read pages 410–413 in Chapter 23. If you'll rely on published sources, read the sections on card catalogs and periodical indexes in Chapter 21 and those on handling quotations and avoiding plagiarism in Chapter 22. As always, follow your instructor's guidelines for documenting sources.

ILLUSTRATION: MAKING YOURSELF CLEAR

"It doesn't pay to fight City Hall. For example, my friend Josie . . ."

"Many intelligent people lack common sense. Take Dr. Brandon . . ."

"Top-notch women tennis players are among the biggest moneymakers in sports. Last year, for instance, Martina Hingis . . ."

"Predicting the weather is far from an exact science. Two winters ago, a surprise snowstorm . . ."

Have you ever noticed how often people use *illustrations* (examples) to clarify general statements?

Ordinary conversations teem with "for example . . ." and "for instance . . . ," often in response to a furrowed brow or puzzled look. A local character, Hank Cassidy, might serve as the perfect example of a "good old boy" or Chicago's Water Tower Place illustrate a vertical shopping mall. But illustration is not limited to concrete items. Teachers, researchers, and writers often present an abstract principle or natural law, then supply concrete examples that bring it down to earth. An economics instructor might illustrate compound interest by an example showing how much $100 earning 5 percent interest would appreciate in ten years. Examples can also persuade, as when advertisers trot out typical satisfied users of their products to induce us to buy.

Many classroom writing assignments can benefit from the use of illustration. A business student writing a paper on effective management can provide a better grasp of the topic by including examples of successful managers and how they operate. A paper defining democracy for a political science course will be more effective if it offers examples of several democratic governments. An explanation of irony for a literature course will gain force and clarity through examples taken from stories and poems. Illustration plays a similarly important role in work-related writing. A teacher wanting a bigger student-counseling staff might cite students who need help but can't get it. An advertising copywriter urging that new copiers be bought might mention different instances of copier breakdown and the resulting delays in customer service. A union steward wanting a better company safety program might call attention to several recent accidents.

The old saying that a picture is worth a thousand words best explains the popularity of illustration. The concrete is always easier to grasp than the abstract, and examples add flavor and clarity to what might otherwise be flat and vague.

Selecting Appropriate Examples

Make sure that your examples stay on target, that is, actually support your general statement and do not veer off into an intriguing side issue. For instance, if you're making the point that the lyrics in a rock group's latest album are not in good taste, don't inject comments on the fast lifestyle of one of its members. Instead, provide examples of lyrics that support your claim, chosen from different songs in the album to head off objections that your examples aren't representative.

Furthermore, see that your examples display all the chief features of whatever you're illustrating. Don't offer Hank Cassidy as an example of a typical good old boy unless he fits the general mold by being a fun-loving, easy-going beer guzzler who likes to hang out with other men. Alternatively, consider this example of a hacker, a compulsive computer programmer:

> Bob Shaw, a 15-year-old high-school student, is a case in point. Bob was temporarily pulled off the computers at school when he began failing his other courses. But instead of hitting the books, he continues to sulk outside the computer center, peering longingly through the glass door at the consoles within.
>
> Pale and drawn, his brown hair unkempt, Bob speaks only in monosyllables, avoiding eye contact. In answer to questions about friends, hobbies, school, he merely shrugs or mumbles a few words aimed at his sneakered feet. But when the conversation turns to the subject of computers, he brightens—and blurts out a few full sentences about the computer he's building and the projects he plans.
>
> Dina Ingber, "Computer Addicts"

Clearly, Shaw fits Ingber's description of hackers as programmers who have "a drive so consuming it overshadows nearly every other part of their lives and forms the focal point of their existence."

Number of Examples

How many examples will you need? One long one, several fairly brief ones, or a large number of very short ones? Look to your topic for the answer. To illustrate the point that a good nurse must be compassionate, conscientious, and competent, your best bet would probably be one example, since one person must possess all these traits.

When dealing with trends, however, you'll need several examples. To show that parents have been raising children more and more permissively over the last half century, at least three examples are called for: one family from around

1955, a second from about 1980, and a third from the present time. Sometimes topics that do not involve trends require more than one example, as when you demonstrate the sharp differences between Japanese and American attitudes toward work.

Finally, some topics require a whole series of examples. If you were contending that many everyday expressions have their origins in the world of gambling, you'd need many examples to demonstrate your point.

EXERCISES

1. **Choose one of the following topic sentences. Select an appropriate example and write the rest of the paragraph.**

   a. Sometimes a minor incident drastically changes a person's life.
   b. _____'s name exactly suits (her/his) personality.
   c. I still get embarrassed when I remember _____.
   d. Not all education goes on in the classroom.
   e. I learned the value of _____ the hard way.

2. **Explain why you would use one extended illustration, several shorter ones, or a whole series of examples to develop each of the following statements. Suggest appropriate illustrations.**

   a. Many parents I know think for their children.
   b. The hamburger isn't what it used to be.
   c. The ideal pet is small, quiet, and affectionate.
   d. Different college students view their responsibilities differently.
   e. The hotels in Gotham City run the gamut from sumptuous to seedy.
   f. Modern English includes any number of words taken directly from foreign languages.

Organizing the Examples

A single extended example often assumes the narrative form, presenting a series of events in time sequence. One person's unfolding experience might show that "doing your thing" doesn't always work out for the best. Sets of examples that trace trends also rely on time sequence, moving either forward or backward. This arrangement would work well for the paper on the growing permissiveness in child rearing.

On the other hand, a paper showing that different individuals exhibit some characteristic to different extents would logically be organized by order of climax (from the least to the greatest extent) or perhaps the reverse order. To demonstrate how salesclerks differ in their attitudes toward customers, you might first describe a hostile clerk, then a pleasant one, and finally an outstandingly courteous and helpful one.

Sometimes any arrangement will work equally well. Suppose you're showing that Americans are taking various precautions to ward off heart attacks. Although you might move from a person who exercises to one who diets and finally to one who practices relaxation techniques, no special order is preferable.

Large numbers of examples might first be grouped into categories and the categories then arranged in a suitable order. For example, the expressions from the world of gambling could be grouped according to types of gambling: cards, dice, horse racing, and the like. Depending upon the specific categories, one arrangement may or may not be preferable to another.

Ethical Issues

In writing an illustration, we try to show readers something truthful about our understanding of the world. They wouldn't read what we've written if they suspected we were unusually careless in our thinking or knew we were trying to deceive them. Deception may stem from prejudice, which causes people to distort examples. For instance, parents trying to talk their teenager out of a career in acting will probably cite only examples of failed or struggling performers who have miserable lives, and they will fail to mention many successful performers. Such a distortion isn't fair to the acting profession or the teenager. Some distortions can be outright lies. In the past debate about welfare, some commentators wrote about people who lived like millionaires while on welfare. It turned out the examples were falsified, and no real instances of such massive abuse could be found. To avoid ethical pitfalls, ask and answer the following questions.

- Have I given adequate thought to the point I'll make and the examples I'll use?
- Are the examples supporting my point truthful, or are they slanted to deceive the reader?
- Could my illustrations have harmful consequences? Do they stereotype an individual or group? Harm someone's reputation unjustly?
- Will my examples promote desirable or undesirable behavior?

Writing an Illustration

Planning and Drafting the Illustration

Assertions, unfamiliar topics, abstract principles, natural laws—as we've seen, all of these can form the foundation for your paper. If you have a choice, you should experience little difficulty finding something suitable. After all, you've observed and experienced many things—for example, how people can be TV junkies and the ways students manage the stresses of college life. As always, the strategies on pages 27–33 can help generate some possibilities, which you can then evaluate by asking these questions:

Exactly what point am I trying to make? (Write it down in precise terms.)

Why do I want to make this point? To show how bad something is? To encourage something? To scare people into or away from something?

Who is my prospective audience?

Should I use one extended example, or will I need more? Why?

Once you've picked your topic, ask yourself, "What example(s) will work best with my audience?" Then brainstorm each one for supporting details. Use a chart patterned after the one below to help you.

Example 1	Example 2	Example 3
First supporting detail	First supporting detail	First supporting detail
Second supporting detail	Second supporting detail	Second supporting detail

Review your details carefully and add any new ones you think of; then make a new chart and re-enter the details into it, arranged in the order you intend to present them.

Your introduction should identify your topic and draw your reader into the paper. If you're illustrating a personal belief, you might indicate how you developed it. If you're trying to scare the reader into or away from something, you might open with an arresting statement.

Present your examples in the body of your paper, keeping your purpose firmly in mind as you plan your organization. If you have many brief examples, perhaps group them into related categories for discussion. The paper on expressions from gambling, for instance, might devote one paragraph each to terms from the worlds of cards, dice, and horse racing. If you're dealing with a few relatively brief examples—say to show a trend—put each in its own paragraph. For a single extended example, use the entire body of the paper, suitably paragraphed. Thus, an extended example of someone with an eccentric lifestyle might include paragraphs on mode of dress, living accommodations, and public behavior.

Conclude in whatever way seems most appropriate. You might express a hope or recommendation that the reader implement or avoid something, or you might issue a personal challenge that grows out of the point you've illustrated.

Revising the Illustration

Think about the following questions and the general guidelines in Chapter 4 as you revise your paper:

Exactly what idea am I trying to put across? Have I used the examples that best typify it?

Do my examples illuminate my idea without introducing irrelevant material?

Are my examples interesting?

Have I used an appropriate number of examples?

Have I organized my paper effectively?

Have I considered appropriate ethical issues?

◖ SAMPLE STUDENT ESSAY OF ILLUSTRATION

If It Is Worth Doing....

Janice Carlton

1   Everyone should keep a slogan in his or her back pocket to pull out at difficult times. Mine may seem a bit ridiculous, but I have found it to be a life saver: "If it is worth doing, it is worth doing badly." This slogan turns my parent's phrase—If it is worth doing, it is worth doing well—completely upside down. To be clear, I am not suggesting that anyone should deliberately do things badly. No one wants to be operated on by a surgeon whose hand shakes. Hopefully, accountants know their subject and offer sound advice. Still, some activities are so worth doing that the fact that we might do them badly is no reason not to take up the task. Far too often we are tempted to give up art because our paintings are bad, avoid writing because our spelling is poor, or avoid helping a friend build a pole barn because we might make mistakes. My slogan reminds me that my possible failure is no reason to avoid a worthwhile project.

2   Consider singing for a moment. Singing can be tremendous fun. A good song can lift the heart. Singing with others can offer a delightful sense of sharing. My only problem is that I have a terrible voice. It cracks, soars when it should sink, and rises when it should drop. Usually, I hit the right pitch, but sometimes I have to wiggle into it as though it were a pair of excessively tight jeans. My more musically gifted friends usually cringe when they hear me sing and mutter something under their breath about "the tone deaf." Should I stop singing just because I do it badly? To me, I sound like a great rock singer, at least when I sing in the shower. Sometimes I sing while I walk from class to class, and I feel, as a result, that I am in an exciting musical. I can even sing with my friends, who only insist that I sing a little more quietly and try, try, try to stay on tune. Probably it would be unfair of me to log in hours at a Karaoke bar, and I usually keep from singing around those who tend to stuff their fingers in their ears. But, with some reasonable precautions, the fact that I sing badly should not prevent me from enjoying the obvious pleasures of singing.

3   Writing poetry is another practice that is worth doing even if we do it badly. What makes poetry worth writing? Writing poetry involves taking time out of the rush of life to reflect on what you're feeling, to perceive more clearly, to hunt for the right word. When it works, you feel like everything in your life has come together.

As I raced through the forest,
I stopped to smell a flower,
a violet, perhaps, a purple pause
Between home and grandmother's house.
The flower didn't have any smell,
But that didn't matter any.
For a moment, I contemplated
The breath of a flower,
And avoided, in the process,
Meeting any unexpected wolves.

4   The above poem isn't very good, I admit. No one would want to publish it. Most readers may not understand how, feeling like Little Red Riding Hood, I rush from place to place to avoid meeting stray wolves. None of that is the point. When writing the poem, I felt in touch with my life while savoring a creative joy. There is no reason to let anything get in the way of such a delight, not even the poor quality of the resulting poem.

5   Of course, it is easy to sing in the shower and write poetry no one ever sees, even if the results, to put it mildly, stink. What about where others are involved? Imagine my predicament when my big brother called and asked me if I would help him put up a pole barn. "Me," I pleaded, "I'm all thumbs." And I meant it, but somehow he needed my help, so despite my complete lack of construction experience, I chanted my mantra three times and said "yes." For a day I held up beams, sawed boards (sometimes off the measured line), and hammered in nails (bending more than a few). But I did help my brother. He said that he couldn't have done it without me; and while he probably could have built the barn without me, it would have been harder for him. Besides, working side by side for a day, we got to reconnect in ways that I hadn't thought possible. I also learned some construction skills. Without being willing to help badly, I would have missed a tremendous opportunity.

6   There are times when doing something badly is significantly better than doing nothing at all. Our local newspaper featured a story about a hiker who was miles from anywhere on the trail when he came across another hiker who was choking on his lunch. What could he do? He couldn't run for help. He was out of his cell phone region. And he didn't know CPR. What he did know was that the man in front of him was starting to turn blue. He pounded the man on the back, but that didn't work. Finally, in desperation he pushed down underneath the man's rib cage. The pressure popped something out of his windpipe and he started breathing again. The point of the article was the importance of learning CPR, the Heimlich

Maneuver, and other life-saving skills. The hiker, of course, knew none of those skills and could have done tremendous damage, perhaps breaking the victim's ribs. Clearly, it would be worthwhile to be expert at life-saving skills. But what should the hiker have done? If he had just stood there paralyzed by his lack of expertise, the man would have choked to death. Fortunately, he seems to have believed in my slogan and did what was worth doing, saving a life, even if he did it badly.

7   There are lots of pressure in our culture to "leave it to the experts." We can listen to CDs instead of sing ourselves. We can call towing services that are glad to change our flats for us. We can watch soccer instead of play it. With so many skilled people, it is easy to be embarrassed by our own lack of expertise and abandon everything except what we do well. Unfortunately, our lives would be significantly poorer for such a surrender. Instead, we would be better off adapting the adage that "if it is worth doing, it is worth doing badly" and step up to the plate at a softball game, grab a sketch pad and draw what we see, write a poem, sing, cook a meal for a friend. In the end, we have nothing to lose but our false pride.

DISCUSSION QUESTIONS

1. What is the writer trying to illustrate?
2. How is this particular illustration developed?
3. Why did the writer include a poem in her essay?
4. What does the paragraph on the use of CPR add to the essay?
5. In the last paragraph, why does the writer use the pronoun "we"?

SUGGESTIONS FOR WRITING

Use one of the following ideas or another that your instructor approves for your illustration essay. Select appropriate examples, determine how many you will use, and decide how you will organize them.

1. "I don't have enough time" is a common complaint of many people today.
2. Many people appear obsessed with exercise (or diet).
3. Incivility has become quite common in public places.
4. Racial and ethnic minorities are becoming increasingly prominent in _____ .
5. Dedication is the secret of success for many athletes (or use any other field or occupation).
6. People have many strange remedies for hangovers.
7. Sometimes actions can have unintended consequences.

8. A good nurse must be compassionate, conscientious, and competent (or use another occupation with appropriate characteristics).

9. Campus gambling assumes various forms.

10. Many intelligent people lack common sense.

11. Sleep deprivation is causing problems for many young people.

12. Talk show hosts often leave much to be desired (or stimulate listeners to think).

13. "Doing your own thing" does not always work out for the best.

14. _____ is the most (or least) effective teacher I have ever had.

15. Not to decide is to decide.

16. How we react to circumstances, not the circumstances themselves, often makes us unhappy.

17. Today's college student is _____ .

18. Sometimes we need to take risks.

19. Wanting more than we need can be destructive.

20. Many people become obsessed with appearance.

CRITICAL EDGE When we write an illustration paper, we don't always draw our examples from personal experience. As we reflect on a topic, we may talk with other people and read various source materials to broaden our understanding. We explore differing perspectives and determine the connections between them en route to arriving at our own views and insights. Take, for instance, the topic of racism in America. "For My Indian Daughter" (page 437), "Momma's Encounter" (page 433), and "Black Men and Public Space" (page 527) offer poignant illustrations of how racism affects people's personal lives. Reading these essays, drawing upon your own observations, and perhaps questioning minority students could lead you to an important insight: for example, that racism can have personal effects that are very different from the more widely discussed kinds of institutional discrimination. You might then synthesize (see pages 82–83) others' illustrations and your own to produce a paper that presents this insight.

Sometimes illustrations don't reflect reality. An author trying to make the point that many college students are irresponsible might offer examples of students who skip classes, fail to hand in assignments, and party constantly. These examples, however, overlook the many students who hold part-time jobs while taking a full load of classes, participate in professional organizations, and function successfully as spouses, and even parents, while earning good grades. Because published material can paint an inaccurate picture, develop the habit of judging the examples you read in the light of what your knowledge, further investigation, and other sources reveal. Critical thinking is one of the most important skills a writer can cultivate.*

*Because this type of paper draws upon published information, it is important to read the sections on card catalogs and periodical indexes in Chapter 21 and those on handling quotations and avoiding plagiarism in Chapter 22. As always, follow your instructor's guidelines for documenting sources.

SUGGESTIONS FOR WRITING

1. Examine the Reader essays on racism cited above. Then, drawing upon examples from the essays and perhaps the observations of minority students you know, write a paper presenting your own conclusions about the personal effects of racism.

2. Read several issues of a magazine such as *Sports Illustrated* or *Working Woman* and determine what the articles suggest about American life. Then write an essay that illustrates your conclusions and incorporates relevant material from the articles.

3. Martin Gottfried, author of "Rambos of the Road," concludes by noting, "It seems to me that it is a new America we see on the road now. It has the mentality of a hoodlum and the backbone of a coward" (page 476). Write an essay that includes both your own illustrations and one or more of Gottfried's and that agrees or disagrees with his assessment.

CLASSIFICATION: GROUPING INTO CATEGORIES

H*elp Wanted, Situations Wanted, Real Estate, Personal.* Do these terms look familiar? They do if you've ever scanned the classified ads of the newspaper. Ads are grouped into categories, and each category is then subdivided. The people who assemble this layout are *classifying.* Figure 9.1 (see page 120) shows the main divisions of a typical classified ad section and a further breakdown of one of them.

As this figure indicates, grouping allows the people who handle ads to divide entries according to a logical scheme and helps readers find what they are looking for. Imagine the difficulty of checking the real estate ads if all the entries were run in the order the ads were placed.

Our minds naturally sort information into categories. Within a few weeks after their birth, infants can tell the faces of family members from those of outsiders. Toddlers learn to distinguish between cats, dogs, and rabbits. In both cases the classification rests solely on physical differences. As we mature we start classifying in more abstract ways, and by adulthood we are constantly sorting things into categories: dates or mates, eating places, oddballs, friends, investments, jobs, political views.

Classification also helps writers and readers come to grips with large or complex topics. It breaks a broad topic into categories according to some specific principle, presents the distinctive features of each category, and shows how the features vary among categories. Segmenting the topic simplifies the discussion by presenting the information in small, neatly sorted piles rather than in one jumbled and confusing heap.

Furthermore, classification helps people make choices. Identifying which groups of consumers—students, accountants, small-business owners—are most likely to buy some new product allows the manufacturer to advertise in appropriate media. Knowing the engine size, maneuverability, seating capacity, and

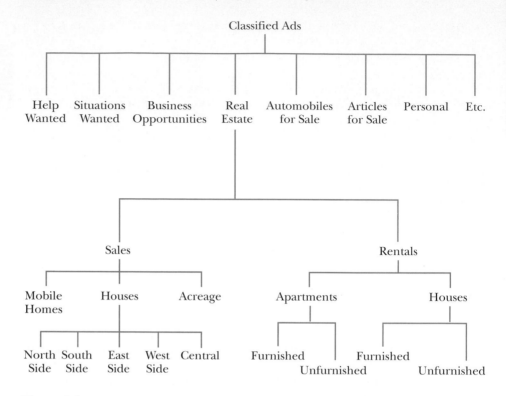

Figure 9.1

gas mileage of typical subcompact, compact, and intermediate-size cars helps customers decide which one to buy. Examining the features of term, whole-life, and endowment insurance enables prospective buyers to select the policy that best suits their needs.

Because classification plays such an important part in our lives, it is a useful writing tool in many situations. Your accounting instructor may ask you to categorize accounting procedures for retail businesses. In a computer class, you may classify computer languages and then specify appropriate applications for each grouping. For an industrial hygiene class, you might categorize types of respiratory protective equipment and indicate when each type is used. On the job, a state health department employee may prepare a brochure grouping illegal drugs into categories based on their effects. The communications director of an investment firm might write a customer letter categorizing investments according to their degree of risk. An employee of a textbook publisher might prepare a catalog grouping new books by field of study.

Selecting Categories

People classify in different ways for different purposes, which generally reflect their interests. A clothing designer might classify people according to their fashion sense, a representative of the National Organization for Women according to their views on women's rights, and the Secretary of Labor according to their occupations. A college's director of housing might classify students according to their type of residence, the dean of students according to their behavior problems, and the financial aid officer according to their sources of income.

When you write a classification paper, choose a principle of classification that's suited not only to your purpose but also to your audience. To illustrate, if you're writing for students, don't classify instructors according to their manner of dress, body build, or cars they drive. These breakdowns probably wouldn't interest most students and certainly wouldn't serve their needs. Instead, develop a more useful principle of classification—perhaps by teaching styles, concern for students, or grading policies.

Sometimes it's helpful or necessary to divide one or more categories into subcategories. If you do, use just one principle of classification for each level. Both levels in Figure 9.2 meet this test because each reflects a single principle: place of origin for the first, number of cylinders for the second.

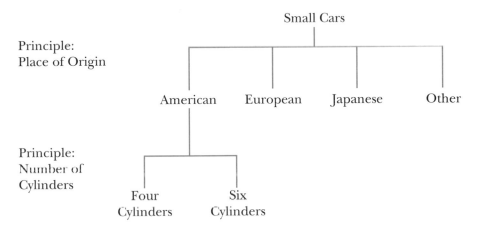

Figure 9.2 Proper Classification of Small Cars

Now examine Figure 9.3. This classification is *improper* because it groups cars in two ways—by place of origin and by kind—making it possible for one car to end up in two categories. For example, the German Porsche is both a European car and a sports car. When categories overlap in this way, confusion reigns and nothing is clarified.

Figure 9.3 Improper Classification of Small Cars

EXERCISES

1. **How would each of the following people be most likely to classify the families in Anytown, USA?**

   a. The bishop of the Roman Catholic diocese in which the city is located
   b. The state senator who represents the city
   c. A field worker for the NAACP
   d. The director of the local credit bureau

2. **The following lists contain overlapping categories. Identify the inconsistent item in each list and explain why it is faulty.**

Nurses	Pictures	Electorate in Midville
Surgical nurses	Oil paintings	Republicans
Psychiatric nurses	Magazine illustrations	Democrats
Emergency room nurses	Lithographs	Nonvoters
Terminal care nurses	Watercolors	Independents
Night nurses	Etchings	

Number of Categories

Some classification papers discuss every category included in the topic. Others discuss only selected categories. Circumstances and purpose dictate the scope of the discussion. Suppose you work for the commerce department of your state and are asked to write a report that classifies the major nonservice industries in a certain city and assesses their strengths and weaknesses. Your investigation shows that food processing, furniture making, and the production of auto parts account for more than 95 percent of nonservice jobs. Two minor industries, printing and toy making, provide the rest of the jobs. Given these circumstances, you'd probably focus on the first three industries, mentioning the others only in passing. But if printing and toy making were significant industries, they too would require detailed discussion.

Developing Categories

Develop every category you include with specific, informative details that provide a clear picture of each one and help the reader grasp the distinctions and relationships among them. The following excerpt from a student paper classifying public restrooms for women discusses two of the writer's three categories:

> Luxurious restrooms are found in top-drawer business establishments such as fancy department stores, chic boutiques, and the better restaurants. This aristocrat of public facilities usually disdains the term <u>restroom,</u> masquerading instead under the alias of <u>lounge</u> or <u>powder room.</u> Upon entering

its plush environs, the user is captivated by its elegance. Thick carpet reaches up to cushion tired feet, wood paneled or brocade velvet walls beckon invitingly, and dimly twinkling chandeliers or wall sconces soothe the eyes. Narrow little divans and gold-and-velvet tables add to the restful, welcoming atmosphere, and the latest issues of upscale magazines like Vogue, The New Yorker, and Vanity Fair entice resters into their pages. Mirrors in carved frames, designer lavatories with richly ornamented faucets, and creamy scented soap go hand in hand with the attendant who quietly dispenses thick, white towels as soft as suede. Her detached air deserts her only when she sneaks a furtive glance toward the silver tip dish as the patron passes it on the way out.

The adequate restroom offers utility without the swankiness of its lavish cousin. Typically located in a large shopping mall or mass-market department store, it is a stark world of hard, unadorned surfaces—tile floors, tile walls, and harshly glaring fluorescent lights recessed in the ceiling. For those who wish to rest, there is a garishly colored Naugahyde couch and next to it a battered metal or wood table holding a few tattered copies of Family Circle, People, Reader's Digest, and similar publications. The mirrors have steel frames, the lavatories, set in a formica counter, have plain chrome faucets, and the soap dispenser emits a thin stream of unscented liquid. Paper toweling pulled from a wall-mounted metal holder replaces the cloth article, and no maid stands by to offer her help or to exact tips from departing visitors.

Student Unknown

The concrete details in these paragraphs effectively characterize each category and clearly distinguish between them. Imagine how vague and indistinct the categories would be without these details.

Ethical Issues

Classification can seem quite innocent, and yet it can cause great harm. In India, an entire group numbering millions of people was once classified as "untouchables" and so was denied the jobs and rights of other citizens. Although political progress has considerably improved the lot of these people, discrimination still hobbles their lives. In this country, many high school students have suffered the sting of being classified as "nerds" or "geeks." Clearly you'll have to evaluate the appropriateness and consequences of your classification scheme. To avoid problems, ask and answer these questions:

■ Is my classification called for by the situation? It may be appropriate to classify students in a school environment according to their reading skills, but classifying factory workers in this fashion may well be inappropriate and unfair to the people involved.

- Have I avoided the use of damaging classifications? We resent stereotyping because it unjustly reduces us to some distorted general idea. No one is simply a "hillbilly" or a "jock."

- Have I applied my classification without resorting to overgeneralization? In a paper classifying student drinkers, it would be a mistake, and even harmful, to imply that all college students drink excessively.

- Could my classification promote harmful behavior? When classifying the behavior patterns of young urban dwellers, it would be unethical to present favorably the lifestyle of a group that uses hard drugs and engages in disruptive behavior at sporting events.

We are ethically responsible for the classification systems that we use in our writing. Always examine the one you use for suitability, fairness, and potential harm.

Writing a Classification

Planning and Drafting the Classification

Many topics that interest you are potential candidates for classification. If you're selecting your own topic, you might explain different kinds of rock music to novices, take a humorous look at types of teachers, or, in a more serious vein, identify types of discrimination. As always, use one or more of the narrowing strategies on pages 27–33 to stimulate your thinking. As possibilities come to mind, examine each one in light of these questions:

What purpose will this classification serve?

Who is my audience and what will interest them?

What are the categories of this topic?

What features distinguish my categories from one another?

Next, determine whether you'll discuss every category or only selected ones, and then set up a classification chart similar to the one following.

Category 1	Category 2	Category 3
First distinguishing feature	First distinguishing feature	First distinguishing feature
Second distinguishing feature	Second distinguishing feature	Second distinguishing feature

Such a chart helps you see the relationships among categories and provides a starting point for developing your specific details. Proceed by jotting down the details that come to mind for each distinguishing feature of every category. Then prepare a second chart with the distinguishing features and details arranged in the order you want to present them.

Begin your paper by identifying your topic and capturing your reader's attention in some way. A paper classifying hair dyes might point out their growing popularity among both men and women. One classifying snobs might offer an anecdote showing how far snobbery can go. Or you could cite a personal experience that relates to your topic. As always, circumstances dictate your choice.

In the body discuss your categories in whatever order best suits your purpose. Order of climax—least important, more important, most important— often works well. Or perhaps your topic will suggest arranging the categories by behavior, income, education, or physical characteristics. Whatever your arrangement, signal it clearly to your reader. Don't merely start the discussions of your categories by saying first . . . , second . . . , another . . . , next . . . , and the like. These words offer no hint of the rationale behind your order.

In addition, make sure the arrangement of material within the categories follows a consistent pattern. Recall the two categories of restrooms discussed on pages 122–123. In each case, after noting where the restroom can be found, the writer discusses its floor, walls, and lighting, moves to the furniture, and ends by discussing the lavatories, soap, and toweling.

The strategies for ending a classification paper are as varied as those for starting it. A paper on hair dyes might conclude by predicting their continued popularity. One on snobs might end with your recommendations for dealing with them. In other cases, you might express a hope of some kind or advise your reader to do something.

Revising the Classification

Revise your paper by following the guidelines in Chapter 4 as well as by pondering these questions:

Does my classification have a clear sense of purpose and audience?

Does my principle of classification accord with my purpose?

Do any of my categories overlap?

Have I chosen an appropriate number of categories?

Are these categories developed with sufficient details?

Are the categories and details arranged in an effective order?

Have I considered appropriate ethical issues?

◖ SAMPLE STUDENT ESSAY OF CLASSIFICATION
• •

Undesirable Produce Market Customers

Clarence DeLong

1   You will find almost as large a variety of customers at a produce market as you will find fruits and vegetables. Undesirable produce market customers fall into three main categories—those who squeeze the fruit, those who complain constantly, and those who try to cheat the market—and

when you meet them all in one day, you have one big headache. Perhaps you will recognize these people as I describe them.

2   "Sammy Squeezer" is the least annoying of these undesirables. He wants to make sure that everything he buys is "just right." He pokes his thumbs into the top of a cantaloupe. If they penetrate very deeply, he won't buy this particular specimen, considering it to be overripe. He squeezes the peaches, plums, nectarines, and any other fruit he can get his hands on. After ten of these people squeeze one piece of fruit, it will surely be soft, even if it wasn't originally. Moving on to the corn, Sammy carefully peels back the husk to examine the kernels inside. If they don't suit him, he doesn't bother to fold the husk back to protect the kernels; he simply tosses the ear back into the basket. The problems he creates for the employees are primarily physical—removing the damaged items after he leaves.

3   A more annoying customer is "Betty Bitcher." She is never satisfied with the quality of the produce: The bananas are too green, the lettuce has brown spots, the berries are too ripe, and the potatoes have green spots. Sometimes you wonder if Betty would have been satisfied with the fruit grown in the Garden of Eden.

4   The produce has no monopoly on her complaints, however. Betty also finds fault with the service she receives from the employees. Talking to other customers or directly to the clerks, she can be heard saying such things as "Why is this the only place I ever have to wait in line? They must have trouble getting good help here." Even as she leaves the market, which is none too soon, she must make one last complaint: "You mean I have to carry my own potatoes to the car?" The problems she creates for the employees are primarily mental—she can make your nerves quite active.

5   Perhaps the most annoying customer of all is "Charlie Cheater." You have to keep your eye on him constantly because he knows all the tricks of cheating. He will add berries to an already full basket. He will take 6/79¢ oranges and tell you they're the 6/59¢ ones. He will put expensive grapes in the bottom of a sack and add cheaper ones on top. Then he'll tell you that they are all the cheaper variety. Likewise, he will put expensive nectarines in a sack, place a few cheaper peaches on top, and try to pass them all off as peaches. If he is caught, he usually says, "I don't know how that happened. My little girl (or boy) must have put them in there." The child usually looks dumbfounded.

6   The problem Charlie creates for the market is twofold: financial and legal. If you don't catch him, your profits suffer. If you do catch him, you

almost have to prosecute, usually for amounts of only a dollar or two, or you'll have every Charlie in town at your door.

7   Did you recognize any of these customers? If you didn't and would like to see some of them in action, stop in at Steve's Produce Market. That's where I work, and that's where I meet them.

DISCUSSION QUESTIONS

1. What is the writer's purpose in developing this classification? Where does he state it?
2. In what order has he arranged his categories? Refer to the essay when answering.
3. Demonstrate that the writer has avoided overlapping categories.
4. How do you know he hasn't discussed every category of undesirable customers?

SUGGESTIONS FOR WRITING

Write a classification paper on one of the topics below or one approved by your instructor. Determine your purpose and audience, select appropriate categories, decide how many you'll discuss, develop them with specific details, and arrange them in an effective order.

1. College teachers (or college pressures)
2. Pet owners (or types of pets)
3. Herbal remedies
4. Kinds of extreme sports
5. Churchgoers
6. Computer languages
7. Patrons of singles bars
8. Reasons for surfing the Internet
9. Talk show hosts
10. Sports announcers (or fans)
11. Television judges (or sitcoms or discussion groups)
12. Alternative medicines
13. Laundromat users
14. People waiting in line
15. Bores
16. Dangerous males (or females)
17. Web pages
18. Advertisements
19. Cheating (or lies)
20. Leaders

CRITICAL EDGE

Classification provides an effective tool for organizing material into categories. But you won't always rely exclusively on your own knowledge or experience to determine or develop categories. At times you'll supplement what you bring to a writing assignment with information gained through outside reading.

Suppose that for an introductory business course, you're asked to prepare a paper that explores major types of investments. You realize that some research will be necessary. After consulting a number of books and magazines, you conclude that stocks, bonds, and real estate represent the three main categories of investments and that each category can be divided into several subcategories. Bonds, for example, can be grouped according to issuer: corporate, municipal, and U.S. Treasury securities.

At this point, you recognize that the strategy of classification would work well for this assignment. Reading further, you learn about the financial risks, rewards, and tax consequences associated with ownership. For example, U.S. Treasury securities offer the greatest safety, while corporate and municipal bonds, as well as stocks and real estate, entail varying degrees of risk depending on the financial condition of the issuer and the state of the economy. Similarly, the income from the different categories and subcategories of investments is subject to different kinds and levels of taxation. Thus, income from municipal bonds is generally tax free, income from U.S. Treasury securities is exempt from state and local taxes, and income from other kinds of investments does not enjoy such exemptions.

After assimilating the information you've gathered, you could synthesize (see pages 82–83) the views expressed in your sources as well as your own ideas about investments. You might organize your categories and subcategories according to probable degree of risk, starting with the least risky investment and ending with the most risky. For your conclusion you might offer purchase recommendations for different groups of investors such as young workers, wealthy older investors, and retirees.

Before using the material of others in your writing, examine its merits. Do some sources seem more convincing than others? Why? Do any recommendations stem from self-interest? For example, a writer who seems overly enthusiastic about one type of investment may be associated with an organization that markets it. Are any sources overloaded with material irrelevant to your purpose? Which sources offer the most detail? Asking and answering questions such as these will help you write a more informed paper.*

SUGGESTIONS FOR WRITING

1. Examine the Reader essays on women's issues or health and then write a paper that draws upon these sources and classifies their content.

2. Read several authors' views on success and then write a paper that draws on these sources and classifies their content.

3. Reflect on the Reader essays that you've studied and then write a paper that presents an appropriate classification system for them, perhaps based on the writers' levels of diction, tone, or reliance on authorities.

---

*Because you'll rely on published sources, it is important to read the sections on card catalogs and periodical indexes in Chapter 21 and those on handling quotations and avoiding plagiarism in Chapter 22 before you start to write. As always, follow your instructor's guidelines for documenting sources.

CHAPTER 10

COMPARISON: SHOWING RELATIONSHIPS

Which candidate for senator should get my vote, Ken Conwell or Jerry Mander?

Let me know whether this new shipment of nylon thread meets specs.

Doesn't this tune remind you of an Anne Murray song?

How does high school in Australia stack up against high school in this country?

Everyone makes *comparisons*, not just once in a while but day after day. When we compare, we examine two or more items for likenesses, differences, or both.

Comparison often helps us choose between alternatives. Some issues are trivial: whether to plunk the first quarter into Star Wars or Space Ace, whether to order pizza or a sub sandwich. But comparison also influences our more important decisions. We weigh majoring in chemistry against majoring in physics, buying against renting, working for Microsoft against working for IBM. An instructor may ask us to write a paper comparing the features of two word-processing systems. An employer may have us weigh two proposals for decreasing employee absenteeism and write a report recommending one of them.

Comparison also acquaints us with unfamiliar things. To help American readers understand the English sport of rugby, a sportswriter might compare its field, team, rules, and scoring system with those for football. To teach students about France's government, a political science textbook might discuss the makeup and election of its parliament and the method of picking its president and premier, using our own government as a backdrop.

Both your classes and your job will call for comparison writing. Your humanities instructor may ask you to compare baroque and classical music and their contributions to later musical developments. Your psychology instructor may want you to compare two types of psychosis and assess the legal and medical ramifications of each. Your biology instructor may have you consider how the features of two kinds of body cell enable them to perform their functions. Comparisons in the workplace are common because they help people make decisions. An office manager may compare several phone systems to determine which one the company should install, a nurse assesses the condition of a patient before and after a new medicine is given, an insurance agent points out the features of two insurance policies to highlight the advantages of one.

"WE'D LIKE TO TAKE YOU UPSTAIRS AND SHOW YOU THE REAL GRACIOUSNESS OF FRATERNITY LIFE, BUT IT'S SORT OF A RULE AROUND HERE TO WAIT UNTIL THE 'RUSHEE' IS PLEDGED."

Reprinted by permission of Richard N. Bibler.

Selecting Items for Comparison

Any items you compare must share some common ground. For example, you could compare two golfers on driving ability, putting ability, and sand play, or two cars on appearance, gas mileage, and warranty; but you can't meaningfully compare a golfer with a car, any more than you could compare guacamole with Guadalajara or chicken with charcoal. There's simply no basis for comparison.

Any valid comparison, on the other hand, presents many possibilities. Suppose you head the music department of a large store and have two excellent salespeople working for you. The manager of the store asks you to prepare a one- or two-page report that compares their qualifications for managing the music department in a new branch store. Assessing their abilities becomes the guiding purpose that motivates and controls the writing. On the spot you can rule out points such as eye color, hair style, and religion, which have no bearing on job performance. Instead, you must decide what managerial traits the job will require and the extent to which each candidate possesses them. Your thinking might result in a list like this.

Points of Similarity or Difference	Pat	Mike
1. Ability to deal with customers, sales skills	Excellent	Excellent
2. Effort: regular attendance, hard work on the job	Excellent	Excellent
3. Leadership qualities	Excellent	Good
4. Knowledge of ordering and accounting procedures	Good	Fair
5. Musical knowledge	Excellent	Good

This list tells you which points to emphasize and suggests Pat as the candidate to recommend. You might briefly mention similarities (points 1 and 2) in an introductory paragraph, but the report would focus on differences (points 3, 4, and 5), since you're distinguishing between two employees.

EXERCISE *Say you want to compare two good restaurants in order to recommend one of them. List the points of similarity and difference that you might discuss. Differences should predominate because you will base your decision on them.*

Developing a Comparison

Successful comparisons rest upon ample, well-chosen details that show just how the items under consideration are alike and different. Such support helps the reader grasp your meaning. Read the following two student paragraphs and note how the concrete details convey the striking differences between south and north 14th Street:

> On 14th Street running south from P Street are opulent department stores, such as Woodward and Lothrop and Julius Garfinkle, and small but expensive clothing stores with richly dressed mannequins in the windows. Modern skyscraping office buildings harbor banks and travel bureaus on the ground floors and insurance companies and corporation headquarters in the upper stories. Dotting the concretescape are high-priced movie theaters, gourmet restaurants, multilevel parking garages, bookstores, and candy-novelty-gift shops, all catering to the prosperous population of the city. This section of 14th Street is relatively clean: The city maintenance crews must clean up after only a nine-to-five populace and the Saturday crowds of shoppers. The pervading mood of the area is one of bustling wealth during the day and, in the night, calm.
>
> Crossing P Street toward the north, one notes a gradual but disturbing change in the scenery of 14th Street. Two architectural features assault the eyes and automatically register as tokens of trouble: the floodlights that

leave no alley or doorway in shadows and the riot screens that cage in the store windows. The buildings are old, condemned, decaying monoliths, each occupying an entire city block. Liquor stores, drugstores, dusty television repair shops, seedy pornographic bookstores that display photographs of naked bodies with the genital areas blacked out by strips of tape, discount stores smelling perpetually of stale chocolate and cold popcorn, and cluttered pawnshops—businesses such as these occupy the street level. Each is separated from the adjoining stores by a littered entranceway that leads up a decaying wooden stairway to the next two floors. All the buildings are three stories tall; all have most of their windows broken and blocked with boards or newspapers; and all reek of liquor, urine, and unidentifiable rot. And so the general atmosphere of this end of 14th Street is one of poverty and decay.

Student Unknown

Vivid details depict with stark clarity the economic differences between the two cultures.

Organizing a Comparison

You can use either of two basic patterns to organize a comparison paper: block or alternating. The paper may deal with similarities, differences, or some combination of them.

The Block Pattern   The block pattern first presents all of the points of comparison for one item and then all of the points of comparison for the other. Here is the comparison of the two salespeople, Pat and Mike, outlined according to the block pattern:

    I. Introduction: mentions similarities in sales skills and effort but recommends Pat for promotion.
    II. Specific points about Mike
       A. Leadership qualities
       B. Knowledge of ordering and accounting procedures
       C. Musical knowledge
    III. Specific points about Pat
       A. Leadership qualities
       B. Knowledge of ordering and accounting procedures
       C. Musical knowledge
    IV. Conclusion: reasserts that Pat should be promoted.

The block pattern works best with short papers or ones that include only a few points of comparison. The reader can easily remember all the points in the first block while reading the second.

The Alternating Pattern   The alternating pattern presents a point about one item, then follows immediately with a corresponding point about the other. Organized in this way, the Pat-and-Mike paper would look like this:

I. Introduction: mentions similarities in sales skills and effort but recommends Pat for promotion.
II. Leadership qualities
    A. Mike's qualities
    B. Pat's qualities
III. Knowledge of ordering and accounting procedures
    A. Mike's knowledge
    B. Pat's knowledge
IV. Musical knowledge
    A. Mike's knowledge
    B. Pat's knowledge
V. Conclusion: reasserts that Pat should be promoted.

For longer papers that include many points of comparison, use the alternating method. Discussing each point in one place highlights similarities and differences; your reader doesn't have to pause and reread in order to grasp them. The alternating plan also works well for short papers.

Once you select your pattern, arrange your points of comparison in an appropriate order. Take up closely related points one after the other. Depending on your purpose, you might work from similarities to differences or the reverse. Often, a good writing strategy is to move from the least significant to the most significant point so that you conclude with punch.

EXERCISE   *Using the points of comparison you selected for the exercise on page 131, prepare outlines for a paper organized according to the block and then the alternating pattern.*

Using Analogy

An *analogy*, a special type of comparison, calls attention to one or more similarities underlying two kinds of item that seem to have nothing in common. While some analogies stand alone, most clarify concepts in other kinds of writing. Whatever their role, they follow the same organizational pattern as ordinary comparisons.

An analogy often explains something unfamiliar by likening it to something familiar. Here is an example:

> The atmosphere of Earth acts like any window in serving two very important functions. It lets light in, and it permits us to look out. It also serves as a shield to keep out dangerous or uncomfortable things. A normal glazed window lets us keep our houses warm by keeping out cold air, and it prevents rain, dirt, and unwelcome insects and animals from coming in. . . . Earth's atmospheric window also helps to keep our planet at a comfortable temperature by holding back radiated heat and protecting us from dangerous levels of ultraviolet light.
>
> Lester del Ray, *The Mysterious Sky*

Conversely, an analogy sometimes highlights the unfamiliar in order to help illuminate the familiar. The following paragraph discusses the qualities and obligations of an unfamiliar person, the mountain guide, to shed light on a familiar practice—teaching:

> The mountain guide, like the true teacher, has a quiet authority. He or she engenders trust and confidence so that one is willing to join the endeavor. The guide accepts his leadership role, yet recognizes that success (measured by the heights that are scaled) depends upon the close cooperation and active participation of each member of the group. He has crossed the terrain before and is familiar with the landmarks, but each trip is new and generates its own anxiety and excitement. Essential skills must be mastered; if they are lacking, disaster looms. The situation demands keen focus and rapt attention: slackness, misjudgment, or laziness can abort the venture.
>
> Nancy K. Hill, "Scaling the Heights: The Teacher as Mountaineer"

When you develop an analogy, keep these points in mind:

1. Your readers must be well acquainted with the familiar item. If they aren't, the point is lost.
2. The items must indeed have significant similarities. You could develop a meaningful analogy between a kidney and a filter or between cancer and anarchy but not between a fiddle and a flapjack or a laser and limburger cheese.
3. The analogy must truly illuminate. Overly obvious analogies, such as one comparing a battle to an argument, offer few or no revealing insights.
4. Overextended analogies can tax the reader's endurance. A multipage analogy between a heart and a pump would likely overwhelm the reader with all its talk of valves, hoses, pressures, and pumping.

Ethical Issues

Although an old adage declares that "comparisons are odious," most people embrace comparisons except when they are unfair. Unfortunately, this situation occurs all too often. For example, advertisers commonly magnify trivial drawbacks in competitive products while exaggerating the benefits of their own merchandise. Politicians run attack ads that distort their opponents' views and demean the opponents' character. And when scientific theories clash, supporters of one view have been known to alter their findings in order to undermine the other position. Your readers expect any comparison to meet certain ethical standards. Ask and answer these questions to help ensure that those you write measure up.

- Have I avoided skewing one or both of my items in order to ensure a particular outcome?
- Are the items I'm comparing properly matched? It would be unethical to compare a student essay to a professional one in order to demonstrate the inadequacy of the former.

- If I'm using an analogy, is it appropriate? Comparing immigration officials to Nazi storm troopers is ethically odious: It trivializes the suffering and deaths of millions of Nazi victims and taints the officials with a terrible label.

Writing a Comparison

Planning and Drafting the Comparison

Don't write merely to fulfill an assignment; if you do, your paper will likely ramble aimlessly and fail to deliver a specific message. Instead, build your paper around a clear sense of purpose. Do you want to show the superiority of one product or method over another? Do you want to show how sitcoms today differ from those twenty years ago? Purpose governs the details you choose and the organization you follow.

Whether you select your own topic or write on an assigned one, answer these questions:

What purpose will my comparison serve?

Who will be my audience and why will they want to read the essay?

What points of similarity or difference will I discuss?

To develop the comparison, draw up a chart similar to this one.

Item A	Item B
First point of comparison	First point of comparison
Second point of comparison	Second point of comparison

Next, brainstorm each point in turn, recording appropriate supporting details. When you finish, stand back and ask these questions:

Do all the details relate to my purpose?

Do any new details come to mind?

In what order should I organize the details?

When you decide upon an order, copy the points of comparison and the details, arranged in the order you will follow, into a chart like the one below.

Item A	Item B
First point of comparison	First point of comparison
First detail	First detail
Second detail	Second detail
Second point of comparison	Second point of comparison

Use the introduction to identify your topic and arouse the reader's interest. If you intend to establish the superiority of one item over the other, you might call attention to your position. If you're comparing something unfamiliar with something familiar, you might explain the importance of understanding the unfamiliar item.

Organize the body of your paper according to whichever pattern—block or alternating—suits its length and the number of points you're planning to take up. If you explain something familiar by comparing it with something unfamiliar, start with the familiar item. If you try to show the superiority of one item over another, proceed from the less to the more desirable one. Note that both of the Pat-and-Mike outlines (pages 132–133) put Mike ahead of Pat, the superior candidate.

Write whatever kind of conclusion will round off your discussion effectively. Many comparison papers end with a recommendation or a prediction. A paper comparing two brands of stereo receivers might recommend purchasing one of them. A paper comparing a familiar sport, such as football, with an unfamiliar one, such as rugby, might predict the future popularity of the latter. Unless you've written a lengthy paper, don't summarize the likenesses and differences you've presented. If you've done a proper writing job, your reader already has them clearly in mind.

Revising the Comparison

Revise your paper in light of the general guidelines in Chapter 4 and the questions that follow:

- Have I accomplished my purpose, whether to choose between alternatives or acquaint the reader with something unfamiliar?
- For something unfamiliar, have I shown clearly just how it is like and unlike the familiar item?
- Have I consistently written with my audience in mind?
- Have I considered all points of similarity and difference that relate to my purpose?
- Have I included appropriate supporting details?
- Are my comparisons arranged effectively?
- Have I considered appropriate ethical issues?

◖ SAMPLE STUDENT ESSAY OF COMPARISON

Different Shifts, Different Actions

Claire Mutter

1   The nursing team in a small hospital meets the routine and special daily needs of patients. A registered professional nurse usually leads the team, and members often include registered and practical nurses, nurse's aides, and attendants. Although all nurses care for patients, the duties and working conditions of team members on the first and second shifts differ considerably.

2   The first shift begins at 7:00 A.M., when nurses awaken patients and prepare them for laboratory tests, X-rays, or medications. Additional nursing

duties include taking temperatures, pulses, and respirations and giving enemas or preoperative injections. Team members also serve breakfast and then administer medications such as pain pills.

3   By this time doctors have arrived to visit their patients. The nursing station swirls with activity. Doctors write new orders at desks cluttered with their patients' charts. Laboratory and X-ray technicians explain test results. The pharmacist brings medications and inquires about any new orders for drugs. Inhalation and physical therapists check charts for their new orders. The dietitian asks why Mr. Bowers is not eating his prescribed foods. Telephones ring and patients' signal lights flash continually. The members of the nursing team, all with their own duties, try desperately to keep up with these frenzied activities, which leaves little time to spend with their patients. This pace continues through most of the first shift.

4   Second shift team members, starting work at 3:00 P.M., usually can devote more attention to their patients' personal needs. To prepare for supper, nurses clear flowers and cards from tables, wash faces and hands where necessary, and position patients for eating comfort. After supper, when visitors have departed, team members inform patients about their conditions and teach them how to care for themselves after discharge. For example, they show diabetic patients how to administer insulin injections and to care for their skin, and tell them what foods to eat.

5   To prepare patients for the night, nurses straighten and change beds and give last medications. By 10:00 most patients are asleep. Calmness and quiet prevail at the nursing station, with only two or three nurses doing their charting—recording how patients have tolerated treatment and medication. Except for an occasional signal light from a patient, activities cease for the night.

6   Although both shifts have the same responsibilities, the care and welfare of the patient, the second shift usually works in a much more relaxed atmosphere. Fewer staff people and a slower pace result in more personalized treatment.

Discussion Questions

1. Comment on the significance of the phrase "the duties and working conditions" in paragraph 1.
2. Point out effective supporting details in the essay. What do they accomplish?
3. What pattern of organization does the writer use?

4. Explain why the writer ends the third sentence of paragraph 5 as follows: "recording how patients have tolerated treatment and medication." What can you learn from this explanation?

SUGGESTIONS FOR WRITING

1. Write a properly focused comparison essay on one of the topics below or another that your instructor approves. Determine the points you will discuss and how you will develop and arrange them. Emphasize similarities, differences, or both.

   a. Two sportscasters (or news commentators or talk show hosts)
   b. The physical or mental demands of two jobs
   c. Male and female responses to stress
   d. Online and traditional shopping
   e. Something natural and something artificial
   f. The playing styles of two NBA or WNBA superstars
   g. Two computer languages
   h. A high-pressure and a no-pressure salesperson
   i. Online and traditional dating
   j. The business, residential, or slum districts of two cities or a wealthy and a working-class residential district in the same city
   k. A favorite social spot during the day and during the evening
   l. Conventional and digital photography
   m. The effectiveness of two pieces of writing
   n. Traditional and extreme sports
   o. Two techniques for doing something in your field
   p. Two musical groups
   q. Two managers (or styles of managing)
   r. Authoritarian vs. permissive parenting
   s. Two products being considered for purchase
   t. Two video games

2. Develop an analogy based on one of the following sets of items or another set that your instructor approves. Proceed as you would for any other comparison.

   a. The offerings in a college catalog and a restaurant
   b. A conquering army and a swarm of locusts
   c. Driving on certain highways and gambling
   d. A heart and a pump
   e. Writing and gardening
   f. A teacher and a merchant
   g. Cancer and anarchy
   h. A parent and a farmer
   i. A brain and a computer
   j. Developing an idea and building a house
   k. Succeeding at school and winning a military campaign
   l. A workaholic and an alcoholic

m. A mob and a storm

n. A kidney and a filter

o. A cluttered attic and a disorderly mind

p. Reading a book and exploring a new place

q. A rock concert and a circus

r. A party and a circus

s. Casinos and robbery

t. Contemporary America and an amusement park

CRITICAL EDGE   Although you rely on your own knowledge or findings to develop many comparisons, in some cases you'll synthesize (see pages 82–83) material from other sources.

Let's say that your business management instructor has asked you to prepare a report on the management styles of two high-profile chief executive officers (CEOs) at Fortune 500 companies that manufacture the same kinds of products. You realize that you'll need to do some reading in business periodicals like *Forbes, Fortune,* and the *Wall Street Journal* in order to complete this assignment. Your sources reveal that the first CEO favors a highly centralized managerial structure with strict limits on what can be done by all employees except top executives. The company has pursued foreign markets by establishing factories overseas and has aggressively attempted to merge with or acquire its domestic competitors. The second CEO has established a decentralized managerial structure that allows managers at various levels of the company to make key decisions. The company has also established a strong foreign presence, but it has done so primarily by entering into joint ventures with foreign firms. Most of its domestic expansion has resulted from the construction of new plants rather than from mergers or takeovers. Both CEOs have borrowed heavily to finance their companies' expansion. These three differences and one similarity are your points of comparison, which you can organize using either the block or alternating pattern. You might conclude by indicating why you prefer one of the two management styles.

After you've read the views expressed by your sources, examine them critically. Does any of the information about the two CEOs seem slanted so that it appears to misrepresent their management styles? For example, do any of the writers seem to exaggerate the positive or negative features of centralized or decentralized management? Do appropriate examples support the writers' contentions? Does any relevant information appear to be missing? Does any source contain material that isn't related to your purpose? Judging the works of others in this fashion will help you write a better report.*

---

*Because you'll rely on published sources, it is important to read the sections on card catalogs and periodical indexes in Chapter 21 and those on handling quotations and avoiding plagiarism in Chapter 22 before you start to write. As always, follow your instructor's guidelines for documenting sources.

Suggestions for Writing

1. Read "Close the Borders to All Newcomers" (pages 579–582) and "Give Us Your Best, Your Brightest" (pages 583–587) and then compare the views of these two writers.
2. Read several reviews of the same movie and then compare what the critics have written.
3. Write a criticism of a comparison you recently read that you thought was unreasonable.

CHAPTER 11

CAUSE AND EFFECT: EXPLAINING WHY

Cause and effect, like the two sides of a coin, are inseparably linked and together make up *causation*. Cause probes the reasons why actions, events, attitudes, and conditions exist. Effect examines their consequences. Causation is important to us because it can explain historical events, natural happenings, and the actions and attitudes of individuals and groups. It can help us anticipate the consequences of personal actions, natural phenomena, or government policies.

Everyone asks and answers questions of causation. Scott wonders why Sue *really* broke off their relationship, and Jennifer speculates on the consequences of changing her major. People wonder why child abuse and homelessness are on the rise, and millions worry about the effects of corporate cost cutting and violence in our schools.

Inevitably, therefore, you will need to write papers and reports that employ causation. Your instructors might ask you to write on topics such as the causes of the American Revolution, the consequences of white-collar crime, the reasons why so many couples are divorcing, or the effects of different fertilizers on plant growth. An employer may want a report on why a certain product malfunctions, what might happen if a community redesigns its traffic pattern, or how a school closing might affect business.

Patterns in Causal Analysis

Several organizational patterns are possible for a causal analysis. Sometimes, a single cause produces several effects. For instance, poor language skills prevent college students from keeping up with required reading, taking adequate notes, and writing competent papers and essay exams. To explore such a single cause—multiple effect relationship, construct outlines similar to the following two:

I. Introduction: identifies cause	I. Poor language skills
II. Body	II. Body
A. Effect number 1	A. Can't keep up with required reading
B. Effect number 2	B. Can't take adequate notes
C. Effect number 3	C. Can't write competent papers or exams
III. Conclusion	III. Conclusion

Alternatively, you might discuss the cause after the effects are presented.

On the other hand, several causes may join forces to produce one effect. Zinc production in the United States, for example, has decreased over the last few years because it can be produced more cheaply abroad than it can here, it is being replaced on cars by plastics and lighter metals, and it cannot be recycled. Here's how you might organize a typical multiple cause–single effect paper:

I. Introduction: identifies effect	I. Decrease in U.S. zinc production
II. Body	II. Body
A. Cause number 1	A. Produced more cheaply abroad
B. Cause number 2	B. Replaced on cars by plastics, lighter metals
C. Cause number 3	C. Cannot be recycled
III. Conclusion	III. Conclusion

Sometimes discussion of the effect follows the presentation of causes.

At times a set of events forms a causal chain, with each event the effect of the preceding one and the cause of the following one. For example, a student sleeps late and so misses breakfast and ends up hungry and distracted, which in turn results in a poor performance on an exam. Interrupting the chain at any point halts the sequence. Such chains can be likened to a row of upright dominoes that fall one after the other when the first one is pushed. Belief in a domino theory, which held that if one nation in Southeast Asia fell to the communists all would, one after the other, helped bring about U.S. entry into the Vietnam War. Causal chains can also help explain how devices function and some social changes proceed. The following outlines typify the arrangement of a paper explaining a causal chain:

I. Introduction	I. Introduction
II. Body	II. Body
A. Cause	A. Sleep late
B. Effect	B. Miss breakfast
C. Cause	C. Become hungry and distracted
D. Effect	D. Perform poorly on exam
III. Conclusion	III. Conclusion

Papers of this kind resemble process analyses, but process is concerned with *how* the events occur, cause and effect with *why*.

In many situations the sequence of causes and effects is too complex to fit the image of a chain. Suppose you are driving to a movie on a rainy night. You approach an intersection screened by bushes and, because you have the right-of-way, start across. Suddenly a car with unlit headlights looms directly in your path. You hit the brakes but skid on the slippery pavement and crash into the other car, crumpling its left fender and damaging your own bumper. Later, as you think about the episode, you begin to sense its complexities.

Obviously, the *immediate cause* of the accident was the other driver's failure to heed the stop sign. But other causes also played roles: the bushes and unlit headlights that kept you from seeing the other car sooner; the starts and stops, speedups and slowdowns that brought the two cars to the intersection at the same time; the wet pavement you skidded on; and the movie that brought you out in the first place.

You also realize that the effects of the accident go beyond the fender and bumper damage. After the accident, a police officer ticketed the other driver. As a result of the delay, you missed the movie. Further, the accident unnerved you so badly that you couldn't attend classes the next day and therefore missed an important writing assignment. Because of a bad driving record, the other driver lost his license for sixty days. Clearly, the effects of this accident rival the causes in complexity.

Here's how you might organize a multiple cause–multiple effect essay:

I. Introduction	I. The accident
II. Body	II. Body
A. Cause number 1	A. Driver ran stop sign
B. Cause number 2	B. Bushes and unlit headlights
C. Cause number 3	impaired vision
D. Effect number 1	C. Wet pavement caused skidding
E. Effect number 2	D. Missed the movie
F. Effect number 3	E. Unnerved so missed classes
III. Conclusion	next day
	F. Other driver lost license
	III. Conclusion

In some situations, however, you might first present the effects, then turn to the causes.

EXERCISES

1. **Read the following selection and then arrange the events in a causal chain:**

   Although some folk societies still exist today, similar human groups began the slow process of evolving into more complex societies many millennia ago, through settlement in villages and through advances in technology and organizational structure. This gave rise to the second level of organization: civilized preindustrial, or "feudal," society. Here there is a surplus of food because of the selective cultivation of grains—and also because of the practice of animal husbandry. The food surplus permits both the specialization of labor and the kind of class structure that can, for instance, provide the leadership and command the manpower to develop and maintain extensive irrigation systems (which in turn makes possible further increases in the food supply). . . .

Gideon Sjöberg, "The Origin and Development of Cities"

2. Trace the possible effects of the following occurrences:

    a. You pick out a salad at the cafeteria and sit down to eat. Suddenly you notice a large green worm on one of the lettuce leaves.

    b. As you leave your composition classroom, you trip and break your arm.

    c. Your boss has warned you not to be late to work again. You are driving to work with ten minutes to spare when you get a flat tire.

Reasoning Errors in Causal Analysis

Ignoring Multiple Causes

An effect rarely stems from a single cause. The person who believes that permissive parents have caused the present upsurge of venereal disease or the one who blames television violence for the climbing numbers of emotionally disturbed children oversimplifies the situation. Permissiveness and violence perhaps did contribute to these conditions. Without much doubt, however, numerous other factors also played important parts.

Mistaking Chronology for Causation

Don't assume that just because one event followed another that the first necessarily caused the second. This kind of faulty thinking feeds many popular superstitions. Horace walks under a ladder, later stubs his toe, and thinks that his path caused his pain. Sue breaks a mirror just before Al breaks their engagement; then she blames the cracked mirror. Many people once believed that the election of Herbert Hoover as President in 1928 brought on the Great Depression in 1929. Today some people believe that the testing of atomic weapons has altered our weather patterns. Don't misunderstand: One event *may* cause the next; but before you go on record with your conclusion, make sure that you're not dealing with mere chronology.

Confusing Causes with Effects

Young children sometimes declare that the moving trees make the wind blow. Similarly, some adults may think that Pam and Paul married because they fell in love, when in reality economic necessity mandated the vows, and love came later. Scan your evidence carefully in order to avoid such faulty assertions.

‹EXERCISES›

1. **Which of the following statements point toward papers that will focus on causes? Which point toward papers focusing on effects? Explain your answers.**

    a. Most of the problems that plague newly married couples are the direct outgrowth of timidity and pride.

    b. The Marshall Plan was designed to aid the economic recovery of Europe after World War II.

    c. The smoke from burning poison ivy can bring on a skin rash and lung irritation.

    d. Popularity in high school stems largely from good looks, a pleasing personality, participation in school activities, the right friends, and frequent dates.

2. **Identify which of the following paragraphs deals with causes, which with effects. List the causes and effects.**

    a.   Color filters offer three advantages in black-and-white photography. First, a particular color will be lightened by a filter of the same color. For example, in a photograph of a red rose in a dark blue vase, both will appear almost the same shade of gray if no filter is used. However, when photographed through a red filter, the rose will appear much lighter than the vase; and through a blue filter the vase will appear much lighter than the rose. This effect can be useful in emphasizing or muting certain objects in a photograph. Second, a particular color filter will darken its complementary color in the scene. Consequently, any orange object will appear darker than normal if a blue filter is used. Finally, color filters can reduce or increase atmospheric haze. For example, in a distant aerial shot there will often be so much haze that distant detail is obscured. To eliminate haze almost entirely, the photographer can use a deep red filter. On the other hand, if more haze is desired in order to achieve an artistic effect, varying shades of blue filters can be used.

    Timothy Kelly

    b.   Overeating, which has become a national pastime for millions of Americans, has several roots. For example, parents who are concerned that their children get enough to eat during the growing years overfeed them and thereby establish a lifetime overeating habit. The child who is constantly praised for cleaning up his plate experiences a sort of gratification later on as he cleans up all too many plates. The easy availability of so much food is a constant temptation for many people, especially the types of food served at fast-food restaurants and merchandised in the frozen food departments of supermarkets. Equally tempting are all the snack foods constantly advertised on TV. But many people don't need temptation from the outside; their overeating arises from such psychological factors as nervousness, boredom, loneliness, insecurity, an overall discontent with life, or an aversion to exercise. Thus, overeating can actually be a symptom of psychological surrender to, or withdrawal from, the complexities and competition of modern life.

Kenneth Reichow

Ethical Issues

Causation is not immune from abuse, either accidental or deliberate. Imagine the consequences of an article that touts a new herbal remedy but fails to mention several potentially serious side effects that could harm many users. Think about the possible strain on your relationship with a friend if she unjustly suspected you of starting a vicious rumor about her. Writing cause-and-effect papers creates an ethical responsibility. Asking and answering these questions will help you meet that obligation.

- Have I tried to uncover all of the causes that might result in a particular outcome? A report blaming poor instruction alone for a high student failure rate in a certain town's public schools almost certainly overlooks such factors as oversized classes, inadequate facilities, and poor home environments.
- Have I carefully weighed the importance of the causes I've uncovered? If a few, but not most, of the classes in the school system with problems are oversized, then the report should not stress their significance.
- Have I tried to uncover and discuss every important effect, even one that might damage a case I'm trying to make? A report emphasizing the beneficial effects of jogging would be dangerously negligent if it failed to note the potential for injury.
- What would be the consequences if people act on my analysis?

Careful evaluation of causes and effects not only fulfills your writing obligation but also your ethical one.

Writing a Causal Analysis

Planning and Drafting the Causal Analysis

Because you have probably speculated about the causes and effects of several campus, local, state, or national problems, writing this type of paper should pose no great difficulty. If you choose your own topic, perhaps your personal experience will suggest something promising. Topics such as "Why I Dislike (or

Like) Foreign Cars" and "How My Father's (or Someone Else's) Death Has Changed My Life" might work well. Nonpersonal topics also offer writing possibilities. For instance, "What's Behind Teenage Suicides?" and "The Impact of Global Markets on American Corporations" would allow you to draw on library resources.

The strategies on pages 27–33 can also help you find several topics. Answer these questions about each candidate:

What purpose will guide this writing?

Who is my audience? Will the topic interest them? Why or why not?

Shall I focus on causes, effects, or both?

Brainstorming your topic for supporting details should be easy. If you're dealing with causes, pose these questions about each one:

How significant is this cause?

Could it have brought about the effect by itself?

Does it form part of a chain?

Precisely how does it contribute to the effect?

For papers dealing with effects, substitute the following questions for the ones above:

How important is this effect?

What evidence will establish its importance?

Charting your results can help you prepare for writing the paper. To tabulate causes, use an arrangement like this one:

Cause	Contribution to Effect
First cause	Specific contribution
Second cause	Specific contribution

For effects, use this chart:

Effect	Importance
First effect	Why important
Second effect	Why important

Once your items are tabulated, examine them carefully for completeness. Perhaps you've overlooked a cause or effect or have slighted the significance of one you've already mentioned. Think about the order in which you'd like to discuss your items and prepare a revised chart that reflects your decision.

Use the opening of your paper to identify your topic and indicate whether you plan to discuss causes, effects, or both. You can signal your intention in a number of ways. To prepare for a focus on causes, you might use the words *cause, reason,* or *stem from,* or you might ask why something has occurred. To signal a paper on effects, you might use *effect, fallout,* or *impact,* or you might ask what has happened since something took place. Read these examples:

Signals causes: Midville's recent decrease in street crime stems primarily from its expanded educational program, growing job opportunities for young people, and falling rate of drug addiction.

Signals effects: Since my marriage to Rita, how has my social life changed?

At times you may choose some dramatic attention-getter. For a paper on the effects of radon, a toxic radioactive gas present in many homes, you might note that "Although almost everyone now knows about the hazards associated with smoking, eating high-cholesterol foods, and drinking excessively, few people are aware that just going home could be hazardous to one's health." If you use an arresting statement, be sure the content of your paper warrants it.

How you organize the body of the paper depends on your topic. Close scrutiny may reveal that one cause was indispensable; the rest merely played supporting roles. If so, discuss the main cause first. In analyzing your automobile mishap, which fits this situation, start with the failure of the other driver to yield the right-of-way; then fan out to any other causes that merit mentioning. Sometimes you'll find that no single cause was essential but that all of them helped matters along. Combinations of this kind lie at the heart of many social and economic concerns: inflation, depression, and urban crime rates, to name just a few. Weigh each cause carefully and rank them in importance. If your topic and purpose will profit from building suspense, work from the least important cause to the most important. Otherwise, reverse the order. For analyzing causal chains, chronological order works effectively.

If space won't permit you to deal adequately with every cause, pick out the two or three you consider most important and limit your discussion to them. To avoid giving your reader an oversimplified impression, note that other causes exist. Even if length poses no problem, don't attempt to trace every cause to some more remote cause and then to a still more remote one. Instead, determine some sensible cutoff point that accords with your purpose, and don't go beyond it.

Treat effects as carefully as you do causes. Keep in mind that effects often travel in packs, and try to arrange them in some logical order. If they occur together, consider order of climax. If one follows the other in a chainlike sequence, present them in that fashion. If space considerations dictate, limit your discussion to the most interesting or significant effects. Whatever order you choose for your paper, don't jump helter-skelter from cause to effect to cause in a way that leaves your reader bewildered.

As you write, don't restrict yourself to a bare-bones discussion of causes and effects. If, for instance, you're exploring the student parking problem on your campus, you might describe the jammed lots or point out that students often miss class because they have to drive around and look for spots. Similarly, don't simply assert that the administration's insensitivity contributes to the problem. Instead, cite examples of the college's refusal to answer letters about the situation or to discuss it. To provide statistical evidence of the problem's seriousness, you might note the small number of lots, the limited spaces in each, and the approximate number of student cars on campus.

It's important to remember, however, that you're not just listing causes and effects; you're showing the reader their connection. Let's see how one student handled this connection. After you've read "Why Students Drop Out of College," the student essay that follows in this chapter, carefully re-examine paragraph 3. Note how the sentence beginning "In many schools" and the two following it show precisely how poor study habits develop. Note further how the sentence beginning "This laxity produces" and the three following it show precisely how such poor habits result in "a flood of low grades and failure." Armed with this information, readers are better able to avoid poor study habits and their consequences.

Causal analyses can end in several ways. A paper discussing the effects of acid rain on America's lakes and streams might specify the grave consequences of failing to deal with the problem or express the hope that something will be done. Frequently, writers use their conclusions to evaluate the relative importance of their causes or effects.

Revising the Causal Analysis

Follow the guidelines in Chapter 4 and answer these questions as you revise your causal analysis:

- Have I made the right decision in electing to focus on causes, effects, or both?
- Have I ferreted out all important causes and effects? Mistakenly labeled something as an effect merely because it follows something else? Confused causes with effects?
- Am I dealing with a causal chain? An immediate cause and several supporting causes? Multiple causes and effects?
- Have I presented my causes and effects in an appropriate order?
- Have I supported my discussion with sufficient details?
- Have I considered appropriate ethical issues?

◖ SAMPLE STUDENT ESSAY OF CAUSE AND EFFECT

Why Students Drop Out of College

Diann Fisher

1   Each fall a new crop of first-year college students, wavering between high hopes for the future and intense anxiety about their new status, scan college maps searching for their classrooms. They have been told repeatedly that college is the key to a well-paying job, and

they certainly don't want to support themselves by flipping hamburgers or working at some other dead-end job. So, notebooks at the ready, they await what college has in store. Unfortunately many of them—indeed, over 30 percent—will not return after the first year. Why do so many students leave? There are several reasons. Some find the academic program too hard, some lack the proper study habits or motivation, others fall victim to the temptations of the college environment, and a large group leave for personal reasons.

2   Not surprisingly, the academic shortcomings of college students have strong links to high school. In the past, a high school student who lacked the ability or desire to take a college-preparatory course could settle for a diploma in general studies and afterward find a job with decent pay. Now that possibility scarcely exists, so many poorly prepared students feel compelled to try college. Getting accepted by some schools isn't difficult. Once in, though, the student who has taken nothing beyond general mathematics, English, and science faces serious trouble when confronted with college algebra, first-year composition, and biological or physical science. Most colleges do offer remedial courses and other assistance that may help some weaker students to survive. In spite of everything, however, many others find themselves facing ever-worsening grade-point averages and either fail or just give up.

3   Like academic shortcomings, poor study habits have their roots in high school, where even average students can often breeze through with a minimum of effort. In many schools, outside assignments are rare and so easy that they require little time or thought to complete. To accommodate slower students, teachers frequently repeat material so many times that slightly better students can grasp it without opening their books. And when papers are late, teachers often don't mark them down. This laxity produces students who can't or don't want to study, students totally unprepared for the rigorous demands of college. There, courses may require several hours of study each week in order to be passed with even a <u>C</u>. In many programs, outside assignments are commonplace and demanding. Instructors expect students to grasp material after one explanation, and many won't accept late papers at all. Students who don't quickly develop disciplined study habits face a flood of low grades and failure.

4   Poor student motivation aggravates faulty study habits. Students who thought high school was boring find even less allure in the more challenging college offerings. Lacking any commitment to do well, they shrug off

assigned papers, skip classes, and avoid doing required reading. Over time, classes gradually shrink as more and more students stay away. With final exams upon them, some return in a last-ditch effort to salvage a passing grade, but by then it is too late. Eventually, repetition of this scenario forces the students out.

5   The wide range of freedoms offered by the college environment can overwhelm even well-prepared newcomers. While students are in high school, parents are on hand to make them study, push them off to class, and send them to bed at a reasonable hour. Once away from home and parents, however, far too many students become caught up in a constant round of parties, dates, bull sessions, and other distractions that seem more fascinating than school work. Again, if such behavior persists poor grades and failure result.

6   Personal reasons also take a heavy toll on students who might otherwise complete their programs successfully. Often, money problems are at fault. For example, a student may lose a scholarship or grant, fail to obtain needed work, or find that the family can no longer afford to help out. Some students succumb to homesickness; some are forced out by an illness, injury, or death in the family; and yet others become ill or injure themselves and leave to recuperate. Finally, a considerable number become disillusioned with their programs or the size, location, or atmosphere of their schools and decide not to return.

7   What happens to the students who drop out? Some re-enroll in college later, often in less demanding two- and four-year schools that offer a better chance of academic success. Of the remainder, the great bulk find civilian jobs or enlist in the armed forces. Most, whatever their choice, go on to lead productive, useful lives. In the meantime, campus newcomers need to know about the dangers that tripped up so many of their predecessors and make every effort to avoid them.

Discussion Questions

1. Identify the thesis statement in this essay.
2. Trace the causal chain that makes up paragraph 2.
3. What is the function of the first sentence in paragraph 3?
4. In which paragraphs does the writer discuss causes? Effects?

Suggestions for Writing

Use one of the following topics, or another that your instructor approves, to develop a causal analysis. Determine which causes and/or effects to consider. Scrutinize your analysis for errors in reasoning, settle on an organization, and write the essay.

1. Reasons that relationships fail
2. The effect of some friend, acquaintance, public figure, or writer on your life
3. Causes, effects, or both of road rage
4. Effects of divorce on children
5. Why you are a _____ major
6. Causes, effects, or both of the popularity of the Internet
7. Causes of school violence
8. Effects of the popularity of casino gambling
9. Causes, effects, or both of the cell phone phenomenon
10. Reasons that you have a particular habit or participate in a particular sport
11. Causes or effects of sleep deprivation
12. Reasons that _____ is a popular celebrity
13. Effects of some recent Supreme Court decision or change in public policy
14. Causes, effects, or both of some family crisis in your life
15. Causes, effects, or both of our hunger for heroes
16. Reasons that herbal medicines enjoy widespread popularity
17. Effects of drinking on college students
18. Causes of procrastination
19. Reasons that the national crime rate has decreased
20. Causes and effects of violence at sporting events

CRITICAL EDGE

Although nearly everyone recognizes the role of causation in human affairs, differences of opinion often surface about the causes and effects of important matters. What lies behind the widespread incivility in the United States today? Why are women more likely than men to leave management jobs? How do video games affect children? What impact does the high divorce rate have on American society? Obviously such questions lack simple answers; and as a result investigators, even when they agree on the causes and effects involved, often debate their relative importance.

Suppose your women's studies instructor has asked you to investigate the departure of women from managerial positions. A library search reveals several articles on this topic as well as a number of reasons for resigning. Some women leave because they find it harder to advance than men do, and as a result they seldom attain senior positions. Others leave because they receive lower salaries than their male counterparts. Still others leave because of the stifling effects of corporate rigidity, unrealistic expectations, the demands of raising a family, or possibly diminished chances of marriage. Although most articles cite these causes, their relative importance is debatable. One writer, for example, emphasizes family concerns by discussing them last and at greatest length. Another puts the chief blame on obstacles to upward mobility—the existence of a "glass ceiling" that blocks women from upper-level positions along with an "old-boy network" of entrenched executives that parcels out jobs among its members.

Once you've finished your research, you're ready to synthesize (see pages 82–83) the views of your sources as well as your own views. Before you start to write, though, take some time to consider carefully each cause and effect you've uncovered. Obviously you should ground your paper on well-supported and widely acknowledged causes and effects, but you might also include more speculative ones as long as you clearly indicate their secondary nature. To illustrate, one writer, while mentioning corporate rigidity as a reason that women leave management jobs, clearly labels this explanation as a theory and backs it with a single example. As you examine your material, ask yourself these critical questions as well as any others that occur to you: Does any writer exhibit obvious bias? Do the studies cited include a sufficient number of examples to be meaningful? Do the statistics appear reliable, or are some out of date, irrelevant, or skimpy? Have the writers avoided the reasoning errors discussed on page 144? Whenever you find a flaw, note where the problem lies so that you can discuss it in your writing if you choose. Such discussions often clear up common misconceptions. There are various possibilities for organizing your paper. If your sources substantially agree on the most important cause, you might begin with that one and then take up the others. A second possibility, the order-of-climax arrangement, reverses the procedure by starting with secondary causes and ending with the most significant one. You can use the same options for organizing effects. When no clear consensus exists about the relative importance of the different causes and effects, there is no best arrangement of the material.*

SUGGESTIONS FOR WRITING

1. Read three articles on the causes of a major social problem such as domestic violence and incorporate those causes and your own views in a paper.
2. Read two articles that disagree about the effects of a proposed government program such as oil and gas drilling on public land and write a paper that incorporates the writers' views and presents your own conclusions.
3. Write an essay that corrects a common misconception about the causes or effects of a matter about which you feel strongly. Possibilities might include the causes of homelessness or the impact of capital punishment on murder rates in different states.

*Because this type of paper draws upon published information, it is important to read the sections on card catalogs and periodical indexes in Chapter 21 and those on handling quotations and avoiding plagiarism in Chapter 22 before you start to write. As always, follow your instructor's guidelines for documenting sources.

DEFINITION: ESTABLISHING BOUNDARIES

That movie was egregious.

Once the bandage is off the wound, swab the proud flesh with the disinfectant.

Speaking on statewide television, Governor Blaine called his opponent a left-winger.

Do you have questions? You're not alone. Many people would question the sentences above: "What does *egregious* mean?" "How can flesh be *proud*?" "What does the governor mean by *left-winger*? What specific policies does the opponent support that warrant this label?" To avoid puzzling and provoking your own readers, you'll often need to explain the meaning of some term. The term may be unfamiliar *(egregious)*, used in an unfamiliar sense *(proud flesh)*, or mean different things to different people *(left-winger)*. Whenever you clarify the meaning of some term, you are *defining*.

Humans are instinctively curious. We start asking about meanings as soon as we can talk, and we continue to seek, as well as supply, definitions all through life. In school, instructors expect us to explain all sorts of literary, historical, scientific, technical, and social terms. On the job, a member of a company's human resources department might prepare a brochure that explains the meaning of such terms as *corporate responsibility* and *product stewardship* for new employees. An accountant might define *statistical sampling inventory* in a report calling for a change in the inventory system. A special education teacher might write a memo explaining *learning disabled* to the rest of the staff.

When you define, you identify the features that distinguish a term, thereby putting a fence around it, establishing its boundaries, and separating it from all others. Knowing these features enables both you and your reader to use the term appropriately.

Sometimes a word, phrase, or sentence will settle a definition question. To clear up the mystery of "proud flesh," all you'd need to do is insert the parenthetical phrase "(excessively swollen and grainy)" after the word *proud*. But when you're dealing with new terms—*information superhighway* and *virtual reality* are examples—brief definitions won't provide the reader with enough information for proper understanding.

Abstract terms—those standing for things we can't see, touch, or otherwise detect with our five senses—often require extended definitions, too. It's impossible to capture the essence of *democracy* or *hatred* or *bravery* in a single sentence: The terms are too complex, and people have too many differing ideas about what they mean. The same holds true for some concrete terms—those standing for actions and things we can perceive with our five senses. Some people, for instance, limit the term *drug pusher* to full-time sellers of hard drugs like cocaine and heroin. Others, at the opposite extreme, extend the term to full- and part-time sellers of any illegal drug. Writing an argument recommending life sentences for convicted drug pushers would require you to tell just what you mean by the term so that the reader would have solid grounds for judging your position.

Types of Definitions

Three types of definition—synonyms, essential definitions, and extended definitions—serve writers' needs. Although the first two seldom require more than a word or a sentence, an extended definition can run to several pages. The three types, however, are related. Synonyms and essential definitions share space between the covers of dictionaries, and both furnish starting points for extended definitions.

Synonyms

Synonyms are words with very nearly the same meanings. *Lissome* is synonymous with *lithe* or *nimble,* and *condign* is a synonym of *worthy* and *suitable.* Synonyms let writers clarify meanings of unfamiliar words without using cumbersome explanations. To clarify the term *expostulation* in a quoted passage, all you'd have to do is add the word *objection,* in brackets, after it. Because synonyms are not identical twins, using them puts a slightly different shade of meaning on a message. For example, to "protest" and to "object" are certainly similar in many ways. Yet the claim that we "object" to the establishment of a nuclear waste site in our area fails to capture the active and sustained commitment implied in our willingness to "protest" against such a site. Still, synonyms provide a convenient means of breaking communications logjams.

Essential Definitions

An essential definition does three things: (1) names the item being defined, (2) places it in a broad category, and (3) distinguishes it from other items in that category. Here are three examples:

Item Being Defined	Broad Category	Distinguishing Features
A howdah	is a covered seat	for riding on the back of an elephant or camel.
A voiceprint	is a graphical record	of a person's voice characteristics.
To parboil	is to boil meat, vegetables, or fruits	until they are partially cooked.

Writing a good essential definition requires careful thought. Suppose your instructor has asked you to write an essential definition of one of the terms listed in an exercise, and you choose vacuum cleaner. Coming up with a broad category presents no problem: A vacuum cleaner is a household appliance. The hard part is pinpointing the distinguishing features. The purpose of a vacuum cleaner is to clean floors, carpets, and upholstery. You soon realize, however, that these features alone do not separate vacuum cleaners from other appliances. After all, carpet sweepers also clean floors, and whisk brooms clean upholstery. What then does distinguish vacuum cleaners? After a little thought, you realize that, unlike the other items, a vacuum cleaner works by suction. You then write the following definition:

> A vacuum cleaner is a household appliance that uses suction to clean floors, carpets, and upholstery.

The same careful attention is necessary to establish the distinguishing features of any essential definition.

Limitations of Essential Definitions   Essential definitions have certain built-in limitations. Because of their brevity, they often can't do full justice to abstract terms such as *cowardice, love, jealousy, power.* Problems also arise with terms that have several settled meanings. To explain *jam* adequately, you'd need at least three essential definitions: (1) a closely packed crowd, (2) preserves, and (3) a difficult situation. But despite these limitations, an essential definition can be useful by itself or as part of a longer definition. Writers often build an extended definition around an essential definition.

Pitfalls in Preparing Essential Definitions   When you prepare an essential definition, guard against these flaws:

Circular definition. Don't define a term by repeating it or changing its form slightly. Saying that a psychiatrist is "a physician who practices psychiatry" will only frustrate someone who's never heard of psychiatry. Repress circularity and provide the proper insight by choosing terms the reader can relate to, for example, "A psychiatrist is a physician who diagnoses and treats mental disorders."

Overly broad definition. Shy away from definitions that embrace too much territory. If you define a skunk as "an animal that has a bushy tail and black fur with white markings," your definition is not precise. Many cats and dogs also fit this description. But if you add "and that ejects a foul-smelling secretion when threatened," you will clear the air—of any misconceptions at least.

Overly narrow definition. Don't hem in your definition too closely, either. "A kitchen blender is a bladed electrical appliance used to chop foods" illustrates this error. Blenders perform other operations, too. To correct the error, add the missing information: "A kitchen blender is a bladed electrical appliance used to chop, mix, whip, liquefy, or otherwise process foods."

Omission of main category. Avoid using "is where" or "is when" instead of naming the main category. Here are examples of this error: "A bistro is where food and wine are served" and "An ordination is when a person is formally recognized as a minister, priest, or rabbi." The reader will not know exactly what sort of thing (a bar? a party?) a *bistro* is and may think that *ordination* means a time. Note the improvement when the broad categories are named: "A bistro is a small restaurant where both food and wine are served" and "An ordination is a ceremony at which a person is formally recognized as a minister, priest, or rabbi."

EXERCISES

1. **Identify the broad category and the distinguishing traits in each of these essential definitions:**

   a. Gangue is useless rock accompanying valuable minerals in a deposit.

   b. A catbird is a small American songbird with a slate-colored body, a black cap, and a catlike cry.

   c. A soldier is a man or woman serving in an army.

   d. Myelin is a white, fatty substance that forms a sheath around some nerve fibers.

   e. A gargoyle is a waterspout carved in the likeness of a grotesque animal or imaginary creature and projecting from the gutter of a building.

   f. A magnum is a wine bottle that holds about two-fifths of a gallon.

2. **Indicate which of the following statements are acceptable essential definitions. Explain what is wrong with those that are not. Correct them.**

   a. A scalpel is a small knife that has a sharp blade used for surgery and anatomical dissections.

   b. A puritan is a person with puritanical beliefs.

   c. A kraal is where South African tribes keep large domestic animals.

   d. A rifle is a firearm that has a grooved barrel and is used for hunting large game.

   e. A motorcycle is a two-wheeled vehicle used mainly for human transportation.

   f. Fainting is when a person loses consciousness owing to inadequate flow of blood to the brain.

3. **Write an essential definition for each of the following terms:**

   a. groupie   c. hit man   e. pushover

   b. happy hour   d. jock   f. hard grader ◀

Extended Definitions

Sometimes it's necessary to go beyond an essential definition and write a paragraph or whole paper explaining a term. New technical, social, and economic terms often require extended definitions. To illustrate, a computer scientist might need to define *data integrity* so that computer operators understand the importance of maintaining it. Terms with differing meanings also frequently require extended definitions. To let voters know just what he means by *left-winger,* Governor Blaine might detail the kinds of legislation his opponent favors and opposes. Furthermore, extended definition is crucial to interpretation of the law, as we see when courts clarify the meaning of concepts such as obscenity.

Extended definitions are not merely academic exercises; they are fundamental to your career and your life. A police officer needs to have a clear understanding of what counts as *reasonable grounds for search and seizure;* an engineer must comprehend the meaning of *stress;* a nuclear medical technologist had better have a solid grasp of *radiation.* And all of us are concerned with the definition of our basic rights as citizens.

Extended definitions are montages of other methods of development— narration, description, process analysis, illustration, classification, comparison, and cause and effect. Often, they also define by negation: explaining what a term *does not* mean. The following paragraphs show how one writer handled an extended definition of *sudden infant death syndrome.* The student began by presenting a case history (illustration), which also incorporated an essential definition and two synonyms.

> Jane and Dick Smith were proud, new parents of an eight-pound, ten-ounce baby girl named Jenny. One summer night, Jane put Jenny to bed at 8:00. When she went to check on her at 3:00 A.M., Jane found Jenny dead. The baby had given no cry of pain, shown no sign of trouble. Even the doctor did not know why she had died, for she was healthy and strong. The autopsy report confirmed the doctor's suspicion—the infant was a victim of "sudden infant death syndrome," also known as SIDS or crib death. SIDS is the sudden and unexplainable death of an apparently healthy, sleeping infant. It is the number-one cause of death in infants after the first week of life and as a result has been the subject of numerous research studies.

DISCUSSION QUESTIONS

1. What synonyms does the writer use?
2. Which sentence presents an essential definition?

In the next paragraph, the writer turned to negation, pointing out some of the things that researchers have ruled out about SIDS.

> Although researchers do not know what SIDS is, they do know what it is <u>not.</u> They know it cannot be predicted; it strikes like a thief in the night. Crib deaths occur in seconds, with no sound of pain, and they always happen when the child is sleeping. Suffocation is <u>not</u> the cause, nor is aspiration or regurgitation. Researchers have found no correlation between the incidence

of SIDS and the mother's use of birth control pills or tobacco or the presence of fluoride in water. Since it is not hereditary or contagious, only a slim chance exists that SIDS will strike twice in the same family.

Finally, the student explored several proposed causes of SIDS as well as how parents may react to the loss of their child.

> As might be expected, researchers have offered many theories concerning the cause of crib death. Dr. R. C. Reisinger, a National Cancer Institute scientist, has linked crib deaths to the growth of a common bacterium, E. coli, in the intestines of newborn babies. The organisms multiply in the intestines, manufacturing a toxin that is absorbed by the intestinal wall and passes into the bloodstream. Breast milk stops the growth of the organism, whereas cow's milk permits it. Therefore, Dr. Reisinger believes, bottle-fed babies run a higher risk of crib death than other babies. . . .

> The loss of a child through crib death is an especially traumatic experience. Parents often develop feelings of guilt and depression, thinking they somehow caused the child's death. To alleviate such feelings, organizations have been established to help parents accept the fact that they did not cause the death.

Trudy Stelter

Ethical Issues

How we define can have devastating consequences. For centuries, the practice of defining Africans as "subhuman" helped justify the slave trade and slavery. During the 1930s and early 1940s, labeling Jews as "vermin" was used to fuel the attempt to exterminate them both in Nazi Germany and much of Western Europe. Even in the absence of malice, definition can have far-reaching effects, both good and bad. For instance, a change in the federal definition of "poverty" can increase or decrease by millions the number of individuals and households eligible for benefits such as Medicaid. Although the consequences of your writing won't approach those of the above examples, you'll nevertheless need to think about possible ethical implications. Addressing the following questions will help you do this.

- Have I carefully evaluated all of the features of my definition? In clarifying what constitutes "excessive force" by the police, it would be unfair to include the reasonable means necessary to subdue a highly dangerous suspect.
- Have I slanted my definition to reflect some prejudice? Let's say a writer opposed to casino gambling is defining "gambling addicts." The paper should focus on those who spend an excessive amount of time in casinos, bet and often lose large sums of money, and in so doing neglect family, financial,

and personal obligations. It would be unfair to include those who visit casinos occasionally and strictly limit their losses.

■ Have I avoided unnecessary connotations that might be harmful? A definition of teenagers that overemphasized their swift changes in mood might be unfair, perhaps even harmful, since it may influence the reactions of readers.

Writing an Extended Definition

Planning and Drafting the Extended Definition

If you choose your own topic, pick an abstract term or one that is concrete but unfamiliar to your reader. Why, for instance, define *table* when the discussion would likely ease the reader into the Land of Nod? On the other hand, a paper explaining *computer virus* might well prove interesting and informative. Use one of the strategies on pages 27–33 to unearth promising topics. Then answer these questions about them:

Which topic holds the most promise? Why?

What purpose will guide my writing? To clarify a technical or specialized concept? To show what the term means to me? To persuade the reader to adopt my attitude toward it? To discuss some neglected facet of it?

For what audience should I write?

Here's a helpful process to follow as you think your definition through. First, select a clear example that illustrates what you wish to define: the United States could exemplify *democracy*. Then brainstorm to uncover major identifying characteristics. For democracy your list might include majority rule, free elections, a separately elected chief executive, and basic human rights. Next, test these characteristics against other legitimate examples and retain only the characteristics that apply. Britain is clearly a democracy but doesn't have a separately elected chief executive. Finally, test the unfolding definition against a clear counter-example, perhaps the People's Republic of China. If the definition fits the example, something is wrong.

Now evaluate what methods you might use to develop your definition. Each method has its own set of special strengths, as the following list shows:

Narration. Tracing the history of a new development or the changing meaning of a term

Description. Pointing out interesting or important features of a device, an event, or an individual

Process. Explaining what a device does or how it is used, how a procedure is carried out, or how a natural event takes place

Illustration. Tracing changes in meaning and defining abstract terms

Classification. Pointing out the different categories into which an item or an event can be grouped

Comparison. Distinguishing between an unfamiliar and a familiar item

Cause and effect. Explaining the origins and consequences of events, conditions, problems, and attitudes

Negation. Placing limitations on conditions and events and correcting popular misconceptions

Examine your topic in light of this listing and select the methods of development that seem most promising. Don't hesitate to use a method for some purpose not mentioned here. If you think that a comparison will help your reader understand some abstract term, use it.

Chart the methods of development you'll use, and then brainstorm each method in turn to gather the details that will inform the reader. When you've finished, look everything over, rearrange the details as necessary, add any new ones you think of, and prepare a revised chart. The example that follows is for a paper using four methods of development.

Narration	**Classification**	**Process**	**Negation**
First supporting detail	First supporting detail	First supporting detail	First supporting detail
Second supporting detail	Second supporting detail	Second supporting detail	Second supporting detail

Definition papers can begin in various ways. If you're defining a term with no agreed-upon meaning (for example, *conservatism*), you might note some differing views of it and then state your own. If the term reflects some new social, political, economic, or technological development (such as the *wireless Internet*), you might mention the events that brought it into being. A colloquial or slang term often lends itself nicely to an attention-getting opener. A paper defining *chutzpah* might begin by illustrating the brash behavior of someone with this trait. Often an introduction includes a short definition, perhaps taken from a dictionary. If you do include a dictionary definition, use the full name of the dictionary (*Webster's New World Dictionary* says . . .). Several dictionary titles include the word *Webster*, and unless you use the full name your reader won't know which one you mean. Draw on a dictionary definition, however, only as a last resort.

In writing the body of the paper, present the methods of development in whatever order seems most appropriate. A paper defining *drag racing* might first describe the hectic scene as the cars line up for a race, then classify the different categories of vehicles, and finally explain the steps in a race. One defining *intellectual* might start by showing the differences between intellectuals and scholars, then name several prominent intellectuals and note how their insights have altered our thinking, and conclude by trying to explain why many Americans hold intellectuals in low regard.

Definition papers can end, as well as begin, in a number of ways. If you're defining some undesirable condition or event (such as *sudden infant death syndrome*), you might express hope for a speedy solution. If you're reporting on some new development (like *information superhighway*), you might predict its economic or social impact. Often, a summary of your main points is effective. Choose whichever type of ending best supports your main idea.

Revising the Extended Definition

Use the general guidelines in Chapter 4 and these specific questions as you revise your extended definition:

Are my purpose and audience clear and appropriate?

If I've used an essential definition, does it do what it should and avoid the common pitfalls?

Are the methods of development suitable for the topic?

Is the paper organized effectively?

Are there other factors or examples I need to consider?

Have I considered appropriate ethical issues?

SAMPLE STUDENT ESSAY OF DEFINITION

Rediscovering Patriotism

Peter Wing

1   After the horrifying events of September 11, 2001, when terrorists flew jet planes into the World Trade Center and the Pentagon, killing thousands of Americans, there was a surge of patriotism. America was under attack, and as we frequently do when our nation is threatened, we rallied around the flag. Flags were pasted in the back windows of cars and the front windows of homes. So many Americans bought flags that stores were quickly sold out. It was a rare car that didn't have a United We Stand bumper sticker. Rock groups that had built their image around cynicism gleefully partici- pated in patriotic concerts. In short, it became fashionable once again to be a flag-waving, Star Spangled Banner–singing, country-loving patriot.

2   These results were good, but there was also an alarming side to this newfound patriotism. Those who even suggested that American foreign policy might have contributed to the attack were branded *traitor* and were effectively silenced. People, including members of Congress, who criti- cized the way the war on terrorism was being conducted were lambasted as unpatriotic. In my neighborhood, those who didn't fly flags, who didn't have patriotic bumper stickers, who didn't seethe with righteous anger at America's enemy were labeled un-American. All of this raises an obvious question. What is patriotism?

3   The obvious answer is that patriotism is love for one's country. But clearly that answer is too broad. Someone could easily love the skyscrapers of Man- hattan, the gorgeous vistas of the Grand Canyon, and even the cornfields of Iowa and still sell military secrets to an enemy of America, a far from patriotic

act. Timothy McVeigh would probably have said that he loved his country, but it would be troubling to consider his attack on the Alfred P. Murrah Federal Building a patriotic act. Certainly patriotism can include an intense love for the land, an appreciation for the people that make up our nation, and a pride in the accomplishments of our country. Part of the heart-swelling quality of patriotism is the recognition of all that is great and good about our nation: the valiant role of our soldiers in World War II; the innovative spirit that forged new technologies, cured diseases, and allowed Americans to journey to the moon. However, that pride would be incomplete without an appreciation for and dedication to the core principles that define this nation.

4   In the end what is most essential to America is not our industrial wealth, our military power, or artistic works. America is defined by its initial vision, the commitment to democracy, to basic political equality for all Americans, to liberty, to the rights of the individual. Consider how odd it would be if someone's claim to patriotism were a desire for a military coup that toppled democracy to establish a more powerful military. Surely we would find someone seriously misguided who loved American industry but wanted to discard the Constitution and have only the heads of corporations serve in Congress. While there may be many aspects to patriotism, the core of American patriotism would have to be a solid commitment to the core values of the Constitution.

5   What is it then to have a love for and commitment to the core values of a nation? It is easy to confuse patriotism with the symbols of patriotism, the flag waving and anthem singing. Just as a husband who gives his wife a love poem and a diamond ring and then rushes out to cheat on her isn't really the best husband, someone who proudly flies a flag but never votes, refuses to serve on juries, and actively discriminates is not the best patriot. Serving in the military is rightly considered one of the most distinguished acts of patriotism, and properly so. Soldiers don't just say they love their country, they risk their lives to protect the people and the principles of their nation, to preserve liberty. Just as love for a spouse isn't simply a matter of gushy greeting cards but rather concerted day-to-day action, including listening patiently to the other's problems, so patriotism lives and breathes through actions. That doesn't have to be military action but can be participation in anything that preserves and strengthens what is best about a nation. Patriotism then means voting in elections, actively participating in campaigns, writing to legislators, serving on juries, volunteering for schools, building homes for the poor, obeying laws, honoring those who serve, and criticizing things that are wrong.

6   One of the paradoxes of this notion of patriotism is that it makes it essential to criticize and even protest against government policy. It would be a poor friend who let a buddy slide into alcoholism without comment. It would be a poor patriot who would let America move away from the best it can be without action. To really love one's country is to struggle to help make that country realize its best ideals. Those who protested against segregation in America were patriots, recalling America to the fundamental commitment to equality. Many who marched against the Vietnam War were patriotic since they believed that the war violated America's commitment to justice. So too were those who felt the Vietnam War was necessary to American security for they only wanted to protect America from a perceived communist threat. Those who objected to the way the war against terrorism was being conducted also, then, could be considered patriotic, for they also, out of a love for their country, were participating in the democratic process, raising their voice so that America would choose the best course of action. Patriotism doesn't reside in being on one side or the other of a political debate; it exists in the honest struggle to realize the best ideals of the country. Given this view, in a democracy no group has a monopoly on patriotism.

7   That is why some of the bitter slogans of supposed patriotism—*My Country Right or Wrong* or *America: Love It or Leave It*—are just plain wrong. While it is true that patriotism would suggest that we not disown our country when it takes what we consider a misguided direction, it would surely not be patriotic to defend and support a direction we thought wrong. Those who are alarmed by the policies of the government or are deeply dissatisfied with some injustice, such as the horrible conditions of many inner-city schools, are not lacking in patriotism and have no obligation to leave. Those who complain, carp, protest, point out shortcomings are acting out of a profound patriotism. Because of their love for their country, they struggle to move the country to realize its best ideals. If there were any bumper sticker I would want to see for patriotism, it would be *Our Country: Make It the Best It Can Be*.

8   It is heartening to see the revival of patriotism. Hopefully, that patriotism will go beyond simple flag waving and dig deeper to the core meaning of patriotism where Americans together struggle to preserve and develop American ideals. Patriotism will really have taken root in America when citizens become involved in the political process, eagerly serve on juries, work to improve the lives of fellow citizens, and, surprisingly enough, raise their voices in criticism when we, as a government and a people, fall short of the very best we can become.

DISCUSSION QUESTIONS

1. Identify the essay's essential definition.
2. What purpose do the first two paragraphs serve?
3. How does the writer develop his definition?
4. What do the first three sentences of paragraph 6 accomplish?
5. Why might the writer have decided to discuss bumper sticker slogans in the next to the last paragraph?

SUGGESTIONS FOR WRITING

Write a properly focused extended definition using one of the following suggestions or one approved by your instructor. The term you define may be new, misused, or misunderstood or may have a disputed meaning. Develop the essay by any combination of writing strategies.

1. Integrity
2. Campus gambling
3. Depression
4. School violence
5. Stress
6. Human genome
7. Extreme sports
8. Body piercing
9. Tae-Bo
10. Cybervandals
11. Campus security
12. Feminist
13. Hate crimes
14. Family values
15. Some term from your field
16. Senior citizen
17. Addiction
18. The Internet
19. The Christian Right
20. Rap music

CRITICAL EDGE Definitions are always social creations. The way various people and communities understand and use any word determines its definition. As a result, writers who use complex words such as *justice, love,* and *charisma* to convey a message may need to consult a number of sources to determine how others have used the words. With their findings of this research in mind, the writers can stake out their own meanings of those words.

If you were writing a paper defining *dance* for a humanities class, you would probably find several conflicting meanings of the term. Frank Thiess, writing in *The Dance As an Artwork*, defines dance as the use of the body for expressive gesture. But as you mull over that definition, you realize that it is both too broad and too narrow. While some forms of dance, such as ballet, feature expressive gesture, so does pantomime or even a shaken fist; and neither of these qualifies as dance. A square dance clearly qualifies, but does it represent expressive gesture? Susanne Langer, in *Philosophy in a New Key,* defines dance as "a play of Powers made visible," pointing to the way dancers seem to be moved by forces beyond themselves. You recognize that this definition may apply to religious dance forms, that dancers sometimes appear swept away by the music, and that you yourself have experienced a feeling of power when dancing. Nevertheless, upon reflection you decide that often it's the dancer's skill that attracts us, and rarely do we dance to reveal invisible powers. Finally, you discover that Francis Sparshott, in *The Theory of the Arts,* defines dance as a rhythmical, patterned motion that transforms people's sense of their own existence according to the dance they do. As you evaluate Sparshott's contention, you decide that it has considerable merit, although you aren't convinced that every dance transforms our sense of existence. When you think about the kinds of dance you know and the various definitions you have uncovered, you conclude that each of these writers, like the blind men who felt different parts of an elephant and tried to describe it, is only partly correct. For your humanities paper, you decide to synthesize (see pages 82–83) the different definitions. You might explain that all dance involves a rhythmical, patterned movement of the body for its own sake. Sometimes such movement can transform our sense of existence, as in trance dances or even waltzes. Other dances, such as story ballets, use rhythmical movements as expressive gestures that tell stories or convey emotions. Still other dances may suggest the manifestation of powers beyond the dances themselves. You proceed to explain each of these features with details drawn from both your sources and personal experience.

Carrying out this type of project requires you to look critically at the definitions of others. Do they accurately reflect the examples you know about? Do they describe examples that do not fit the definition? Are any parts of the definition questionable? Once you've answered these questions, you can then draw on the appropriate elements of the definitions to formulate your own. You might organize such a paper by developing each definition in a separate section, first presenting it in detail and then pointing out its strengths and weaknesses. In the final section, you could offer your own definition and support it with your reasoning and suitable examples.*

SUGGESTIONS FOR WRITING

1. Read the two essays on national identity cards and privacy in the Reader (pages 563–568 and 560–563) as well as several others on this topic that you find in

---

*Because you'll draw upon published sources, it is important to read the sections on card catalogs and periodical indexes in Chapter 21 and those on handling quotations and avoiding plagiarism in Chapter 22 before you start to write. As always, follow your instructor's guidelines for documenting sources.

the library. Reflect on the different definitions of privacy then, drawing on your reading, offer your own definition.

2. Read "The Sweet Smell of Success . . ." (pages 532–534) and "I Have a Dream" (pages 571–574). Then write your own definition of success, taking into account the views expressed in these essays.

3. Do some reading about an abstract term like *bravery, democracy,* or *hatred* in at least three sources. Use the sources to develop your own definition of the term.

ARGUMENT: CONVINCING OTHERS

"What did you think of that movie?"

"Great!"

"What do you mean, *great?* I thought the acting was wooden and the story completely unbelievable."

"That's about what I'd expect from you. You wouldn't know a good movie if it walked up and bit you."

"Oh yeah? What makes you think you're such a great . . . ?"

Argument or quarrel? Many people would ask, "What's the difference?" To them, the two terms convey the same meaning, both calling to mind two angry people, shouting, trading insults, and sometimes slugging it out. In writing, however, *argument* stands for something quite different: a paper, grounded on logical, structured evidence, that attempts to convince the reader to accept an opinion, take some action, or do both. Argument is also a process during which you explore an issue fully, considering different perspectives, assumptions, reasons, and evidence to reach your own informed position.

The ability to argue effectively will help you succeed both in class and on the job. A business instructor may ask students to defend a particular management style. A political science instructor may want you to support or oppose limiting the number of terms that members of a legislature can serve. A special education instructor may have students make a written case for increased funding for exceptional students. In the workplace, a computer programmer may argue that the company should change its account-keeping program, an automotive service manager call for new diagnostic equipment, and a union president make a case that a company's employees merit raises.

Arguments don't always involve conflicts. Some simply support a previously established decision or course of action, as when a department manager sends her boss a memo justifying some new procedure that she implemented. Others try to establish some common ground, just as you might do when you and your date weigh the pros and cons of two films and pick one to see.

When preparing to write an argument, you need to be aware that certain kinds of topics just aren't arguable. There's no point, for instance, in trying to tackle questions of personal preference or taste (Is red prettier than blue?). Such contests quickly turn into "it is," "it isn't" exchanges that establish nothing except the silliness of the contenders. Questions of simple fact (Was Eisenhower first elected President in 1952?) don't qualify either; one side has all the ammunition. Bickering will never settle these issues; reference books quickly will. We turn to argument when there is room for disagreement.

When you write an argument, you don't simply sit down and dash off your views as though they came prefabricated. Instead, argument represents an opportunity to think things through, to gradually, and often tentatively, come to some conclusions, and then, in stages, begin to draft your position with the support you have discovered. You should try to keep an open mind as you formulate and then express your views. And remember, you rarely start from scratch. Instead, you join a conversation where ideas and evidence have already been exchanged. As a result, you need to be thoughtful and informed.

The most successful arguments rest on a firm foundation of solid, logical support. In addition, many arguments include emotion because it can play an important part in swaying reader opinion. Furthermore, writers often make ethical appeals by projecting favorable images of themselves since readers form conclusions based on their judgments of the writer.

The Rational Appeal

In society, and certainly in professional circles, you are usually expected to reach your conclusions on the basis of good reasons and appropriate evidence. Reasons are the key points or general ideas you'll use to defend your conclusions. If, for instance, you support the needle-exchange program for intravenous drug users, one reason might be the considerable reduction in AIDS-related deaths that could result. If you oppose the program, one reason may be the drug dependency that will continue.

To convince readers, your reasons must be substantiated by evidence. If you favor needle exchange, you could cite figures that project the number of deaths that will be prevented. If you're against the program, you might quote a respected authority who verifies that dependency will become entrenched.

When you appeal to reason in an argument, then, you present your reasons and evidence in such a way that if your readers are also reasonable they will likely agree with you, or at least see your position as plausible. That assumes, of course, that you and your readers start from some common ground about the principles you share and what you count as evidence. Evidence falls into several categories: established truths, opinions of authorities, primary source information, statistical findings, and personal experience. The strongest arguments usually combine several kinds of evidence.

Established Truths

These are facts that no one can seriously dispute. Here are some examples:

Historical fact: The First Amendment to the United States Constitution prohibits Congress from abridging freedom of the press.

Scientific fact: The layer of ozone in the earth's upper atmosphere protects us from the sun's harmful ultraviolet radiation.

Geographical fact: The western part of the United States has tremendous reserves of coal.

Established truths aren't arguable themselves but do provide strong backup for argumentative propositions. For example, citing the abundant coal supply in the western regions could support an argument that the United States should return to coal to supply its energy needs.

Some established truths, the result of careful observations and thinking over many years, basically amount to enlightened common sense. The notion that everyone possesses a unique combination of interests, abilities, and personality characteristics illustrates this kind of truth. Few people would seriously question it.

Opinions of Authorities

An authority is a recognized expert in some field. Authoritative opinions—the only kind to use—play a powerful role in winning readers over to your side. The views of metropolitan police chiefs and criminologists could support your position on ways to control urban crime. Researchers who have investigated the effects of air pollution could help you argue for stricter smog-control laws. Whatever your argument, don't settle for less than heavyweight authorities, and, when possible, indicate their credentials to your reader. This information makes their statements more persuasive. For example, "Ann Marie Forsythe, a certified public accountant and vice-president of North American operations for Touche Ross Accounting, believes that the President's tax cut proposal will actually result in a tax increase for most Americans." You should, of course, also cite the source of your information. Follow your instructor's guidelines.

The following paragraph, from an article arguing that extra-high-voltage electric transmission lines pose a health hazard, illustrates the use of authority:

> Robert Becker, a physician and director of the Orthopedic–Biophysics Laboratory at the Syracuse, New York, Veterans Administration Hospital–Upstate Medical Center, has been researching the effects of low-frequency electric fields (60 Hz) for fifteen years. Testifying at health and safety hearings for proposed lines in New York, he said that exposure to the fields can produce physiological and functional changes in humans—anything from increased irritability and fatigue to raised cholesterol levels, hypertension and ulcers. Studies of rats exposed to low-level electric fields showed tumor growths and abnormalities in development. Dr. Becker believes

we are performing unauthorized medical experiments by exposing people to the electromagnetic fields surrounding the transmission lines.

                              Kelly Davis, "Health and High Voltage: 765 KV Lines"

Beware of biased opinions. The agribusiness executive who favors farm price supports or the labor leader who opposes any restrictions on picketing may be writing merely to guard old privileges or garner new ones. Unless the opinion can stand especially close scrutiny, don't put it in your paper; it will just weaken your case with perceptive readers.

Because authorities don't always see eye to eye, their views lack the finality of established truths. Furthermore, their opinions will convince only if the audience accepts the authority *as* authoritative. Although advertisers successfully present football stars as authorities on shaving cream and credit cards, most people would not accept their views on the safety of nuclear energy.

Primary Source Information

You'll need to support certain types of argument with primary source information—documents or other materials produced by individuals directly involved with the issue or conclusions you reached by carrying out an investigation yourself. To argue whether the United States should have dropped the atom bomb on Japan to end World War II, for example, you would want to examine the autobiographies of those involved in making the decision and perhaps even the documents that prompted it. To take a position on the violence mentioned in some gangster rap, you would want to analyze the actual lyrics in a number of songs. To make a claim about the press coverage of the Persian Gulf War, you would want to read the newspaper and magazine accounts of correspondents who were on the scene. To convince readers to adopt your solution for the homeless problem, you might want to visit a homeless shelter or interview (in a safe place) some homeless people. This type of information can help you reach sound conclusions and build strong support for your position. Most college libraries contain a significant amount of primary source materials. Document the sources you use according to your instructor's guidelines.

Statistical Findings

Statistics—data showing how much, how many, or how often—can also buttress your argument. Most statistics come from books, magazines, newspapers, handbooks, encyclopedias, and reports, but you can use data from your own investigations as well. *Statistical Abstract of the United States* is a good source of authoritative statistics on many topics.

Because statistics are often misused, many people distrust them, so any you offer must be reliable. First, make sure your sample isn't too small. Don't use a one-day traffic count to argue for a traffic light at a certain intersection. City Hall might counter by contending that the results are atypical. To make your case, you'd need to count traffic for perhaps two or three weeks. Take care not to push statistical claims too far. You may know that two-thirds of Tarrytown's factories pollute the air excessively, but don't argue that the same figures probably apply to your town. There's simply no carryover. Keep alert for biased statistics; they can cause as serious a credibility gap as biased opinions. Generally, recent data are better than old data, but either must come from a reliable source. Older information from the *New York Times* would probably be more accurate than current data from some publication that trades on sensationalism. Note how the following writer uses statistics in discussing America's aging population and its impact on the federal budget:

> . . . In 1955 defense spending and veterans benefits accounted for almost 70 percent of federal outlays. By 1995 their share was 19 percent. In the same period social security and Medicare (which didn't exist until 1965) went from 6 percent to 34 percent of the budget. Under present trends, their share would rise to 39 percent by 2005, projects the Congressional Budget Office. . . . Between 2010 and 2020, the older-than-65 population will rise by about a third; in the next decade, it will rise almost another third. Today, about one in eight Americans is older than 65; by 2030, the proportion is projected to be one in five. The older-than-85 population will rise even faster.
>
> Robert J. Samuelson, "Getting Serious"

Again, follow your instructor's guidelines when documenting your sources.

Personal Experience

Sometimes personal experience can deliver an argumentative message more forcefully than any other kind of evidence. Suppose that two years ago a speeder ran into your car and almost killed you. Today you're arguing for stiffer laws against speeding. Chances are you'll rely mainly on expert opinions and on statistics showing the number of people killed and injured each year in speeding accidents. However, describing the crash, the slow, pain-filled weeks in the hospital, and the months spent hobbling around on crutches may well provide the persuasive nudge that wins your reader over.

Often the experiences and observations of others, gathered from books, magazines, or interviews, can support your position. If you argue against chemical waste dumps, the personal stories of people who lived near them and suffered the consequences—filthy ooze in the basement, children with birth defects, family members who developed a rare form of cancer—can sway your reader.

Despite its usefulness, personal experience generally reinforces but does not replace other kinds of evidence. Unless it has other support, readers may reject it as atypical or trivial.

Evaluation of Evidence

Once you have gathered the appropriate type(s) of evidence, certain standards govern the evaluation and use of that evidence. That a piece of information is in some way connected to your topic does not make it good evidence or qualify it for inclusion in your paper. Readers won't be convinced that trains are dangerous merely because you were in a train wreck. You should not reach a conclusion based on such flimsy evidence either. In order to reach a reasonable conclusion and defend a position with suitable evidence, you should apply the following principles.

Evaluation Criteria	Explanation
How credible are the sources of the information? How reliable is the evidence?	Not all sources are created equal. U.S. Census data about population change is more credible than a local newspaper's estimate, though both may be more valid than your own estimate.
How much confirming evidence is there?	With evidence, more is better. One scientific study on the efficacy of high-protein diets would be good, but several would be better. One authority who claims that global warming is a reality becomes more credible when confirmed by several other authorities.
How much contradictory evidence is there?	If several scientific studies or authorities point to the efficacy of high-protein diets and several other studies find such diets harmful, clearly you would need to weigh the evidence more carefully.
How well established is the evidence?	Extremely established evidence, such as the evidence for atoms, becomes the basis for textbooks and is assumed in most other research. This evidence is usually unquestionable, although it also can be overturned.
How well does the evidence actually support or fit the claim?	The fact that most Americans are immigrants or descendents of immigrants has no bearing on whether the country is admitting too many or too few immigrants. To make a case for or against some policy on immigration, the evidence would have to focus on its good or bad results.
What does the evidence actually allow you to conclude?	The evidence shouldn't lead you to reach an exaggerated conclusion. Studies showing that TV violence causes children to play more aggressively do not warrant the conclusion that it causes children to kill others.

Sometimes unwarranted conclusions result because a writer fails to take competing claims and evidence into consideration. For example, evidence shows that children in Head Start programs do better than others during the first three years of school. Other evidence, however, shows that in later years these students do not do significantly better. Yet other evidence shows that they are more likely to stay in school and less likely to get into trouble. Clearly, you shouldn't argue that Head Start ensures continuing success at all grade levels. You would need to weigh the credibility, quantity, reliability, and applicability of the available evidence to reach and defend a more limited conclusion.

Reasoning Strategies

An argument, then, consists of a conclusion you want to support, your reasons for that conclusion, and the evidence that supports your reasons. But how are reasons and evidence fitted together? Rational appeals include three reasoning strategies: induction, deduction, and analogy.

Induction

An argument from induction occurs when a general claim is supported by specific evidence, whether direct observations, statistical data, or scientific studies. Most of our conclusions are supported inductively. When we conclude that a movie is worth watching because our friends liked it, when we decide a college program is effective because most students in it get jobs, or even when we support a scientific hypothesis based on formal experimentation, we are basing a conclusion on bits of evidence. We need to be thoughtful in reaching such conclusions. Are our friends like us and trustworthy? Are the jobs students get good jobs? All the principles for evaluating evidence apply.

Induction makes our conclusions probable but rarely proves them. To prove something by induction, we must check every bit of evidence and often that's just not practical or possible. The greater the number of observations and the larger the populations surveyed, the more strongly the conclusion is supported. Obviously then, just a few observations makes the evidence very weak. If you ask ten of fifteen thousand students whether they like the meal plan, you cannot conclude much if eight of the students liked the plan. These students may just be atypical.

All inductive evidence only makes supported conclusions, likely. It is important to measure the strength of the supporting evidence.

You have several options for organizing an inductive argument. You might begin by posing some direct or indirect question in order to snare your reader's interest, or you might simply state the position you will argue. The body of the paper provides the supporting evidence. In the conclusion you could reaffirm your position or suggest the consequences of that position. You can also raise a general question, evaluate the evidence, and then come to a conclusion.

The following short example illustrates inductive argument:

> Bologna is perhaps the most popular of all luncheon meats. Each day, thousands of individuals consume bologna sandwiches at noontime without ever considering the health consequences. Perhaps they should.
>
> The sodium content of bologna is excessively high. On the average, three ounces contain over 850 milligrams, three times as much as a person needs in a single day. In addition, bologna's characteristic flavor and reddish color are caused by sodium nitrite, which is used to prevent the growth of botulism-causing organisms. Unfortunately, sodium nitrite combines with amines, natural compounds already in most foods, to form nitrosamines,

which have been proved to cause cancer in laboratory animals. Finally, from a nutrition standpoint, bologna is terrible. The fat content is around 28 percent, the water content ranges upward from 50 percent, and the meat includes very little protein.

Health-conscious people, then, will choose better fare for lunch.

Alison Russell

When writing an induction argument, in addition to presenting the available evidence, there are two other important things you should do. It is helpful to demonstrate the credibility of your evidence. Why should the reader find the evidence credible? In the above example, the argument would have been much stronger if the writer had established the source of the evidence.

On the average, as indicated on any store package, three ounces contain over 850 milligrams, three times as much as a person needs in a single day, according to the American Medical Association.

Also, if possible, try to show how the evidence fits the conclusion you want to reach.

Excess sodium and fat, low protein content, and the presence of a possible carcinogen are all considered by nutritionists to be unhealthy. Health-conscious people, then, will choose better fare for lunch.

Deduction

Deduction is a process of argumentation that demonstrates how a specific conclusion follows logically from some initial premises about which people might agree. For example, to convince a friend to study harder, you begin with the assumption that a profitable career requires a good education; proceed to argue that for a good education students must study diligently; and conclude that, as a result, your friend should spend more time with the books. Politicians who assert that we all want to act in ways beneficial to future generations, then point out how the policies they favor will ensure that outcome, argue deductively.

As with induction, you have several options when organizing a deductive argument. You might begin with the position you intend to prove, with a question that will be answered by the argument, or with a synopsis of the argument. The body of the paper works out the implications of your assumption. In the conclusion you could directly state (or restate, in different words) your position, suggest the consequences of adopting or not adopting that position, or pose a question that is easily answered after reading the argument. Here is a short example of deductive argument:

The recent spot-checks of our rooms by the dorm's head advisor are an unacceptable invasion of privacy. This practice should stop immediately.

The United States Constitution prohibits searches by police officers unless these officers have adequate reason. That is why the police need a search warrant before they can search any home. If they fail to obtain one, a case that ends up in court will likely be thrown out. Our right to privacy, then, can't be violated without due cause.

If the police can't search our homes without good reason, why should our head advisor spot-check our rooms for signs of wrongdoing?

Sammy Borchardt

When arguing from deduction, you need to make clear how your conclusions do actually follow from the agreed-upon premises. Those premises may also be questionable and need support, whether by induction or by demonstrating their deductive relationship to other strongly held ideas.

Reductio ad Absurdum   A common and powerful form of deduction called *reductio ad absurdum* ("to reduce to absurdity") is used to question a position by showing that its consequences are problematic if carried to their logical end. To counter the position that the government should impose no restrictions on the public's right to bear arms, you might point out that, carried to its logical extreme, such a policy would allow individuals to own bazookas, cannons, and nuclear bombs. This absurd result makes it clear that certain restrictions should apply to our right to bear arms. The question then becomes where we should draw the ownership line.

Syllogism   Sometimes a deductive argument is built around a categorical syllogism, a set of three statements that follow a fixed pattern to ensure sound reasoning. The first statement, called the *major premise,* names a category of things and says that all or none of them shares a certain characteristic. The *minor premise* notes that a thing or group of things belongs to that category. The *conclusion* states that the thing or group shares the characteristics of the category. Here are two examples:

Major premise:	All persons are mortal.
Minor premise:	Sue Davis is a person.
Conclusion:	Therefore, Sue Davis is mortal.

Major premise:	No dogs have feathers.
Minor premise:	Spot is a dog.
Conclusion:	Therefore, Spot does not have feathers.

Note that in each case both major and minor premises are true and the conclusion follows logically.

Syllogisms frequently appear in stripped-down form, with one of the premises or the conclusion omitted. The following example omits the major premise: "Because Wilma is a civil engineer, she has a strong background in mathematics." Obviously the missing major premise is as follows: "All civil engineers have strong backgrounds in mathematics."

Syllogistic Argument at Work   A syllogism can occur anywhere in an essay: in the introduction to set the stage for the evidence, at various places in the body, even in the conclusion in order to pull the argument together. Here is an example that uses a syllogism in the introduction:

> In 1966, when the Astrodome was completed in Houston, Texas, the managers concluded that it would be impossible to grow grass indoors. To solve their problem, they decided to install a ruglike synthetic playing surface that was fittingly called Astroturf. In the ensuing years, many other sports facilities have installed synthetic turf. Unfortunately, this development has been accompanied by a sharp rise in the number and severity of injuries suffered by athletes—a rise clearly linked to the surface they play upon. <u>Obviously, anything that poses a threat to player safety is undesirable. Because synthetic turf does this, it is undesirable and should be replaced by grass.</u>
>
> Denny Witham

To support his position, the writer then notes that turf, unlike grass, often becomes excessively hot, tiring players and increasing their chances of injury; that seams can open up between sections of turf and lead to tripping and falling; that players can run faster on artificial turf and thus collide more violently; and that the extreme hardness of the turf leads to torn ligaments and tissues when players slam their toes into it.

Avoiding Misuse of Syllogisms   Two cautions are in order. *First,* make sure any syllogism you use follows the proper logical order. The writer of the following passage has ignored this caution:

> And that's not all. Newton has stated openly that he favors federally funded abortions for the poor. Just the other day, the American Socialist party took this same stand. In my book, Newton's position puts him squarely in the Socialist camp. I strongly urge anyone supporting this man's candidacy to reconsider. . . .

Restated in syllogistic form, the writer's argument goes like this:

> Socialists favor federally funded abortions for the poor.
> Newton favors federally funded abortions for the poor.
> Therefore, Newton is a Socialist.

The last two statements reverse the proper logical relationship, and as a result the syllogism proves nothing about Newton's politics: he may or may not be "in the Socialist camp."

Second, make sure the major premise of your syllogism is in fact true. Note this example:

> All conservatives are opposed to environmental protection.
> Mary is a conservative.
> Therefore, Mary is opposed to environmental protection.

But is every conservative an environmental Jack the Ripper? In some communities, political conservatives have led fights against air and water pollution, and most conservatives agree that at least some controls are worthwhile. Mary's sympathies, then, may well lie with those who want to heal, rather than hurt, the environment.

EXERCISE   *Which of these syllogisms is satisfactory, which have false major premises, and which is faulty because the last two statements reverse the proper order?*

1. All singers are happy people.
   Mary Harper is a singer.
   Therefore, Mary Harper is a happy person.

2. All cowards fear danger.
   "Chicken" Cacciatore is a coward.
   Therefore, "Chicken" Cacciatore fears danger.

3. All cats like meat.
   Towser likes meat.
   Therefore, Towser is a cat.

4. No salesperson would ever misrepresent a product to a customer.
   Sabrina is a salesperson.
   Therefore, Sabrina would never misrepresent a product to a customer.

Analogy in Argument

An analogy compares two unlike situations or things. Arguers often use analogies to contend that because two items share one or more likenesses, they are also alike in other ways. Familiar analogies assume that humans respond to chemicals as rats do and that success in school predicts success on the job. You have used analogy if you ever pressed your parents for more adult privileges, such as a later curfew, by arguing that you were like an adult in many ways.

Because its conclusions about one thing rest upon observations about some different thing, analogy is the weakest form of rational appeal. Analogies never prove anything. But they often help explain and show probability and therefore are quite persuasive.

For an analogy to be useful, it must feature significant similarities that bear directly on the issue. In addition, it must account for any significant differences between the two items. It is often helpful to test an analogy by listing the similarities and differences. Here's an effective analogy, used to back an argument that a liberal education is the best kind to help us cope successfully with life:

> Suppose it were perfectly certain that the life and fortune of every one of us would, one day or other, depend upon his winning or losing a game of chess. Don't you think that we should all consider it to be a primary duty to learn at least the names and the moves of the pieces; to have a notion of a gambit, and a keen eye for all the means of giving and getting out of check? Do you not think that we should look with a disapprobation amounting to scorn, upon the father who allowed his son, or the state which allowed its members, to grow up without knowing a pawn from a knight?

Yet it is a very plain and elementary truth, that the life, the fortune, and the happiness of every one of us, and, more or less, of those who are connected with us, do depend upon our knowing something of the rules of a game infinitely more difficult and complicated than chess. It is a game which has been played for untold ages, every man and woman of us being one of the two players in a game of his or her own. The chessboard is the world, the pieces are the phenomena of the universe, the rules of the game are what we call the laws of Nature. The player on the other side is hidden from us. We know that his play is always fair, just, and patient. But also we know, to our cost, that he never overlooks a mistake, or makes the smallest allowance for ignorance. To the man who plays well, the highest stakes are paid, with that sort of overflowing generosity with which the strong shows delight in strength. And one who plays ill is checkmated—without haste, but without remorse. . . .

Well, what I mean by Education is learning the rules of this mighty game. In other words, education is the instruction of the intellect in the law of Nature, under which name I include not merely things and their forces, but men and their ways; and the fashioning of the affections and of the will into an earnest and loving desire to move in harmony with those laws. For me, education means neither more nor less than this. Anything which professes to call itself education must be tried by this standard, and if it fails to stand the test, I will not call it education, whatever may be the force of authority, or of numbers, upon the other side.

Thomas Henry Huxley, "A Liberal Education and Where to Find It"

To develop an argument by analogy, brainstorm the two items being compared for significant similarities and prepare a chart that matches them up. The greater the number and closeness of these similarities, the better the argument by analogy.

The Emotional Appeal

Although effective argument relies mainly on reason, an emotional appeal can lend powerful reinforcement. Indeed, emotion can win the hearts and the help of people who would otherwise passively accept a logical argument but take no action. Each Christmas, newspapers raise money for local charities by running stark case histories of destitute families. Organizations raise funds to fight famine by displaying brochures that feature skeletal, swollen-bellied children. Still other groups use emotion-charged stories and pictures to solicit support for environmental protection, to combat various diseases, and so on. Advertisers use emotion to play upon our hopes, fears, and vanities in order to sell mouthwash, cars, clothes, and other products. Politicians paint themselves as God-fearing, honest toilers for the public good while lambasting their opponents as the uncaring tools of special interests. In evaluating or writing an argument, ask yourself whether the facts warrant the emotion. Is the condition of the destitute family truly cause for pity? Is any politician unwaveringly good, any other irredeemably bad?

The following passage, from a student argument favoring assisted suicide for the terminally ill, represents an appropriate use of emotion:

When I visited Grandpa for the last time, he seemed imprinted on the hospital bed, a motionless, skeleton-like figure tethered by an array of tubes to the droning, beeping machine at his bedside. The eyes that had once sparkled with delight as he bounced grandchildren on his knee now stared blankly at the ceiling, seemingly ready to burst from their sockets. His mouth, frozen in an open grimace, emitted raspy, irregular noises as he fought to breathe. Spittle leaked from one corner of his mouth and dribbled onto the sheet. A ripe stench from the diaper around his middle hung about the bedside, masking the medicinal sickroom smells. As I stood by the bedside, my mind flashed back to the irrepressible man I once knew, and tears flooded my eyes. Bending forward, I planted a soft kiss on his forehead, whispered "I love you, Gramps," and walked slowly away.

Dylan Brandt Chafin

To develop an effective emotional appeal, identify the stories, scenes, or events of the topic that arouse the strongest emotional response within you. Do some thinking about the types of words that will best convey the emotion you feel. Then write the section so that it builds to the kind of emotional conclusion that will help your argument.

The Ethical Appeal

Before logic can do its work, the audience must be willing to consider the argument. If a writer's tone offends the audience, perhaps by being arrogant or mean-spirited, the reasoning will fail to penetrate. But if the writer comes across as pleasant, fair-minded, and decent, gaining reader support is much easier. The image that the writer projects is called the *ethical appeal*.

If you write with a genuine concern for your topic, a commitment to the truth, and a sincere respect for others, you will probably come across reasonably well. When you finish writing, check to see that an occasional snide comment or bitter remark didn't slip unnoticed onto the page. In the following introductory paragraph, from an essay arguing that many universities violate the Constitution by imposing campus rules that restrict freedom of speech, the student establishes an appealing ethical image:

Most of us would agree that educated people should not indulge in name-calling and stereotyping in their speaking and writing. To do so is an essential mark of irrational prejudice. Nevertheless, such speaking and writing are protected by the United States Constitution, which prohibits anyone from abridging freedom of expression. Today, many colleges and universities, in a well-meaning attempt to shield particular groups from unwelcome or insensitive words, are subverting this prohibition. Former Supreme Court Justice William Brennan, noted for his liberal views, has stated, "If there is a bedrock principle underlying the First Amendment, it is that the government may not prohibit the expression of an idea simply because society finds the idea offensive or disagreeable."

Linda Kimrey

The writer opposes on constitutional grounds any attempts to ban the expression of two forms of "irrational prejudice." Nevertheless, she characterizes these attempts as "well-meaning" and acknowledges that they are prompted by worthy motives. As a result, she emerges as fair-minded, decent, sensitive, and concerned, an image she maintains throughout the essay.

Ferreting Out Fallacies

Fallacies are lapses in logic that reflect upon your ability to think clearly, and therefore they weaken your argument. The fallacies described below are among the most common. Correct any you find in your own arguments, and call attention to those used by the opposition.

Hasty Generalization

Hasty generalization results when someone bases a conclusion on too little evidence. The student who tries to see an instructor during one of her office hours, finds her out, and goes away muttering, "She's never there when she should be." is guilty of hasty generalization. Perhaps the instructor was delayed by another student, attended a special department meeting, or went home ill. Even if she merely went shopping, that's not a good reason for saying she always shirks her responsibility. Several more unsuccessful office visits would be needed to make such a charge stick.

Non Sequitur

From the Latin "It does not follow," the *non sequitur* fallacy draws unwarranted conclusions from seemingly ample evidence. Consider this example: "Bill's been out almost every night for the last two weeks. Who is she?" These evening excursions, however numerous, point to no particular conclusion. Bill may be studying in the library, participating in campus organizations, taking night classes, or walking. Of course, he *could* be charmed by a new date, but that conclusion requires other evidence.

Stereotyping

A person who commits this fallacy attaches one or more supposed characteristics to a group or one of its members. Typical stereotypes include "Latins make better lovers," "Blondes have more fun," and "Teenagers are lousy drivers." Stereotyping racial, religious, ethnic, or nationality groups can destroy an argument. The images are often malicious and always offensive to fair-minded readers.

Card Stacking

In card stacking, the writer presents only part of the available evidence on a topic, deliberately omitting essential information that would alter the picture considerably. For instance: "College students have a very easy life; they attend classes for only twelve to sixteen hours a week." This statement ignores the many hours that students must spend studying, doing homework and/or research, writing papers, and the like.

Either/Or Fallacy

The either/or fallacy asserts that only two choices exist when, in fact, several options are possible. A salesperson who wants you to buy snow tires may claim, "Either buy these tires or plan on getting stuck a lot this winter." But are you really that boxed in? You might drive only on main roads that are plowed immediately after every snowstorm. You could use public transportation when it snows. You could buy radial tires for year-round use. If very little snow falls, you might not need special tires at all.

Not all either/or statements are fallacies. The instructor who checks a student's record and then issues a warning, "Make at least a *C* on your final or you'll fail the course," is not guilty of a reasoning error. No other alternatives exist. Most situations, however, offer more than two choices.

Begging the Question

A person who begs the question asserts the truth of some unproved statement. Here is an example: "Vitamin A is harmful to your health, and all bottles should carry a warning label. If enough of us write the Food and Drug Administration, we can get the labeling we need." But how do we know vitamin A does harm users? No evidence is offered. People lacking principles often use this fallacy to hit opponents below the belt: "We shouldn't allow a right-wing sympathizer like Mary Dailey to represent us in Congress." Despite a lack of suitable evidence, voters often accept such faulty logic and vote for the other candidate.

Circular Argument

Circular argument, a first cousin to begging the question, supports a position merely by restating it. "Pauline is a good manager because she runs the company effectively" says, in effect, that "something is because something is." Repetition replaces evidence.

Arguing off the Point

The writer who argues off the point, which is sometimes called "ignoring the question" or "a red herring," sidetracks an issue by introducing irrelevant information. To illustrate: "The Ford Thunderbolt is a much better value than the Honda Harmony. Anyway, far too many foreign cars are coming into the country. As a result, thousands of auto workers have lost their jobs and had to take lower-paying jobs. Many Americans strongly oppose this state of affairs." The writer sets out to convince us that the American car is superior in value but then abruptly shifts to the plight of downsized auto workers—a trend that has no bearing on the argument.

The Argument ad Hominem

The Latin term "to the man" designates an argument that attacks an individual rather than that individual's opinions or qualifications. Note this example: "Sam Bernhard doesn't deserve promotion to personnel manager. His divorce was a disgrace, and he's always writing letters to the editor. The company should find someone more suitable." This attack completely skirts the real issue—whether Sam's job performance entitles him to the promotion. Unless his personal conduct has caused his work to suffer, it should not enter into the decision.

Appeal to the Crowd

An appeal of this sort arouses an emotional response by playing on the irrational fears and prejudices of the audience. Terms like *communists, fascists, bleeding hearts, right-winger, welfare chiselers,* and *law and order* are tossed about freely to sway the audience for or against something. Consider:

> The streets of our country are in turmoil. The universities are filled with students rebelling and rioting. Communists are seeking to destroy our country. Russia is threatening us with her might, and the public is in danger. Yes, danger from within and without. We need law and order. Yes, without law and order our nation cannot survive. Elect us, and we shall by law and order be respected among the nations of the world. Without law and order our republic shall fall.

Tapping the emotions of the crowd can sway large groups and win acceptance for positions that rational thinking would reject. Think what Adolf Hitler, the author of the foregoing excerpt, brought about in Germany.

Guilt by Association

This fallacy points out some similarity or connection between one person or group and another. It tags the first with the sins, real or imagined, of the second. The following excerpt from a letter protesting a speaker at a lecture series illustrates this technique:

> The next slated speaker, Dr. Sylvester Crampton, was for years a member of the Economic Information Committee. This foundation has very strong ties with other ultraright-wing groups, some of which have been labeled fascistic. When he speaks next Thursday, whose brand of Americanism will he be selling?

Post Hoc, ergo Propter Hoc

The Latin meaning, "after this, therefore because of this," refers to the fallacy of assuming that because one event follows another, the first caused the second.

Such shoddy thinking underlies many popular superstitions ("If a black cat crosses your path, you'll have bad luck") and many connections that cannot be substantiated ("I always catch cold during spring break"). Sometimes one event does cause another: A sudden thunderclap might startle a person into dropping a dish. At other times, coincidence is the only connection. Careful thinking will usually lay far-fetched causal notions to rest.

Faulty Analogy

This is the error of assuming that two circumstances or things are similar in all important respects, when in fact they are not. Here's an example: Harvey Thompson, high school football coach, tells his players, "Vince Lombardi won two Super Bowls by insisting on perfect execution of plays and enforcing strict disciplinary measures. We're going to win the conference championship by following the same methods." Thompson assumes that because he and Lombardi are coaches, he can duplicate Lombardi's achievements by using Lombardi's methods. Several important differences, however, mark the two situations:

1. Lombardi had very talented players, obtained through the player draft or trades; Thompson can choose only from the students in his high school.
2. Lombardi's players were paid professionals who very likely were motivated, at least in part, by the financial rewards that came from winning the Super Bowl; Thompson's players are amateurs.
3. "Perfect execution of plays" is probably easier to attain on the professional level than in high school because of the players' experience.
4. Despite Lombardi's rigid disciplinary measures, very few of his players quit, perhaps because they were under contract. Could Thompson expect his players, essentially volunteers, to accept the kind of verbal and physical rigors Lombardi was famous for?

EXERCISE   *Identify and explain the fallacies in the following examples. Remember that understanding the faulty reasoning is more important than merely naming the fallacy.*

1. After slicing a Golden Glow orange, Nancy discovers that it is rotten. "I'll never buy another Golden Glow product," she declares emphatically.
2. A campaigning politician states that unless the federal government appropriates funds to help people living in poverty, they will all starve.
3. A husband and wife see an X-rated movie called *Swinging Wives.* A week later the husband discovers that his wife, while supposedly attending an evening class, has been unfaithful to him. He blames the movie for her infidelity.
4. "Look at those two motorcycle riders trying to pick a fight. All those cycle bums are troublemakers."
5. "Bill really loves to eat. Some day he'll have a serious weight problem."
6. "Because no-fault divorce is responsible for today's skyrocketing divorce rate, it should be abolished."
7. "This is the best-looking picture in the exhibit; it's so much more attractive than the others."

8. "I do not support this school millage proposal. It's sponsored by James McAndrews, who's about the most ill-tempered, quarrelsome person I've ever met. I'd never favor anything he supports."

9. "My position on social and economic issues is easy to state. I am against wooly-brained do-gooders and big-spending, pie-in-the-sky social programs that have brought us to the brink of social disaster. I stand foursquare behind our free-enterprise system, which has given us a standard of living the whole world envies; and if elected, I will defend it with everything at my command."

10. "I am against the proposed ban on smoking in public places. As long as I don't inhale and I limit my habit to ten cigarettes a day, my health won't suffer."

11. "Life today has become far too frenzied and stressful. It was much better a century ago." ◄◼

Ethical Issues

When writing an argument we attempt to alter attitudes or spark some action. These objectives create an ethical responsibility for both the quality and the possible consequences of our arguments. Suppose a doctor writing a nationally syndicated advice column recommends an over-the-counter herbal product but fails to disclose that it may cause a serious reaction in users who also take a certain prescription drug. Clearly this writer has acted irresponsibly and risks legal action if some readers suffer harm. Asking and answering the following questions will help you avoid any breach of ethics.

- Have I carefully considered the issue I'm arguing and the stance I'm taking? Since you're trying to convince readers to adopt your views, you'll need either to make sure they are credible or make very clear that your position is tentative or dependent on certain conditions.
- Am I fair to other positions on the issue? Careless or deliberate distortion of opposing views is ethically dishonest and could raise questions about your credibility.
- Are my reasons and evidence legitimate? Presenting flawed reasons as if they were credible or falsifying evidence are attempts to deceive the reader.
- Do I use fallacies or other types of faulty thinking to manipulate the reader unfairly?
- What consequences could follow if readers adopt my position? Say a writer strongly opposes genetically modified foods and advocates disrupting installations that help develop them. If some who agree act on the recommendation, innocent people could be injured.

Writing an Argument

Planning and Drafting the Argument

Some instructors assign argumentative topics, and some leave the choice of topic to you. If you will be choosing, many options are available. Interesting issues—some local, some of broader importance—crowd our newspapers, magazines, and TV airways, vying for attention. Because several of them have probably piqued your interest, there's a good chance you won't have to rely on the strategies on pages 27–33 for help in choosing your topic.

Focusing Your Question

As you explore your topic you should be prepared to focus your question. You may begin to examine whether you should support or oppose gun control, but you will soon begin to discover there are hundreds of related, narrower questions. Does the right to carry concealed weapons reduce crime? How should the Second Amendment be interpreted? Should guns be registered? Does the Brady Bill work? Do background checks deter criminals from purchasing guns? Should there be a ban on automatic and semiautomatic weapons? You may discover that one of your related questions is more than enough of a subject.

Some students approach an argument with such strong attitudes that they ignore evidence that contradicts their thinking. Don't make this mistake. Instead, maintain an open mind as you research your issue, and then, after careful thought, choose the position you'll take. Often, several possible positions exist. On the question of whether handguns should be banned, the positions might include (1) banning the possession of handguns by anyone except law officers and military personnel, (2) eliminating all restrictions on handgun possession, (3) banning handguns for persons with criminal records or a history of mental problems, and (4) banning certain types of handgun, such as "Saturday night specials" and all-plastic handguns. Even if you don't shift your position, knowing the opposition's strengths allows you to counter or neutralize it, and thus enhance your argument. Suppose you favor the first position. You need to know that half of our state constitutions grant citizens the right to own guns. Unless you acknowledge and somehow counter this fact, your case will suffer and perhaps even founder.

Exploring Your Topic

You never really start an argument with a blank page. There is almost always an ongoing conversation about the issue. Before you enter a conversation, it helps to be informed. You can do research by reading. If your paper is based on sources, you may want to review Chapters 21 and 22 for ideas and information about proper documentation. You may want to talk to others to get their views on the matter. Or you might make your own formal or informal observations; if so, you may be helped by the Chapter 23 about additional research strategies.

As you investigate the various positions, ask and answer the following questions about each:

What are the reasons for the various positions?

What values are at stake, and what conclusions do they imply?

What shared ideas do we accept, and what can be deduced from those ideas?

What kinds of evidence support the position?

If the evidence includes statistics and authoritative opinions, are they reliable or flawed for some reason?

What are the objections to each position, and how can they be countered? If the issue involves taking some action, what might be its consequences?

Some find it useful to create a table like the following to sort out the different positions.

	Ban Handguns	**Allow Possession of Handguns**	**Allow Possession of Handguns but Registered and for Justified Purposes**
Values Related to the Position	■ People have the right to be protected from potential harm from others.	■ Right to self-protection ■ Broad interpretation of Second Amendment	■ Commonly register cars and other significant property.
Reasons	■ Handguns result in accidental shootings. ■ Could cause increase in emotional killings. ■ Could create increased risk to public safety.	■ Persons could protect self and home. ■ Could reduce crime. ■ People have a constitutional right.	■ A combination of the reasons from the first two. ■ Gun owners need to be held responsible. ■ Guns need to be kept out of the hands of unstable or dangerous people.
Evidence	■ Statistics and examples of accidental shootings. ■ Statistics on states with right-to-carry laws. ■ Examples of emotional uses of hand guns.	■ Statistics on overall crime rates. ■ Examples of when guns prevented crimes. ■ Statistics comparing right-to-carry states with other states. ■ Authoritative material on the Second Amendment.	■ The evidence on the first two. ■ Examples and statistics on hand guns used in crimes. ■ Examples and statistics on how such restrictions would have had a positive consequence.
Objections	■ Is the position unconstitutional? ■ Don't criminals get guns anyway? ■ How often are legitimately owned guns misused?	■ Aren't there other interpretations of the Second Amendment? ■ Why do police groups often oppose this position?	■ Who should really get to say who should have handguns? ■ Can't a registration process be misused? ■ Can't criminals or others find illegal ways to get guns?

Obviously, this table is far from complete, and the writer would need to supply the actual evidence and flesh out the reasons. Still, such a table can be a useful device in sorting out and organizing an argument.

Another effective technique for developing an argument is to write a dialogue between two or more people that explores the various sides of an issue without trying to arrive at conclusion. The beginning of such a dialogue on a handgun ban might look like the following:

> *Doug:*   We need a ban on handguns. The United States has the highest murder rate in the industrialized world and the largest number of people owning guns. This is no coincidence. A handgun makes it easy to kill people.
>
> *Leslie:*   Are handguns really the cause of the high murder rate? Just owning a gun doesn't make someone kill. Most legitimate handgun owners will never use their guns on another human being. Many people kill with illegal weapons, including already banned semiautomatic weapons. So it isn't clear that a ban would actually prevent murders.
>
> *Kyra:*   I don't think a ban on handguns would prevent a black market in guns. Drugs are illegal and seem to be readily available.
>
> *Doug:*   I didn't say a ban on handguns would prevent all murders.

Writing such a dialogue can help start your mental juices flowing, help you see the issue from many sides, and help you develop effective material for your paper.

Arguments for Different Purposes

As you contemplate your position and evidence, consider the purpose of your argument and how that might affect the strategies you choose to employ. Arguments are written for several purposes, each requiring a different approach. Some arguments *try to establish that something is a fact*—nursing is hard work, dormitories are poor study places, bologna is an unhealthy food. This type of paper usually relies on assorted evidence, perhaps some combination of statistics, authoritative opinion, and personal experience. To prove that nursing is quite demanding, you might narrate and describe some of the strenuous activities in a typical nursing day, cite hospital nursing supervisors who verify the rigors of the job, and perhaps give statistics on nurses who quit the profession because of stress.

Other arguments *defend or oppose some policy*—for example, whether first-year students should be allowed cars on campus or a company should begin drug-testing its employees—*or support or oppose some action or project,* such as the construction of a study lounge for students or the addition of computer equipment with Internet links to more classrooms. In this type of paper, you usually discuss the need for the policy or action, how it can best be met, the cost or feasibility of your recommendation, and the benefits that will result. For instance, if you believe your college needs more compute-equipped classrooms, you might indicate how computers are currently used in some classrooms (to show Power Point presentations, offer clips from DVDs, demonstrate how to use computer applications, link to the Web to provide important illustrations), compare the number of classrooms equipped with the number not equipped, indicate the costs of equipping classrooms with computers and projectors, calculate the number of classes that would be able to use the new equipment, and demonstrate the ways teachers and students would benefit.

Still other arguments *assert the greater value of someone or something,* as when a supervisor ranks one candidate for promotion ahead of another. To write this type of paper, generally you would indicate what you're trying to prove; identify the points on which the items will be evaluated; and then, using reasons along with details, examples, or statistics, demonstrate that one of the items has greater worth than the other. Often such an argument will be deductive as you show how your conclusions follow from agreed-upon values.

Directing Arguments to Readers

With an argument, as with any essay, purpose and audience are closely linked. For example, imagine that your audience is a group of readers who are neutral or opposed to your position; there's no point in preaching to the converted. Take a little time to analyze these readers so that you can tailor your arguments appropriately. Pose these questions as you proceed:

> What are the readers' interests, expectations, and needs concerning this issue?
>
> What evidence is most likely to convince them?
>
> What objections and consequences would probably weigh most heavily with them?
>
> How can I answer the objections?

To convince an audience of farmers that the federal school lunch program needs expanding, you might stress the added income they would gain. For nutritionists, you might note the health benefits that would result, and for school officials, the improved class performance of the students. Even though you are unlikely to convince everyone, it is best to adopt the attitude that most readers are willing to be convinced if your approach is appealing and your evidence is sound.

Rogerian Arguments

If you're arguing an emotionally charged issue such as gun control or federally funded abortions for the poor, you may want to use *Rogerian argument.* Named for psychologist Carl Rogers, this type of argument attempts to reduce the antagonism that people with opposing views might feel toward your position. To succeed, you must show that you understand and respect the opposing position as well as acknowledge its good points. You try to establish some common point of agreement, then show how the conclusion you want really follows from the reader's own values and assumptions without compromising your own. For example, if you want stricter gun-control laws, you might begin by acknowledging that the Constitution grants citizens the right to bear arms and that you believe anyone with legitimate uses for guns—hunters, target shooters, and the like—should have access to them. Moving on, you might point out that gun owners and those who agree with the Second Amendment support the proper, safe use of firearms and are concerned about firearm abuse. You might then possibly agree with the premise that people, rather than guns themselves, kill people, and for that reason, no one wants criminals to have guns. Finally, you might demonstrate that requiring computer background checks before issuing handgun permits would deprive criminals of such weapons while protecting the constitutional right to bear arms.

Exploratory Argument

You do not always have to write an argument to forcefully convince someone. You can also write more to share with your reader how you came to your conclusion. This form of discussion allows you to indicate your doubts about your own position, explain why certain reasons and evidence have weight for you, include personal reasons that influenced you, and address alternative positions and arguments that may tempt you. The goal in such an argument is really to provide the readers with your thinking on the matter; if they are convinced along the way, so much the better. Below is a short excerpt of what a section of an answer to the sample student argument essay (page 194) might look like.

> While the authors of the Bill of Rights may have intended the Second Amendment to allow all citizens the right to bear arms, the amendment was drafted in a very different period of our history. We had just won a revolutionary war that had depended on a citizen army. Americans faced real threats from the native population and other armed groups. Their weapons were different as well. Citizens mostly owned a muzzle-loading musket that was slow and cumbersome to use, as well as inaccurate. It would seem that understanding the intent of these authors would require us to understand the historical period shaping their vision, a period when a well-ordered militia seemed essential. What would they make, then, of our current situation where the threat we face is almost always from fellow citizens and the power of today's guns would have been unimaginable?

Exploratory essays do not need to be informal or personal. An academic paper that considers the political influences on TV programming may make little use of the personal pronoun and yet still explain tentative ideas and show connections in an exploratory rather than strictly argumentative fashion. Sometimes it can be useful to write out an exploratory essay to find your position before you craft a more focused argument.

Drafting the Argument

When you have a good grasp on your position, reasons, evidence, and the approach you want to take, you're ready to draft your paper. A typical introduction arouses the reader's interest and may also present the proposition—a special thesis statement that names the issue and indicates which position the writer will take. It can declare that something is a fact, support a policy, call for a certain action, or assert that something has greater value than something else. Here are examples:

1. Carron College does not provide adequate recreational facilities for its students. *(Declares something is fact.)*
2. Our company's policy of randomly testing employees for drug use has proved effective and should be continued. *(Supports policy.)*
3. Because the present building is overcrowded and unsafe, the people of Midville should vote funds for a new junior high school. *(Calls for action.)*
4. The new Ford Fire-Eater is superior to the Honda Harmony in performance and economy. *(Asserts value.)*

Any of the techniques on pages 222–224 can launch your paper. For example, in arguing for stepped-up AIDS education, you might jolt your reader by describing a dying victim. If your issue involves unfamiliar terms, you might define them up front; and if the essay will be long, you could preview its main points.

Introductions can also take other tacks. In a Rogerian argument, you may want to start by affirming the reader's core values or beliefs on which you build your argument. In an exploratory essay, you might raise the core question you will discuss without taking position.

After the introduction comes the evidence, arranged in whatever order you think will work best. If one of your points is likely to arouse resistance, hold it back and begin by making points your reader can more easily accept. Argument always goes more smoothly if you first establish some common ground of agreement that recognizes the values of your reader. Where strong resistance is not a factor, you could begin or end with your most compelling piece of evidence.

The strategies discussed in earlier chapters can help you develop an argument. Some papers incorporate one strategy, while others rely on several. Let's see how you might combine several in an argument against legalized casino gambling. You might open with a brief *description* of the frantic way an all-too-typical gambling addict keeps pulling the lever of a slot machine, his eyes riveted on the spinning dials, his palms sweating, as flashing lights and wailing sirens announce winners at other machines. Next, you could offer a brief *definition* of gambling fever so that the writer and reader are on common ground, and, to show the dimensions of the problem, *classify* the groups of people who are especially addicted. Then, after detailing the negative *effects* of the addiction, you might end by *comparing* gambling addiction with drug addiction, noting that both provide a "high" and both kinds of addict know their habits hurt them.

Whatever strategies you use, make sure that substantiating evidence is embedded in them. Strategies by themselves won't convince. To illustrate, in discussing the negative effects of gambling, you might cite statistics that show the extent and nature of the problem. An expert opinion might validate your classification of addicts. Or you might use personal experience to verify gambling's addictive effects.

Besides presenting evidence, use this part of your paper to refute, that is, to point out weaknesses or errors in the opposing position. You might try the following:

■ **Point out any evidence that undermines that position.** If one viewpoint holds that drug testing violates cherished privacy rights, you might note that employers already monitor phone calls, check employees' desks, and violate privacy in other ways.

■ **Identify faulty assumptions and indicate how they are faulty: they don't lead to the implied conclusion, they lack the effectiveness of an alternative, or they are false or unsupported.** If you oppose drug testing, you could point out problems in the assumption that such tests are necessary to protect the public. Closer supervision of work performance might be a better protection; after all, fatigue, stress, negligence, and alcohol abuse can all result in serious problems, and they are not detected by drug tests.

■ **Identify problems in the logic of the argument.** Are there missing premises, faulty connections between reasons, or conclusions that don't follow from the premises? The argument against drug testing usually proceeds by asserting that privacy is a fundamental right, that drug testing violates privacy, and that therefore drug testing should not be allowed. There is a missing premise, however: that because privacy is a fundamental right it should never be violated. This premise is, in fact, at the heart of the dispute and therefore cannot be accepted as a reason to disallow drug testing.

You can place refutations throughout the body of the paper or group them together just ahead of the conclusion. Whatever you decide, don't adopt a gloating or sarcastic tone that will alienate a fair-minded reader. Resist the urge to engage in *straw man* tactics—calling attention to imaginary or trivial weaknesses of the opposing side so that you can demolish them. Shrewd readers easily spot such ploys. Finally, don't be afraid to concede secondary or insignificant points to the opposition. Arguments have two or more sides; you can't have all the ammunition on your side. (If you discover you must concede major points, however, consider switching sides.) Here is a sample refutation from a student paper:

Not everyone agrees with workplace drug testing for employees in public transportation companies, electric utilities, nuclear power plants, and other industries involving public safety. Critics assert that such tests invade privacy and therefore violate one of our cherished freedoms. While the examination of one's urine does entail inspection of something private, such a test is a reasonable exception because it helps ensure public safety and calm public fears. Individuals have a right to be protected from the harm that could be caused by an employee who abuses drugs. An airline pilot's right to privacy should not supersede the security of hundreds of people who could be injured or killed in a drug-induced accident. Thus the individual's privacy should be tempered by concern for the community—a concern that benefits all of us.

Annie Louise Griffith

Conclude in a manner that will sway the reader to your side. Depending on the argument, you might restate your position, summarize your main points, predict the consequences if your position does or doesn't prevail, or make an emotional appeal for support or action.

There can be more than one pattern for an argument. Below are three examples.

Example 1	Example 2	Example 3
Introduction	Introduction	Introduction
Definition of the issue (optional)	Definition of the issue (optional)	Definition of the issue (optional)
Your reasons and evidence (can be a large number of paragraphs)	Alternative positions and reasons for those positions	Common objections or questions and answers to both
	Objections and contrary evidence and reasons to those positions (can be several paragraphs)	
Objections or questions and answers to both (can be several paragraphs)	Restatement of your position and reasons and evidence for that position	Your reasons and evidence
Conclusion	Objections or questions and answers to both	Conclusion
	Conclusion	

You are not limited to these patterns. Alternative positions and objections can be discussed and answered within the context of presenting your own reasons. An argument can be built around answering common questions. A Rogerian argument starts by affirming the reader's core values and beliefs and then shows deductively and by supporting evidence how those values and beliefs yield the conclusion you hope to support.

Revising the Argument

Review the guidelines in Chapter 4 and ponder these questions as you revise your argument paper:

Is my topic controversial? Have I examined all of the main positions? Assessed the evidence supporting each one? Considered the objections to each position and how they can be countered? Weighed the consequences if a position involves taking some action?

Is the paper aimed at the audience I want to reach? Have I tailored my argument to appeal to that audience?

Is my evidence sound, adequate, and appropriate to the argument? Are my authorities qualified? Have I established their expertise? Are they biased? Will my audience accept them as authorities? Do my statistics adequately support my position? Have I pushed my statistical claims too far?

If I've used analogy, are my points of comparison pertinent to the issue? Have I noted any significant differences between the items being compared?

If I've included an emotional appeal, does it center on those emotions most likely to sway the reader?

Have I made a conscious effort to present myself in a favorable light?

Is my proposition clearly evident and of the appropriate type—that is, one of fact, policy, action, or value? If the proposition takes the form of a syllogism, is it sound? If faulty, have I started with a faulty premise? Reversed the last two statements of the syllogism?

Is my evidence effectively structured? Have I adequately refuted opposing arguments? Developed my position with one or more writing strategies?

Is my argument free of fallacies?

Have I considered appropriate ethical issues?

◖ SAMPLE STUDENT ESSAY OF ARGUMENT

The Right to Bear Arms

Brenda Buehrle

1   The right of citizens to bear arms is often discussed in heated tones and emotional language. Political assassinations, for example, inevitably spark an outcry for control of firearms, as do workplace and school shootings. These appeals are frequently countered by jingles such as "When guns are outlawed, only outlaws will have guns." If we bypass such pleas and examine the issue from a constitutional perspective, we find that there is ample legal justification for the right to bear arms.

2   The first thing we should consider is the original intent of the Second Amendment to the United States Constitution, which states: "A well-regulated militia being necessary to the security of a free State, the right of the people to keep and bear arms shall not be infringed." When the purpose of any constitutional provision or law is in question, a good procedure is to return to the thoughts and words of those who originally framed it. For the Second Amendment, it is necessary to examine the ideas of George Mason, the Virginia constitutionalist. Mason wrote several specific safeguards of individual rights into the Virginia constitution of 1776. The Bill of Rights— that is, the first ten amendments added to the United States Constitution in

1791—incorporates many of Mason's safeguards. R. A. Rutland's edition of Mason's papers reveals clearly that his conception of the militia—that group empowered by law to bear arms—went far beyond an organized group of men in uniform. During a debate in Richmond on June 16, 1788, Mason rhetorically said, "I ask, who are the militia?" and then answered his own question with these words: "They consist now of the whole people, except a few public officials." There can be little doubt that George Mason, "father of the Bill of Rights," never intended to restrict the right to bear arms to a relatively few men in uniform. Therefore, the original concept of the Second Amendment was that the militia consisted of all people; and to ensure security of a free country, the people had the right to keep and bear arms.

3   Early in this century Congress interpreted the militia more narrowly than Mason did. On January 23, 1903, Congress defined the militia as all able-bodied male citizens more than eighteen and less than forty-five years of age. These men were divided into two classes: the organized militia, to be known as the National Guard of the State, Territory, or District of Columbia, and the remainder, to be known as the Reserve Militia. Thus, the Congress classified all males within certain age limits, and not in the National Guard, as members of the militia. These men would now seem to be the "people to keep and bear arms" whose right to firearms "shall not be infringed" under the Second Amendment. Furthermore, under the broad doctrine of equal rights, it would appear that women should also be included, if they fall into the proper age groups eligible for military service.

4   Since no provision of the United States Constitution defines the rights of gun owners throughout the fifty states, the state constitutions certainly would seem to be the highest law in such cases, as provided in the Ninth and Tenth Amendments. These reserve to the states and the people all rights and powers not spelled out in the United States Constitution. Because the Second Amendment does not definitely state the rights of gun owners, the federal government cannot alter the rights that are defined in individual state constitutions. At least half of these state constitutions go beyond the Second Amendment by spelling out that the right to bear arms is an individual right for personal protection or defense of home and property and has nothing to do with a "well-regulated militia." Among these states are Arizona, Michigan, and Pennsylvania. For example, Arizona's constitution states, "The right of the individual citizen to bear arms in

defense of himself or the State shall not be impaired. . . ." Michigan's says, "Every person has a right to keep and bear arms for the defense of himself and the State." Pennsylvania's constitution is emphatic: "The right of the citizens to bear arms in defense of themselves and the State shall not be questioned." Given such declarations, the states with these and similar provisions could not possibly prohibit ownership of handguns or any other arms.

5   It should be clear that the Second Amendment was not originally intended to apply only to militia but to the "whole people." In addition, Congress has indicated that the militia consists of all able-bodied young and middle-aged males (and now perhaps females also). Furthermore, 50 percent of the state constitutions define and protect the rights of individual gun owners. Is it not evident that the right to bear arms is rooted in solid legal precedent?

DISCUSSION QUESTIONS

1. Identify the writer's proposition. Is it one of fact, policy, action, or value?
2. What type of evidence does the writer use in her argument?
3. Reread the last two sentences in paragraph 3. Indicate why the phrasing "would now seem" and "it would appear" is appropriate here.
4. What type of conclusion does the writer use? Why is the question that ends it effective?

SUGGESTIONS FOR WRITING

Write a properly focused argument on some topic you feel strongly about. Study all sides of the issue so you can argue effectively and appeal to a particular audience. Support your proposition with logical evidence. Here are some possibilities to consider if your instructor gives you a free choice:

1. Compulsory composition classes in college
2. Requiring safety locks on firearm triggers
3. Prohibiting development of private property to save endangered species
4. Prayer in public schools
5. Some aspect of Native American or Hispanic affairs
6. Filters on Internet stations at public libraries
7. Legalizing marijuana for medical purposes
8. Gay rights
9. Coed military training
10. Bilingual instruction in schools
11. The effectiveness of some kind of alternative medicine (or some particular diet)
12. Coping with school violence
13. Taxpayer funding for professional athletic facilities
14. Use of animals for research

15. A campus, local, or state issue
16. A national missile defense system
17. Privatizing a small portion of social security payroll taxes
18. Publicly funded private school vouchers
19. U.S. participation in peace-keeping missions
20. Virtual universities where all classes are conducted on the Internet

CRITICAL EDGE   A successful argument, by its very nature, requires critical thinking. This chapter has given you the tools you'll need to test the logic and evaluate the evidence offered in support of argumentative positions. After all, rarely will you generate an idea on your own and then argue for it. Instead, because most important issues have already been debated in print, you'll enter a discussion that's already under way. Sometimes it's on a topic of national interest, such as the desirability of politically correct speech and writing or the need to limit the number of terms elected officials can serve. At other times, the topic may be more localized: Should your state outlaw teacher strikes, your company install new equipment to control air pollution, or your college reduce its sports programs? On any of these issues you begin to form your own view as you read and assess the arguments of other writers.

A good way to take stock of conflicting opinions is to make a chart that summarizes key reasons and evidence on each side of the argument. Here is a segment of a chart that presents opposing viewpoints on whether industrial air pollution poses a significant threat of global warming:

Pro-threat side	No-threat side
Industrial emissions of carbon dioxide, methane, and chlorofluorocarbons let sun's rays in but keep heat from escaping. Andrew C. Revkin	Natural sources account for almost 50 percent of all carbon dioxide production. Dixy Lee Ray
Atmospheric levels of carbon dioxide are now 25 percent higher than in 1860. Computer models indicate a continuing rise will cause a temperature increase of 3 9°F. Revkin	The computer models are inaccurate, don't agree with each other, and fail to account for the warming effects of the oceans. H. E. Landsberg

Even though you investigate the reasons and evidence of others, deciding what position to take and how to support it—that is, establishing your place in the debate—is the real work of synthesis. (See pages 82–83.) Therefore, after evaluating your sources, outline the main points you want to make. You can then incorporate material that supports your argument. Let's say that you're considering the issue of global warming. After examining the differing viewpoints, you might conclude that although those who believe that global warming is occurring sometimes overstate their case, those who disagree tend to dismiss important scientific evidence. Because global warming is a serious possibility if not a certainty, you decide to argue for immediate environmental action. You might begin your paper by pointing out the dire consequences that will ensue if global warming becomes a reality, then offer evidence supporting this possibility, acknowledge and answer key opposing viewpoints, and finally offer your recommendations for averting a crisis.*

SUGGESTIONS FOR WRITING

1. Read several sources that explore the problem of spouse abuse and write an argument that incorporates the views expressed in the sources and suggests the extent of the problem.
2. Read several sources that take different positions on the question of whether the United States should be "the world's police officer" and write an argument that draws on those sources.
3. Read several sources that explore the issue of children suing parents or guardians for physical or sexual abuse and then write an argument that incorporates the views expressed in those sources.

*Before starting to write this type of paper, it is important to read the sections on card catalogs and periodical indexes in Chapter 21 and those on handling quotations and avoiding plagiarism in Chapter 22. As always, follow your instructor's guidelines for documenting sources.

MIXING THE WRITING STRATEGIES

Why and How to Mix Strategies

Writing strategies seldom occur in pure form. Writers nearly always mix them in assorted combinations for various purposes, not just in papers of definition and argument, as we've noted in Chapters 12 and 13, but also in papers of narration, description, process analysis, illustration, classification, comparison, and cause and effect. An essay that is primarily narration might contain descriptive passages or note an effect. A comparison might include illustrations or carry an implied argument. The purpose, audience, and occasion of the individual essay dictate the mixture, which can't be predetermined. Your best bet is to familiarize yourself with the individual strategies and use them as needed.

Assignments in other classes and on the job will also require you to mix the writing strategies. Your political science professor might ask for a paper that evaluates the advantages of a democratic state over a totalitarian one. You could open with contrasting *definitions* of the two forms of government and then, to make them more concrete, offer XYZ as an *illustration* of a typical democracy, ABC as a typical totalitarian state. After *describing* the key characteristics of each type, you might *compare* their social, economic, and religious effects on their citizens.

At work, a sales manager might have to write a year-end analysis that *compares* sales trends in the first and second quarters of the year, suggests the *causes* of any areas of weakness, and *classifies* the regions with superior potential in the upcoming year. And almost any employee could be asked to compose a report that *defines* and *illustrates* a problem, examines its *causes*, and *argues* for a particular solution.

When tackling a multistrategy writing assignment, break the project into separate stages. Determine first what you need to accomplish, then which strategies will serve your purpose, and finally how best to implement and organize them. It also helps to list all the strategies before you start reflecting on which ones to use. After a brief consideration of ethical issues, let's apply these guidelines to the writing of a problem/solution report and then to an evaluation report, two common projects that rely on a mix of writing strategies.

Ethical Issues

As you might guess, when your writing includes several strategies, the ethical issues pertinent to each apply. You may, however, need to consider additional issues with problem/solution and evaluation reports.

> *Problem/Solution.* What consequences might follow if my recommendation is adopted? If a college with a grade inflation problem implements a policy that instructors grant no more than 10 percent A's and 20 percent B's, some students who do excellent work could be denied the grades they deserve.
>
> *Evaluation.* Are my evaluation criteria fair? When evaluating the job performance of the clerks in a bookstore, it would seem unfair and discriminatory to include their ability to do heavy lifting if a number of them are older employees.

Problem/Solution Report

Suppose many students have experienced serious delays in getting to use the computers in your college library and you want to report the situation to the administration. Your goal is to eliminate the problem. After a little thought, you realize that you must first demonstrate that a problem exists and that it warrants action.

Before you can write such a report, you need to investigate the extent of the problem (does it really need solving?), look for its causes (possibly hidden causes), and determine the possible effects. Almost always these are your first steps before you decide on any solutions. Often you can find effective solutions by addressing the causes of the problem, but you might also explore new ways of improving the situation. You'll want to consider carefully whether your solution will work. After you review your options, you decide to use illustration and description to demonstrate the problem, and then to examine the effects and their causes.

Here's how you might proceed as you write the report. Your introduction states the problem. Then you portray a typical evening with long lines of students waiting to use the computers, while others mill around, grumble, and sometimes leave in disgust. Next, you take up effects, noting a number of occasions when both you and your friends have turned in late papers due to unavailable computers and received low grades. Turning to causes, you report your findings. Perhaps the library lacks funds to buy more computers. Perhaps it needs to expand its hours, or instructors need to schedule research projects at differing times.

The solution you recommend will, of course, depend on the cause(s). If extending the library hours would solve the problem, then purchasing more computers would just waste funds. The best solution may consist of several actions:

buying a few computers, extending the library hours, and persuading instructors to stagger their research assignments. In some cases, you may have to explain the process of implementing your solution and/or defend (argue) its feasibility by showing that it will not have unacceptable consequences. For instance, in our computer example, you would need to consider the costs of keeping the library open and staffed for longer hours.

Evaluation Report

Imagine that your school has been experimenting with metal whiteboards that use markers instead of chalk. The administration has asked you to assess how effectively these boards serve student and instructor needs and to present your findings in an evaluation report.

As you think the project through, you realize that you first need to determine the key criteria for evaluation, which you decide are glare, the quality of the writing left by the markers, and the effectiveness of erasing. Because these boards compete with conventional blackboards, you decide that you need a comparison of the two that includes a description of the whiteboards and illustrations supporting your observations. You also decide that a discussion of the effects the boards have on students would be in order.

After drawing your conclusions, you begin your report by indicating why it's being written, providing a definition and description of the whiteboards, and noting the criteria you will use. Following this introduction, you discuss each criterion in turn, describing with illustrative examples how well the whiteboard measures up in comparison to conventional blackboards. You also note the effects of any shortcomings on students. In your conclusion, you argue that the irregular performance of the markers, the glare of the whiteboard surfaces, and the difficulty of erasing the marking frustrate students and make classes more difficult for instructors to conduct. You recommend that the college discontinue using whiteboards except in computer classrooms where chalk dust damages the units.

 EXERCISE   *Suggest what combination of writing strategies you might use in each of the situations below.*

1. The company you work for, school you attend, or club you belong to has a serious morale problem. You have been asked to evaluate its various dimensions, propose feasible solutions, and then make a recommendation to the appropriate person.

2. Your company, school, or club is about to purchase some specific type of new equipment. You have been asked to write a report examining the available brands and recommending one.

3. Your local newspaper has asked you to write about your college major or occupation and how you regard it. The article will help high school students decide whether this major or occupation would be appropriate for them.

4. Your general science instructor has asked you to study and report on some industrial chemical. The report must answer typical questions a layperson would likely ask about the chemical.

The margin notes on the following essay show the interplay of several writing strategies.

◖ SAMPLE ESSAY USING SEVERAL WRITING STRATEGIES

• •

BRUCE JAY FRIEDMAN

Eating Alone in Restaurants

Bruce Jay Friedman (born 1930) is a native of New York City and a 1951 graduate of the University of Missouri, where he majored in journalism. Between 1951 and 1953, he served in the U.S. Air Force and for the next decade was editorial director of a magazine management company. He now freelances. A versatile writer, Friedman has produced novels, plays, short stories, and nonfiction, earning critical acclaim as a humorist. In our selection, taken from The Lonely Guy's Book of Life *(1979), he offers the urban male who must dine out alone witty advice on coping with the situation.*

Illustration in narrative form	1 Hunched over, trying to be as inconspicuous as possible, a solitary diner slips into a midtown Manhattan steakhouse. No sooner does he check his coat than the voice of the headwaiter comes booming across the restaurant.

2   "Alone again, eh?"

3   As all eyes are raised, the bartender, with enormous good cheer, chimes in: "That's because they all left him high and dry."

4   And then, just in case there is a customer in the restaurant who isn't yet aware of the situation, a waiter shouts out from the buffet table: "Well, we'll take care of him anyway, won't we fellas!"

5   *Haw, haw, haw,* and a lot of sly winks and pokes in the ribs.

6   Eating alone in a restaurant is one of the most terrifying experiences in America.

Definition Description Effect	7 Sniffed at by headwaiters, an object of scorn and amusement to couples, the solitary diner is the unwanted and unloved child of Restaurant Row. No sooner does he make his appearance than he is whisked out of sight and seated at a thin sliver of a table with barely enough room on it for an hors d'oeuvre. Wedged between busboy stations, a hair's breadth from the men's room, there he sits, feet lodged in a railing as if he were in Pilgrim stocks, wondering where he went wrong in life.

8   Rather than face this grim scenario, most Lonely Guys would prefer to nibble away at a tuna fish sandwich in the relative safety of their high-rise apartments.

9   What can be done to ease the pain of this not only starving but silent minority—to make dining alone in restaurants a rewarding experience? Absolutely
nothing. But some small strategies *do* exist for making the experience bearable.

Before You Get There

10   Once the Lonely Guy has decided to dine alone at a restaurant, a sense of
terror and foreboding will begin to build throughout the day. All the more
reason for him to get there as quickly as possible so that the experience can
soon be forgotten and he can resume his normal life. Clothing should be light
and loose-fitting, especially around the neck—on the off chance of a fainting
attack during the appetizer. It is best to dress modestly, avoiding both the fu-
neral-director-style suit as well as the bold, eye-arresting costume of the gau-
cho. A single cocktail should suffice; little sympathy will be given to the Lonely
Guy who tumbles in, stewed to the gills. (The fellow who stoops to putting
morphine in his toes for courage does not belong in this discussion.) En route
to the restaurant, it is best to play down dramatics, such as swinging the arms
pluckily and humming the theme from *The Bridge on the River Kwai*.

| Step in process |
| Description |

Once You Arrive

11   The way your entrance comes off is of critical importance. Do not skulk
in, slipping along the walls as if you are carrying some dirty little secret. There
is no need, on the other hand, to fling your coat arrogantly at the hatcheck
girl, slap the headwaiter across the cheeks with your gloves and demand to be
seated immediately. Simply walk in with a brisk rubbing of the hands and approach the headwaiter. When asked how many are in your party, avoid cute responses such as "Jes lil ol' me." Tell him you are a party of one; the Lonely
Guy who does not trust his voice can simply lift a finger. Do not launch into a
story about how tired you are of taking out fashion models, night after night,
and what a pleasure it is going to be to dine alone.

| Step in process |
| Comparison |

12   It is best to arrive with no reservation. Asked to set aside a table for one,
the restaurant owner will suspect either a prank on the part of an ex-waiter, or
a terrorist plot, in which case windows will be boarded up and the kitchen
bomb-swept. An advantage of the "no reservation" approach is that you will
appear to have just stepped off the plane from Des Moines, your first night in
years away from Marge and the kids.

| Effect |

13   All eyes will be upon you when you make the promenade to your table.
Stay as close as possible to the headwaiter, trying to match him step for step.
This will reduce your visibility and fool some diners into thinking you are a
member of the staff. If you hear a generalized snickering throughout the restaurant, do not assume automatically that you are being laughed at. The other diners may all have just recalled an amusing moment in a Feydeau farce.

14   If your table is unsatisfactory, do not demand imperiously that one for
eight people be cleared immediately so that you can dine in solitary grandeur.
Glance around discreetly and see if there are other possibilities. The ideal table
will allow you to keep your back to the wall so that you can see if anyone is
laughing at you. Try to get one close to another couple so that if you lean over
at a 45-degree angle it will appear that you are a swinging member of their
group. Sitting opposite a mirror can be useful; after a drink or two, you will
begin to feel that there are a few of you.

15   Once you have been seated, and it becomes clear to the staff that you are
alone, there will follow The Single Most Heartbreaking Moment in Dining Out

Definition

Alone—when the second setting is whisked away and yours is spread out a bit to make the table look busier. This will be done with great ceremony by the waiter—angered in advance at being tipped for only one dinner. At this point, you may be tempted to smack your forehead against the table and curse the fates that brought you to this desolate position in life. A wiser course is to grit your teeth, order a drink and use this opportunity to make contact with other Lonely Guys sprinkled around the room. A menu or a leafy stalk of celery can be used as a shield for peering out at them. Do not expect a hearty greeting or a cry of "huzzah" from these frightened and browbeaten people. Too much excitement may cause them to slump over, curtains. Smile gently and be content if you receive a pale wave of the hand in return. It is unfair to imply that you have come to help them throw off their chains.

Effect   16   When the headwaiter arrives to take your order, do not be bullied into ordering the last of the gazelle haunches unless you really want them. Thrilled to be offered anything at all, many Lonely Guys will say "Get them right out here" and wolf them down. Restaurants take unfair advantage of Lonely Guys, using them to get rid of anything from withered liver to old heels of roast beef. Order anything you like, although it is good to keep to the light and simple in case of a sudden attack of violent stomach cramps.

Some Proven Strategies

Step in process   17   Once the meal is under way, a certain pressure will begin to build as couples snuggle together, the women clucking sympathetically in your direction. Warmth and conviviality will pervade the room, none of it encompassing you. At this point, many Lonely Guys will keep their eyes riveted to the restaurant paintings of early Milan or bury themselves in a paperback anthology they have no wish to read.

Effect

Classification   18   Here are some ploys designed to confuse other diners and make them feel less sorry for you:

19   ■ After each bite of food, lift your head, smack your lips thoughtfully, swallow and make a notation in a pad. Diners will assume you are a restaurant critic.

20   ■ Between courses, pull out a walkie-talkie and whisper a message into it. This will lead everyone to believe you are part of a police stake-out team, about to bust the salad man as an international dope dealer.

21   ■ Pretend you are a foreigner. This is done by pointing to items on the menu with an alert smile and saying to the headwaiter: "Is good, no?"

22   ■ When the main course arrives, brush the restaurant silverware off the table and pull some of your own out of a breastpocket. People will think you are a wealthy eccentric.

23   ■ Keep glancing at the door, and make occasional trips to look out at the street, as if you are waiting for a beautiful woman. Half-way through the meal, shrug in a world-weary manner and begin to eat with gusto. The world is full of women! Why tolerate bad manners! Life is too short.

The Right Way

Step in process   24   One other course is open to the Lonely Guy, an audacious one, full of perils, but all the more satisfying if you can bring it off. That is to take off your dark glasses, sit erectly, smile broadly at anyone who looks in your direction, wave off inferior wines, and begin to eat with heartiness and enormous

Implied argument

confidence. As outrageous as the thought may be—enjoy your own company. Suddenly, titters and sly winks will tail off, the headwaiter's disdain will fade, and friction will build among couples who will turn out to be not as tightly cemented as they appear. The heads of other Lonely Guys will lift with hope as you become the attractive center of the room.

25   If that doesn't work, you still have your fainting option.

CRITICAL EDGE   Most writing, including writing that draws on outside sources, uses a mixture of several strategies. As you determine which strategies will help you present your ideas, you can draw upon the principles of critical thinking that you used with each individual strategy. You can, for example, evaluate the merits of different writers' opinions, look for evidence of bias, weigh the type and amount of support backing each assertion, and select the key points you'll include in your paper.

Let's say that you're taking an elementary education class and are asked to write a paper evaluating the effectiveness of computers as an educational tool in elementary schools. Obviously, this assignment would require you to synthesize (see pages 82–83) the results of your outside reading and very likely the conclusions drawn from one or more observations of computer use in classrooms. It would, in short, require both secondary (that is, library) research and direct observations (see pages 420–423), a form of primary research.

You might begin your paper by describing a typical morning's activities in a computer-equipped classroom, noting particularly the students' responses to computer instruction. Next, you might classify the different uses of computers in the classroom and provide a brief history of the movement toward this type of instruction. You could proceed by citing the positive effects of computers in the classroom, as noted by those who advocate their use, and then evaluate whether these claims are exaggerated or reflect any bias. For example, you might notice some kind of bias in a comparison of classrooms with and without computers and then suggest how to make such a comparison so as to eliminate the bias. Finally, you might also critically examine the objections of those who oppose computer instruction. After you've completed this research and analysis, you could argue for or against the use of computers as an educational tool. Even though this type of assignment may seem overwhelming, you can meet the challenge if you tackle the project one stage at a time.*

SUGGESTIONS FOR WRITING

1. Using a combination of strategies, write a paper that investigates and assesses the placement of students with mental and emotional handicaps in "mainstream"

---

*Because you'll need to consult library sources, it is important to read the sections on card catalogs and periodical indexes in Chapter 21 and those on handling quotations and avoiding plagiarism in Chapter 22 before you start to write. As always, follow your instructor's guidelines for documenting sources.

rather than special classes. You might visit classrooms with and without handi-capped students.

2. Examine several sources that favor or oppose the use of community tax rev-enues to modernize an existing sports stadium or construct a new one. Then use a combination of strategies to write a paper that presents and assesses your findings.

3. Investigate in outside sources a current national phenomenon such as the up-surge in sensationalist television programming, the popularity of diet and exer-cising, or the increase in antismoking sentiment. Then use a combination of strategies to write a paper that presents and assesses these findings.

4. Identify what you consider a problem with some social policy of your college. Discuss this problem with several responsible students and also examine any available printed material that addresses this policy. Then use a combination of strategies to write a paper that identifies the problem and proposes a reason-able solution.

5. Identify what you consider a problem with some local, state, or national law. Perhaps you see it as unjust, unfairly applied, outdated, or the like. Examine several sources that discuss this law and then use a combination of strategies to write a paper that identifies the problem and proposes a reasonable solution.

PARAGRAPHS

Imagine the difficulty of reading a magazine article or book if you were faced with one solid block of text. How could you sort its ideas or know the best places to pause for thought? Paragraphs help guide readers through longer pieces of writing. Some break lengthy discussions of one idea into segments of different emphasis, thus providing rest stops for readers. Others consolidate several briefly developed ideas. Yet others begin or end pieces of writing or link major segments together. Most paragraphs, though, include a number of sentences that develop and clarify one idea. Throughout a piece of writing, paragraphs relate to one another and reflect a controlling purpose. To make paragraphs fit together smoothly, you can't just sit down and dash them off. Instead, you first need to reflect on the entire essay, then channel your thoughts toward its different segments. Often you'll have to revise your paragraphs after you've written a draft.

Characteristics of Effective Paragraphs

Unity

A paragraph with unity develops one, and only one, key controlling idea. To ensure unity, edit out any stray ideas that don't belong and fight the urge to take interesting but irrelevant side trips; they only create confusion about your destination.

The following paragraph *lacks unity:*

> The psychiatric nurse deals with dangerous mental patients, pathological personalities who may explode into violence at any moment. Sigmund Freud was one of the first doctors to study mental disorders. Today psychotherapy is a well-established medical discipline.

What exactly is this writer trying to say? We can't tell. Each sentence expresses a different, undeveloped idea:

1. Job of the psychiatric nurse
2. Freud's pioneering work in studying mental disorders
3. Present status of psychotherapy

In contrast, the following paragraph develops and clarifies only one central idea, the professional responsibilities of a psychiatric nurse:

> Psychiatric nurses deal with dangerous mental patients, pathological personalities who may explode into violence at any moment. For this reason, they must remain on guard at all times. When a patient displays anger or violence, they cannot respond in kind but must instead show tolerance and understanding. Furthermore, they must be able to recognize attempts at deception. Sometimes a mentally ill person, just prior to launching an attack, will act in a completely normal way in order to deceive the intended victim. The nurse must recognize this behavior and be alert for any possible assault.
>
> Peggy Feltman

Because no unrelated ideas sidetrack the discussion of responsibilities, the paragraph has unity. To check your paragraphs for unity, ask yourself what each one aims to do and whether each sentence helps that aim.

EXERCISE   *After reading the next two paragraphs, answer the questions that follow.*

1. The legend—in Africa—that all elephants over a large geographical area go to a common "graveyard" when they sense death is approaching led many hunters to treat them with special cruelty. Ivory hunters, believing the myth and trying to locate such graveyards, often intentionally wounded an elephant in the hopes of following the suffering beast as it made its way to the place where it wanted to die. The idea was to wound the elephant seriously enough so that it thought it was going to die but not so seriously that it died in a very short time. All too often, the process resulted in a single elephant being shot or speared many times and relentlessly pursued until it either fell dead or was killed when it finally turned and charged its attackers. In any case, no wounded elephant ever led its pursuers to the mythical graveyard with its hoped-for booty of ivory tusks.

   Kris Hurrell

2. When I was growing up, I spent many happy hours with my brothers and sisters playing jungle games in the woodlot behind our farm home. This lot,

ten acres of dense-set poplars and birches standing amidst the blackened stumps of an old pine forest, provided a perfect setting for our jungle adventures. At times we acted out African versions of cowboys and Indians; at others we sought the long-lost treasures of fabled diamond mines. Often our adventures pitted Tarzan against tomb robbers and poachers. Besides serving as a playground, our woodlot furnished most of the fuel for the iron stoves in our kitchen and living room. I can still remember the backbreaking work of chopping up stumps and fallen trees and hauling them to the house. In the winter, the woodlot offered fine small-game hunting. In the summer, it provided a cool refuge from the heat that blistered the fields and farmhouse. Today, farm and woodlot are gone, swallowed up by a sprawling suburb. I wonder whether the children who live there ever want to play jungle games or regret that there's no place for them.

Student Unknown

1. Which of these paragraphs lacks unity? Refer to the paragraphs when answering.
2. How would you improve the paragraph that lacks unity?

The Topic Sentence

The topic sentence states the main idea of the paragraph. Think of the topic sentence as a rallying point, with all supporting sentences developing the idea it expresses. A good topic sentence helps you gauge what information belongs in a paragraph, thus ensuring unity. At the same time, it informs your reader about the point you're making.

Placement of the topic sentence varies from paragraph to paragraph, as the following examples show. As you read each, note how supporting information develops the topic sentence, which is italicized.

Topic Sentence Stated First   Many paragraphs open with the topic sentence. The writer reveals the central idea immediately and then builds from a solid base.

> *Starting about one million years ago, the fossil record shows an accelerating growth of the human brain.* It expanded at first at the rate of one cubic inch of additional gray matter every hundred thousand years; then the growth rate doubled; it doubled again; and finally it doubled once more. Five hundred thousand years ago the rate of growth hit its peak. At that time, the brain was expanding at the phenomenal rate of ten cubic inches every hundred thousand years. No other organ in the history of life is known to have grown as fast as this.
>
> Robert Jastrow, *Until the Sun Dies*

Topic Sentence Stated Last   In order to emphasize the support and build gradually to a conclusion, a topic sentence can end the paragraph. This position creates suspense as the reader anticipates the summarizing remark.

> An experience of my own comes handily to mind. Some years ago, when the Restaurant de la Pyramide in Vienne was without question one of the best half-dozen restaurants in the world, I visited it for the first time. After I had ordered my meal, the sommelier[wine steward] appeared to set before me a wine list of surpassing amplitude and excellence. But as I cast my eyes down this unbelievable offering of the world's most tantalizing wines, the sommelier bent over me and pointed out a wine of which I had never heard, ticketed at a price one-fifth that of its illustrious neighbors. "Monsieur," said the sommelier, "I would suggest this one. It is a local wine, a very good wine. It is not a great wine, but after all, monsieur, you are likely to pass this way only once. The great wines you will find everywhere; this wine you will find only in Vienne. I would like you to try it, while you have the opportunity." *This, to my mind, was true sophistication—on the part of M. Point for having the wine and on the part of the waiter for offering it.*
>
> Stephen White, "The New Sophistication: Defining the Terms"

Topic Sentence Stated First and Last   Some paragraphs lead with the main idea and then restate it, usually in different words, at the end. This technique allows the writer to repeat an especially important idea.

> *Everything is changing. . . .* This is a prediction I can make with absolute certainty. As human beings, we are constantly in a state of change. Our bodies change every day. Our attitudes are constantly evolving. Something that we swore by five years ago is now almost impossible for us to imagine ourselves believing. The clothes we wore a few years ago now look strange to us in old photographs. The things we take for granted as absolutes, impervious to change, are, in fact, constantly doing just that. Granite boulders become sand in time. Beaches erode and shape new shorelines. Our buildings become outdated and are replaced with modern structures that also will be torn down. Even those things which last thousands of years, such as the Pyramids and the Acropolis, also are changing. This simple insight is very important to grasp if you want to be a no-limit person, and are desirous of raising no-limit children. *Everything you feel, think, see, and touch is constantly changing.*
>
> Wayne Dyer, *What Do You Really Want for Your Children?*

Topic Sentence Stated in the Middle   On occasion, the topic sentence falls between one set of sentences that provides background information and a follow-up set that develops the central idea. This arrangement allows the writer to shift the emphasis and at the same time preserve close ties between the two sets.

> Over the centuries, China has often been the subject of Western fantasy. In their own way, a number of scholars, journalists, and other travelers have perpetuated this tradition in recent years, rushing to rediscover the country after its long period of isolation. Some of these visitors, justifiably impressed by the Communists' achievements in eliminating the exploitative aspects of pre-1949 mandarin society, propagated the view that the revolution, after its initial successes, had continued to "serve the people," and that China was "the wave of the future"—a compelling alternative to the disorder and materialism of contemporary Western society. Human rights were not at issue, they argued, because such Western concepts were inapplicable to China. *In the past year, however, the Chinese have begun to speak for themselves, and they are conveying quite a different picture.* In the view of many of its own people, China is a backward and repressive nation. "China is Asia's Gulag Archipelago," an elderly Chinese scholar said to me

shortly after I had arrived in China last spring. "I was in Germany right after the Second World War, and I saw the horrors of Buchenwald and other concentration camps. In a way—in its destruction of the human spirit these past two decades—China has been even worse."

David Finkelstein, "When the Snow Thaws"

Topic Sentence Implied   Some paragraphs, particularly in narrative and descriptive writing, have no topic sentence. Rather, all sentences point toward a main idea that readers must grasp for themselves.

> [Captain Robert Barclay] once went out at 5 in the morning to do a little grouse shooting. He walked at least 30 miles while he potted away, and then after dinner set out on a walk of 60 miles that he accomplished in 11 hours without a halt. Barclay did not sleep after this but went through the following day as if nothing had happened until the afternoon, when he walked 16 miles to a ball. He danced all night, and then in early morning walked home and spent a day partridge shooting. Finally he did get to bed—but only after a period of two nights and nearly three days had elapsed and he had walked 130 miles.

John Lovesey, "A Myth Is As Good As a Mile"

The details in this paragraph collectively suggest a clear central idea: that Barclay had incredible physical endurance. But writing effective paragraphs without topic sentences challenges even the best writers. Therefore, control most of your paragraphs with clearly expressed topic sentences.

EXERCISE   *Identify the topic sentences in each of the following paragraphs and explain how you arrived at your decisions. If the topic sentence is implied, state the central idea in your own words.*

1. Last winter, while leafing through the <u>Guinness Book of World Records</u>, I came across an item stating that the tallest sunflower ever had been grown by G. E. Hocking, an Englishman. Fired by a competitive urge, I planted a half acre of sunflower seeds. That half acre is now a magnificent 22,000 square feet of green and gold flowers. From the elevated rear deck of my apartment, I can look out over the swaying mass of thick, hairy green stalks and see each stalk thrusting up through the darker heart-shaped leaves below and supporting an ever-bobbing imitation of the sun. In this dwarf forest, some of the flower heads measure almost a foot in diameter. Though almost all my plants are now blooming, none will top the sixteen feet, two inches reached by Hocking's plant. My tallest is just thirteen feet even, but I don't think that's too bad for the first attempt. Next year, however, will be another matter. I plan to have an automatic watering system to feed my babies.

Joseph Wheeler

2. What my mother never told me was how fast time passes in adult life. I remember, when I was little, thinking I would live to be at least as old as my grandmother, who was dynamic even at ninety-two, the age at which she died. Now I see those ninety-two years hurtling by me. And my mother never told me how much fun sex could

be, or what a discovery it is. Of course, I'm of an age when mothers really didn't tell you much about anything. My mother never told me the facts of life.

Joyce Susskind, "Surprises in a Woman's Life"

3. The UN's International Labor Organization estimates that as many as 200 million children go to work rather than to school. They are in developing nations throughout the world, making everything from clothing and shoes to handbags and carpets. These children are the dark side of the new global economy, an international underclass working 12 or more hours a day, six or seven days a week. In the carpet factories of India, they are often separated from their families for years at a time. In the leather-handbag plants of Thailand, children report being forced to ingest amphetamines just to keep up their strength. In the charcoal industry of Brazil, tens of thousands of children work in a soot-drenched hell producing ingredients for steel alloys used in the manufacture of American cars. Child laborers everywhere develop arthritis and carpal tunnel syndrome from the repetitive work; their respiratory systems are damaged by inhaling toxic chemicals in poorly ventilated workshops; their posture is permanently altered by the long hours in cramped conditions. And the products they make are in homes across America, serving as a bitterly ironic commentary on what we consider a child's right to a carefree youth.

Mark Schapiro, "Children of a Lesser God"

4. The first hostage to be brought off the plane was a dark little man with a bald head and a moustache so thick and black that it obliterated his mouth. Four of the masked terrorists were guarding him closely, each with a heavy rifle held ready for fire. When the group was about fifty feet from the plane, a second hostage, a young woman in flowered slacks and a red blouse, was brought out in clear view by a single terrorist, who held a pistol against the side of her head. Then the first four pushed the dark little man from them and instructed him to kneel on the pavement. They looked at him as they might an insect. But he sat there on his knees, seemingly as indifferent as if he had already taken leave of his body. The shots from the four rifles sounded faintly at the far end of the field where a group of horrified spectators watched the grisly proceedings.

Bradley Willis

EXERCISES

1. **Develop one of the ideas below into a topic sentence. Then write a unified paragraph that is built around it.**

   a. The career (or job or profession) I want is _____.
   b. The one quality most necessary in my chosen field is _____.
   c. The most difficult aspect of my chosen field is _____.
   d. One good example of the American tendency to waste is _____.
   e. The best (or worst) thing about fast-food restaurants is _____.
   f. The college course I find most useful (or interesting) is _____.
   g. Concentration (or substitute your own term here) is an important part of a successful golf game (or substitute your own sport).

    h. The one place where I feel most at home is _____.

    i. More than anything else, owning a pet (or growing a garden) involves _____.

2. Write a topic sentence that would control a paragraph on each of the following:

    a. Preparations for traveling away from home

    b. Advantages of having your own room

    c. Some landmark of the community in which you live

    d. The price of long-distance telephone calls

    e. Registering for college courses

    f. A cherished memento or souvenir

    g. High school graduation

    h. New Year's resolutions

Adequate Development

Students often ask for guidelines on paragraph length: "Should I aim for fifty to sixty words? Seven to ten sentences? About one-fourth of a page?" The questions are natural, but the approach is wrong. Instead of targeting a particular length, ask yourself what the reader needs to know. Then supply enough information to make your point clearly. Developing a paragraph inadequately is like inviting guests to a party but failing to tell them when and where it will be held. Skimpy paragraphs force readers to fill in the gaps for themselves, a task that can both irritate and stump them. On the other hand, a paragraph stuffed with useless padding dilutes the main idea. In all cases, the reader, the information being presented, and the publication medium determine the proper amount of detail. A newspaper might feature short paragraphs including only key facts, whereas a scientific journal might have lengthy paragraphs that offer detailed development of facts.

The details you supply can include facts, figures, thoughts, observations, steps, lists, examples, and personal experiences. Individually, these bits of information may mean little, but together they clearly illustrate your point. Keep in mind, however, that development isn't an end in itself but instead advances the purpose of the entire essay.

Here are two versions of a paragraph, the first inadequately developed:

Underdeveloped Paragraph

    Most of the delegates to the Constitutional Convention of 1787 feared too much democracy. As a result, they drafted the Constitution as a document outlining a limited democracy. Indeed, some of the provisions were simply undemocratic. But despite reflecting the delegates' distrust of popular rule, the Constitution did provide a framework in which democracy could evolve.

Adequately Developed Paragraph

    Most of the delegates to the Constitutional Convention of 1787 feared too much democracy. As a result, they drafted the Constitution as a document outlining a limited democracy. Indeed, some of the provisions were simply undemocratic: *universal suffrage was denied; voting qualifications were left to the states; and women, blacks,*

and persons without property were denied the federal franchise. Until the passage of the Seven-
teenth Amendment in 1913, senators were not popularly elected but were chosen by state legis-
lators. But despite reflecting the delegates' distrust of popular rule, the Constitution
did provide a framework in which democracy could evolve.

The first paragraph lacks examples of undemocratic provisions, whereas the second one provides the needed information.

Readability also helps set paragraph length. Within a paper, paragraphs signal natural dividing places, allowing the reader to pause and absorb the material presented up to that point. Too little paragraphing overwhelms the reader with long blocks of material. Too much creates a choppy Dick-and-Jane effect that may seem simplistic, even irritating. To counter these problems, writers sometimes use several paragraphs for an idea that needs extended development, or they combine several short paragraphs into one.

⊂EXERCISES

1. **Indicate where the ideas in this long block of material divide logically; explain your choices.**

   During the summer following graduation from high school, I could hardly wait to get to college and "be on my own." In my first weeks at State University, however, I found that independence can be tough and painful. I had expected raucous good times and a carefree collegiate life, the sort depicted in old beach movies and suggested by the selective memories of sentimental alumni. Instead, all I felt at first was the burden of increasing responsibilities and the loneliness of "a man without a country." I discovered that being independent of parents who kept at me to do my homework and expected me to accomplish certain household chores did not mean I was free to do as I pleased. On the contrary, living on my own meant that I had to perform for myself all the tasks that the family used to share. Studying became a full-time occupation rather than a nightly duty to be accomplished in an hour or two, and my college instructors made it clear that they would have little sympathy for negligence or even for my inability to do an assignment. But what was more troubling about my early college life than having to do laundry, prepare meals, and complete stacks of homework was the terrifying sense of being entirely alone. I was independent, no longer a part of the world that had seemed to confine me, but I soon realized that confinement had also meant security. I never liked the feeling that people were watching over me, but I knew that my family and friends were also watching out for me—and that's a good feeling to have. At the university no one seemed particularly to be watching, though professors constantly evaluated the quality of my work. I felt estranged from people in those first weeks of college life, desperately needing a confidant but fearful that the new and tenuous friendships I had made would be damaged if I were to confess my fears and problems. It was simply too early for me to feel a part of the university. So there I was, independent in the fullest sense, and thus "a man without a country."

2. **The following short, choppy units are inadequately developed. List some details you could use to expand one of them into a good paragraph.**

> I like living in a small town because the people are so friendly. In addition, I can always get the latest gossip from the local busybody.
>
> In a big city, people are afraid to get too friendly. Everything is very private, and nobody knows anything about anybody else.

3. **Scan the compositions you have written in other classes for paragraphs that are over- or underdeveloped. Revise any you find.** ◖◗

Organization

An effective paragraph unfolds in a clear pattern of organization so that the reader can easily follow the flow of ideas. Usually when you write your first draft, your attempt to organize your thoughts will also organize your paragraphs. Writers do not ordinarily stop to decide on a strategy for each paragraph. But when you revise or are stuck, it's useful to understand the available choices. Here are some options:

1. The strategies discussed in Chapters 5–13
2. Order of climax

The choice you make depends upon your material and purpose in writing.

Writing Strategies   These include all of the following patterns:

Time sequence (narration)
Space sequence (description)
Process analysis
Illustration
Classification
Comparison
Cause and effect
Definition
Argument

Four example paragraphs follow. The first, organized by *time sequence,* traces the final years of the Model T Ford, concluding with a topic sentence that sums up its impact.

In 1917 the Model T lost much of its attraction when its exterior appearance was drastically altered. The famous flat-sided brass radiator disappeared and the new style featured (in the words of the catalogue) "The stream-lined hood, large radiator and enclosed fan, crown fenders, black finish and nickel trimmings" ("crown fenders" would be described in England as domed mud-guards). Electric lighting and starting followed in 1919, and the model then continued with little alteration until 1927, when it was finally withdrawn. After a considerable pause it was replaced by the Model A, a very conventional machine with wire wheels, three-speed gearbox and four-wheel brakes (the "T" had never made this concession to progress and continued to the last with two minute brake drums on the back wheels only). While it was in preparation, others had taken the lead and the "A" never replaced the immortal "T" in the public fancy. Indeed, the "Tin Lizzy" or "Flivver" had become almost a national characteristic, and at the end of its eighteen years in production the total number sold was fifteen million.

Cecil Clutton and John Stanford, *The Vintage Motor-Car*

The next paragraph, organized by *space sequence*, describes a ceramic elf, starting from the bottom and working up to the top. Other common spatial arrangements include top to bottom, left to right, right to left, nearby to far away, far away to nearby, clockwise, and counterclockwise.

The ceramic elf in our family room is quite a character. His reddish-brown slippers, which hang over the mantel shelf, taper to a slender point. Pudgy, yellow-stockinged legs disappear into a wrinkled tunic-style, olive-green jacket, gathered at the waist with a thick, brown belt that fits snugly around his roly-poly belly. His short, meaty arms hang comfortably, one hand resting on the knapsack at his side and the other clutching the bowl of an old black pipe. An unkempt, snow-white beard, dotted by occasional snarls, trails patriarch-fashion from his lower lip to his belt line. A button nose capped with a smudge of gold dust, mischievous black eyes, and an unruly snatch of hair peeking out from under his burnt-orange stocking cap complete Bartholomew's appearance.

Maria Sanchez

Although descriptive paragraphs, like those developed by narration, often lack topic sentences, our example leads off with the central idea.

Here is a paragraph showing *process* development.

Making beer nuts is a quick, simple procedure that provides a delicious evening snack. You'll need six cups of raw peanuts, three cups of sugar, and one-and-one-half cups of water. To begin, combine the sugar and water in a two-quart saucepan and stir to dissolve the sugar. Next, add the peanuts and stir again until all of the peanuts are covered by the sugar-water solution. Leave the pan, uncovered, on a burner set at medium-high heat for ten to twelve minutes, until the sugar crystallizes and coats the peanuts thoroughly. Stay at the stove during the heating process and stir the mixture every two or three minutes to ensure even coating of the nuts. When the peanuts are thoroughly coated, pour them onto an ungreased cookie sheet and bake at 350 degrees for about thirty minutes, stirring and lightly salting at ten-minute intervals. Serve your beer nuts fresh out of the oven or eat them at room temperature.

Kimberlee Walters

Again, the topic sentence comes first.

The final example illustrates development by *comparison* and also proceeds from an opening topic sentence.

There is an essential difference between a news story, as understood by a newspaperman or a wire-service writer, and the newsmagazine story. The chief purpose of the conventional news story is to tell what happened. It starts with the most important information and continues into increasingly inconsequential details, not only because the reader may not read beyond the first paragraph but because an editor working on galley proofs a few minutes before press time likes to be able to cut freely from the end of the story. A newsmagazine is very different. It is written to be read consecutively from beginning to end, and each of its stories is designed, following the critical theories of Edgar Allan Poe, to create one emotional effect. The news, what happened that week, may be told in the beginning, the middle, or the end; for the purpose is not to throw information at the reader but to seduce him into reading the whole story, and into accepting the dramatic (and often political) point being made.

Otto Friedrich, "There Are 00 Trees in Russia"

Order of Climax   Climactic order creates a crescendo pattern, starting with the least emphatic detail and progressing to the most emphatic. The topic sentence can begin or end the paragraph, or it can remain implied. This pattern holds the reader's interest by building suspense. On occasion, writers reverse the order, landing the heaviest punch first; but such paragraphs can trail off, leaving the reader dissatisfied.

Here is a paragraph illustrating climactic order:

The speaking errors I hear affect me to different degrees. I'm so conditioned to hearing "It don't make any difference" and "There's three ways to solve the problem" that I've almost accepted such usage. However, errors such as "Just between you and I, Arnold loves Edna" and "I'm going back to my room to lay down" still offend my sensibility. When hearing them, I usually just chuckle to myself and walk away. The "Twin I's"—irrevelant and irregardless—are another matter. More than any other errors, they really grate on my ear. Whenever I hear "that may be true, but it's irrevelant" or "Irregardless of how much I study, I still get C's," I have the urge to correct the speaker. It's really surprising that more people don't clean up their language act.

Valerie Sonntag

From a magazine or newspaper article, select four paragraphs that illustrate different patterns of organization. Identify the topic sentence in each case; or if it is implied, state it in your own words. Point out the organization of each paragraph.

Coherence

Coherent writing flows smoothly and easily from one sentence and paragraph to another, clarifying the relationships among ideas and thus allowing the reader to grasp connections. Because incoherent writing fails to do this, it confuses, and sometimes even irritates, the reader.

Here is a paragraph that lacks coherence:

> I woke up late. I had been so tired the night before that I had forgotten to set the alarm. All I could think of was the report I had stayed up until 3 A.M. typing, and how I could possibly get twenty copies ready for next morning's 9 o'clock sales meeting. I panicked and ran out the door. My bus was so crowded I had to stand. Jumping off the bus, I raced back up the street. The meeting was already under way. Mr. Jackson gestured for me to come into the conference room. Inserting the first page of the report into the copier, I set the dial for twenty copies and pressed the print button. The sign started flashing CALL KEY OPERATOR. The machine was out of order. Mr. Jackson asked whether the report was ready. I pointed to the flashing red words. Mr. Jackson nodded grimly without saying anything. He left me alone with the broken machine.

This paragraph has some degree of unity: most of its sentences relate to the writer's disastrous experience with the sales report. Unfortunately, though, its many gaps in logic create rather than answer questions, and in very bumpy prose, at that. Note the gap between the third and fourth sentences. Did the writer jump out of bed and rush right out the door? Of course not, but the reader has no real clue to the actual sequence of events. Another gap occurs between the next two sentences, leaving the reader to wonder why the writer had to race up the street upon leaving the bus. And who is Mr. Jackson? The paragraph never tells, but the reader will want to know.

Now read this rewritten version, additions italicized:

> I woke up late *because* I had been so tired the night before that I had forgotten to set the alarm. All I could think of was the report I had stayed up until 3 A.M. typing, and how I could possibly get twenty copies ready for next morning's 9 o'clock sales meeting. *When I realized it was 8:30,* I panicked. *Jumping out of bed, I threw on some clothes, grabbed the report,* and ran out the door. My bus was so crowded I had to stand *and could not see out the window. Two blocks beyond my stop, I realized I should have gotten off. "Stop!" I cried and,* jumping off the bus, raced back up the street. *When I reached the office, it was 9:15, and* the meeting was already under way. Mr. Jackson, *the sales manager, saw me and* gestured for me to come into the conference room. *"One moment," I said as calmly as I could and hurried to the copier.* Inserting the first page of the report into it, I set the dial for twenty copies and pressed the print button. *Immediately,* the sign started flashing CALL KEY OPERATOR. The machine was out of order. *The next thing I knew,* Mr. Jackson *was at my side* asking whether the report was ready. I pointed to the flashing

red words, *and* Mr. Jackson nodded grimly without saying anything. *Turning on his heel,* he *walked away and* left me alone with the broken machine.

As this example shows, correcting an incoherent paragraph may call for anything from a single word to a whole sentence or more.

Coherence derives from a sufficient supply of supporting details and your firm sense of the way your ideas go together. If you brainstorm your topic thoroughly and think carefully about the relationships between sentences, incoherence isn't likely to haunt your paragraphs.

As you write, and especially when you revise, signal connections to the reader by using *transitions*—devices that link sentences to one another. These are the most common transitional devices:

1. Connecting words and phrases
2. Repeated key words
3. Pronouns and demonstrative adjectives
4. Parallelism

You can use them to furnish links both within and between paragraphs.

Connecting Words and Phrases   Connectors clarify relationships between sentences. The following list groups them according to function:

Showing similarity: in like manner, likewise, moreover, similarly

Showing contrast: at the same time, but, even so, however, in contrast, instead, nevertheless, still, on the contrary, on the other hand, otherwise, yet

Showing results or effects: accordingly, as a result, because, consequently, hence, since, therefore, thus

Adding ideas together: also, besides, first (second, third . . .), furthermore, in addition, in the first place, likewise, moreover, similarly, too

Drawing conclusions: as a result, finally, in brief, in conclusion, in short, to summarize

Pointing out examples: for example, for instance, to illustrate

Showing emphasis and clarity: above all, after all, again, as a matter of fact, besides, in fact, in other words, indeed, nonetheless, that is

Indicating time: at times, after, afterward, from then on, immediately, later, meanwhile, next, now, once, previously, subsequently, then, until, while

Conceding a point: granted that, of course, to be sure, admittedly

Don't overload your paper with connectors. In well-planned prose, your message flows clearly with only an occasional assist from them.

In the following excerpt, which clarifies the difference between workers and workaholics, the connectors are italicized:

My efforts to define workaholism and to distinguish workaholics from other hard workers proved difficult. *While* workaholics do work hard, not all hard workers are workaholics. Moonlighters, *for example,* may work 16 hours a day to make ends meet, but most of them will stop working when their financial circumstances permit. Accountants, *too,* seem to work non-stop, but many slow down after the April 15 tax deadline. Workaholics, *on the other hand,* always devote more time and thought to their work than their situation demands. Even in the absence of deadlines to meet, mortgages to pay, promotions to earn, or bosses to please, workaholics still work hard. What sets them apart is their attitude toward work, not the number of hours they work.

Marilyn Machlowitz, "Workaholism: What's Wrong with Being Married to Your Work?"

DISCUSSION QUESTIONS

1. What ideas do each of the italicized words and phrases connect?
2. What relationship does each show?

Repeated Key Words   Repeating key words, especially those that help convey a paragraph's central idea, can smooth the reader's path. The words may appear in different forms, but their presence keeps the main issues before the reader. In the following paragraph, the repetition of *majority, minority,* and *will* aids coherence, as does the more limited repetition of *government* and *interests.*

Whatever fine-spun theories we may devise to resolve or obscure the difficulty, there is no use blinking the fact that the *will* of the *majority* is not the same thing as the *will* of all. *Majority* rule works well only so long as the *minority* is *willing* to accept the *will* of the *majority* as the *will* of the *nation* and let it go at that. Generally speaking, the *minority* will be *willing* to let it go at that so long as it feels that its essential *interests* and rights are not fundamentally different from those of the current *majority,* and so long as it can, in any case, look forward with confidence to mustering enough votes within four or six years to become itself the *majority* and so redress the balance. But if it comes to pass that a large *minority* feels that it has no such chance, that it is a fixed and permanent *minority* and that another group or class with rights and *interests* fundamentally hostile to its own is in permanent control, then *government* by *majority* vote ceases in any sense to be *government* by the *will* of the people for the good of all, and becomes *government* by the *will* of some of the people for their own *interests* at the expense of the others.

Carl Becker, *Freedom and Responsibility in the American Way of Life*

EXERCISE   *Write a paragraph using one of the following sentences as your topic sentence. Insert the missing key word and then repeat it in your paragraph to help link your sentences.*

1. _____ is my favorite relative.
2. I wish I had (a, an, some, more) _____.
3. _____ changed my life.
4. _____ is more trouble that it's worth.
5. A visit to _____ always depresses me.
6. Eating _____ is a challenge.
7. I admire _____.

Pronouns and Demonstrative Adjectives   Pronouns stand in for nouns that appear earlier in the sentence or in previous sentences. Mixing pronouns and their nouns throughout the paragraph prevents monotony and promotes clarity.

We have italicized the pronouns in the following excerpt from an article about the writer's first visit to a gambling casino.

> There are three of *us* on this trip, two veterans of Atlantic City and *I*, a neo-phyte, all celebrating the fact that *we* have recently become grandmothers. One of *my* companions is the canny shopper in *our* crowd; as a bargain-hunter *she* knows the ways of the world. *I* have followed *her* through discount shops and outlet stores from Manhattan's Lower East Side to the Secaucus, New Jersey, malls. . . . Without saying a word, *she* hands *me* a plastic container of the kind that might hold two pounds of potato salad, and takes one *herself*. *She* drags *me* off to the change booth, where *she* exchanges bills for tubes of silver, careful not to let *me* see just how much. *I* do the same. Then *she* leads *me* to a clattering corner, where a neon sign winks on and off, *Quartermania*. "Let's try to find a couple of machines that only have handles," *she* says. . . .
>
> Eileen Herbert Jordan, "My Affair with the One-Armed Bandit"

All the pronouns in the excerpt refer to the writer, her bargain-hunting friend, or the whole group.

Four demonstrative adjectives—*this, that, these,* and *those*—also help hook ideas together. Demonstratives are special adjectives that identify or point out nouns rather than describe them. Here is an example from the Declaration of Independence:

> We hold *these* truths to be self-evident, that all men are created equal, that they are endowed by their Creator with certain unalienable Rights, that among *these* are Life, Liberty, and the pursuit of Happiness. That to secure *these* rights, Governments are instituted among Men, deriving their just powers from the consent of the governed. That whenever any Form of Government becomes destructive of *these* ends, it is the Right of the People to alter or to abolish it, and to institute new Government, laying its foundation on such principles and organizing its power in such form, as to them shall seem most likely to effect their Safety and Happiness.

> **EXERCISE**   *In a magazine, newspaper, textbook, or some other written source, find two paragraphs that use pronouns and demonstrative adjectives to increase coherence. Copy the paragraphs, underline the pronouns and demonstrative adjectives, and explain what each refers to.* ◄

Parallelism   Parallelism uses repetition of grammatical form to express a series of equivalent ideas. Besides giving continuity, the repetition adds rhythm and balance to the writing. Note how the following italicized constructions tie together the unfolding definition of poverty:

> *Poverty is staying* up all night on cold nights to watch the fire, knowing one spark on the newspaper covering the walls means your sleeping children die in flames. In summer *poverty is watching* gnats and flies devour your baby's tears when he cries. The screens are torn and you pay so little rent you know they will never be fixed. *Poverty means* insects in your food, in your nose, in your eyes, and crawling over you when you sleep. *Poverty is hoping* it never rains because diapers won't dry when it rains and soon you are using newspapers. *Poverty is seeing* your children forever with runny noses. Paper handkerchiefs cost money and all your rags you

need for other things. Even more costly are antihistamines. *Poverty is cooking* without food and cleaning without soap.

Jo Goodwin Parker, "What Is Poverty?"

Paragraphs with Special Functions

Special-function paragraphs include introductions, transitional paragraphs, and conclusions. One-paragraph introductions and conclusions appear in short, multiparagraph essays. Transitional paragraphs occur primarily in long compositions.

Introductions

A good introduction acquaints and coaxes. It announces the essay's topic and may directly state the thesis. In addition, it sets the tone—somber, lighthearted, angry—of what will follow. An amusing anecdote would not be an appropriate opening for a paper about political torture.

With essays, as with people, first impressions are important. If your opening rouses interest, it will draw the reader into the essay and pave the way for your ideas. If, instead, you'd like to try your hand at turning the reader away, search for a beginning that is mechanical, plodding, and dull. Your success will astonish you. Here are some bad openings:

In this paper I intend to . . .

Wars have always afflicted humankind.

As you may know, having too little time is a problem for many of us.

In the modern world of today . . .

How would you respond to these openings? Ask yourself that same question about every opening you write.

Gear the length of the introduction to that of the essay. Although longer papers sometimes begin with two or more introductory paragraphs, generally the lead-in for a short essay is a single paragraph. Here are some possibilities for starting an essay. The type you select depends on your purpose, subject, audience, and personality.

A Directly Stated Thesis   This is a common type of opening, orienting the reader to what will follow. After providing some general background, the writer of our example narrows her scope to a thesis that previews the upcoming sections of her essay.

An increasing number of midlife women are reentering the workforce, pursuing college degrees, and getting more involved in the public arena. Several labels besides "midlife" have been attached to this type of person: the mature woman, the older woman, and, more recently, the re-entry woman. By definition, she is between thirty-five and fifty-five years old and has been away from the business or academic scene anywhere from fifteen to thirty years. The academic community, the media, marketing people, and employers are giving her close scrutiny, and it is apparent that she is having a greater impact on our society than she realizes.

Jo Ann Harris

A Definition   This kind of introduction works particularly well in a paper that acquaints the reader with an unfamiliar topic.

You are completely alone in a large open space and are struck by a terrifying, unreasoning fear. You sweat, your heart beats, you cannot breathe. You fear you may die of a heart attack, although you do not have heart disease. Suppose you decide you will never get yourself in this helpless situation again. You go home and refuse to leave its secure confines. Your family has to support you. You have agoraphobia—a disabling terror of open spaces.

"Controlling Phobias Through Behavior Modification"

A Quotation   A beginning quotation, particularly from an authority in the field, can be an effective springboard for the ideas that follow. Make sure any quote you use relates clearly to your topic.

The director of the census made a dramatic announcement in 1890. The Nation's unsettled area, he revealed, "has been so broken into by isolated bodies of settlement that there can hardly be said to be a frontier line." These words sounded the close of one period of America's history. For three centuries before, men had marched westward, seeking in the forests and plains that lay beyond the settled areas a chance to begin anew. For three centuries they had driven back the wilderness as their conquest of the continent went on. Now, in 1890, they were told that a frontier line separating the settled and unsettled portions of the United States no longer existed. The west was won, and the expansion that had been the most distinctive feature of the country's past was at an end.

Ray Allen Billington, "The Frontier Disappears"

An Anecdote or Personal Experience   A well-told personal anecdote or experience can lure readers into the rest of the paper. Like other introductions, this kind should bear on what comes afterward. Engle's anecdote, like the stories she reviews, demonstrates that "women also have dark hearts."

My mother used to have a little china cream and sugar set that was given to her by a woman who later killed her children with an axe. It sat cheerfully in the china cabinet, as inadequate a symbol as I have ever seen of the dark mysteries within us. Yet at least it was there to remind us that no matter how much Jesus wanted us for a sunbeam, we would still have some day to cope with a deeper reality than common sense could explain. It stood for strange cars not to get into, running shoes to wear when you were out alone at night and the backs of Chinese restaurants you were not supposed to go into.

Marian Engle, review of *The Goddess and Other Women* by Joyce Carol Oates.

An Arresting Statement   Sometimes you can jolt the reader into attention, using content, language, or both, particularly if your essay develops an unusual or extreme position.

It's like Pearl Harbor. The Japanese have invaded, and the U.S. has been caught short. Not on guns and tanks and battleships—those are yesterday's weapons—but on mental might. In a high-tech age where nations increasingly compete on brainpower, American schools are producing an army of illiterates. Companies that cannot hire enough skilled workers now realize they must do something to save the public schools. Not to be charitable, not to promote good public relations, but to survive.

Nancy Perry, "Saving the Schools: How Business Can Help"

Interesting Details   These details pique curiosity and draw the reader into the paper.

It is Friday night at any of the ten thousand watering holes of the small towns and crossroads hamlets of the South. The room is a cacophony of the ping-pong-ding-ding ding of the pinball machine, the pop-fizz of another round of Pabst, the refrain of "Red Necks, White Socks and Blue Ribbon Beer" on the juke box, the insolent roar of a souped-up engine outside and, above it all, the sound of easy laughter. The good ole boys have gathered for their fraternal ritual—the aimless diversion that they have elevated into a life-style.

Bonnie Angelo, "Those Good Ole Boys"

A Question   A provocative question can entice the reader into the essay to find the answer.

When you leave your apartment or house, do you begin to feel better? If you leave for a week-long trip, do you find your head clears, your migraine disappears, dizziness stops, your aches and pains subside, depression fades away, and your entire attitude is better? If so, chemical pollution of the atmosphere in your home may be making you ill.

Marshall Mandell, "Are You Allergic to Your House?"

EXERCISES

1. **Explain why each of the preceding introductions interests or does not interest you. Does your response stem from the topic or the way the author introduces it?**

2. **Find magazine articles with effective introductory paragraphs illustrating at least three different techniques. Write a paragraph explaining why each impresses you.**

Transitional Paragraphs

In the midst of a lengthy essay, you may need a short paragraph that announces a shift from one group of ideas to another. Transitional paragraphs summarize previously explained ideas, repeat the thesis, or point to ideas that follow. In our example, Bruno Bettelheim has been discussing a young boy named Joey who has turned into a kind of human machine. After describing Joey's assorted delusions, Bettelheim signals his switch from the delusions to the fears that caused them.

What deep-seated fears and needs underlay Joey's delusional system? We were long in finding out, for Joey's preventions effectively concealed the secret of his autistic behavior. In the meantime we dealt with his peripheral problems one by one.

Bruno Bettelheim, "Joey: 'A Mechanical Boy'"

The following transitional paragraph looks back as well as ahead:

> Certainly these three factors—exercise, economy, convenience of short-cuts—help explain the popularity of bicycling today. But a fourth attraction sometimes overrides the others: the lure of the open road.

Mike Bernstein

Conclusions

A conclusion rounds out a paper and signals that the discussion has been completed. Not all papers require a separate conclusion; narratives and descriptions, for example, generally end when the writer finishes the story or concludes the impression. But many essays benefit from a conclusion that drives the point home a final time. To be effective, a conclusion must mesh logically and stylistically with what comes earlier. A long, complex paper often ends with a summary of the main points, but any of several other options may be used for shorter papers with easy-to-grasp ideas. Most short essays have single-paragraph conclusions; longer papers may require two or three paragraphs.

Here are some cautions about writing your conclusion:

1. Don't introduce new material. Draw together, round out, but don't take off in a new direction.
2. Don't tack on an ending in desperation when the hour is late and the paper is due tomorrow—the so-called midnight special. Your reader deserves better than "All in all, skiing is a great sport" or "Thus we can see that motorcycle racing isn't for everyone."
3. Don't apologize. Saying that you could have done a better job makes a reader wonder why you didn't.
4. Don't moralize. A preachy conclusion can undermine the position you have established in the rest of your composition.

The following examples illustrate several common types of conclusion.

Restatement of the Thesis   The following conclusion reasserts Jordan's thesis that "a mood of antisocial negativism is creeping through the structure of American life, corroding our ideals, and suffocating the hopes of poor people and minorities."

> There is room for honest differences about each of these key issues, but the new negativism's overt greed and the implicit racism of its loud "No" to minority aspirations indicate that this is a poisonous movement that denies the moral ideals and human values that characterize the best in America's heritage.

Vernon E. Jordan, Jr., "The New Negativism"

A Summary   A summary draws together and reinforces the main points of a paper.

There are, of course, many other arguments against capital punishment, including its high cost and its failure to deter crime. But I believe the most important points against the death penalty are the possibility of executing an innocent man, the discriminatory manner in which it is applied, and the barbaric methods of carrying it out. In my opinion, capital punishment is, in effect, premeditated murder by society as a whole. As the old saying goes, two wrongs don't make a right.

Diane Trathen

A Question   The paragraph below concludes an argument that running should not be elevated to a religion, that its other benefits are sufficient. A final question often prompts the reader to think further on the topic. If your essay is meant to be persuasive, be sure to phrase a concluding question so that the way a reasonable person would answer emphasizes your point of view.

Aren't those gifts enough? Why ask running for benefits that are plainly beyond its capacity to bestow?

James Fixx, "What Running Can't Do for You"

A Quotation   A quotation can capture the essence of your thought and end the essay with authority.

"We had no idea of the emotional involvement and the commitment of these women," Richard says. "Suddenly a constituency arose. Suddenly there are thousands and thousands of women who don't care about your moral position or mine—they want a baby."

David Zimmerman, "Are Test-Tube Babies the Answer for the Childless?"

Ironic Twist or Surprising Observation   These approaches prompt the reader to think further about a paper's topic. The following paragraph points out the ironic refusal of the government to confront poverty that exists a mere ten blocks away from its offices:

Thus, a stark contrast exists between the two cultures of 14th Street, which appears to be like an earthworm with half of its body crushed by poverty but the other half still alive, wriggling in wealth. The two are alike only in that each communicates little with the other because of the wide disparity between the lives of the people and the conditions of the environments. The devastating irony of the situation on 14th Street lies in the fact that only ten blocks away sit the very government institutions that could alleviate the poverty—the Senate, the House of Representatives, and the White House.

Student Unknown

Clever or Lighthearted Ending   In our example, the writer, capitalizing on the essay's topic, ends by exaggerating the fault being criticized.

Because using clichés is as easy as falling off a log, it goes without saying that it would be duck soup to continue in this vein till hell freezes over.

However, since that would be carrying coals to Newcastle, let's ring down the curtain and bid adieu to the fair topic of the cliché. (No use beating a dead horse.)

Student Unknown

Personal Challenge   A challenge often prompts the reader to take some action.

And therein lies the challenge. You can't merely puff hard for a few days and then revert to the La-Z-Boy recliner, smugly thinking that you're "in shape." You must sweat and strain and puff regularly, week in and week out. They're your muscles, your lungs, your heart. The only caretaker they have is you.

Monica Duvall

Hope or Recommendation   Both a hope and a recommendation may restate points already made in the essay or suggest actions to take in order to arrive at a solution.

Periodically my pilot and I climb into our aircraft and head out over the Minnesota wilderness, following a succession of electronic beeps that lead to some of the last remaining wolves in the lower 48 states. We hope that the data we collect will provide a better understanding of the wolf. We especially hope that our work will help guide authorities into a management program that will insure the perpetuation of the species in the last vestiges of its former range.

L. David Mech, "Where Can the Wolves Survive?"

I who am blind can give one hint to those who can see—one admonition to those who would make full use of the gift of sight: Use your eyes as if tomorrow you would be stricken blind. And the same method can be applied to the other senses. Hear the music of voices, the song of the bird, the mighty strains of an orchestra, as if you would be stricken deaf tomorrow. Touch each object you want to touch as if tomorrow your tactile sense would fail. Smell the perfume of flowers, taste with relish each morsel, as if tomorrow you could never smell and taste again. Make the most of every sense; glory in all the facets of pleasure and beauty which the world reveals to you through the several means of contact which Nature provides. But of all the senses, I am sure that sight must be the most delightful.

Helen Keller, "Three Days to See"

EXERCISES

1. **Explain why each of the foregoing conclusions does or does not interest you. Does your response stem from the topic or from the author's handling of it?**

2. **Copy effective concluding paragraphs, illustrating at least three different techniques, from magazine articles. Then write a paragraph explaining why each impresses you.**

CHAPTER 16

EFFECTIVE SENTENCES

A sentence is a group of words that begins with a capital letter; ends with a period, question mark, or exclamation point; and makes sense by itself. The elements that comprise sentences include subjects, predicates, direct objects, indirect objects, subject complements, object complements, phrases, and clauses.

Sentences take many forms, some straightforward and unadorned, others intricate and ornate, each with its own stylistic strengths. Becoming familiar with these forms and their uses gives you the option to

- emphasize or de-emphasize an idea
- combine ideas into one sentence or keep them separate in more than one sentence
- make sentences sound formal or informal
- emphasize the actor or the action
- achieve rhythm, variety, and contrast.

Effective sentences bring both exactness and flair to your writing. You may wish to read the Handbook section for review if you are not familiar with the sentence elements or how to identify and correct sentence errors effectively.

Sentence Strategies

Effective sentences are not an accident; they require work. There are several strategies you can employ, including avoiding unnecessary wordiness; varying sentence length, complexity, and word order; building a rhythm for your reader; and selecting the right verb voice. Usually it's best to work on these different strategies as you revise rather than pausing to refine each sentence after you write it.

Avoiding Unnecessary Wordiness

Sometimes in first drafts we write flabby sentences.

- It is my considered opinion that you will make an excellent employee.
- Joan will give a presentation on our latest sales figures to the CEO.
- Mr. Headly, who was my seventh-grade biology teacher, recently was honored for the research he had done over the years with his classes.
- My neighbor's Subaru that was old and rusty still could navigate the winter streets better than most other cars.

Although there may be stylistic reasons for these sentences, such as creating variety or adding a particular emphasis, a writer could sharpen them by reordering the sentence structure and eliminating unnecessary words.

- You will make an excellent employee. (The fact that you write it makes it clear that it is your opinion.)
- Joan will present our latest sales figures to the CEO. (Many times we use verbs as nouns with a filler verb—"have a meeting," "give a talk," "go running." Change these nouns back to verbs and dragging sentences can be energized.)
- Mr. Headly, my seventh-grade biology teacher, recently was honored for the research he had done over the years with his classes. (The rules of English let you delete some redundant phrases, even repeated subjects, to tighten your language.)
- My neighbor's rusty, old Subaru still could navigate the winter streets better than most other cars. (Changing a relative clause to simple adjectives makes this sentence crisper. Often you can change word order to produce more emphatic sentences.)

The actual rules for tightening sentences are discussed in the Handbook. How do most writers do it? Cut out words that seem unnecessary, organize sentences different ways, let verbs bear the brunt of the burden.

EXERCISES   *Rewrite the sentences to avoid unnecessary wordiness.*

1. The principal will give a talk to the parents at the PTA meeting about how important it is for their children to get to school on time.
2. I would like to say that no playwright has ever used language as effectively as Shakespeare.
3. Mozart, who was a musical prodigy, is best known for his operas.
4. The jewelry store sold me a watch that was stolen.
5. The meeting that was scheduled for 3 P.M. was cancelled because Mr. Rushton, the consultant who was giving the presentation about the results on our computer security, was arrested for creating computer viruses that were very destructive.

Varying Sentence Complexity and Length

Sentences that are all the same length yield a repetitive, tedious prose.

> Janice hated pain. She had her nose pierced. She had her bellybutton pierced. She had her tongue pierced. She wanted to be different. She ended up just like her friends.

This string of simple sentences unnecessarily repeats word phrases and gives the reader a bumpy ride. Combining these sentences results in a smoother and more varied prose style.

> Although Janice hated pain, she had her nose, bellybutton, and tongue pierced in order to be different. She ended up, however, just like her friends.

> Simple sentences of one subject and predicate—"The audience was young"—can be combined through coordinate and subordinate conjunctions, as well as the use of relative clause structures and other techniques. The result is not only a smoother style but a combination that more effectively shows the relationship of your ideas.

Coordination

Discussed more fully in the Handbook, coordinating conjunctions include *and, but, or, nor, for, yet, so,* and can combine clauses or phrases in a way that makes them equal.

- The audience was young, friendly, *and* responsive; *so* it cheered for each speaker.
- *Either* we hang together *or* we hang separately.
- A tornado ripped through our town but fortunately it spared our house.

Subordination

Subordinate conjunctions such as *because, since, while, before, during, after,* and *instead of* can link dependent clauses to the main independent clause in a way that shows logical relationship.

- Millicent swam 400 laps today ***because*** *she was feeling unusually strong.*
- Arthur collapsed on the sofa ***after*** *the dance was over.*
- ***Once*** *they had reached the lakeshore,* the campers found a level spot ***where*** *they could pitch their tent.*

Relative Clauses

Nouns can often be modified by relative clauses, which use a **relative pronoun** that substitutes for a noun and binds ideas together.

- Students ***who*** *work hard* usually succeed.
- The books on the history of Crete ***that*** *you ordered* have finally arrived.

There are certainly other ways to combine sentences and vary sentence length, including the use of prepositional phrases, participle phrases, and infinitive phrases.

- The crook raced **around** *the corner,* **down** *the alley,* **into** *the arms* **of** *the waiting police officers.* (prepositional phrases)

- Some people handle a crisis by avoiding it, **ignoring** *the problem until someone else solves it.* (participle phrase)

- The early settlers moved west **to escape** *an unsavory or difficult past,* **to forge** *a new life,* **to realize** *dreams.* (infinitive phrases)

The point is to find ways to vary your sentences to increase interest and rhythm.

Intentional Fragments

A fragment is a part of a sentence that is capitalized and punctuated as if it were a complete sentence.

Although fragments are seldom used in formal prose, they form the backbone of most conversations. Here's how a typical bit of dialogue might go:

"Where are you going tonight?" *(sentence)*
"To Woodland Mall." *(fragment)*
"What for?" *(fragment)*
"To buy some shoes." *(fragment)*
"Alone?" *(fragment)*
"No, with Maisie Perkins." *(fragment)*
"Can I come too?" *(sentence)*
"Sure." *(fragment)*

As with most conversations, the sprinkling of complete sentences makes the fragments clear.

Writers of nonfiction use fragments to create special effects. In the following passage, the fragment emphasizes the importance of the question it asks and varies the pace of the writing:

> Before kidney transplants, people had an ethical unease about renal dialysis—the artificial kidney machine. Unquestionably it was a great technical advance making it possible to treat kidney dysfunctions from which thousands die. But the machine was, and is, expensive and involves intensive care of the patient by doctors and nurses. For whom the machine? In the United States the dilemma was evaded but not solved by having lay panels, like juries, making life-or-death choices. In Britain, where the National Health Service entitles everyone, rich or poor, to have access to any necessary treatment, the responsibility rests on the medical staff. It was (and still is) a difficult decision.
>
> Lord Ritchie-Calder, "The Doctor's Dilemma"

Once in a while, as in the following example, a writer will use a whole series of fragments. In the following paragraph, they create a kaleidoscopic effect that mirrors the kaleidoscopic impressions offered by the Jazz Age itself.

> The Jazz Age offers a kaleidoscope of shifting impressions. Of novelties quickly embraced and quickly discarded. Of flappers flaunting bobbed hair and short skirts. Of hip flasks and bootleg whisky, fast cars and coonskin coats, jazz and dancing till dawn. And overall a sense of futility, an uneasy conviction that all the gods were dead.
>
> Elliott L. Smith and Andrew W. Hart,
> *The Short Story: A Contemporary Looking Glass*

Before using any fragment in your own writing, think carefully about your intended effect and explore other ways of achieving it. Unless only a fragment will serve your needs, don't use one; fragments are likely to be viewed as unintentional—and thus errors—in the work of inexperienced writers.

 The following passage includes one or more fragments. Identify each and explain its function.

> He [Richard Wagner] wrote operas; and no sooner did he have the synopsis of a story, but he would invite—or rather summon—a crowd of his friends to his house and read it aloud to them. Not for criticism. For applause. When the complete poem was written, the friends had to come again, and hear *that* read aloud. Then he would publish the poem, sometimes years before the music that went with it was written. He played the piano like a composer, in the worst sense of what that implies, and he would sit down at the piano before parties that included some of the finest pianists of his time, and play for them, by the hour, his own music, needless to say. He had a composer's voice. And he would invite eminent vocalists to his house, and sing them his operas, taking all the parts.
>
> Deems Taylor, "The Monster"

Working together, these techniques provide varied sentences that create interest. In the following paragraph, the sentences differ considerably in length.

> To protest that some fairly improbable people, some people who could not possibly respect themselves, seem to sleep easily enough is to miss the point entirely, as surely as those people miss it who think that self-respect has necessarily to do with not having safety pins in one's underwear. There is a common superstition that "self-respect" is a kind of charm against snakes, something that keeps those who have it locked in some unblighted Eden, out of strange beds, ambivalent conversations, and trouble in general. It does not at all. It has nothing to do with the face of things, but concerns instead a separate peace, a private reconciliation.
>
> Joan Didion, "On Self-Respect"

Much of the appealing rhythm of this passage stems from varied sentence length. The first two rather long sentences (forty-nine and thirty-six words) are followed by the very brief "It does not at all," which gains emphasis by its position. The last sentence adds variety by means of its moderate length (nineteen words), quite apart from its interesting observation on the real nature of self-respect.

Varying sentence length can help you emphasize a key idea. If a key point is submerged in a long sentence, highlight it as a separate thought, giving it the recognition it deserves.

Original Version

Employers find mature women to be valuable members of their organizations. They are conscientious, have excellent attendance records, and stay calm when things go awry, *but unfortunately many employers exploit them.* Despite their desirable qualities, most remain mired in clerical, sales, and elementary teaching positions. On the average they earn two-thirds as much as men.

Revised Version

Employers find mature women to be valuable members of their organizations. They are conscientious, have excellent attendance records, and stay calm when things go awry. *Unfortunately, though, many employers exploit them.* Despite their desirable qualities, most remain mired in clerical, sales, and elementary teaching positions. On the average they earn two-thirds as much as men.

EXERCISE *Using coordination and subordination, rewrite the following passages to reduce words and/or improve smoothness.*

1. He played the piano. He played the organ. He played the French horn. He did not play the viola.
2. The weather was icy cold and windy. Lee was wearing only a T-shirt and athletic shorts.
3. Life on Venus may be possible. It will not be the kind of life we know on Earth. Life on Mars may be possible. It will not be the kind of life we know on Earth.
4. He felt his classmates were laughing at his error. He ran out of the room. He vowed never to return to that class.
5. Albert lay in bed. He stared at the ceiling. Albert thought about the previous afternoon. He had asked Kathy to go to dinner with him. She is a pretty, blonde-haired woman. She sits at the desk next to his. They work at Hemphill's. She had refused.
6. I went to the store to buy a box of detergent. I saw Bill there, and we talked about last night's game.
7. Tim went to the newsstand. He bought a magazine there. While he was on the way home, he lost it. He had nothing to read.

Varying Word Order

What other tools do you have to create more interesting prose? One powerful technique is to vary word order in a sentence.

Word Order in Independent Clauses

Most independent clauses follow a similar arrangement. First comes the subject, then the verb, and finally any other element needed to convey the main message.

Barney blushed. *(subject, verb)*

They built the dog a kennel. *(subject, verb, indirect object, direct object)*

Samantha is an architect. *(subject, verb, subject complement)*

This arrangement puts the emphasis on the subject, right where it's usually wanted.

But the pattern doesn't work in every situation. Occasionally, a writer wants to emphasize some element that follows the verb, create an artistic effect, or give the subject unusual emphasis. Enter inverted order and the expletive construction.

Inverted Order   To invert a sentence, move to the front the element you want to emphasize. Sometimes the rest of the sentence follows in regular subject-then-verb order; sometimes the verb precedes the subject.

Lovable he isn't. *(subject complement, subject, verb)*

This I just don't understand. *(direct object, subject, verb)*

Tall grow the pines in the mountains. *(subject complement, verb, subject)*

Sentences that ask questions typically follow an inverted pattern.

Is this your coat? *(verb, subject, subject complement)*

Will you let the cat out? *(verb, subject, verb, direct object)*

Most of your sentences should follow normal order: Readers expect it and read most easily through it. Furthermore, don't invert a sentence if the result would sound strained and unnatural. A sentence like "Fools were Brett and Amanda for quitting college" will only hinder communication.

Expletives   An expletive fills a vacancy in a sentence without contributing to the meaning. English has two common expletives, *there* and *it*. Ordinarily, *there* functions as an adverb, *it* as a pronoun, and either can appear anywhere in a sentence. As expletives, however, they alter normal sentence order by beginning sentences and anticipating the real subjects or objects.

Expletives are often used unnecessarily, as in the following example:

There were twenty persons attending the sales meeting.

This sentence errs on two counts: Its subject needs no extra emphasis, and it is very clumsy. Notice the improvement without the expletive and the unneeded words:

Twenty persons attended the sales meeting.

When the subject or object needs highlighting, leading off with an expletive will, by altering normal order, call it more forcefully to the reader's attention.

Normal order:	A fly is in my soup.
	He seeks her happiness.
Expletive construction:	There is a fly in my soup. *(expletive anticipating subject)*
	It is her happiness he seeks. *(expletive anticipating object)*

Once in a while you'll find that something just can't be said unless you use an expletive.

There is no reason for such foolishness.

No other construction can express exactly the same thought.

EXERCISE   *Indicate which of these sentences follow normal order, which are in-*
verted, and which have expletive constructions. Rewrite so that all
will be in normal order.

1. Dick Lewis is a true friend.
2. It was her car in the ditch.
3. An intelligent person is she.
4. May I go to the movie with you?
5. A sadder but wiser man he became.
6. There are many dead fish on the beach.
7. The instructor gave the class a long reading assignment.
8. The Willetts have bought a new house.
9. It is Marianne's aim to become a lawyer.
10. Harry works at a supermarket.

Positioning of Movable Modifiers

Movable modifiers can appear on either side of the main statement or within it.

Modifiers after Main Statement   Sentences that follow this arrangement, frequently called *loose sentences*, occur more commonly than either of the others.
They mirror conversation, in which a speaker first makes a statement and then
adds further thoughts. Often, the main statement has just one modifier.

> Our company will have to file for bankruptcy *because of this year's huge
> losses. (phrase as modifier)*

Or it can head up a whole train of modifiers.

> He burst suddenly into the party, *loud, angry, obscene. (words as modifiers)*

> The family used to gather around the hearth, *doing such chores as polishing
> shoes, mending ripped clothing, reading, chatting, always warmed by one another's
> presence as much as by the flames. (words and phrases as modifiers)*

A sentence may contain several layers of modifiers. In the following exam
ple, we've indented and numbered to show the different layers.

1. The men struggled to the top of the hill,
    2. thirsty,
    2. drenched in sweat,
    2. and cursing in pain
        3. as their knapsack straps cut into their raw, chafed shoulders
            4. with every step.

In this sentence, the items numbered 2 refer to *men* in the item numbered 1. Item
3 is linked to *cursing* in the preceding item 2, and item 4 is linked to *cut* in item 3.

The modifiers-last arrangement works well for injecting descriptive details into narratives and also for qualifying, explaining, and presenting lists in other kinds of writing.

Modifiers before Main Statement   Sentences that delay the main point until the end are called *periodic*. In contrast to loose sentences, they lend a formal note to what is said, slowing its pace, adding cadence, and making it more serious.

> *If you can keep your head when everyone around you is panicking,* you probably don't understand the situation. *(clauses as modifiers)*

> *The danger of sideswiping another vehicle, the knowledge that a hidden bump or hole could throw me from the dune buggy,* both of these things added to the thrill of the race. *(noun plus phrase and noun plus clause as modifiers)*

> 1. *When the public protests,*
>   2. *confronted with some obvious evidence of the damaging results of pesticide applications,* it is fed little tranquilizing pills of half truth. *(clause and phrase as modifiers)*
>
> Rachel Carson, *Silent Spring*

As shown in the Carson example, periodic sentences can also have layers of modifiers.

Positioning the modifiers before the main point throws the emphasis to the end of the sentence, adding force to the main point. The delay also lets the writer create sentences that, like the first example, carry stings, ironic or humorous, in their tails.

Modifiers within Main Statement   Inserting one or more modifiers into a main statement creates a sentence with *interrupted order*. The material may come between the subject and the verb or between the verb and the rest of the predicate.

> The young girl, *wearing a tattered dress and looking anything but well-off herself,* gave the beggar a ten-dollar bill. *(phrases between subject and verb)*

> The evolutionists, *piercing beneath the show of momentary stability,* discovered, *hidden in rudimentary organs,* the discarded rubbish of the past. *(one phrase between subject and verb, another between verb and rest of predicate)*

By stretching out the main idea, inserted modifiers slow the forward pace of the sentence, giving it some of the formality and force of a periodic sentence.

 Identify each sentence as loose, periodic, or interrupted. Rewrite each as one of the other kinds.

1. Victoria, rejected by family and friends, uncertain where to turn next, finally decided to start a new life in Chicago.
2. When told that she had to have her spleen removed, the woman gasped.
3. The first graders stood in line, talking and giggling, pushing at one another's caps and pencil boxes and kicking one another's shins, unmindful of the drudgery that awaited them within the old schoolhouse.

4. Good health, warm friends, a beautiful summer evening—the best things cannot be purchased.
5. A customer, angry and perspiring, stormed up to the claims desk.
6. Stopping just short of the tunnel entrance, the freight train avoided a collision with the crowded commuter train stalled inside.
7. The new kid hammered away at the fading champ, determination in his eyes and glory in his fists.
8. The new tract house sparkled in the sunlight, pink and trim, its lawn immaculate, its two bushes and newly planted crab apple tree, by their very tininess, making the yard look vaster than its actual size. ◄

Building Rhythm

Effective sentences have patterns of organization that help convey meaning while assisting the readers in following the text. Poor organization, even if grammatical, is usually awkward.

Using Parallelism

Parallelism presents equivalent ideas in grammatically equivalent form. Dressing them in the same grammatical garb calls attention to their kinship and adds smoothness and polish. The following sentence pairs demonstrate the improvement that parallelism brings:

> *Nonparallel:*   James's outfit was *wrinkled, mismatched,* and *he needed to wash it. (words and independent clause)*
>
> *Parallel:*   James's outfit was *wrinkled, mismatched,* and *dirty. (words)*
>
> *Nonparallel:*   Oscar likes *reading books, attending plays,* and *to search for antiques. (different kinds of phrases)*
>
> *Parallel:*   Oscar likes *reading books, attending plays,* and *searching for antiques. (same kind of phrases)*
>
> *Nonparallel:*   Beth performs her tasks *quickly, willingly,* and *with accuracy. (words and phrase)*
>
> *Parallel:*   Beth performs her tasks *quickly, willingly,* and *accurately. (words)*

As the examples show, revising nonparallel sentences smooths out bumpiness, binds the ideas together more closely, and lends them a more finished look.

Parallelism doesn't always stop with a single sentence. Writers sometimes use it in a series of sentences:

> He had never lost his childlike innocence. He had never lost his sense of wonder. He had never lost his sense of joy in nature's simplest gifts.

For an example of parallelism that extends over much of a paragraph, see pages 221–222.

Balance, a special form of parallelism, positions two grammatically equivalent ideas on opposite sides of some pivot point, such as a word or punctuation mark.

Hope for the best, and prepare for the worst.

Many are called, but few are chosen.

When I'm right, nobody ever notices; when I'm wrong, nobody ever forgets.

The sheep are in the meadow, and the cows are in the corn.

Like regular parallel sentences, balanced sentences sometimes come in series:

The tension in this city is not between white people and Negro people. The tension is, at bottom, between justice and injustice, between the forces of light and the forces of darkness. And if there is a victory, it will be a victory not merely for fifty thousand Negroes, but a victory for justice and the forces of light.

Martin Luther King, Jr., "Pilgrimage to Nonviolence"

Balance works especially well for pitting contrasting or clashing ideas against each other. It sharpens the difference between them while achieving compactness and lending an air of insight to what is said.

 Identify each sentence as nonparallel, parallel, or balanced; then rewrite each nonparallel sentence to make it parallel.

1. Professor Bartlett enjoys helping students, counseling advisees, and participation in faculty meetings.
2. I can still see Aunt Alva striding into the corral, cornering a cow against a fencepost, try to balance herself on a one-legged milking stool, and butt her head into the cow's belly.
3. The city plans on building a new fishing pier and on dredging the channel of the river.
4. Elton plans on vacationing in New York, but Noreen wants to raft down the Colorado River.
5. Being half drunk and because he was already late for work, Tom called his boss and said he was too ill to come in that day.
6. The novel's chief character peers through a tangle of long hair, slouches along in a shambling gait, and gets into trouble constantly.
7. You can take the boy out of the country, but you can't take the country out of the boy.
8. Joe's problem is not that he earns too little money but spending it foolishly.
9. The room was dark, gloomy, and everything was dusty.
10. The apparition glided through the wall, across the room, and up the fireplace chimney.

Choosing the Right Verb Voice

A sentence's verb voice derives from the relationship between the subject and the action. A sentence in the *active voice* has a subject that does something plus a verb that shows action.

The boy hit the target.

The girl painted the garage.

This pattern keeps the key information in the key part of the sentence, making it strong and vigorous and giving the reader a close-up look at the action.

The *passive voice* reverses the subject–action relationship by having the subject receive, rather than perform, the action. It is built around a form of the verb *to be,* for example, *is, are, was, were.* Some sentences identify the actor by using a prepositional phrase; others don't mention the actor at all.

The target was hit by the boy. *(actor identified)*

The federal debt limit is to be increased. *(actor unidentified)*

Demoting or banishing the actor dilutes the force of the sentence, puts greater distance between the action and the reader, and almost always adds extra words to the message.

Most writers who overuse the passive voice simply don't realize its effects on their writing. Read the following paragraph, written mainly in the passive voice:

> Graft becomes possible when gifts are given to police officers or favors are done for them by persons who expect preferential treatment in return. Gifts of many kinds may be received by officers. Often free meals are given to them by the owners of restaurants on their beats. During the Christmas season, they may be given liquor, food, or theater tickets by merchants. If favored treatment is not received by the donors, no great harm is done. But if traffic offenses, safety code violations, and other infractions are overlooked by the officers, corruption results. When such corruption is exposed by the newspapers, faith is lost in law enforcement agencies.

This impersonal, wordy passage plods across the page and therefore lacks any real, persuasive impact. Now note the livelier, more forceful tone of this rewritten version.

> Graft becomes possible when police officers accept gifts or favors from persons who expect preferential treatment in return. Officers may receive gifts of many kinds. Restaurant owners often provide free meals for officers on the beat. During the Christmas season, merchants may give them liquor, food, or theater tickets. If donors do not receive favored treatment, no great harm is done. But if officers overlook traffic offenses, safety code violations, and other infractions, corruption results. When the newspapers expose such corruption, citizens lose faith in law enforcement agencies.

Don't misunderstand: The passive voice does have its uses. It can mask identities—or at least try to. A child may try to dodge responsibility by saying, "Mother, while you were out, the living room lamp got broken." Less manipulatively, reporters may use it to conceal the identity of a source.

Technical and scientific writing customarily uses the passive voice to explain processes.

> In the production of steel, iron ore is first converted into pig iron by combining it with limestone and coke and then heating the mixture in a blast furnace. Pig iron, however, contains too many impurities to be useful to industry, and as a result must be refined and converted to steel. In the refining process, manganese, silicon, and aluminum are heated with the pig iron in order to degas it, that is, to remove excess oxygen and impurities from it. The manganese, silicon, and aluminum are vaporized while the iron remains in the liquid state and the impurities are carried away by the vapors. Once this step has been completed, the molten

steel is poured into ingots and allowed to cool. The steel is now ready for further processing.

Putting such writing in the passive voice provides a desirable objective tone and puts the emphasis where it's most important: on the action, not the actor. On occasion, everyday writing also uses the passive voice.

The garbage is collected once a week, on Monday.

These caves were formed about 10 million years ago.

In the first case, there's no need to tell who collects the garbage; obviously, garbage collectors do. In the second, the writer may not know what caused the formation, and saying "Something formed these caves about 10 million years ago" would sound ridiculous. In both situations, the action, not the actor, is paramount.

Unless special circumstances call for the passive voice, however, use the active voice.

EXERCISE *After determining whether each sentence below is in active or passive voice, rewrite the passive sentences as active ones.*

1. Mary's parents gave her a sports car for her sixteenth birthday.
2. Fires were left burning by negligent campers.
3. The new ice arena will be opened by the city in about two weeks.
4. Harry left the open toolbox out in the rain.
5. Corn was introduced to the Pilgrims by friendly American Indians.
6. Maude took a trip to Sante Fe, New Mexico.
7. We have just installed a new computer in our main office.
8. The club president awarded Tompkins the Order of the Golden Mace.
9. The sound of war drums was heard by the missionaries as they floated down the river.
10. Objections were raised by some members of the legislature to the ratification of the proposed amendment.

Beyond the Single Sentence

What makes a team successful? Skilled players, to be sure, but teamwork as well. Likewise, your sentences need to work together to produce the desired effect. Your content and purpose will guide you in determining how your sentences will work together. You will need to vary sentence length, word order, and rhythms to produce your desired effect; but in a way that is not obvious or clumsy. This takes work. A good place to start is by studying the essays in the Reader to see what kinds of combinations they use—a series of questions that are then answered; long sentences with modifiers that lead to a short sentence that gains emphasis; a series of fragments followed by a long sentence. In your own writing, keep an eye on what kind of sentences you are creating and how those sentences create a pattern. Once you have finished a draft of your paper, read it over, see how its rhythms strike your inner ear, and put check marks by sections that "sound" wrong. Play with your sentences to get the results that you want.

EXERCISE   *Revise the following passages to improve their style.*

1. Andrew Carnegie came to America from Scotland. He worked as a factory hand, a telegrapher, and a railway clerk to support himself. His savings from these jobs were invested in oil and later in the largest steel works in the country. Historians do not agree in their assessments of Carnegie. Some have considered him a cruel taskmaster and others a benevolent benefactor. His contributions to American society, however, cannot be denied. He established public libraries all across the country and spent much time in promoting peace. Good or bad, he ranks as one of our most noteworthy nineteenth-century immigrants.

2. She went to the seashore. She found some seashells. She picked up the seashells. She put the seashells into a basket. She had a whole basketful of seashells. She went home with the basket. She took the shells out of the basket. She put the shells on a dinette table. She brought jeweler's tools to the table. She pierced holes in the shells. She strung the shells on small chains. The chains were gold and silver. She made twenty necklaces. The selling price of the necklaces was $10 apiece. She earned $175 profit. She used her profits to go to the shore again. She could afford to stay for a week this time.

DICTION, TONE, STYLE

Your decisions about words and sentences set the tone and style of your writing. Not only do you choose sentence strategies for correctness and effectiveness, but you also choose words for accuracy and effect. Sentences must be clear and effective; so must words. Diction deals broadly with words, not in isolation but as parts of sentences, paragraphs, and essays. Every time you write and revise, diction comes into play.

Toward Clear Diction

Clear diction stems from choosing words with the right meanings, using abstract and concrete words appropriately, and picking terms that are neither too specific nor too general. Dictionaries and thesauruses can guide your choices.

Word Meanings

Make sure the words you use mean what you think they do, so that inaccurate words will not distort your message. Sound-alike word pairs often trip up unwary writers. Take *accept* and *except* for example. *Accept* means "to approve." *Except*, when used as a verb, means "to exclude or omit." If you want to indicate approval but you say, "The following new courses were *excepted* by the committee," think of the obvious consequences. Likewise, consider the distinction between *continual* (frequently or regularly repeated) and *continuous* (uninterrupted). If you illustrate your popularity by saying "My phone rings *continuously*," your reader will wonder why you never answer it and how you ever sleep.

Concrete and Abstract Words

A concrete word names or describes something that we can perceive with one or more of our five senses. A thing is concrete if we can weigh it, measure it, hold it in our hands, photograph it, taste it, sniff it, add salt to it, drop it, smash into it, or borrow it from a neighbor. If it's abstract, we can't do any of these things. *Eric Clapton* is a concrete term, as are *Swiss cheese, petroleum, maple syrup,* and *Dallas.* On the other hand, *jealousy, power, conservatism, size,* and *sadness* are abstract terms.

Concrete words evoke precise, vivid mental images and thus help convey a message. The images that abstract terms create differ from person to person. Try this test: Ask several of your friends to describe what comes to mind when they think of *joy, hatred, fear,* or some other abstract term. To illustrate, the word *hatred* might call up images of a person with cold, slitted eyes, and a grimly set jaw, for one person and another image for a different person. As you can see, concrete terms help us specify what we mean and thus enhance communication.

In the following passage, the concrete diction is italicized:

> To do without self-respect . . . is to be an unwilling *audience of one* to an interminable *documentary* that details one's failings, both real and imagined, with *fresh footage spliced* in for every *screening.* There's *the glass you broke* in anger, there's *the hurt on X's face; watch now, this next scene, the night Y came back from Houston,* see how you muff this one. To live without self-respect is to *lie awake some night,* beyond the reach of *warm milk, phenobarbital,* and *the sleeping hand on the coverlet,* counting up the sins of commission and omission, the trusts betrayed, the promises subtly broken, the gifts irrevocably wasted through sloth or cowardice or carelessness. However long we postpone it, we eventually lie down alone in that notoriously *uncomfortable bed,* the one we make ourselves. Whether or not we sleep in it depends, of course, on whether or not we respect ourselves.
>
> Joan Didion, "On Self-Respect"

Now note how vague and colorless the passage becomes without the concrete diction:

> To do without self-respect is to be continuously aware of your failings, both real and imagined. Incidents stay in your mind long after they are over. To live without self-respect means being bothered by intentional or unintentional failings, trusts betrayed, promises subtly broken, and gifts irrevocably wasted through sloth or cowardice or carelessness. However long we postpone it, we eventually must come to terms with who we are. How we respond to this situation depends, of course, on whether or not we respect ourselves.

EXERCISE *Underline the concrete terms in the following passage:*

> The fog which rises from the river has no color, no texture, no taste, smell, or sound. It is sheer vision, a vision of purity, a slow, mesmeric, inexorable erasure of the slate. You see fog mushrooming along the river's course. Gently, it obliterates the alders tangled on the banks, wipes out the road. Buildings without foundations, trees without trunks, hang in the air like mirages. Sun may be shining brightly on them, or rain drenching them, or stars twinkling above or among them. Slowly the fog reaches higher and spreads. Ridgepoles, small topmost branches, and your own dooryard vanish. There is nothing left now but shining

mist. It is all, and you float on it, utterly alone, as one imagines he might in empty space if flung off by earth; as the mind does, drifting into sleep; as the spirit does, having escaped its mortal frame.

Gladys Hasty Carroll, *Sing Out the Glory*

Specific and General Terms

One concrete term can be more specific or more general than another. As we move from *Lassie* to *collie* to *dog* to *mammal* and finally to *animal,* we become less and less specific, ending with a term that encompasses every animal on earth. With each step we retain only those features that fit the more general term. Thus, when we move from *collie* to *dog,* we leave out everything that makes collies different from terriers, greyhounds, and other breeds.

The more specific the term, the less difference among the images it calls to mind. If you say *animal* to a group of friends, one may think of a dog, another of a horse, and a third of a gorilla. *Collie,* on the other hand, triggers images of a large, long-haired, brown and white dog with a pointed muzzle.

Ask yourself how specific you need to be and then act accordingly. Often, the more specific term will be the better choice. If, for instance, you're describing a wealthy jet-setter, noting that he drives a Ferrari, not just a car, helps establish his character. But if you're writing a narrative about your flight to New Orleans and your experience at Mardi Gras, nothing is gained by naming the make of car you rented and used uneventfully during your stay.

EXERCISES

1. **Arrange each set of words from less specific to more specific.**

   a. man, ex-President, human being, Bill Clinton, American
   b. Forest Hills Apartments, building, structure, condominium, dwelling

2. **Expand each of the following words into a series of four or more that become progressively more specific. Use 1a or 1b as a pattern.**

   a. activity
   b. event
   c. political party
   d. institution
   e. device
   f. reading matter

Dictionaries and Thesauruses

Get the dictionary habit and learn to use a thesaurus. These will increase your vocabulary as well as your skill at using words you already know.

Dictionaries   Dictionaries are storehouses of word meanings. In general, dictionary makers do not try to dictate how words should be used. Instead, they note current and past meanings. When a word gains or loses a meaning or a newly minted word enjoys wide circulation, dictionary makers observe and record. Most users, however, regard dictionaries as authorities on correctness.

Dictionaries supply much more than word meanings. Figure 17.1, an annotated entry from a college-level dictionary, shows what they can provide. Some dictionary entries include idioms, irregular forms of words, usage labels, and supplementary information, as well.

Idioms   Idioms express meanings that differ from those of the words that make them up. Here are two examples.

I won't *put up with* any foolishness.

The dowager *gave me the cold shoulder.*

Put up with means "tolerate"; *gave me the cold shoulder* means "snubbed me." Looking up the most prominent word of an unfamiliar idiom may lead you to a listing and a definition.

Irregular Forms   Any irregular forms are indicated. In *Webster's New World Dictionary*, the entry for the verb *spring* notes that the other forms are *sprang*, *sprung*, and *springing*. This information helps you use correct forms in your writing.

Usage Labels   Usage labels help you determine whether a word suits the circumstances of your writing. Here are the most common labels:

Label	Meaning
Colloquial	Characteristic of informal writing and speaking; should not be considered nonstandard.
Slang	Informal, newly coined words and expressions or old expressions with new meanings.
Obsolete	No longer in use but found in past writing.
Archaic	Still finds restricted use, for example, in legal documents; otherwise not appropriate.
Poetic	Used only in poetry and in prose with a poetic tone.
Dialect	Used regularly only in a particular geographical location such as the southeastern United States or the Scottish Lowlands.

Supplementary Information   While focusing primarily on individual words, college-level dictionaries often provide several other kinds of information. They may include a history of the language, lists of standard abbreviations and of colleges and universities, biographical notes on distinguished individuals, and geographical notes on important locations.

Any dictionary is better than none, but some clearly outrank others in usefulness. A pocket dictionary is handy but not as comprehensive as a desk dictionary. Excellent desk-sized dictionaries include the following:

The American Heritage Dictionary
Funk and Wagnall's Standard College Dictionary
The Random House Dictionary of the English Language
Webster's Merriam-Collegiate Dictionary
Webster's New World Dictionary of the American Language

Spelling, Syllabication. When a word has variant spellings, some dictionaries indicate a preferred version. Alphabetically close variants appear in the same entry. Dots or hyphens separate syllables and tell where to divide a word written on two lines.

Parts of Speech. Each word is classified by grammatical function. Usually, abbreviations such as *n* (noun), *adj.* (adjective), and *vt.* (transitive verb) identify the part of speech.

Pronunciation. Dictionaries indicate preferred as well as secondary pronunciations. Accent marks (') show which syllable gets the primary stress and which the secondary stress, if any. To determine the pronunciation, follow the key at the bottom of the page.

Etymology. This term means the origin and development of words. Most college dictionaries limit the entry to the root (original) word and an abbreviation for the original language. The abbreviation key near the front of the dictionary identifies the language.

man-i-fold (man´ ə fōld´) *adj.* [ME. < OE. *manigfeald:* see MANY & -FOLD] 1. having many and various forms, features, parts, etc. *[manifold wisdom]* 2. of many sorts; many and varied; multifarious: used with a plural noun *[manifold duties.]* 3. being such in many and various ways or for many reasons *[a manifold villain]* 4. comprising, consisting of, or operating several units or parts of one kind: said of certain devices —*n.* 1. something that is manifold 2. a pipe with one inlet and several outlets or with one outlet and several inlets, for connecting with other pipes, as, in an automobile, for conducting exhausts from each cylinder into a single exhaust pipe —*vt.* 1. to make manifold; multiply 2. to make more than one copy of *[to manifold a letter with carbon paper]* —*SYN.* see MANY — **man´i-fold´er** *n.* —**man´i-fold´ly** *adv.* —**man´i-fold´ness** *n.*

MANIFOLD
(A. manifold; B. cylinders)

Additional Word Formations. These are words derived from the one being defined. Their parts of speech are also indicated. Because they have the same basic meaning as the parent word, definitions are omitted.

Meanings. Meanings are grouped by parts of speech. Sometimes usage is briefly illustrated (*manifold* duties). Some dictionaries list meanings in historical order, others according to frequency of use. The front part of the dictionary specifies the arrangement.

Synonyms. These are words close in meaning to the one being defined. Although no synonym carries exactly the same meaning as the original, the two may be interchangeable in some situations.

Figure 17.1 From *Webster's New World Dictionary of the American Language,* Third College Edition

Unabridged (complete) dictionaries such as *Webster's Third New International Dictionary* and the *Oxford English Dictionary* can be found in college and public libraries. There you'll also find a variety of specialized dictionaries. Your librarian can direct you to dictionaries that list terms in particular fields.

EXERCISE   *Use a good desk dictionary to look up the specified information for each of the following lists of words:*

1. Variant spellings:

| airplane | aesthete | gray | tornadoes |
| color | gaily | theater | usable |

2. Syllabication and the syllable that receives the main stress:

| anacrusis | cadenza | harbinger | misanthrope |
| baccalaureate | exclamation | ionize | sequester |

3. Parts of speech:

| before | fair | separate | to |
| deep | here | then | where |

4. Etymology:

| carnival | Icarian | phenomenon | supercilious |
| fiduciary | lethargy | sabotage | tawdry |

5. Idiomatic phrases:

| beat | get | jump | put |
| cat | high | make | set |

6. Synonyms:

| attack | ghastly | mercy | plot |
| distress | keep | object | range |

Thesauruses   Thesauruses list synonyms for words but omit the other elements in dictionary entries. Figure 17.2 shows a typical entry. Note that the items are grouped according to parts of speech, and some are cross-indexed.

A thesaurus will help you find a word with just the right shade of meaning or a synonym when you want to avoid repetition. But synonyms are never exactly equal, nor are they always interchangeable. To illustrate, *old* means "in existence or use for a long time"; *antiquated* conveys the notion that something is old-fashioned or outdated. Therefore, use the thesaurus along with the dictionary. Only then can you tell which synonym fits a specific sentence.

Excellent guides to synonyms include the following:

Roget's International Thesaurus

Webster's New Dictionary of Synonyms

Modern Guide to Synonyms and Related Words

Toward Rhetorical Effect

Rhetorical effect refers to the response that the manner of writing, not the message, generates in the reader. Successful writers create a desired response through the level of their diction and the tone of their writing.

Level of Diction

What level of diction is best? The answer depends on the writer's audience and purpose. Think about a safety engineer who investigates a serious industrial accident on which she must write two reports, one for the safety director of the

247. FORMLESSNESS

.1 NOUNS **formlessness, shapelessness;** amorphousness, amorphism, amorphia; **chaos,** confusion, messiness, orderlessness; disorder 62; entropy; anarchy 740.2; **indeterminateness, indefiniteness,** indecisiveness, vagueness, mistiness, haziness, fuzziness, blurriness, unclearness, obscurity.

.2 unlicked cub, diamond in the rough.

.3 VERBS **deform, distort** 249.5; unform, unshape; disorder, jumble, mess up, muddle, confuse; obfuscate, obscure, fog up, blur.

.4 ADJS **formless, shapeless,** featureless, characterless, nondescript, inchoate, lumpen, blobby *or* baggy [both informal], inform: amorphous, amorphic, amorph(o)-: **chaotic, orderless,** disorderly 62.13, unordered, unorganized, confused, anarchic 740.6; kaleidoscopic; **indeterminate, indefinite,** undefined, indecisive, vague, misty, hazy, fuzzy, blurred *or* blurry, unclear, obscure.

.5 **unformed, unshaped,** unshapen, unfashioned, unlicked; uncut, unhewn.

Figure 17.2   From *Roget's International Thesaurus,* 5th edition, Peter Mark Roget. Copyright © 1992 by HarperCollins Publishers, Inc. Reprinted by permission of HarperCollins Publishers, Inc.

company, who represents a technical audience, and another for the local newspaper, read by a general audience. Although the two accounts would deal with the same matter, clearly they would use very different language: specialized and formal in the first case, everyday and more relaxed in the second. In each case, the language would reflect the background of the audience. As you write, always choose language suited to your audience and purpose.

Edited American English follows the familiar grammatical rules maintained in most formal and academic writing. Generally, everything you write for college courses or on the job should be in edited American English. *Nonstandard English* refers to any version of the language that deviates from these rules. Here is an example from Mark Twain's famous novel *The Adventures of Huckleberry Finn:*

> You don't know about me without you have read a book by the name of *The Adventures of Tom Sawyer,* but that ain't no matter. That book was made by Mr. Mark Twain, and he told the truth, mainly. There was things which he stretched, but mainly he told the truth. That is nothing. I never seen anybody but lied one time or another, without it was Aunt Polly, or the widow, or maybe Mary. Aunt Polly—Tom's Aunt Polly, she is—and Mary, and the Widow Douglas is all told about in that book, which is mostly a true book, with some stretchers, as I said before.

Nonstandard English does have a place in writing. Fiction writers use it to narrate the talk of characters who, if real, would speak that way. Journalists use it to report eyewitness reactions to accidents and crimes, and people who compile oral histories use it to record the recollections of people they interview.

Edited American English includes four levels of usage: formal, informal, formal–informal and technical. Another commonly recognized category is colloquial language and slang.

Formal Level   The formal level, dignified and serious, is suitable for important political, business, and academic occasions. Its vocabulary is marked by many abstract and multisyllabic words but no slang or contractions. Long sentences and deliberately varied sentence patterns help give it a strong, rhythmic flow. Sentences are often periodic, and many have parallel or balanced structures. (See pages 237–238.) Overall, formal prose impresses the reader as authoritative, stately, and graceful.

The following excerpts from John F. Kennedy's inaugural address illustrate the formal level:

> Now the trumpet summons us again—not as a call to bear arms, though arms we need; not as a call to battle, though embattled we are; but a call to bear the burden of a long twilight struggle, year in and year out, "rejoicing in hope, patient in tribulation," a struggle against the common enemies of man: tyranny, poverty, disease, and war itself. . . .
>
> In the long history of the world, only a few generations have been granted the role of defending freedom in its hour of maximum danger. I do not shrink from this responsibility; I welcome it. I do not believe that any of us would exchange places with any other people or any other generation. The energy, the faith, the devotion which we bring to this endeavor will light our country and all who serve it, and the glow from that fire can truly light the world.
>
> And so, my fellow Americans, ask not what your country can do for you; ask what you can do for your country.

The first sentence opens with parallelism to show contrast: "not as a call to bear arms, though arms we need" and "not as a call to battle, though embattled we are." In the second paragraph, parallelism in the second sentence shows contrast; in the last sentence it does not. Except for the second sentence in paragraph 2, all of the sentences are periodic rather than loose. Thus, not until the end of the opening sentence do we learn the nature of the "long twilight struggle" to which "the trumpet summons us." Time and again Kennedy uses elevated diction—polysyllabic words like *embattled, rejoicing, tribulation, tyranny, poverty, generations, devotion,* and *endeavor,* along with shorter abstract words like *hope, freedom,* and *faith.* These carefully controlled sentence patterns, along with this wording, lend rhythmical dignity to the whole passage.

Informal Level   Informal writing resembles orderly, intelligent conversation. Earmarked by relatively ordinary words, loose sentences, and numerous shorter, less varied sentence structures than formal prose, informal writing may include contractions or even slang, and it is more likely than formal writing to use the pronouns *I, me, my, you,* and *yours.* Casual and familiar rather than dignified and rhythmic, informal writing does not usually call attention to itself. Nevertheless, the language is precise and effective. Here is an example:

> There was a distressing story in the paper a few months ago. I wish I'd clipped it out and saved it. As it is, I can only hope I remember it fairly accurately. There

was a group of people who wanted a particular dictionary removed from the shelves of the local library because it contained a lot of obscenity. I think they said there were sixty-five or so dirty words in it. Some poor woman who was acting as a spokesman for the group had a list of offending words, which she started to read aloud at a hearing. She managed to read about twenty of them before she started sobbing uncontrollably and couldn't continue.

Thomas H. Middleton, "The Magic Power of Words"

Unlike the Kennedy excerpt, this one has relatively uncomplicated sentences. Three of them—the fourth, sixth, and seventh—are loose rather than periodic. The passage includes two contractions, *I'd* and *couldn't,* one casual expression, *a lot of,* and the pronoun *I.* Most of the words are very short, and none would be out of place in an ordinary conversation.

Formal–Informal Level   As life has become less formal, informal diction has become increasingly widespread. Today many articles and books, even ones on relatively serious topics, mix informal and formal elements. Here is an example:

. . . faith in sports has been vigorously promoted by industry, the military, government, the media. The value of the arena and the locker room has been imposed on our national life. Coaches and sportswriters are speaking for generals and businessmen, too, when they tell us that a man must be physically and psychologically "tough" to succeed, that he must be clean and punctual and honest, that he must bear pain, bad luck, and defeat without whimpering or making excuses. A man must prove his faith in sports and the American Way by whipping himself into shape, playing by the rules, being part of the team, and putting out all the way. If his faith is strong, he will triumph. It's his own fault if he loses, fails, remains poor.

Robert Lipsyte, *Sports World*

All these sentences except the next to last are loose. Two are quite long, four quite short, and only two have parallel phrases or clauses. Although a few expressions—"bear," "the American Way," "triumph"—echo formal diction, most of the words have an informal ring, and two expressions, "whipping himself into shape" and "putting out all the way," skirt the edges of slang.

Technical Level   A specialist writing for others in the same field or for sophisticated nonspecialists writes on the technical level, a cousin to the formal level. Technical language uses specialized words that may be unfamiliar to a general audience. Its sentences tend to be long and complex, but unlike formal diction it doesn't lean toward periodic sentences, parallelism, and balance. Read this example from the field of entomology, the study of insects:

The light organs of fireflies are complex structures, and recent studies using the electron microscope show them to be even more complex than once supposed. Each is composed of three layers: an outer "window," simply a transparent portion of the body wall; the light organ proper; and an inner layer of opaque, whitish cells filled with granules of uric acid, the so-called "reflector." The light organ proper contains large, slablike light cells, each of them filled with large granules and much smaller, dark granules, the latter tending to be concentrated around the numerous air tubes and nerves penetrating the light organ. These smaller granules were once assumed by some persons to be luminous bacteria, but we now know that they are mitochondria, the source of ATP [adenosine triphosphate] and therefore of the energy of light production. The much larger granules that fill most of the light cells are still of unknown function; perhaps they serve as the source of luciferin.

Howard Ensign Evans, *Life on a Little-Known Planet*

Note the specialized vocabulary—*granules, uric acid, mitochondria,* and *luciferin*—as well as the length and complexity of the sentences. Five sentences make up the passage, the shortest having twenty-four words. None is periodic, and none has a parallel or balanced structure.

Every field has *jargon*, specialized terms or inside talk that provides a convenient shorthand for communication among its members. For an audience of biologists, you may write that two organisms have a *symbiotic relationship,* meaning "mutually beneficial"; for psychology majors, you might use *catalepsy* instead of "a temporary loss of consciousness and feeling, often accompanied by muscular rigidity." As a general rule, use technical terms only if your audience will know their meanings. If you must use unfamiliar words when writing for a general audience, define them the first time they appear.

Colloquial Language and Slang   *Colloquial* originally meant "the language of ordinary conversation between people of a particular region." *Slang*, according to *Webster's Tenth New Collegiate Dictionary*, is "an informal nonstandard vocabulary composed typically of coinages, arbitrarily changed words, and extravagant, forced, or facetious figures of speech." These two categories shade into each other, and even authorities sometimes disagree on whether to label a term *colloquial* or *slang*. The word *bender,* meaning "a drinking spree," seems firmly in the colloquial camp, and *bummer,* a term recently used by young people to mean "a bad time," is just as clearly slang. *Break a leg* is theater slang used to wish a performer success. But what about *guy* and *kid*? Once they were slang, but so many people have used them for so long that they have now become colloquial.

Regardless of their labels, colloquial and slang terms are almost never appropriate in formal writing. They sometimes serve a useful purpose in informal writing by creating a special effect or increasing audience appeal. Even so, careful writers use them sparingly. Some readers may not understand some colloquial language, and slang usually becomes dated quickly. The following paragraph uses colloquial and slang expressions successfully:

. . . When I was just a kid on Eighth Avenue in knee pants . . . [Big Bill] was trying to get himself killed. He was always in some fight with a knife. He was always cutting or trying to cut somebody's throat. He was always getting cut or getting shot. Every Saturday night that he was out there, something happened. If you heard on Sunday morning that somebody had gotten shot or stabbed, you didn't usually ask who did it. You'd ask if Big Bill did it. If he did it, no one paid much attention to it, because he was always doing something like that. They'd say, "Yeah, man. That cat is crazy."

Claude Brown, *Manchild in the Promised Land*

Kid, yeah, and *cat* reflect the speech of Brown's characters and thus add authenticity to his account. Despite the informal diction, Brown uses parallelism in the second, third, and fourth sentences; repetition of "he was always" emphasizes the single-minded self-destructiveness of Big Bill's behavior.

 EXERCISE   *Identify the level of diction in each of the following passages. Support your answers with examples from the passages. Point out slang or colloquial expressions.*

1. We may now recapitulate the reasons which have made it necessary to substitute "space-time" for space and time. The old separation of space and time rested upon the belief that there was no ambiguity in saying that two events in distant places happened at the same time; consequently it was thought that we could describe the topography of the universe at a given instant in purely spatial terms. But now that simultaneity has become relative to a particular observer, this is no longer possible. What is, for one observer, a description of the state of the world at a given instant, is, for another observer, a series of events at various different times, whose relations are not merely spatial but also temporal.

   Bertrand Russell, *The ABC of Relativity*

2. In some ways I am an exceptionally privileged woman of thirty-seven. I am in the room of a private, legal abortion hospital, where a surgeon, a friend of many years, is waiting for me in the operating room. I am only five weeks pregnant. Last week I walked out of another hospital, unaborted, because I had suddenly changed my mind. I have a husband who cares for me. He yells because my indecisiveness makes him anxious, but basically he has permitted the final choice to rest in my hands: "It would be very tough, especially for you, and it is absolutely insane, but yes, we could have another baby." I have a mother who cares. I have two young sons, whose small faces are the most moving arguments I have against going through with this abortion. I have a doctorate in psychology, which among other advantages, assures me of the professional courtesy of special passes in hospitals, passes that at this moment enable my husband and my mother to stand in my room at a nonvisiting hour and yell at each other over my head while I sob.

   Magda Denes, *In Necessity and Sorrow: Life and Death in an Abortion Hospital*

3. I have just spent two days with Edward T. Hall, an anthropologist, watching thousands of my fellow New Yorkers short-circuiting themselves into hot little twitching death balls with jolts of their own adrenalin. Dr. Hall says it is overcrowding that does it. Overcrowding gets the adrenalin going, and the adrenalin gets them queer, autistic, sadistic, barren, batty, sloppy, hot-in-the-pants, charred-in-the-flankers, leering, puling, numb—the usual in New York, in other words, and God knows where else. Dr. Hall has the theory that overcrowding has already thrown New York into a state of behavioral sink. Behavioral sink is a term from ethology, which is the study of how animals relate to their environment. Among animals, the sink winds up with a "population collapse" or "massive die-off." O rotten Gotham.

   Tom Wolfe, *The Pump House Gang*   ◄

Tone

Tone reveals the author's attitude toward the topic and the reader. Every piece of writing has a tone, intended or otherwise, that stems from the meanings and connotations of words, the sentence patterns, and the rhythm of the prose.

Denotation and Connotation   The denotation of a word is its direct, essential meaning: what the word always stands for. The word *book*, for example, denotes "a set of printed or blank sheets bound together along one edge to form a volume." This definition is objective and neutral: It does not assign any special value or convey any particular attitude toward the word or what the word stands for. Connotations are the values and emotional associations that accompany a word. When the self-made man snorts "book learnin'" at his better-educated junior partner, he assigns a value and an attitude—that he ranks experience higher than the knowledge gained from books.

Some words—*death*, for instance—almost always carry strong connotations or emotional associations. *Webster's Tenth New Collegiate Dictionary* defines it as "a permanent cessation of all vital functions" or "the end of life," but it means much more. All of us have hopes, fears, and memories about death, feelings that color our responses whenever we hear or read the word. Likewise, we have personal responses to words like *sexy, cheap, radical, politician,* and *mother.* Experience, to a considerable extent, conditions how we think and feel about a word. To an Olympic swimmer who has won a gold medal, *swimming* may stir pleasant memories of the victory and the plaudits that went with it. The victim of a near-drowning, however, might react to the same word with something approaching horror.

Nonetheless, cultural connotations are more important than personal ones. Cultural connotations develop the way individual ones do, but on a much larger scale, growing out of the common experiences of many speakers and writers and changing with usage and circumstances.

Context, the parts of a passage that precede and follow a word, also affects connotation. Note, for instance, the different associations of *dog* in these sentences:

That movie is a real dog.

I sure am putting on the dog!

It's a dog-eat-dog world.

Your dog-in-the-manger attitude makes you very unpopular.

Denotation is sometimes called the language of science and technology, connotation, the language of art. But we need both to communicate effectively. Denotation allows us to convey precise, essential meanings. Connotation adds richness, warmth, and bite. Without these qualities our language would be bland and sterile, our lives bleak and mechanical.

Objective Tone   An objective tone keeps the writer's personality and opinions out of the message. Here is an example:

Myopia is a condition of the eye that makes distant vision blurry. In brief, the myopic individual is nearsighted. When the eye is normal, rays of light pass through it and come to focus on the retina, located at the back of the eye. In the myopic eye, however, the rays of light come together a little in front of the retina. As a result, the distant image is not seen clearly. Myopia may result from the eye itself being too long or the lens of the eye being too flat. In either case, the rays converge in front of the retina, and the near-sighted individual is likely to have difficulty making out distant objects.

Janine Neumann

This tone suits a popular explanation of a medical condition. The prose is businesslike and authoritative, the sentence patterns uncomplicated, and nothing reveals the person behind the words.

Other Attitudes   Sometimes you write merely to inform, sometimes to persuade. In persuasive writing, let your attitude toward your topic set the tone. Decide how subtle, flamboyant, or formal your writing should be and what special tone—satiric, cynical, serious, mock pompous, bawdy, playful—will win your reader over.

Every essay has combined characteristics that give it a special tone. The following excerpts illustrate some of tone's many dimensions:

> Unless you have led an abnormally isolated adulthood, the chances are excellent that you know many people who have at one time or another committed an act, or consorted with someone who was committing an act, for which they might have been sent to prison. We do not consider most of these people, or ourselves, criminals; the act is one thing, the criminality of it quite something else. Homicide, for example, is in our law not a crime; murder only is proscribed. The difference between the two is the intention, or to be more accurate, society's decision about the nature of that intention.
>
> Bruce Jackson, "Who Goes to Prison: Caste and Careerism in Crime"

Here we have a sophisticated and rather formal tone. Terms like *consorted* and *proscribed,* while exactly suited to Jackson's meaning, do not form part of most people's word kits. The complexity of the first sentence and the varied patterns of the others add to the air of sophistication. The emphatic *quite,* meaning "entirely," is cultivated usage; and along with *society's decision,* it lends the tone a wry touch.

> Cans. Beer cans. Glinting on the verges of a million miles of roadways, lying in scrub, grass, dirt, leaves, sand, mud, but never hidden. Piels, Rheingold, Ballantine, Schaeffer, Schlitz, shining in the sun or picked by moon or the beams of headlights at night; washed by rain or flattened by wheels, but never dulled, never buried, never destroyed. Here is the mark of savages, the testament of wasters, the stain of prosperity.
>
> Who are these men who defile the grassy borders of our roads and lanes, who pollute our ponds, who spoil the purity of our ocean beaches with the empty vessels of their thirst? Who are the men who make these vessels in millions and then say, "Drink and discard"? What society is this that can afford to cast away a million tons of metal and to make a wild and fruitful land a garbage heap?
>
> Marya Mannes, "Wasteland"

Rhythm and word choice contribute equally to the tone of this passage. The excerpt opens with imagistic sentence fragments that create a panoramic word picture of our littered roadways. Then complete sentences and somber commentary follow. Words and patterns are repeated, mixing the dignified language of epic and religion with common derogatory terms—*testament, purity, vessels,* and *fruitful* set against *savages, wasters, defile,* and *garbage heap*—to convey the contradictions Mannes deplores. The rhetorical questions, used instead of accusations, add a sense of loftiness to her outrage, helping create a tone both majestic and disdainful.

> *Erethizon dorsatus,* an antisocial character of the Northern U.S. and Canadian forest, commonly called a porcupine, looks like an uncombed head, has a grumpy personality, fights with his tail, hides his head when he's in trouble, attacks backing up, retreats going ahead, and eats toilet seats as if they were Post Toasties. It's a sad commentary on his personality that people are always trying to do him in.
>
> R. T. Allen, "The Porcupine"

The tone of this passage is affectionately humorous. Allen sets this tone by noting the porcupine's tousled appearance, testy personality, and peculiar habits, such as eating outdoor toilet seats (for their salt content, as Allen later explains). The net effect is to personify porcupines, making them seem like the eccentric reprobate human that others regard with amused toleration.

The final passage begins by referring to a "promissory note": the Constitution and the promise of life, liberty, and the pursuit of happiness spelled out in the Declaration of Independence.

> It is obvious today that America has defaulted on this promissory note in so far as her citizens of color are concerned. Instead of honoring this sacred obligation, America has given the Negro people a bad check; a check which has come back marked "insufficient funds." But we refuse to believe that the bank of justice is bankrupt. We refuse to believe that there are insufficient funds in the great vaults of opportunity of this nation. And so we've come to cash this check, a check that will give us upon demand the riches of freedom and the security of justice.
>
> We have also come to this hallowed spot to remind America of the fierce urgency of now. This is no time to engage in the luxury of cooling off or to take the tranquilizing drug of gradualism. Now is the time to make real the promises of democracy, now is the time to rise from the dark and desolate valley of segregation to the sunlit path of racial justice; now is the time to lift our nation from the quicksands of racial injustice to the solid rock of brotherhood; now is the time to make justice a reality for all of God's children.
>
> Martin Luther King, Jr., "I Have a Dream"

This writing speaks passionately for freedom and justice. Its most obvious rhetorical strategy is metaphor, first the extended one of the promissory note, then brief separate metaphors that make the same point. The repetition of *now* sharpens the insistent tone. Eloquence comes through parallelism, repetition, and words like *sacred* and *hallowed,* vividness through figures of speech like "vaults of opportunity" and "sunlit path of racial justice." Like George Orwell, Mark Twain, Joseph Conrad, and other masters of tonal effects whose work appears in this book, King uses both rhythm and diction to create a tone that infuses and invigorates his message.

EXERCISE   *Characterize the tone of each of the following paragraphs. Point out how word choice, sentence structure, rhythm, and other elements contribute to it.*

1. When I awoke, dimly aware of some commotion and outcry in the clearing, the light was slanting down through the pines in such a way that the glade was lit like

some vast cathedral. I could see the dust motes of wood pollen in the long shaft of light, and there on the extended branch sat an enormous raven with a red and squirming nestling in its beak.

The sound that awoke me was the outraged cries of the nestling's parents, who flew helplessly in circles around the clearing. . . . And he, the murderer, the black bird at the heart of life, sat there, glistening in the common light, formidable, unperturbed, untouchable. The sighing died. It was then I saw the judgment. It was the judgment of life against death. I will never see it again so forcefully presented. I will never hear it again in notes so tragically prolonged. For in the midst of protest, they forgot the violence. There, in that clearing, the crystal note of a song sparrow lifted hesitantly in the hush. And, finally, after painful fluttering, another took the song, and then another, the song passing from one bird to another, doubtfully at first, as though some evil thing was being slowly forgotten. Till suddenly they took heart and sang from many throats joyously together as birds are known to sing. They sang under the brooding shadow of the raven. In simple truth they had forgotten the raven, for they were the singers of life, and not of death.

Loren Eiseley, "The Judgment of the Birds"

2. America, which leads the world in almost every economic category, leads it above all in the production of schlock. Christmas toys broken before New Year's, wash-n-wear suits that neither wash well nor wear well, appliances that expire a month after the guarantee, Barbie dolls, frozen pizza—these are but a few of the shoddy goods whose main contribution to our civilization, apart from a momentary satisfaction to the purchaser, is to swell the sanitary-fill schlock heaps that are the feces of our Gross (and how!) National Product.

Robert Claiborne, "Future Schlock"

3.   Babe Ruth was *** The Sultan of Swat ***
Babe Ruth was *** THE BAMBINO ***
Babe Ruth was what you came to see!!!!

It was like going to a carnival, with Babe as both the star performer and the side-show attraction. Hell, that's what we called him: "You big ape." He was what a home-run hitter was supposed to look like. Wide, flat nose. Big feet. Little ankles. Belly hanging over his belt. All he had to do was walk on to the field and everybody would applaud. The air became charged with electricity. You just felt that something great was going to happen.

He'd twirl that big 48-ounce bat around in little circles up at the plate as if he were cranking it up for the Biggest Home Run Ever Hit—*you felt that*—and when he'd hit one he would hit it like nobody has hit it before or since. A mile high and a mile out. I can see him now, as I did so many times, just look up, drop the bat and start to trot, the little pitter-patter pigeon-toed, high-bellied trot that seemed to say, I've done it before and I'll do it again, but this one was for you.

Leo Durocher, *Nice Guys Finish Last*

Special Stylistic Techniques

The style of a piece of writing is its character or personality. Like people, writing can be many things: dull, stuffy, discordant, sedate, lively, flamboyant, eccentric, and so on. Figurative language and irony can contribute to your own distinctive writing style.

Figurative Language

Figurative language uses concrete words in a nonliteral way to create sharply etched sensory images that catch and hold the reader's attention. Besides energizing the writing, figurative language strengthens the reader's grip on the ideas. Five figurative devices are especially important: simile, metaphor, personification, overstatement, and understatement.

Simile and Metaphor   A *simile* directly compares two unlike things by the use of *like* or *as*. "Todd is as restless as an aspen leaf in a breeze" and "Her smile flicked on and off like a sunbeam flashing momentarily through a cloud bank" are similes. A *metaphor* also compares unlike things, but without using *like* or *as*. Some metaphors include a linking verb (*is, are, were,* and so on); others do not. "The moon was a wind-tossed bark" and "The curtain of darkness fell over the land" are both metaphors. Here is an excerpt that contains similes and metaphors:

> The field is a sea of deep, dark green, a sea made up of millions of small blades of grass blended together as one. Each blade is a dark green spear, broad at the bottom and narrowing to a needle point at the tip. Its full length is arched so that, viewed from one end, it looks like a shallow trough with paper-thin sides. On the inner side of this trough, small ridges and shallow valleys run from base to tip. To a finger rubbed across them, they feel like short, bristly hairs.
>
> Daniel Kinney

DISCUSSION QUESTIONS

1. Locate the similes in this passage and explain how they help the reader.
2. Locate the metaphors and point out how each heightens the sensory impact of the writing.

Writers too often snatch hastily at the first similes and metaphors that come to mind and end up strewing their pages with overused and enfeebled specimens. Johnny is "as blind as a bat," Mary runs around "like a chicken with its head cut off"—and the writing slips into trite gear. Other comparisons link items that are too dissimilar. For example, "The wind whistled through the trees like a herd of galloping horses" would only puzzle a reader.

Personification   This is a special sort of metaphor that assigns human qualities or traits to something nonhuman: a plant, an abstraction, a nonliving thing. Here are some examples:

The vine clung stubbornly to the trunk of the tree.

May fortune smile upon you.

The waves lapped sullenly against the base of the cliff.

Each of these sentences assigns its subject a different emotional quality—stubbornness, friendliness, gloom—each figurative rather than literal: Vines aren't stubborn, fortune doesn't smile, and waves aren't sullen.

Personification sometimes extends beyond a single sentence. To illustrate, the following passage carries a single image through two paragraphs:

> "I figured when my legislative program passed the Congress," [Lyndon] Johnson said in 1971, "that the Great Society had a real chance to grow into a beautiful woman. And I figured her growth and development would be as natural and inevitable as any small child's. In the first year, as we got the laws on the books, she'd begin to crawl. Then in the second year, as we got more laws on the books, she'd begin to walk, and the year after that, she'd be off and running, all the time growing bigger and healthier and fatter. And when she grew up, I figured she'd be so big and beautiful that the American people couldn't help but fall in love with her, and once they did, they'd want to keep her around forever, making her a permanent part of American life, more permanent than the New Deal.
>
> "But now Nixon has come along and everything I've worked for is ruined. There's a story in the paper every day about him slashing another one of my Great Society programs. I can just see him waking up in the morning, making that victory sign of his and deciding which program to kill. It's a terrible thing for me to sit by and watch someone else starve my Great Society to death. She's getting thinner and thinner and uglier and uglier all the time; now her bones are beginning to stick out and her wrinkles are beginning to show. Soon she'll be so ugly that the American people will refuse to look at her; they'll stick her in a closet to hide her away and there she'll die. And when she dies, I too will die."
>
> Doris Kearns, "Who *Was* Lyndon Baines Johnson?"

Through personification, Johnson expresses affection for his social program, disapproval of Nixon's policies, and sorrow over the coming demise of the "child" he has so carefully nurtured.

Personification works best when it is used in moderation and doesn't make outrageous comparisons. Dishes don't run away with spoons except in nursery rhymes.

Overstatement   Overstatement, sometimes called hyperbole, deliberately and drastically exaggerates in order to make a point. An example is "Wilfred is the world's biggest fool."

One of the best examples of sustained overstatement is Mark Twain's essay "Fenimore Cooper's Literary Offences." In it, Twain claims, "In one place in *Deerslayer,* and in the restricted space of two-thirds of a page, Cooper has scored 114 offences against literary art out of a possible 115." Twain also asserts, "There have been daring people in the world who claimed that Cooper could write English, but they are all dead now. . . ." Through such exaggerations, Twain mocks the shortcomings of Cooper's novels.

Used sparingly, overstatement is emphatic, adding real force to an event or situation. Writers who consistently exaggerate, however, risk losing their credibility.

Understatement   Understatement makes an assertion in a humble manner without giving something its due, as when a sportscaster calls a team's 23–2 record "pretty fair." By drawing attention to the thing it appears to slight, this soft-spoken approach offers writers an effective strategy. Here is an example:

To assume that Heidi Mansfield lacks the qualifications for this position is not unwarranted.

Without ever actually calling Mansfield unqualified, the statement suggests that she is. Similarly, when a meat company executive says, "It is not unlikely that beef prices will jump ten cents a pound in the next two months," we might as well count on spending another dime. As these statements show, understatement not infrequently has an ulterior motive.

EXERCISE   *Identify the similes, metaphors, personifications, overstatements, or understatements in these sentences.*

1. The old table greedily sucked up the linseed oil.
2. Russia's social and economic system is a giant staircase that leads nowhere.
3. Stanley has the bile of human meanness by the quart in every vein.
4. Their music sounds like the drumming of an infant's fists against the sides of a crib.
5. The foundations of our divorce are as strong as ever.
6. It is not unlike Muriel to be late.
7. You're the world's biggest liar!
8. "Fashion, though folly's child, and guide of fools, Rules e'en the wisest, and in learning rules."
9. Einstein's theories have had some impact on modern science.
10. I'm as tired as a farm horse at sunset.

Irony

Irony occurs when a writer intentionally states one thing but actually means something different or even opposite. A certain point is thus highlighted. The sportswriter who refers to the "ideal conditions" for a tennis tournament when rain has drenched the courts and forced cancellation of matches speaks ironically. Here is a longer example of the same sort of irony.

> The baron, though a small man, had a large soul, and it swelled with satisfaction at the consciousness of being the greatest man in the little world about him. He loved to tell long stories about the dark old warriors whose portraits looked grimly down from the walls around, and he found no listeners equal to those that fed at his expense. He was much given to the marvellous, and a firm believer in all those supernatural tales with which every mountain and valley in Germany abounds. The faith of his guests exceeded even his own; they listened to every tale of wonder with open eyes and mouths, and never failed to be astonished, even though repeated for the hundredth time. Thus lived the Baron Von Landshort, the oracle of his table, the absolute monarch of his little territory, and happy, above all things, in the persuasion that he was the wisest man of the age.
> Washington Irving, "The Spectre Bridegroom"

Irving never directly states the baron's shortcomings. Rather, suggestive details such as the swelling of the baron's soul, his belief in the supernatural, and his deception by the sponging guests portray one who, far from being "the wisest man of the age," is pompous, superstitious, and gullible.

Eliminating Flawed Diction

Diction flaws include wordiness, euphemisms, clichés, mixed metaphors, and sexist language. As you revise, stay alert for these culprits and eliminate any that you find.

Wordiness

Wordiness is verbal obesity, and like physical obesity it has more than one cause. Some writers overnourish their prose to make it sound more impressive, some to pad an assignment, and some simply because they don't realize they're doing it. Whatever the reason, the results are the same: ponderous, slow-moving papers that lack punch. To inject vigor, strip your prose down to fighting weight by cutting out every word that doesn't serve a purpose. If five words are doing the work of one, drop four.

The two major forms of wordiness, deadwood and gobbledygook, often occur together. *Deadwood,* which does nothing but take up space and clutter the writing, is bracketed in the following sentence:

> Responsible parents [of today] neither allow their children [to have] absolute freedom [to do as they please] nor severely restrict their children's activities.

Now read the sentence without the deadwood:

> Responsible parents neither allow their children absolute freedom nor severely restrict their children's activities.

Careful revision has increased the clarity and reduced the words from twenty-three to fourteen.

Gobbledygook consists of long, abstract, or technical words that help create unnecessarily long and complex sentences. Some people who write it mistakenly believe it "dignifies" their thoughts. Others want to conceal their meanings by clouding their statements. And some naively think that long words are better than short ones. All of these writers use gobbledygook, but none of their readers appreciates it. Here are some samples of gobbledygook followed by revised versions in plain English:

Original Version	**Revised Version**
The fish exhibited a 100 percent mortality response.	All the fish died.
We have been made cognizant of the fact that the experiment will be terminated in the near future.	We have learned that the experiment will end soon.

Euphemisms

Euphemisms take the sting out of something unpleasant or add stature to something humble. Familiar expressions include *pass away* for *die, preowned* for *used,* and *sanitation engineer* for *garbage collector.*

In most cases, the writer simply intends to cushion reality. But euphemisms also have grisly uses. Mobsters don't *beat up* merchants who refuse *protection* (itself a euphemism); they *lean on* them. Hitler didn't talk about *exterminating the Jews* but about *the final solution to the Jewish problem.* These euphemisms don't just blur reality; they blot out images of horror. Of merchants with broken limbs and bloodied faces. Of cattle cars crammed with men, women, and children en route to death camps. Of barbed wire and gas ovens and starved corpses in the millions.

Any euphemism, however well-intentioned, probably obscures an issue. On occasion you may need one in order to protect the sensitive reader, but usually you will serve readers best by using direct expressions that present reality, not a tidied-up version.

Clichés and Mixed Metaphors

Clichés   Clichés are expressions that have become flat and stale from overuse. Rather than respond to experience with their own perceptions, writers sometimes resort to oft-repeated words or phrases that stem from patterned thinking. Dullness follows. Daily conversation abounds with stale, trite expressions because talk is unplanned, but writing allows you time to find invigorating and effective language. Your individual response is what draws the reader's interest, and only fresh thinking will produce that response. The following list of clichés barely "scratches the surface":

acid test	burn the midnight oil	green with envy
almighty dollar	chip off the old block	last but not least
beat a hasty retreat	clear as a bell	nipped in the bud
better late than never	cool as a cucumber	rears its ugly head
black sheep	easier said than done	set the world on fire
blind as a bat	goes without saying	sick as a dog

Mixed Metaphors   Clichéd writing often suffers as well from mixed metaphors—inappropriate combinations that startle or amuse the reader. How would you respond if you came across this example?

> When he opened that can of worms, he bit off more than he could chew.

Can you visualize someone chewing a mouthful of worms? The point is obvious.

Sexist Language

Sexist language can assume several guises. Sometimes it appears as unneeded information that dilutes or even demeans someone's accomplishments. It can occur when the writer uses gender-exclusive pronouns like *he* and *she* inappropriately. And it may attach arbitrary gender labels to persons and groups. All U.S. government agencies, most businesses, and most academic publications prohibit sexist language. Deliberate or accidental, such language has no place in your writing. These guidelines will help you avoid it.

1. Don't unnecessarily mention a person's appearance, spouse, or family.

   Sexist: The cute new loan officer at the Godfather Finance Company is a real hit with customers.

   Sexist: Craig Helmond, husband of nationally known cardiologist Dr. Jennifer Helmond, won election to the Beal City Board of Education.

   Sexist: After eight years of attending college part time, Angelica Denham, a three-time grandmother, was awarded a bachelor of science degree.

   Nonsexist: The efficient new loan officer at the Godfather Finance Company is a real hit with customers.

   Nonsexist: Craig Helmond, an accountant at Oakwood Growth Enterprise, won election to the Beal City Board of Education.

   Nonsexist: After eight years of attending college part time, Angelica Denham was awarded a bachelor of science degree.

   Note how, in each case, the sentence has been rewritten to include only relevant information.

2. Use the pronouns *he, him, his,* and *himself* only when referring to antecedents that are clearly masculine and *she, her, hers,* or *herself* only when their antecedents are clearly feminine.

   Sexist: Each tourist must carry his passport with *him* at all times.

   Sexist: If a collector wishes to find an out-of-print book, she should try http://www.bibliofind.com on the Web.

   Correct this type of error by substituting plural antecedents and pronouns for the singular ones or by rewriting the sentence to eliminate the pronouns.

   Nonsexist: Tourists must carry their passports with *them* at all times.

   Nonsexist: Any collector wishing to find an out-of-print book should try http://www.bibliofind.com on the Web.

3. Don't use occupational labels that imply the positions are held only by one sex.

Sexist	Nonsexist
chairwoman	chair
draftsman	drafter
fireman	fire fighter
policeman	police officer
postman	letter carrier
weatherman	weather reporter

   A word of caution here. To avoid sexism, some writers substitute the suffix *-person* for *-man* in many job titles (such as *handyperson* for someone who does odd jobs). Such attempts, however, often create awkward expressions that you should avoid.

EXERCISE   *The following sentences are flawed by wordiness, euphemisms, clichés, mixed metaphors, and sexist language. When you have identified the faults, revise the sentences.*

1. The American eagle will never, in the face of foreign threats, pull in its horns or draw back into its shell.
2. Last summer, I was engaged in the repair of automobiles.
3. You're looking as bright as a button this morning.
4. My mother was called to her heavenly reward last winter.
5. Any student wishing to attend summer school at Burns State College must pay his tuition one week before registration day.
6. My brother is in the process of pursuing a curriculum of industrial chemistry.
7. The ball's in your court, and if you strike out, don't expect me to pick up the pieces.
8. The beautiful, sultry-voiced clerk quickly filled the order.
9. Winning first prize for her essay was a real feather in Peggy's cap.
10. Our company plans to confer retirement on 200 employees by year's end.

THE ESSAY EXAMINATION

Instructors use essay examinations to gauge your grasp of ideas, noting how well you apply, analyze, challenge, compare, or otherwise handle them. Facts and figures, on the other hand, are more often tested by objective examinations. Writing essay answers under pressure and with minimal time to rethink and revise differs from writing at home. Instructors expect reasonably complete and coherent answers but not models of style or neatness. They do expect legibility. An effective presentation increases your chances for success; the skills learned in composition class can help you achieve it. A plan, a thesis, specific support, staying on track, and the pointers presented in this chapter—all are grade boosters.

Studying for the Examination

Here are some pointers for studying:

1. Allow adequate preparation time. For a comprehensive test, start reviewing several days in advance. For one that covers a small segment of the course, a day or two should be enough.
2. Reread the key points you've marked in your class notes and textbook. Use them to develop a set of basic concepts.
3. Make up a set of sample questions related to these concepts and do some freewriting to answer them. Even if none of the questions appears on the test, your efforts will ease pretest jitters and supply insights that apply to other questions.
4. Answer your questions by drawing on your concepts and supplying details from your notes and textbook.

Types of Test Questions

Some instructors favor narrow, highly focused test questions with detailed answering instructions. Others like broad items, perhaps with simple directions such as "Write for twenty minutes." The sample questions below range from very broad to very narrow. Note how when answering them you can often use the writing strategies discussed in Chapters 5–13.

1. Analyze the *influences* of the industrial revolution on European society.
2. Discuss the most important *causes* of the Spanish–American War.
3. *Compare and contrast* the David statues of Michelangelo and Bernini.
4. Select three different camera shots used in the movie *Titanic*. Identify at least one scene that *illustrates* each shot; then explain how each shot functions by *describing* the relationship between the shot and the action or dialogue.
5. Discuss the stock market plunge of October 27, 1997. Consider the major *factors* involved, such as the liberal lending practices of international banks, the growth in global manufacturing capacity, the severe recessions and monetary turmoil in Pacific Rim countries like Thailand and Malaysia, the concerns of Wall Street, and how these *factors* interacted. Use a thesis statement that signals the points you will discuss.

A highly focused question such as item 5 suggests how to organize and develop the essay. If you know the answer, you can begin writing quickly. In contrast, item 1 forces you to focus and narrow the subject before you respond. Answering this type of item requires careful planning.

Preparing to Write

You can't get from Pocatello to Poughkeepsie without knowing and following an appropriate route. The same principle applies to exam writing. Often students fail to read general directions or to answer what is asked. Low grades follow. To avoid penalizing yourself, scan the test items, noting how many must be answered and which ones, if any, are optional. When you have a choice, select the questions you can answer most thoroughly. Pay attention to any suggestions or requirements concerning length (one paragraph, two pages) or relative weight (25 points, 30 minutes, 40 percent), and budget your time accordingly.

The first requirement for most essay tests is to read the question for *key words*. Does the instructor want you to analyze, compare, criticize, defend, describe, discuss, evaluate, illustrate, explain, justify, trace, or summarize? If you are asked to explain how Darwin's theory of evolution affected nineteenth-century thinking, do just that; you won't like your grade if, instead, you summarize the theory. Merely putting ideas on paper, even perceptive ideas, does not substitute for addressing the question.

Indicate what each of the following questions calls for. What is required? By what methods—arguing, describing, or the like—would you develop the answer?

1. Distinguish between mild depression and severe depression. You might focus on the nature, the symptoms, or the potential treatments of each condition.
2. Support or refute the following statement: Because waste incineration generates stack gases and ash that contain high levels of toxic substances, it is not an acceptable solution to waste-disposal problems.
3. Explain how to clean an automobile carburetor.
4. Briefly relate the events in the Book of Job and then explain the significance of the tale. Could the tale be called symbolic? Why or why not? ◄

When you have the essay question clearly in mind, don't immediately start writing. A jackrabbit start spells trouble. Instead, take a few moments to plan your answer. Following these steps will help you do this:

1. Jot down specific supporting information from your reading and lecture notes.
2. Make a rough outline that sketches the main points you'll cover and an effective order for presenting them.
3. Prepare a thesis statement that responds to the question and will control your answer.

Writing an essay exam, like writing an essay, is a front-end-loaded process. Much of the brain work occurs before you put your answer on paper. You won't get to Poughkeepsie just by starting to drive.

Writing the Examination Answer

Here are some guidelines that will help you write a successful exam:

1. Position your thesis statement at the beginning of your answer. Make sure each paragraph is controlled by a topic sentence tied to the thesis statement.
2. Don't become excessively concerned about your wording. Focus on content and, if time permits, make stylistic changes later.
3. Fight the impulse to jot down everything you know about the general subject. The grader doesn't want to plow through verbiage to arrive at your answer.

The following essay illustrates these guidelines:

Question:	Discuss the various appeals described by classical rhetoric that an orator can use. Give a brief example of each kind of appeal.
Answer: *Thesis statement previews* *focus and order of answer*	Classical rhetoric defines three major appeals—logical, emotional, and ethical—that orators may use to win support from their audience.

Topic sentence:	Most rhetoricians agree that any argument must be based on logic; that is, it must appeal to the intellect of the listeners. Unless it does,
Example 1:	the orator will fail to convince them. For example, a speaker who is urging the election of a candidate and presents the candidate's voting record is appealing to logic, asking the audience to understand that the voting record predicts how the candidate will continue to vote if
Example 2:	elected. Likewise, a candidate for public office who describes how a tax cut will stimulate the economy and create new jobs is using a logical appeal.
Topic sentence:	In addition to logic, emotional appeals are a powerful means of swaying people, especially groups. Though emotional appeals work along with logical appeals, they are quite different because they are directed at the listener's hopes,
Example 1:	fears, and sympathies. The presidential candidate who indicates that a vote for an opponent is a vote to increase government spending and risk a financial crisis is making an emotional
Example 2:	appeal. So, too, is the gubernatorial candidate who asserts that her state's industry can be revitalized and serve as a model for all other states.
Topic sentence:	The ethical appeal is more subtle than either of the other two but probably just as important. The orator must strike the audience as a sensible, good person if they are to believe the
Example 1:	message. Sometimes the speaker's logic and also the tone—moderate, sensible, or wise—
Example 2:	will convey sufficient ethical appeal. At other times, a speaker will use statements that are deliberately intended to create ethical appeal. "In developing this program, I will work closely with both houses of the legislature, including the members of both political parties" and "Despite our differences, I believe my opponent to be a decent, honest person" are examples of such statements.
Restatement of thesis:	In any speech, all these appeals—logical, emotional, and ethical—work together to convince an audience.

Student Unknown

In contrast, the next two responses to the same question illustrate common faults of examination essays.

Answer A

1   There are three basic appeals that a speaker can make to captivate an audience. These are the ethical appeal, the logical appeal, and the emotional appeal.

2   The first of these—the ethical appeal—includes all the speaker's efforts to be viewed as rational, wise, good, and generous. Needless to say, the ethical appeal is very important. Without it, no one would pay attention to the speaker's argument.

3   The second appeal—logical—is also extremely important. It carries the burden of the argument from speaker to listener and appeals to the intellect of the audience.

4   Emotional appeal—the third and final one—is made to the passions and feelings of the listeners. The significance of such an appeal is obvious.

5   A speaker often uses all three appeals to win an audience over.

Answer *A* starts with a thesis statement and includes brief definitions of the three appeals; however, it omits any concrete examples and includes no specific details. As a result, the significance of the emotional appeal is not "obvious," as paragraph 4 claims, nor does the answer offer any hints as to why the other appeals are important. This response resembles an outline more than an answer and suggests the student lacked the knowledge to do a good job.

Answer B

1   Orators may make three different kinds of appeals to win favor from an audience: emotional appeal, logical appeal, and ethical appeal.

2   Let's start with emotional appeal because this is the one that is not essential to a speech. Logical and ethical appeals are always included; emotional appeal may be used to help sway an audience, but without logical and ethical appeals no argument is accepted. This simply makes sense: If there is no logic, there is no argument; and if the speaker doesn't come across as an ethical person—someone to be relied upon—then no one will accept the message. But emotional appeal is different. Unemotional arguments may be accepted.

3   Nevertheless, emotional appeal is important. It includes whatever a speaker does to move the feelings of the audience. The speaker asks, "Don't you want to protect your families?" Such an appeal is emotional. A speaker may appeal to the prejudices or biases of listeners. Someone at a Ku Klux Klan rally does that. So does a minister who exhorts people to be "saved." Both speakers address the emotions of the groups they talk to.

4   There is a very fine use of emotional appeal in the "Letter from Birmingham Jail" by Martin Luther King, Jr. At one point King asks his audience of white clergy how they would feel if, like blacks, they had to deny their children treats such as amusement parks and had to fear for the lives of their families, and so on. He also describes the bombings and burnings that blacks are subjected to. All the details move readers emotionally, so that they come to sympathize with blacks who live in fear.

5   Logical appeal, as noted earlier, is crucial. The speaker must seem to have an intelligent plan. The listeners want the plan to meet their needs.

6   The other appeal is the ethical one. It is made when speakers make themselves seem generous, good, and wise.

7   All three appeals can be used in one speech, although the logical and ethical
appeals are essential to it.

Although the writer opens with an acceptable thesis statement, this answer
shows little evidence of advance planning. Does it make sense to begin in paragraph 2 with an appeal tagged "not essential"? And note how the paragraph drifts
from the emotional appeal to the other two types, despite its topic sentence. Paragraphs 3 and 4 do focus on the emotional appeal and ironically, through specific
examples, make a good case for its importance. Paragraphs 5 and 6 shortchange
logical and ethical appeals by saying next to nothing about them. The essay contradicts itself: If logical and ethical appeals are the essential ones and emotional appeals "not essential," why is more than half of the essay about emotional appeal?

> EXERCISE   *Read the examination questions and answers below. Then respond to
> the questions that follow the answers.*

A. Question

Living organisms are composed of cells. On the basis of structure, biologists categorize cells into two groups: the prokaryotic cells and the eukaryotic cells. What are the
major differences between prokaryotic cells and eukaryotic cells, and in which living organisms are these cells found?

Answer

1   Eukaryotic cells have a true nucleus and their genetic material, the DNA-contain-
ing chromosomes, is located within this nucleus, which is surrounded by a nuclear
membrane. Prokaryotic cells lack a true nucleus, and their genetic material lies
free in the cytoplasm of the cell.

2   Eukaryotic cells are also much more complex than prokaryotic cells. Eukaryotic
cells commonly contain organelles such as mitochondria, a Golgi complex, lyso-
somes, an endoplasmic reticulum, and in photosynthetic cells, chloroplasts. These
organelles are typically lacking in the simpler prokaryotic cells.

3   Prokaryotic cells make up the structure of all bacteria and the blue-green algae.
These are the simplest of all known cellular organisms. All other cellular organisms, including humans, are composed of eukaryotic cells.

                                                                    Scott Wybolt

a. Does the response answer the question that was asked? Discuss.

B. Question

Analyze the significant relationships between imagination and reality in Coleridge's
"This Lime-Tree Bower My Prison." In your answer, you might consider some of the following questions: What is the importance of setting in the poem? Is the speaker's mind
a form of setting? How is reality implicitly defined in the poem? How, and through what
agencies, can reality be transmitted? What relationship is finally perceived between the
spiritual and the concrete? How does friendship or fellow feeling trigger the essential insights revealed in the poem?

Answer

1   Coleridge's "This Lime-Tree Bower My Prison" shows imagination to be a powerful force that can control one's perception of reality and that is, in itself, a kind of reality—perhaps the most important reality. Thus, imagination and reality are more intimately linked and more similar in Coleridge's poem than they are ordinarily thought to be.

2   The relationship between imagination and reality is revealed by the speaker of "Lime-Tree Bower," although he doesn't openly state it. The technique for revelation is dramatic monologue, with the speaker seemingly talking spontaneously as his situation gives rise to a series of thoughts.

3   As the poem begins, the speaker finds himself "trapped" at home in his lime-tree bower, while his friends go on a walk he had hoped to take with them. This situation at first bothers the speaker, causing him to feel imprisoned. As the poem progresses, however, the speaker begins to imagine all the places his friends are visiting on their walk. Though he laments not being with them, he shows excitement as he describes the scenes his friends are viewing: the "roaring dell," the sea, and so on. Thus the speaker recognizes that he is able to participate imaginatively in the walk and, in doing so, to escape his "prison" reality and enter the reality of his friends.

4   The moment of recognition occurs at the beginning of stanza three: "A delight/ Comes sudden on my heart, and I am glad/As I myself was there!" Interestingly, however, this point marks a turn in the speaker's thoughts. Once again he realizes where he actually is—the lime-tree bower. But now he appreciates its beauties. The natural beauties he imagined have taught him to appreciate the beauties of nature right before him. He has learned that there is "No plot so narrow, be but Nature there." The lime-tree bower is no longer a prison but a rich and beautiful, if somewhat small, world.

5   Imagination has again shaped the speaker's perceptions of reality. It controls the perception of circumstances—whether one views a place as a prison or a microcosm of a larger world, with beauties and possibilities in its own right. The use of imagination can teach one about reality, as it has Coleridge's speaker. And, if one surrenders to it completely—as the speaker does when he envisions the world of the walkers—imagination is a delightful reality, as valid as the reality of the place in which one sits.

6   Imagination and reality are merged in "This Lime-Tree Bower My Prison," and though this identification is apparently temporary, one may learn through imagination how to cope with and enjoy reality. Thus, imagination is intimately involved in shaping the perception of reality.

Lori McCue

   a. Which of the possible approaches suggested in the question does the student select?

   b. Which of the other questions does she indirectly answer? Which ones are not addressed?

   c. Identify the thesis statement and explain how it controls the answer.

   d. Show how the answer demonstrates careful planning.

   e. Point out some effective supporting details.

WRITING ABOUT LITERATURE

Teachers of literature generally expect you to write about what you've read. Typically they might ask you to

- show how an author handled one element of a short story, play, or poem
- compare how two different works treat a particular element
- weigh several elements and then determine the writer's intention
- air your reactions to some work.

Writing about literature offers several benefits. Weighing and recording your thoughts on the different elements sharpen your critical thinking ability. Literary papers also pay artistic dividends, as careful reading and subsequent writing deepen your appreciation of the writer's craft. Furthermore, you'll feel a sense of accomplishment as you coherently express your perceptions. Finally, writing a literature paper offers yet another opportunity to apply the writing guidelines discussed in Chapters 1–4. Focusing, gathering information, organizing, writing, revising, and editing—the old familiar trail leads to success here too.

The Elements of Literature

Most writing assignments on literature will probably feature one or more of the following elements:

Plot	Symbols
Point of view	Irony
Character	Theme
Setting	

Depending on the work, some of these will be more important than others. Read the following story by Stephen Crane, "The Bride Comes to Yellow Sky."

The discussions that follow it point out the basic features of each element and offer useful writing suggestions.

The Bride Comes to Yellow Sky

Stephen Crane

I

The great Pullman was whirling onward with such dignity of motion that a glance from the window seemed simply to prove that the plains of Texas were pouring eastward. Vast flats of green grass, dull-hued spaces of mesquit and cactus, little groups of frame houses, woods of light and tender trees, all were sweeping into the east, sweeping over the horizon, a precipice.

A newly married pair had boarded this coach at San Antonio. The man's face was reddened from many days in the wind and sun, and a direct result of his new black clothes was that his brick-colored hands were constantly performing in a most conscious fashion. From time to time he looked down respectfully at his attire. He sat with a hand on each knee, like a man waiting in a barber's shop. The glances he devoted to other passengers were furtive and shy.

The bride was not pretty, nor was she very young. She wore a dress of blue cashmere, with small reservations of velvet here and there, and with steel buttons abounding. She continually twisted her head to regard her puff sleeves, very stiff, straight, and high. They embarrassed her. It was quite apparent that she had cooked, and that she expected to cook, dutifully. The blushes caused by the careless scrutiny of some passengers as she had entered the car were strange to see upon this plain, under-class countenance, which was drawn in placid, almost emotionless lines.

They were evidently very happy. "Ever been in a parlor-car before?" he asked, smiling with delight.

"No," she answered; "I never was. It's fine, ain't it?"

"Great! And then after a while we'll go forward to the diner, and get a big layout. Finest meal in the world. Charge a dollar."

"Oh, do they?" cried the bride. "Charge a dollar? Why, that's too much—for us—ain't it, Jack?"

"Not this trip, anyhow," he answered bravely. "We're going to go the whole thing."

Later he explained to her about the trains. "You see, it's a thousand miles from one end of Texas to the other; and this train runs right across it and never stops but four times." He had the pride of an owner. He pointed out to her the dazzling fittings of the coach; and in truth her eyes opened wider as she contemplated the sea-green figured velvet, the shining brass, silver, and glass, the wood that gleamed as darkly brilliant as the surface of a pool of oil. At one end a bronze figure sturdily held a support for a separated chamber, and at convenient places on the ceiling were frescos in olive and silver.

To the minds of the pair, their surroundings reflected the glory of their marriage that morning in San Antonio; this was the environment of their new estate; and the man's face in particular beamed with an elation that made him appear ridiculous to the negro porter. This individual at times surveyed them from afar with an amused and superior grin. On other occasions he bullied them with skill in ways that did not make it exactly plain to them that they were being bullied. He subtly used all the manners of the most unconquerable kind of snobbery. He oppressed them; but of this oppression they had small knowledge, and they speedily forgot that infrequently a number of travelers covered them with stares of derisive enjoyment. Historically there was supposed to be something infinitely humorous in their situation.

"We are due in Yellow Sky at 3:42," he said, looking tenderly into her eyes.

"Oh, are we?" she said, as if she had not been aware of it. To evince surprise at her husband's statement was part of her wifely amiability. She took from a pocket a little silver watch; and as she held it before her, and stared at it with a frown of attention, the new husband's face shone.

"I bought it in San Anton' from a friend of mine," he told her gleefully.

"It's seventeen minutes past twelve," she said, looking up at him with a kind of shy and clumsy coquetry. A passenger, noting this play, grew excessively sardonic, and winked at himself in one of the numerous mirrors.

At last they went to the dining car. Two rows of negro waiters, in glowing white suits, surveyed their entrance with the interest, and also the equanimity, of men who had been forewarned. The pair fell to the lot of a waiter who happened to feel pleasure in steering them through their meal. He viewed them with the manner of a fatherly pilot, his countenance radiant with benevolence. The patronage, entwined with the ordinary deference, was not plain to them. And yet, as they returned to their coach, they showed in their faces a sense of escape.

To the left, miles down a long purple slope, was a little ribbon of mist where moved the keening Rio Grande. The train was approaching it at an angle, and the apex was Yellow Sky. Presently it was apparent that, as the distance from Yellow Sky grew shorter, the husband became commensurately restless. His brick-red hands were more insistent in their prominence. Occasionally he was even rather absent-minded and far-away when the bride leaned forward and addressed him.

As a matter of truth, Jack Potter was beginning to find the shadow of a deed weigh upon him like a leaden slab. He, the town marshal of Yellow Sky, a man known, liked, and feared in his corner, a prominent person, had gone to San Antonio to meet a girl he believed he loved, and there, after the usual prayers, had actually induced her to marry him, without consulting Yellow Sky for any part of the transaction. He was now bringing his bride before an inno-cent and unsuspecting community.

Of course people in Yellow Sky married as it pleased them, in accordance with a general custom; but such was Potter's thought of his duty to his friends, or of their idea of his duty, or of an unspoken form which does not control men in these matters, that he felt he was heinous. He had committed an extraordinary crime. Face to face with this girl in San Antonio, and spurred by his sharp impulse, he had gone headlong over all the social hedges. At San Antonio he was like a man hidden in the dark. A knife to sever any friendly duty, any form, was easy to his hand in that remote city. But the hour of Yellow Sky—the hour of daylight— was approaching.

He knew full well that his marriage was an important thing to his town. It could only be exceeded by the burning of the new hotel. His friends could not for-give him. Frequently he had reflected on the advisability of telling them by tele-graph, but a new cowardice had been upon him. He feared to do it. And now the train was hurrying him toward a scene of amazement, glee, and reproach. He glanced out of the window at the line of haze swinging slowly in toward the train.

Yellow Sky had a kind of brass band, which played painfully, to the delight of the populace. He laughed without heart as he thought of it. If the citizens could dream of his prospective arrival with his bride, they would parade the band at the station and escort them, amid cheers and laughing congratulations, to his adobe home.

He resolved that he would use all the devices of speed and plainscraft in making the journey from the station to his house. Once within that safe citadel, he could issue some sort of vocal bulletin, and then not go among the citizens until they had time to wear off a little of their enthusiasm.

The bride looked anxiously at him. "What's worrying you, Jack?"

He laughed again. "I'm not worrying, girl; I'm only thinking of Yellow Sky." She flushed in comprehension.

A sense of mutual guilt invaded their minds and developed a finer tenderness. They looked at each other, with eyes softly aglow. But Potter often laughed the same nervous laugh; the flush upon the bride's face seemed quite permanent.

The traitor to the feelings of Yellow Sky narrowly watched the speeding landscape. "We're nearly there," he said.

Presently the porter came and announced the proximity of Potter's home. He held a brush in his hand, and, with all his airy superiority gone, he brushed Potter's new clothes as the latter slowly turned this way and that way. Potter tumbled out a coin and gave it to the porter, as he had seen others do. It was a heavy and muscle-bound business, as that of a man shoeing his first horse.

The porter took their bag, and as the train began to slow they moved forward to the hooded platform of the car. Presently the two engines and their long string of coaches rushed into the station of Yellow Sky.

"They have to take water here," said Potter, from a constricted throat and in mournful cadence, as one announcing death. Before the train stopped his eye had swept the length of the platform, and he was glad and astonished to see there was none upon it but the station-agent, who, with a slightly hurried and anxious air, was walking toward the water-tanks. When the train had halted, the porter alighted first, and placed in position a little temporary step.

"Come on, girl," said Potter, hoarsely. As he helped her down they each laughed on a false note. He took the bag from the negro, and bade his wife cling to his arm. As they slunk rapidly away, his hang-dog glance perceived that they were unloading the two trunks, and also that the station-agent, far ahead near the baggage-car, had turned and was running toward him, making gestures. He laughed, and groaned as he laughed, when he noted the first effect of his marital bliss upon Yellow Sky. He gripped his wife's arm firmly to his side, and they fled. Behind them the porter stood, chuckling fatuously.

II

The California express on the Southern Railway was due at Yellow Sky in twenty-one minutes. There were six men at the bar of the Weary Gentleman saloon. One was a drummer[1] who talked a great deal and rapidly; three were Texans who did not care to talk at that time; and two were Mexican sheepherders, who did not talk as a general practice in the Weary Gentleman saloon. The barkeeper's dog lay on the boardwalk that crossed in front of the door. His head was on his paws, and he glanced drowsily here and there with the constant vigilance of a dog that is kicked on occasion. Across the sandy street were some vivid green grass-plots, so wonderful in appearance, amid the sands that burned near them in a blazing sun, that they caused a doubt in the mind. They exactly resembled the grass mats used to represent lawns on the stage. At the cooler end of the railway station, a man without a coat sat in a tilted chair and smoked his pipe. The fresh-cut

[1]Traveling salesman

bank of the Rio Grande circled near the town, and there could be seen beyond it a great plum-colored plain of mesquit.

Save for the busy drummer and his companions in the saloon, Yellow Sky was dozing. The new-comer leaned gracefully upon the bar, and recited many tales with the confidence of a bard who has come upon a new field.

"—and at the moment that the old man fell downstairs with the bureau in his arms, the old woman was coming up with two scuttles of coal, and of course—"

The drummer's tale was interrupted by a young man who suddenly appeared in the open door. He cried: "Scratchy Wilson's drunk, and has turned loose with both hands." The two Mexicans at once set down their glasses and faded out of the rear entrance of the saloon.

The drummer, innocent and jocular, answered: "All right, old man. S'pose he has? Come in and have a drink, anyhow."

But the information had made such an obvious cleft in every skull in the room that the drummer was obliged to see its importance. All had become instantly solemn. "Say," said he, mystified, "what is this?" His three companions made the introductory gesture of eloquent speech; but the young man at the door forestalled them.

"It means, my friend," he answered, as he came into the saloon, "that for the next two hours this town won't be a health resort."

The barkeeper went to the door, and locked and barred it; reaching out of the window, he pulled in heavy wooden shutters, and barred them. Immediately a solemn, chapel-like gloom was upon the place. The drummer was looking from one to another.

"But say," he cried, "what is this, anyhow? You don't mean there is going to be a gun-fight?"

"Don't know whether there'll be a fight or not," answered one man, grimly; "but there'll be some shootin'—some good shootin'."

The young man who had warned them waved his hand. "Oh, there'll be a fight fast enough, if any one wants it. Anybody can get a fight out there in the street. There's a fight just waiting."

The drummer seemed to be swayed between the interest of a foreigner and a perception of personal danger.

"What did you say his name was?" he asked.

"Scratchy Wilson," they answered in chorus.

"And will he kill anybody? What are you going to do? Does this happen often? Does he rampage around like this once a week or so? Can he break in that door?"

"No; he can't break down that door," replied the barkeeper. "He's tried it three times. But when he comes you'd better lay down on the floor, stranger. He's dead sure to shoot at it, and a bullet may come through."

Thereafter the drummer kept a strict eye upon the door. The time had not yet been called for him to hug the floor, but, as a minor precaution, he sidled near to the wall. "Will he kill anybody?" he said again.

The men laughed low and scornfully at the question.

"He's out to shoot, and he's out for trouble. Don't see any good in experimentin' with him."

"But what do you do in a case like this? What do you do?"

A man responded: "Why, he and Jack Potter—"

"But," in chorus the other men interrupted, "Jack Potter's in San Anton'."

"Well, who is he? What's he got to do with it?"

"Oh, he's the town marshal. He goes out and fights Scratchy when he gets on one of these tears."

"Wow!" said the drummer, mopping his brow. "Nice job he's got."

The voices had toned away to mere whisperings. The drummer wished to ask further questions, which were born of an increasing anxiety and bewilderment; but when he attempted them, the men merely looked at him in irritation and motioned him to remain silent. A tense waiting hush was upon them. In the deep shadows of the room their eyes shone as they listened for sounds from the street. One man made three gestures at the barkeeper; and the latter, moving like a ghost, handed him a glass and a bottle. The man poured a full glass of whisky, and set down the bottle noiselessly. He gulped the whisky in a swallow, and turned again toward the door in immovable silence. The drummer saw that the barkeeper, without a sound, had taken a Winchester from beneath the bar. Later he saw this individual beckoning to him, so he tiptoed across the room.

"You better come with me back of the bar."

"No, thanks," said the drummer, perspiring: "I'd rather be where I can make a break for the back door."

Whereupon the man of bottles made a kindly but peremptory gesture. The drummer obeyed it, and, finding himself seated on a box with his head below the level of the bar, balm was laid upon his soul at sight of various zinc and copper fittings that bore a resemblance to armorplate. The barkeeper took a seat comfortably upon an adjacent box.

"You see," he whispered, "this here Scratchy Wilson is a wonder with a gun—a perfect wonder; and when he goes on the wartrail, we hunt our holes—naturally. He's about the last one of the old gang that used to hang out along the river here. He's a terror when he's drunk. When he's sober he's all right—kind of simple—wouldn't hurt a fly—nicest fellow in town. But when he's drunk—whoo!"

There were periods of stillness. "I wish Jack Potter was back from San Anton'," said the barkeeper. "He shot Wilson up once—in the leg—and he would sail in and pull out the kinks in this thing."

Presently they heard from a distance the sound of a shot, followed by three wild yowls. It instantly removed a bond from the men in the darkened saloon. There was a shuffling of feet. They looked at each other. "Here he comes," they said.

III

A man in a maroon-colored flannel shirt, which had been purchased for purposes of decoration, and made principally by some Jewish women on the East Side of New York, rounded a corner and walked into the middle of the main street of Yellow Sky. In either hand the man held a long, heavy, blue-black revolver. Often he yelled, and these cries rang through a semblance of a deserted village, shrilly flying over the roofs in a volume that seemed to have no relation to the ordinary vocal strength of a man. It was as if the surrounding stillness formed the arch of a tomb over him. These cries of ferocious challenge rang against walls of silence. And his boots had red tops with gilded imprints, of the kind beloved in winter by little sledding boys on the hillsides of New England.

The man's face flamed in a rage begot of whisky. His eyes, rolling, and yet keen for ambush, hunted the still doorways and windows. He walked with the creeping movement of the midnight cat. As it occurred to him, he roared menacing information. The long revolvers in his hands were as easy as straws; they were moved with an electric swiftness. The little fingers of each hand played sometimes in a musician's way. Plain from the low collar of the shirt, the cords of his neck straightened and sank, straightened and sank, as passion moved him. The only sounds were his terrible invitations. The calm adobes preserved their demeanor at the passing of this small thing in the middle of the street.

There was no offer of fight—no offer of fight. The man called to the sky. There were no attractions. He bellowed and fumed and swayed his revolvers here and everywhere.

The dog of the barkeeper of the Weary Gentleman saloon had not appreciated the advance of events. He yet lay dozing in front of his master's door. At sight of the dog, the man paused and raised his revolver humorously. At sight of the man, the dog sprang up and walked diagonally away, with a sullen head, and growling. The man yelled, and the dog broke into a gallop. As it was about to enter an alley, there was a loud noise, a whistling, and something spat the ground directly before it. The dog screamed, and, wheeling in terror, galloped headlong in a new direction. Again there was a noise, a whistling, and sand was kicked viciously before it. Fear-stricken, the dog turned and flurried like an animal in a pen. The man stood laughing, his weapons at his hips.

Ultimately the man was attracted by the closed door of the Weary Gentleman saloon. He went to it and, hammering with a revolver, demanded drink.

The door remaining imperturbable, he picked a bit of paper from the walk, and nailed it to the framework with a knife. He then turned his back contemptuously upon this popular resort and, walking to the opposite side of the street and spinning there on his heel quickly and lithely, fired at the bit of paper. He missed it by a half-inch. He swore at himself, and went away. Later he comfortably fusilladed the windows of his most intimate friend. The man was playing with this town: it was a toy for him.

But still there was no offer of fight. The name of Jack Potter, his ancient antagonist, entered his mind, and he concluded that it would be a glad thing if he should go to Potter's house, and by bombardment induce him to come out and fight. He moved in the direction of his desire, chanting Apache scalp-music.

When he arrived at it, Potter's house presented the same still front as had the other adobes. Taking up a strategic position, the man howled a challenge. But this house regarded him as might a great stone god. It gave no sign. After a decent wait, the man howled further challenges, mingling with them wonderful epithets.

Presently there came the spectacle of a man churning himself into deepest rage over the immobility of a house. He fumed at it as the winter wind attacks a prairie cabin in the North. To the distance there should have gone the sound of a tumult like the fighting of two hundred Mexicans. As necessity bade him, he paused for breath or to reload his revolvers.

IV

Potter and his bride walked sheepishly and with speed. Sometimes they laughed together shamefacedly and low.

"Next corner, dear," he said finally.

They put forth the efforts of a pair walking bowed against a strong wind. Potter was about to raise a finger to point the first appearance of the new home when, as they circled the corner, they came face to face with a man in a maroon-colored shirt, who was feverishly pushing cartridges into a large revolver. Upon the instant the man dropped his revolver to the ground and, like lightning, whipped another from its holster. The second weapon was aimed at the bridegroom's chest.

There was a silence. Potter's mouth seemed to be merely a grave for his tongue. He exhibited an instinct to at once loosen his arm from the woman's grip, and he dropped the bag to the sand. As for the bride, her face had gone as yellow as old cloth. She was a slave to hideous rites, gazing at the apparitional snake.

The two men faced each other at a distance of three paces. He of the revolver smiled with a new and quiet ferocity.

"Tried to sneak up on me," he said. "Tried to sneak up on me!" His eyes grew more baleful. As Potter made a slight movement, the man thrust his revolver venomously forward. "No; don't you do it, Jack Potter. Don't you move a finger toward a gun just yet. Don't you move an eyelash. The time has come for me to settle with you, and I'm goin' to do it my own way, and loaf along with no interferin'. So if you don't want a gun bent on you, just mind what I tell you."

Potter looked at his enemy. "I ain't got a gun on me, Scratchy," he said. "Honest, I ain't." He was stiffening and steadying, but yet somewhere at the back of his mind a vision of the Pullman floated: the sea-green figured velvet, the shining brass, silver, and glass, the wood that gleamed as darkly brilliant as the surface of a pool of oil—all the glory of the marriage, the environment of the new estate. "You know I fight when it comes to fighting, Scratchy Wilson; but I ain't got a gun on me. You'll have to do all the shootin' yourself."

His enemy's face went livid. He stepped forward, and lashed his weapon to and fro before Potter's chest. "Don't tell me you ain't got no gun on you, you whelp. Don't tell me no lie like that. There ain't a man in Texas ever seen you without no gun. Don't take me for no kid." His eyes blazed with light, and his throat worked like a pump.

"I ain't takin' you for no kid," answered Potter. His heels had not moved an inch backward. "I'm takin' you for a damn fool. I tell you I ain't got a gun, and I ain't. If you're goin' to shoot me up, you better begin now; you'll never get a chance like this again."

So much enforced reasoning had told on Wilson's rage; he was calmer. "If you ain't got a gun, why ain't you got a gun?" he sneered. "Been to Sunday-school?"

"I ain't got a gun because I've just come from San Anton' with my wife. I'm married," said Potter. "And if I'd thought there was going to be any galoots like you prowling around when I brought my wife home, I'd had a gun, and don't you forget it."

"Married!" said Scratchy, not at all comprehending.

"Yes, married. I'm married." said Potter, distinctly.

"Married?" said Scratchy. Seemingly for the first time, he saw the drooping, drowning woman at the other man's side. "No!" he said. He was like a creature allowed a glimpse of another world. He moved a pace backward, and his arm, with the revolver, dropped to his side. "Is this the lady?" he asked.

"Yes; this is the lady," answered Potter.

There was another period of silence.

"Well," said Wilson at last, slowly, "I s'pose it's all off now."

"It's all off if you say so, Scratchy. You know I didn't make the trouble." Potter lifted his valise.

"Well, I 'low it's off, Jack," said Wilson. He was looking at the ground. "Married!" He was not a student of chivalry; it was merely that in the presence of this foreign condition he was a simple child of the earlier plains. He picked up his starboard revolver, and, placing both weapons in their holsters, he went away. His feet made funnel-shaped tracks in the heavy sand.

Plot

Plot Factors   Plot is the series of events that moves a narrative along. The opening of a story with a conventional plot introduces important characters and sets the stage for what happens. Then one or more conflicts develop, some pitting person against person, others setting characters against society, nature, fate, or themselves. Action gradually builds to a climax, where events take a decisive turn. The ending can do a number of things—clear up unanswered questions, hint at the future, state a theme, or reestablish some sort of relationship between two foes. In "The Bride," Potter experiences two conflicts: one with Scratchy Wilson and the other within himself over his marriage. The climax comes when Potter and Scratchy meet face to face, and Scratchy learns about his old adversary's marriage. As Scratchy walks away, we sense that the two old foes have had their last confrontation, that Potter's marriage has altered forever the relationship between them.

To organize plots, writers use a number of techniques. In foreshadowing, for example, the writer hints at later developments, thus creating interest and building suspense. In H. H. Munro's short story "The Open Window," a visitor to a country house observes that "An undefinable something about the room seemed to suggest masculine habitation." Yet he accepts the story of a young girl that her uncle, the man of the house, had lost his life in a bog three years before. Because he ignores his observation and accepts the girl's story at face value, the visitor is terrified by the sudden appearance of the uncle, who seems to be a ghost. The careful reader, however, senses what's coming and enjoys the trick more for having been in on it.

When using a flashback, another organizational technique, the writer interrupts the flow of events to relate one or more happenings that occurred before the point at which the story opened, then resumes the narrative at or near the point of interruption. Ernest Hemingway's short story "The Short Happy Life of Francis Macomber" provides an illustration. As the story opens, we meet characters who hint that Macomber displayed cowardice by running from, rather than shooting, a charging, wounded lion. A bit later the story flashes back to detail the actual incident. Flashbacks supply essential information and either create or resolve suspense.

Not every plot unfolds in clear stages. Many modern stories lack distinct plot divisions and focus on psychological, not physical, conflicts. In extreme cases, writers may abandon the traditional plot structure and present events in a disorganized sequence that helps accomplish some literary purpose, such as reflecting a character's disturbed state of mind. Joyce Carol Oates's short story "How I Contemplated the World from the Detroit House of Correction and Began My Life Over Again" fits this mold. To dramatize her chief character's mental turmoil, Oates presents the story as a series of notes for an English composition. These notes, labeled "Events," "Characters," "Sioux Drive," "Detroit," and "That Night," are internally disorganized and arranged in a jumbled sequence.

A poem sometimes includes a series of actions and events, as Edwin Arlington Robinson's "The Miller's Wife" illustrates:

> The miller's wife had waited long,
>   The tea was cold, the fire was dead;
> And there might yet be nothing wrong
>   In how he went and what he said:
> "There are no millers any more,"
>   Was all that she had heard him say:

And he had lingered at the door
    So long that it seemed yesterday.

Sick with a fear that had no form
    She knew that she was there at last;
And in the mill there was a warm
    And mealy fragrance of the past.
What else there was would only seem
    To say again what he had meant;
And what was hanging from a beam
    Would not have heeded where she went.

And if she thought it followed her,
    She may have reasoned in the dark
That one way of the few there were
    Would hide her and would leave no mark;
Black water, smooth above the weir
    Like starry velvet in the night,
Though ruffled once, would soon appear
    The same as ever to the sight.

Most poems, however, present a series of images, building statements that make a philosophical point rather than tell a conventionally plotted story.

Writing About Plot   Unless your instructor asks for a plot summary, don't merely repeat what happens in the story. Instead, help your reader understand what's special about the plot and how it functions. Does it build suspense, mirror a character's confusion, shape a conflict, show how different lives can intersect, or help reveal a theme?

Before starting to write, answer the following questions:

What are the key events of the story? Do they unfold in conventional fashion or deviate from it in some way?

Does the writer use foreshadowing or flashback? If so, for what purpose?

Is the plot believable and effective, or does it display weakness of some sort?

Does it include any unique features?

Is it similar to the plot of another story or some type of story?

What plot features could I write about? What examples from the story would support my contentions?

As you prepare your analysis, determine the important events and how they relate to your topic. If the story is disjointed or incoherent, arrange the events so that they make sense and ask yourself why the writer chose that sequence. To mirror the main character's disordered state of mind? To show that life is chaotic and difficult to understand? Similarly, assess the reason for any use of foreshadowing or flashback. Does it build, create, or resolve suspense?

Not all plots are successful. A character's actions may not fit his or her personality or the situation. The plot might be too hard to follow or fail to produce the desired effect, as in a mystery where the clues are too obvious to create suspense. Or a writer might rely on chance or coincidence to resolve a conflict or problem: It's unacceptable to have the cavalry charge in gallantly out of nowhere and rescue the hero.

If there's something unique about the plot—perhaps a surprise event that works well—describe it and tell how it functions in the story, or perhaps you can compare the plot with one in another story in order to show how both develop some key insight.

The organization of a paper on plot is simple: You'll either present a thesis and then support it with examples taken from the text, or you'll write a comparison. Writing about "The Bride Comes to Yellow Sky," you could show how foreshadowing moves the story toward an inevitable showdown. As support, you could cite the deliberate, forward motion of the train, the repeated emphasis on clocks and time, the repeated suggestions of Potter's anxiousness, and Scratchy's ongoing conflict with Potter. As a more ambitious project, you might compare the plot of "The Bride" to that of a conventional western showdown, noting any important differences and what they accomplish. A more critical approach would be to argue that the plot is implausible, citing Potter's unplanned marriage and the coincidence of his return to Yellow Sky precisely when Scratchy Wilson was drunk and shooting up the town.

EXERCISE   *In a short story with a strong plot line, identify conflicts and climax and tell what the ending accomplishes. Point out any use of foreshadowing or flashback.*

Point of View

Point-of-View Factors   The point of view is the vantage point from which the writer of a literary work views its events. A writer may adopt either a first-person or a third-person point of view. In *first-person* narration, someone in the work tells what happens and is identified by words like *I, me, mine,* and *my.* A *third-person* narrator stays completely out of the story and is never mentioned in any way. "The Bride Comes to Yellow Sky" illustrates third-person narration.

The most common form of first-person narration features a narrator who takes part in the action. This technique puts the readers directly on the scene and is excellent for tracing the growth or deterioration of a character. Instead of participating in the action, the narrator may view it from the sideline, an approach that preserves on-the-scene directness and allows the narrator to comment on the characters and issues. The narrator, however, cannot enter the mind and reveal the unspoken thoughts of anyone else.

Third-person narrators don't participate in the action but can survey the whole literary landscape and directly report events that first-person narrators would know only by hearsay. Most third-person narrators reveal the thoughts of just one character. Others, with *limited omniscience,* can enter the heads of several characters, while still others display *full omniscience* and know everything in the literary work, including all thoughts and feelings of all characters. Omniscience allows the narrator to contrast two or more sets of thoughts and feelings and draw general conclusions from them. The narrator of Stephen Crane's "The Open Boat" is fully omniscient. The story is about four shipwrecked sailors adrift in a lifeboat, and the narrator, knowing what they all think, traces their developing awareness that nature is completely indifferent to their plight.

Yet another type of third-person narration, *dramatic,* has emerged in contemporary fiction. A dramatic narrator, like a motion-picture camera, moves about recording the characters' actions and words but without revealing anyone's thoughts. Stories with surprise endings often use this technique.

Writing About Point of View   For a paper about point of view, ask and answer these questions:

> What point of view is used? Why is it used?
>
> Is it suitable for the situation? Why or why not?
>
> If the story uses first-person narration, is the narrator reliable? What textual evidence supports my answer?
>
> What focus would produce an effective paper? What textual evidence could support its discussion?

Various reasons might prompt the choice of a particular point of view. For example, an author might use the first person to show a character's mental deterioration. A third-person narrator might enter two minds to contrast opposing attitudes toward some incident or enter no minds at all to heighten the emotional impact of a story's climax.

If a point of view seems unsuitable, say so and suggest why. Suppose a man is planning an elopement that will create a surprising ending. A point of view that revealed the man's thoughts would give away that ending.

First-person narrators are sometimes unreliable; that is, they offer the reader a warped view of things. To gauge reliability, compare the narrator's version of the facts with what the work otherwise reveals. The narrator may come off as stupid, psychologically warped, or too biased to view events fairly. If so, speculate on the reasons. A mentally unreliable narrator may be meant, for example, to heighten the horror of events.

Although organization can vary, papers on point of view basically follow a cause-and-effect format, first identifying the point of view used and then demonstrating, with examples, its effect on the story and reader. In "The Bride," the third-person point of view allows Crane to shift from Potter and his new wife to the men in the saloon to the rampaging Scratchy and then to Potter and Scratchy as they confront each other. Shifting scenes in this way builds a sense of impending conflict, which would be difficult to produce with a first-person narrator, who could not move about in this fashion.

EXERCISE   *Read the following two excerpts and answer the questions that follow them:*

Max shook his head no at the mugger, his mouth in a regretful pout.

The teenager lunged at Max's chest with the blade. Instinctively, Max moved one step to his right. He didn't shift far enough. The knife sank into him. Max lowered his head and watched as the metal disappeared into his arm and chest. He felt nothing. With the blade all the way in, the teenager's face was only inches from Max's; he stared at the point of entry, stunned, his mouth sagging open. The mugger's eyes were small and frightened. Max didn't like him. He put his hand on the kid's chest and pushed him away. He didn't want to die looking into scared eyes.

The mugger stumbled back, tripped over his feet and fell. . . . Max felt the point of the blade in his armpit. He realized he wasn't cut. The stupid kid had stuck the knife in the space below Max's armpit, the gap between his arm and chest. He had torn Max's polo shirt, but missed everything else. For a moment the knife hung there, caught by the fabric. Max raised his arm and the switchblade fell to the ground.

The teenager jumped to his feet and ran away, heading uptown.

Rafael Yglesias, Fearless

"Now!" I cry, aloud or to myself I don't know. Everything has boiled down to this instant. There's nothing in the world except the hand of the gate judge, lowering in slow motion to the catch that contains us. I see each of his fingers clearly, separately, as they fold around the lever, I see the muscles in his forearm harden as he begins to push down.

Wheeling and spinning, tilting and beating, my breath the song, the horse the dance. Time is gone. All the ordinary ways of things, the gettings from here to there, the one and twos, forgot. The crowd is color, the whirl of a spun top. The noises blend into a waving band that flies around us like a ribbon on a string. Beneath me four feet dance, pounding and leaping and turning and stomping. My legs flap like wings. I sail above, first to one side, then the other, remembering more than feeling the slaps of our bodies together. Things happen faster than understanding, faster than ideas. I'm a bird coasting, shot free into the music, spiraling into a place without bones or weight.

Michael Dorris, A Yellow Boat in Blue Water

1. In this third-person excerpt, Yglesias depicts the climax of an unsuccessful mugging, entering one character's mind but not the other's. Whose mind does he enter, and how does he convey the other person's mental state?
2. What does Dorris accomplish by using the first-person point of view? ◄

Character

Character Factors   The characters in a literary work function in various ways. Some are centers of physical and mental action. Others furnish humor, act as narrators, provide needed information, act as *foils* who highlight more important characters by contrast, serve as symbols, or simply populate the landscape. In "The Bride," the drummer helps funnel information to the reader. He asks questions, the bartender answers them, and the reader learns all about Scratchy.

Writers present characters in several ways. Some tell the reader point-blank that a person is brave, stupid, self-serving, or the like. But most authors take an indirect approach by indicating how their characters look and act, what they think and say, how they live, and how other characters regard them.

Beware of uncritically accepting Character X's assessment of Character Y. X may be prejudiced, simpleminded, a deliberate liar, or too emotionally involved or disturbed to be objective. To illustrate, Scratchy Wilson, despite the bartender's fearful comments, proves to be something less than a real terror. He makes no real attempt to break down any doors and toys with, rather than shoots, the dog and Potter.

In picturing Potter, Crane first notes his appearance and self-conscious behavior, then delves into his mind to show the turmoil his marriage has stirred. Somewhat later, the bartender adds his brush strokes to Potter's portrait. At the confrontation, we again observe Potter's thoughts and behavior, as well as what he says to Scratchy. From all this, Potter emerges not as a mere one-dimensional lawman but as someone with a recognizably lifelike personality.

Some characters remain static; others mature, gain insight, or deteriorate in some telling way. Potter changes. As the story unfolds he abandons his doubts about the course he's charted and ends up fully committed to "the environment of the new estate." Scratchy, on the other hand, ends just as he started, "a simple child of the earlier plains."

Writing About Character   Start the process by asking yourself these questions:

What characters offer the potential for a paper?

What are their most important features, and where in the story are these features revealed?

Do the characters undergo any changes? If so, how and why do the changes occur?

Are the characters believable, true to life? If not, why?

What focus would produce an effective paper?

What textual evidence could support the discussion?

Usually, you'll write about the main character, but at times you might choose the chief adversary or some minor character. For a lesser character, point out how that person interacts with the main one.

Most main characters change; most lesser ones do not. But sometimes a main character remains frozen, allowing the writer to make an important point. To show that a certain social group suffers from paralysis of the will, an author might create a main character who begins and ends weak and ineffectual. Whatever the situation, when you determine what purpose your character serves, tell the reader.

Think hard about your character's credibility. Ask yourself if he or she is true to life. Cruel stepmothers, brilliant but eccentric detectives, mad scientists, masked seekers after justice—these and other stereotyped figures don't square with real-life people, who are complex mixtures of many traits. Inconsistent acts or unexplained and unmotivated personality changes don't ring true: Most people behave the same in similar situations and change only when properly motivated. Not every character needs to be a full-dress creation, but all require enough development to justify their roles.

Start your paper by identifying your character's role or personality; then back your contention with illustrations that support it, possibly following the sequence in which the writer presents them. If a character changes, say so, tell why, and indicate the results of the change, again using supporting examples.

Such a paper is usually a cause-and-effect analysis. Papers that evaluate two characters are essentially comparisons.

For an example of a paper analyzing a character, see pages 295–297.

EXERCISE *Write a paragraph describing the personality of the character in the following passage:*

> The thousand injuries of Fortunato I had borne as I best could, but when he ventured upon insult, I vowed revenge. You, who so well know the nature of my soul, will not suppose, however, that I gave utterance to a threat. *At length* I would be avenged; this was a point definitely settled—but the very definiteness with which it was resolved precluded the idea of risk. I must not only punish, but punish with impunity. A wrong is unredressed when retribution overtakes its redresser. It is equally unredressed when the avenger fails to make himself felt as such to the one who has done the wrong.
>
> Edgar Allan Poe, "The Cask of Amontillado"

Setting

Setting Factors Setting locates characters in a time, place, and culture so they can think, feel, and act against this background. Writers can generate feelings and moods by describing settings. Sunny spring landscapes signal hope or happiness, dark alleys are foreboding, and thunderstorms suggest violent possibilities. Poetry, especially, uses setting to create mood. In "Cannery Town in August," Lorna Dee Cervantes combines images of tired, work-stained employees, a noisy workplace, and dismal streets to evoke an unpleasant setting.

> All night it humps the air.
> Speechless, the steam rises
> from the cannery columns. I hear
> the night bird rave about work
> or lunch, or sing the swing shift
> home. I listen, while bodyless
> uniforms and spinach specked shoes
> drift in monochrome down the dark
> moon-possessed streets. Women
> who smell of whiskey and tomatoes,
> peach fuzz reddening their lips and eyes—
> I imagine them not speaking, dumbed
> by the can's clamor and drop
> to the trucks that wait, grunting
> in their headlights below.
> They spotlight those who walk
> like a dream, with no one
> waiting in the shadows
> to palm them back to living.

Setting can also help reveal a character's personality. In this excerpt from Amy Tan's novel *The Joy Luck Club,* the size and contents of the wealthy merchant Wu Tsing's house reflect the owner's love of wealthy display:

As soon as we walked into that big house, I became lost with too many things to see; a curved staircase that wound up and up, a ceiling with faces in every corner, then hallways twisting and turning into one room then another. To my right was a large room, larger than I had ever seen, and it was filled with stiff teakwood furniture: sofas and tables and chairs. And at the other end of this long, long room, I could see doors leading into more rooms, more furniture, then more doors. To my left was a darker room, another sitting room, this one filled with foreign furniture: dark green leather sofas, paintings with hunting dogs, armchairs, and mahogany desks. And as I glanced in these rooms I would see different people. . . .

Settings sometimes function as symbols, reinforcing the workings of the other elements. A broad, slowly flowing river may stand for time or fate, a craggy cliff for strength of character, a blizzard-swept plain for the overwhelming power of nature. The following section, a discussion of symbols, points out some symbolic settings in "The Bride."

At times, setting provides a clue to some observation about life. At one point in Stephen Crane's story "The Open Boat," the men spot a nearby flock of seagulls sitting comfortably on the turbulent waves. Juxtaposing the complacent gulls and the imperiled men suggests the philosophical point of the story: that the universe is indifferent to human aspirations and struggles.

Shifts in setting often trigger shifts in a character's emotional or psychological state. Jack Potter, typically calm and assured in Yellow Sky, displays great awkwardness and embarrassment in the unfamiliar environment of the Pullman car.

Writing About Setting   Begin your search for a topic by identifying the settings in the story and then asking these questions about each one:

What are its key features?

What does it accomplish? Does it create a mood? Reveal a character? Serve as a symbol? Reinforce the story's point? How does it accomplish these things?

In what ways does it support or interfere with the story?

Does the setting seem realistic? If not, why not?

What focus would produce an effective paper? What textual evidence would support it?

Check the impact of setting on mood by seeing how well the two match up for each setting. Sometimes, as in "The Bride," the two bear little or no relationship to each other. In other cases, the two intertwine throughout the work.

Try to establish connections between settings and characters. If an emotionally barren individual always appears against backdrops of gloomy furnished rooms, cheerless restaurants, and decaying slums, you can assume that the writer is using setting to convey character. Look for links between changes in characters and changes in settings. If the setting remains the same, point out any shifts in the way the character views it.

Occasionally, a writer drums home settings so insistently that they overpower the characters and story line. A novel about the super rich may linger so lovingly over their extravagant surroundings that the plot lacks force and the characters seem mere puppets. If the setting hobbles the other elements, identify this flaw in your analysis.

When you write about setting, describe it and discuss its impact on the story's other elements, supporting your claims with specific examples. In writing about "The Bride," you might argue that Crane used as his chief setting a pulp fiction cliché of a western town in order to heighten the atypical nature of the showdown. As support, you could cite such stock features as the train station, saloon, dog, and dusty streets, all of which point toward an actual shootout rather than Scratchy Wilson's backdown.

> **EXERCISE**   *What mood does the following description of a room generate? What does it suggest about the situation of the room's inhabitants, two women in an Old Ladies' Home?*

> Marian stood enclosed by a bed, a washstand, and a chair; the tiny room had altogether too much furniture. Everything smelled wet—even the bare floor. She held onto the back of the chair, which was wicker and felt soft and damp. . . . How dark it was! The window shade was down, and the only door was shut. Marian looked at the ceiling. . . . It was like being caught in a robbers' cave. . . .
>
> Eudora Welty, "A Visit of Charity"

Symbols

Symbol Factors   To strengthen and deepen their messages, writers use symbols: names, persons, objects, places, colors, or actions that have a significance beyond their surface meaning. A symbol may be very obvious—as a name like Mr. Grimm, suggesting the person's character—or quite subtle, as an object representing a universal human emotion.

Some symbols are private and others conventional. A private symbol has special significance within a literary work but not outside it. Conventional symbols are deeply rooted in our culture, and almost everyone knows what they represent. We associate crosses with Christianity and limousines with wealth and power. In "The Bride," the plains pouring eastward past the Pullman windows, Scratchy's eastern clothing, and the mirage-like grass plots in front of the saloon are all private symbols that stand for the passing of the Old West. Because people of Crane's time associated Pullman cars with an urbane, eastern lifestyle, the Pullman is a conventional symbol that represents the new order of things. Like the Pullman, a symbol may appear more than once in a literary work.

Whether or not a recurring item is a symbol depends upon its associations. In Ernest Hemingway's novel *A Farewell to Arms*, rain may fairly be said to symbolize doom because it consistently accompanies disasters, and one of the main characters says that she has visions of herself lying dead in the rain. But if rain is randomly associated with a rundown lakeside resort, a spirited business meeting, a cozy weekend, and the twentieth-anniversary celebration of a happy marriage, the writer probably intends no symbolism.

Writing About Symbols When you examine the symbols in a literary work, think about these questions:

> What symbols are used and where do they appear?
>
> Are they private or conventional?
>
> What do they appear to mean?
>
> Do any of them undergo a change in meaning? If so, how and why?
>
> Which symbol(s) could I discuss effectively?
>
> What textual evidence would support my interpretation?

To locate symbols, read the literary work carefully, looking for items that seem to have an extended meaning. You might, for example, discover that the cracked walls of a crumbling mansion symbolize some character's disordered mental state or that a voyage symbolizes the human journey from birth to death. Several symbols often mean the same thing; writers frequently use them in sets. In "Bartleby the Scrivener," for instance, Herman Melville uses windows that look upon walls, a folding screen, and a prison to symbolize Bartleby's alienated condition, that is, his mental separation from those around him. Determining whether each symbol is private or conventional can provide clues to its meaning.

Sometimes a symbol changes meaning during the course of a work. A woman who regards her lover's large, strong hands as symbols of passion may, following an illness that leaves him a dangerous madman, view them as symbols of danger and brute strength. Note any changes you discover, and suggest what they signify.

A word of caution: Don't let symbol hunting become an obsession. Before you assert that something has a different and deeper meaning than its surface application, make sure the evidence in the work backs your claim.

For each symbol you discuss, state what you think it means and then support your position with appropriate textual evidence. You could argue, for example, that the Pullman car in "The Bride" symbolizes the Eastern civilization that is encroaching on the West, offering as evidence the car's "figured velvet . . . shining brass, silver, and glass" and darkly gleaming wood appointments.

 Read the following poem and answer the questions that follow:

Heritage

Margaret Abbott

> We were building there together,
> Two children playing blocks,
> And I debated whether
> To copy your cautious scheme
> That would withstand the knocks
> Of a careless hand or try
> My own impracticable plan
> Of block on block until a high
> Column, random and unsure, would stand
> Memento to my dream.
> I looked at you and planned

My tower. Each block fanned
My zeal. The shaft rose higher
And higher, like a spire
To my joy. I knew it could not last at all,
And yet—yet, when I saw it fall,
Some nameless hope came tumbling, too.
I crept, forlornly, close to you
And laid a finger on your solid square
And wished my heart would learn to care
For safety. Then, within that selfsame hour,
My traitor hands began another tower.

1. What does the "high / Column, random and unsure" symbolize? The "solid square"?
2. What is the significance of the final statement? ◀

Irony

Irony Factors   Irony features some discrepancy, some difference between appearance and reality, expectation and outcome. Sometimes a character says one thing but means something else. The critic who, tongue in cheek, says that a clumsy dancer is "poetry in motion" speaks ironically.

Irony also results when the reader or a character recognizes something as important, but another character does not. In "The Bride" this situation occurs when Potter, not knowing that Scratchy is on a rampage, flees the station agent, who tries to let him know. A character's behavior sometimes offers ironic contrasts, too. There's high irony in the contrast between Potter's unflinching face-off with Scratchy and his fear of telling the townsfolk about his marriage.

At times the ending of a work doesn't square with what the reader expects: the confrontation between Potter and Scratchy ends not in a fusillade of bullets but a flurry of words. To add to the irony, Potter wins because he is armed with a new and unfamiliar weapon—his wife. The emotional impact of an ironic ending depends upon the circumstances of plot and character. As Scratchy walks off, we're likely to view matters with amusement. In other cases, we might register joy, horror, gloom, or almost anything else.

Writing About Irony   Start by answering these questions:

Where does irony occur?

What does it accomplish?

What could my thesis be, and how could I support it?

In probing for irony, check for statements that say one thing and mean something else, situations in which one character knows something that another doesn't, and contrasts between the ways characters should and do behave. Review the plot to see whether the outcome matches the expectations.

To prove that irony is intended, examine the context in which the words are spoken or the events occur. Also, tell the reader what the irony accomplishes. In "The Bride," it is ironic that someone as wild as Scratchy Wilson would be awed by, and retreat from, Potter's wife; yet this irony is central to the idea that the Old West, despite its violence, was no match for the civilizing forces of the East.

 Discuss the irony in this poem:

Yet Do I Marvel

Countee Cullen

> I doubt not God is good, well-meaning, kind,
> And did He stoop to quibble could tell why
> The little buried mole continues blind,
> Why flesh that mirrors Him must some day die,
> Make plain the reason tortured Tantalus[1]
> Is baited by the fickle fruit, declare
> If merely brute caprice dooms Sisyphus[2]
> To struggle up a never-ending stair.
> Inscrutable His ways are, and immune
> To catechism by a mind too strewn
> With petty cares to slightly understand
> What awful brain compels His awful hand.
> Yet do I marvel at this curious thing:
> To make a poet black, and bid him sing!

Theme

Theme Factors   The theme of a literary work is its controlling idea, some observation or insight about life or the conditions and terms of living, such as the prevalence of evil, the foolishness of pride, or the healing power of love. Many literary works suggest several themes: sometimes one primary motif and several related ones, sometimes a number of unrelated motifs. Theme is central to a work of literature; frequently all of the other elements help develop and support it.

On occasion, the writer or a character states the theme directly. Mrs. Alving, the main character in Henrik Ibsen's play *Ghosts*, notes that the dead past plays a powerful and evil role in shaping human lives:

> . . . I am half inclined to think that we are all ghosts, Mr. Manders. It is not only what we have inherited from our fathers and mothers that exists again in us, but all sorts of old dead ideas and all kinds of old dead beliefs and things of that kind. They are not actually alive in us; but there they are dormant, all the same, and we can never be rid of them.

Ordinarily, though, the theme remains unstated and must be deduced by examining the other elements of the literary work.

---

[1]In Greek mythology, a king confined to hell who is teased by water and fruit trees forever beyond his reach.
[2]In Greek mythology, a king confined to hell who must continually roll a heavy rock up a hill and then see it roll back down.

Writing About Theme   Before you begin writing, ask and answer these questions:

What are the themes of this work? Which of these should I write about?
  Are they stated or unstated?

If stated, what elements support them?

If unstated, what elements create them?

What, if any, thematic weaknesses are present?

Check the comments of the characters and the narrator to see whether they state the themes directly. If they don't, assess the interaction of characters, events, settings, symbols, and other elements to determine them.

Let's see how the elements of Nathaniel Hawthorne's short story "Young Goodman Brown" work together to yield the primary theme. The story has four characters—Goodman Brown; his wife, Faith; Deacon Gookin; and Goody Cloyse—whose names symbolically suggest that they are completely good. Another symbol, Faith's pink hair ribbon, at first suggests innocence and later its loss. The story relates Brown's nighttime journey into a forest at the edge of a Puritan village and subsequent attendance at a baptismal ceremony for new converts to the Devil. He proceeds into the forest, suggestive of mystery and lawlessness, during a dark night, suggestive of evil, where he meets his guide, the Devil in the guise of his grandfather. As he proceeds, Brown vacillates between reluctance to join the Devil's party and fascination with it. Innocent and ignorant, he is horrified when he finds that the deacon and Goody Cloyse seem to be in league with the Devil. Brown tries to preserve his pure image of his wife, Faith, but her pink ribbon falls out of a tumultuous sky seemingly filled with demons, and Brown sees her at the baptismal ceremony. He shrieks out to her to "resist the wicked one" and is suddenly alone in the woods, not knowing whether she obeyed. The end of the story finds Brown back in his village, unable to view his wife and neighbors as anything but totally evil.

In light of these happenings, it's probably safe to say that the primary theme of the story is somewhat as follows:

> Human beings are a mixture of good and evil, but some individuals can't accept this fact. Once they realize that "good" people are susceptible to sin, they decide that everyone is evil, and they become embittered for life.

Point out any thematic weakness that you find. Including a completely innocent major character in a story written to show that people are mixtures of good and evil would contradict the writer's intention.

A paper on theme is basically an argument, first presenting your interpretation and then supporting it with textual evidence. You might argue that the primary theme of "The Bride" is the demise of the Old West under the civilizing influence of the East. You could cite the luxurious Pullman car in contrast to the drab town, Potter's uncomfortable submission to the waiter and porter, and Scratchy Wilson's retreat at the story's end. In addition, you could suggest a related theme: People out of their element often founder—sometimes even appear ridiculous. As support, you might point to Potter's behavior on the train, the drummer's subdued attitude when Scratchy's arrival is imminent, and Scratchy's reaction when told about Potter's wife.

EXERCISE   *State the controlling idea of this poem by Emily Dickinson:*

'Twas like a Maelstrom, with a notch,
That nearer, every Day,
Kept narrowing its boiling Wheel
Until the Agony

Toyed coolly with the final inch
Of your delirious Hem—
And you dropt, lost,
When something broke—
And let you from a Dream—

As if a Goblin with a Gauge—
Kept measuring the Hours—
Until you felt your Second
Weigh, helpless, in his Paws—

And not a Sinew—stirred—could help,
And sense was setting numb—
When God—remembered—and the Fiend
Let go, then, Overcome—

As if your Sentence stood—pronounced—
And you were frozen led
From Dungeon's luxury of Doubt
To Gibbets, and the Dead—

And when the Film had stitched your eyes
A Creature gasped "Reprieve"!
Which Anguish was the utterest—then—
To perish, or to live?

Ethical Issues

When you write about literature, you'll need to be aware of certain ethical considerations. Imagine someone reading only part of a short story and then writing a scathing analysis that suggests he has read the entire work. Imagine a thematic analysis of a novel that deliberately ignores large sections of the text in order to develop a twisted interpretation about the evils of capitalism. Imagine citing atypical quotations from the heroine of a play that deliberately create a distorted impression of her character. To help fulfill your ethical responsibility, ask and answer the following questions.

- Have I read the entire work carefully?
- Is my interpretation supported by the preponderance of textual evidence? Does it avoid deliberate distortion? A student who emphasizes a story's passing description of the pleasant feelings that accompany cocaine use while downplaying the drug's progressive effects that destroy a character could send a dangerous message.

- Have I avoided using quotations that are atypical or taken out of context?
- Is my interpretation fair to the text and the author rather than distorting events to promote an agenda?

Writing a Paper on Literature

The Writing Procedure

Focusing, gathering information, organizing, writing, revising, and editing—the same procedure leads to success in a literature paper as in any other type.

First, make sure you *understand the assignment.* Let's assume you have been asked to do the following:

> Write a 750-word essay that analyzes one of the elements in Stephen Crane's "The Bride Comes to Yellow Sky." Take into account all the pertinent factors of whatever element you choose.

For this assignment you could focus on plot, point of view, character, setting, symbols, irony, or theme.

Next, *decide on a suitable topic.* For papers on literature, your best approach is to reread the work carefully and then reflect on it. As you do this for the assignment on "The Bride," you rule out a paper centering on plot, setting, irony, point of view, or theme. Because your class has discussed the first three so thoroughly, you doubt you can offer anything more. The matter of the narrator stumps you; you can understand why Crane uses a third-person narrator who airs Potter's thoughts, but you can't see what's accomplished by the brief looks into other characters' minds. Regarding theme, you doubt you can do justice to the topic in 750 words. As you mentally mine character and symbolism for possible topics, your thoughts turn to the many gunfighters you've watched in the movies and read about in western fiction. Because gunfighters have always fascinated you and Scratchy Wilson seems an intriguing example of the breed, you decide to analyze his character.

To complete the next stage, *gathering information,* reread the story again and as you do, list all pertinent information about Scratchy that might help develop a character analysis. Your efforts might yield these results:

1. Scratchy "a wonder with a gun."
2. "about the last one of the old gang that used to hang out along the river here."
3. "He's a terror when he's drunk," the opposite otherwise.
4. Potter "goes out and fights Scratchy when he gets on one of these tears."
5. Has shot Scratchy once, in the leg.
6. Does nothing to stop "tears" from happening.
7. On street, Scratchy "in a rage begot of whisky." Neck works angrily.

8. Utters "Cries of ferocious challenge."
9. Moves with "the creeping movement of the midnight cat."
10. Guns move "with an electric swiftness."
11. Clothes—maroon shirt, gilded red-topped boots—not adult western garb.
12. Doesn't shoot dog.
13. Doesn't try breaking down doors.
14. Warns Potter not to go for gun rather than shooting him.
15. Says he'll hit Potter with gun, not shoot him, if Potter doesn't "mind what I tell you."
16. Only sneers when Potter calls him "damn fool," and when Potter says, "If you're goin' to shoot me up, you better begin now; you'll never get a chance like this again."
17. Backs down and walks away when confronted with Potter's marriage.

List in hand, you are now ready to *organize your information*. As you examine your items and answer the questions about character on page 284, you start to realize that Scratchy is not merely a one-dimensional gunslinging menace. To reflect your discovery, you prepare a formal topic outline.

I. I. Bartender's assessment
   A. Evidence that Scratchy is a menace
      1. A wonder with a gun
      2. Former outlaw gang member
      3. A terror when drunk
   B. Contradictory evidence
      1. Mild when sober
      2. Only one actual shootout with Potter
II. Scratchy's behavior
   A. Evidence that Scratchy is a menace
      1. Rage
      2. Wary movements
      3. Skillful handling of guns
   B. Contradictory evidence
      1. Mode of dress
      2. Failure to shoot dog
      3. Failure to try breaking down doors
      4. Behavior during confrontation
      5. Final retreat

The next stage, *developing a thesis statement,* presents few difficulties. After examining the outline and thinking about its contents, you draft the following sentence:

A close look at Scratchy Wilson shows that he has much more depth than his pulp fiction counterparts.

Drawing on your notes and following your outline, you now *write a first draft* of your essay, and then follow up with the necessary revising and editing. In addition, you review the story and verify your interpretation.

As you *prepare your final draft,* follow these guidelines.

Handling Quotations   Like aspirin, quotations should be used when necessary, but not to excess. Cite brief, relevant passages to support key ideas, but fight the urge to quote huge blocks of material. Place short quotations, fewer than five lines, within quotation marks and run them into the text. For longer passages, omit the quotation marks and indent the material ten spaces from the left-hand margin. When quoting poetry, use a slash mark (/) to show the shift from one line to the other in the original: "A honey tongue, a heart of gall, / Is fancy's spring, but sorrow's fall." Pages 402–404 provide added information on handling quotations.

Documentation   Document ideas and quotations from outside sources by following the guidelines on pages 396–401.

If your instructor wants you to document quotations from the work you're writing about, include the information within parentheses following the quotations. For fiction, cite the page number on which the quotation appeared: (83). For poetry, cite the word "line" or "lines" and the appropriate numbers: (lines 23–24). For plays, cite act, scene, and line numbers, separated by periods: (1.3.18–19). When discussing a work of fiction not in your textbook, identify the book you used as your source. Your instructor can then easily check your information. In short papers like the following student essay, internal documentation is often omitted.

Tense   Write your essay in the present rather than the past tense. Say "In *The Sound and the Fury,* William Faulkner uses four narrators, each of whom provides a different perspective on the events that take place," not ". . . William Faulkner used four narrators, each of whom provided a different perspective on the events that took place."

◖ SAMPLE STUDENT ESSAY ON LITERATURE

Scratchy Wilson: No Cardboard Character

Wendell Stone

Stephen Crane's "The Bride Comes to Yellow Sky" is artful on several counts. For one thing, the story is rich in irony. It makes use of an elaborate set of symbols to get its point across. It is filled with vivid language, and in Jack Potter and Scratchy Wilson it offers its readers two very unusual characters. Potter's actions and thoughts clearly show that he is a complex person. In fact, his complexity is so conspicuous that it becomes easy to regard Scratchy as nothing more than a one-dimensional badman. But this judgment is mistaken. A close look at Scratchy shows that he, like Potter, has much more depth than his pulp fiction counterparts.

Nothing in what the bartender says about Scratchy hints that there is anything unusual about the old outlaw. We learn that Scratchy is "a wonder with a gun," that he is "about the last one of the old gang that used to hang out along the river here," and that "He's a terror when he's drunk" but mild-mannered and pleasant at other times. One thing may strike the careful reader as a little odd, though. Although Potter "goes out and fights Scratchy when he gets on one of these tears," he has wounded Scratchy just once, and then only in the leg. Apparently, Potter has been able to talk the supposed terror out of a shootout each of the other times. Nor has Potter apparently tried doing anything to stop Scratchy's "tears."

As he steps onto the main street of Yellow Sky, Scratchy seems every bit as menacing as the bartender has described him. His face flames "in a rage begot of whisky," the cords in his neck throb and bulge with anger, and he hurls "cries of ferocious challenge" at the barricaded buildings. Scratchy is clearly no stranger to either weapons or shootouts. He walks with "the creeping movement of the midnight cat," moves his revolvers with "an electric swiftness," and keeps constantly on the alert for an ambush.

Nevertheless, Scratchy comes across as less than totally menacing. For one thing, his maroon shirt and gilded, red-topped boots make him look not like a westerner but like some child's notion of one. When he sees the dog, he deliberately shoots to frighten rather than to kill it. And in spite of all his bluster, he makes no real attempt to break down any doors and get at the people hiding behind them. Scratchy's clothing shows that eastern ways have touched even this "child of the earlier plains." But one could easily argue that eastern gentleness has had some slight softening influence on him, too. Be that as it may, it seems evident that Scratchy, perhaps without quite realizing it himself, is mainly play-acting when he goes on his rampages and that Potter knows this.

During the whole final confrontation, Scratchy seems more of an actor than a gunman wanting revenge against his "ancient antagonist." Instead of shooting when Potter makes a slight movement, Scratchy warns him not to go for a gun and says that he intends to take his time settling accounts, to "loaf along with no interferin.'" Significantly, he threatens to hit Potter with a gun, not shoot him, if the marshal does not "mind what I tell you."

Even when Potter, recovered from his brief fright, calls Scratchy a "damn fool" and says "If you're goin' to shoot me up, you better begin now: you'll never get a chance like this again," Scratchy does nothing except sneer. This confrontation, like all but one of the others, ends with no shots fired. But one thing is different. Potter's marriage has forced Scratchy to realize that something unstoppable is changing the Old West forever. When he drops his revolver to his side, stands silent for a while, and then says, "I s'pose it's all off now," we sense that he means not just this episode but any future clashes as well.

Scratchy is not a cardboard creation. His behavior is by no means as easily explainable as it at first seems, and he is capable of some degree of insight. Nonetheless, Scratchy remains very much a creature of the past, something that time has passed by. As he leaves, his feet make "funnel-shaped tracks," reminiscent of hourglasses, in the sand. Soon these tracks, along with Scratchy and his way of life, will disappear.

Including the Views of Others

Obviously you are not the first one to write about an established piece of literature. To help deepen your understanding, your instructor may ask you to draw upon various sources that analyze the work you are discussing.

As you read these secondary sources, jot down any insights you find helpful. Be sure to record the name of the author and the source so that you can document appropriately and therefore avoid plagiarism. (For an explanation of plagiarism and when you need to document a source, see "Avoiding Plagiarism" in Chapter 22.) Keep track of where you disagree or have a different insight. Some students keep a reading journal in which they record useful quotes or information about both the piece of literature and the secondary source.

When you write the paper, you can synthesize (see pages 82–83) the views of the critics you've read and offer them as additional support for your view. Alternatively, you might summarize the conclusions, or perhaps the conflicting views, of critics and then offer your own observations along with appropriate support. Think of writing in response to others' views as entering a conversation with friends about a good book; they have their opinions, but your insights will add something to the discussion.

EXERCISE *Using the guidelines offered in this chapter, write a short essay comparing and contrasting the two writers' assessments of the women in the following poems. (You might find it helpful to review pages 129–136 on comparison.) Limit your focus and back any general statements you make with appropriate support from the poems.*

There Is a Garden in Her Face

Thomas Campion (1617)

There is a garden in her face,
Where roses and white lilies grow;
A heavenly paradise is that place,
Wherein all pleasant fruits do flow.
There cherries grow which none may buy
Till "Cherry ripe" themselves do cry.

Those cherries fairly do inclose
Of orient pearl a double row,
Which when her lovely laughter shows,
They look like rosebuds filled with snow;
Yet them nor peer nor prince can buy,
Till "Cherry ripe" themselves do cry.

Her eyes like angels watch them still;
Her brows like bended bows do stand.
Threat'ning with piercing frowns to kill
All that attempt with eye or hand
Those sacred cherries to come nigh,
Till "Cherry ripe" themselves do cry.

Sonnet 130

William Shakespeare (1609)

My mistress' eyes are nothing like the sun;
Coral is far more red than her lips red;
If snow be white, why then her breasts are dun;
If hairs be wires, black wires grow on her head.
I have seen roses damask'd, red and white,
But no such roses see I in her cheeks;
And in some perfumes there is more delight
Than in the breath that from my mistress reeks.
I love to hear her speak, yet well I know
That music hath a far more pleasing sound;
I grant I never saw a goddess go;
My mistress, when she walks, treads on the ground.
And yet, by heaven, I think my love as rare
As any she belied with false compare.

CHAPTER 20

BUSINESS LETTERS AND RÉSUMÉS

Businesspeople aren't the only ones who write business letters. You write quite a few yourself, or soon will, especially to request information, place orders, register complaints, and apply for jobs. There's nothing mysterious or difficult about business correspondence. True, it follows its own special format, but otherwise it breaks no new writing ground. As always, deciding what to say and how to say it is vital to your success.

As you turn to business writing, pay particular attention to audience. Ask yourself these questions: To whom should I write? Why that person? What is his or her position in the organization? How will this person likely receive the communication? What action can he or she take? After all, you wouldn't write the president of a large company to inquire about a recent order you haven't received.

Letter Language

Effective letter language weaves conciseness, informality, and courtesy into a three-strand finished fabric.

Conciseness Concise writing avoids word clutter and gets directly to the point, saving the reader time and enlivening the message. As you write and revise, guard against two kinds of wordiness: deadwood and gobbledygook. *Deadwood* repeats the same thing or uses excess words to deliver its message. Here are some examples of deadwood and ways of correcting them:

Deadwood	Correction
in view of the fact that, due to the fact that	because
had the effect of causing	caused
would you be kind enough to	would you please

I want to take this opportunity to thank you	thank you
in the event that	if
personally, I believe	I believe
I want to make it clear that	[simply state what you want known]

Gobbledygook uses inflated, elaborately polite expressions that make writing stiff, stuffy, and distant. Note how the corrections soften the standoffish tone:

Gobbledygook	**Correction**
enclosed please find	I am enclosing
subsequent to the purchase of your	after buying your
in accordance with the terms of your warranty	your warranty provides
reference is made herewith	I am referring to
the said lawnmower	this lawnmower

Informality   Informal language is everyday language. Friendly and relaxed, it has the air of face-to-face conversation between writer and reader. To achieve it, use simple words and sentence structures; personal pronouns like *I, me, you,* and *your* are appropriate. At the same time, though, don't go overboard and resort to slang or overly casual expressions. Saying "When you guys packed my radio, you must have goofed; when I got it, it was busted" raises questions about your seriousness.

Courtesy   In your business letters, as in your direct dealings with others, courtesy plays a key role in accomplishing your objective. Here are some guidelines to keep in mind.

First, try to adopt what is sometimes called the "you" approach. That is, focus on the reader's concerns and values while avoiding expressions of sarcasm, anger, or disappointment. Assume, for example, that a well-established landscaping company has done a poor job of seeding your lawn, and the work has to be repeated. Nothing would be gained by attacking the company's integrity and declaring "I am not going to pay you until you redo your shoddy work." Indeed, the letter could spark an angry refusal or result in an unwarranted delay. If, however, you stress how the job reflects poorly on the company's excellent reputation and note that "You will receive the final $500 payment when the lawn is reseeded consistent with your high-quality work," you are much more likely to achieve your goal.

Sarcasm and anger aren't the only forms of discourtesy. Curt demands and writing with negative implications can also be offensive to readers. Consider these examples:

Curt:	I want you to send me . . . I need a copy of . . .
Negative:	I take the position that . . .

Note how rewriting has eliminated the discourtesy.

Courteous:	Would you please send me . . .
Courteous:	I think you'll find that . . .

As you prepare your letter, try changing places with your reader. How would you react to the message? If you're pleased with what you see, courtesy should be no problem.

Parts of the Business Letter

The letter in Figure 20.1, labeled to show the parts of a business letter, is set up in the modified block format, a very common one for business correspondence.

Heading   Spell out every word except the two-letter state abbreviation used by the postal service. Begin the heading at the center of the sheet.

Inside Address   *Ms.* is an acceptable personal title for both married and single women. If you don't know the name of the person you want to reach, begin the inside address with the job title or name of the department, for example, *Vice-President for Research* or *Sales Department.* If you don't know the job title or department, start with the company name. Use abbreviations only if they are part of the company name. Begin the inside address two spaces below the heading in long letters and three to eight spaces in shorter letters. The shorter the letter, the more space should be left.

Salutation   Standard practice calls for addressing individuals by both personal title and last name: *Dear Ms. Barnes.* If the inside address begins with a job title or the name of a department, use that title or department name for the salutation, for instance, *Vice-President for Research* or *Sales Department.* If the inside address begins with the name of the company, try to determine which department would answer it and use the department name as a salutation. The letters throughout the chapter illustrate these conventions. The salutation comes two spaces below the inside address.

Recently, a more informal salutation for individuals has been gaining popularity. This salutation uses the recipient's full name without a personal title, and the letter also omits the title from the inside address. Here is an example.

Leslie Avery
Calmath Chemical Company
239 Dorman Drive
Birmingham AL 35207

Dear Leslie Avery:

Before using this new form of salutation, check with your instructor.

Body   Most letters are one page or less. Try to keep your paragraphs short—about seven lines at most. Begin the body two spaces below the salutation. If the letter contains only one brief paragraph, double-space the typing. Otherwise use single spacing with double spacing between paragraphs.

Heading ─────────────►

Inside ─────────────►
address

Salutation ─────────►

Body ─────────►

Complimentary ──────►
close

Signature ──────────►

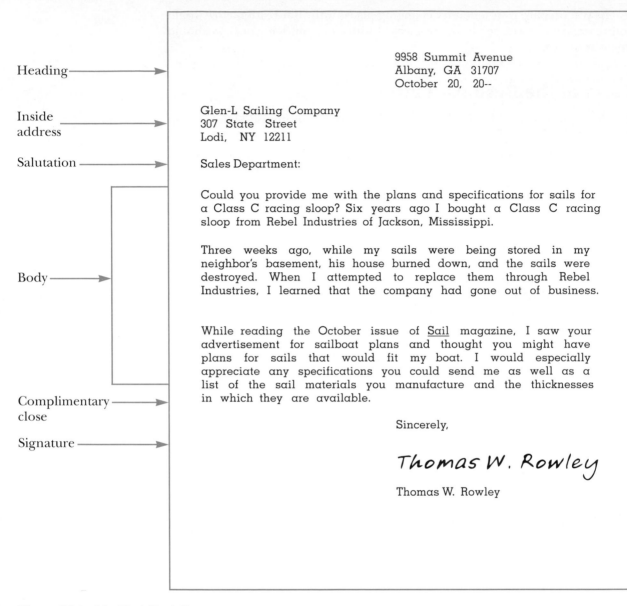

9958 Summit Avenue
Albany, GA 31707
October 20, 20--

Glen-L Sailing Company
307 State Street
Lodi, NY 12211

Sales Department:

Could you provide me with the plans and specifications for sails for a Class C racing sloop? Six years ago I bought a Class C racing sloop from Rebel Industries of Jackson, Mississippi.

Three weeks ago, while my sails were being stored in my neighbor's basement, his house burned down, and the sails were destroyed. When I attempted to replace them through Rebel Industries, I learned that the company had gone out of business.

While reading the October issue of Sail magazine, I saw your advertisement for sailboat plans and thought you might have plans for sails that would fit my boat. I would especially appreciate any specifications you could send me as well as a list of the sail materials you manufacture and the thicknesses in which they are available.

Sincerely,

Thomas W. Rowley

Thomas W. Rowley

Figure 20.1   Modified Block Form

Complimentary Close   Acceptable closings are *Sincerely*, *Sincerely yours*, and *Yours truly*. Type the complimentary close two spaces below the last line of the body and line it up with the center of the sheet.

Signature   Both typewritten and handwritten signatures are necessary. Leave four spaces between the complimentary close and the typed signature. Line the typed signature up with the center of the sheet.

Enclosure Notation   The abbreviation *Enc.,* used in several of our sample letters, indicates that a brochure, drawing, check, money order, or other document accompanies the letter. It starts at the left margin. If more than one item accompanies a letter, the notation should indicate how many there are. Important documents are often named:

Enc. 3

Enc. Money Order

Type business letters on $8\frac{1}{2} \times$ 11-inch unlined white paper and center them on the page. For full-page letters, make the side margins one inch wide; for shorter letters, make wider margins. In all cases, establish top and bottom margins of roughly equal depth.

Preparation for Mailing

To ensure that the Post Office's optical scanners can read your envelope, type the address entirely in capital letters and without punctuation. Position the address between one-half and three inches from the bottom of the envelope and at least one inch from the right edge. Figure 20.2 shows a properly typed address. Use the standard state abbreviations, which are readily available.

Proofread your letter carefully, sign it, and then fold it neatly in thirds (Figure 20.3) so that it will fit into a number 10 size business envelope.

```
DJ ASSOCIATES
230 PARK AVE S
NEW YORK NY 10003-1502


                    MS SHARON CUSTOMER
                    806 S ARLINGTON MILL DRIVE APT 1A
                    ARLINGTON VA 22204-2921
```

Figure 20.2

Figure 20.3

E-Mail Correspondence

E-mail is quick, can carry a number of attachments, allows for prompt responses, and saves paper. As a result, many students now use e-mail to communicate with friends and faculty as well as for business purposes, including job applications.

E-mail is usually more informal than conventional business correspondence but should follow good business writing practices. Because it is so easy to send and the receiver can promptly ask follow-up questions, writers may be tempted to dash off incomplete, error-riddled messages. Remember that both you and your reader are busy; try to write clearly so that follow-up exchanges are unnecessary. Remember also that your e-mail can be forwarded to other people, so make sure your messages reflect well on you.

Types of Letters

Of the many kinds of business letter, the ones you'll most likely write are inquiries, orders, complaints, and job applications. Here are guidelines and models.

Letters of Inquiry

Your letters of inquiry may be written to request information about a vacation spot, a hobby, or a project that you are working on; or you may write for data to be used in a research paper (see Figure 20.4). Here's how to proceed:

1. Identify yourself, indicate the kind of information you're after, and explain why you need it.
2. To avoid inconveniencing your reader, keep your questions to a minimum, make them clear, and word them so they can be answered briefly.
3. If you have three or more questions, set them up in a numbered list so the reader is less likely to miss answering one.
4. If you're using the information for a research paper and it's appropriate to do so, offer to supply a copy of your paper. Acknowledge the source of information when you write the paper.
5. Close by expressing appreciation for any help the reader can give.

 EXERCISE   *Write a letter of inquiry that requests one of the following kinds of information:*

1. More details about a project reported in a magazine or newspaper article
2. Performance data for something you might buy
3. Detailed information about the credit policies of a company
4. Information for a research paper
5. Your congressional representative's, mayor's or other public official's position on an issue you're concerned about
6. Membership information for a club or professional organization   ◀◣

325 Darrin Hall
Prentice College
Barstow, ME 04611
January 3, 20--

Mr. John Antwerp
Antrim Industries, Inc.
6431 Honeysuckle Avenue
Modesto, CA 95355

Dear Mr. Antwerp:

Your article in the December issue of <u>Modern Health</u>, in which you describe the features of your company's new comprehensive medical program, greatly interested me.

I am an environmental health student investigating the benefits that small companies have realized by instituting such programs. Can you help me by answering the following questions?

1. To what extent has the number of employees calling in sick increased or decreased since your program began?

2. To what extent has the program affected worker productivity and efficiency?

3. How do the costs of the program compare with those of the medical insurance you used to provide through a private insurance company?

Thank you for any information you can supply. If you wish, I will be happy to send you a copy of my finished report.

Sincerely,

René M. Hewitt

René M. Hewitt

Figure 20.4 The Pointers Applied: Sample Inquiry Letter

Order Letters

Order letters, used to order sports equipment, hobby supplies, appliances, furniture, clothing, and the like, must be brief and to the point (see Figure 20.5). Write the letter as follows:

1. Identify the merchandise by name, model or catalog number, size, weight, color, finish, or whatever else is needed.

2. To order a single item, write the letter in paragraph form. Otherwise set up a numbered list.

3. Specify how many items of each sort you want, the cost of a single item, and the total cost of the order.

4. Indicate when you wish to pay and how: by check, money order, or credit card. If you are enclosing payment, say so.

5. If you're ordering a gift to be shipped to someone at another address, be sure to include that address in the body of your letter.

420 Bayshore Drive
Durham, NC 27701
October 30, 20--

Order Department
Fitzpatrick Manufacturing Company
123 Getty Street
Philadelphia, PA 19141

Order Department:

Please ship the following merchandise as advertised in the October 20-- issue of <u>Better Homes and Gardens</u>:

1	Model 979-14/ES Luxury Kitchen Center. Unit price: $141.77	$141.77
1	Model 5109/WN Whippet five-quart Automatic Oriental Wok. Unit price: $35.67.	35.67
	TOTAL	$177.44

Please send the order at your earliest convenience to the above address. I have enclosed a check for the total amount.

Sincerely yours,

Cheryl A. Forrest

Cheryl A. Forrest

Enc. Check

Figure 20.5 The Pointers Applied: Sample Order Letter

EXERCISE *Write one of the following letters:*

1. Order one or more pieces of furniture, household appliances, garden implements, or automobile accessories.
2. Order a gift to be shipped to a friend or relative. ◧

Claim Letters

Writing a claim (complaint) letter is unpleasant but sometimes necessary. An improperly filled order, damaged or shoddy merchandise, a misunderstanding about prices—these and many other situations can result in claims. The letter points out the problem and asks that it be corrected.

When writing your letter, don't let anger make you discourteous. Remember, you're trying to settle a problem, not antagonize your reader. These guidelines will help you get a quick, favorable response:

1. If you are writing to a large company and don't know the name of the department that handles claims, address your letter to "Customer Adjustments Department" or "Claims Department." For small companies, write to the sales department. Your letter should then quickly reach someone who can help you.
2. Begin the body of the letter by identifying the problem precisely. Tell what happened and when, giving size, colors, model numbers, order number, prices—whatever the reader needs to investigate and make an adjustment.
3. If you've suffered serious inconvenience, mentioning it may speed the settlement.
4. Clearly state the adjustment you want.
5. Back your position with supporting evidence or arguments, positioned at whatever point in the letter seems most appropriate.
6. End courteously by expressing hope for a speedy settlement or offering any further information needed to reach that settlement.

Figure 20.6 shows a typical claim letter.

EXERCISE *Write a claim letter calling attention to one of the following:*

1. An improperly or incompletely filled order
2. An order that was delivered late
3. Merchandise damaged in transit because of improper packing
4. Improper billing by a credit card company or utility ◧

Memos

Although memorandums, or memos, are rarely written by students, they will almost certainly be an important part of your on-the-job writing. The most common

815 Buckaroo Lane
Dallas, TX 75226
July 10, 20--

Customer Relations   Department
Carlson Craft
P.O. Box 87
Mankato, MN 56001

Customer Relations   Department:

On June 12, I sent a check for $15.19 and an order for 150 imprinted white luncheon napkins, style 7219. These napkins were intended for my wedding reception.

The napkins came today, but instead of saying "Kathleen and Ward" they have the wrong imprint--"Kathleen and Lard." I am enclosing one of them to show you the mistake.

My wedding is less than five weeks off, and I'd like to settle the details of the reception well before then. Therefore, I'd appreciate a replacement order as soon as possible.

My fiancé and I both hope you'll take care of this matter promptly.

Yours truly,

Kathleen M. Van Meer

Kathleen M. Van Meer

Enc.

Figure 20.6   The Pointers Applied: Sample Claim Letter

kind of business correspondence, memos are used to present data, announce meetings or their results, announce or suggest policy changes, request action, ask for recommendations, explain procedures, and perform many other functions.

Because memos are so common, most word processing programs such as Word have a template. Most companies, however, send memos using e-mail which quickly and efficiently distributes the message to the intended readers. A memo consists of two parts: the heading and the body. A basic heading includes spaces for the names of the receiver and sender, the date, and the subject.

To: _____

From: _____

Date: _____

Subject: _____

To ensure that you write effective memos, follow these guidelines.

1. Make sure that your subject line states precisely what you're writing about. For example, if you're announcing a meeting, be sure to indicate its exact purpose. If you merely say "special meeting," you lessen the chance that your message will be read.

2. Consider how much background information you'll need to supply for the reader. Perhaps the subject line will provide all the background that's necessary. If this is not the case, however, include whatever is required in an introduction.

3. When you write the body of the memo, ask yourself what kinds of information the reader will need and how detailed it should be. Here are several kinds of memo and the basic information you might provide.

   Announcement of a Meeting: Date, time, and place; details concerning matters to be discussed; indication of any materials participants need to bring.

   Announcement of an Appointment: Name of appointee and position; appointee's background and qualifications; duties of job if unfamiliar to readers.

   Report of Safety Violations: Location and nature of violations; unless the information is obvious, the regulations violated; why violations are dangerous and how to correct them.

   Report of Minor Mishap: When, where, and why mishap occurred; results of mishap; how to prevent recurrence.

4. Determine the need for a conclusion. Among the most common endings are those that offer to provide more information, make recommendations, and set starting dates for procedures and policies. Don't provide a conclusion unless one is clearly needed.

Figure 20.7 illustrates a typical memo.

EXERCISE   *Write a memorandum that does the following:*

1. Announces an appointment
2. Reports a safety violation
3. Reports a minor mishap

To: All Department Supervisors
From: Gregory Conti, Production Planner
Date: July 5, 20--

Subject: Special meeting to draft flow chart
        for production of Data Star unit

Engineering has recently introduced a number of changes in the
design of the Data Star unit. As all of you know by now, these
changes have made it necessary for us to rework all of the
I/O and CPU boards in stock as well as the sensor packages and
purge systems of the last eight units. Consequently, we
have fallen behind our schedule for completing the twenty
units needed for the Russian shipment this October.

In an effort to correct this situation, I am calling a special
meeting for the purpose of drawing up a new production
flow chart. This chart will be my primary tool for producing
a new, and speedier, production schedule. The meeting will be
held in the main conference room on July 9. It will begin at
1:30 p.m. and end when the objective has been met. All department supervisors are required to attend as the outcome
will affect all departments. At the meeting, you will be
asked to submit a status report on all jobs currently listed
in your work areas.

If you need further information about this meeting, call me
at extension 356.

Figure 20.7   The Pointers Applied: Sample Memorandum

Job Application Letters

Once you've finished your academic preparation and started looking for a permanent job, you'll have to write one or more job application letters. In the
meantime, you may need to write one to apply for a summer job (see Figures
20.8 and 20.9).

Take great care to do a first-rate job. Companies scan applications carefully
and immediately discard those that fail to measure up. Grammatical or punctuation errors, misspellings, strikeovers, obvious erasures, smudge marks, beverage stains—all can earn your letter a quick trip to the reject pile. Be sure to
include enough information for the employer to evaluate your qualifications.
Here are some guidelines:

1. If you know an opening exists, begin by naming the position and how
   you heard of it—through an advertisement or from an instructor, for
   example. Using a name implies a recommendation by that person. If
   you're writing to ask whether an opening exists, specify exactly what

1407 East Elm Street
Big Rapids, MI 49307
February 24, 20-—

Ms. Helen Thompson
Medical Records Administrator
St. Luke's Hospital
411 West Cooper Street
Saginaw, MI 48602

Dear Ms. Thompson:

Ms. Leslie Goldstein, director of your nursing department, has informed me that you intend to hire an assistant administrator. I believe that my formal training in medical records administration and my hospital experience qualify me for this position. Please regard this letter as my formal application.

On May 24, 20-—, I will receive a bachelor of science degree in medical records administration from Ferris State University. This program offers a thorough background in medical terminology, health science, technical skills, and personnel management, and emphasizes health administration.

As an intern, I served three months in the medical records department of a large hospital, learning the day-to-day operations of such a department and the managerial skills necessary to hold a supervisory position. To help pay for my education, I have worked three summers as a server. This job has provided experience in meeting and dealing with people on a one-to-one basis.

While in college, I have been social chairman of the Ferris Medical Records Association and a member of the American Medical Records Association. The enclosed résumé provides further information about my experience and background.

May I arrange an interview to discuss my qualifications in greater detail? You can reach me by writing to the above address or by calling (231) 796-7791 Monday through Friday from 2 to 5 P.M.

Sincerely,

Karen K. Auernhamer

Karen K. Auernhamer

Enc.

—— Attracts interest

—— Establishes superiority

—— Requests interview

Figure 20.8   The Pointers Applied: Sample Job Application Letter [Permanent Job]

2439 South Lake Road
Fenton, MI 48438
March 27, 20—

Mr. Roger Updike
General Manager
Martin Buick-Olds,   Inc.
Fenton, MI 48439

Dear Mr. Updike:

According to the weekly bulletin of the Drake College Placement
Bureau, you have several summer openings for automotive
technicians. I believe my academic training and practical
experience have provided me with the qualifications needed to
fill one of these positions.

I am a second-year student in the automotive service program at
Drake College and expect to receive my bachelor of science
degree in May 20--.   My overall academic average is 3.08 on a
4.0 scale.

I have worked nine months as a co-op auto mechanic, and I owned
a lawn-care service for one year. The co-op position has given
me hands-on experience working with automobiles, and both positions have taught me the value of teamwork. I am hardworking,
responsible, and quick to learn, and I will do an effective job
for you.

If you desire further information concerning my background and
qualifications, the Drake Placement Bureau can supply you with
my college transcripts. Just call (231) 892-2319, extension 2607,
and request them.

I will be happy to come in for an interview at some mutually
convenient time. My number is (231) 892-9531, or you can reach
me at the above address.

Sincerely yours,

Philip Thomas Dieck

Philip Thomas Dieck

Figure 20.9   The Pointers Applied: Sample Job Application Letter [Summer Job]

position you're after. In either case, proceed by naming one or two of
your qualifications or mentioning some service you can provide.

2. Establish your superiority over other candidates. Elaborate on the
qualities mentioned at the start and present others that suit you for

the position. If you have earned the money for some or all of your college expenses or had on-the-job supervisory experience, note these facts; employers like candidates who are ambitious and possess leadership potential.

3. Don't take a "hard-sell" approach. Assertions such as "I'm just the person you're looking for" or "You'll be making a mistake if you bypass me" will likely backfire. On the other hand, don't sell yourself short with statements such as "Although I have little on-the-job experience, I think I can probably handle your job." Instead, say something like "I'm confident my academic training has prepared me to handle this job successfully." In short, don't cast yourself in a negative light; accentuate the positive without bragging.

4. Keep your letter short by referring the reader to your résumé for further information. (Summer jobs often don't require résumés.)

5. End by requesting an interview. Provide a phone number and e-mail address so the employer can contact you quickly. If you can be reached only at certain times, specify them.

Résumés

The résumé, sent with the application letter, elaborates on the qualifications mentioned in that letter and presents others that the employer is likely to find useful (see Figure 20.10). Since it, like the letter, helps to sell you as a candidate, spare no effort to ensure that it's attractive, well-organized, and easy to read. Here are some tips:

1. Capitalize the main headings to make them stand out on the page.

2. To condense information, use phrases and clauses rather than complete sentences.

3. List your most recent education and employment experience first and then work backward so the employer can quickly gauge what you've done recently.

4. Don't try to cram too much material onto a page. Ample white space is important.

5. Center the heading at the top of the page.

Typically, information is grouped under the six headings below. If you are a recent graduate with little or no full-time work experience, list education before work experience. If you've worked for a number of years, however, reverse the order.

1. *Heading.* Include your name, address, phone number, and e-mail address and Web page address if you have one. Don't date the résumé; it will then become obsolete more quickly than it otherwise would.

2. *Employment Objective.* State your immediate work goal and the direction you hope your career will take. Avoid any impression that you will soon

Karen   K.   Auernhamer

1407 East Elm Street   Home tPhone: (231) 796-7791
Big Rapids, MI 49307   E-mail: Auernh@aol.com

Employment Objective
>To work in a technical or an assistant managerial position in a medical records department, gain experience, and eventually assume an administrative position

Education
>Bachelor of science in Medical Records Administration. Ferris State University, Big Rapids, MI. May 2001

>**Academic Honors**
>Grade Point Average 3.85 (of 4.0) in Medical Records Courses

>**Selected Course Work**
>Legal Aspects of Health Care   Health Data and Analysis
>Quality Assurance   Principles of Information Systems

>**Familiar with the Following Computer Programs**
>Office 97 (all features)   3M Coding Software
>Visio   E and M Calculator

Employment Experience
>Technical Trainee (Internship Program). Entered new patient information into computer systems, processed insurance claims, assisted in managing patient charts, and assisted in other technical duties in the medical records department. Saginaw Osteopathic Hospital, Saginaw, MI 48602. June 2000 to August 2000

>Server at Zehnder's of Frankenmuth. 215 South Main Street, Frankenmuth, MI 48734. Summers of 1997, 1998, 1999

Professional Interests
>Member, American Medical Records Association, Ferris Medical Records Association (Social Chair)

References will be furnished upon request

Figure 20.10   The Pointers Applied: Sample Résumé

move on to another organization or try for the boss's job. If you can't specify your objective in a believable manner, leave it out.

3. *Education.* List pertinent facts of your college education. Note any academic honors, such as a good (above 3.0) grade-point average, a scholarship, or a certificate of commendation. If you've taken elective courses in your major or have a minor in a closely related field, so indicate.

4. *Employment Experience.* Highlight your full-time, part-time, volunteer, and summer work experience. If a job was seasonal, note this fact to avoid the impression that you were fired. Mention any promotions or raises you've received and any supervisory experience you've had. Don't mention any job duties unless they are similar to those of the job you're after.

5. *Professional Interests.* Cite membership in professional organizations. In addition, note special skills such as training in lifesaving, fluency in a foreign language, or familiarity with some specialized form of communication.

6. *References.* List references only if you are answering an advertisement that asks for them. Otherwise, indicate that they will be furnished on request. Typical references include instructors, supervisors, and prominent community leaders who know you. Never use names of relatives or name anyone as a reference without first obtaining permission. For each reference, give the person's name, including a personal title, position, business address, and telephone number. An example follows:

> Ms. Brenda Pretzer
> Director, Medical Records Department
> Saginaw Osteopathic Hospital
> 515 North Michigan Avenue
> Saginaw, MI 48602
> Telephone: (517) 776-2682

EXERCISES

1. Write a letter applying for an advertised job or one that someone has told you about.
2. Write a letter applying for a position for which there may or may not be a vacancy.
3. Prepare a résumé to accompany your letter.

Ethical Issues

Businesses depend on the ethical behavior of their employees. Employers need accurate reports, credible claims about an employee's work and abilities, and much more to make reasonable decisions. In business, unethical communication can result in a law suite. It should be no surprise then that employers can fire you for violating communication ethics. Ethics in business communication can be very complex, but there are several rules that do apply.

1. State facts and describe events honestly and in a manner appropriate to the situation. It is considered acceptable to exaggerate in advertisements but only when it is clear that the claims are exaggerations.

2. Represent your own abilities and the work that you have done fairly without exaggeration.

3. Take responsibility for your actions, even when that could have serious consequences for your career. Do not claim credit for the work of others.

4. Write clearly so that the designate readers can readily understand your text.

5. Write so that your work reflects positively on your employer and the company.

6. Write with a clear respect for all your possible readers.

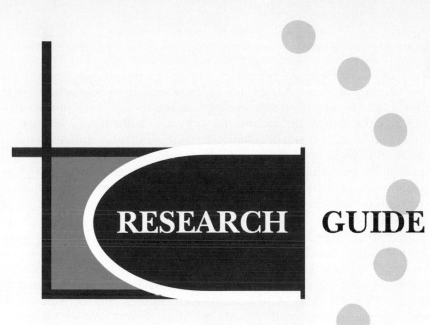

RESEARCH GUIDE

Much of your college and workplace writing will require some type of research—obtaining information from one or more sources to help achieve your writing purpose. The nature of your writing task and the demands of the situation determine the format you use and the way you document your sources.

This section of the text explores in detail the research tools and procedures you will use to develop various types of papers and reports. Sometimes you'll draw upon books, magazines, newspapers, and other printed sources, as well as electronic sources, in order to prepare a longer library research paper; at other times you'll do the same for shorter papers. Still other situations call for using primary research—the type in which you develop the information you use—to accomplish your purpose. The three chapters in this section will help you to meet these writing demands.

Chapter 21 explains how to choose a suitable library research topic and then focuses on carrying out the necessary steps to write a research paper. The chapter includes a continuing case history that leads to a finished paper complete with margin notes that will provide guidance as you prepare your own paper.

Chapter 22 shows how to prepare correct references for your paper's bibliography. It also shows the correct formats for references within the body of the paper, explains how to handle quotations, and offers guidelines for avoiding plagiarism.

Chapter 23 explains and illustrates the most common primary research strategies—interviews, questionnaires, and direct observations. In each case, student models, annotated with margin notes, embody the key features of that strategy.

Together, the material in these three chapters should provide all the information you'll need to complete writing assignments that require research.

CHAPTER 21

THE RESEARCH PAPER

Scene: A dark, sinister-looking laboratory. In the center of the stage stands a large laboratory bench crowded with an array of mysterious chemistry apparatus. Tall, cadaverous, and foreboding, Dr. Frankenslime leers as he pours the contents of a tube through a funnel and into a bubbling flask. A short, hunched-over figure looks on with interest. Suddenly the doctor spreads his arms wide and flashes a sardonic smile.

Frankenslime: Igor! At last! At last I've got it! With this fluid, I can control . . .

Research yes. But not all researchers are mad scientists, or scientists, or even mad. You might not be any of these things, but no doubt you'll be asked to prepare a *library research paper* for your composition class. This assignment calls for you to gather information from a variety of sources and then to focus, organize, and present it in a formal paper that documents your sources. The procedure will familiarize you with the mechanics of documentation, and when you finish you'll have a solid grasp of your topic and pride in your accomplishment. In addition, the experience will help you learn how to meet the research demands of other courses and your job.

For many students, the thought of writing a research paper triggers feelings of anxiety and fears of drudgery. Some feel overwhelmed by the amount of material in a college library and the need to make a lengthy search for useful information. Others doubt that they could have anything more to say about any topic they might choose: What's the point of simply rehashing what experts have already said much better? Still others are daunted by how much there might actually be to say about their topic.

But writing a research paper really isn't so formidable. You can acquaint yourself with the various library resources that will provide easy access to the information you need. Reading what others have written on a topic will give you a chance to draw your own conclusions. And as a writer you can limit your topic so that it doesn't balloon out of control.

Research writing is common both in the classroom and on the job. A history professor might require a long report on the causes of the Vietnam War. A business instructor might ask you to trace the history of a company, evaluate an advertising campaign, or review the latest styles of management. A building trades instructor might call for a short report that compares the effectiveness of several new insulating materials. At work, a marketing analyst might report on the development costs, sales potential, and competition for a product the company is considering introducing. An engineer might write a journal article that summarizes recent developments in plastic fabrication. A physical therapist might prepare a seminar paper that evaluates different exercise programs to follow arthroscopic surgery.

Whatever the writing project, let your purpose guide your research and determine the information you elect to use. When you write, the conclusions you have reached from thinking about what you have read and your purpose in communicating, not your notes, should dictate what you say.

Learning About Your Library

Before starting a library research paper, take time to familiarize yourself with your library. Many college libraries offer guided tours, and almost all of them display floor plans that show where and how the books are grouped. If your library doesn't have tours, browse through it on your own and scan its contents. As you do, note the following features:

Card Catalog: The card catalog indexes the library's books and often most of its other holdings as well. Most colleges now have computerized card catalogs. Pages 327–332 discuss computerized catalogs.

Computerized Databases: These databases, like printed periodical indexes, provide listings of articles in magazines and newspapers, and some even provide the full text of the article. Information may be on compact discs or transmitted to the library by wire from another location. Pages 334–339 discuss databases.

Computers with Internet Access: These computers connect users to a worldwide network of organizations and individuals, providing access to an almost endless variety of information. Pages 339–346 discuss the Internet.

Stacks: These are the bookshelves that hold books and bound periodicals (magazines and newspapers). Stacks are either open or closed. Open stacks allow you to go directly to the books you want, take them off the shelf, and check them out. Closed stacks do not allow you direct access to shelved material. Instead, a staff member brings you what you want.

Periodical Area: Here you'll find current and recent issues of magazines and newspapers. If your topic calls for articles that have appeared within the last few months, you're likely to find them in this area.

Microfilm and Microfiche Files: Microfilm is a filmstrip bearing a series of photographically reduced printed pages. Microfiche is a small card with a set of photographically reduced pages mounted on it. Often, most of a library's magazine and newspaper collection is on film. Ask a librarian how to work the viewing machines. Once you can run them, you'll have access to many library resources.

Circulation Desk: Here's where you check materials in and out, renew books you want to keep longer, and pay overdue fines. If you can't find something you want, the desk clerk will tell you whether it's missing, on reserve, or checked out. If it's out, fill out a hold card, and the library will notify you when it is available.

Reserve Area: This area contains books that instructors have had removed from general circulation so students can use them for particular courses. Ordinarily, you can keep these books for only a few hours or overnight.

Reference Area: This area houses the library's collection of encyclopedias, periodical indexes, almanacs, handbooks, dictionaries, and other research tools that you'll use as you investigate your topic. You'll also find one or more reference guides—Eugene P. Sheehy's *Guide to Reference Books* (1996), for example—that direct you to useful reference tools. To ensure that these books are always available, they must be used in the library. Someone is usually on duty to answer questions.

Choosing a Topic

Instructors take different approaches to assigning library research papers. Some want explanatory papers, other want papers that address a two-sided question, and still others allow students a free choice. An explanatory paper takes no position but provides information that gives the reader a better grasp of the topic. For example, it may explain the key advantages of solar heating, thereby clearing up popular misconceptions. An argument paper, on the other hand, attempts to sway the reader toward one point of view—for instance, that solar heat is commercially feasible. Some instructors specify not only the type of paper but also the topic. Others restrict students to a general subject area, ask them to pick topics from lists, or give them free choice. If you have little to say in the selection, take a positive view: At least you won't have to wrestle with finding a topic.

Whatever the circumstances, it's a good idea to follow a pacing schedule that establishes completion dates for the various stages of your paper. Such a timetable encourages you to plan your work, clarifies both your progress and the work remaining, and provides an overview of the project. You can use the following sample schedule as a guide, modifying the stages or adding other ones as necessary.

Sample Schedule for a Library Research Paper

Activity	Targeted Completion Date		
Topic Selection		_____	
Working Bibliography		_____	
Research Question and Tentative Thesis		_____	
Note Taking		_____	
Working Outline		_____	
First Draft		_____	
Revised Drafts	_____	_____	_____
Date Due:		_____	

Topics to Avoid

If you have free rein to pick your topic, how should you proceed? To begin, rule out certain types of topic.

- Those based entirely on personal experience or opinion such as "The Thrills I Have Enjoyed Waterskiing" or "Colorado Has More [or Less] Scenic Beauty than New Mexico." Such topics can't be supported by library research. Don't hesitate, however, to include personal judgments and conclusions that emerge from your reading.

- Those fully explained in a single source. An explanation of a process, such as cardiopulmonary resuscitation, or the description of a place, such as the Gobi Desert, does not require coordination of materials from various sources. Although you may find several articles on such topics, basically they all contain the same information.

- Those that are brand new. Often it's impossible to find sufficient source material about such topics.

- Those that are overly broad. Don't try to tackle such elephant-sized topics as "The Causes of World War II" or "Recent Medical Advances." Instead, slim them down to something like "How Did Germany's Depression Contribute to the Rise of Hitler?" or "Eye Surgery with Laser Beams."

- Those that have been worked over and over, such as abortion and the legal drinking age. Why bore your reader with information and arguments that are all too familiar already?

EXERCISE *Using the advice on topics to avoid, explain why each of the following would or would not be suitable for a library research topic:*

1. Genetic counseling
2. Neoconservatism
3. The fiber optics revolution
4. How last night's riot got started
5. Building a rock garden
6. A Third World hot spot as described on the evening news
7. Reforming the financing of presidential election campaigns

Drawing on Your Interests

Let your interests guide your choice. A long-standing interest in basketball might suggest a paper on the pros and cons of expanding the number of teams in the National Basketball Association. An instructor's lecture might spark your interest in a historical event or person, an economic crisis, a scientific development, a sociological trend, a medical milestone, a political scandal, or the influences on an author. An argument with a friend might spur you to investigate latch-key children. A television documentary might arouse your curiosity about a group of primitive people. A recent article or novel might inspire you to explore the occult or some taboo.

Be practical in selecting a topic. Why not get a head start on a particular aspect of your major field by researching it now? Some management, marketing, or advertising strategy; the beginnings of current contract law; medical ethics—all of these topics, and many others, qualify. Think about your audience, the availability of information, and whether you can fit it into the guidelines for your paper.

To develop a focus for your paper, it's often helpful to brainstorm, skim encyclopedia articles and other materials, and use the branching or clustering technique. If you're exploring the topic of child abuse, preparing a clustering diagram like the one in Figure 21.1 can help you decide how to narrow your topic as well as provide a rough map of areas to research. The more you brainstorm, the richer your map will be. Brainstorming often results in a series of questions, perhaps based on the writing strategies discussed in Chapters 5–13, that will help guide your research. Often it is helpful to state your main research question, followed by a series of related questions that elaborate on it. From our cluster example, a student wishing to explore the topic of psychological abuse might develop the following set of questions:

What can be done to help victims of psychological abuse?
    What is psychological abuse?
    What long-term and short-term effects does it have on a child?
    How can a child living at home be helped?
       Are there services to help limit the abuse?
       Is family therapy an option?
          What is family therapy, and what does it do?
    What psychological help is available for an adult who experienced
       childhood abuse?
       What therapies work best?
       What do they do?
       How effective are they?

These questions make research easier. After all, the purpose of research is to answer questions. Later, as you examine source material, you will be seeking specific answers, not just randomly searching for information.

Encyclopedias are usually neither current enough nor sufficiently detailed to be major sources for a paper. They can, however, provide an overview of a topic's essential points and alert you to areas of controversy that you'll need to investigate in order to produce a thoughtful paper. You can consult both general and specialized encyclopedias, and other specialized publications are also available. If, for instance, you need material on a historical figure, you can check the *Dictionary of American Biography* for deceased American figures, the *Dictionary of National Biography* for deceased British figures, and the *McGraw-Hill Encyclopedia of World Biography.* Your librarian can suggest other useful resources. Once you've found your focus, the branching technique will allow you to expand the list of items obtained by brainstorming.

More often than not, things won't fall neatly into place as you probe for a topic and then a focus. Don't be discouraged by false starts and blind alleys. Think of yourself as an explorer who will gradually become well-versed in your chosen topic.

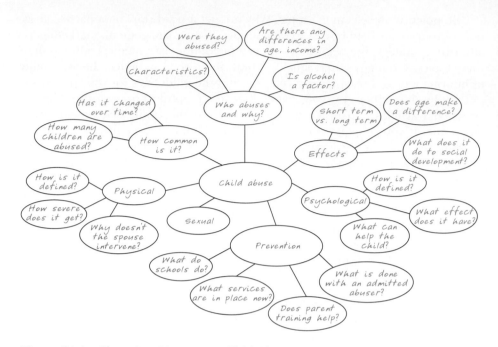

Figure 21.1   Clustering Diagram on Child Abuse

CASE HISTORY

Keith Jacque was a first-year composition student majoring in criminal justice when he wrote the library research paper at the end of this chapter. The assignment was to write about a recent technological development or an innovative solution to a social problem. Intrigued by the possible solutions to the problem of prison overcrowding, Keith decided to explore several options: building more prisons, developing early release programs for the least dangerous criminals, setting up house-arrest programs verified by electronic monitoring systems, utilizing halfway houses, converting empty military bases into prisons, and re-evaluating legal codes to determine which offenses should require incarceration. After a little thought, Keith realized that in order to develop his paper properly he would need to concentrate on only one option. Because he had recently watched a televised report on electronic monitoring and found it interesting, he decided to investigate this alternative.

To establish a focus for his paper, Keith drafted a series of questions suggested by the writing strategies discussed in Chapters 5–13. Here are the questions he developed:

Could I *narrate* a brief history of electronic monitoring?
Could I *describe* how a monitoring system works?

Could I *classify* monitoring systems?
Could I *compare* monitoring systems to anything?
Could I explain the *process* involved in monitoring?
What *causes* led to the development of monitoring?
What *effects* is monitoring likely to have?
What systems best *illustrate* the essence of monitoring?
Is there a widely accepted *definition* of electronic monitoring?
Could I *argue* for or against the expanded use of monitoring?

These writing strategies can often help you narrow a subject down to a manageable topic.

For background reading, Keith consulted two general encyclopedias: the *Encyclopedia Americana* and the *Encyclopaedia Britannica*. After preparing a list of possible entries that included "electronic monitoring," "electronic surveillance," "electronic incarceration," "home incarceration," and "house arrest," he began searching for those entries but found none of them. Next, he decided to look in more specialized publications. Not knowing how to proceed, he asked a reference librarian, who directed him to the latest editions of the *Encyclopedia of Crime and Justice* and the *McGraw-Hill Encyclopedia of Science and Technology*. These sources also contained no useful information.

At this point, drawing on what he had learned from his criminal justice instructor and the television report, Keith brainstormed in order to determine a possible focus for his paper. He came up with the following list:

1. Brief history of electronic monitoring
2. Technical problems in developing systems
3. Types of monitoring systems
4. Benefits of monitoring
5. Problems associated with monitoring

Upon reflection, Keith eliminated the second item because it would require reading highly technical material, which he might not understand. The other items were interesting to him, and he believed that they would also interest his audience—fellow students at the vocationally oriented school he attended.

Next, Keith used branching to expand his list and guide his library search, concentrating on what he knew at this stage.

Benefits of monitoring
— reduces jail population
— less expensive than prison
— effective for non-violent offenders
— several systems available

Problems associated with monitoring
— signal interference problems
— legal concerns

This case history continues on page 346.

Assembling a Working Bibliography

Once you have a topic, you're ready to see whether the library has the resources you'll need to complete the project. This step requires you to check additional reference tools and compile a working bibliography—a set of cards that list promising sources of information. This section discusses these reference tools and how to use them.

Encyclopedias

What They Are   Encyclopedias fall into two categories, general and specialized. General encyclopedias, the *Encyclopedia Americana* and the *Encyclopaedia Britannica,* for instance, offer articles on a wide range of subjects. Specialized encyclopedias cover one particular field, such as advertising or human behavior. Here's a sampling of specialized encyclopedias:

> *Encyclopedia of Advertising*
> *Encyclopedia of Education*
> *Encyclopedia of Environmental Science*
> *Encyclopedia of Human Behavior: Psychology, Psychiatry, and Mental Health*
> *Encyclopedia of Social Work*
> *Encyclopedia of World Art*
> *Harper's Encyclopedia of Science*
> *International Encyclopedia of the Social Sciences*
> *McGraw-Hill Encyclopedia of Science and Technology*

How to Use Them   Encyclopedias are sometimes a convenient launching pad for your investigation because they provide an overview of the broad field your topic fits into. For a nonspecialized topic, like the impact of commercial television during the 1950s, check the articles on television in one or more general encyclopedias. For a specialized aspect of television, say the development of the picture tube, consult one or more specialized encyclopedias, such as *Harper's Encyclopedia of Science* and the *McGraw-Hill Encyclopedia of Science and Technology,* along with the general encyclopedias. During this search you'll re-encounter material you scanned while trying to focus on a topic.

Some instructors allow you to acknowledge encyclopedias as a source; others prohibit their use; and still others allow material from specialized, but not general, encyclopedias. As always, follow your instructor's wishes.

If you will be using encyclopedia sources, jot down the following information for each note you take:

Title of article

Author(s) of article (Not always available. Sometimes only initials at the end of an article identify an author. In that case, check the list of contributors at the front of the first volume for the full name.)

Name of encyclopedia

Year of publication

For specialized encyclopedias, also include the number of volumes in the set, the encyclopedia editor, and the place of publication.

Most important, check for bibliographies at the ends of articles and copy down any reference that looks promising.

Computer-Based Encyclopedias   Today, a number of encyclopedias, both general and specialized, are available on computer compact discs or over the Internet. They are easy to search and often allow you to search for a key phrase such as "Greek architecture." The results will guide you not only to articles devoted to your topic but also to others that refer to it, even if only in a paragraph. If you use an electronic encyclopedia, write down, in addition to the other source information, the publication medium, the name of the vendor (Microsoft, for example, for a Microsoft product), and the name and date of the electronic publication.

When you've finished your exploratory reading in encyclopedias, turn to the card catalog and periodical indexes—the prime sources of information for library research papers.

Computerized Card Catalog

What It Is   A computerized card catalog lists all the books in the library, usually along with other holdings like magazines, newspapers, government documents, and electronic recordings. It may also provide additional information, such as whether a book has been checked out and, if so, the return date. Some catalogs even include the holdings of nearby libraries. Books are usually cataloged using Library of Congress call numbers, although some libraries use the Dewey decimal system.

Several catalog systems are available, all having similar terminals that consist essentially of a viewing screen and a keyboard on which to enter requests for information. Some terminals also have printers for copying material shown on the screen. To use the unit properly, read the instructions at the terminal or ask a librarian. Remember, a computer can't think. It can only match the string of letters you type to similar strings of letters in its database. If you misspell a word, you will not find any matches.

Most systems let you conduct searches by key terms (those appearing in book titles and descriptions), author, title, and subject (based on the Library of Congress's cataloging system). Most systems now let you select the kind of search by a menu or icons as in Figure 21.2. Older systems have you type in a code such as—A for "author" or KT for "key term" and then, in some cases, an equal sign and your specific search request. Searching may require you to view a series of screens having increasingly specific instructions, with the final screen providing information from a single book. Figure 21.3 illustrates a keyword search. Figure 21.4 shows the list of works discovered by the search, including the publication date; Figure 21.5 one specific work, including the call number to locate the book in your library stacks, an indication of the availability of the book, a brief description of the contents, and a list of subjects that could be used in additional searches. Most libraries have handouts and training programs that explain the different symbols and options of their specific symbols.

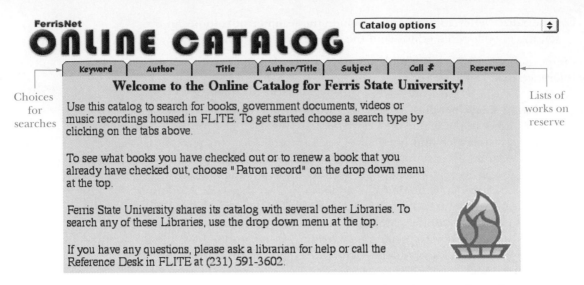

Figure 21.2   The Online Catalog's opening screen allows you to select the type of search.
Software of Innovative Interface, Inc. Screens presented by permission of Innovative Interfaces, Inc.

Figure 21.3   Keyword Search

Figure 21.4 Results Screen. Click on the blue underlined terms to display more information.

Often, a key term search (see Figure 21.5) can be the most helpful way to approach a topic. In this type of search, the computer checks the titles and descriptions of books for the key terms you enter and lists any that it finds. Different key terms will produce varying strings of articles, so it is a good idea to try different words or phrases for the same topic. For example, if you're searching for material on "electric cars," you might also try "electronic cars," "alternative fuels," and so on. Because such searches are very rapid, you can experiment with different combinations of terms to focus your search. If, for instance, you're asked to write a paper on some aspect of Japanese culture, you might investigate such combinations as "Japanese business," "Japan and education," and "Japanese feminists." Because key term searches allow you to use logical terms like *and, or, but,* and *not,* they are especially useful for narrowing a broad focus.

Obtaining the Books   Most researchers start with a key term search. Following the instructions in the above paragraph, type in one or several terms, using the appropriate logical terms. Advanced search functions will allow you to limit the dates of your search if you are only looking for more recent texts.

Successful key term and subject searches often turn up more book titles than a single screen can accommodate. In this case, using a key designated at the bottom of the screen will let you review the rest of the list. With especially long lists, you may need to narrow your focus and start a new search.

Sometimes it is useful to conduct a subject search because such a search can produce different works and often a more focused list. If you find a book under term search, the screen will suggest related subjects, as in Figure 21.5. If you found a promising title in an encyclopedia or another source, enter the title exactly using

Figure 21.5   Detailed Search Results

the "title" code. The resulting title screen will also show possible subject headings. Usually you will start a subject search based on headings suggested by a term or title search. There are also reference tools to help. If your library uses the Library of Congress system, turn to the *Library of Congress Subject Headings.* If it uses the Dewey decimal system, consult the *Sears List of Subject Headings.*

When you have found a promising title, entering its number, or a command and the number, will call up a screen with relevant information. This is illustrated in Figure 21.5. With some systems, this screen indicates whether the book is in the library or checked out and tells you how to proceed if you can't find it on the shelf. With other systems, you can get the information by entering a command. Some systems even allow you to reserve a book by entering the request into the computer.

If your terminal has a printer, use it to make a copy of each promising reference. Otherwise, record the following information on a 3 × 5-inch note card:

Author(s)
Title
Editor(s) and translator(s), as well as author(s) of any supplementary material

Total number of volumes (if more than one) and the number of the
specific volume that you want to use
City of publication
Name of publisher
Date of publication

Also, copy the book's call number in the upper left corner of the card.

Next, scan the books themselves. If your library stacks are closed, give the librarian a list of your call numbers and ask to see the books. If you can enter the stacks, locate the general areas where your books are shelved. Once you find a number range that includes one of your call numbers, follow the trail of guides on the book spines until you find your book. Spend a few extra minutes browsing in the general area of each book; you may discover useful sources that you overlooked in the card catalog.

Skim each book's table of contents and any introductory material, such as a preface or introduction, to determine its scope and approach. Also check the index and note the pages with discussions that relate to your topic. Finally, thumb through portions that look promising. If the book won't help you, throw away the note card.

If a book is missing from the shelf and the computer hasn't indicated that someone has checked it out, then it's probably on reserve. Check at the circulation desk; if the book is on reserve, go to that section and examine it there. If someone has checked the book out and the due date is some time away, perhaps a library nearby will have a copy.

How to Use It   Follow the procedure given on pages 327–331 for computerized card catalogs, making any needed modifications.

EXERCISES

1. **Select five of the following subjects. Go to the online card catalog and find one book about or by each. List each book's call number, author, title, publisher, and date of publication. Because subject headings may vary, investigate related categories, if necessary, to find an entry. To illustrate, if you find nothing under "mountaineering," check "mountain climbing" or "backpacking."**

   1. AIDS research
   2. The American family
   3. The American workplace
   4. Campaign reform
   5. Cancer research
   6. Charter schools
   7. Children and divorce
   8. Hillary Clinton
   9. Diets
   10. Electric cars
   11. Gloria Estefan
   12. Bill Gates
   13. Genetic research
   14. Global warming
   15. HMOs
   16. Home schooling
   17. The Internet and business
   18. The Internet and games
   19. Stephen King
   20. Bobby Knight
   21. Barbara Mandrell
   22. Mountaineering

23.	Colin Powell	**27.**	Tupac Shakur
24.	Robots	**28.**	Telecommunication
25.	Laura Schlessinger	**29.**	Andrew Weil
26.	School vouchers	**30.**	Oprah Winfrey

2. **Provide your instructor with a list of the books you found that appear useful for developing your paper's topic. For each book, furnish the information specified in Exercise 1, along with a brief note indicating why you think the book will be useful.** ◀

Periodical and Database Indexes

What They Are Periodical indexes catalog articles in magazines and newspapers. Indexes may be in book form, on microfilm or microfiche, or computerized. Some are offered in two or more forms. Computerized indexes, called *databases,* are available to libraries through subscription. Depending upon the particular database, information may be furnished on compact discs or transmitted via wire from a mainframe computer to the library. The term *CD-ROM* (compact disc, read-only memory) designates the first type of system, and *online* designates the second type. Databases are accessed through terminals equipped with a keyboard and a viewing screen. Some have printers that can supply lists of references and even copies of articles.

In some cases, terminals are intended for student operation; others are operated by library personnel. If you use a database, you may have to pay a service fee, but it's likely to be small.

Updated frequently, sometimes every week, periodical indexes provide access to information that hasn't yet found its way into books and perhaps never will. Their listings allow you to examine new topics, follow developments in older ones, and explore your topic in greater depth than you could by using books alone. In short, indexes help you avoid doing a superficial paper.

The *Readers' Guide to Periodical Literature,* available since 1900 in printed form, is now available online and on compact discs. The *Guide* indexes the material in more than 200 widely circulated magazines—*Harper's, Newsweek, Scientific American,* and the like. Articles are indexed by subject and author, and other categories are indexed by title and author. The *Guide* is especially useful for finding material on historical events (say the Persian Gulf War or the Iran-Contra hearings) and on social, political, and economic developments (for instance, the assisted-suicide movement and the drive to limit the terms of political officeholders). The *Guide* also includes scientific, technical, and even literary articles intended for a general audience rather than specialists, but such articles do not include all the available research.

The first pages in the printed version of the *Guide* identify the abbreviations used for the magazines indexed. Figure 21.6 shows the arrangement of the index and the "see also" cross-references that direct you to related subject headings.

The *Magazine Index,* available on microfilm or online, indexes some four hundred popular publications by author, title, and subject. Updated monthly, it covers a five-year period and includes references to articles no more than two weeks old. The viewing machines for units using microfilm resemble small television sets

Subject heading ——— **Europe and the United States**
           See also
       Europe, Western—Foreign opinion—American
Cross-references ——— United States—Foreign opinion—European
European American Bancorp
    A six-sided stalemate at European American Bank, il *Bus Week* p88-9 F 20 '84
European artificial satellites *See* Artificial satellites, European
European communications satellites *See* Communications satellites, European
European Economic Community
    Close to collision on trade, il *Bus Week* p22-3 Mr 12 '84
    Deficits may force Buy Europe policy [aerospace trade] M. Feazel. il *Aviat Week Space Technol* 120:135 + F 13 '84
    Economics in the Common Market. R. Ball. *Current* 260:34-9 F '84
Subject subheading   Europeans back computer plan [Esprit] D. Dickson. *Science* 223:1159 Mr 16 '84
    Test of wills in the Common Market. N. Gelb. il *New Leader* 67:5-7 Ja 9 '84
    —— **Conferences**
Title of article   Battling against a breakdown [agricultural policy] M. McDonald. il *Macleans* 97:32 Mr 26 '84
    The Community faces a crisis [Britain's contribution] M.
Author ——— McDonald. il *Macleans* 97:41 Ap 2 '84 ———
                                 Bracketed notation indicating topic
Notation indicating   Name of   Volume number Page number   Date
article is illustrated   magazine   of magazine   of article

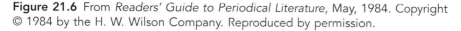

Figure 21.6 From *Readers' Guide to Periodical Literature*, May, 1984. Copyright © 1984 by the H. W. Wilson Company. Reproduced by permission.

and have motorized controls that allow swift movement through the filmstrip. Accompanying the viewer are coded reels of microfilm containing the indexed articles, together with a reader/printer that allows you to read articles and obtain printed copies. Your librarian will demonstrate how these machines work. The producers of the index also publish a list of recent articles on twenty to thirty current topics.

The *National Newspaper Index* covers five national newspapers: the *Christian Science Monitor,* the *Los Angeles Times,* the *New York Times,* the *Wall Street Journal,* and the *Washington Post.* It is available on microfilm, on compact discs, and online. Each monthly issue covers two-and-one-half years of references, and back issues can be obtained on microfiche cards. Microfilm units have the same kind of viewer as the microfilm version of the *Magazine Index.*

The *New York Times Index* comes in printed and online form. It indexes, by subject, all news articles, book reviews, commentaries, and features that have appeared in the paper and briefly summarizes each listing. The index entries refer to the "late city edition" of the paper, the one most libraries have on microfilm. If your library subscribes to a regional edition, an article may appear on another page or not at all.

NewsBank may be your best bet for a topic of regional interest. This CD-ROM database covers more than five hundred newspapers in all fifty states and Canada, indexing articles on politics, economics, business, the environment, and the entertainment world. It also offers the full text of many articles. A loose-leaf notebook version of *NewsBank,* accompanied by the articles on microfiche cards, is also available.

Database Indexes

Database indexes allow you to search quickly and effectively for articles in journals, magazines, and newspapers. Some databases such as *ERIC* (Educational Resources Information Center) and *Medline* (National Library of Medicine) give you access to citations of articles appearing in professional journals in a specific area. These articles, however, are usually aimed at a specialized audience and may be difficult to comprehend. Perhaps the best place to start a search is with a general periodical database such as *First Search* or *InfoTrac*. These databases provide access to listings of articles, arranged and subdivided by subject and key word, that have appeared in over a thousand magazines and newspapers, including the entries in various other indexes. Articles are sometimes accompanied by abstracts—brief summaries of the articles' main points—and in some cases the full articles are available on screen. *A word of caution: Don't mistake an abstract for the full article; an abstract is a 200–300-word summary of a journal article and should not be used as a source. Always take notes on the full article.* These databases are easy to operate. Your library probably has handouts that explain how to use your school's system and probably offers training sessions as well.

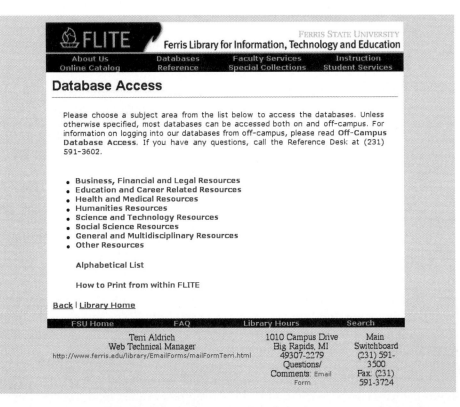

Figure 21.7   Initial Library Screen. From this list of database topics, choose the database that best matches the subject of your research.
Software by Innovative Interface, Inc.

Figure 21.8 Second Library Screen. From this list of databases, you can choose those that are most likely to have resources you can use in your research papers.

Subject Search   If a periodical index is organized around subject headings, it's a good idea to try a variety of subject terms because each will yield different articles. If your entry matches a subject heading or you are referred to a cross-reference, the computer will use a series of screens to direct you to a list of articles.

Along the way, one of the screens may list subdivisions of the request being searched, as in the following example:

Acquaintance Rape, subdivisions of

—analysis

—cases

—investigation

—laws, regulations, etc.

—media coverage

—moral and ethical aspects
—personal narratives
—prevention
—psychological aspects
—research
—social aspects
—statistics
—studying and teaching
—usage

Such a list can uncover facets of your topic that you hadn't considered and that might enrich your final paper. For example, the subdivision "personal narratives" might contain an experience that would provide a powerful opening for the paper. Similarly, articles cataloged under "statistics" could provide information on the scope of the acquaintance rape problem.

Key Word Search   Most databases now use the key term search (see page 330). Some search services, such as Research Navigator (Figure 21.9), allow you to search several databases at once. It is helpful to include as many databases as may be relevant to your project. Just follow the instructions for beginning

EBSCO's
ContentSelect

View Journal List

Exclusive to instructors and students using Pearson Education textbooks, the ContentSelect Research Database gives students instant access to thousands of academic journals and periodicals from any computer with an Internet connection!

Search by Keyword
You must select a database to search. To select multiple databases, hold down the Control (Ctrl) or Command key.

| Accounting |
| Anthropology |
| Biology |
| Business Law |

Select database

Enter Keyword   ⚠ Log in to search.   Enter search term

Search by Article number
Enter the article number in the following format: 123456

⚠ Log in to search.

Figure 21.9   Search Screen for EBSCO's Content Select.

the search and then enter your key term. If, for example, your topic is "teenage suicide," type "teenagers and suicide" onto the screen that's already showing and press the search or enter key. The computer will check titles and abstracts for the key terms and provide a list of the corresponding articles. Allow ample time to explore a number of possibilities. If you try several terms related to your topic, you will find a wider variety of articles that serve your purpose.

Search Results   The final result of any search is a list of articles like the following one, obtained through Research Navigator, for the search term "acquaintance rape."

Figure 21.10   List of Results. Click on the blue underscored "Text" to see the complete article.

Sometimes the result of a search may be formatted like the following list of magazine articles from an older version of Infotrac:

An open letter to a rape victim. Gail Elizabeth Wyatt. *Essence*, April 1992 v22 n12 p80(3). Mag. Coll.: 64B0749.
—Abstract Available—
Holdings: AS Magazine Collection

Between seduction and rape. (date rape) Kathy Dobie. *Vogue*, Dec 1991 v181 n12 p154(4). Mag. Coll.: 62G6035.
Abstract Available
Holdings: AS Magazine Collection

Rape on campus: is your daughter in danger? Kate Fillion. *Chatelaine*, August 1991 v64 n8 p33(5). Mag. Coll.: 61A5794.
Holdings: AS Magazine Collection

This list shows that all three magazines are available in the library and that two articles are abstracted in the computer. (If the database provides the full text of an article, the notation "full text available" will appear after the citation.) The coded notation "Mag. Coll." indicates that the magazine is available on microfilm. The first two numbers and the letter in the code identify the number of the microfilm cassette. The remaining numbers indicate the microfilm page on which the article starts. The exact listings of your system may be somewhat different from what's shown here; the same kind of information, however, should be available.

Besides the previously mentioned specialized indexes, many others are available that you could use to supplement your search of general indexes. Here is a brief sampling of them:

Applied Science and Technology Index, 1958–date (indexed by subject)
Education Index, 1929–date (indexed by subject and author)
Humanities Index, 1974–date (indexed by subject and author)
International Index to Periodicals, 1907–1964 (indexed by subject and author; titled *Social Sciences and Humanities Index*, 1965–1974, and then separated into the *Humanities Index* and the *Social Sciences Index*)
Social Sciences and Humanities Index, 1965–1974 (indexed by subject and author)
Social Sciences Index, 1975–date (indexed by subject and author)

All come in printed form, and most are also available on compact discs and online.

With periodical indexes, as with the card catalog, don't give up if a subject heading you're exploring yields few or no entries. Instead, explore related headings. For example, if your topic is teenage marriages, look also under "adolescence," "divorce," "teen pregnancies," and the like. Browse through the system and try a variety of options. Use this as an opportunity to gain different perspectives on your research project.

Obtaining the Articles   If the index is computerized and provides printouts, print a copy of each promising reference you find. Otherwise, copy the following information on a 3×5-inch note card.

Author(s), if identified

Title of article

Name of periodical

Volume or issue number (for professional and scholarly journals only)

Date of periodical

For newspapers, the edition name (city, metro) if more than one published, and section letter

The page range of the entire article

Obtain printouts of whatever articles you can and check the topic sentences of paragraphs for essential points. Also, scan any accompanying abstracts or summaries. If an article appears useful, check to see whether it has a bibliography, which might include additional useful sources. Keep the note cards for articles that seem promising—and any useful articles—and throw away the others.

Check the remaining references, including the ones from encyclopedia bibliographies, against the library's periodical catalog to see which periodicals are available and where they are located. Libraries frequently keep current issues in a periodical room or some other special section. Back issues of magazines are often kept on microfilm or bound into hardcover volumes and shelved. Most newspapers are on microfilm. Check the articles for which you don't have printouts in the same manner that you checked the others.

EXERCISE *Select five of the following subjects and find one magazine article about each. Use at least three periodical indexes to locate the articles. List the author, if given; the title of the article; the name of the magazine; its date; the page range; and the name of the index used. Because subject categories may vary, investigate related categories, if necessary, to find an entry. To illustrate, if you find nothing under "bioengineered foods," check "genetically modified foods" or "bioaltered foods."*

1. Animal rights
2. Bandwidth technology
3. Bioengineered foods
4. Black holes
5. Tony Blair
6. Campaign funds
7. Campus drinking
8. Cellular phones
9. Corporate mergers
10. DNA testing
11. Fiber optics
12. Alan Greenspan
13. Hedge funds
14. Laser surgery
15. NASDAQ stock exchange
16. National missile defense system
17. Rosie O'Donnell
18. Shaquille O'Neal
19. Oral history
20. Racial profiling
21. John Rocker
22. Sport utility vehicles
23. Telemarketing
24. Televangelism
25. Unemployment
26. Vegetarianism
27. Venus or Serena Williams
28. Wiretapping
29. X-ray astronomy
30. Yale University

The Internet

What It Is   The Internet is a worldwide network that links the computer systems of educational institutions, government agencies, businesses, professional organizations, and individuals. The Internet offers a number of services, including the World Wide Web, electronic mail (e-mail), newsgroups, and listservs. It allows you to check the holdings of college libraries; obtain information from online books, magazines, and newspapers; access research and government documents; gather viewpoints and information from numerous organizations and individuals; and communicate with people around the world or at the next computer station. This abundance of information and perspectives, sometimes not more than a day old, can greatly enhance your research. But remember that you'll still need to consult traditional sources in addition to using the Internet.

You can easily learn how to access the Internet and World Wide Web if you don't already know how. Your school may offer training sessions that you can attend. In addition, a number of excellent, easy-to-follow books are available. Whether enrolled in a training session or learning on your own, you'll need to obtain a log-on name, your own password, and an e-mail address if you plan to use your school's computers. If you encounter problems, personnel in the computer labs can probably answer many of your questions.

World Wide Web   During the 1990s the World Wide Web exploded into national prominence. The Web gained quick popularity because it is easy to use and offers visuals, including many sites dedicated to art, and hypertext, that is, text with color-coded words that can link you to other related sites. Web pages can include text, graphics, sound, video clips, entire computer programs, files that can be downloaded, and even animated images.

To use the World Wide Web, you need access to a computer with a Web browser such as *Netscape Navigator* or *Microsoft Internet Explorer,* and an Internet service provider such as *America Online, CompuServe,* or another provider to connect you to the Web. The format of these services is user-friendly and, in addition, most colleges have training programs. The top of the screen on any browser features a tool bar that you can click on to save locations for future reference, stop the transfer of data, or initiate a search.

Each Web page has an address called a URL (uniform resource locator), which allows the browser to locate that page. Here is a sample address:

http://www.whitehouse.gov

How to Use It   The Internet includes millions of computers and offers a stupendous amount of information. As a result, finding just the material you want can be quite difficult. To solve this problem, several indexes, or *search engines,* have been developed that can connect any search term or terms with potentially millions of sites that include the key words. The easiest way to connect with these search engines is to simply select the search command or its nearest equivalent on your browser or Internet service. This will connect you with a specific search engine but also give you a choice of several others. You can also enter the direct address (URL) in the address window. Figure 21.11 provides the addresses of several

Search Engine	Address
Google	http://www.google.com
Yahoo	http://www.yahoo.com
WebCrawler	http://webcrawler.com
Alta Vista	http://www.altavista.com
Excite	http://www.excite.com

Figure 21.11   Popular Search Engines

popular search engines. Because the various search engines often select differently and produce different results, it's a good idea to use several engines while conducting your search.

While each search engine works in a slightly different manner, they all provide similar sorts of information. When prompted by the key words you enter, the engine searches and returns lists of links to information containing these words. Such engines simplify the job of finding what you want on the Internet. Still, expect the job to require patience since search engines often provide information that isn't useful. For that reason, you'll often want to narrow your search when you begin. Single terms such as "health," "cancer," or "crime" could give you a million possible sites; instead, you may want to search for "ovarian cancer" or even "ovarian cancer cures." Most search engines also let you add key words that will further narrow what has already been found. Different words or phrases can produce different results, so try a variety of words for the same topic.

You can scroll through the list of sites the engine has found. The sites are usually accompanied by a short description that may help you decide whether they are useful. If you select any highlighted words, the search engine will transfer the data from that site and will connect you to the selected Web page.

Figures 21.12, 21.13, and 21.14 show the results of searching the subject "robotic advances." Figure 21.12 shows a search engine screen with the search subject entered, Figure 21.13 shows some of the Web sites found during the search, and Figure 21.14 shows a Web page with potentially useful information.

When viewing a Web page, you may notice menus, highlighted words, or specially marked graphics. These features, called *hyperlinks,* will usually take you to a different location: another section within the original page, a different page within the same domain, or even a new page on a computer in a different country. Following these hyperlinks allows you to explore related information from a variety of sources. As you move from Web page to Web page, browsers provide an easy way to navigate. *Netscape,* for example, has "back" and "forward" buttons that allow you to move to other sites. If you move back far enough, you will eventually get back to your main search site or even your home page. When you find an interesting site, you can print it out, or you can "bookmark" the site, allowing you easy future reference to the page. You'll need to keep track of site addresses that you use so you can include them in your bibliography.

Figure 21.12   Screen Showing Search Entry
Google, Inc. used by permission.

Figure 21.13   Search Screen Showing Results of Search *(continues)*

ROBOTIC-ASSISTED SURGICAL INTERVENTION: RECENT **ADVANCES** AND ...
... And now, recent **advances** in **robotic**-assisted surgery are revolutionizing contemporary
medicine by increasingly bringing technology into a more human role. ...
www.hospitalmanagement.net/informer/technology/tech6/ - 18k - Cached - Similar pages

Sebastian Thrun's Homepage
Recent **Advances** in **Robot** Learning. ... Recent **Advances** in **Robot** Learning contains seven
papers on **robot** learning written by leading researchers in the field. ...
www.cs.cmu.edu/~thrun/papers/franklin.book.html - 11k - Cached - Similar pages

[PDF] **Advances** in Doppler-Based Navigation of Underwater **Robotic** ...
File Format: PDF/Adobe Acrobat
Page 1. **Advances** in Doppler-Based Navigation of Underwater **Robotic** Vehicles Louis
Whitcomb * , Dana Yoerger † , Hanumant Singh ‡ Abstract New low-cost ...
robotics.me.jhu.edu/dscl/ps/ICRA99_nav_preprint.pdf - Similar pages

RAM Database - Search Page
... This is done by just adding the symbol * to the stem. Example: **robot*** will
retrieve records containing **robot, robots, robotic** and **robotics.** ...
www.eevl.ac.uk/ram/index.php - 10k - Dec 17, 2003 - Cached - Similar pages

Goooooooooogle ▶

Result Page: **1** 2 3 4 5 6 7 8 9 10   **Next**

| robotic advances | Google Search | Search within results |

Dissatisfied with your search results? Help us improve.

Google Home - Advertise with Us - Business Solutions - Services & Tools - Jobs, Press, & Help

©2003 Google

Figure 21.13   *(continued)*

Evaluating Internet Material   Because anyone can post virtually anything on
the Internet, it is crucial that you check the accuracy and validity of information
you obtain from it. A source that sounds like a research center, for example, the
Institute for Social Justice, could be a political or even a cult organization giving out one-sided or false information for its own purposes. While articles for
professional journals are reviewed by experts to ensure that the information is
reliable, no such safeguard exists on the Internet. Carelessly researched or ethically questionable material can and does appear. Here are some guidelines for
checking the validity of an Internet source:

1. Is the source identified as a reputable professional organization, such
   as the American Cancer Society, a university like MIT, or a government
   agency like the Department of Justice? Keep in mind that anyone can
   use a professional-sounding name, so be alert.
2. Is there an identified author whose credentials you can check and who
   speaks with some authority? If there is no e-mail contact listed or you
   can't find another way to verify the contents of the Web site, don't use it.
3. Is the tone of the site professional? Does it maintain an objectice stance
   and support its position with credible evidence?
4. Is the information consistent with the other material you have found?
   If the site disagrees with the standard information, does it offer adequate support for its claims?

APPLIANCE MANUFACTURER

FEATURES - NEWS - SUBSCRIBE NOW! - FREE PRODUCT INFO - PRODUCTS - HOME

Thursday, Dec 18

SEARCH AM!

Design and Engineering Solutions for the Global Appliance Industry

Inside AM Online

About AM
Advertiser Index
Article Archives
Association Listings
Books
Breaking News
NEW! Bulletin Board
Buyers Guide
Calendar of Events
Classifieds
Contact Us
Editorial Guidelines
Excellence in Design
Feature Articles
FREE Product Info
Industry Research
Let Us Know
List Rental
Media Kit
New Products
NEW! Online
Showrooms
Product Innovations
Reprints
Shipments/Forecasts
Subscribe
Home

Want to use this article? <u>CLICK HERE</u> for options!

Software Breakthrough Advances Robotic Painting
Complex breakthrough makes automation simpler.

Albert L. Harlow, Jr.

Posted on: 06/01/2000

Listing of controllable spray painting or coating variables

Whether wet or powder, variables in spray painting that influence painting results, such as color and thickness, include many things. A list of the controllable or measurable variables in an ARTomation system is given below:

- Temperature:
  a. Coating / viscosity.
  b. Atmosphere.

- Humidity.

- Speed at which nozzle passes over the part's surface.

- Angle of inference relative to a surface, or part's position relative to the gun.

- Spray gun nozzle and cap.

- Fluid or powder's delivery rate.

- Spray gun settings:
  Wet: Atomization and Fan Air.
  Powder: Conveying Air and
  Fluidizing Air

Figure 21.14   Online Article

5. Does the site explain how the data were obtained?
6. Does the site appear to misuse any data? For instance, is the sample too small? Are the claims pushed too far? Are the statistics biased?

Look at the selected Web page. The address of this Web site in Figure 21.14 is normally at the bottom of the Web page (not shown here). This article has an author, which increases the credibility of the report. However, research shows that the author is founder and vice-president of a robotics technology company, which though it demonstrates a clear expertise suggests a bias in favor of such technologies. A check of the home page shows that Appliance Manufacturer is an established organization promoting applied technologies. This group would have the professional expertise to make certain the article is credible. However, they might also have a slight bias to stress the effectiveness of such technologies rather than dwell on the negatives.

Sometimes, of course, you may want to check out pages that present the views of individuals or organizations with strong but slanted positions to gain a better understanding of their thinking, but don't consider such pages to be reliable sources. When using the Internet, "Reader beware" is a prudent attitude.

E-Mail   You probably have your own e-mail address. You may also have an address provided to you by your University. In some cases, your professor may be using a Web based instructional program that includes e-mail specific to your class. It is a good idea to jot down the e-mail addresses of other students in your class, making certain it is the one they actually are using, so that you can exchange ideas. Your professor, however, may prefer that you use the class or university e-mail.

You can also use e-mail to ask knowledgeable people about your research topic and get swift answers to your questions. Use this approach, however, as a last resort since busy people have limited time. If you must contact experts, don't bother them with questions that you could easily answer by reading background material. Reserve e-mail for specific queries that defy answer after extensive research. Most search engines have clearly identified directories that allow you to look up an e-mail address if you know a person's name. Sometimes you can find the name of an expert through the Web pages of major universities. If you do get a response to your query, evaluate it carefully; an overburdened expert may dash off a quick response while doing something else.

Newsgroups   A newsgroup is a group of people who discuss a common interest by posting their responses to a common address for everyone to read. These discussions can be informal and often are not monitored; as a result, they leave something to be desired as a source for research. Still, your university system will likely give you access to newsgroups, so ask your computer center for an instruction sheet. A word of caution: Many newsgroups are intolerant of uninformed people intruding upon their conversation. Common netiquette (the etiquette of the Internet) calls for you to read what has already been written and to think before you write.

Listservs   A listserv consists of numerous e-mail addresses that make up a mailing list of people interested in a particular topic. Once you sign up, everything posted to that listserv will be sent to your e-mail address. People who subscribe to three or four listservs may receive thirty or forty e-mail messages every day. If you post a question on a listserv, you may get dozens of responses from professionals interested in the topic, and sorting out the validity of the different responses can be difficult. As with newsgroups, netiquette calls for you to acquire an understanding of your subject and follow the discussions on the listserv for some time before you post a question or a response. Your university computer professionals can probably supply you with instructions on how to find and sign up for a listserv. You can access a subject index of listservs at http://www.liszt.com.

FAQs   Whenever you find a promising Web site, newsgroup, or listserv, you will often see a line for FAQs (frequently asked questions). It's a good idea to read the FAQs first since they may well answer your questions.

EXERCISES

1. **Using an appropriate search engine, find information on each of the following topics:**
   a. the Vietnam War
   b. current crime statistics
   c. sexual harassment
   d. current government immigration policy

2. **Enter the name of a major university into a search engine and then search. You should find that university's home page. Try to access the university's library to find what books are available on a topic of your choice. You might try schools like Harvard, Duke, or Notre Dame.**

Primary Research Findings

Besides relying on library materials, you may wish to use information obtained by conducting primary research. Chapter 23 provides detailed instructions for interviewing specialists, sending out questionnaires, and making direct observations. Before doing any type of primary research, always get your instructor's permission.

Adjusting Your Topic

After finishing your search for sources, you may need to adjust the scope and emphasis of your topic. If you start with "America's First Nuclear-Powered Submarine" but fail to turn up enough sources, you might expand your emphasis to "America's First Nuclear-Powered Warships." On the other hand, if you're working with "America's First Nuclear-Powered Warships" and find yourself floundering in an ocean of sources, you might zero in on one type of vessel. Gathering evidence helps to develop your judgment about how many sources you need to do the job.

CASE HISTORY

(Continued from page 325)

Once Keith Jacque had selected a focus for his paper on electronic monitoring, he began compiling his working bibliography. First he turned to the computerized card catalog and began his search for books and government documents by typing in the subject entry "house arrest," but he found nothing. Next he tried "electronic monitoring of prisoners." This entry yielded a cross-reference directing him to the entries "punishment—United States" and "criminal statistics—analysis." These two entries yielded a list of seven books and eleven government documents. Further examination revealed that three of the books and four of the documents appeared promising.

Keith's search for periodical articles took him to the college's *InfoTrac* database. Using this system, he found three useful subject headings: "home detention," "electronic monitoring of prisoners," and "criminal statistics—analysis." A search of these subjects turned up twenty-four journal articles, all of which were available in the library. Eight looked as if they would be useful. Three newspaper articles seemed suitable, and a search of *NewsBank* revealed another promising newspaper article.

Since his library offered access to the Internet, Keith also searched the World Wide Web. He used the Lycos and Yahoo search engines and entered complete phrases such as "electronic incarceration," "home detention," "electronic monitoring," and "incarceration, electronic." Many of the Web sites he found were not relevant to his topic, but he persisted and finally found two that seemed promising. One, from an organization concerned with public policy, discussed the indirect costs of incarceration. The other, from the Probation Division of Georgia's Department of Corrections, discussed alternatives to jail sentences.

After completing his search for library and Internet sources, Keith sought and obtained his instructor's permission to conduct primary research on his topic. Unsure of how to proceed, he talked to his advisor in the criminal justice department. She suggested that he ask the director of Michigan's electronic surveillance program for a personal interview. (See pages 410–412). He was able to obtain the interview, which provided information on the scope, operation, and success rate of the program as well as the savings it has achieved.

Satisfied that ample information was available, Keith carefully evaluated the content of the articles and of pertinent sections of the books and government documents he had located. His instructor had suggested that one good way to approach a topic is to pose a question about it and then draft a *tentative* answer, if possible. Here's how Keith proceeded:

Q. What benefits does electronic monitoring offer jurisdictions that adopt it?

A. Electronic monitoring is less expensive than incarceration, presents no serious problems, and offers a choice among several systems.

This answer provided a *tentative thesis,* an informed opinion that guided Keith's later note taking, giving him a sense of direction and indicating what information would probably prove useful and what was likely to be useless. Tentative theses can be altered slightly or changed completely if necessary. If later reading indicated that electronic monitoring can sometimes be more expensive than incarceration, Keith could alter his thesis accordingly.

This case history continues on page 354.

Taking Notes

To take notes, read your references carefully and record significant information. You might review or even expand your original research questions (page 325) so that you can read with a better sense of purpose. Notes are the raw materials for your finished product, so develop them accurately.

Evaluating Your Sources

Evaluate your sources by considering these factors.

The Expertise of the Author   Judge an author's expertise by examining his or her professional status. Say you're searching for information on some new cancer-treating drug. An article by the director of a national cancer research center would be a better bet than one by a staff writer for a magazine. Similarly, a historian's account of a national figure will probably have more balance and depth than a novelist's popularized account of that person's life. Gauging a writer's credentials is not difficult. Articles in periodicals often note authors' job titles along with their names. Some even supply thumbnail biographies. For a book, check its title page, preface, or introduction, and—if it's been left on—the dust jacket. Finally, notice whether the writer has other publications on this general subject. If your sources include two or more items by one person or if that person's name keeps cropping up as you take notes, you're probably dealing with an expert.

The Credibility of the Publication   A book's credibility hinges on its approach and its reception by reviewers. Cast a cautious eye on books that take a popular rather than a scholarly approach. For research papers, scholarly treatments provide more solid fare. Weigh what reviewers said when a book first appeared. Two publications excerpt selected reviews and provide references to others. The *Book Review Digest* (1905–date) deals mainly with nontechnical works, while the *Technical Book Review Index* (1935–date) covers technical and scientific books. Turn first to the volume for the year the book came out. If you don't find any reviews, scan the next year's index. Often books published in the fall are not reviewed until the following year.

Periodical articles can also take a scholarly or popular tack. Editors of specialized journals and of some wide-circulation magazines—for example, *Scientific American* and *The Atlantic Montly*—publish only in-depth, accurate articles. Most newsstand publications, however, popularize to some extent, and some deliberately strive for sensationalism. Popularizing may result in broad, general statements, skimpy details, and a sensational tone.

Don't automatically reject a source because the writer lacks expertise or offers a popularized treatment. Often, especially when writing about a current topic, you'll need to use material that falls short in some way. Remember, though, that you undertake research to become more knowledgeable than general readers are about a topic. When information in popular periodicals provides less than adequate coverage, candidly acknowledge the shortcomings.

Mechanics of Note Taking

Generally your most effective approach to note taking is to use note cards. Copy each note on a 4 × 6-inch card to avoid confusion with the smaller bibliography cards. Record only one note per card, even when you take several notes from a single page; you may use the notes at different points. If you can't fit a note on a single card, continue the note on a second card and paper-clip or staple the two together. Cards allow you to test different arrangements of notes and use the best one to write the paper.

Before you take a note, indicate its source at the bottom of the card. You will then have all the details necessary for documenting the information if you use it in your paper. Usually, the author's last name and the page number suffice, since your bibliography card contains all other details. To distinguish between two authors with the same last name or between two works by the same author, add initials or partial titles. *Don't forget to include the page number or numbers for each note.* Otherwise, you'll have to waste time looking them up when you cite your sources in the paper.

Summarize briefly the contents of the note at the top of the card. Later, when you construct an outline, these notations will help you sort your cards into categories and subcategories.

Responding to Notes

As you take notes, reflect on your topic and try to come up with new ideas, see connections to other notes, and anticipate future research. Think of yourself as having a conversation with your sources, and jot down your responses on the backs of your note cards. Ask yourself these questions: Does this information agree with what I have learned so far? Does it suggest any new avenues to explore? Does it leave me with questions about what's been said? Although it may take a few minutes to record your responses to a note, this type of analysis will help you write a paper that reflects *your* opinions, decisions, and evaluations, not one that smacks of notes merely patched together from different sources.

Types of Notes

A note can be a summary, paraphrase, or quotation. *Whenever you use any kind of note in your paper, give proper credit to your source. Failure to do so results in plagiarism—that is, literary theft—a serious offense even when committed unintentionally.* Pages 404–406 discuss plagiarism, and pages 381–402 explain proper documentation of sources.

Summary A summary condenses original material, presenting its core ideas *in your own words.* In order to write an effective summary, you must have a good grasp of the information, and this comprehension ensures that you are ready to use the material in your paper. You may include brief quotations if you enclose them in quotation marks. A properly written summary presents the main points in their original order without distorting their emphasis or meaning, and it omits supporting details and repetition. Summaries, then, serve up the heart of the matter.

Begin the summarizing process by asking yourself, "What points does the author make that have an important bearing on my topic and purpose?" To answer, note especially the topic sentences in the original, which often provide essential information. Copy the points in order; then condense and rewrite them in your own words. Figure 21.15 summarizes the Bertrand Russell passage that follows. We have underscored key points in the original.

Necessity for law

About a century and a half ago, there began a still-existing preference for impulsive actions over deliberate ones. Those responsible for this development believed that people are naturally good but institutions have perverted them. Actually, unfettered human nature breeds violence and brutality, and law is our only protection against anarchy. The law assumes the responsibility for revenge and settles disputes equitably. It frees people from the fear of being victimized by criminals and provides a means of catching them. Without it, civilization could not endure.

Russell, pp. 63-65

Figure 21.15 Summary

Under the influence of the romantic movement, a process began about a hundred and fifty years ago, which has continued ever since—a process of revaluing the traditional virtues, placing some higher on the scale than before, and others lower. The tendency has been to exalt impulse at the expense of deliberation. The virtues that spring from the heart have come to be thought superior to those that are based upon reflection: a generous man is preferred to a man who is punctual in paying his debts. *Per contra*, deliberate sins are thought worse than impulsive sins: a hypocrite is more harshly condemned than a murderer. The upshot is that we tend to estimate virtues, not by their capacity for providing human happiness, but by their power of inspiring a personal liking for the possessors, and we are not apt to include among the qualities for which we like people, a habit of reflecting before making an important decision.

The men who started this movement were, in the main, gentle sentimentalists who imagined that, when the fetters of custom and law were removed, the heart would be free to display its natural goodness. Human nature, they thought, is good, but institutions have corrupted it; remove the institutions and we shall all become angels. Unfortunately, the matter is not so simple as they thought. Men who follow their impulses establish governments based on pogroms, clamour for war with foreign countries, and murder pacifists and Negroes. Human nature unrestrained by law is violent and cruel. In the London Zoo, the male baboons fought over the females until all the females were torn to pieces; human beings, left to the ungoverned impulse, would be no better. In ages that have had recent experience of anarchy, this has been obvious. All the great writers of the middle ages were passionate in their admiration of the law; it was the Thirty Years' War that led Grotius to become the first advocate of international law. <u>Law, respected and enforced, is in the long run the only alternative to violent and predatory anarchy</u>; and it is just as necessary to realize this now as it was in the time of Dante and Grotius.

<u>What is the essence of law? On the one hand, it takes away from private citizens the right of revenge</u>, which it confers upon the government. If a man steals your money, you must not steal it back, or thrash him, or shoot him; you must establish the facts before a neutral tribunal, which inflicts upon him such punishment as has seemed just to the disinterested legislators. On the other hand, <u>when two men have a dispute, the law provides a machinery for settling it</u>, again on principles laid down in advance by neutrals. The advantages of law are many. It diminishes the amount of private violence, and settles disagreements in a manner more nearly just than that which would result if the disputants fought it out by private war. <u>It makes it possible for men to work without being perpetually on the watch against bandits. When a crime has been committed it provides a skilled machine for discovering the criminal.</u>

<u>Without law, the existence of civilized communities is impossible.</u> In international law, there is as yet no effective law, for lack of an international police force capable of overpowering national armies, and it is daily becoming more evident that this defect must be remedied if civilization is to survive. Within single nations there is a dangerous tendency to think that moral indignation excuses the extralegal punishment of criminals. In Germany an era of private murder (on the loftiest grounds) preceded and followed the victory of the Nazis. In fact, nine-tenths of what appeared as just indignation was sheer lust for cruelty; and this is equally true in other countries where mobs rob the law of its functions. In any civilized community, toleration of mob rule is the first step towards barbarism.

Bertrand Russell, "Respect for Law," *San Francisco Review,* Winter 1958, 63–65.

EXERCISES

1. **Select two passages that your instructor approves from an essay in the Reader and prepare summary note cards for them.**

2. **Submit summaries of three pieces of information that you plan to use in writing your paper; also submit complete versions of the original.**

Paraphrase   To paraphrase is to restate material *in your own words* without attempting to condense it. Unlike a summary, a paraphrase allows you to present an essentially complete version of the original material. A note of caution, however: Don't copy the original source nearly verbatim, changing only a word here and there. To do so is to plagiarize. To avoid this offense, follow a read, think, and write-without-looking-at-the-original strategy when you take notes so that you concentrate on recording the information in your own words. Then verify the accuracy of your notes by checking them against the original source. Here is a sample passage; Figure 21.16 is its paraphrase.

Over time, more and more of life has become subject to the controls of knowledge. However, this is never a one-way process. Scientific investigation is continually increasing our knowledge. But if we are to make good use of this knowledge, we must not only rid our minds of old, superseded beliefs and fragments of magic, but also recognize new superstitions for what they are. Both are generated by our wishes, our fears, and our feelings of helplessness in difficult situations.

Margaret Mead, "New Superstitions for Old,"
A Way of Seeing, New York: McCall, 1970. 266.

Combatting Superstitions

As time has passed, knowledge has asserted its sway over larger and larger segments of human life. But the process cuts two ways. Science is forever adding to the storehouse of human knowledge. Before we can take proper advantage of its gifts, however, we must purge our minds of old and outmoded convictions, while recognizing the true nature of modern superstitions. Both stem from our desires, our apprehensions, and our sense of impotence under difficult circumstances.

Mead, p. 266

Figure 21.16   Paraphrase

EXERCISE *Paraphrase a short passage from one of your textbooks. Submit a complete version of the passage with the assignment.*

Quotation   A quotation is a copy of original material. Since your paper should demonstrate that you've mastered your sources, don't rely extensively on quotations. You need practice in expressing yourself. As a general rule, avoid quotations except when

- the original displays special elegance or force
- you really need support from an authority
- you need to back up your interpretation of a passage from a literary work.

Paraphrasing a passage as well-written as the one below would rob it of much of its force.

Man is himself, like the universe he inhabits, like the demoniacal stirring of the ooze from which he sprang, a tale of desolation. He walks in his mind from birth to death the long resounding shores of endless disillusionment. Finally, the commitment to life departs or turns to bitterness. But out of such desolation emerges the awful freedom to choose beyond the narrowly circumscribed circle that delimits the rational being.

Loren Eiseley, *The Unexpected Universe*

Special rules govern the use of quotations. If, for clarity, you need to add an explanation or substitute a proper name for a personal pronoun, enclose the addition in *brackets*.

> The Declaration of Independence asserts that "the history of the present King of Great Britain [George III] is a history of repeated injuries and usurpations. . . ."

If your keyboard doesn't have brackets, insert them neatly with a dark pen.

Reproduce any grammatical or spelling errors in a source exactly as they appear in the original. To let your reader know that the original author, not you, made the mistake, insert the Latin word *sic* (meaning "thus") within brackets immediately after the error.

> As Wabash notes, "The threat to our enviroment [sic] comes from many directions."

If you're using the MLA documentation system and exclude an unneeded part of a quotation, show the omission with three spaced periods. Indicate omissions *within sentences* as follows:

> Writing in *The Age of Extremes*, Eric Hobsbawm observed, "What struck both the opponents of revolution and the revolutionists was that, after 1945, the primary form of revolutionary struggle . . . seemed to be guerilla warfare."

When an omission comes *at the end of a sentence* and what is actually quoted can also stand as a complete sentence, use an unspaced period followed by an ellipsis.

> In his second inaugural address, Lincoln voiced his hopes for the nation: "With malice toward none, with charity for all, with firmness in the right as God gives us to see the right, let us strive on to finish the work we are in. . . ."

Do the same when you drop *a whole sentence* within a quoted passage.

> According to newspaper columnist Grace Dunn, "Williamson's campaign will undoubtedly focus primarily on the legalized gambling issue because he hopes to capitalize on the strong opposition to it in his district. . . . Nonetheless, commentators all agree he faces an uphill fight in his attempt to unseat the incumbent."

Don't change or distort when you delete. Tampering like the following violates ethical standards:

Original passage: This film is poorly directed, and the acting uninspired; only the cameo appearance by Laurence Olivier makes it truly worth seeing.

Distorted version: This film is . . . truly worth seeing.

If the original passage you are quoting already includes ellipsis, place your own ellipsis in brackets [. . .] to distinguish your ellipsis from the one in the original. Some instructors may require you to enclose all ellipses in brackets. Follow your instructor's directions.

If you're using the APA documentation system, never enclose ellipsis within brackets.

You can summarize or paraphrase original material but retain a few words or phrases to add vividness or keep a precise shade of meaning. Simply use quotation marks but no ellipsis.

> Presidential spokesperson Paula Plimption notes that because of the "passionate advocacy" of its supporters, the push to roll back property taxes has been gaining momentum across the country.

When you copy a quotation onto a note card, put quotation marks at the beginning and the end so you won't mistake it for a paraphrase or a summary when you write the paper. If the quoted material starts on one page and ends on the next, use a slash mark (/) to show exactly where the shift comes. Then if you use only part of the quotation in your paper, you'll know whether to use one page number or two.

Don't expect to find a bonanza on every page you read. Sometimes one page will yield several notes, another page nothing. If you can't immediately gauge the value of some material, take it down. Useless information can be discarded later. Place a rubber band around your growing stack of note cards. Store them in a large envelope closed with a snap or string and labeled with your name and address. Submit them with your completed paper if your instructor requests.

CASE HISTORY

(Continued from page 347)

Working bibliography in hand, Keith Jacque prepared note cards. Most of his notes were summaries of the source material, but in a few cases he chose quotations because of the importance of the source or the significance of the material. For example, one quotation cited a former U.S. Attorney General who pointed out the disproportionate number of crimes committed by habitual violent offenders. Another quotation cited a key reason for the growing use of electronic monitoring: the high cost of prisons. Still another detailed various difficulties encountered in transmitting signals.

As Keith took notes, a plan for his paper began to emerge. The introduction would explain the reasons behind the growing use of electronic monitoring. The body would present a brief history of monitoring and then detail the different kinds of systems, examine the problems encountered when using them, and point out their effectiveness.

This case history continues on page 356.

Organizing and Outlining

Next comes your formal outline, the blueprint that shows the divisions and subdivisions of your paper, the order of your ideas, and the relationships between ideas and supporting details. An outline is a tool that benefits both writer and reader.

A formal outline follows the pattern shown below:

I.
   A.
   B.
      1.
      2.
         a.
         b.
II.

You can see the significance of an item by its numeral, letter, or number designation and by its distance from the left margin; the farther it's indented, the less important it is. All items with the same designation have roughly the same importance.

Developing Your Outline

Developing an outline is no easy job. It involves arranging material from various sources in an appropriate manner. Sorting and re-sorting your note cards is a good way to proceed. First, determine the main divisions of your paper by checking the summarized notations at the tops of your cards, and then make one stack of cards for each division. Next, review each stack carefully to determine further subdivisions and sort it into smaller stacks. Finally, use the stacks to prepare your outline.

There are two types of formal outline: *topic* and *sentence*. A topic outline presents all entries as words, short phrases, or short clauses. A sentence outline presents them as complete sentences. To emphasize the relationships among elements, items of equal importance have parallel phrasing. Although neither is *the* preferred form, a sentence outline includes more details and also your attitude toward each idea. Many students first develop a topic outline, do additional research, and then polish and expand this version into a sentence outline. While it's easy to be sloppy in a topic outline, forming a sentence outline requires you to reach the kinds of conclusions that will be the backbone of your paper. The following segments of a topic and a sentence outline for a paper on tranquilizer dependence illustrate the difference between the two:

Topic Outline

II. The tranquilizer abuse problem
   A. Reasons for the problem
      1. Overpromotion
      2. Overprescription
      3. Patient's misuse
         a. Dosage
         b. Length of usage
   B. Growth of the problem

Sentence Outline

    II. Tranquilizers are widely abused.
        A. Several factors account for the abuse of tranquilizers.
            1. Drug companies overpromote their product.
            2. Doctors often unnecessarily prescribe tranquilizers.
            3. Patients often do not follow their doctors' instructions.
                a. Some patients take more than prescribed doses.
                b. Some continue to use tranquilizers beyond the prescribed time.
        B. The problem of tranquilizer abuse appears to be growing.

Note that the items in the sentence outline are followed by periods, but those in the topic outline are not.

Keying Your Note Cards to Your Outline

When your outline is finished, key your note cards to it by writing at the top of each card the letters and numbers—such as IIA or IIIB2—for the appropriate outline category. Now arrange the cards into one stack, following the order shown in the outline. Finally, start with the top card in the stack and number all of them consecutively. If they later fall off the table or slide out of place, you can easily put them in order again. You might have a few stragglers left over when you complete this keying. Some of these may be worked into your paper as you write or revise it.

CASE HISTORY   *(Continued from page 354)*

Sorting and re-sorting was challenging and at times frustrating for Keith. Since some of his material could be arranged in different ways, he found himself experimenting, evaluating, and rearranging as he tried various options. After much thought and some trial and error, the following *initial draft* of his outline emerged:

    I. Reasons why monitoring used
       A. Serious crime problem and number of people in prisons
       B. High cost of prisons
   II. Brief history of electronic monitoring
  III. Types of monitoring systems
       A. Programmed-contact systems
       B. Continuous-contact systems
       C. Hybrid systems
  IV. Problems with these systems
       A. Practical problems
          1. Offenders' problems
          2. Transmission difficulties
       B. Legal problems
          1. Do the systems violate constitutional rights?
          2. "Net-widening" effect

V. Effectiveness of electronic monitoring
    A. Effectiveness with low-risk offenders
    B. Cost effectiveness
VI. Expanded use of monitoring likely

This version is marked by nonparallel structure and inadequate attention to some points. Despite these weaknesses, it provided an adequate blueprint for the first draft of Keith's paper.

This case history concludes on page 360.

Ethical Issues

When you present the information you've gathered from a variety of sources, you'll want to proceed in an ethically responsible way. Asking and answering the following questions will help you do just that.

- Have I carefully researched my topic so that my conclusions are well-founded? Imagine the consequences if slipshod testing by an auto company led to the erroneous conclusion that the steering mechanism on one of its models met current safety standards.

- Have I adequately acknowledged any evidence that runs counter to the conclusions I draw? A paper that stresses the advantages of charter schools but deliberately avoids mentioning their disadvantages could be a form of deception.

- Have I properly documented my sources? Using someone else's words or ideas without giving proper credit is a form of academic dishonesty (see pages 404–406).

- Have I honestly represented the authority of my sources? If you read an article touting almond extract as a cure for cancer that was written by a practicing foot doctor, it would be dishonest to suggest that the article was written by a "prominent research scientist." Refer to someone as an "expert" only when that person's credentials warrant the label.

- Could my information have an undesirable effect on readers? If so, how can I address their concerns? A report describing a new antibiotic-resistant strain of tuberculosis might alarm some readers, and therefore the writer could provide appropriate reassurances of the limited risk to most people.

Writing Your Research Paper

Some students think of a library research paper as a series of quotations, paraphrases, and summaries, one following the other throughout the paper. Not so. Without question, you use the material of others, but *you* select and organize it according to *your purpose. You* develop insights, and *you* draw conclusions about what you've read. You can best express your conclusions by setting your notes aside, stepping back to gain some perspective, and then expressing your sense of what you've learned. Many students find it helpful to write two or three pages on which they summarize what they want to say as well as whom they want to reach with their message and why. Like all forms of writing, research papers are written for some purpose and aimed at some audience.

Writing the First Draft

Your final research results will be expressed in a thesis. You've already drafted a tentative thesis (see page 347), and now you'll probably refine or revise it to accommodate any changes in your perspective on the topic. Position the thesis in the introductory part of your paper unless you're analyzing a problem or recommending a solution; then you might hold back the thesis until later in the essay. If you do hold it back, state the problem clearly at the outset. Because of the paper's length, it's a good idea to reveal your organizational plan in your introductory section.

Write the paper section by section, following the divisions of your outline. But keep in mind that you're not locked into its pattern. If you see an opportunity to develop an important idea that you omitted from your outline, try it. If you discover that it might be better to introduce an item earlier than you intended, go ahead. Just be sure to check your organization later. As you write, think of yourself as supporting the conclusions you have reached with the appropriate material on your note cards, not just as stringing these cards together. You will then incorporate the material on your note cards with your own assessments and with transitional elements that clarify your information and orient the reader. As you proceed, here again you'll use the writing strategies presented earlier in the book.

Because of this paper's length, you will probably need to connect its major sections with transitional paragraphs that pull together the material already covered and prepare the reader for what follows. Don't fret if the style bumps along or connections aren't always clear. These problems can be smoothed out when you revise. You will, of course, need to know how to document your sources properly, handle quotations, and avoid plagiarism. Chapter 22 presents guidelines on these important subjects.

On occasion you may want to include supplementary information that would interrupt the flow of thought if you placed it in the paper. When this happens, use an *explanatory note.*[1] A typical explanatory note might clarify or elaborate on a point, discuss some side issue, or define a term used in a specialized way.

When you finish writing, let this version sit for a day or two. Then revise it, just as you would with a shorter essay. Keep track of all sources so that preparing the bibliography will go smoothly.

---

[1]This is an explanatory note. Position it at the bottom of the page, spaced four lines away from the main text. If more than one note occurs on a page, double-space between them. If the note carries over to the next page, separate it from your text with a solid, full-length line. Put two spaces above the line and two spaces below it.

Preparing Your Finished Copy

Follow the revision guidelines in Chapter 4. In addition, verify that you have

- included all key information
- clearly organized your material
- not overloaded your paper with quotations
- worked in your own observations
- put in-text documentation and source information in proper form.

Prepare your final draft with a word processing program. Be sure you have access to a laser or inkjet printer that produces dark, readable copy. Double-space throughout, including indented block quotations and the list of works you used to prepare the paper.

Two systems for formatting and documenting library research papers are in common use: the Modern Language Association (MLA) system, favored by many English and humanities instructors, and the American Psychological Association (APA) system, used by many social science and psychology instructors.

MLA System for Preparing Papers

- Number each page in the upper right corner, one-half inch from the top. Precede each page number with your last name.
- Starting one inch from the top of the first page, type your full name, the instructor's name, the course designation, and the date, all flush with the left margin.
- Double-space below the date, and center the title; then double-space before starting the first paragraph.
- Leave one-inch margins on all four sides except at the top of the first page. Indent the first line of each paragraph five spaces or one-half inch.
- The MLA system does not require a title page. If your instructor wants one, however, center (1) the title of the paper about two inches below the top of the sheet, (2) your name in the middle of the sheet, and (3) the instructor's name, course designation, and date about two inches from the bottom. Use capital and lowercase letters for everything. Repeat the title, again in capital and lowercase letters, on the first text page, centered about two inches from the top.
- Begin the bibliography on a new page that follows the text of the paper, and give it the heading "Works Cited," without quotation marks. Center the heading on the page.
- List each bibliographic entry alphabetically according to the author's last name or, if no author is given, by the first significant word in the title. For a work with more than one author, alphabetize by the name that comes first. If there's more than one entry for an author, substitute

three unspaced hyphens, followed by a period and a double space, for the author's name in the second and subsequent entries.

■ Begin the first line of each entry at the left margin and indent subsequent lines five spaces.

APA System for Preparing Papers

■ The APA system requires a title page. Center (1) the title of the paper about four inches from the top and (2) your name, two spaces below the title. About three-fourths of the way from the top, provide the course designation, the name of your instructor, and the date, typed double-spaced and flush with the right margin. Two inches from the top of the page, type the words "Running Head," without quotation marks, flush with the left margin; then type a colon and a word or phrase that identifies the paper's topic. Type the running head in capital letters; type everything else in capital and lowercase letters.

■ Repeat the title of the paper on the first text page, centered about one-and-a-half inches from the top and typed in capital and lowercase letters.

■ Number every page of the text in the upper right corner, starting with the title page. Position the first two or three words of the title five spaces to the left of the page number.

■ Leave one-inch margins at the bottom and at both sides of each page. Indent the first line of each paragraph five spaces.

■ Begin the bibliography on a new page that follows the text of the paper, and give it the heading "References," without quotation marks. Center this heading on the page. Follow the alphabetizing and positioning guidelines for the MLA system except that if the listing includes more than one entry for an author, repeat the author's name.

■ Indent the first line of each entry five spaces and begin subsequent lines at the left margin.

◖ SAMPLE STUDENT RESEARCH PAPER

● ●

CASE HISTORY   *(Concluded)*

Using his outline and thesis statement as a guide, Keith prepared a first draft of his paper, following the MLA format required by his instructor. It didn't all come easily. In order to ensure an effective presentation, he checked his note cards carefully to determine which material would provide the strongest support for his conclusions. He was careful to use his own words except when he was quoting. To achieve smoothness, he tried to connect his major sections with transitions, aware that he could polish these connections when he revised the paper.

When he had completed the first draft, Keith set it aside for two days in order to distance himself from his writing. Then he returned to it and revised it carefully. Reading the paper from the perspective of a slightly skeptical critic, he looked for unsupported claims, questions that readers might have, sections that might be confusing or poorly organized, and weak transitions. Like most writers, Keith found sections that could be improved. Next, he revised his initial topic outline and followed it when drafting the sentence outline that appears on pages 361–362. Keith then prepared the final draft of the paper itself, which is on pages 363–374. Direct your attention to its noteworthy features, which include italicized notations next to the paper indicating where Keith used the writing strategies discussed earlier in the text.

Sentence Outline

Thesis statement: House arrest offers a choice of several monitoring systems, presents no insurmountable problems, proves effective in controlling low-risk offenders, and costs less than incarceration.

  I. The use of house arrest stems from the country's serious crime problem.

    A. Violent crimes are committed by a small number of repeat offenders.

    B. These crimes have led to tougher crime-control legislation.

    C. This legislation has increased the country's prison population and the cost of incarceration.

    D. As a result, many jurisdictions have adopted house-arrest programs for low-risk offenders.

  II. Electronic monitoring has a short history.

    A. The idea first appeared in the comic Spiderman.

    B. A New Mexico judge asked computer companies to develop an electronic bracelet.

    C. Monitoring was first used in 1984 to control offenders, and the concept quickly spread across the country.

  III. Electronic monitoring devices fall into three categories.

    A. A programmed-contact system calls the offender's home during curfew periods and reports absences.

      1. A computer may simply record the offender's voice.

Sentence outline: Note use of complete sentences throughout, use of periods following section and subsection markers, and the indentation arrangement.

        2. A computer may compare the voice heard over the phone to a recording of the offender's voice.

        3. The offender may wear an encoded bracelet and insert it into a special telephone transmitter.

        4. A camera may transmit photos of the offender over telephone lines.

    B. A continuous-signal system requires the offender to wear a transmitter that sends uninterrupted electronic signals.

    C. A hybrid system combines programmed-contact and continuous-signal techniques.

        1. The programmed-contact component usually includes voice- and photo-transmission units.

        2. Jurisdictions can tailor systems to their needs.

IV. Electronic systems have created practical and legal problems.

    A. Practical problems include both difficulties experienced by offenders and transmission difficulties.

        1. Encoded bracelets can cause offenders discomfort and embarrassment.

        2. Telephone lines and objects in the offender's home can interfere with signal pickup.

    B. Legal problems include possible constitutional infringements and the net-widening effect.

        1. Charging surveillance fees and limiting surveillance to the least dangerous persons may infringe on offenders' equal-protection rights.

        2. Monitoring may violate the right to privacy of others in offenders' homes.

        3. Net-widening can result in an excessive number of individuals under house arrest.

V. Electronic monitoring has proved effective with low-risk offenders.

    A. The great majority of offenders successfully complete monitoring programs.

    B. Monitoring costs less than incarceration.

VI. The advantages of house arrest should increase its use.

Jacque 1

Keith Jacque

Professor Reinking

English 250

May 4, 2001

House Arrest: An Attractive Alternative to Incarceration

Few of us would deny that crime is a serious national problem. Almost daily, newspapers and television screens offer accounts of "white-collar crimes" such as embezzlement and tax evasion and violent crimes such as aggravated assault, rape, and murder. Unlike nonviolent crimes, most violent ones are committed by chronic offenders. As former U.S. Attorney General William Barr notes, "Study after study shows that there is a tiny fraction of the population who [. . .] commit a disproportionate amount—a vast amount—of predatory violence in our society" (B3).

These violent crimes have hardened society's attitude toward criminals and brought about a demand for "get-tough" policies in dealing with all kinds of offenses. The result has been federal legislation like the Crime Control Act of 1984 and the Anti-Drug Abuse Act of 1986. The first of these makes incarceration mandatory for certain habitual offenders; the second does the same for persons convicted of specified drug offenses (United States, Prison Projections 12). The introduction of mandatory sentencing guidelines, now common on the state as well as the federal level, provides consistent punishment for similar crimes. It has led, however, to an explosion in the number of prison inmates, which by mid-1999 totaled over 1.8 million, including a 4.4 percent increase between mid-1997 and mid-1998 (Gearan A1). Between 1980 and 1995, the nation's prison population grew 242 percent ("Inmate Populations" 10). Many of these inmates are guilty of nonviolent offenses. In 1997, three-fourths of all prisoners fell into the nonviolent category (Richey 3).

1"

1/2"

1"

1"

1"

Paper is double-spaced throughout

Title reflects main thrust of paper

Opening paragraph cites *cause:* nonviolent and violent crimes

Omission within sentence, ellipsis within brackets

Effect of nonviolent and violent crimes

Causal chain

Jacque 2

It is likely that the prison population will continue to grow. The National Council on Crime and Delinquency has estimated that the total number of prisoners might reach 1.4 million by the year 2000, a jump of 24 percent over the 1995 level ("Inmate Populations" 10). The Bureau of Prisons has projected construction costs of some four billion dollars for new federal prisons scheduled to open in the 1996–2006 decade and between ten billion and fourteen billion dollars for the new state prisons required to house the anticipated increase in prisoners ("Inmate Populations" 10).

Even these figures don't tell the whole story. Director of the Federal Bureau of Prisons J. Michael Quinlan comments that over the lifetime of a prison, "construction costs are only 5–7 percent of the total expense. This means that from 15–20 times the construction costs will have to be budgeted over the life of each prison now being built" (114). Underestimating operating costs can result in unused facilities as in Florida where, in 1992, two newly constructed 900-person prisons and a 336-person death-row facility remained empty because the state lacked the money to operate them (Katel 63).

Overcrowding and the high costs of prisons have seriously undermined state spending on public services and created a number of hidden expenses. In Michigan, for example, corrections spending increased over 300 percent between 1979 and 1989, as compared to a 98 percent increase in social services spending and a 40 percent increase in education spending (Baird 122). And these figures do not include hidden costs such as welfare payments to the families of imprisoned offenders and the loss of tax revenues from prisoners removed from the job market (Lynch).

Faced with the social and educational consequences of current policy, many state legislators have recommended using prison space only for violent offenders and developing, for nonviolent ones, low-cost alternatives that provide adequate public

Statistics, forecasts of prisoner increases, costs provide interest, depth

Author's name introduces short run-in quote within quotation marks; page number follows quote

Effect of underestimating costs

Comparison of spending figures

Jacque 3

protection. At times, results have been mixed. In the early
1980s, for example, the state of Georgia attempted to relieve severe prison overcrowding by greatly expanding the use of
closely supervised probation. While significant cost savings
were realized, tremendous work overloads on the probation
staff resulted, according to the Georgia Probation Division.

House arrest—a strategy that confines nonviolent offenders
to their homes and monitors their compliance with electronic
devices—avoids the drawbacks of other approaches. It offers a
choice of several monitoring systems, presents no insurmountable problems, is effective in controlling low-risk offenders,
and costs less than incarceration.

Electronic monitoring[1] has curious roots—the comic
<u>Spiderman</u>. The idea first occurred in 1979 to New Mexico Judge
Jack Love, who observed that Kingpin, Spiderman's nemesis,
used an electronic bracelet to control his crime-fighter enemy.
Love asked computer companies to develop a similar device
(Scaglione, "Jails" 32; Sullivan 51). The first house-arrest program using electronic monitoring was implemented in 1984,
and five years later programs had been established in over a
hundred jurisdictions across more than thirty states (Peck 26;
Scaglione, "Under Arrest" 26). By 1993, the number of offenders
being electronically monitored totaled 65,650 nationwide (Carey
and McLean 1).

The U.S. Department of Justice classifies electronic monitoring systems according to their signaling characteristics (United
States, <u>Electronic Monitoring</u> 1). Types include programmed
contact, continuous signal, and hybrid systems—a combination
of the first two.

With a programmed-contact system, a computer calls an
offender's residence on a random basis during established
curfew periods and reports any unauthorized absence to

---

[1]This alternative is sometimes called electronic tethering, electronic surveillance, electronic house arrest, or electronic incarceration.

Definition of term

Thesis statement reflects
paper's content, previews
organization

Narrative relates brief history
of monitoring

Double citations show two
sources with essentially identical information, shortened titles distinguish between
separate articles by same
author

Classification of monitoring
systems

Definition of system

Explanatory note

Jacque 4

correctional authorities. Various levels of sophistication are possible depending upon how much certainty is desired. In the simplest system, the computer merely records the offender's voice. Correctional authorities then review the taped responses the next day to determine any curfew violations. A variant approach uses a prerecording of the offender's voice, which the computer compares to the voice heard during random calls. If the two do not match, the computer can immediately notify authorities of a violation. Voice systems are comparatively inexpensive as no special equipment needs to be installed in the offender's home or worn by the individual (Hofer and Meierhoefer 36–37).

Comparison of systems

A more sophisticated means of checking on offenders makes use of an encoded bracelet worn by the offender. Again, a computer calls randomly during curfew. Instead of answering in the usual manner, however, the offender responds by inserting the bracelet into a special transmitter attached to the telephone. The bracelets can be made in such a way that unauthorized attempts to remove them will damage their transmitting ability (Hofer and Meierhoefer 36–37).

Process explained

Visual verification probably offers the best assurance against curfew violation. A special camera that can transmit photographs over telephone lines is installed in the offender's home. During calls, the computer can request the monitored individual to provide a variety of poses to the camera. These photographs can then be stored in the computer for later review or compared immediately to a reference key for the individual (Hofer and Meierhoefer 37).

Comparison of systems; definition of system

Continuous-signal systems, unlike programmed-contact systems, require the offender to wear a transmitter that sends a continuous sequence of electronic signals, often several times a minute, to his or her home telephone. If a break in transmission occurs during a detention period, the monitoring

Jacque 5

computer notifies authorities. The transmitters are relatively small and generally worn on a tamper-resistant strap around the ankle. Attempts to remove the strap could cause the unit to stop sending signals or could be detected during periodic inspections. These systems provide a greater degree of supervision than programmed-contact systems, which check on offenders only intermittently (Hofer and Meierhoefer 38–39).

Comparison of systems

Hybrid systems combine programmed-contact and continuous-signal techniques in order to realize the advantages of each (United States, <u>Electronic Monitoring</u> 1). Typically, the programmed-contact component includes both voice and video units. This component can function as a backup for continuous-signal monitoring or as a supplement to it. In the first case, the computer is programmed to call for voice-video identification whenever the offender's transmitter fails to send a continuous signal. In the second case, the computer randomly calls for voice-video verification as well as receives transmitter signals (Scaglione, "Jails" 36).

Jurisdictions can develop hybrid systems tailored to their individual needs. For example, a house-arrest program for drunk drivers could employ a continuous-signal transmitter supplemented by random telephone verification. Home monitoring equipment could even include a Breathalyzer to determine and transmit to the computer the offender's blood-alcohol level during telephone verification calls (Scaglione, "Jails" 36). A variation of this type of system is used in Annapolis, Maryland, where video cameras have been installed in the homes of some convicted drunk drivers. The offenders are called periodically and required to give themselves a blood-alcohol test in front of the camera (Peck 28).

Not surprisingly, electronic monitoring has resulted in some practical problems and legal concerns. Most problems arise with those who wear encoded verification bracelets or

Jacque 6

transmitters. These offenders complain that the devices cause physical discomfort or embarrassment. Correction officials can adjust the fit of the device or suggest that offenders wear a cut-off tube sock, tennis-type wrist band, or other type of padding under the strap. Wearers, however, must find their own ways of coping with embarrassment. In studying the electronic monitoring of federal parolees, Beck, Klein-Saffran, and Wooten found that offenders could be quite innovative in explaining why they were wearing units. When questioned by strangers, "the majority told the truth, while other parolees stated that [the unit] was a heart monitor, pager, battery charger for a video camera, or a fish caller" (29).

> *Cites article with three authors; page number follows quotation*

> *Brackets enclose explanatory words inserted into quotation*

Transmitting difficulties have created other practical problems. In some areas, existing telephone lines may be inadequate or incompatible with the transmitting characteristics of certain monitoring systems. In other cases, the offender's home may cause difficulties. Ford and Schmidt, who conducted research for the National Institute of Justice, point out that

> *Extended quotation indented ten spaces, without quotation marks, double spaced*

> The typical room has dead space in which the receiver cannot pick up the transmitter's signal. In particular, metal tends to limit the range of the transmitter; kitchens are therefore an especially difficult environment.
>
> Transmission breaks have also been attributed to metal furniture, faulty wiring, other electronic devices, bathroom fixtures, waterbeds, and even certain sleeping positions. Mobile homes constitute a problem for offenders trying to do yard chores: The range outside the building is as little as ten feet, as compared to as much as 200 feet from a mainframe building. (3)

> *Period precedes citation*

Jacque 7

Other researchers have noted similar interference problems. In one situation, authorities suspected noncompliance
when they discovered breaks in an offender's continuous signal
transmissions. These breaks always occurred during the same
time period and only on Sundays. Investigation revealed that a
large rock and metal coffee table was blocking the signal from
the transmitter on the offender's ankle while he was watching
football on television (Beck, Klein-Saffran, and Wooten 27).

Most practical problems associated with electronic monitoring pose no serious challenge. Troublesome bracelets and
transmitters can be adjusted or padded. Offenders often develop ingenious explanations for the units they wear. Difficulties in signal transmission can often be overcome by having
trained technicians install equipment or by having offenders
slightly modify their routine. Legal problems, on the other
hand, pose a greater challenge.

> Transition paragraph summa-
> rizes solutions to practical
> problems, looks ahead to legal
> problems

Electronic surveillance programs necessarily involve some
type of entry into offenders' homes. Therefore, they need careful
examination to ensure that they don't violate the equal protection and right to privacy provisions of the Constitution. The
American Civil Liberties Union is concerned that two common
practices—charging a fee to cover surveillance costs and restricting surveillance to classes of offenders least likely to violate house arrest—may infringe on the equal protection clause of
the Constitution. The first practice, the ACLU notes, can discriminate against young and indigent offenders by imprisoning them
because they cannot pay their fees. The second, by singling out
persons guilty only of property crimes and without serious criminal records or histories of drug abuse, may target disproportion-
ately high numbers of white-collar offenders (Petersilia 3).

These concerns can be answered. Because electronic monitoring programs are always voluntary, participants essentially
waive their right to privacy. By agreeing to a program in lieu

Jacque 8

of prison, they have indicated their willingness to undergo surveillance. Still, as the Bureau of Justice Assistance notes, court rulings may uphold a convicted person's right to privacy if electronic surveillance "cannot be justified in terms of an articulated security interest, ability to deter future criminal conduct or ability to reduce the risk of flight" (United States, <u>Electronic Monitoring</u> 5). Furthermore, electronic monitoring can invade the privacy of others in the offender's home. Family members who have not committed an offense and have not waived their right to privacy can accidentally be photographed or recorded. To prevent such intrusions, Kentucky, Nevada, and West Virginia have banned the use of equipment that might accidentally record extraneous sights and sounds. And because North Carolina prohibits photographing juveniles, visual verification cannot be used in that state (Scaglione, "Jails" 34).

> Quotation indicates precise conditions that justify monitoring

Besides protecting an offender's constitutional rights, correction officials must try to avoid a "net-widening" effect when electronic monitoring is used. This effect occurs when a judge approves surveillance for offenders who would formerly have received probation but denies it to anyone who would formerly have gone to prison. The result is a "widening of the net of social control" to encompass more individuals. When such abuses take place, the system does not provide an option for those who would otherwise have gone to prison, and it serves as a new form of punishment for those who would otherwise have been placed on probation. Prison overcrowding is not reduced, and the costs of punishment actually rise because of the excess number of individuals under surveillance (Morris and Tonry 225). The net-widening effect has been avoided in some jurisdictions by establishing strict rules for the selection of participants. New Jersey, for instance, restricts alternative punishment programs to offenders who have already been sentenced to prison (Hofer and Meierhoefer 22).

> Definition of term

Jacque 9

A personal interview with Richard N. Irrer, who supervises the Michigan Department of Corrections electronic monitoring program, has provided convincing evidence that monitoring works well in supervising low-risk prisoners. Monitoring began experimentally in 1986, and the following year the program was expanded to include the entire state. Offenders monitored by the department include circuit-court probationers, prison parolees, and prisoners released from halfway houses. By mid-2000, some twenty-nine hundred offenders were being monitored.

The department uses the continuous-signal monitoring system exclusively. Before being fitted with bracelets, offenders are fully briefed on the operation of the system and must read and sign a set of rules and regulations that includes a list of possible penalties for violations. These preliminaries and the fact that the program includes only carefully screened offenders with minimum-security status have undoubtedly helped the program achieve its high success rate. For 2000, according to Irrer, only 2.2 percent of the offenders were arrested for new felonies, and just 6.7 percent disappeared. The penalty for program violators depends on the status of the violator and the nature of the crime. For example, parolees and probationers who commit serious violations may go to prison, while prisoners on furlough from halfway houses may be returned there. Minor violations could result in extended curfew hours.

The Michigan program has also been a financial success. Imprisoning offenders costs the state an average of $65 a day. In contrast, Irrer notes, electronic monitoring costs just $7.30 a day, and financially able offenders must reimburse the state. Those who can't pay must perform community service. Earlier findings reported by Hofer and Meierhoefer also reveal wide spreads between the costs of imprisoning and monitoring offenders (54–55). Clearly, electronic monitoring can significantly reduce the country's enormous prison costs.

Interview supplements library research

Classification of offenders

Classification of punishments

Arguments in favor of monitoring

Comparison of costs

Independent conclusion concerning savings in prison costs

Jacque 10

Electronic monitoring is not a cure-all for prison overcrowding. But it does offer a number of advantages that deserve serious consideration: Several systems are available; no insurmountable problems are evident; low-risk offenders are effectively controlled; and the costs are less than those for incarceration. As we move on into the twenty-first century, authorities in increasing numbers can be expected to establish house-arrest programs that monitor compliance with electronic devices.

Independent conclusion draws together and reinforces main points of paper; predicts future of house-arrest programs

Works Cited

Entry for collection containing several authors' contributions compiled by three editors

Baird, Christopher. "Building More Prisons Will Not Solve Prison Overcrowding." <u>America's Prisons: Opposing Viewpoints.</u> Ed. David Bender, Bruno Leone, and Stacey Tipp. San Diego: Greenhaven, 1991. 118–24.

Entry for newspaper article

Barr, William. "Corraling the Hard-Core Criminal." <u>Detroit News and Free Press</u> 18 Oct. 1992, state ed.: B3.

Entry for occupational journal article with three authors

Beck, James L., Jody Klein-Saffran, and Harold B. Wooten. "Home Confinement and the Use of Electronic Monitoring with Federal Parolees." <u>Federal Probation</u> Dec. 1990: 22–31.

Entry for newspaper item with two authors

Carey, Anne R., and Elys A. McLean. "Electronic Prison Bars." <u>USA Today</u> 30 Sept. 1993: A1.

Entry for government document, two authors given

Ford, Daniel, and Annesley K. Schmidt. <u>Electronically Monitored Home Confinement.</u> United States. National Institute of Justice, Department of Justice. Washington: GPO, 1989.

Gearan, Anne. "1.8M in U.S. Prisons, the Most Ever." <u>USA Today</u> 15 March 1999: A1.

Entry for Internet report, no author given

Georgia State. Probation Division of the Georgia Department of Corrections. <u>Alternatives to Incarceration.</u> 1 July 1997. 3 Feb. 1998 <http://www.harvard.edu/~innovat/ aiga87. html>.

Jacque 11

Hofer, Paul J., and Barbara S. Meierhoefer. <u>Home Confinement:</u>
     <u>An Evolving Sanction in the Federal Criminal Justice Sys-</u>
     <u>tem.</u> Washington: Federal Judicial Center, 1987.

"Inmate Populations, Costs and Projection Models." <u>Corrections</u>
     <u>Compendium</u> Jan. 1997: 10–11.

Irrer, Richard N. Personal interview. 20 Feb. 2001.

Katel, Peter. "New Walls, No Inmates." <u>Newsweek</u> 18 May 1992: 63.

Lynch, Allen. <u>Cost Effectiveness of Incarceration.</u> Leroy Collins
     Institute for Public Policy. 1 July 1997
     <http://www.dos.state.fl.us/fgils/agencies/fcc/
     reports/crime.html>.

Morris, Norval, and Michael Tonry. <u>Between Prison and Proba-</u>
     tion: Intermediate <u>Punishments in a Rational Sentencing</u>
     <u>System.</u> New York: Oxford UP, 1990.

Peck, Keenan. "High-Tech House Arrest." <u>Progressive</u> July 1988:
     26–28.

Petersilia, Joan. <u>House Arrest.</u> United States. National Institute
     of Justice, Department of Justice. Washington: GPO, 1988.

Quinlan, J. Michael. "Building More Prisons Will Solve Prison
     Overcrowding." <u>America's Prisons: Opposing Viewpoints.</u>
     Ed. David Bender, Bruno Leone, and Stacey Tipp. San
     Diego: Greenhaven, 1991. 112–16.

Richey, Warren. "Bulging Cells Renew Debate Over Prisons as
     Tools to Fight Crime." <u>Christian Science Monitor</u> 22 Jan.
     1997: 3.

Scaglione, Fred. "Jails Without Walls." <u>American City & County</u>
     Jan. 1989: 32–40.

Entry for book with two authors

Entry for interview

Entry for popular magazine article with one author

Entry for Internet report, one author given

Entry for government document, one author given

Entry for occupational journal article with one author

Jacque 12

Second entry for author; three unspaced hyphens substitute for author's name

———. "You're Under Arrest—At Home." <u>USA Today</u> Nov. 1988: 26–28.[1]

Sullivan, Robert E. "Reach Out and Guard Someone: Using Phones and Bracelets to Reduce Prison Overcrowding." <u>Rolling Stone</u> 29 Nov. 1990: 51.

Entry for government document, no author given

United States. Department of Justice. Bureau of Justice Assistance, Office of Justice Programs. <u>Electronic Monitoring in Intensive Probation and Parole Programs</u>. Washington: GPO, 1989.

United States. Senate. Subcommittee on Federal Spending, Budget, and Accounting of the Committee on Governmental Affairs. <u>Prison Projections: Can the United States Keep Pace?</u> 100th Cong., 1st. sess. Washington: GPO, 1987.

[1]The magazine *USA Today*, not the newspaper of that name.

Using a Computer

Word-processor software programs can help you with the various stages of library research. Several guidelines will enhance your efficiency as you proceed.

Taking Notes

Students with laptop computers or notebooks sometimes take them into the library and enter notes as they read their sources, despite the inconvenience that often results. In most cases, though, you will find it works best to take notes on cards, then afterward enter them and your bibliographical references into your word processor. You can type notes into one central file and distribute them later to separate files by topic or distribute them as you go along.

As you proceed, take great care to distinguish between your notes and your thoughts about them. One good way to do this is to establish some system, such as typing notes in boldface and putting brackets around your thoughts. To avoid inadvertently using the exact words of others without giving proper credit, always put quotation marks around directly quoted material. As an added safeguard you might also use different spacing for quotations. To identify the sources of your notes, you could number them to match the number of the source or end each note with the author's name. For an anonymous source use a shortened title. Finally, don't neglect to keep printouts of your notes and bibliography to guard against accidental erasure or a power surge.

Outlining

Many word-processing programs provide options that facilitate outlining. With some programs you can compare two arrangements side by side; others enable you to call up your stored and organized notes on one side of the screen and create your outline on the other side.

Don't let limitations of your software cramp your explorations of possibilities. If your program lets you compare two outlines but you'd like to check more, make a second and if necessary a third printout; then examine them side by side. Similarly, if an outline includes more items than a single screen can accommodate, continue on a second screen and use printouts to check the complete product.

Drafting

Students follow different approaches when drafting on a computer. Some follow the outline section by section, entering their notes and any thoughts that previously occurred to them, then go through everything again and add material. Others finish off one section before moving on to the next, some by focusing on their notes and then developing thoughts that elaborate on them, others by developing their thoughts and working in their notes afterward. Follow the procedure that works best for you.

When you write the paper, fight the urge simply to string your notes together. Such an approach results in a draft that lurches from one bit of information to another without consistent style or proper attention to the underlying thesis. If you find yourself merely typing in notes, stop, open a separate file, read each note carefully, and then enter your thoughts concerning it. When you've examined all the notes, begin the drafting process over again, integrating your notes and your thoughts in the new file.

As you compose, don't overfill any of your files; too many words leave little room for revision. You can avoid this problem by establishing a separate file for each section of your paper.

Revising and Formatting

Students often hesitate to revise research papers because of their length. A word processor gives you an edge. You can isolate sections and experiment with them; move large sections of the text around; or, if you used separate files for different sections, change transitions to reflect different orders. When you make such changes, check to see that you maintain the flow of the paper. An adjustment in one section must mesh logically and stylistically with what precedes and follows. Reviewing a printout offers the best opportunity to check your paper's continuity. As you revise, always keep copies of earlier versions. Some part that seemed ineffective may fill a gap or take on a new look in view of your changes.

Finally, the formatting capabilities of word-processor software can be a powerful asset. Most programs will position page numbers, set margins properly, and add your name at the top of each page. Some programs will also indent bibliographic entries properly. Don't, however, neglect your instructor's specifications with regard to spacing, print style, and the like.

Using Images, Illustrations, and Graphs

Computer programs make it easy to import photographs, illustrations, and graphs into an essay and report. Visuals can be useful. An essay on different kinds of cats would be enhanced by pictures of cats. The best way to explain the bones in the skull is a labeled drawing. Complicated numbers can be presented best through the appropriate graphs or charts.

General Principles for Using Visuals

- **Use visuals only when they help.** Excess visuals detract from a text; visuals should be used when they are the best way of presenting the information. Clichéd clip art only detracts from important messages.

- **Visuals should fit the text.** Visuals shouldn't be just thrown in. Instead, they should have a connection to nearby text so that the meanings are related.

- **Visuals need to be explained.** Visuals don't always stand on their own. You need to explain to readers why they should look at the visual and direct their attention to what they should notice. With graphs and tables, it is helpful to explain first what to look for in the visual and then, after the visual, identify the major conclusion the readers could reach from the visual.

- **Visuals often need a title.** To direct the reader's attention, label all visuals. The title should tell the story of the visual.

- **Place visuals so they don't break up the text.** You want your page to be attractive but not distracting. Visuals need to be positioned so the page looks good but the flow of the text is not seriously interrupted.

- **Visuals should be honest.** It is important to represent the data fairly and not distort the image or graph to slant the information.

Pictures   The use of a scanner or digital camera makes it easy to import pictures, which can spice up the text. We have used pictures of the authors in the Reader so that they will come alive for you. If you use pictures, make certain they are clear and simple. Readers shouldn't have to spend time trying to decipher the picture.

Tables Including tables with columns and rows is an excellent way of comparing information such as the features of different computers, the quantity of sales, or even the quality of different employees. Make certain your table is clearly labeled. See Table 21.1 for an example.

Table 21.1   Use Different Classroom Media for Different Purposes

Features	Blackboard	Overhead	PowerPoint
Class Time Used	Extensive; text written out in class	Minimal; prepared before class	Minimal; prepared before class
Equipment Required	Usually in every classroom	In most classrooms or easily obtained	Limited by limited number of computers and screens
Information Presented	Text and handdrawn images or low-resolution graphs	Text and images or graphs; variable resolutions	All text and visuals with good resolution
Flexibility in Classroom Environment	Plans can be easily changed; readily accepts new direction and student input	Limited flexibility: order can be varied between overheads; can write on blank overheads	Limited; hard to change order of presentation or enter new input

Pie Charts Pie charts are an excellent way to present percentages or quantities of a whole. Figure 21.17 is a sample pie chart.

Figure 21.17   How Teachers Use Their Time

Bar Graphs Bar graphs can help you present and compare data that isn't a continuous trend, as Figure 21.18 shows.

Line Graphs Line graphs are an excellent way to show data that are continuous over time and shows trends effectively. See Figure 21.19 for an example.

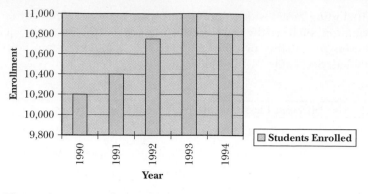

Figure 21.18   Student Enrollment Grows

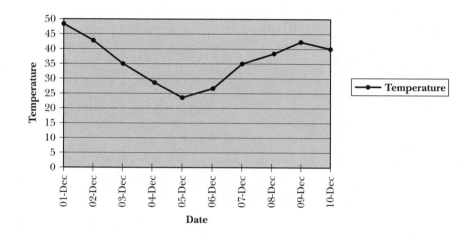

Figure 21.19   Temperatures at Noon Show Cold Spell

Headers, Numbered Lists, and Bullets

Information in longer reports is not always presented in an unbroken stream of text. You can use a number of devices to help readers.

- **Bold headings and subheadings can guide the reader to different sections of the text.** When the sections of a longer report, or even a shorter business memo, can be broken into distinct sections, it can be helpful to label those sections with bold words or phrases that will direct the reader's attention. This text uses headings and subheadings and so do some of the articles in the Reader such as "Blur: Cheetahs. Ranchers. Hope" (pages 588–592).

- **Lists can be a useful way to present organized information.** Steps in a process, several recommendations, the identification of important qualities can all be well represented by an indented list. The discussion questions in this text are all presented as numbered lists.

- **Bullets are used when listed information shouldn't be numbered because there is no implied sequence.** The recommendations for using visuals in this section are presented as a bulleted list. Lists and bullets should use parallelism, the same grammatical form, discussed on pages 665–666.

Writing Your Research Paper Checklist

Search Checklist

- Brainstorm to focus your topic.
- Get an overview by searching general references such as encyclopedias.
- Search your library for books.
    Use either key term or subject searches using a computer catalog.
    Copy or print out the call number that locates the book.
    Scan the books in your located section for unexpected finds.
- Search your periodical indexes and databases.
    Select an index or database that fits your topic.
    InfoTrac and Wilson Select are often useful starting indexes.
    Use either key term or subject searches.
    Use the headings you find to narrow or guide your search.
    Print or copy the title of the articles, the author, the magazine, the volume number, the page number, and the date.
    If you use a full text of an online article, be sure to copy the reference information.
    Find the hard copy, microfiche, or microfilm version of your article.
- Search the Internet.
    Use an appropriate search engine such as Google or Yahoo.
    Try several combinations of terms or modify them to narrow a search.
    Assess the credibility of all Internet sources based on the source for the site, author, quality of the Web pages, consistency with other credible information.
    Be sure to copy or print the URL, author (if any), and title (if any).

Taking Notes Checklist

- Evaluate your source by author's qualification, publication's credibility, and obvious bias.
- Take notes using cards, yellow pad, or computer file.
    Keep track of source and page number for each note.
    You may want to cross-reference notes with bibliography cards.
    Give a title to each note card that identifies the notes topic.
- Respond as you take notes with your own thoughts and observations.
- Consciously decide to summarize, paraphrase, or quote in your notes.
    If you paraphrase, it must be completely in your own words.
    If you quote, be sure to mark your quotes so you don't forget.

- Always consciously work to avoid plagiarism.
    Always carefully record your sources for notes.
    Do not simply change a few words in a paraphrase.
    Do not forget to mark quotes when you quote.
    Ask you teacher or a tutor if you are not sure of the rules.

Drafting Your Paper Checklist

- Take steps to integrate your information.
    Read over your notes.
    Possibly write a brief draft without looking at your notes.

- Write an outline.
    Determine the main divisions of your paper.
    Read note cards for subdivisions.
    Detail either a sentence or topic outline.

- Key your note cards to your outlines.

- Determine if you need to perform additional research.

- Draft your paper in sections.
    Work to keep the paper in your own voice.
    Don't get stuck on the introduction. Just write.
    Use your notes to support your claims but don't just cut and paste.
    Be sure to document as you write.
    Avoid plagiarism.
    Create deliberate transitions between sections.
    Go back and rework the introduction and conclusion.
    Carefully document using the material from the next chapter.

Revising Your Draft Checklist

- Do not be afraid to make extensive changes.

- Read and change the paper with an eye to your original purpose.

- Get feedback from other readers.

- Check for material that doesn't fit and needs to be cut.

- Check for holes that may require additional research and do it if needed.

- Check your notes to see that you didn't leave out something important.

- Check to see that the paper is easy to follow.

- Smooth your transitions and add transition paragraphs where needed.

- Make certain the draft is in a consistent voice.

CHAPTER 22

DOCUMENTING SOURCES

In order to acknowledge and handle sources, you must know how to (1) prepare proper bibliographical references, (2) document sources within your text, (3) handle quotations, and (4) avoid plagiarism.

The kind of information included in bibliographical references depends on the type of source and the documentation system. Two systems are in common use: the Modern Language Association (MLA) system and the American Psychological Association (APA) system. The entries that follow illustrate basic MLA and APA conventions. For more information, consult the *MLA Handbook for Writers of Research Papers,* 6th ed., 2003, and the *Publication Manual of the American Psychological Association,* 5th ed., 2001. When documenting online sources, consult the Web site noted on page 390 to supplement the information in the *Manual.*

Preparing Proper MLA and APA Bibliographic References

Books

The basic bibliographic reference for a book includes the name of the author, the title of the book, the place of publication, the name of the publisher, and the date of publication. Other information is added as necessary. The order of presentation depends on which system of listing sources, the MLA or APA, is used. Note that the APA system uses initials rather than first and middle names for authors, editors, and translators.

■ *A Book with One Author*

MLA   Wilk, Max. <u>Every Day's a Matinée</u>. New York: Norton, 1975.

APA   Wilk, M. (1975). *Every day's a matinée*. New York: W. W. Norton.

■ *A Book with Two Authors*

MLA   Duncan, Dayton, and Ken Burns. <u>Lewis & Clark</u>. New York: Knopf, 1997.

APA   Duncan, D., & Burns, K. (1997). *Lewis & Clark*. New York: Alfred Knopf.

Note that the APA system reverses the name of the second author and uses "&" instead of "and" between the names. In titles and subtitles, only the first word and proper nouns and adjectives are capitalized. Both the MLA and APA systems use the hanging indent for entries in the reference list. Start the first line of each entry flush to the left margin and indent all subsequent lines five spaces.

■ *A Book with More Than Three Authors*

MLA   Alder, Roger William, et al. <u>Mechanisms in Organic Chemistry</u>. New York: Wiley, 1971.

APA   Alder, R. W., Finn, T., Bradley, M. A., & Li, A. W. (1971). *Mechanisms in organic chemistry*. New York: John Wiley.

The MLA system permits the use of "et al." for four or more authors or editors (listing all authors is also permitted); the APA system gives up to and including six author or editor names in the reference list. Substitute "et al." for the seventh or more.

■ *A Book with a Title That Includes Another Title*

The MLA offers two options: You may omit underlining the embedded title, or you may set it off with quotation marks.

MLA   Tanner, John. <u>Anxiety in Eden: A Kierkegaardian Reading of</u> Paradise Lost. Oxford: Oxford UP, 1992.

MLA   Tanner, John. <u>Anxiety in Eden: A Kierkegaardian Reading of "Paradise Lost."</u> Oxford: Oxford UP, 1992.

The APA offers no guidelines for this specific situation. However, the general guidelines for italics apply if you use the first option.

APA   Tanner, J. (1992). *Anxiety in Eden: A Kierkegaardian reading of* Paradise Lost. Oxford: Oxford University Press.

■ *A Book with Corporate or Association Authorship*

United Nations, Public Administration Division. <u>Local Government Training</u>. New   MLA
    York: UN, 1968.

United Nations, Public Administration Division. (1968). *Local government training*.   APA
    New York: Author.

When the author of the work is also the publisher, the APA system uses the word "Author" following the place of publication. If the work is published by another organization, its name replaces "Author."

■ *An Edition Other Than the First*

Turabian, Kate L. <u>A Manual for Writers of Term Papers, Theses, and Dissertations</u>.   MLA
    6th ed. Chicago: U of Chicago P, 1996.

Turabian, K. L. (1996). *A manual for writers of term papers, theses, and*   APA
    dissertations (6th ed.). Chicago: University of Chicago Press.

■ *A Book in Two or More Volumes*

Bartram, Henry C. <u>The Cavalcade of America</u>. 2 vols. New York: Knopf, 1959.   MLA

Bartram, H. C. (1959). *The cavalcade of America* (Vols. 1–2). New York: Alfred Knopf.   APA

■ *A Reprint of an Older Work*

Matthiessen, F. O. <u>American Renaissance: Art and Expression in the Age of</u>   MLA
    <u>Emerson and Whitman</u>. 1941. New York: Oxford UP, 1970.

Matthiessen, F. O. (1970). *American renaissance: Art and expression in the age of*   APA
    Emerson and Whitman. New York: Oxford University Press. (Original work
    published 1941)

■ *A Book with an Editor Rather Than an Author*

Deetz, James, ed. <u>Man's Imprint from the Past: Readings in the Methods of</u>   MLA
    <u>Archaeology</u>. Boston: Little, 1971.

Deetz, J. (Ed.). (1971). *Man's imprint from the past: Readings in the methods of*   APA
    archaeology. Boston: Little, Brown.

■ *A Book with Both an Author and an Editor*

MLA   Melville, Herman. <u>The Confidence Man</u>. Ed. Hershel Parker. New York: Norton,
1971.

APA   Melville, H. (1971). *The confidence man* (H. Parker, Ed.). New York: W. W. Norton.
(Original work published 1857)

■ *A Translation*

MLA   Beauvoir, Simone de. <u>All Said and Done</u>. Trans. Patrick O'Brian. New York:
Putnam, 1974.

APA   Beauvoir, S. de. (1974). *All said and done* (P. O'Brian, Trans.). New York: G. P.
Putnam. (Original work published 1972)

■ *An Essay or Chapter in a Collection of Works by One Author*

MLA   Woolf, Virginia. "The Lives of the Obscure." <u>The Common Reader, First Series</u>.
New York: Harcourt, 1925. 111–18.

APA   Woolf, V. (1925). The lives of the obscure. In V. Woolf, *The common reader, first
series* (pp. 111–118). New York: Harcourt Brace.

■ *An Essay or Chapter in an Anthology*

MLA   Angell, Roger. "On the Ball." <u>Subject and Strategy</u>. Ed. Paul Eschholz and Alfred
Rosa. New York: St. Martin's, 1981. 34–41.

APA   Angell, R. (1981). On the ball. In P. Eschholz & A. Rosa (Eds.), *Subject and strategy*
(pp. 34–41). New York: St. Martin's Press.

Periodicals

Periodicals include newspapers, popular magazines, and specialized occupational and scholarly journals. The basic information for a periodical article includes the name of the article's author, the name of the periodical, the title of
the article, the date of publication, the page range of the entire article, and, for
scholarly journals, the volume number of the periodical. Again, the order of
presentation depends on the documentation system used. The MLA and APA
systems capitalize periodical titles identically; however, the MLA style omits an
introductory *the* from these titles. As illustrated by our example for a signed article in a daily newspaper, the two systems follow different formats for showing

when an article does not appear on consecutive pages. Note also that the systems capitalize the titles of articles differently and that the APA system precedes page numbers for newspaper articles with "p." or "pp."

■ *An Article in a Scholarly Journal Consecutively Paged through the Entire Volume*

Pfennig, David. "Kinship and Cannibalism." <u>Bioscience</u> 47 (1997): 667–75.   MLA

Pfennig, D. (1997). Kinship and cannibalism. *Bioscience, 47,* 667–675.   APA

■ *An Article in a Scholarly Journal That Pages Each Issue Separately*

Block, Joel W. "Sodom and Gomorrah: A Volcanic Disaster." <u>Journal of Geological Education</u> 23.5 (1976): 74–77.   MLA

Block, J. W. (1976). Sodom and Gomorrah: A volcanic disaster. *Journal of Geological Education, 23*(5), 74–77.   APA

■ *An Unsigned Article in a Scholarly Journal*

"Baby, It's Cold Inside." <u>Science</u> 276 (1997): 537–38.   MLA

Baby, it's cold inside. (1997). *Science, 276,* 537–538.   APA

■ *A Signed Article in an Occupational or a Popular Magazine*

Gopnik, Adam. "The Good Soldier." <u>New Yorker</u> 24 Nov. 1997: 106–14.   MLA

Gopnik, A. (1997, November 24). The good soldier. *The New Yorker, 73,* 106–114.   APA

■ *An Unsigned Article in an Occupational or a Popular Magazine*

"Robot Productivity." <u>Production Engineering</u> May 1982: 52–55.   MLA

Robot productivity. (1982, May). *Production Engineering, 29,* 52–55.   APA

■ *A Signed Article in a Daily Newspaper*

Wade, Nicholas. "Germ Weapons: Deadly but Hard to Use." <u>New York Times</u> 26 Nov. 1997, national ed.: A13+.   MLA

Wade, N. (1997, November 26). Germ weapons: Deadly but hard to use. *The New York Times,* pp. A13, A15.   APA

■ *An Unsigned Article in a Daily Newspaper*

MLA "The Arithmetic of Terrorism." <u>Washington Post</u> 14 Nov. 1997: A26.

APA The arithmetic of terrorism. (1997, November 14). *The Washington Post*, p. A26.

Encyclopedia Articles

When documenting familiar works, such as the *Encyclopedia Americana*, the basic information for the MLA system includes the name of the article's author if known, the title of the article, the name of the encyclopedia, and the date of the edition.

MLA Sobieszek, Robert A. "Photography." <u>World Book Encyclopedia</u>. 1991 ed.

The APA system requires additional information for all encyclopedia citations, as does the MLA system when less familiar publications are documented. Again, the order of presentation differs for the two systems.

MLA Fears, J. Rufus. "Emperor's Cult." <u>Encyclopedia of Religion</u>. Ed. Mircea Eliade. 16
     vols. New York: Macmillan, 1987.

APA Fears, J. R. (1987). Emperor's cult. In *The encyclopedia of religion* (Vol. 5, pp. 101–102).
     New York: Macmillan.

For an anonymous article, references for both the MLA and APA systems begin with the article's title. With the APA system, position the publication date, within parentheses, after this title. The remaining format is identical to the citations with an author.

Government Documents

The basic information for a federal, state, or foreign government publication that is documented using the MLA system includes the name of the author, the title of the publication, the name of the government and the agency issuing the publication, the place of publication, the name of the printing group, if known, and the date. If no author is named, begin by identifying the government and then cite the government agency as the author. The APA system presents similar information but omits the government name, adds a cataloging code where one exists, and follows a different order of presentation.

MLA Carpenter, Russell D. <u>Defects in Hardened Timber</u>. United States. U.S. Department
     of Agriculture, Forest Service. Washington: GPO, 1989.

APA Carpenter, R. D. (1989). *Defects in hardened timber* (UCLC No. 20504424). U.S.
     Department of Agriculture, Forest Service. Washington, DC: U.S.
     Government Printing Office.

United States. Environmental Protection Agency, Consumer Products Safety
    Commission. <u>Asbestos in the Home</u>. Washington: GPO, 1989.

MLA

U.S. Environmental Protection Agency, Consumer Products Safety Commission.
    (1989). *Asbestos in the home* (SUDOCS No. Y3.C76/3:2/A51/989). Washington,
    DC: U.S. Government Printing Office.

APA

United States. Cong. Office of Technology Assessment. <u>The Biology of Mental
    Disorders</u>. 102nd Cong., 2nd sess. Washington: GPO, 1992.

MLA

U.S. Congress, Office of Technology Assessment. (1992). *The biology of mental
    disorders* (SUDOCS No. Y3.T22/2:2/B57/10). Washington, DC: U.S.
    Government Printing Office.

APA

Other Sources

The information presented and the order of presentation depend on the type
of source and the documentation system.

■ Book Reviews

Koenig, Rhoda. "Billy the Kid." Rev. of <u>Billy Bathgate</u>, by E. L. Doctorow. <u>New York</u>
    20 Feb. 1989: 20–21.

MLA

Koenig, R. (1989, February 20). Billy the Kid [Review of the book *Billy Bathgate*].
    New York, 21, 20–21.

APA

If the review is untitled, follow the above formats but omit the missing element.

■ Published Interviews

Noriega, Manuel. "A Talk with Manuel Noriega." By Felipe Hernandez. News
    <u>Report</u> 20 March 1997: 28–30.

MLA

The APA system does not include a documentation format for published interviews. If you are using the APA format and your paper includes material from a
published interview, we suggest that you document as follows:

Hernandez, F. (1997, March 20). A talk with Manuel Noriega. [Interview with
    Manuel Noriega]. *News Report, 15*, 28–30.

APA

If the interview is untitled, use, in place of a title, the word "Interview," without
quotation marks or underlining, for the MLA system. For the APA system, follow the example above, omitting mention of a title.

■ *Personal Interviews*

If you conducted the interview yourself and are using the MLA system, start with the name of the person interviewed and follow it with the kind of interview and the date conducted.

MLA   Newman, Paul. Personal interview. 18 May 2001.

For the APA system, a personal interview is considered personal correspondence and is not included in the References list. Instead, use an in-text parenthetical citation. Include the name of the person interviewed, the notation "personal communication," and the date: (P. Newman, personal communication, May 18, 2001).

■ *Audiovisual Media*

MLA   <u>Frankenstein</u>. Dir. James Whale. Perf. Boris Karloff, John Boles, Colin Clive, and
        Mae Clarke. Universal, 1931.

If you are interested in the contribution of a particular person, start with that person's name. Use the term *film* in MLA format, and use the same model for vidoecassette and DVD recordings.

MLA   Whale, James, dir. <u>Frankenstein</u>. Perf. Boris Karloff, John Boles, Colin Clive, and
        Mae Clarke. Universal, 1931.

In the APA format, the citation begins with an individual's name and his or her contribution to the *motion picture* (use this term, not *film*). The country of origin (where it was made and released) is now required.

APA   Whale, J. (Director). (1931). *Frankenstein* [Motion Picture]. United States: Universal.

■ *Television and Radio Programs*

Basic citations follow the formats below:

MLA   <u>Washington Week in Review</u>. Prod. S. Ducat. PBS. WKAR, East Lansing. 6 Jan. 1995.

APA   Ducat, S. (Producer). (1995, January 6). *Washington week in review* [Television
        Broadcast]. Washington, DC: Public Broadcasting Service.

Use these formats when additional information is pertinent:

MLA   Peril at End House. By Agatha Christie. Dir. Renny Rye. Prod. Brian Eastman. Perf.
        David Suchet and Hugh Fraser. Mystery. Introd. Diana Rigg. PBS. WKAR,
        East Lansing. 12 Aug. 1993.

APA   Exton, C. (Script Writer). (1993). *Peril at end house* [Television Series Episode] (R.
        Rye, Director). In B. Eastman (Producer), *Mystery*. Washington, DC: Public
        Broadcasting Service.

With the APA system, the name of the script writer appears in the author's position. Any in-text references begin with the first name in the bibliographical reference (for example, Exton, 1993).

■ Music and Sound Recordings

Smith, Bessie. The World's Greatest Blues Singer. LP. Columbia, 1948. | MLA |

In MLA style, list the medium (Audiocassette, LP, etc.) only when the recording is not a CD. If you mention the name of a particular item on the recording, set it off with quotation marks, as shown below. If the recording date is important, place it before the medium.

Smith, Bessie. "Down Hearted Blues." The World's Greatest Blues Singer. LP. | MLA |
    Columbia, 1948.

The APA format requires indetification of all formats, including a CD:

Smith, B. (1997). *The Essential Bessie Smith* [CD]. New York: Columbia Records. | APA |

Smith, B. (1948). Down hearted blues. On *The world's greatest blues singer* [CD]. | APA |
    New York: Columbia Records. (Original recording February 17, 1923)

Recording dates, if different from the copyright year, follow the entry, enclosed in parentheses, with no final period.

■ Computer Software

Data Desk. Computer software. Vers. 6.0. Data description, 1997. | MLA |

Data Desk (Version 6.0) [Computer software]. (1997). Ithaca, NY: Data Description, | APA |
    Inc.

In the APA system, only specialized software or computer programs are listed in the References. Standard commercial software and languages should be cited by their proper name and version in the text itself.

■ CD-ROMs and Other Databases

Norman, J. L. "Barcelona." Software Toolworks Multimedia Encyclopedia. CD- | MLA |
    ROM. Disc 1. Danbury, CT: Grolier, 1996.

Norman, J. L. (1996). Barcelona. *Software Toolworks Multimedia Encyclopedia* [CD- | APA |
    ROM]. Boston: Grolier.

The APA *Manual* (5th ed.) takes the view that all aggregated databases are the same type of source, regardless of the format or manner of access (CD-ROM, library or university server, or online Web supplier). Follow the model above when you need to cite an entire CD-ROM (not a document from it). In a reference to information taken from a database (even a CD-ROM), give a "retrieval statement" containing the date you retrieved the document, article, piece of data, as well as the full, correct name of the database. When you retrieve information from an online database, end the entry with a correct and complete URL for the specific document or version. In this case, the name of the database is omitted, unless this information will help in retrieval from a large or complex site. (See online models in the next section.)

Online Sources

The most recent edition of the *Publication Manual of the American Psychological Association* provides the APA's newest guidelines for documenting online sources. You can also consult the association's Web site for its most up-to-date information about citing electronic sources:

> http://www.apastyle.org/elecref.html

The examples here follow the published guidelines for the MLA (2003) and the APA (2001). Be sure to ask your instructor which format to follow and then use that format consistently. Often, data from the Internet are incomplete, perhaps lacking an author, a title, or any recognizable page or paragraph number. Include all the available information. The recommendation from APA is that you cite document locations rather than home pages and that the referenced address actually works for that file. Remember: Your goal is to allow your reader to find the source. When the actual address is extremely long or unusable, the MLA allows you to use the home page for your source.

■ Books

The basic information for a book documented by the MLA system includes the name(s) of the author(s), if known; the title of the book; the place and date of original publication, if applicable; the electronic site, if named; the date of electronic publication if the online version has never been published in print, or if it is part of a scholarly project; the sponsor of the site; the date the material was retrieved; and the online address.

MLA Locke, John. <u>An Essay Concerning Human Understanding</u>. London, 1690. Institute

of Learning Technologies. 1995. Columbia U. 24 June 2000

<http://www.ilt.columbia.edu/projects/digitexts/locke/understanding/

title.html>.

The APA *Publication Manual* does not show a model for documenting online books; however, the *Manual* treats all nonperiodical Internet documents in one category, including multipage or multipart documents such as books or reports. Follow the general guidelines for a printed book and conclude with appropriate electronic source information, as modeled here.

Locke, J. (1995). *An essay concerning human understanding.* New York: Columbia

    University. (Original work published 1690). Retrieved June 24, 2000, from

    http://www.ilt.columbia.edu/projects/digitexts/locke/understanding/title.html

> APA

When some of the basic information is not provided, use whatever is available.

Chaney, Walter J., William J. Diehm, and Frank Seeley. The Second 50 Years: A

    Reference Manual for Senior Citizens. Weed, CA: London Circle, 1999. 8

    August 2000 <http://londoncircle.com/2d50html>.

> MLA

Chaney, W. J., Diehm, W. J., & Seeley, F. (1999). *The second 50 years: A reference*

    manual for senior citizens. Weed, CA: London Circle. Retrieved August 8,

    2000, from http://www.londoncircle.com/2d50.html

> APA

To cite part of an electronic book, place the part's title after the name(s) of the author(s) or, in APA format, after the date of publication. APA also cites a chapter or section identifier following the title of the complete document.

Dawson, Marie. Introduction. Methods of Sociological Investigation. New York:

    Harmon, 1997. 6 Sept. 2000 <http://www.harmon.edu/edu-books.html>.

> MLA

Trochim, W. M. K. Language of research. In *The research methods knowledge base*

    (Foundations sec.). Cincinnatti, OH: Atomic Dog. Retrieved September 6,

    2001, from http://www.trochim.human.cornell.edu/kb/language.htm

> APA

■ Periodicals on the World Wide Web

Periodicals online include specialized occupational and scholarly journals, popular magazines, newspapers, and newsletters. The basic information for a periodical includes the author's name, if known; the title of the article; the title of the periodical; the volume number; the date the article was published; the number of paragraphs in the article or its page numbers; the date the material was retrieved; and the online address.

    The APA recommends using the models for print periodicals when documenting online articles that do not vary from their printed versions. In such cases, add [Electronic version] after the title and before the period to complete the citation. When the electronic format alters the printed version (e.g., no pagination, added data or links), then cite as an online document, using a retrieval statement and the name of the database and/or the URL. APA guidelines ask for the identification of the server or the Web site in a retrieval statement only when it would be helpful in finding the source; for example, it is not necessary to state "Retrieved from the World Wide Web" since it is the most common access point to the Internet.

Cervetti, Nancy. "In the Breeches, Petticoats, and Pleasures of Orlando." Journal

    of Modern Literature 20.2 (1996): 32 pars. 8 Jan. 1998

    <http://www.indiana.edu/~iupress/journals/mod-art2.html>.

> MLA

APA   Cervetti, N. (1996). In the breeches, petticoats, and pleasures of Orlando. *Journal of Modern Literature*, 20(2). Retrieved January 8, 1998, from http://www.indiana.edu/~iupress/journals/mod-art2.html

MLA   Navarro, Mireya. "Women in Sports Cultivating New Playing Fields." New York Times on the Web 13 Feb. 2001. 22 Feb. 2001 <http://www.nytimes.com>.

APA   Navarro, M. (2001, February 13). Women in sports cultivating new playing fields. *The New York Times on the Web*. Retrieved February 22, 2001, from http://www.nytimes.com

MLA   "No Link Found in Violence, Videos." Boston Globe Online 8 Aug. 2000. 27 Aug. 2000. <http://www.boston.com>.

APA   No link found in violence, videos. (2000, August 8). *Boston Globe Online*, p. A14. Retrieved August 27, 2000, from http://www.boston.com/dailyglobe2/ . . .nk_found_in_violence_videos+.shtml

MLA   Oakes, Jeannie. "Promotion or Retention: Which One Is Social?" Harvard Education Letter. Jan.–Feb. 1999. 7 pars. 8 Aug. 2000 <http://www.edletter.org>.

APA   Oakes, J. (1999, January–February). Promotion or retention: Which one is social? *Harvard Education Letter*. Retrieved August 8, 2000, from http://www.edletter.org/past/issues/1999-jf/promotion.shtml

■ *Periodicals Accessed through an Online Library Service or Large Network Provider*

Increasingly, full-text articles are available online at libraries or at home through services such as Lexis-Nexis, ProQuest Direct, and America Online. These services may or may not provide an online address for accessed material. If you know the service's home page, and you're documenting by the MLA system, cite the author's name, if known; the title of the article; the title of the periodical; the date the article was published; the page numbers for the article (If the service identifies only the initial page of the article, indicate the page followed by a hyphen, 132-); the name of the database; the name of the library service; the name of the library; the date the material was accessed; and the online address of the service's home page.

MLA   Clemetson, Lynette. "A Ticket to Private School." Newsweek 27 Mar. 2000. Lexis-Nexis. Ferris State University Library Web Database Access. 5 May 2000 <http://library.ferris.edu/databaseframes.html>.

The APA documentation system provides the same information but omits online addresses except World Wide Web addresses.

Clemetson, L. (2000, March 27). A ticket to private school. *Newsweek*. Retrieved

  May 5, 2000, from Ferris State University Library Web Database Access

  (Lexis-Nexis)

APA

For MLA style, when no online address is provided, it is necessary to identify the keyword or keywords (the path) you used to find the material.

Mayo Clinic Health Information: Lung Cancer. 21 Feb. 2000. America Online. 10

  June 2000. Keywords: Cancer; Lung Cancer.

MLA

Mayo Clinic health information: Lung cancer. (2000, February 21). Retrieved June

  10, 2000, from America Online. Keywords: Cancer; Lung Cancer.

APA

If you had accessed this source through a library, you would name the library after you named the service. APA style prefers that the URL that leads directly to the document file be provided, following the word *from*.

■ *Encyclopedia Articles*

The basic information for an encyclopedia article accessed through the World Wide Web includes the author's name, if known; the title of the article; the name of the encyclopedia; the date of the edition; and the online address. MLA style also names the vendor. For encyclopedia articles accessed through a CD-ROM, name this media after the title of the database for MLA format. The format is not required information in APA style, unless this information is needed for retrieval.

Daniel, Ralph Thomas. "The History of Western Music." Britannica Online:

  Macropaedia. 1995. Encyclopaedia Britannica. 14 June 1995

  <http://www.eb.com:180/cgi-bin/g:DocF=macro/5004/45/0.html>.

MLA

Daniel, R. T. (1995). The history of western music. In *Britannica Online:*

  Macropaedia. Retrieved June 14, 1995, from http://www.eb.com:180/cgi-bin/

  g:DocF=macro/5004/45/0.html

APA

■ *Government Documents*

The basic information for a government document includes the name of the author, if known; the title; the name of the government and agency issuing the document; the place of publication and printing group, if known; the date of publication; the date the material was retrieved; and the online address. If no author is given, begin by identifying the government and then give the government agency as the author. For the APA system, omit the government name, and add a cataloging code if one is available.

MLA   Georgia State. Probation Division of the Georgia Department of Corrections.

Alternatives to Incarceration. 1 July 1997. 3 Feb. 1998

<http://www.harvard.edu/~innovat/aiga87.html>.

APA   Probation Division of the Georgia Department of Corrections. (1997, July 1).

Alternatives to Incarceration. (CSP No. 239875). Retrieved February 3, 1998,

from http://www.harvard.edu/~innovat/aiga87.html

■ *Personal Home Page*

The basic information for a personal home page documented according to the
MLA system includes the name of its originator, if known; the title of the site, if
any (use *Home page* or other such description if no title is given); the date the
material was retrieved from the site; and the online address.

MLA   Lanthrop, Olin. Home page. 24 June 2000

<http://www.cognivis.com/olin/photos.htm>.

The APA *Manual* offers no specific guidelines for personal home pages. We suggest that you follow the following pattern, which conforms to general APA practice. Note that the APA system, unlike the MLA, includes the date of the latest
Web page revision, if known, in parentheses.

APA   Lanthrop, O. (2000, May 28). Home page. Retrieved June 24, 2000, from

http://www.cognivis.com/ olin/photos.htm

■ *Newsgroups, Electronic Mailing Lists, and E-mail*

MLA gives guidelines for including newsgroups, electronic mailing lists (sometimes called listservs), and e-mail within the Works Cited list. APA format treats
e-mail as personal communications, which are cited in parentheses in the text
only. Newsgroups, online forums, discussion groups, and electronic mailing
lists that maintain archives can be cited in the References, but the APA cautions that there must be a scholarly purpose. When in doubt, treat as a personal
communication.

MLA   Corelli, Aldo. "Colleges and Diversity." Online posting. 20 Apr. 1993. 25 Apr. 1993

<learninghouse.michigan.edu>.

MLA   Nicholson, Brad. "Casino Gambling." E-mail to author. 2 Feb. 2001. . . . as reported

in his study (B. Nicholson, personal communication, February 2, 2001).

APA   Trehub, A. (2002, January 28). The conscious access hypothesis [Msg. 18]. Message

posted to University of Houston Psyche Discussion Forum:

http://listserv.uh.edu/cgi-bin/wa?A2=ind0201&L=psyche-b&F=&S=&P=2334

EXERCISES

1. Using the MLA system, write a proper reference for each of the unstyled information sets that follow:

a. A book titled Gas Conditioning Fact Book. The book was published in 1962 by Dow Chemical Company in Midland, Michigan. No author is named.

b. An unsigned article titled Booze Plays a Big Role in Car Crashes. The article was published in the November 28, 1997, state edition of the Detroit News. It appears on page 2 of section C.

c. An essay written by C. Wright Mills and titled The Competitive Personality. The essay appeared in a collection of Mills's writings entitled Power, Politics, and People. The collection was published in 1963 by Ballantine Books in New York. The book is edited and introduced by Irving Louis Horowitz. The essay appears on pages 263 through 273.

d. An unsigned article titled Global Warming Fears on Rise. The article was published in the October 25, 1997, issue of Newswatch magazine. It appears on pages 29 to 31.

e. A book written by Paul Theroux and titled The Kingdom by the Sea. The book was published in 1983 by the Houghton Mifflin Company in Boston.

f. A book written by Kate Chopin and titled The Awakening. The book, edited by Margaret Culley, was published in 1976 by W. W. Norton and Company in New York.

g. An article written by James E. Cooke and titled Alexander Hamilton. The article appears on pages 31 and 32 of the World Book Encyclopedia, Volume 9, published in 1996.

h. An article written by Sarah McBride and titled Young Deadbeats Pose Problems for Credit-Card Issuers. The article was published in the November 28, 1997, midwest edition of the Wall Street Journal. It appears on pages 1 and 6 of section B.

i. A book written by Magdalena Dabrowski and Rudolph Leopold and titled Egon Schiele. The book was published in 1997 by the Yale University Press in New Haven, Connecticut.

j. A book written by Jean Descola and titled A History of Spain. The book, translated by Elaine P. Halperin, was published in 1962 by Alfred A. Knopf in New York.

k. An article written by John T. Flanagan and Raymond L. Grimer and titled Mexico in American Fiction to 1850. The article was published in 1940 in a journal called Hispania. It appears on pages 307 through 318. The volume number is 23.

l. A United States government document titled Marine Fisheries Review. It was published by the National Marine Fisheries Service of the U.S. Department of Commerce in 1993. No author is given.

m. A book written by David Kahn and titled The Codebreakers. The second edition of the book was published in 1996 by Scribner's in New York.

n. A book written by Joseph Blotner and titled Faulkner: A Biography. The book was published in two volumes in 1974 by Random House in New York.

o. An article written by Calvin Tompkins and titled The Importance of Being Elitist. The article was published in the November 24, 1997, issue of the New Yorker. It appears on pages 58 through 69.

p. A book written by Thomas Beer and titled Stephen Crane: A Study in American Letters. The book was published in 1923 and reprinted in 1972 by Octagon Books in New York.

q. A review of a book written by Jacques Barzun and titled The Culture We Deserve. The review, by Beth Winona, appeared in the March 1989 issue of American Issues magazine and was titled Barzun and Culture. It appeared on pages 46 through 50.

r. An interview of playwright Neil Simon. The interview was titled Neil Simon on the New York Theater and appeared in the September 3, 1997, issue of the Long Island News, on pages C4–5. The interviewer was Pearl Barnes.

s. A film titled Casablanca. The film was directed by Michael Curtiz and starred Humphrey Bogart, Ingrid Bergman, Claude Rains, and Paul Henreid. It was released in 1942 by Warner Brothers.

t. A television program titled Grizzly. It appeared on WNTR, New York, on February 3, 1997. The station is part of the CBS network.

u. An online article with no author titled Robert Frost: A Reader Response Perspective. The article appears on the online journal Off the Wall and had a location of http://www.offthewall.com/articles/backdated_bin_RobertFrost_archive.html. The article is listed with the date May 8, 2003, but you found it on January 4, 2004.

v. An article accessed through a library data base by May Gottchalk titled Reconsidering Dyslexia. The article was published in the May 24, 2002, issue of Education Matters and you retrieved the article using Wilson Select on November 22, 2003, on the Ferris State Library Web Database Access with the address http://library.ferris.edu/-databaseframes.html.

w. A personal page by Randy Cordial titled My Best Science Fiction Movies Ever. You found the webpage on May 4, 2004 at http://www.cordial.com/bestscifi.htm.

2. Prepare a proper MLA entry for each of the works you plan to use in writing your paper. ◄▣

Handling In-Text Citations

Both the MLA and APA systems use notations that appear within the text and are set off by parentheses. The systems are illustrated by the following examples.

Basic Citation Form

For the MLA system, the citation consists of the last name of the author and the page numbers of the publication in which the material originally appeared. The APA system adds the year to the citation. At the writer's option, the items may be grouped in parentheses or separated, as shown in the following examples. The bibliographic references preceding the passages follow the MLA format.

■ *Bibliographic Reference*

Rothenberg, Randall. "Life in Cyburbia." Esquire Feb. 1996: 56–63.

■ *Passage and Citation*

MLA   A mania for the Internet has invaded many important aspects of our culture.

Newspapers run stories on it, businesses have rushed to set up Web sites, and the Speaker of the House of Representatives has stated that even our poorest children have a stake in the Internet (Rothenberg 59).

Rothenberg states that a mania for the Internet has invaded many important   MLA

aspects of our culture. Newspapers run stories on it, businesses have rushed to set up Web sites, and the Speaker of the House of Representatives has stated that even our poorest children have a stake in the Internet (59).

. . . our poorest children have a stake in the Internet (Rothenberg, 1996, p. 59).   APA

Rothenberg (1996) states . . . have a stake in the Internet (p. 59).   APA

■ *Bibliographic Reference*

Weider, Benjamin, and David Hapgood. <u>The Murder of Napoleon</u>. New York: Congdon, 1982.

■ *Passage and Citation*

Four different autopsy reports were filed. All the reports agreed that there was a   MLA

cancerous ulcer in Napoleon's stomach, but none of them declared that the cancer was the cause of death. Nevertheless, cancer has become accepted as the cause (Weider and Hapgood 72).

. . . Nevertheless, cancer has become accepted as the cause (Weider & Hapgood,   APA

1982, p. 72).

If a source has more than three authors (more than six for the APA), use "et al.," meaning "and others," for all but the first-named one.

■ *Bibliographic Reference*

Baugh, Albert C., et al. <u>A Literary History of England</u>. New York: Appleton, 1948.

■ *Passage and Citation*

Although no one knows for certain just when Francis Beaumont and John Fletcher   MLA

started collaborating, by 1610 they were writing plays together (Baugh et al. 573).

. . . writing plays together (Baugh et al., 1948, p. 573).   APA

Authors with the Same Last Name

If your citations include authors with the same last name, use the initials of their first names to distinguish them.

■ *Bibliographic References*

Adler, Jerry. "Search for an Orange Thread." <u>Newsweek</u> 16 June 1980: 32–34.

Adler, William L. "The Agent Orange Controversy." <u>Detroit Free Press</u> 18 Dec. 1979, state ed.: B2.

■ *Passage and Citation*

<table>
<tr><td>MLA</td><td>As early as 1966, government studies showed that dioxin-contaminated 2,4,5-T caused birth defects in laboratory animals. Later studies also found that this herbicide was to blame for miscarriages, liver abscesses, and nerve damage (J. Adler 32).</td></tr>
<tr><td>APA</td><td>. . . miscarriages, liver abscesses, and nerve damage (J. Adler, 1980, p. 32).</td></tr>
</table>

Separate Works by the Same Author

If your references include two or more works by the same author, add shortened forms of the titles to your in-text citation if you follow the MLA system. Underline shortened book titles and use quotation marks around article and essay titles. For the APA system, use the conventional name–date–page number entry.

■ *Bibliographic References*

Mullin, Dennis. "After U.S. Troops Pull Out of Grenada." <u>U.S. News & World Report</u> 14 Nov. 1983: 22–25.

——. "Why the Surprise Move in Grenada—and What Next." <u>U.S. News & World Report</u> 7 Nov. 1983: 31–34.

■ *Passage and Citation*

<table>
<tr><td>MLA</td><td>As the rangers evacuated students, the marines launched another offensive at Grand Mal Bay, then moved south to seize the capital and free the governor (Mullin, "Why the Surprise" 33).</td></tr>
<tr><td>APA</td><td>. . . and free the governor (Mullin, 1983b, p. 33).</td></tr>
</table>

As the APA example illustrates, if the two works appeared in the same year, put an "a" or a "b," without quotes, after the date to identify whether you are referring to the first or second entry for that author in the bibliography.

Two Sources for the Same Citation

If two sources provide essentially the same information and you wish to mention both in one parenthetical citation, alphabetize them according to their authors' last names, give them alphabetically with a semicolon between them, and position the citation as you would any other citation.

■ *Bibliographic References*

Bryce, Bonnie. "The Controversy over Funding Community Colleges." <u>Detroit Free Press</u> 13 Nov. 1988, state ed.: A4.

Warshow, Harry. "Community College Funding Hits a Snag." <u>Grand Rapids Press</u> 15 Nov. 1988, city ed.: A2.

■ *Passage and Citation*

In contending that a 3 percent reduction in state funding for community colleges would not significantly hamper their operations, the governor overlooked the fact that community college enrollment was expected to jump by 15 percent during the next year (Bryce A4; Warshow A2).

MLA

. . . enrollment was expected to jump by 15 percent during the next year (Bryce, 1988, p. A4; Warshow, 1988, p. A2).

APA

Unsigned References

When you use a source for which no author is given, the in-text citation consists of all or part of the title, the appropriate page numbers, and, for the APA system, the date.

■ *Bibliographic Reference*

"Money and Classes." <u>Progressive</u> Oct. 1997: 10.

■ *Passage and Citation*

According to the General Accounting Office, repairing the country's dilapidated school buildings would carry a price tag of over 110 billion dollars

MLA

> Furthermore, constructing the 6,000 buildings needed to end classroom overcrowding would cost many billions more ("Money and Classes" 10).

APA   . . . many billions more ("Money and classes," 1997, p. 10).

Citing Quotations

When the quotation is run into the text, position the citation as shown below.

■ Bibliographic Reference

Schapiro, Mark. "Children of a Lesser God." <u>Harper's Bazaar</u> Apr. 1996: 205–6+.

■ Passage and Citation

MLA   U.N. investigators who have studied the extent of child labor in third-world countries estimate that "as many as 200 million children go to work rather than to school [. . .] making everything from clothing and shoes to handbags and carpets" (Schapiro 205).

APA   ". . . handbags and carpets" (Schapiro, 1996, p. 205).

With longer, indented quotations, skip two horizontal spaces after the end punctuation and type the reference in parentheses.

■ Bibliographic Reference

Newhouse, John. "The Diplomatic Round: A Freemasonry of Terrorism." <u>New Yorker</u> 8 July 1985: 46–63.

■ Passage and Citation

MLA   One commentator offers this assessment of why foreign terrorist groups don't operate in this country:

> The reason that America has been spared so far, apparently, is that it is less vulnerable than Europe, especially to Middle Eastern extremists. Moving in and out of most European countries isn't difficult for non-Europeans; border controls are negligible. But American customs and immigration authorities, being hyper-alert to drug traffic, tend to pay attention to even marginally doubtful people, and a would-be terrorist [. . .] could come under surveillance for the wrong reason. (Newhouse 63)

APA   . . . come under surveillance for the wrong reason. (Newhouse, 1985, p. 63)

Indirect Citations

If you use a quotation from person A that you obtained from a book or article written by person B, or you paraphrase such a quotation, put "qtd. in" before the name of the publication's author in the parenthetical reference.

■ *Bibliographic Reference*

Klein, Joe. "Ready for Rudy." New York 6 Mar. 1989: 30–37.

■ *Passage and Citation*

Rudolph Giuliani favors the death penalty for "the murder of a law-enforcement   MLA
   officer, mass murder, a particularly heinous killing" but would impose it
   only "when there is certainty of guilt well beyond a reasonable doubt" (qtd.
   in Klein 37).

". . . there is certainty of guilt well beyond a reasonable doubt" (qtd. in Klein, 1989,   APA
   p. 37).

Authors Identified in Text

Sometimes you'll want to introduce a paraphrase, summary, or quotation with the name of its author. In this case the page number may be positioned immediately after the name or follow the material cited.

■ *Bibliographic Reference*

Jacoby, Susan. "Waiting for the End: On Nursing Homes." New York Times
   Magazine 31 Mar. 1974, city ed.: 80.

■ *Passage and Citation*

Susan Jacoby (80) sums up the grim outlook of patients in bad nursing homes by   MLA
   noting that they are merely waiting to die.

Susan Jacoby sums up the grim outlook of patients in bad nursing homes by   MLA
   noting that they are merely waiting to die (80).

Susan Jacoby (1974, p. 80) sums up . . .   APA

Susan Jacoby (1974) sums up . . . waiting to die (p. 80).   APA

> *EXERCISE*   *Using the MLA system, write a proper in-text citation for each of the bibliographic references you prepared for part 2 on page 396. Assume that you have not used the author's name to introduce the material you cite.* ◄▬

Handling Quotations

Set off quotations fewer than five lines long (fewer than forty words long for the APA system) with quotation marks and run them into the text of the paper. For longer quotes, omit the quotation marks and indent the material ten spaces from the left margin (five spaces for the APA system). Double-space the typing. If you quote part or all of one paragraph, don't further indent the first line. If you quote two or more consecutive paragraphs, indent each one's first line three additional spaces (five for the APA system). Use single quotation marks for a quotation within a shorter quotation and double marks for a quotation within a longer, indented quotation. The following examples illustrate the handling of quotations. The documentation and indentation follow the MLA guidelines.

■ *Short Quotation*

Ellen Goodman offers this further observation about writers who peddle formulas for achieving success through selfishness: "They are all Doctor Feelgoods, offering placebo prescriptions instead of strong medicine. They give us a way to live with ourselves, perhaps, but not a way to live with each other" (16).

■ *Quotation within Short Quotation*

The report further stated, "All great writing styles have their wellsprings in the personality of the writer. As Buffon said, 'The style is the man'" (Duncan 49).

■ *Quotation within Longer, Indented Quotation*

Barbara Tuchman's <u>The Proud Tower</u> presents a somewhat different view of the new conservative leaders:

> Besides riches, rank, broad acres, and ancient lineage, the new government also possessed, to the regret of the liberal opposition, and in the words of one of them, "an almost embarrassing wealth of talent and capacity." Secure in authority, resting comfortably on their electoral majority in the House of Commons and on a permanent majority in the House of Lords, of whom four-fifths were

conservatives, they were in a position, admitted the same opponent, "of unassailable strength." (4)

Always provide some context for material that you quote. Various options
exist. When you quote from a source for the first time, you might provide the
author's full name and the source of the quotation, perhaps indicating the author's expertise as well. The passage just above omits the author's expertise; the
passage below includes it.

> Writing in <u>Newsweek</u> magazine, Riena Gross, chief psychiatric social
> worker at Illinois Medical Center in Chicago, said, "Kids have no real
> sense that they belong anywhere or to anyone as they did ten or fifteen
> years ago. Parents have loosened the reins, and kids are kind of floun-
> dering" (74).

Or you might note the event prompting the quotation and then the author's
name.

> Addressing a seminar at the University of Toronto, Dr. Joseph Pomeranz
> speculated that "acupuncture may work by activating a neural pain
> suppression mechanism in the brain" (324).

On other occasions you might note only the author's full name and expertise.

> Economist Richard M. Cybert, president of Carnegie-Mellon University, of-
> fers the following sad prediction about the steel industry's future: "It will
> never be as large an industry as it has been. There are a lot of plants that
> will never come back and many laborers that will never be rehired" (43).

When quoting from a source with no author given, introduce the quotation
with the name of the source.

> Commenting upon the problems that law enforcement personnel have
> in coping with computer crime, <u>Credit and Financial Management</u> mag-
> azine pointed out, "A computor crime can be committed in three hun-
> dredths of a second, and the criminal can be thousands of miles from
> the 'scene,' using a telephone" ("Computer Crime" 43).

After first citing an author's full name, use only the last name for subsequent
references.

> In answering the objections of government agencies to the Freedom of
> Information Act, Wellford commented, "Increased citizen access should
> help citizens learn of governmental activities that weaken our First
> Amendment freedoms. Some administrative inconvenience isn't too
> large a price to pay for that" (137).

Page numbers are not helpful when you cite passages from plays and poems since these literary forms are available in many editions. When you quote from a play, identify the act, scene, and line numbers. Use Arabic numbers separated by periods. Here's how to cite Act 2, Scene 1, lines 295–300 of Shakespeare's *Othello*:

> That Cassio loves her, I do well believe it;
>
> That she loves him, 'tis apt, and of great credit:
>
> The Moor, how be it that I endure him not,
>
> Is of a constant, loving, noble nature;
>
> And I dare think he'll prove to Desdemona
>
> A most dear husband. (<u>Othello</u> 2.1. 295–300)

When quoting from a short poem, use "line" or "lines" and the line number(s).

> In "Dover Beach," Matthew Arnold offers this melancholy assessment of the state of religion:
>
>> The Sea of Faith
>>
>> Was once, too, at the full, and round earth's shore
>>
>> Lay like the folds of a bright girdle furl'd.
>>
>> But now I only hear
>>
>> Its melancholy, long, withdrawing roar. (lines 21–25)

In quoting poetry that has been run into the text, use a slash mark (/) to indicate the shift from one line to the next in the original:

> In his ode "To Autumn," Keats says that Autumn is the "Season of mists and mellow fruitfulness, / Close bosom-friend of the maturing sun" (lines 1–2).

Avoiding Plagiarism

Plagiarism occurs when a writer uses another person's material without properly acknowledging the debt. Sometimes plagiarism is deliberate, but often it happens because students simply don't understand what must be acknowledged and documented. Deliberate or not, plagiarism is absolutely unacceptable. *Any summary, paraphrase, or quotation you include in your paper must be documented as must statistics and graphics.* The only types of information escaping this requirement are those listed below:

1. Common knowledge. Common knowledge is information that most educated people would know. For instance, there's no need to document a statement that the Disney theme parks in California and Florida attract thousands of visitors each year. However, if you include precise daily, monthly, or yearly figures, then documentation is necessary.

2. Your own conclusions. As you write your paper, you'll incorporate your own conclusions at various points. (See the margin notes accompanying Keith Jacque's library research paper, page 372, for examples.) Such comments require no documentation. The same holds true for your own research. If you polled students on a campus issue, simply present the findings as your own.

3. Facts found in many sources. Facts such as the year of Shakespeare's death, the size of the 2001 national budget surplus, and the location of the Taj Mahal need not be documented.

4. Standard terms. Terms widely used in a particular field require no documentation. Examples include such computer terms as *mouse, floppy disk,* and *download.*

Any piece of information not set off with quotation marks must be in your own words. Otherwise, even though you name your source, you plagiarize by stealing the original phrasing.

The following passages illustrate the improper and proper use of source material.

Original Passage

One might contend, of course, that our country's biological diversity is so great and the land is so developed—so criss-crossed with the works of man—that it will soon be hard to build a dam anywhere without endangering some species. But as we develop a national inventory of endangered species, we certainly can plan our *necessary* development so as to exterminate the smallest number possible. [. . .]

James L. Buckley, "Three Cheers for the Snail Darter,"
National Review, September 14, 1979: 1144–45.

■ *Plagiarism*

Our country's biological diversity is so great and the land is so developed that it will soon be hard to build a dam anywhere without endangering some species. But as we develop a national inventory of endangered species, we certainly can plan our necessary development so as to exterminate the smallest number possible.

This writer clearly plagiarizes. The absence of Buckley's name and the failure to enclose his words in quotation marks create the impression that this passage is the student's own work.

■ *Plagiarism*

Our country's biological diversity is so great and the land so developed that in the near future we may pose a threat to some creature whenever we construct a dam. By developing a national inventory of endangered species, however, we can plan necessary development so as to preserve as many species as possible (Buckley 1144).

This version credits the ideas to Buckley, but the student has plagiarized by failing to put quotation marks around the phrasing (underlined here) that was copied from the original. As a result, readers will think that the passage represents the student's own wording.

■ *Proper Use of Original*

> America has so many kinds of plants and animals, and it is so built up, that in the near future we may pose a threat to some living thing just by damming some waterway. If, however, we knew which of our nation's plants and animals were threatened, we could use this information to preserve as many species as we can (Buckley 1144).

This student has identified the author and used her own words. As a result, no plagiarism occurs.

Plagiarism is a serious offense because it robs the original writer of recognition. Students caught plagiarizing risk failure in the course or perhaps suspension from school. Whenever you are unsure whether material requires documentation, supply a reference. And always handle direct quotations by following the guidelines beginning on page 402.

ADDITIONAL RESEARCH STRATEGIES: INTERVIEWS, QUESTIONNAIRES, DIRECT OBSERVATIONS

The library isn't the only source of information for research writing. Investigators also gather information through *primary research,* which includes such activities as consulting public records in local, state, and federal archives, performing experiments, conducting interviews, sending out questionnaires, and making direct observations of various kinds.

This chapter focuses on the latter three types, the most common primary research strategies.

The Value of Primary Research

What makes primary research so valuable? First, it allows individuals and organizations to collect recent information, often unavailable elsewhere, that precisely suits their needs. A company that has developed a new product can't turn to published data to estimate its sales prospects; such information simply doesn't exist. But polling test users with a well-crafted questionnaire could suggest some answers and perhaps also some tips for improving the product. Similarly, someone wanting to gauge the success of an ongoing clothing drive by a local charitable organization might interview its director.

Even when published material exists, it may not contain desired information. Although numerous articles discuss student attitudes about required courses, you probably wouldn't find a report that explores student reaction to a new general-education requirement at your school. You could, however, assemble this information by distributing a questionnaire. The findings might even contradict, and therefore cause you to question, the conclusions of others.

Primary research can also yield unexpected and significant material. Suppose you're investigating adult illiteracy, and you interview a professor with a specialty in this area of study. She explains the reasons why people who can't read resist help and supplies several relevant examples. Such information might not appear anywhere in print. Certainly the resulting report would carry more weight and elicit more interest than one without such insights.

You can integrate primary research into a report that consists largely of *secondary research,* the kind that depends on library materials. The student who wrote the research paper on electronic monitoring (see pages 363–374) incorporated the results of a personal interview with the director of Michigan's electronic monitoring program. This interview provided information on the scope, operation, success rate, and cost advantage of the program. Often, however, writers detail the findings of primary research in separate reports. This would be the case if, for example, your employer asked you to interview users of a new computer system in order to determine their degree of satisfaction with it.

General Principles for Primary Research

Primary research, like all research, requires well-formulated questions. Such questions must be specifically focused, contain clearly defined terms, and be answerable by the actual research. A vague, general question such as "What attitudes do Americans have about their government?" lacks the necessary precision and therefore can't be resolved. What kind(s) of attitudes? What level or branch of government? Which Americans? How would you gather their opinions? A more realistic question might be "According to the Mason College faculty, how adequate is the new congressional proposal for funding academic research in this country?" You could easily develop and distribute to faculty members a questionnaire addressing the different provisions of the proposal. In addition, you can't resolve ethical or philosophical questions through primary research. While you could use a questionnaire to determine student attitudes about the police using sobriety check lanes, such information won't decide the ethical issue of whether the police should use such check lanes.

For valid results, conduct your primary research in an impartial manner. Always aim to determine facts rather than to justify some belief you hold. This means, first of all, that you must develop questions that have no built-in bias. If you poll other students and ask them to tell you "how core-course teachers on this campus marked their papers unreasonably hard," those responding might falsify their answers to give you what you want. Instead, use neutral phrasing such as "Do you believe core-course teachers on this campus mark your papers fairly or unfairly? Explain." Second, don't rely on atypical sources and situations for your data. If you investigate the adequacy of parking space on campus, don't deliberately observe the parking lots on a day when some special event has flooded the campus with visitors. Careful readers will see what you have done and reject your findings.

Just as you avoid bias when gathering information, so also do you report your results fairly. For one thing, don't use inaccurate interpretations of your findings to make them agree with the conclusions you're after. If you believe peer editing produces questionable results, don't claim that the students in a class you observed spent their time sneering at one another's work when in fact they offered constructive criticism. While such criticism can sometimes be straightforward, certainly most people wouldn't consider it sneering. Similarly, don't report conclusions that are unsupported by your actual research. If you observe a large number of violent acts while watching Saturday cartoons, don't leap to the conclusion that the violence in the cartoons causes violent behavior in children. You simply don't have the evidence to support that assertion. Finally, don't cover up results that you don't like. If your survey of teachers' marking practices shows that most of your respondents believe core-course instructors mark fairly, don't hide the fact because it doesn't match what you expected to discover. Instead, report your findings accurately and rethink your original position. The following section further explores ethical matters.

Ethical Issues

Today most people chuckle at an advertisement for a product recommended by "nine out of ten doctors." We recognize that the doctors were hand picked and don't represent an objective sample of adequate size. As a result, little harm occurs. With primary research, however, distorted investigating and reporting are sometimes hard to detect and can have significant consequences.

Say the officials of Anytown, USA, alarmed at a sharp rise in auto accidents caused by distracted drivers, schedule a special meeting attempting to ban cell phone calls by those driving within city limits. It would be unethical for a reporter opposed to the ban to write a supposedly objective feature article on the issue but include interviews only with people who share his views. Now suppose a presumably neutral group in the city of Lost Wages distributes a questionnaire to residents to gauge their reaction to a proposed gambling casino. It would be unethical to include a biased question such as "Should the city deprive its citizens of the revenue that a casino can provide?" Finally, imagine that a city manager, concerned by reports of motorists running the red light at a major intersection, gets the Department of Public Safety to investigate. A department employee conducts a twenty-minute observation, then writes a report concluding that surveillance cameras are not needed there. Clearly, the employee has acted unethically in drawing a conclusion after such a limited observation. To help ensure that your primary research reports are ethically responsible, ask and answer the following questions.

- Have I attempted to avoid bias in gathering and evaluating information?
- Are my data based on an adequate sample size? If not, have the limitations of the sample been clearly indicated?
- Is my information presented objectively and completely with no intentional effort to omit findings that run counter to my position?
- Are the people involved, whether I'm preparing an interview, questionnaire, or direct observation report, aware that they are part of a study and how the information will be used? Are they protected from harm that might result from their inclusion?
- Do I have permission to name in my report persons interviewed or observed?
- In an interview report, would the interviewee recognize and accept statements attributed to him or her?

- Have I noted any apparent bias in the interviewee?
- In a questionnaire report, have I avoided any biased questions?

Interviews

During an interview, questions are asked and answered. Some interviews amount to little more than brief, informal chats. Others, like those discussed here, may feature extended conversations, involve a series of questions, and require careful preparation. Interviewing an informed person provides you with firsthand answers to your queries, lets you ask follow-up questions, and gives you access to the most up-to-date thinking.

If you major in a business program, an instructor may require you to question a personnel manager about the company's employee relations program. If your field is social work, you might have to interview a case worker as part of your study of some kind of family problem. On the job, you might have to talk with prospective employees and then assess their suitability for a position in the company. Police officers routinely interview witnesses to accidents and crimes, and journalists do the same in pursuit of stories.

Choosing the Interviewee

Professional and technical personnel are a rich source of interview candidates. The faculty of any university can provide insights into a wide range of subjects. Doctors, pharmacists, and other health professionals can draw upon their expertise to help you, as can lawyers, engineers, researchers, corporation managers, and employees at every level of government—federal, state, and local.

Whom you interview depends, of course, on what you wish to know. For information on the safe disposal of high-level nuclear waste, you might consult a physics professor. If you want an expert view on the causes of homelessness, contact an authority such as a sociologist, who could provide objective information. If, however, you want to gain a sense of what it's like to be homeless, you might interview the manager of a shelter or (in a safe place) one or more homeless people.

Preparing for the Interview

If you don't relish the thought of phoning to request an interview, keep in mind that most interviewees are eager to discuss their areas of expertise and are often flattered by the opportunity. The worst that can happen is a turndown, and in that event you can always find someone else in the same field.

Before you phone, review your own upcoming commitments and try to determine which ones you could reschedule if necessary. You may need to make an adjustment to accommodate the schedule of a busy person. When you call, indicate who you are, that you are requesting an interview, the subject of the interview, and how much time you'd like.

If the person agrees to meet with you, then ask when it would be convenient. Carefully record the time, day, and place of the interview, and if for any reason you need to cancel be sure to call well in advance.

Before the interview, do as much background reading as possible. This reading will help you develop a list of key questions and avoid those with obvious and readily available answers. Write out your questions to help ensure that the interview will proceed smoothly.

Good questions permit elaboration and don't call for simple "yes" or "no" answers. To illustrate:

Poor: Is it difficult to work with adult illiterates? (The obvious answer is "yes.")

Better: What have you found most challenging about working with adult illiterates?

On the other hand, don't ask overly broad questions that can't be answered in a relatively brief interview.

Poor: What's wrong with primary-school education?

Better: Why do you think so many children have trouble learning to read?

Avoid questions that are biased and may insult the interviewee.

Poor: Why do you bother to work with adult illiterates?

Better: Why did you decide to work with adult illiterates?

Likewise, avoid questions that restrict the interviewee's options for answering.

Poor: What do you think accounts for the poor academic performance of so many American secondary-school students—too much TV watching or overly large classes?

Better: People often blame the poor academic performance of so many American students on too much TV watching or overly large classes. What importance do you attach to these factors? Do you think other factors contribute to the problem?

The number of questions you prepare depends on the length of the interview. It's a good idea to draft more questions than you think you'll have time to ask, then arrange them from most to least important. If the interviewee keeps to the schedule, you'll obtain your desired information. If the interviewee grants you extra time, your written follow-up will have even more substance.

Conducting the Interview

Naturally you'll want to arrive on time and to bring a notepad and a pen. Sometimes you can tape-record an interview but only if you ask permission first. Because most people warm up slowly, you might start with one or two brief, general questions that provide you with useful background. Possibilities include

"What is the nature of your specialty?" and "How long have you been employed in this field?"

Proceed by asking your most important questions first. If you believe that a question hasn't been answered or that an answer is incomplete, don't hesitate to ask follow-up questions.

As the interview unfolds, take notes but don't attempt to copy everything that's said. Instead, jot down key phrases and ideas that will serve as memory prompts. If you want to capture an essential explanation or some other important material in the interviewee's own words, ask the person to go slowly while you copy them down. When the interview is over, thank the person for talking to you. You may also offer to supply a copy of the finished report. Write a personal note thanking the person for his or her time. With the answers to your questions fresh in your mind, expand on your notes by filling in details, supplying necessary connections between points that were made, and noting your reactions.

Writing About the Interview

The project you're working on determines how to handle your interview information. If you're preparing a library research paper, include the material, suitably presented, at the appropriate spot and document it according to whatever system, MLA or APA, you're using (see page 381).

Often, however, you'll be asked to prepare a separate report of the interview. Then, as with any other report, you'll need to organize and present the material in an effective order. Your topic, purpose, and audience will determine the arrangement you select. In any event, remember to establish the context for the report, identify the interviewee and his or her position, and present the information accurately.

◖ SAMPLE STUDENT INTERVIEW REPORT

● ●

Budget Cuts Affect State Police: An Interview Report with Officer

Robert Timmons

Holly Swain

Paragraph 1: establishes context for interview

Confronted with a billion-dollar budget deficit, the state legislature and the governor have been forced to make sharp budget cuts. One of these cuts is the allocation to the state police. This decision has threatened the loss of some police jobs and aroused considerable controversy. How, many ask, will the police, who were already on a tight budget, be able to provide the public with adequate protection when they have even less money and fewer personnel?

Sentence 1, paragraph 2: identifies interviewee and his position

When Trooper Robert Timmons, a state police officer based in Marywood County, first heard that the governor might call for police cutbacks, he didn't believe they would become a reality. Timmons thought the governor was just making "political noise." Actually, the state police head did at first propose cutting 350 jobs, Timmons's among them, to help meet a $19 million cutback. This proposal was rejected in favor of one that combined demotions, pay cuts, and the elimination of special programs. In addition, the amounts allotted for other purposes were also cut.

Remainder of report: presents information provided by interviewee

All of these actions, Timmons says, have had an unfortunate effect on the operations of the state police. As an example, he mentions a sergeant who was demoted to "accident reconstructionist," a job requiring him to review severe accidents and reconstruct what happened for the court. This demotion, Timmons says, has taken an excellent police officer out of the field, where he's most needed, and put him behind a desk.

Timmons notes several bad effects of cuts in the allocation for gasoline. Because of these cuts, troopers are expected to drive just ninety miles a night. Timmons thinks this limitation has a "direct effect on the public." A motorist stranded on a freeway might not be spotted and aided by a trooper who is unable to make another run through that territory. Late-night accidents might go undiscovered, with serious or fatal consequences for those involved. Many more speeders and drunk drivers will escape being caught.

As of now, Timmons says, there are only 3,000 state police, about 400 fewer than needed. Each year, 100 to 200 officers retire. These vacancies need to be filled, but according to Timmons the state academy has been closed for over a year. The personnel shortages that already exist and the cutbacks resulting from the state's budget troubles are making it harder and harder for the state police to do an adequate job of protecting the public.

Officer Timmons understands that the state government needs to control its spending. However, he believes that the present budget cutbacks for a department that is already understaffed are very unwise. "I feel the governor should have given the matter more thought," he says.

Questionnaires

A questionnaire consists essentially of a series of statements or questions to which recipients are asked to respond. Questionnaires help individuals and organizations determine what select groups of people think about particular products, services, issues, and personal matters. You yourself have probably completed a variety of questionnaires, including teacher evaluations and market surveys.

Questionnaires are used extensively both on campus and in the workplace. A social science instructor might ask you to prepare a survey that explores community reaction to a recently implemented curfew for teenagers. A business instructor might want you to survey a test-market group to determine its response to some new product. In fact, some marketing classes focus on survey techniques. But even if marketing isn't your specialty, learning how to construct questionnaires can serve you well in your career. If you work in the hotel, restaurant, or health service field, you could use a questionnaire to gauge customer satisfaction. The same holds true if you manage or own a small repair service. As a landscape specialist, you might survey the people in your community to learn what planting and maintenance services they desire.

Developing the Questionnaire

When you develop a questionnaire, you need to target precisely what you want to know and what group you intend to survey. You could survey restaurant customers to determine their attitudes about the service and the quality of the food or to assess the types of food they prefer. Zero in on only one area of interest and then explore it with appropriate questions.

Begin the questionnaire with a clear explanation of what you intend to accomplish, and supply brief but clear instructions on how to respond to each part. Keep the questionnaire as short as possible, preferably no longer than a page or two. The longer the survey, the less likely that people will answer all the questions.

As you draw up your questions, take care to avoid these common errors:

1. Don't ask two questions in the same sentence. Their answers may be different.

   Unacceptable: Do you find that this year's Ford Taurus has better acceleration and fuel economy than last year's model?

   To correct this fault, use separate sentences.

   Better: Do you find that this year's Ford Taurus has better acceleration than last year's model?

   Better: Do you find that this year's Ford Taurus has better fuel economy than last year's model?

2. Don't include vague or ambiguous questions. Since people won't understand your intent, their answers may not reflect their beliefs.

   Unacceptable: Is assisted suicide a good idea?

   Better: Should assisted suicide be permitted for terminally ill patients?

3. Avoid biased questions. They might antagonize those who don't share your views and cause them not to complete the questionnaire.

   Unacceptable: Should Century City taxpayers continue to waste money on renovating the North Park Bridge?

   Better: Should Century City taxpayers spend an additional $100,000 to complete the North Park Bridge renovation?

Most questionnaire items fall into the categories that follow. The information you want determines which you choose. Often you'll need to include several or all of the categories in your questionnaire.

Two-Choice Items   Some items have two possible responses: yes/no, true/false, male/female.

Example: Do you plan to repaint your house during the summer months?

☐ yes
☐ no

Multiple-Choice Items   Often there are several possible responses to a questionnaire item. When you prepare this type of item, make sure that you include all significant choices and that the choices share some common ground. Don't ask if someone's primary vehicle is a subcompact, compact, full-size, or foreign car as size and place of manufacture are unrelated. To determine whether the vehicle is domestic or foreign, use a separate item.

Example: Check the income group that describes your combined family income.

☐ less than $10,000 a year
☐ $10,000–$20,000 a year
☐ $20,000–$30,000 a year
☐ $30,000–$40,000 a year
☐ $40,000–$50,000 a year
☐ over $50,000 a year

Checklists   Checklists allow respondents to mark more than one option. They can help you determine the range of factors that led to a decision.

Example: Please check any of the following factors that help explain why you decided not to re-enroll your child in Good Growth Private School:

☐ can no longer afford tuition
☐ moved
☐ dissatisfaction with child's progress
☐ disagree with school's educational approach
☐ conflict with teacher
☐ conflict with other staff
☐ child unhappy with school
☐ child had conflict with other children

Ranking Lists   Sometimes you may need to ask people to rank their preferences. This information will help you select the most suitable option from among several possibilities.

Example: Designating your first choice as "1," please rank your preferences in music from 1 through 5.

☐ classical
☐ country and western
☐ jazz
☐ rock and roll
☐ heavy metal
☐ rap

Using the responses to this item, the manager of a local radio station could broadcast the type of music that listeners clearly prefer.

Scale Items   When you are trying to determine the extent to which members of a group support or oppose some issue, using a scale can be helpful. Be sure to have people respond to a statement, *not* a question.

Example: Please circle the response that best reflects your feelings about the statement below.

SA = strongly agree, A = agree, N = no opinion, D = disagree, SD = strongly disagree
Women should be allowed to fly combat aircraft in time of war.
SA   A   N   D   SD

Open-Ended Items   When you want to gather ideas from other people, you might turn to open-ended items—those that don't limit the reader's response. If you do, keep such items narrow enough to be manageable. You should know, however, that readers are less likely to complete open-ended items and that they are difficult to sort and tally.

Example: Please list the three improvements that you would most like to see in Lowden's high school curriculum.

_____

_____

_____

_____

_____

_____

◖ SAMPLE STUDENT QUESTIONNAIRE

• •

Survey on Public Smoking

Please take a few minutes to fill out this questionnaire. Your responses will help Bartram College ensure that its smoking policies are sensitive to the smoking habits and attitudes toward public smoking of Bartram College male smokers.

1. Do you smoke cigarettes? (check one) yes/no item

   _____ yes (If you checked yes, please go on to the next question.)

   _____ no (If you checked *no*, please go on to question 4.)

   Multiple-choice item

2. If you smoke, indicate how many cigarettes each day. (check one)

   _____ less than half a pack

   _____ between a half and a whole pack

   _____ between one and two packs

   _____ more than two packs

3. If you smoke, what are you likely to do upon entering a public place with no posted smoking restrictions? (check one)

   _____ smoke freely

   _____ check to see whether your smoking is bothering others

   _____ ask others whether they would be bothered if you smoke

   _____ not smoke

4. Check the statements you believe are true.

   Checklist

   _____ My health is at risk only if I am a smoker.

   _____ Secondhand smoke contains the same ingredients as directly inhaled smoke.

   _____ Secondhand smoke poses no health risk to nonsmokers.

   _____ Secondhand smoke poses a health risk to nonsmokers.

   _____ Secondhand smoke poses less of a health risk than directly inhaled smoke.

5. Please rate each of the statements below, using the following scale:

   Scale items

   SA = strongly agree, A = agree, N = no opinion, D = disagree,

   SD = strongly disagree.

   _____ There should be no restrictions on public smoking.

   _____ Smoking should be prohibited in stores, banks, offices, and workshops.

   _____ Smoking and nonsmoking sections in restaurants should be separated by a barrier that smoke cannot penetrate.

   _____ Smokers and nonsmokers should have separate workplace lounges.

   _____ All public smoking should be prohibited.

6. Please add one or two comments you might have regarding public smoking. Open-ended item

   _____

   _____

   _____

Testing and Administering the Questionnaire

When you have finished creating the questionnaire, ask several people to respond to the items and gauge their effectiveness. Are any items vague, ambiguous, biased, or otherwise faulty? If so, rewrite and retest them.

To ensure that you obtain an accurate assessment, make certain that you select an appropriate cross-section of recipients. To illustrate, assume that you and many of your campus friends dislike early morning classes. You decide to draw up a questionnaire to sample the attitudes of other students. You suspect that many students share your dislike, and you plan to submit your findings to the college president for possible action. To obtain meaningful results, you'll have to sample a sizable group of students. Furthermore, this group will need to include representative numbers of first-year students, sophomores, juniors, and seniors because these classes may not share a uniform view. Failure to sample properly can call your results into question and cause the administration to disregard them. Proper sampling, on the other hand, pinpoints where dissatisfaction is greatest and suggests a possible response. Thus if first-year students and sophomores register the most objections, the administration might decide to reduce the number of 100- and 200-level classes meeting at 8 A.M.

Totaling the Responses

When the recipients have finished marking the questionnaire, you will need to total the responses. Even without computer scoring, this job is easier than you might think. Simply prepare a table that lists the questionnaire items and the possible responses to each; then go through the questionnaire and add up the number of times each response is marked.

When you finish, turn your numbers into percentages, which provide an easier-to-understand comparison of the responses. Simply divide the number of times each possible response is checked by the total number of questionnaires and then multiply the result by 100.

Writing the Questionnaire Report

When you write your report, don't merely fill it with numbers and responses to the questionnaire items. Instead, look for patterns in the responses and try to draw conclusions from them. Follow the order of the questionnaire items in presenting your findings.

Typically, a report consists of two or three sections. The first, "Purpose and Scope," explains why the survey was performed, how many questionnaires were distributed and returned, and how the recipients were contacted. The second section, "Results," reports the conclusions that were drawn. Finally, if appropriate, a "Recommendations" section offers responses that seem warranted based on the survey findings.

SAMPLE STUDENT QUESTIONNAIRE REPORT

● ●

Findings from Smoking Questionnaire
Distributed to Bartram College Students

Kelly Reetz

Purpose and Scope of Survey

This survey was carried out to determine the smoking habits and attitudes toward public smoking of Bartram College's male students. The assignment was one of my requirements for completing Public Health 201. Each of the 240 male students in Crandall Hall received a copy of the questionnaire in his mailbox, and 72 completed questionnaires were returned. This latter number equals 10 percent of the college's male student population and therefore can be considered a representative sample. Of those responding, 37, or 51 percent, were cigarette smokers. Thirty-five, or 49 percent, were nonsmokers. Of the smokers, all but 11 percent smoked over a pack of cigarettes a day.

> Provides background details on project, profile of respondents

Results of Survey

Smokers seemed fairly considerate of nonsmokers in public places. Only 16 percent said they would smoke freely. In fact, 51 percent said they wouldn't smoke at all. The remaining 33 percent indicated they would either look around to see whether they were bothering others or ask others whether they objected to cigarette smoke.

> Discusses responses to questionnaire item 3

In general, respondents seemed aware that secondhand smoke poses a health risk. Seventy-six percent believe that such smoke contains the same ingredients as directly inhaled smoke, and an amazing 96 percent believe that anyone exposed to secondhand smoke may be at risk. Only 3 percent think no health risk is involved.

> Discusses responses to questionnaire item 4

Opinions were strongly divided on the matter of banning all public smoking, with 79 percent strongly opposed and 21 percent strongly in favor. As might be expected, all of the smokers fell in the first group, but a surprising 51 percent of the nonsmokers did too. A sharp division was equally apparent between supporters and opponents of restaurant barriers, with 81 percent for or strongly for them and 19 percent against or strongly against them. In contrast to the findings on a smoking ban, all of the smokers favored barriers. Respondents overwhelmingly endorsed, 90 percent to 10 percent, prohibiting smoking in stores and banks and providing separate workplace lounges. Nobody registered a "no opinion" vote on any of the statements under item 5.

> Discusses responses to questionnaire item 5

Discusses patterns in responses to items 3–5

Responses to items 3–5 reveal an awareness among smokers of the dangers posed by secondhand cigarette smoke, a concern for the well-being of nonsmokers, and a willingness to accept restrictions, though not an outright ban, on public smoking. This attitude was consistent for both light and heavy smokers. For their part, about half the nonsmokers showed a tolerant attitude by supporting smoking restrictions but rejecting an outright ban.

Discusses responses to item 6

No smokers, but 71 percent of the nonsmokers, responded to the request to provide one or two additional comments. All of these comments dealt with how the respondents would act if bothered by someone else's smoke. Two-thirds said they would move to another spot, half of the remainder said they would ask the smoker to stop, and the other half said they would remain silent rather than risk an argument.

Recommendations

As noted previously, this survey included only male students. To determine how its results compare with those for females, the same questionnaire should be administered to a similar group of female students.

Direct Observations

Often direct observation is the most effective means of answering research questions. If you want to know the extent and nature of violence in children's TV cartoons, watching a number of shows will tell you. Similarly, a researcher who seeks information about living conditions in an inner-city area of some metropolis can obtain it by visiting that locale. Such observations furnish firsthand answers to our questions.

In college and on the job, you may need to report your own observations. If you're majoring in business, an instructor might require a report on the work habits of employees at a small local company. If your field is biology, you might need to assess and report on the environmental health of a marsh, riverbank, or other ecological area. On the job, a factory superintendent might observe and then discuss in writing the particulars of some problem-plagued operation. Police officers routinely investigate and report on accidents, and waste-management specialists inspect and report on potential disposal sites.

The following suggestions will help you make your observations, record them, and then write your report.

Preparing to Make the Observations

First, determine the purpose of your observations and keep the purpose firmly in mind as you proceed. Otherwise, you'll overlook important details and record less-than-helpful information. Obviously, observing a classroom to assess the interaction of students calls for a different set of notes than if you were observing the teacher's instructional style or the students' note-taking habits.

Next, establish the site or sites that will best supply you with the information you need. If you're trying to determine how college students interact in the classroom, then the time of day, kind of class, and types of students will all make a difference. You might have to visit more than one class in order to observe the different types of behavior.

If your observations will take place on private property or will involve an organized group such as a class or a legislative body, you'll need to obtain permission and to make an appointment. Also, you might want to supplement your observations with an interview. Ordinarily, the interview will take place after you make your observations so that you can ask about what you've seen. If technical information is needed in advance, the interview should precede the observations. However, you should have done research first so that you do not waste the expert's time and goodwill by asking about information that is reasonably available.

Because you'll probably be making a great many individual observations, try to develop a chart and a code for recording them. Suppose you're comparing the extent to which students interact with one another and with the instructor in remedial and nonremedial composition courses. After much thought, you might develop a chart like the one following:

Class Designation: Composition 100				
Minutes into observation when interaction occurred	Classroom location of interacting students	Number and sex of students	Subject of interaction	Length of interaction

With certain kinds of observations, using a chart will not be possible.

In developing your code, you would undoubtedly use M = male and F = female to distinguish the sexes. To show the location of the interacting students, FC = front of class, MC = middle of class, and BC = back of class would probably work quite well. Coding the kinds of interaction presents a more difficult task. Here, after considering several possibilities, you might decide upon these symbols: CR = class related, SR = school related, SP = sports, D = dating, O = other matters. To save writing time, you'd probably want to use "min." for "minutes" and "sec." for "seconds" when recording the lengths of the interactions.

Making the Observations

If your visit involves a scheduled appointment, be sure to arrive on time and be ready to take notes. Select a location where you can observe without interfering. If you are observing people or animals, remember that they need to adjust to you before they will behave naturally.

Before you begin taking notes, record any pertinent general information. If you're observing a class, you might note the time it is meeting, its size, the name of the instructor, and whether he or she is present when you arrive. If you're observing an apartment, pertinent information would include the location and condition of the building, the time of the visit, and the general nature of the environment. Note also whether the landlord as well as the tenant knew you were coming: It is amazing how much cleanup landlords can carry out when they know an observer will soon arrive.

Don't feel as though you must take extensive notes. Do, however, record enough details to ensure that you won't forget any events, activities, or features that are important. If you have a chart and coding system, rely on it as much as possible when recording information. Refer to the chart at the bottom of this page for how the coded notes for part of a classroom visit might look.

If you haven't developed a chart, take enough notes so that you can produce a thorough report. Try to follow some note-taking pattern. When observing the condition of an apartment, you could proceed from room to room, jotting down observations such as "Front hallway, entranceway: paint peeling in large strips from wall, paint chips on floor. Hallway dark, bulb burned out. Linoleum curling up along sides. Cockroaches running along lower molding." Remain as objective as possible as you take notes. Record what you see, hear, and smell, and avoid loaded language. If you must record a subjective impression, identify it as such.

Ask questions if necessary, but rely primarily on what you observe, not what you're told. If the landlord of a run-down apartment you're visiting tells you that he's repainting the building but you see no signs that this is happening, ignore what he says or report it along with an appropriate cautionary comment. When you finish, thank the person(s) who made your observations possible or helped you in other ways.

When you leave the observation site, expand your notes by adding more details. Supply any needed connections and record your overall impressions. To illustrate, suppose you are expanding your notes on student interactions in a composition class. You might note that the greatest number of interactions occurred before and immediately after the instructor arrived, that all student–student interactions involved individuals seated together, that student–instructor interactions included students in all parts of the room, and that all the latter interactions were about subject–related matters. This information might stimulate interesting speculation concerning the student–student and student–teacher relationships in the class, causing you to conclude that the students were hesitant about having exchanges with the instructor. As you proceed, record only what you actually observed, not what you wanted or expected to observe.

Class Designation: Composition 100

Minutes into observation when interaction occurred	Classroom location of interacting students	Number and sex of students	Subject of interaction	Length of interaction
0	FC	M-M	SP	1 min. 30 sec.
3	MC	F-F	D	
Instructor arrived				
5	FC, MC, BC	M-M-M-F-F	CR	3 min. 45 sec.
20	FC, MC	M-F-M	CR	1 min.

If upon reviewing your notes you find that you require more information, you may need to arrange a second or even a third visit to the observation site.

Writing the Report

Once your notes are in final form, you can start writing your report. On the job your employer may specify a certain form to follow. As a general rule, all such reports reflect their purposes, focus on relevant information, and remain objective.

Usually you begin by explaining the reason for the investigation, noting any preliminary arrangements that were made, and if appropriate, providing an overview of the observation site. Depending on the nature of the report, the primary means of organization may be as follows:

1. *Narration.* A report on the changing conduct of a child over a three-hour period in a day-care center would probably be organized by narration.
2. *Description.* A report assessing the tornado damage in a large urban area could present its details in spatial order.
3. *Classification.* A visit to a toxic-waste dump suspected of violating state regulations might produce a report classifying the types of waste improperly stored there.
4. *Point-by-point comparison.* If you're comparing two possible sites for a baseball stadium, shopping mall, or other structure, a point-by-point comparison will probably best suit your purpose.
5. *Cause and effect.* This pattern works well for reporting events whose effects are of special concern, such as the testing of a new siren intended to scare birds from an airport runway.
6. *Process.* This arrangement is indicated when readers will want to know step-by-step how some process—for example, a new test for determining the mineral content of water—is carried out.

Conclude the report by discussing the significance of the findings and making any other comments that seem justified.

SAMPLE STUDENT OBSERVATION REPORT

Observations of an Inner-City Apartment Building

Caleb Thomas

To fulfill part of the requirements for Social Service 321, I observed the housing conditions in an inner-city residential area. The building I selected is located in the city of Grand Mound, at the corner of Division Avenue and Hall Street, an area where most of the residents hold minimum-wage jobs or receive some form of public assistance.

> Gives reason for visit, location of site

Notes preliminary arrangements, provides overview of site location

I met the building supervisor, who had agreed to this visit, at 9:30 A.M. on Friday, April 13, 2001. The brick sides of the three-story apartment building appeared to be in good repair, but one second-story window was broken out and boarded up. Most windows had standard window shades, but a few were blocked with sheets or black plastic bags. Two had no coverings of any kind. Overall, the building's appearance was similar to that of several nearby apartment buildings.

Continues overview of site location

Heavy traffic clogged Division Avenue at the time of my visit. Next to the apartment building stood three single-story wooden buildings housing an adult video store, a bar, and a novelty shop, all with boarded windows and peeling paint. Across the street, a single-story Goodwill Store occupied the entire block. In front of it, three women in short skirts walked slowly back and forth, eyeing the cars that passed. Two men sat on crates, their backs to the building, drinking something out of paper bags.

Describes building's hallway

The supervisor opened the unlocked metal door of the apartment building, and we went in. The hallway was lighted by a single dim bulb located on the wall toward the rear. Other bulbs along the wall and in two light fixtures hanging from the ceiling appeared burned out. Scraps of newspaper and chips of paint that had peeled from the ceiling and walls littered the floor. A strong urine-like smell pervaded the air.

Describes apartment hallway

Stating that he couldn't show me an occupied apartment because he "respected the privacy of the tenants," the supervisor took me to an unoccupied apartment on the first floor. He had trouble unlocking the wooden door; the key appeared to stick in the lock. The inside of the door had two bolt locks, one a few inches above the door handle and the other one near the floor. The door opened into a short hall with rooms off either side. Here, as in the building entrance, paint chips from the peeling walls and ceiling littered the floor. A battered socket on the wall held a single bulb, but when I flicked its switch, the bulb did not light. On the hall floor, linoleum curled at the edges. When I bent down to examine it more closely, several cockroaches scurried under the curl.

Describes apartment living room

The first door on the right-hand side of the hall led into a 10-by-12-foot room that the supervisor identified as the living room. Here the walls had been recently painted—by a former tenant, the supervisor said—and a strong paint smell was still apparent. However, nothing else had been done to the rest of the room. The radiator was unshielded, several nail heads protruded from the stained and uncovered wooden floor, and the sagging ceiling had several long cracks. Plaster chips dotted the floor.

A small kitchen was situated behind the living room. Again, linoleum floor covering curled from the baseboard, and cockroaches scurried for cover. The kitchen was furnished with a battered-looking gas stove, but there was no refrigerator (the supervisor said one was on order). The surface of the sink was chipped and had many brownish stains. When I turned on the faucet, a rusty brown stream of water spurted out. I asked for a sample to be tested for lead content, but the supervisor refused.

The bathroom, located at the end of the hall, had no radiator. Its floor tiles, broken in a number of places, exposed a foot-long section of rotted wood. The toilet, with seat missing, would not flush when I tried it but simply made a hissing noise. A brown stain spread over the bottom of the bathtub and a large portion of its sides. The wall tiles around the tub bulged outward and appeared ready to collapse into the tub. The supervisor offered the observation that there had been "some trouble with the plumbing."

Two small bedrooms opened off the left side of the hall. Like the living room both had unprotected radiators, uncovered wooden floors, and cracked ceilings. Walls were papered rather than painted, but long strips of the wallpaper were missing. In one bedroom a piece of plasterboard hung on the wall as if covering a hole. The windows in both bedrooms were covered with sheets tacked to the wall.

When I had finished looking at the bedrooms, the supervisor quickly escorted me from the apartment and the building, declaring that he was too busy to show me any other vacant apartments. He also said he had no time to answer any questions.

Clearly the building I visited fails to meet city housing code: The living conditions are not what most people would consider acceptable. A careful investigation, including a test of the water and of the paint for lead content, seems called for to determine whether this apartment constitutes a health risk.

| Describes apartment kitchen |

| Describes apartment bathroom |

| Describes apartment bedrooms |

| Discusses significance of findings |

NARRATION

Reading Strategies

1. Read the narrative rapidly to get a feel for the story and identify the main point.
2. Identify the main conflict that moves the story forward. Identify the major characters and what they may represent.
3. Read the narrative more slowly with the main point in mind. Keep an eye on how the narrative supports the main point.

Reading Critically

1. Consider if the narrative would seem different if told from another person's point of view. Consider that point of view.
2. Ask whether the narrative really supports the author's main point. Consider what other narratives could be told about the issue and determine whether they might undermine the writer's claims.

Reading As a Writer

1. Determine the setting, conflict, characters, and development of the narrative. You might want to outline the plot to determine how it was organized.
2. Notice any particularly effective movements in the plot. If you find a useful strategy, jot it down.
3. Observe how the writer used dialogue. Make a note of any especially effective uses.

JAMES ALEXANDER THOM

The Perfect Picture[1]

James Alexander Thom (born 1933) is a native of Gosport, Indiana, where his parents were physicians, and a graduate of Butler University. Before becoming a freelance writer in 1973, he worked as an editor for the Indianapolis Star *and the* Saturday Evening Post *and as a lecturer at Indiana University. He has authored one volume of essays and several historical novels, one of which,* Panther in the Sky, *earned the Best Novel Award from the Western Writers of America. His latest novel,* The Red Heart, *appeared in 1998. He is a contributor to many magazines.* "The Perfect Picture" *depicts an incident and an ethical dilemma that Thom experienced as a cub reporter.*

1　　It was early in the spring about 15 years ago—a day of pale sunlight and trees just beginning to bud. I was a young police reporter, driving to a scene I didn't want to see. A man, the police-dispatcher's broadcast said, had accidentally backed his pickup truck over his baby granddaughter in the driveway of the family home. It was a fatality.

> Introduction: notes time, locale, and cause of action; first-person point of view

2　　As I parked among police cars and TV-news cruisers, I saw a stocky white-haired man in cotton work clothes standing near a pickup. Cameras were trained on him, and reporters were sticking microphones in his face. Looking totally bewildered, he was trying to answer their questions. Mostly he was only moving his lips, blinking and choking up.

> Body: paragraphs 2–12; action begins

3　　After a while the reporters gave up on him and followed the police into the small white house. I can still see in my mind's eye that devastated old man looking down at the place in the driveway where the child had been. Beside the house was a freshly spaded flower bed, and nearby a pile of dark, rich earth.

> Time signal
> Key event

4　　"I was just backing up there to spread that good dirt," he said to me, though I had not asked him anything. "I didn't even know she was outdoors." He stretched his hand toward the flower bed, then let it flop to his side. He lapsed back into his thoughts, and I, like a good reporter, went into the house to find someone who could provide a recent photo of the toddler.

> Dialogue

5　　A few minutes later, with all the details in my notebook and a three-by-five studio portrait of the cherubic child tucked in my jacket pocket, I went toward the kitchen where the police had said the body was.

> Time signal
> Secondary event

6　　I had brought a camera in with me—the big, bulky Speed Graphic which used to be the newspaper reporter's trademark. Everybody had drifted back out of the house together—family, police, reporters and photographers. Entering the kitchen, I came upon this scene:

7　　On a Formica-topped table, backlighted by a frilly curtained window, lay the tiny body, wrapped in a clean white sheet. Somehow the grandfather had managed to stay away from the crowd. He was sitting on a chair beside the table, in profile to me and unaware of my presence, looking uncomprehendingly at the swaddled corpse.

> Key event

8　　The house was very quiet. A clock ticked. As I watched, the grandfather slowly leaned forward, curved his arms like parentheses around the head and feet of the little form, then pressed his face to the shroud and remained motionless.

> Time signal

9　　In that hushed moment I recognized the makings of a prize-winning news photograph. I appraised the light, adjusted the lens setting and distance, locked a bulb in the flashgun, raised the camera and composed the scene in the viewfinder.

10　　Every element of the picture was perfect: the grandfather in his plain work clothes, his white hair backlighted by sunshine, the child's form wrapped in the sheet, the atmosphere of the simple home suggested by black iron trivets and World's Fair souvenir plates on the walls flanking the window. Outside, the police could be seen inspecting the fatal rear wheel of the pickup while the child's mother and father leaned in each other's arms.

11　　I don't know how many seconds I stood there, unable to snap that shutter. I was keenly aware of the powerful story-telling value that photo would have, and my professional conscience told me to take it. Yet I couldn't make my hand fire that flashbulb and intrude on the poor man's island of grief.

> Conflict

12　　At length I lowered the camera and crept away, shaken with doubt about my suitability for the journalistic profession. Of course I never told the city editor or any fellow reporters about that missed opportunity for a perfect news picture.

> Time signal
> Action ends

Conclusion: paragraphs 13 and 14; indirectly states point; notes writer's reaction

13   Every day on the newscasts and in the papers, we see pictures of people in extreme conditions of grief and despair. Human suffering has become a spectator sport. And sometimes, as I'm watching news film, I remember that day.

14   I still feel right about what I did.

DISCUSSION QUESTIONS

1. Thom notes in his opening paragraph that he is "driving to a scene I didn't want to see." How does this statement help explain what happens later?
2. Paragraph 10 contains numerous descriptive details. What bearing do these details have on Thom's decision?
3. Do you think that Thom made the right decision? Why or why not?

TOWARD KEY INSIGHTS

How have the media affected our sense of privacy?

Is their influence good or bad?

To answer these questions, consider the role of the newspaper photographer in "The Perfect Picture," TV crews at disasters, and talk shows built around very personal revelations.

SUGGESTION FOR WRITING

Write a personal narrative that features a conflict over a choice between an advantageous and a morally satisfying decision. State your point directly or indirectly, and use time signals and dialogue as necessary.

DAN GREENBURG

Sound and Fury

Dan Greenburg is a native of Chicago who holds a bachelor of fine arts from the University of Illinois and a master of fine arts from UCLA. A prolific writer, he has authored over forty books, including such best sellers as How to Be a Jewish Mother, How to Make Yourself Miserable, How to Avoid Love and Marriage, *and a series of more than twenty-four children's books,* The Zack Files. *His articles have appeared in a wide and diverse range of popular magazines and been reprinted in many anthologies of humor and satire. He has been a guest on* The Today Show, Larry King Live, Late Night with David Letterman, *and other major TV talk shows. In this selection, Greenburg relates a situation in which soft words defused a potentially explosive situation.*

1   We carry around a lot of free-floating anger. What we do with it is what fascinates me.

2   My friend Lee Frank is a stand-up comedian who works regularly in New York comedy clubs. Not long ago I accompanied him to one of these places, where he was to be the late-night emcee and where I myself had once done a stand-up act in a gentler era.

3   The crowd that night was a typical weekend bunch—enthusiastic, hostile and drunk. A large contingent of inebriated young men from Long Island had decided that a comedian named Rusty who was currently on stage was the greatest thing since pop-top cans and began chanting his name after almost everything he said: "Rus-TEE! Rus-TEE!"

4   My friend Lee knew he had a tough act to follow.

5   Indeed, the moment Lee walked on stage, the inebriated young men from Long Island began chanting "Rus-TEE! Rus-TEE!" and didn't give him a chance. Poor Lee, the flop sweat running into his eyes, tried every trick he knew to win them over, and finally gave up.

6   When he left the stage I joined him at the bar in the back of the club to commiserate.

7   "You did the best you could," I told him.

8   "I don't know," he said, "I could have handled it better."

9   "How?"

10   "I don't know," he said.

11   As we spoke, the young men who'd given him such a tough time trickled into the bar area. One of them spotted Lee and observed to a companion that Lee might want to do something about their heckling.

12   Lee thought he heard the companion reply, "I'm down," a casual acknowledgment that he was willing to have a fistfight. Lee repeated their remarks to me and indicated that he, too, was "down."

13   Though slight of frame, Lee is a black belt in Tae Kwon Do, has had skirmishes with three-card monte con men in Times Square, and once even captured a robber-rapist. I am also slight of frame but have had no training in martial arts. I did have one fistfight in my adult life (with a movie producer), but as Lee's best friend, I assumed that I was "down" as well.

14   Considering that there were more than a dozen of them and only two of us, the period of time that might elapse between our being "down" and our being down seemed exceedingly brief.

15   The young man who'd made the remark drifted toward Lee.

16   The eyes of everyone in the bar shifted slightly and locked onto the two men like heat-seeking missiles. Fight-or-flight adrenaline and testosterone spurted into dozens of male cardiovascular systems. Safeties snapped off figurative weapons. Red warning lights lit up dozens of DEFCON systems; warheads were armed and aimed. In a moment this bar area might very well resemble a saloon in a B grade western.

17   "How ya doing?" said Lee, his voice flat as unleavened bread, trying to make up his mind whether to be friendly or hostile.

18   "Okay," said the guy, a pleasant-looking, clean-cut kid in his mid-20s.

19   I was fascinated by what was going on between the two of them, each feeling the other out in a neutral, unemotional, slightly bemused manner. I saw no

hostility here, no xenophobic loathing, just two young males jockeying for position, going through the motions, doing the dance, willing to engage at the slightest provocation. I had seen my cat do this many times when a stranger strayed onto his turf.

20   And then I had a sudden flash of clarity: These guys could either rip each other's heads off now or they could share a beer, and both options would be equally acceptable to them.

21   I'd felt close to critical mass on many occasions myself. But here, feeling outside the action, I could see clearly that it had to do with the enormous reservoir of rage that we men carry around with us, rage that seethes just under the surface and is ready to be tapped in an instant, with or without just provocation.

22   "What're you in town for?" asked Lee casually.

23   The guy was watching Lee carefully, making minuscule adjustments on his sensing and triggering equipment.

24   "It's my birthday," said the guy.

25   Lee mulled over this information for a moment, still considering all his options. Then he made his decision.

26   "Happy birthday," said Lee finally, sticking out his hand.

27   The guy studied Lee's hand a moment. Then, deciding the gesture was sincere, he took the hand and shook it.

28   "Thanks," he said, and walked back to his buddies.

29   All over the room you could hear safeties snapping on, warheads being unarmed. The incident was over, and in a moment it was as if it had never happened.

30   I felt I had just witnessed in microcosm the mechanism that triggers most acts of aggression, from gang fights to international conflagrations. It was so simple: a minor act of provocation. A decision on how to interpret it. Whether or not to escalate. And, in this particular case, a peaceful outcome. What struck me was how absolutely arbitrarily it had all been decided.

DISCUSSION QUESTIONS

1. Discuss the appropriateness of Greenburg's title.
2. Does this essay have a stated or an unstated point? If it is stated, indicate where. If it is unstated, express it in your own words.
3. The expression "our being down" occurs twice in paragraph 14. Explain what it means in each instance.
4. Discuss the effectiveness of the figurative language in paragraph 16.
5. In paragraph 21 Greenburg credits "feeling outside the action" for helping him understand the rage involved in this situation as well as in others. Explain what he means.
6. How often do you think that the "equally acceptable" options mentioned in paragraph 20 occur in confrontations?

TOWARD KEY INSIGHTS

What reasons can you give for the "free-floating anger" that Greenburg mentions at the outset of the essay?

How frequently and in what ways is this anger manifested?

What are some effective strategies for coping with this anger?

SUGGESTION FOR WRITING

Write a narrative about a small incident that turned into a serious confrontation. Possible incidents might include an improper or reckless action of another driver, a minor disagreement with a friend or spouse, or a retaliation for an action at a sporting event. The outcome can be peaceful or otherwise.

MAYA ANGELOU

Momma's Encounter[1]

Maya Angelou has earned a reputation as one of this country's foremost black writers. Born (1928) Marguerite Johnson in St. Louis, Missouri, she spent much of her childhood in Stamps, Arkansas, the locale of our selection, where her grandmother ran a general store. Angelou has written plays, poems, and a six-part autobiography that includes I Know Why the Caged Bird Sings *(1970), from which our selection is taken. She has acted in numerous plays and has served as a television narrator, interviewer, and poet. At the January 1993 inauguration of President William Clinton, she recited a poem, "On the Pulse of Morning," that she had written especially for the occasion. In our selection, Angelou tells about an encounter in which her grandmother, whom she calls Momma, triumphs over a pack of taunting neighborhood children.*

1   "Thou shall not be dirty" and "Thou shall not be impudent" were the two commandments of Grandmother Henderson upon which hung our total salvation.

2   Each night in the bitterest winter we were forced to wash faces, arms, necks, legs and feet before going to bed. She used to add, with a smirk that unprofane people can't control when venturing into profanity, "and wash as far as possible, then wash possible."

3   We would go to the well and wash in the ice-cold, clear water, grease our legs with the equally cold stiff Vaseline, then tiptoe into the house. We wiped the dust from our toes and settled down for schoolwork, cornbread, clabbered milk, prayers and bed, always in that order. Momma was famous for pulling the quilts off after we had fallen asleep to examine our feet. If they weren't clean enough for her, she took the switch (she kept one behind the bedroom door for emergencies) and woke up the offender with a few aptly placed burning reminders.

4   The area around the well at night was dark and slick, and boys told about how snakes love water, so that anyone who had to draw water at night and then stand there alone and wash knew that moccasins and rattlers, puff adders and

boa constrictors were winding their way to the well and would arrive just as the person washing got soap in her eyes. But Momma convinced us that not only was cleanliness next to Godliness, dirtiness was the inventor of misery.

5   The impudent child was detested by God and a shame to its parents and could bring destruction to its house and line. All adults had to be addressed as Mister, Missus, Miss, Auntie, Cousin, Unk, Uncle, Buhbah, Sister, Brother and a thousand other appellations indicating familial relationship and the lowliness of the addressor.

6   Everyone I knew respected these customary laws, except for the powhite-trash children.

7   Some families of powhitetrash lived on Momma's farm land behind the school. Sometimes a gaggle of them came to the Store, filling the whole room, chasing out the air and even changing the well-known scents. The children crawled over the shelves and into the potato and onion bins, twanging all the time in their sharp voices like cigarbox guitars. They took liberties in my Store that I would never dare. Since Momma told us that the less you say to whitefolks (or even powhitetrash) the better, Bailey and I would stand, solemn, quiet, in the displaced air. But if one of the playful apparitions got close to us, I pinched it. Partly out of angry frustration and partly because I didn't believe in its flesh reality.

8   They called my uncle by his first name and ordered him around the Store. He, to my crying shame, obeyed them in his limping dip-straight-dip fashion.

9   My grandmother, too followed their orders, except that she didn't seem to be servile because she anticipated their needs.

10   "Here's sugar, Miz Potter, and here's baking powder. You didn't buy soda last month, you'll probably be needing some."

11   Momma always directed her statements to the adults, but sometimes, Oh painful sometimes, the grimy, snotty-nosed girls would answer her.

12   "Naw, Annie . . ."—to Momma? Who owned the land they lived on? Who forgot more than they would ever learn? If there was any justice in the world, God should strike them dumb at once!—"Just give us some extry sody crackers, and some more mackerel."

13   At least they never looked in her face, or I never caught them doing so. Nobody with a smidgen of training, not even the worst roustabout, would look right in a grown person's face. It meant the person was trying to take the words out before they were formed. The dirty little children didn't do that, but they threw their orders around the Store like lashes from a cat-o'-nine tails.

14   When I was around ten years old, those scruffy children caused me the most painful and confusing experience I had ever had with my grandmother.

15   One summer morning, after I had swept the dirt yard of leaves, spearmint-gum wrappers and Vienna-sausage labels, I raked the yellow-red dirt, and made half-moons carefully, so that the design stood out clearly and mask-like. I put the rake behind the Store and came through the back of the house to find Grandmother on the front porch in her big, wide white apron. The apron was so stiff by virtue of the starch that it could have stood alone. Momma was admiring the yard, so I joined her. It truly looked like a flat redhead that had been raked with a big-toothed comb. Momma didn't say anything but I knew she liked it. She looked over toward the school principal's house and to the right at Mr. McElroy's. She was hoping one of those community pillars would see the design before the day's business wiped it out. Then she looked upward to the school. My head had swung with hers, so at just about the same time we saw a troop of the powhitetrash kids marching over the hill and down by the side of the school.

16   I looked to Momma for direction. She did an excellent job of sagging from her waist down, but from the waist up she seemed to be pulling for the top of the oak tree across the road. Then she began to moan a hymn. Maybe not to moan, but the tune was so slow and the meter so strange that she could have been moaning. She didn't look at me again. When the children reached halfway down the hill, halfway to the Store, she said without turning, "Sister, go on inside."

17   I wanted to beg her, "Momma, don't wait for them. Come on inside with me. If they come in the Store, you go to the bedroom and let me wait on them. They only frighten me if you're around. Alone I know how to handle them." But of course I couldn't say anything, so I went in and stood behind the screen door.

18   Before the girls got to the porch I heard their laughter crackling and popping like pine logs in a cooking stove. I suppose my lifelong paranoia was born in those cold, molasses-slow minutes. They came finally to stand on the ground in front of Momma. At first they pretended seriousness. Then one of them wrapped her right arm in the crook of her left, pushed out her mouth and started to hum. I realized that she was aping my grandmother. Another said, "Naw, Helen, you ain't standing like her. This here's it." Then she lifted her chest, folded her arms and mocked that strange carriage that was Annie Henderson. Another laughed, "Naw, you can't do it. You mouth ain't pooched out enough. It's like this."

19   I thought about the rifle behind the door, but I knew I'd never be able to hold it straight, and the .410, our sawed-off shotgun, which stayed loaded and was fired every New Year's night, was locked in the trunk and Uncle Willie had the key on his chain. Through the fly-specked screen-door, I could see that the arms of Momma's apron jiggled from the vibrations of her humming. But her knees seemed to have locked as if they would never bend again.

20   She sang on. No louder than before, but no softer either. No slower or faster.

21   The dirt of the girls' cotton dresses continued on their legs, feet, arms and faces to make them all of a piece. Their greasy uncolored hair hung down, uncombed, with a grim finality. I knelt to see them better, to remember them for all time. The tears that had slipped down my dress left unsurprising dark spots, and made the front yard blurry and even more unreal. The world had taken a deep breath and was having doubts about continuing to revolve.

22   The girls had tired of mocking Momma and turned to other means of agitation. One crossed her eyes, stuck her thumbs in both sides of her mouth and said, "Look here, Annie." Grandmother hummed on and the apron strings trembled. I wanted to throw a handful of black pepper in their faces, to throw lye on them, to scream that they were dirty, scummy peckerwoods, but I knew I was as clearly imprisoned behind the scene as the actors outside were confined to their roles.

23   One of the smaller girls did a kind of puppet dance while her fellow clowns laughed at her. But the tall one, who was almost a woman, said something very quietly, which I couldn't hear. They all moved backward from the porch, still watching Momma. For an awful second I thought they were going to throw a rock at Momma, who seemed (except for the apron strings) to have turned into stone herself. But the big girl turned her back, bent down and put her hands flat on the ground—she didn't pick up anything. She simply shifted her weight and did a hand stand.

24   Her dirty bare feet and long legs went straight for the sky. Her dress fell down around her shoulders, and she had on no drawers. The slick pubic hair made a brown triangle where her legs came together. She hung in the vacuum of that lifeless morning for only a few seconds, then wavered and tumbled. The other girls clapped her on the back and slapped their hands.

25   Momma changed her song to "Bread of Heaven, bread of Heaven, feed me till I want no more."

26   I found that I was praying too. How long could Momma hold out? What new indignity would they think of to subject her to? Would I be able to stay out of it? What would Momma really like me to do?

27   Then they were moving out of the yard, on their way to town. They bobbed their heads and shook their slack behinds and turned, one at a time:

28   "'Bye, Annie."

29   "'Bye, Annie."

30   "'Bye, Annie."

31   Momma never turned her head or unfolded her arms, but she stopped singing and said, "'Bye, Miz Helen, 'bye, Miz Ruth, 'bye, Miz Eloise."

32   I burst. A firecracker July-the-Fourth burst. How could Momma call them Miz? The mean nasty things. Why couldn't she have come inside the sweet, cool store when we saw them breasting the hill? What did she prove? And then if they were dirty, mean and impudent, why did Momma have to call them Miz?

33   She stood another whole song through and then opened the screen door to look down on me crying in rage. She looked until I looked up. Her face was a brown moon that shone on me. She was beautiful. Something had happened out there, which I couldn't completely understand, but I could see that she was happy. Then she bent down and touched me as mothers of the church "lay hands on the sick and afflicted" and I quieted.

34   "Go wash your face, Sister." And she went behind the candy counter and hummed, "Glory, glory, hallelujah, when I lay my burden down."

35   I threw the well water on my face and used the weekday handkerchief to blow my nose. Whatever the contest had been out front, I knew Momma had won.

36   I took the rake back to the front yard. The smudged footprints were easy to erase. I worked for a long time on my new design and laid the rake behind the wash pot. When I came back in the Store, I took Momma's hand and we both walked outside to look at the pattern.

37   It was a large heart with lots of hearts growing smaller inside, and piercing from the outside rim to the smallest heart was an arrow. Momma said, "Sister, that's right pretty." Then she turned back to the Store and resumed, "Glory, glory, hallelujah, when I lay my burden down."

DISCUSSION QUESTIONS

1. Does this narrative have a stated or an unstated point? If it is stated, indicate where. If it is unstated, express it in your own words.
2. Point out the contrast between Angelou's upbringing and that of the "powhite-trash" children. How does this contrast prepare the reader for the events that follow?
3. Explain what Angelou means in paragraph 22 when she says " . . . but I knew I was as clearly imprisoned behind the scene as the actors outside were confined to their roles."

4. Discuss the significance of the dialogue in paragraphs 28–31.

5. Suggest the significance of the pattern of hearts that Angelou draws in the front yard. Of Momma singing "Glory, glory, hallelujah, when I lay my burden down."

6. Angelou recalls that she was "around ten years old" when the encounter took place. Explain why her age was significant. How would her perception have differed had she been, say, eighteen?

7. Angelou uses the first-person point of view. Explain why third-person narration would have been inappropriate for this narrative.

TOWARD KEY INSIGHTS

Was Momma's strategy for enduring the children's taunts the most effective approach? Why or why not?

What else could she have done?

Has she really won?

Some argue that racism should always be actively confronted since passive endurance only perpetuates it. Do you agree? If not, when and how should racism be confronted and when should it be endured?

SUGGESTION FOR WRITING

Write a narrative that illustrates how a friend, an acquaintance, or a family member achieved a personal triumph through turning the other cheek.

LEWIS SAWAQUAT

For My Indian Daughter

Lewis Sawaquat (born 1935), a Native American who numbers an Indian chief among his ancestors, is an active participant in the affairs of his tribe and in securing scholarships for Native American students. While serving in the U.S. Army, he completed a program in surveying and then spent the remainder of his enlistment in Korea. Later, he attended the Art Institute of Chicago. He is now a retired U.S. government surveyor. In "For My Indian Daughter," Sawaquat addresses anti-Indian prejudice and the development of his sense of "what it means to be Indian."

1   My little girl is singing herself to sleep upstairs, her voice mingling with the sounds of the birds outside in the old maple trees. She is two and I am nearly 50, and I am very taken with her. She came along late in my life, unexpected and unbidden, a startling gift.

2   Today at the beach my chubby-legged, brown-skinned daughter ran laughing into the water as fast as she could. My wife and I laughed watching her, until we heard behind us a low guttural curse and then an unpleasant voice raised in an imitation war whoop.

3   I turned to see a fat man in a bathing suit, white and soft as a grub, as he covered his mouth and prepared to make the Indian war cry again. He was middle-aged, younger than I, and had three little children lined up next to him, grinning foolishly. My wife suggested we leave the beach, and I agreed.

4   I knew the man was not unusual in his feelings against Indians. His beach behavior might have been socially unacceptable to more civilized whites, but his basic view of Indians is expressed daily in our small town, frequently on the editorial pages of the county newspaper, as white people speak out against Indian fishing rights and land rights, saying in essence, "Those Indians are taking our fish, our land." It doesn't matter to them that we were here first, that the U.S. Supreme Court has ruled in our favor. It matters to them that we have something they want, and they hate us for it. Backlash is the common explanation of the attacks on Indians, the bumper stickers that say, "Spear an Indian, Save a Fish," but I know better. The hatred of Indians goes back to the beginning when white people came to this country. For me it goes back to my childhood in Harbor Springs, Mich.

5   **Theft:** Harbor Springs is now a summer resort for the very affluent, but a hundred years ago it was the Indian village of my Ottawa ancestors. My grandmother, Anna Showanessy, and other Indians like her, had their land there taken by treaty, by fraud, by violence, by theft. They remembered how whites had burned down the village at Burt Lake in 1900 and pushed the Indians out. These were the stories in my family.

6   When I was a boy my mother told me to walk down the alleys in Harbor Springs and not to wear my orange football sweater out of the house. This way I would not stand out, not be noticed, and not be a target.

7   I wore my orange sweater anyway and deliberately avoided the alleys. I was the biggest person I knew and wasn't really afraid. But I met my comeuppance when I enlisted in the U.S. Army. One night all the men in my barracks gathered together and, gang-fashion, pulled me into the shower and scrubbed me down with rough brushes used for floors, saying, "We won't have any dirty Indians in our outfit." It is a point of irony that I was cleaner than any of them. Later in Korea I learned how to kill, how to bully, how to hate Koreans. I came out of the war tougher than ever and, strangely, white.

8   I went to college, got married, lived in La Porte, Ind., worked as a surveyor and raised three boys. I headed Boy Scout groups, never thinking it odd when the Scouts did imitation Indian dances, imitation Indian lore.

9   One day when I was 35 or thereabouts I heard about an Indian powwow. My father used to attend them and so with great curiosity and a strange joy at discovering a part of my heritage, I decided the thing to do to get ready for this big event was to have my friend make me a spear in his forge. The steel was fine and blue and iridescent. The feathers on the shaft were bright and proud.

10   In a dusty state fairground in southern Indiana, I found white people dressed as Indians. I learned they were "hobbyists," that is, it was their hobby and leisure pastime to masquerade as Indians on weekends. I felt ridiculous with my spear, and I left.

11   It was years before I could tell anyone of the embarrassment of this weekend and see any humor in it. But in a way it was that weekend, for all its silliness, that was my awakening. I realized I didn't know who I was. I didn't have an Indian name. I didn't speak the Indian language. I didn't know the Indian customs. Dimly I remembered the Ottawa word for dog, but it was a baby word, *kahgee,* not the full word, *muhkahgee,* which I was later to learn. Even more hazily I remembered a naming ceremony (my own). I remembered legs dancing

around me, dust. Where had that been? Who had I been? "Suwaukquat," my mother told me when I asked, "where the tree begins to grow."

12   That was 1968, and I was not the only Indian in the country who was feeling the need to remember who he or she was. There were others. They had powwows, real ones, and eventually I found them. Together we researched our past, a search that for me culminated in the Longest Walk, a march on Washington in 1978. Maybe because I now know what it means to be Indian, it surprises me that others don't. Of course there aren't very many of us left. The chances of an average person knowing an average Indian in an average lifetime are pretty slim.

13   **Circle:** Still, I was amused one day when my small, four-year-old neighbor looked at me as I was hoeing in my garden and said, "You aren't a real Indian, are you?" Scotty is little, talkative, likable. Finally I said, "I'm a real Indian." He looked at me for a moment and then said, squinting into the sun, "Then where's your horse and feathers?" The child was simply a smaller, whiter version of my own ignorant self years before. We'd both seen too much TV, that's all. He was not to be blamed. And so, in a way, the moronic man on the beach today is blameless. We come full circle to realize other people are like ourselves, as discomfiting as that may be sometimes.

14   As I sit in my old chair on my porch, in a light that is fading so the leaves are barely distinguishable against the sky, I can picture my girl asleep upstairs. I would like to prepare her for what's to come, take her each step of the way saying, there's a place to avoid, here's what I know about this, but much of what's before her she must go through alone. She must pass through pain and joy and solitude and community to discover her own inner self that is unlike any other and come through that passage to the place where she sees all people are one, and in so seeing may live her life in a brighter future.

DISCUSSION QUESTIONS

1. After reflecting on the entire essay, try to account for Sawaquat's choice of title.
2. Why, according to Sawaquat, are so many whites prejudiced against Indians?
3. The man who ridicules Sawaquat's daughter is described in paragraph 3 as being "white and soft as a grub." What does this description reveal about Sawaquat's attitude toward him?
4. Why was the "powwow" that Sawaquat discusses in paragraphs 9–10 an important event in his life?
5. What is accomplished by the repetition of "I didn't" in four consecutive sentences of paragraph 11?
6. Discuss the significance of the dialogue in paragraph 13.
7. Reflecting on his daughter's future, Sawaquat says in paragraph 14 that "much of what's before her she must go through alone." Explain what he means.

TOWARD KEY INSIGHTS

Many Native Americans say that they maintain their Indian identity only in their community—for example, by belonging to a tribe. With that in mind, is Sawaquat correct when he asserts that solving the Indian identity problem lies in discovering an "inner self that is unlike any other" and in seeing that "all people are one"? Why or why not?

> *Write a narrative that relates an instance when you experienced some form of prejudice and how you coped with it. Your thesis may be stated or unstated.*

DESCRIPTION

Reading Strategies

1. Identify a thesis statement (possibly first or last paragraph) and/or a statement of purpose. Read the essay with an anticipation of what the description is intended to accomplish.
2. Don't get lost in the details. Note, possibly write in the margins, the overall impression or mood the description is evoking.
3. Decide how much of the description you need to remember. If the description is intended to create a mood, you may read quickly. If you are reading a description of rock formations for a geology class, you might want to take notes that organize the key features you need to remember under the appropriate headings.
4. Note if there is a pattern to the organization of the description. Recognizing the organizational pattern can make even dense writing easier to read.

Reading Critically

1. Identify the point of view of the description. The scene described might look very different from a different vantage point.
2. Look for how the details were selected. An emphasis on different details might have painted a very different picture.
3. Check to see if the conclusion of the essay really follows from the description. Just because a wilderness can be described as pristine doesn't mean that careful logging should be entirely banned.

Reading As a Writer

1. Identify and note down the organizational pattern if it is effective.
2. Jot down any phrases or sections that you find especially effective.
3. Examine the essay for word choice. Notice how the writer obtained the effects he or she did.

JOHN V. YOUNG

When the Full Moon Shines Its Magic over Monument Valley

John V. Young (1909–1999) was born in Oakland, California. After attending San Jose State Teachers College, he spent twelve years as a reporter and editor for several rural California newspapers, then

Title identifies dominant impression: magic

held a series of personnel and public relations positions. In 1966, he became a full-time freelance writer, specializing in western travel pieces. His books include The Grand Canyon *(1969),* Ghost Towns of the Santa Cruz Mountains *(1979, 1984),* Hot Type and Pony Wire *(1980),* State Parks of New Mexico *(1984),* State Parks of Arizona *(1986), and* State Parks of Utah *(1989). His articles have appeared in the* New York Times *as well as in numerous travel publications. In the article that follows, he focuses on the sensations generated first by his surroundings and then by the moonrise.*

1　We were camped here in early spring, by one of those open-faced shelters that the Navajos have provided for tourists in this part of their vast tribal park on the Arizona–Utah border, 25 miles north of Kayenta. It was cool but pleasant, and we were alone, three men in a truck.

Introduction: paragraphs 1 and 2; identifies when, where, who, why
Touch impression

2　We were here for a purpose; to see the full moon rise over this most mysterious and lonely of scenic wonders, where fantastically eroded red and yellow sandstone shapes soar to the sky like a giant's chess pieces and where people—especially white strangers—come quickly to feel like pretty small change indeed.

Sight impression
Comparisons

3　Because all Navajo dwellings face east, our camp faced east—toward the rising sun and the rising moon and across a limitless expanse of tawny desert, that ancient sea, framed by the towering nearby twin pinnacles called The Mittens. We began to feel the magic even before the sun was fully down. It occurred when a diminutive wraith of a Navajo girl wearing a long, dark, velvet dress gleaming with silver ornaments drifted silently by, herding a flock of ghostly sheep to a waterhole somewhere. A bell on one of the rams tinkled faintly, and then its music was lost in the soft rustle of the night wind, leaving us with an impression that perhaps we had really seen nothing at all.

Body: paragraphs 3–8
Fixed vantage point
Sight impressions
Time signal
Sound impressions
Sight impressions

4　Just then, a large woolly dog appeared out of the gloom, seeming to materialize on the spot. It sat quietly on the edge of the glow from our campfire, its eyes shining like mirrors. It made no sound but when we offered food, it accepted the gift gravely and with much dignity. The dog then vanished again, probably to join the girl and her flock. We were not certain it was not part of the illusion.

Time signal
Sight impression
Comparison

5　As the sun disappeared entirely, the evening afterglow brush tipped all the spires and cliffs with magenta, deepening to purple, and the sand ripples stood out like miniature ocean waves in darkening shades of orange. Off to the east on the edge of the desert, a pale saffron glow told us the moon was about to rise behind a thin layer of clouds, slashed by the white contrail of an invisible jet airplane miles away.

Time signal
Sight impressions
Comparison
Sight impressions

6　We had our cameras on tripods and were fussing with light meters, making casual bets as to the exact place where the moon would first appear, when it happened—instant enchantment. Precisely between the twin spires of The Mittens, the enormous globe loomed suddenly, seeming as big as the sun itself, behind a coppery curtain on the rim of creation.

Sight impressions
Comparison
Vivid language

7　We were as totally unprepared for the great size of the moon as we were for its flaming color, nor could we have prepared ourselves for the improbable setting. We felt like the wizards of Stonehenge, commanding the planets to send their light through the magic orifices in line at the equinox. Had the Navajo medicine men contrived this for our benefit?

Sight impressions
Comparison

8　The massive disk of the moon seemed to rise very fast at first, an optical effect magnified by the crystalline air and the flatness of the landscape between us and the distant, ragged skyline. Then it seemed to pause for a moment, as if it were

Sight impressions

Vivid language

Absent sound

Impression

Conclusion: time signal; renames dominant impression

Notes writer's reaction

Touch impression

pinioned on one of the pinnacles or impaled on a sharply upthrusting rocky point. Its blazing light made inky shadows all around us, split by the brilliant wedge of the moon's path between the spires. The wind had stopped. There was not a sound anywhere, nor even a whisper. If a drum had sounded just then, it would not have been out of place, I suppose, but it would have frightened us half to death.

9   Before the moon had cleared the tops of The Mittens, the show was over and the magic was gone. A thin veil of clouds spread over the sky, ending the spell as suddenly as it had come upon us. It was as if the gods had decided that we had seen enough for mere mortals on one spring night, and I must confess it was something of a relief to find ourselves back on mundane earth again, with sand in our shoes and a chill in the air.

DISCUSSION QUESTIONS

1. How does the last sentence in paragraph 7 ("Had the Navajo medicine men contrived this for our benefit?") relate to the purpose of the essay?
2. This description takes the form of a narrative. Where does the climax occur, and how does it affect the viewers?

TOWARD KEY INSIGHTS

What makes certain experiences seem magical?

How important are such magical experiences, and how might they shape our perceptions of the everyday world?

SUGGESTION FOR WRITING

Select a place you know well and describe it by conveying some dominant impression that emerges during daylight hours. Settle on an appropriate vantage point and either identify the impression or allow readers to determine it for themselves.

ROBERT RAMIREZ

The Barrio

Robert Ramirez was born (1949) in Edinburg, Texas. After graduating from the University of Texas–Pan American, he taught freshman composition and worked as a photographer. He worked as a salesman, a reporter, the anchor for the CBS affiliate station in Harlingen, Texas, and as the development officer for fundraising at Texas-Pan American. In our selection, originally titled "The Woolen Sarape" and appearing in Pain and Promise: The Chicano Today, *Mr. Ramirez paints a vivid picture of the barrio, a close-knit Chicano community.*

1   The train, its metal wheels squealing as they spin along the silvery tracks, rolls slower now. Through the gaps between the cars blinks a streetlamp, and this pulsing light on a barrio streetcorner beats slower, like a weary heartbeat, until the train shudders to a halt, the light goes out, and the barrio is deep asleep.

2   Throughout Aztlán (the Nahuatl term meaning "land to the north"), trains grumble along the edges of a sleeping people. From Lower California, through the blistering Southwest, down the Rio Grande to the muddy Gulf, the darkness and mystery of dreams engulf communities fenced off by railroads, canals, and expressways. Paradoxical communities, isolated from the rest of the town by concrete columned monuments of progress, and yet stranded in the past. They are surrounded by change. It eludes their reach, in their own back-yards, and the people, unable and unwilling to see the future, or even touch the present, perpetuate the past.

3   Leaning from the expressway or jolting across the tracks, one enters a different physical world permeated by a different attitude. The physical dimensions are impressive. It is a large section of town which extends for fifteen blocks north and south along the tracks, and then advances eastward, thinning into nothingness beyond the city limits. Within the invisible (yet sensible) walls of the barrio are many, many people living in too few houses. The homes, however, are much more numerous than on the outside.

4   Members of the barrio describe the entire area as their home. It is a home, but it is more than this. The barrio is a refuge from the harshness and the coldness of the Anglo world. It is a forced refuge. The leprous people are isolated from the rest of the community and contained in their section of town. The stoical pariahs of the barrio accept their fate, and from the angry seeds of rejection grow the flowers of closeness between outcasts, not the thorns of bitterness and the mad desire to flee. There is no want to escape, for the feeling of the barrio is known only to its inhabitants, and the material needs of life can also be found here.

5   The *tortillería* [tortilla factory] fires up its machinery three times a day, producing steaming, round, flat slices of barrio bread. In the winter, the warmth of the tortilla factory is a wool *sarape* [blanket] in the chilly morning hours, but in the summer, it unbearably toasts every noontime customer.

6   The *panadería* [bakery] sends its sweet messenger aroma down the dimly lit street, announcing the arrival of fresh, hot sugary *pan dulce* [sweet rolls].

7   The small corner grocery serves the meal-to-meal needs of customers, and the owner, a part of the neighborhood, willingly gives credit to people unable to pay cash for foodstuffs.

8   The barbershop is a living room with hydraulic chairs, radio, and television, where old friends meet and speak of life as their salted hair falls aimlessly about them.

9   The pool hall is a junior level country club where *'chucos* [young men], strangers in their own land, get together to shoot pool and tap, while veterans, unaware of the cracking, popping balls on the green felt, complacently play dominoes beneath rudely hung *Playboy* foldouts.

10   The *cantina* [canteen or snackbar] is the night spot of the barrio. It is the country club and the den where the rites of puberty are enacted. Here the young become men. It is in the taverns that a young dude shows his *machismo* through the quantity of beer he can hold, the stories of *rucas* [women] he has

had, and his willingness and ability to defend his image against hardened and scarred old lions.

11   No, there is no frantic wish to flee. It would be absurd to leave the familiar and nervously step into the strange and cold Anglo community when the needs of the Chicano can be met in the barrio.

12   The barrio is closeness. From the family living unit, familial relationships stretch out to immediate neighbors, down the block, around the corner, and to all parts of the barrio. The feeling of family, a rare and treasurable sentiment, pervades and accounts for the inability of the people to leave. The barrio is this attitude manifested on the countenances of the people, on the faces of their homes, and in the gaiety of their gardens.

13   The color-splashed homes arrest your eyes, arouse your curiosity, and make you wonder what life scenes are being played out in them. The flimsy, brightly colored, wood-frame houses ignore no neon-brilliant color. Houses trimmed in orange, chartreuse, lime-green, yellow, and mixtures of these and other hues beckon the beholder to reflect on the peculiarity of each home. Passing through this land is refreshing like Brubeck, not narcoticizing like revolting rows of similar houses, which neither offend nor please.

14   In the evenings, the porches and front yards are occupied with men calmly talking over the noise of children playing baseball in the unpaved extension of the living room, while the women cook supper or gossip with female neighbors as they water the *jardines* [gardens]. The gardens mutely echo the expressive verses of the colorful houses. The denseness of multicolored plants and trees gives the house the appearance of an oasis or a tropical island hideaway, sheltered from the rest of the world.

15   Fences are common in the barrio, but they are fences and not the walls of the Anglo community. On the western side of town, the high wooden fences between houses are thick, impenetrable walls, built to keep the neighbors at bay. In the barrio, the fences may be rusty, wire contraptions or thick green shrubs. In either case you can see through them and feel no sense of intrusion when you cross them.

16   Many lower-income families of the barrio manage to maintain a comfortable standard of living through the communal action of family members who contribute their wages to the head of the family. Economic need creates interdependence and closeness. Small bare-footed boys sell papers on cool, dark Sunday mornings, deny themselves pleasantries, and give their earnings to *mamá*. The older the child, the greater the responsibility to help the head of the household provide for the rest of the family.

17   There are those, too, who for a number of reasons have not achieved a relative sense of financial security. Perhaps it results from too many children too soon, but it is the homes of these people and their situation that numbs rather than charms. Their houses, aged and bent, oozing children, are fissures in the horn of plenty. Their wooden homes may have brick-pattern asbestos tile on the outer walls, but the tile is not convincing.

18   Unable to pay city taxes or incapable of influencing the city to live up to its duty to serve all the citizens, the poorer barrio families remain trapped in the nineteenth century and survive as best they can. The backyards have well-worn paths to the outhouses, which sit near the alley. Running water is considered a luxury in some parts of the barrio. Decent drainage is usually unknown, and when it rains, the water stands for days, an incubator of health hazards and an

avoidable nuisance. Streets, costly to pave, remain rough, rocky trails. Tires do not last long, and the constant rattling and shaking grind away a car's life and spread dust through screen windows.

19   The houses and their *jardines,* the jollity of the people in an adverse world, the brightly feathered alarm clock pecking away at supper and cautiously eyeing the children playing nearby, produce a mystifying sensation at finding the noble savage alive in the twentieth century. It is easy to look at the positive qualities of life in the barrio, and look at them with a distantly envious feeling. One wishes to experience the feelings of the barrio and not the hardships. Remembering the illness, the hunger, the feeling of time running out on you, the walls, both real and imagined, reflecting on living in the past, one finds his envy becoming more elusive, until it has vanished altogether.

20   Back now beyond the tracks, the train creaks and groans, the cars jostle each other down the track, and as the light begins its pulsing, the barrio, with all its meanings, greets a new dawn with yawns and restless stretchings.

DISCUSSION QUESTIONS

1. What perspective does the author use in starting his description of the barrio? What does the opening demonstrate? How is it related to the concluding paragraph?
2. The essay uses both concrete descriptions and a more general account. Identify examples of each and explain the purpose of these two approaches.
3. What senses does the writer target? Identify examples, including specific words, that are aimed at those senses.
4. In some paragraphs, such as paragraph 14, the writer does not simply focus on a single feature. What technique does the writer employ and why?
5. Identify some metaphors and similes that the author uses in this essay. What does the figurative language accomplish?
6. Identify the thesis of the essay. How is this thesis supported by the details in the description?

TOWARD KEY INSIGHTS

Ramirez describes a specific place that is a fundamental part of a community. How do the places where we live shape our lives? How do our lives, in turn, shape the places?

SUGGESTION FOR WRITING

Write an essay describing a place that has been an important part of your life. As part of that essay, show how the qualities of that place have been important to the quality of your life.

LESLEY HAZLETON

Assembly Line Adventure[1]

Lesley Hazleton (born 1945) is a native of England who earned a B.A. degree from Manchester University and an M.A. degree from the Hebrew University of Jerusalem before emigrating to the United States in 1979. Hazleton is a nationally known automotive journalist with wide-ranging interests that include baseball, psychology, and politics. She has authored six nonfiction books, and her numerous shorter pieces have appeared in a variety of major newspapers and popular magazines. Our essay is excerpted from her latest book, Driving to Detroit *(1998). In it she describes her brief introduction to auto assembly line work and the lessons she learned from the experience.*

1   I'd toured many auto plants before, and physically this was not much different. That is, it was an assault on the senses: an enclosed, windowless world of harsh artificial light and hard concrete floors ringing with the discordant cacophony of industrial production. Metal rang on metal. Stamping presses clanked, power tools whined, pulleys groaned, hoists clanged, welding robots whooshed, sparks crackled, lasers beeped, compressed air hissed, bolts banged into place, trolleys rumbled down the aisles, and all the while, conveyor belts carrying cars in one stage or another of production, from bare metal frames to fully painted bodies, clattered and clanketed beside us and behind us and even over our heads.

2   At five in the afternoon, I started work, joining three other workers stationed around a huge rotating machine. Our job was to feed a robot.

3   Officially, we were preparing dashboard molds for foam injection. In fact, we were simply loading and unloading the machine for the robot, which injected the foam and then wiped its own nozzle as though it were wiping its nose—one of those infuriatingly human gestures that make you think, "Cute," and then hate yourself for having thought it.

4   This was one of the simplest tasks on the whole assembly line. Squirt some filler release into a hole. Lift a light plastic mold and place it on a protruding lip of the machine. Bang a board with your knee to drop three locks to hold the mold in place. Check the locks. Push a black button to bring the lip down into the right position for the next guy. Wait for the machine to rotate and present you with a new lip. And that was it. A ten-second job to be repeated ad infinitum.

5   Two hours later, I moved from one of the simplest jobs on the line to one of the most complicated: assembling the whole instrument panel. Steering wheel, indicator and wiper wands, gauges, dashboard line, the lot.

[1]Editors' title.

6　　Audrey, the woman whose task it was to teach me this job, had a tough challenge ahead of her.

7　　I guessed she was in her mid-thirties. Despite a mass of long brown curly hair, she had a boyish way to her, maybe because of the leather builder's apron she was wearing, its pockets so full of connectors and screws and bolts that it took me a while to realize she was six months pregnant.

8　　"Is this your first?" I asked.

9　　She burst out laughing. "Honey, I'm forty-three years old. And a grandmother. I married again not long ago, and"—she spread her arms wide and stared at her belly—"just look what happened. This sure is the last thing I ever expected."

10　　"How long will you go on working?"

11　　She laughed again. "Do you know how much kids cost? I'm staying right here till the day I pop."

12　　She hadn't stopped working for a moment as we talked. She couldn't. The line was rolling, and it was either keep up or bring everything to a halt. We were standing *on* the line, a wide conveyor belt rumbling past an array of shelves piled high with parts, and beneath an overhead rack dangling power tools and bins of screws. On the line with us, every six feet or so, was a workstand holding an empty dashboard shell, placed upside down on the stand so that it was easy to work on. Audrey's job was to make it into a complete instrument panel.

13　　For the first few moments, standing on the moving belt was almost childishly fun. The world was reversed: you stood still and it went past you. Your mind knew it was you moving, not the world, but your senses told you otherwise. And all the time, the belt vibrated gently underfoot; if it weren't for the noise, it might even have been pleasantly sexy.

14　　"Watch your head," Audrey said, and I ducked as a power wrench came dangling past my right ear. Followed by another. And yet another. Even though I reminded myself that it was me moving, not them, every time I looked up they seemed to be aiming for my brains with a certain inexorable malevolence.

15　　I spent the first half-hour watching Audrey and figuring out how to stay out of the way. So far as I could make out, she had a total of some fifty separate procedures to complete in a logic-defying sequence of about three minutes. Each step had to be performed in perfect timing, so that the right parts and tools were at hand exactly when she needed them. And to add to the pressure, this job was what they called a "show-stopper."

16　　Farther on down the line, the completed instrument panel would be lowered into the "smile joint"—a large lazy U going from side to side of the car's frame. If it didn't fit, the line would stop, and the whole plant would start running behind. "You can't go back and do it again," Audrey said. "You got to do it perfect the first time."

17　　I knew I'd never be able to do this job. Yet Audrey seemed convinced that I was educable. She talked each movement out loud as she worked, with me following her around like a pet dog. Somehow, she convinced me to do a bit here and a bit there, until within an hour, I had the beginning of it down pat:

18　　Walk six stands down the line, past other team members at different stages of the job, and read the manifest hanging on the dashboard shell. Pick up different parts from the shelves alongside the line, depending on whether this is to be a sedan or a wagon, an automatic or a manual shift. Jam a leather sheath over the sharp metal edge to the side of the module. Ease the parts into place. Snap-connect electrical wires: gray to the right, blue to the middle, white to the left.

19   So far so good. I was feeling quite proud of myself. Trouble was, this was only the beginning of the beginning.

20   The rest began to blur: Snap-connect a black fastener, then a yellow one. Don't delay. If you go too slow, the line will take you past the parts you need, and you'll have to start running back and forth for them. Pick up the steering shaft from a shelf and ease its thirty-pound weight down through the center of the module. Arrange the wires to run over the top of the shaft. Slip on and snap a green fastener . . .

21   Or were those last two steps the other way round? "Here," said Audrey, re-doing my work.

22   Okay, now pick up two bronze-colored bolts and screws, two black bolts, a circular piece, and two silver bolts from those big bins alongside the line. Insert the silver bolts. Fine. Place the bronze-colored ones in one place, the black ones in another. Great. Pull down a power wrench from the overhead line . . .

23   I grabbed for it and missed. It began to recede from me. I stretched and yanked it down just in time to tighten the bolts. I had no idea of what I was bolting to what, or why. Neither, it turned out, did Audrey.

24   Right, you've got those bolts nice and tight. Now pick different bronze-colored bolts from another bin. No, not alongside the line—right here, hanging overhead. Fine. Insert them and tighten them by hand for now. What about the wrench? Not there yet, that comes soon. First, thread the electrical wires through the back of the module and out through this flap, then loop them over and under the shaft like so, and then . . .

25   Then what? I couldn't remember. And I was only a third of the way through the job.

26   "Don't worry," said Audrey. "It takes most people four days to learn this job. You're doing real good."

27   That was sweet of her, but it didn't feel real good to me. My attention strayed for a moment, I lost a beat, and suddenly the power tools and screw bins were bearing down on me way before I was ready for them. I worked as fast as I could, one eye on my hands, the other on the dangling wrench going past. I swore, lunged for it, and yanked at the cord as though if I pulled hard enough I could pull back the whole line and slow things down to my pace. I remembered Charlie Chaplin's desperation in *Modern Times,* and suddenly there was nothing remotely funny about it. I dropped a bolt, reached for the wrong wrench, and watched pathetically as Audrey stepped in and put everything to rights. I hadn't felt quite this incompetent since I was a kid trying to thread a sewing machine at school. I never did master that.

28   Every time I thought I had the hang of it all, another two steps somehow reversed themselves in my mind, or one slipped out of existence altogether. My ears were ringing, my mind was reeling, and my hands had never felt clumsier. I began to fumble the screws, inserting them at an angle so that they wouldn't tighten properly and had to be taken out and inserted anew. Audrey was working as hard as I was by now; we stood shoulder to shoulder, me fouling things up, her fixing them.

29   And suddenly it was ten o'clock, and there was a half-hour break for lunch. Ten at night, that is. By now, I was squinting to stop from seeing double. I was

convinced that if I could just work through to the end of the shift, I'd get this job down pat. But as the line came to a halt and everything stopped moving, some remote part of my brain managed to signal a weak but just decipherable message that the pressure was getting to me. It was time to call it quits before I damaged a car, or myself, or worse still, somebody else.

30   "Don't you want some lunch before you go?" said Audrey. But I was too exhausted to even look at food. I needed fresh air. And solitude. And silence. I made my excuses, stuffed my yellow Kevlar gloves into my pocket as a memento, got lost twice trying to find the way out, and finally emerged into the parking lot.

31   Never had a parking lot seemed so beautiful: so quiet, so peaceful, so serene. Even the buzzing yellow of the sodium vapor lights seemed soothing. Behind me, the plant hummed gently, its skylights glowing into the night. Midshift, I was the only person out here, and I had a flash of guilt mixed with giddy freedom, the kind that comes from playing hooky.

32   I found the truck, climbed in, made to start it up. Then stopped, hand in midair, and sat staring at the instrument panel. Something was wrong. I took a moment to figure it out: I'd spent the past few hours working on upside-down instrument panels, and now I was seeing this one the right way up.

33   I reached out and examined it for its component parts, thinking of the man or the woman who'd put it together, and appreciating the way it had been done. This thing I usually took so for granted that I'd never before paid a moment's attention to it, was now an astounding piece of man-made—woman-made—complexity.

34   I started the truck and drove slowly out of the lot, wondering how long I'd keep this awareness that cars are not merely machines, but things put together by human beings, products of real men and real women doing the kind of work that would drive most people crazy. Not long enough, for sure.

DISCUSSION QUESTIONS

1. Comment on the effectiveness of the essay's title.
2. Which of the five sensory impressions does Hazleton include? Refer to specific paragraphs when answering.
3. What is the dominant impression of this essay?
4. What time signals does Hazleton use? Refer to specific paragraphs when answering.
5. This description takes the form of a narrative with the action moving forward until a turning point is reached. Where does this turning point occur?
6. Identify the conclusion of the essay and what it accomplishes.
7. After reading Hazleton's description, how do you think you would tolerate working on an assembly line as a summer job? Discuss.

TOWARD KEY INSIGHTS

What jobs have you done or heard about that you would consider unbearable? What characteristics make them unbearable?

What jobs have you done or heard about that you would find enjoyable? What characteristics make them enjoyable?

Write an essay describing your introduction to some new job. Use an appropriate number of sensory details that create a dominant impression and indicate your reaction to what you learned.

E. B. WHITE

Once More to the Lake

E. B. White (1899–1985) was born in Mount Vernon, New York, and was a graduate of Cornell University. In 1927, he joined the staff of The New Yorker, *launched just two years before, and for several decades produced a steady flow of short pieces for it. Between 1937 and 1943, he also wrote a column, "One Man's Meat," for* Harper's. *He is the author of three critically acclaimed children's books,* Stuart Little *(1945),* Charlotte's Web *(1952), and* The Trumpet of the Swan *(1970), as well as numerous adult works, including several collections of his essays and poems. In "Once More to the Lake," White creates a vivid and memorable word picture of a summer vacation that had great meaning for him and that brought him a sobering insight.*

1   One summer, along about 1904, my father rented a camp on a lake in Maine and took us all there for the month of August. We all got ringworm from some kittens and had to rub Pond's Extract on our arms and legs night and morning, and my father rolled over in a canoe with all his clothes on; but outside of that the vacation was a success and from then on none of us ever thought there was any place in the world like that lake in Maine. We returned summer after summer—always on August 1st for one month. I have since become a salt-water man, but sometimes in summer there are days when the restlessness of the tides and the fearful cold of the sea water and the incessant wind which blows across the afternoon and into the evening make me wish for the placidity of a lake in the woods. A few weeks ago this feeling got so strong I bought myself a couple of bass hooks and a spinner and returned to the lake where we used to go, for a week's fishing and to revisit old haunts.

2   I took along my son, who had never had any fresh water up his nose and who had seen lily pads only from train windows. On the journey over to the lake I began to wonder what it would be like. I wondered how time would have marred this unique, this holy spot—the coves and streams, the hills that the sun set behind, the camps and the paths behind the camps. I was sure the tarred road would have found it out and I wondered in what other ways it would be desolated. It is strange how much you can remember about places like that once you allow your mind to return into the grooves which lead back. You remember one thing, and that suddenly reminds you of another thing. I guess I

remembered clearest of all the early mornings, when the lake was cool and motionless, remembered how the bedroom smelled of the lumber it was made of and the wet woods whose scent entered through the screen. The partitions in the camp were thin and did not extend clear to the top of the rooms, and as I was always the first up I would dress softly so as not to wake the others, and sneak out into the sweet outdoors and start out in the canoe, keeping close along the shore in the long shadows of the pines. I remembered being very careful never to rub my paddle against the gunwale for fear of disturbing the stillness of the cathedral.

3   The lake had never been what you would call a wild lake. There were cottages sprinkled around the shores, and it was in farming country although the shores of the lake were quite heavily wooded. Some of the cottages were owned by nearby farmers, and you would live at the shore and eat your meals at the farmhouse. That's what our family did. But although it wasn't wild, it was a fairly large and undisturbed lake and there were places in it which, to a child at least, seemed infinitely remote and primeval.

4   I was right about the tar: it led to within half a mile of the shore. But when I got back there, with my boy, and we settled into a camp near a farmhouse and into the kind of summertime I had known, I could tell that it was going to be pretty much the same as it had been before—I knew it, lying in bed the first morning, smelling the bedroom, and hearing the boy sneak quietly out and go off along the shore in a boat. I began to sustain the illusion that he was I, and therefore by simple transposition, that I was my father. This sensation persisted, kept cropping up all the time we were there. It was not an entirely new feeling, but in this setting it grew much stronger. I seemed to be living a dual existence. I would be in the middle of some simple act, I would be picking up a bait box or laying down a table fork, or I would be saying something, and suddenly it would be not I but my father who was saying the words or making the gesture. It gave me a creepy sensation.

5   We went fishing the first morning. I felt the same damp moss covering the worms in the bait can, and saw the dragonfly alight on the tip of my rod as it hovered a few inches from the surface of the water. It was the arrival of this fly that convinced me beyond any doubt that everything was as it always had been, that the years were a mirage and there had been no years. The small waves were the same, chucking the rowboat under the chin as we fished at anchor, and the boat was the same boat, the same color green and the ribs broken in the same places, and under the floor-boards the same fresh-water leavings and debris—the dead hellgramite,[1] the wisps of moss, the rusty discarded fishhook, the dried blood from yesterday's catch. We stared silently at the tips of our rods, at the dragonflies that came and went. I lowered the tip of mine into the water, tentatively, pensively dislodging the fly, which darted two feet away, poised, darted two feet back, and came to rest again a little farther up the rod. There had been no years between the ducking of this dragonfly and the other one—the one that was part of memory. I looked at the boy, who was silently watching his fly, and it was my hands that held his rod, my eyes watching. I felt dizzy and didn't know which rod I was at the end of.

6   We caught two bass, hauling them in briskly as though they were mackerel, putting them over the side of the boat in a businesslike manner without any

[1]Insect used as bait.

landing net, and stunning them with a blow on the back of the head. When we got back for a swim before lunch, the lake was exactly where we had left it, the same number of inches from the dock, and there was only the merest suggestion of a breeze. This seemed an utterly enchanted sea, this lake you could leave to its own devices for a few hours and come back to, and find that it had not stirred, this constant and trustworthy body of water. In the shallows, the dark, water-soaked sticks and twigs, smooth and old, were undulating in clusters on the bottom against the clean ribbed sand, and the track of the mussel was plain. A school of minnows swam by, each minnow with its small individual shadow, doubling the attendance, so clear and sharp in the sunlight. Some of the other campers were in swimming, along the shore, one of them with a cake of soap, and the water felt thin and clear and unsubstantial. Over the years there had been this person with the cake of soap, this cultist, and here he was. There had been no years.

7   Up to the farmhouse to dinner through the teeming, dusty field, the road under our sneakers was only a two-track road. The middle track was missing, the one with the marks of the hooves and the splotches of dried, flaky manure. There had always been three tracks to choose from in choosing which track to walk in; now the choice was narrowed down to two. For a moment I missed terribly the middle alternative. But the way led past the tennis court, and something about the way it lay there in the sun reassured me; the tape had loosened along the backline, the alleys were green with plantains and other weeds, and the net (installed in June and removed in September) sagged in the dry noon, and the whole place steamed with midday heat and hunger and emptiness. There was a choice of pie for dessert, and one was blueberry and one was apple, and the waitresses were the same country girls, there having been no passage of time, only the illusion of it as in a dropped curtain—the waitresses were still fifteen; their hair had been washed, that was the only difference—they had been to the movies and seen the pretty girls with the clean hair.

8   Summertime, oh summertime, pattern of life indelible, the fade-proof lake, the woods unshatterable, the pasture with the sweetfern and the juniper forever and ever, summer without end; this was the background, and the life along the shore was the design, the cottages with their innocent and tranquil design, their tiny docks with the flagpole and the American flag floating against the white clouds in the blue sky, the little paths over the roots of the trees leading from camp to camp and the paths leading back to the outhouses and the can of lime for sprinkling, and at the souvenir counters at the store the miniature birch-bark canoes and the post cards that showed things looking a little better than they looked. This was the American family at play, escaping the city heat, wondering whether the newcomers in the camp at the head of the cove were "common" or "nice," wondering whether it was true that the people who drove up for Sunday dinner at the farmhouse were turned away because there wasn't enough chicken.

9   It seemed to me, as I kept remembering all this, that those times and those summers had been infinitely precious and worth saving. There had been jollity and peace and goodness. The arriving (at the beginning of August) had been so big a business in itself, at the railway station the farm wagon drawn up, the first smell of the pine-laden air, the first glimpse of the smiling farmer, and the great importance of the trunks and your father's enormous authority in such matters, and the feel of the wagon under you for the long ten-mile haul,

and at the top of the last long hill catching the first view of the lake after eleven months of not seeing this cherished body of water. The shouts and cries of the other campers when they saw you, and the trunks to be unpacked, to give up their rich burden. (Arriving was less exciting nowadays, when you sneaked up in your car and parked it under a tree near the camp and took out the bags and in five minutes it was all over, no fuss, no loud wonderful fuss about trunks.)

10   Peace and goodness and jollity. The only thing that was wrong now, really, was the sound of the place, an unfamiliar nervous sound of the outboard motors. This was the note that jarred, the one thing that would sometimes break the illusion and set the years moving. In those other summertimes all motors were in-board; and when they were at a little distance, the noise they made was a sedative, an ingredient of summer sleep. They were one-cylinder and two-cylinder engines, and some were make-and-break and some were jump-spark, but they all made a sleepy sound across the lake. The one-lungers throbbed and fluttered, and the twin-cylinder ones purred and purred, and that was a quiet sound too. But now the campers all had outboards. In the daytime, in the hot mornings, these motors made a petulant, irritable sound; at night, in the still evening when the afterglow lit the water, they whined about one's ears like mosquitoes. My boy loved our rented outboard, and his great desire was to achieve singlehanded mastery over it, and authority, and he soon learned the trick of choking it a little (but not too much), and the adjustment of the needle valve. Watching him I would remember the things you could do with the old one-cylinder engine with the heavy flywheel, how you could have it eating out of your hand if you got really close to it spiritually. Motor boats in those days didn't have clutches, and you would make a landing by shutting off the motor at the proper time and coasting in with a dead rudder. But there was a way of reversing them, if you learned the trick, by cutting the switch and putting it on again exactly on the final dying revolution of the flywheel, so that it would kick back against compression and begin reversing. Approaching a dock in a strong following breeze, it was difficult to slow up sufficiently by the ordinary coasting method, and if a boy felt he had complete mastery over his motor, he was tempted to keep it running beyond its time and then reverse it a few feet from the dock. It took a cool nerve, because if you threw the switch a twentieth of a second too soon you would catch the flywheel when it still had speed enough to go up past center, and the boat would leap ahead, charging bull-fashion at the dock.

11   We had a good week at the camp. The bass were biting well and the sun shone endlessly, day after day. We would be tired at night and lie down in the accumulated heat of the little bedrooms after the long hot day and the breeze would stir almost imperceptibly outside and the smell of the swamp drift in through the rusty screens. Sleep would come easily and in the morning the red squirrel would be on the roof, tapping out his gay routine. I kept remembering everything, lying in bed in the mornings—the small steamboat that had a long rounded stern like the lip of a Ubangi, and how quietly she ran on the moonlight sails, when the older boys played their mandolins and the girls sang and we ate doughnuts dipped in sugar, and how sweet the music was on the water in the shining night, and what it had felt like to think about girls then. After breakfast we would go up to the store and the things were in the same place—the minnows in a bottle, the plugs and spinners disarranged and pawed over by the youngsters from the boys' camp, the fig newtons and

the Beeman's gum. Outside, the road was tarred and cars stood in front of the store. Inside, all was just as it had always been, except there was more Coca-Cola and not so much Moxie and root beer and birch beer and sarsaparilla. We would walk out with a bottle of pop apiece and sometimes the pop would backfire up our noses and hurt. We explored the streams, quietly, where the turtles slid off the sunny logs and dug their way into the soft bottom; and we lay on the town wharf and fed worms to the tame bass. Everywhere we went I had trouble making out which was I, the one walking at my side, the one walking in my pants.

12   One afternoon while we were there at the lake a thunderstorm came up. It was like the revival of an old melodrama that I had seen long ago with childish awe. The second-act climax of the drama of the electrical disturbance over a lake in America had not changed in any important respect. This was the big scene, still the big scene. The whole thing was so familiar, the first feeling of oppression and heat and a general air around camp of not wanting to go very far away. In mid-afternoon (it was all the same) a curious darkening of the sky, and a lull in everything that had made life tick; and then the way the boats suddenly swung the other way at their moorings with the coming of a breeze out of the new quarter, and the premonitory rumble. Then the kettle drum, then the snare, then the bass drum and cymbals, then crackling light against the dark, and the gods grinning and licking their chops in the hills. Afterward the calm, the rain steadily rustling in the calm lake, the return of light and hope and spirits, and the campers running out in joy and relief to go swimming in the rain, their bright cries perpetuating the deathless joke about how they were getting simply drenched, and the children screaming with delight at the new sensation of bathing in the rain, and the joke about getting drenched linking the generations in a strong indestructible chain. And the comedian who waded in carrying an umbrella.

13   When the others went swimming my son said he was going in too. He pulled his dripping trunks from the line where they had hung all through the shower, and wrung them out. Languidly, and with no thought of going in, I watched him, his hard little body, skinny and bare, saw him wince slightly as he pulled up around his vitals the small, soggy, icy garment. As he buckled the swollen belt suddenly my groin felt the chill of death.

DISCUSSION QUESTIONS

1. In paragraph 4 White says that while doing or saying things "suddenly it would be not I but my father who was saying the words or making the gesture." Explain what he means.
2. White supplies relatively little information about his son except to mention that his actions resemble White's own as a child. How do you account for this brief treatment?
3. What is the significance of the missing middle track of the road (paragraph 7) and the "nervous sound of the outboard motors" (paragraph 10)?
4. Throughout the essay White spices his descriptions with precise sensory impressions of sight, hearing, touch, taste, and smell. How do these sensory details enhance his writing?
5. On what audience would this essay likely have the largest impact?
6. White's final sentence provides an indirect statement of his main point. What is the point?

TOWARD KEY INSIGHTS

In what ways is the lake part of E. B. White's sense of personal identity?

How and to what extent can places become part of our lives?

What kinds of circumstances or events are likely to become part of our identity?

SUGGESTION FOR WRITING

Write an essay describing a place you have revisited after being absent for a number of years. Indicate what was similar and what was different and describe your reactions to the changes. Appeal to at least three of the five senses.

PROCESS ANALYSIS

Reading Strategies

1. Determine the reason you are reading the process essay. If it is to follow instructions you will need to read in one way; if it is to understand a process, you will need to proceed differently.

2. If you are going to follow the instructions, read over the process first to get an understanding of the whole. Look for specific warnings or feedback you should consider. Get an idea of what the end result should look like. Gather any equipment you will need. Then follow the process step by step, checking after each step to make certain the results you are obtaining match those described in the process.

3. If you hope to understand the process, read first quickly to get an overview of the process. As you read through more slowly, it can be very helpful to take notes outlining the major steps of the process.

Reading Critically

1. Check to see if the process could be completed differently or more effectively. Are there any cautions that are not included in the essay that might be reasonable to observe?

2. If the writer is explaining a process, is there evidence that his account is correct? Check to see that there is good reason to believe the given account. Research could show that there are competing accounts.

Reading As a Writer

1. Observe how the writer uses verbs to indicate actions.

2. Notice how the writer gets from step to step in the process. If there is a strategy you could use, make note of it.

Ian Dunbar

Fast Track to Perfection

Ian Dunbar is a veterinarian and behaviorist who has an international reputation for his "lure and reward" method of training animals. Born in England, he holds degrees from the Royal Veterinarian College of London University and in psychology from the University of California. He now heads the Center for Applied Animal Behavior at his California alma mater. Dunbar has written extensively about his speciality, coauthoring a series of volumes on different breeds of dog. In this selection, he shows readers how to apply his methods to training puppies.

Introduction

Warning

Notes requirements, rewards of training a perfect dog

1   Puppies mature at an astounding rate. Don't let yours fall behind on the developmental curve. Nearly everything a puppy needs to learn must be taught in 12 weeks—between the ages of 2 and 5 months. You can buy yourself time by knowing what and how to teach the puppy before you bring it home. Go to puppy classes, read behavior and training books, watch instructional videos and consult your veterinarian. Then raise your puppy perfectly by meeting these six training deadlines.

Deadline 1: Before You Bring Home a Puppy

Body: paragraphs 2–19

First step and its actions

Reason for action

2   Your puppy should be accustomed to a domestic environment before you bring it home—at around 8 weeks of age. Make sure it has been raised indoors and in close contact with people. It should be prepared for the clamor of everyday life—the noise of the vacuum cleaner, the hoopla surrounding sports programs on the television, children crying, adults arguing. Early exposure—before the pup's eyes and ears have fully opened—allows the puppy to gradually assimilate sights and sounds that otherwise might frighten.

3   The window for socializing begins to close by the time the pup turns 3 months of age, and its most impressionable learning period starts to fade by its fifth month.

Deadline 2: Puppy's First Day at Home

Second step and its actions

4   Misbehavior is the most common reason dogs end up in shelters. This is especially sad because owners can prevent most behavior problems. For instance, if you avoid leaving the pup unsupervised, it won't chew furniture and belongings or soil your house; while teeny accidents do little damage in themselves, they may set a precedent for habits in months to come.

Uses polite command, addressing reader as "you"

5   When you cannot watch your pup, confine it to a crate or a puppy-proofed room, which should contain:

- a comfortable bed.
- a bowl of fresh water.
- a doggie toilet placed away from the bed and which simulates the outdoors. Lay down a sheet of linoleum and cover it with a disposable plastic sheet. Next lay newspaper or something absorbent. Top the three layers with dirt or sod to teach the pup to relieve itself on grass (or concrete slabs for city pups that relieve themselves curbside).

Mini-process within process

- Hollow chew toys with kibble inside to reward your puppy for chewing toys rather than furniture. During its first few weeks at home, a marvelous training ploy is to serve your puppy's food only in chew toys. After it's a chew toy-aholic—and has not had a chewing mishap for at least three months—begin to serve its dinner in a bowl.

6   At least every hour, release your puppy from its crate, quickly leash it and hurry it to its outdoor toilet area. Stand still and give the pup three minutes to produce. When it does, lavishly praise and offer *three* extra special treats. Freeze-dried liver treats work well because dogs love their strong smell.

7   If your puppy eliminates, it may be allowed supervised exploration of the house. If it does not eliminate, lead it back to its crate or puppy-proof room and try again in half an hour.

8   Keep up the once an hour schedule until your pup is at least 3 months old to make certain it never eliminates indoors. After 3 months of age pups start to develop the bladder control necessary for longer waits between potty breaks, but you must still be vigilant. One mistake can set a bad precedent.

> Reason for action

> Warning

9   Always reward your puppy for using its outdoors toilet area, but wait until it has completed its shots before taking it to public property; otherwise it can pick up other dogs' diseases. A pup must not walk or sniff where other dogs have been until it has developed sufficient immunity (between 3 and 4 months old).

> Reason for action
> Warning

Deadline 3: Puppy at 3 Months

10   By 3 months your pup must master socialization and basic manners. Pups that do not will have a hard time picking up these skills later in life. Unfortunately, the risk of disease means dog-to-dog socialization must wait. Meanwhile, teach your pup to be people-friendly.

> Third step and its actions

> Warning

11   As a general rule, your pup should socialize with at least 100 people before it is 3 months old. This is easier than it sounds. Invite eight friends over each Sunday to watch sports on the television. Each Monday invite eight different friends to watch *Ally McBeal* and *Dateline*. Catch up on outstanding social obligations by inviting family, friends and neighbors to weekly puppy parties. On another night, invite some neighborhood children. Socializing a puppy is great because it does wonders for *your* social life.

> Reason for action

12   Show your guests how to hand feed the puppy's kibble to encourage and reward it for coming, sitting and lying down. Ask your puppy to come. Praise profusely as it approaches and offer a piece of kibble when it arrives. Back up, then do it again—and again and again. Then say "Puppy, Sit" and slowly move a piece of kibble from in front of the puppy's nose to between its eyes. As the puppy raises its nose to sniff, it will lower its rear and sit. If the puppy jumps up, you're holding the food too high. When your puppy sits, say "Good dog" and offer the kibble. Now say "Puppy, Down" and lower a piece of kibble from in front of the puppy's nose to between its forepaws. As the puppy lowers its head to follow the food, it will usually lie down. If your puppy stands, hide the kibble in your palm until it lies down. Then say "Good dog" and offer the food. Coach your guests until each can get the puppy to come, sit and lie down three times for a piece of kibble.

> Reason for action

> Feedback tells reader what to expect, how to react

13   When a puppy approaches promptly and happily, it is a sign the dog is people-friendly. Sitting and lying down on request indicates respect for the person issuing instructions. If your puppy is regularly hand-fed by guests, it will learn to enjoy people's company.

> Feedback explains significance of behavior

Fourth step and its actions

Reason for action

Reason for action

Deadline 4: Puppy at 4 1/2 Months

14   Seemingly overnight, puppies become adolescents. Enroll in a training class before yours is 14 weeks old—that is, before it starts to test your limits. A professional will teach it to stop nipping and other behavior no-no's, as well as temper its hyper-turbo energy.

15   Most puppies can start classes at 3 months. Classrooms are generally safe places; the puppies are vaccinated, the floors regularly sterilized. I advise delaying walks in public places until your puppy is 4 months old because of the risk of disease.

16   Puppy classes develop canine social savvy through play with other puppies in a controlled setting. Most classes are family-oriented, offering pups opportunities to socialize with all sorts of people—men, women and children. The number of behaviors your pup learns in its first training lesson will amaze you. Shy and fearful pups gain confidence. Bullies tone it down and become gentle. All dogs learn to come, sit and lie down when requested and listen to their owners and ignore distractions.

Fifth step and its actions

Deadline 5: Puppy at 5 Months

17   Take your dog everywhere—errands around town, car trips to visit friends, picnics in the park and especially to explore the neighborhood. And bring a little bag of kibble. Give a couple of pieces to each stranger who wants to meet your dog. Ask each person to offer the kibble only after your pup sits to say hello.

18   At this point, you may come to believe the canine weight-pulling record exceeds 10,000 pounds. Your dog also may begin to ignore you. A few tips:

Feedback tells reader what to expect

- **Make your dog walk for its dinner.** With kibble in hand, stand still and wait for the dog to sit. Ignore everything else your dog does; it will sit eventually. When it does, say "Good dog," offer the kibble, take one giant step forward, stand still and wait for your dog to sit again. Repeat this until your dog sits each time you stop. Now take two giant steps before your stop. Then three steps, five, eight, 10, 20 and so on. *Voilà*, your dog walks calmly and attentively by your side and sits each time you stop.
- **Take a few time-outs on each walk.** Sit down, relax and allow the dog to settle down and watch the world go by. If your pup is not the sit-still type, take along a treat-stuffed chew toy as an incentive.

Warning

- **Never take your dog's sound temperament for granted.** Outdoors can be scary and offer the occasional surprise. Give your dog a piece of kibble every time a big truck, noisy motorcycle or child on a skateboard whizzes by and your dog doesn't overreact.

Warning

- **Don't make a habit of letting your dog off-leash to run and play with other dogs;** your dog may eventually refuse to come when called. Instead, take your dog's dinner to the park and, throughout its play session, call your dog every minute or so and have it sit for a couple of pieces of kibble. It will soon get the idea and its enthusiastic response will be the talk of the park.

Feedback tells reader what to expect

Sixth step and its actions

Deadline 6: Now and Forever

19   Continue walking your dog at least once a day and take it to a dog park several times a week. Find different walks and dog parks to meet a variety of dogs and people. If your dog always sees the same people and dogs, it may regress socially and become intolerant of strangers.

Reason for actions

20   Now enjoy life with your good-natured, well-mannered companion. Give your dog a special bone—Good dog!—and yourself a pat on the back—Good owner!

> Conclusion: indicates results to expect

DISCUSSION QUESTIONS

1. Point out why Dunbar's title is appropriate. Refer to the essay when answering.
2. In paragraph 18 Dunbar states that the owner might "believe the canine weight-pulling record exceeds 10,000 pounds." Explain what he means.

TOWARD KEY INSIGHTS

Given the choice, what animal would you prefer to train? Why?
What animal would you least like to train? Why?

SUGGESTION FOR WRITING

Write an essay that provides directions for training a riding horse, hunting dog, or guard dog. Be sure to include the reason for any action whose purpose is not obvious and provide cautionary warnings whenever necessary.

ALEXANDER PETRUNKEVITCH

From The Spider and the Wasp[1]

Alexander Petrunkevitch (1875–1964) was a professor of zoology at Yale University for over a third of a century. He was born in Russia and emigrated to the United States in 1903, holding teaching positions at several universities before going to Yale. He gained international recognition for his investigations of spiders and his writings on them, in particular his Index Catalogue of Spiders of North, Central, and South America *(1911) and* An Inquiry into the Natural Classification of Spiders *(1933). A man of wide-reaching interests, Petrunkevitch also produced historical and philosophical works as well as translations of Russian poetry. The following selection, excerpted from a 1952* Scientific American *article, describes a natural process and analyzes the behavior of its two participants.*

1   In the adult stage the [pepsis] wasp lives only a few months. The female produces but a few eggs, one at a time at intervals of two or three days. For each

egg the mother must provide one adult tarantula, alive but paralyzed. The mother wasp attaches the egg to the paralyzed spider's abdomen. Upon hatching from the egg, the larva is many hundreds of times smaller than its living but helpless victim. It eats no other food and drinks no water. By the time it has finished its single Gargantuan meal and become ready for wasphood, nothing remains of the tarantula but its indigestible chitinous skeleton.

2   The mother wasp goes tarantula-hunting when the egg in her ovary is almost ready to be laid. Flying low over the ground late on a sunny afternoon, the wasp looks for its victim or for the mouth of a tarantula burrow, a round hole edged by a bit of silk. The sex of the spider makes no difference, but the mother is highly discriminating as to species. Each species of pepsis requires a certain species of tarantula, and the wasp will not attack the wrong species. In a cage with a tarantula which is not its normal prey, the wasp avoids the spider and is usually killed by it in the night.

3   Yet when a wasp finds the correct species, it is the other way about. To identify the species the wasp apparently must explore the spider with her antennae. The tarantula shows an amazing tolerance to this exploration. The wasp crawls under it and walks over it without evoking any hostile response. The molestation is so great and so persistent that the tarantula often rises on all eight legs, as if it were on stilts. It may stand this way for several minutes. Meanwhile the wasp, having satisfied itself that the victim is of the right species, moves off a few inches to dig the spider's grave. Working vigorously with legs and jaws, it excavates—like a machine—a hole 8 to 10 inches deep with a diameter slightly larger than the spider's girth. Now and again the wasp pops out of the hole to make sure that the spider is still there.

4   When the grave is finished, the wasp returns to the tarantula to complete her ghastly enterprise. First she feels it all over once more with her antennae. Then her behavior becomes more aggressive. She bends her abdomen, protruding her sting, and searches for the soft membrane at the point where the spider's legs join its body—the only spot where she can penetrate the horny skeleton. From time to time, as the exasperated spider slowly shifts ground, the wasp turns on her back and slides along with the aid of her wings, trying to get under the tarantula for a shot at the vital spot. During all this maneuvering, which can last for several minutes, the tarantula makes no move to save itself. Finally the wasp corners it against some obstruction and grasps one of its legs in her powerful jaws. Now at last the harassed spider tries a desperate but vain defense. The two contestants roll over and over on the ground. It is a terrifying sight and the outcome is always the same. The wasp finally manages to thrust her sting into the soft spot and holds it there for a few seconds while she pumps in the poison. Almost immediately the tarantula falls paralyzed on its back. Its legs stop twitching; its heart stops beating. Yet it is not dead, as is shown by the fact that if taken from the wasp it can be restored to some sensitivity by being kept in a moist chamber for several months.

5   After paralyzing the tarantula, the wasp cleans herself by dragging her body around the ground and rubbing her feet, sucks the drop of blood oozing from the wound in the spider's abdomen, then grabs a leg of the flabby, helpless animal in her jaws and drags it down to the bottom of the grave. She stays there for many minutes, sometimes for several hours, and what she does all that time in the dark we do not know. Eventually she lays her egg and attaches it to the side of the spider's abdomen with a sticky secretion. Then she emerges, fills the

grave with soil carried bit by bit in her jaws, and finally tramples the ground all around to hide any trace of the grave from prowlers. Then she flies away, leaving her descendant safely started in life.

6   In all this the behavior of the wasp evidently is qualitatively different from that of the spider. The wasp acts like an intelligent animal. This is not to say that instinct plays no part or that she reasons as man does. But her actions are to the point; they are not automatic and can be modified to fit the situation. We do not know for certain how she identifies the tarantula—probably it is by some olfactory or chemo-tactile sense—but she does it purposefully and does not blindly tackle a wrong species.

7   On the other hand, the tarantula's behavior shows only confusion. Evidently the wasp's pawing gives it no pleasure, for it tries to move away. That the wasp is not simulating sexual stimulation is certain because male and female tarantulas react in the same way to its advances. That the spider is not anesthetized by some odorless secretion is easily shown by blowing lightly at the tarantula and making it jump suddenly. What, then, makes the tarantula behave as stupidly as it does?

8   No clear, simple answer is available. Possibly the stimulation by the wasp's antennae is masked by a heavier pressure on the spider's body so that it reacts as when prodded by a pencil. But the explanation may be much more complex. Initiative in attack is not the nature of tarantulas; most species fight only when cornered so that escape is impossible. Their inherited patterns of behavior apparently prompt them to avoid problems rather than attack them. For example, spiders always weave their webs in three dimensions, and when a spider finds that there is insufficient space to attach certain threads in the third dimension, it leaves the place and seeks another, instead of finishing the web in a single plane. This urge to escape seems to arise under all circumstances, in all phases of life, and to take the place of reasoning. For a spider to change the pattern of its web is as impossible as for an inexperienced man to build a bridge across a chasm obstructing his way.

9   In a way the instinctive urge to escape is not only easier but often more efficient than reasoning. The tarantula does exactly what is most efficient in all cases except in an encounter with a ruthless and determined attacker dependent for the existence of her own species on killing as many tarantulas as she can lay eggs. Perhaps in this case the spider follows its usual pattern of trying to escape, instead of seizing and killing the wasp, because it is not aware of its danger. In any case, the survival of the tarantula species as a whole is protected by the fact that the spider is much more fertile than the wasp.

DISCUSSION QUESTIONS

1. Into how many steps is this natural process divided? In which paragraph or paragraphs is each discussed?
2. Characterize Petrunkevitch's attitude toward his topic. Is it completely objective, or does Petrunkevitch sometimes reveal his personal feelings? If he does, indicate where.
3. Petrunkevitch uses a number of transitional words and phrases to ensure a smooth flow of ideas. Indicate those transitional devices and the paragraphs in which they are found.
4. Where does the conclusion begin and what is its purpose?

TOWARD KEY INSIGHTS

When you read this essay, did you sympathize with the spider, the wasp, or neither? How do you account for your feelings?

Critics of overly violent TV and movie dramas charge that such spectacles deaden our capacity for human sympathy. Might televised nature programs depicting the struggle for existence have a similar effect? Why or why not?

SUGGESTION FOR WRITING

Write an essay explaining some process you perform frequently. Possibilities include flossing your teeth, brewing a pot of coffee, and preparing for a date.

BETH WALD

Let's Get Vertical!

Beth Wald (born 1960) first felt the attraction of the mountains when, at age sixteen, she took a backpacking trip to Canada. A native of Minnesota, she studied botany and Russian at the University of Minnesota and then, in the mid-1980s, began a dual career as a freelance writer and photographer. Her career and her love of climbing have taken her around the world. Her articles have appeared in a variety of climbing and outdoor magazines, as have her photographs, which include environmental and cultural subjects as well as sports and travel. From 1988 to 1992, she was a contributing editor for Climbing Magazine. *In our selection, Wald acquaints potential recruits with the sport of rock climbing.*

1   Here I am, 400 feet up on the steep west face of Devil's Tower,[1] a tiny figure in a sea of petrified rock. I can't find enough footholds and handholds to keep climbing. My climbing partner anxiously looks up at me from his narrow ledge. I can see the silver sparkle of the climbing devices I've jammed into the crack every eight feet or so.

2   I study the last device I've placed, a half-inch aluminum wedge 12 feet below me. If I slip, it'll catch me, but only after a 24-foot fall, a real "screamer." It's too difficult to go back; I have to find a way up before my fingers get too tired. I must act quickly.

3   Finding a tiny opening in the crack, I jam two fingertips in, crimp them, pull hard, and kick my right foot onto a sloping knob, hoping it won't skid off. At the same time, I slap my right hand up to what looks like a good hold. To my horror, it's round and slippery.

4   My fingers start to slide. Panic rivets me for a second, but then a surge of adrenalin snaps me back into action. I scramble my feet higher, lunge with my

---

[1]A large, flat-topped rock formation, 876 feet high, in northeastern Wyoming.

left hand, and catch a wider crack. I manage to get a better grip just as my right hand pops off its slick hold. My feet find edges, and I regain my balance. Whipping a chock (wedge) off my harness, I slip it into the crack and clip my rope through a carabiner (oblong metal snaplink). After catching my breath, I start moving again, and the rest of the climb flows upward like a vertical dance.

5　　　　*The Challenges and Rewards*　I've tried many sports, but I haven't found any to match the excitement of rock climbing. It's a unique world, with its own language, communities, controversies, heroes, villains, and devoted followers. I've lived in vans, tepees, tents, and caves; worked three jobs to save money for expenses; driven 24 hours to spend a weekend at a good rock; and lived on beans and rice for months at a time—all of this to be able to climb. What is it about scrambling up rocks that inspires such a passion? The answer is, no other sport offers so many challenges and so many rewards.

6　　　　The physical challenges are obvious. You need flexibility, balance, and strength. But climbing is also a psychological game of defeating your fear, and it demands creative thinking. It's a bit like improvising a gymnastic routine 200 feet in the air while playing a game of chess.

7　　　　Climbers visit some of the most spectacular places on earth and see them from a unique perspective—the top! Because the sport is so intense, friendships between climbers tend to be strong and enduring.

8　　　　*Anyone Can Climb*　Kids playing in trees or on monkey bars know that climbing is a natural activity, but older people often have to relearn to trust their instincts. This isn't too hard, though. The ability to maintain self-control in difficult situations is the most important trait for a beginning climber to have. Panic is almost automatic when you run out of handholds 100 feet off the ground. The typical reaction is to freeze solid until you fall off. But with a little discipline, rational thinking, and/or distraction tactics such as babbling to yourself, humming, or even screaming, fear can change to elation as you climb out of a tough spot.

9　　　　Contrary to popular belief, you don't have to be superhumanly strong to climb. Self-confidence, agility, a good sense of balance, and determination will get you farther up the rock than bulging biceps. Once you've learned the basics, climbing itself will gradually make you stronger, though many dedicated climbers speed up the process by training at home or in the gym.

10　　　　Nonclimbers often ask, "How do the ropes get up there?" It's quite simple; the climbers bring them up as they climb. Most rock climbers today are "free climbers." In free climbing, the rope is used only for safety in case of a fall, *not* to help pull you up. (Climbing without a rope, called "free soloing," is a *very* dangerous activity practiced only by extremely experienced—and crazy—climbers.)

11　　　　First, two climbers tie into opposite ends of a 150-foot-long nylon rope. Then one of them, the belayer, anchors himself or herself to a rock or tree. The other, the leader, starts to climb, occasionally stopping to jam a variety of aluminum wedges or other special gadgets, generically referred to as protection, into cracks in the rock. To each of these, he or she attaches a snaplink, called a carabiner, and clips the rope through. As the leader climbs, the belayer feeds out the rope, and it runs through the carabiners. If the leader falls, the belayer holds the rope, and the highest piece of protection catches the leader. The belayer uses special techniques and equipment to make it easy to stop falls.

12　　　　When the leader reaches the end of a section of rock—called the pitch— and sets an anchor, he or she becomes the belayer. This person pulls up the slack of the rope as the other partner climbs and removes the protection.

Once together again, they can either continue in the same manner or switch leaders. These worldwide techniques work on rock formations, cliffs, peaks, even buildings.

13   ***Rocks, Rocks Everywhere***   Some of the best climbing cliffs in the country are in the Shawangunk Mountains, only two hours from New York City. Seneca Rocks in West Virginia draws climbers from Washington, D.C., and Pittsburgh, Pennsylvania. Chattanooga, Tennessee, has a fine cliff within the city limits. Most states in the U.S. and provinces in Canada offer at least one or two good climbing opportunities.

14   Even if there are no large cliffs or rock formations nearby, you can climb smaller rocks to practice techniques and get stronger. This is called bouldering. Many climbers who live in cities and towns have created climbing areas out of old stone walls and buildings. Ask someone at your local outdoor shop where you can go to start climbing.

15   ***Get a Helping Hand***   There's no substitute for an expert teacher when it comes to learning basic techniques and safety procedures. One of the best (and least expensive) ways to learn climbing is to convince a veteran climber in your area to teach you. You can usually meet these types at the local crag or climbing shop.

16   As another option, many universities and colleges, some high schools, and some YMCAs have climbing clubs. Their main purpose is to introduce people to climbing and to teach the basics. Other clubs, such as the Appalachian Mountain Club in the eastern U.S. and the Mountaineers on the West Coast, also provide instruction. Ask at your outdoor shop for the names of clubs in your area.

17   If you live in a place completely lacking rocks and climbers, you can attend one of the fine climbing schools at the major climbing area closest to you. Magazines like *Climbing, Rock & Ice,* and *Outside* publish lists of these schools. Once you learn the basics, you're ready to get vertical.

18   In rock climbing, you can both lose yourself and find yourself. Life and all its troubles are reduced to figuring out the puzzle of the next section of cliff or forgotten in the challenge and delight of moving through vertical space. And learning how to control anxiety, how to piece together a difficult sequence of moves, and how to communicate with a partner are all skills that prove incredibly useful back on the ground!

DISCUSSION QUESTIONS

1. Discuss the effectiveness of Wald's title.
2. At the beginning of the essay, Wald notes that she is 400 feet up one side of Devil's Tower and positioned above her climbing partner. What do you think these statements accomplish?
3. In which paragraphs does Wald detail the actual process of climbing? What do the remaining paragraphs in the body of the essay accomplish?
4. Point out two places in the first four paragraphs where Wald cites reasons for her actions.
5. What attributes does Wald believe a rock climber must have? Refer to the essay when answering.
6. After reading this essay, are you ready to begin rock climbing? Does your answer stem from Wald's content, the manner of presentation, or both? Discuss.

What challenging activities appeal to you?
What level of risk are you willing to accept in an activity?
How do you account for your attitude about taking risks?

Write a process paper in which you explain the attributes required and the steps involved in one of your recreational activities.

SHARI CAUDRON

Can Generation Xers Be Trained?

Shari Caudron earned a B.A. in journalism and a master's degree in human communication. She is currently pursuing an MFA in creative nonfiction. She has been a full-time freelance journalist since 1989. In this selection she presents the procedures that many businesses have found effective in training members of "Generation X."

1   If you want to know how to reach Generation Xers, eavesdrop on a training seminar conducted by Pencom International, a Denver-based company that provides training products to such restaurant chains as Denny's and Pizza Hut. You won't hear the trainers referring to restaurant patrons as "prospective customers." Instead, they're "hot targets." The trainers don't encourage new employees to "recognize and serve customers quickly." They're told to "lock on and fire." The language isn't what you'd typically find at a corporate training seminar. But, then, Generation Xers (a term they detest) aren't typical employees.

2   "These people grew up with Sonic the Hedgehog and Atari, so training has to be attention-grabbing," says Christopher O'Donnell, vice president of Pencom. "Or as Beavis would say, 'The training can't suck.'"

3   Suck indeed. Members of Generation X, those 40 million or so Americans age 20 to 33, are forcing companies to rethink and reengineer their training programs drastically. Gen Xers' values, communication styles, and life experiences are so different from those of baby boomers that traditional training doesn't stand a chance. To connect with these young employees, forget *Father Knows Best;* bring on MTV.

3   Now, before you grumble about catering to a fringe element, here's an incentive: Training geared to the needs of Generation Xers may actually be better for training all workers.

4   "This generation is spearheading change," says O'Donnell. "They're teaching us a lot about how to manage and train everyone in the workforce."

5   Granted, not all companies experience generational differences. At Dallas-based Texas Instruments, for example, employees are hired based on certain values and characteristics. That keeps TI's corporate culture harmonious and minimizes any discrepancies between workers of different generations.

6   "We don't see generational learning differences," says Ray Gumpert, manager of training and organizational effectiveness for TI's Semiconductor Group. "We recruit a certain kind of individual, so there is great consistency among TIers."

7   In *Twentysomething: Managing and Motivating Today's New Workforce* (Master Media, 1992), Claire Raines writes that companies such as Texas Instruments are the exception, not the rule. "(Though) all generations have things in common," she says, "research on Generation Xers shows that this group typically learns very differently from those that came before them."

Who Are These People Anyway?

8   To understand why and how Xers' learning styles are so different, you have to understand the characteristics that set them apart from older workers.

9   To begin with, they are the first generation to grow up with many of their parents both working. As "latchkey kids," many learned to become self-reliant. Consequently, they tend to be independent problem solvers, who are remarkably good at getting a job done on their own.

10   Many, if not most, grew up with computers at home, in school, and at arcades on weekends, so they are amazingly technoliterate. From the Internet to CD-ROMs, familiarity with new technology is just a mouse-click away.

11   In addition, Xers have been conditioned by the American culture to expect immediate gratification. Such things as automatic teller machines, pagers, and microwave ovens have taught them that they can have what they want, when they want it. In the workplace, that can mean that they expect answers and feedback now.

12   Xers came of age in an era that began with the Watergate scandal and ended with massive corporate layoffs, so they tend to distrust institutions. They don't have to be taught that there is no such thing as lifetime employment; they never expected it. Such distrust, combined with an inherent self-reliance, means that they're more likely to regard companies as places to grow, not places to grow old.

13   So, what do all of those characteristics mean for HRD professionals? Bruce Tulgan—founder of Rainmaker, a firm in New Haven, Connecticut, that helps companies recruit, motivate, and retain Generation X workers—reminds us that in the old days, the corporate approach to training was paternalistic.

14   "It used to be 'welcome to the family,'" says Tulgan. "Companies would tell employees, 'Here is your training agenda, this is the training we'll provide, and this is what you need to know.'" That approach just doesn't work with Xers. They want to know why they must learn something, before they will take the time to learn how.

15   Says Tulgan, "I'm not saying you must change the learning objectives; you must change the process." He recommends focusing on outcomes more than techniques and on what Xers are going to be able to do, not what they need to know.

16   For example, at the Orlando-based Olive Garden restaurants, training for servers had them memorize the menu and ingredients of the dishes. Now, training director Marty Fisher says that training emphasizes what servers are supposed to do with that information.

17   "We tell servers we want them to be tour guides for the menu," says Fisher. Through role play, servers can practice telling customers about each dish in appealing terms. That way, employees not only know why they are learning the ingredients, but they also know how to put the information to work.

18   At Chicago-based Anderson Consulting, trainers spend a lot of time up-front getting trainees' buy-in. According to Joe Kotey, a manager in the consulting education department, young employees have to see value in the training, or they aren't motivated to learn new skills. "Training results vary greatly, depending on how motivated a group is to learn new skills," says Kotey. "By focusing on outcomes, we show up-front why [employees] need this information."

Pushing the Right Buttons

19   Once you have the attention of Generation Xers, keep it by making training experiences meaningful, memorable, and fun. Xers are used to being entertained, having been weaned on portable CD players and Game Boy™. "We can't just pour knowledge into their heads," says Fisher. "We need to combine education with entertainment."

20   One way to keep their attention is to make training experiential. As much as possible, use all six senses, role play, and simulation learning—similar to the approaches used by NASA. Astronauts aren't expected to pilot a space shuttle without having practiced. Don't expect Xers to perform without practice.

21   For example, Andersen Consulting uses CD-ROMs during training to simulate client meetings. Using audio and video clips stored on disc, trainees can interview clients, receive phone calls, obtain advice from senior consultants, and review internal memos.

22   At the end of the computerized course, trainees have an opportunity to deliver a presentation with the findings and recommendations usually delivered to a client. "We want employees to see and feel what a client call is really like," says Roberta Menconi, training manager.

23   Classroom learning can also be made experiential. Pencom's O'Donnell remembers a training session he conducted for young employees of a Denver restaurant.

24   "I was trying to communicate the importance of seating [customers] right away, but getting nowhere. When I asked employees how long [customers] could wait comfortably before being seated, their responses ranged from three minutes to several more."

25   Frustrated, O'Donnell asked the group to time him for one minute. "I acted fidgety for a full 60 seconds while they watched. That minute went on forever and drove home the point that [customers] need to be seated immediately."

26   For a generation that grew up with more remote controls than rattles, the need to control learning is important. Xers need buttons to push. They are independent, and they're used to managing their own time. Because they're accustomed to calling the shots, they tend to resent and resist efforts to force-feed them training. To give Xers a sense of control over their learning, it's wise to provide as many options as possible where and when they can participate. That means a choice of locations and times.

27   "Because this generation is stubborn, we can't be," says O'Donnell.

28   It's even better to let Xers decide how they can learn. Tulgan tells the story of a Big Six accounting firm with a series of outstanding training courses. But they were so popular that no one could get into them.

29   Says Tulgan, "I suggested that the firm put course content on videotapes, audiotapes, and interactive CDs, and in self-paced manuals and workbooks. That puts the information into employees' hands right away and makes them accountable for learning. Generation Xers like that kind of structured self-study." Given Gen Xers' penchant for technology, computers are a natural choice for delivering training. But their ability to control has to be built into the technological solutions.

30   Menconi says that Andersen tested its first CD-ROM courses with younger employees to gauge their responses. "We discovered that they click around a lot. They want control over the paths they take. They want to stop and start at will."

31   To accommodate those needs, Andersen built sophisticated navigation systems into all of its CD-ROM–based courses.

32   Gen Xers' propensity to jump around—unlike older workers who tend to go step by step—doesn't necessarily signify a lack of attention. It's more an ability to assimilate information quickly and to focus on multiple ideas at once—called, "parallel thinking."

33   "Look at MTV or commercials," says Raines, "and you'll see four or five things going on at the same time. That drives me crazy, but these kids are used to it."

34   Companies can appeal to younger workers by developing training materials that provide multiple sources of information at once. *USA Today* and *Wired* are good examples of how to present information to Xers. Those publications combine charts, photos, text, graphics, and cartoons on a single page.

35   When making your materials more eye-catching, make sure you also keep the information simple. Don't make Gen Xers have to guess what you're trying to say. Raines recommends highlighting key points to make the information highly scannable.

36   A note of caution: Don't go overboard and be too trendy. A few years back, the Wendy's restaurant chain created a training video, "Grill Skills," that featured a rap singer in gold lamé reviewing food-grilling techniques. The video won awards. But, after a year, it lost its effectiveness; employees saw it as outdated.

Prime Targets

37   Generation Xers—more than other employee groups—tend to make job decisions based on whether training is available. So, it may be more important that you provide them with training than how you provide it.

38   Says Tulgan, "Training departments are the ace in the hole for retaining and motivating today's workforce." That's because young employees don't envision long-term relationships with their employers, he says. They know that they must keep growing in order to stay marketable. If they don't receive training, they tend to start looking around at other jobs in other companies.

39   "In today's job market, you want to train employees to leave at any time," says Tulgan. "They won't, because they'll see working for your company as an incredible opportunity to grow and develop."

40   Terri Wolfe, director of HR at Patagonia—a Ventura, California–based clothing retailer—agrees that the biggest emerging trend among younger workers is their desire for continuous education. "We have an extensive continuing education program that a majority of our younger workers take advantage of. They're taking classes not only to advance their careers, but also because they are inherently curious."

What Generation Gap

41   What is perhaps most remarkable about training Generation Xers is that the training approaches that work well with them make sense for almost everyone, regardless of age. Here are some tips for training workers of all ages.

42   **Focus.** Training should emphasize end results and place learners in control. Such training helps prepare employees for challenges on the job. After all, isn't the goal of empowerment for employees to focus on business objectives and make the necessary and appropriate decisions to achieve them? Fewer managers

means that all employees have to take more responsibility for their work; learner-directed training is a great way to get them used to that.

43   **Be flexible.** Large-scale corporate cutbacks mean that more people are overworked and are juggling multiple demands. A flexible training schedule and choice of training resources (such as CD-ROMS, videos, and so forth) help employees fit training into their work schedules.

44   **Emphasize visuals.** Create eye-catching, highly scannable training materials. Most people don't have time to read through pages of materials. Like it or not, most of us have been conditioned by the media to expect a point to be made quickly.

45   **Provide continuous education.** Though younger workers have never counted on cradle-to-grave employment, older employees are also getting the message that they must prepare for unexpected events. The companies that provide continuous education are in a better position to retain productive employees.

46   "If you want to see the future of work, look into the eyes of a Generation Xer," says Tulgan. "We were shaped by the same forces that have shaped the (current) workplace and economy. We're comfortable with the new workplace because we never got accustomed to the old management style."

47   But whatever you do, don't call them "Generation Xers."

DISCUSSION QUESTIONS

1. This process essay starts by defining Generation Xers and identifying their place in the workplace. Why is this important to the purposes of the essay?
2. Instead of offering simple concrete steps in a process, how does this essay present the process of training Generation Xers? Why is this approach most likely used?
3. Identify the key elements of the process recommended by the author. Discuss whether this approach would or would not be appealing to you.
4. What is the purpose of the writer using many different businesses as examples?
5. In the end, the author identifies some specific key principles for training Generation Xers. What are the advantages of this approach?

TOWARD KEY INSIGHTS

To what extent are different training methods appropriate to different populations? Explore what kind of job training has been most effective for you. What were the features of that training?

SUGGESTION FOR WRITING

Write a paper explaining to new employees the process of the job training they might receive at one of the places you have worked.

Select some activity you're familiar with—perhaps planning a party, programming a computer, or dieting successfully—and describe the steps involved, using appropriate comparisons and figurative language.

ILLUSTRATION

Reading Strategies

1. Read the introductory and concluding paragraphs quickly to determine the thesis for the illustration. Then read the essay quickly to get the main point of the essay. Jot down the key points of the illustration.
2. Determine, based on your own purpose for reading and the level of the essay, if it is necessary to read the essay more carefully.
3. If a more careful reading is warranted, read slowly, noticing and jotting down any key details of the illustration that make a more general point.

Reading Critically

1. Test whether the illustration really demonstrates the main point.
2. Determine whether the illustrations are typical or atypical.
3. Test the point by seeing if there are illustrations that would illuminate a different position.

Reading As a Writer

1. Identify and evaluate the kinds of examples used in the illustration.
2. Notice the strategies used to link the illustrations to a main point.
3. Identify and evaluate how the illustrations were organized (as short narratives, as descriptions) and jot down any strategies you found useful.

SABRINA RUBIN ERDELY

Binge Drinking, A Campus Killer

Sabrina Rubin Erdely is an award-winning investigative journalist based in Philadelphia. She is a Senior Writer at Philadelphia *magazine, where she has been on staff since 1995, and has contributed to a wide array of other magazines. Erdely's feature writing has earned her a number of awards, including a prestigious National Magazine Award nomination. Our selection focuses on a serious and growing problem at American colleges and universities.*

> Introduction: identifies serious problem, point to be illustrated

1   Pregame tailgating parties, post-exam celebrations and Friday happy hours—not to mention fraternity and sorority mixers—have long been a cornerstone of the collegiate experience. But on campuses across America, these indulgences have a more alarming side. For some of today's college students, binge drinking has become the norm.

> Body: paragraphs 2–39

2   This past February I headed to the University of Wisconsin–Madison, rated the No. 2 party school in the nation by the college guide *Princeton Review*, to see

Illustration   **471**

the party scene for myself. On Thursday night the weekend was already getting started. At a raucous off-campus gathering, 20-year-old Traccy Middler struggled to down her beer as fist-pumping onlookers yelled, "Chug! Chug! Chug!"

End of paragraph 2, paragraphs 3 and 5: first examples support main point, as do all examples

3   In the kitchen, sophomore Jeremy Budda drained his tenth beer. "I get real wasted on weekends," he explained. Nearby, a 19-year-old estimated, "I'll end up having 17, 18 beers."

4   Swept up in the revelry, these partyers aren't thinking about the alcohol-related tragedies that have been in the news. All they're thinking about now is the next party. The keg is just about empty.

5   As the 19-year-old announces loudly, these college students have just one objective: "to get drunk!"

6   The challenge to drink to the very limits of one's endurance has become a celebrated staple of college life. In one of the most extensive reports on college drinking thus far, a 1997 Harvard School of Public Health study found that 43 percent of college students admitted binge drinking in the preceding two weeks. (Defined as four drinks in a sitting for a woman and five for a man, a drinking binge is when one drinks enough to risk health and well-being.)

7   "That's about five million students," says Henry Wechsler, who co-authored the study. "And it's certainly a cause for concern. Most of these students don't realize they're engaging in risky behavior." University of Kansas Chancellor Robert Hemenway adds, "Every year we see students harmed because of their involvement with alcohol."

8   Indeed, when binge drinking came to the forefront last year with a rash of alcohol-related college deaths, the nation was stunned by the loss. There was Scott Krueger, the 18-year-old fraternity pledge at the Massachusetts Institute of Technology, who died of alcohol poisoning after downing the equivalent of 15 shots in an hour. There was Leslie Baltz, a University of Virginia senior, who died after she drank too much and fell down a flight of stairs. Lorraine Hanna, a freshman at Indiana University of Pennsylvania, was left alone to sleep off her night of New Year's Eve partying. Later that day her twin sister found her dead—with a blood-alcohol content (BAC) of 0.429 percent. (Driving with a BAC of 0.1 percent and above is illegal in all states.)

Brief examples feature different students, as do all examples, providing more evidence supporting paper's point

9   Experts estimate that excessive drinking is involved in thousands of student deaths a year. And the Harvard researchers found that there has been a dramatic change in why students drink: 39 percent drank "to get drunk" in 1993, but 52 percent had the same objective in 1997.

10   "What has changed is the across-the-board *acceptability* of intoxication," says Felix Savino, a psychologist at UW–Madison. "Many college students today see not just drinking but being *drunk* as their primary way of socializing."

11   The reasons for the shift are complex and not fully understood. But researchers surmise that it may have something to do with today's instant-gratification life-style—and young people tend to take it to the extreme.

12   In total, it is estimated that America's 12 million undergraduates drink the equivalent of six million gallons of beer a week. When that's combined with teenagers' need to drink secretly, it's no wonder many have a dangerous relationship with alcohol.

13   The biggest predictor of bingeing is fraternity or sorority membership. Sixty-five percent of members qualified as binge-drinkers, according to the Harvard study.

14   August 25, 1997, was meant to be a night the new Sigma Alpha Epsilon pledges at Louisiana State University in Baton Rouge would never forget, and by 8 P.M. it was certainly shaping up that way. The revelry had begun earlier with

Extended example: paragraphs 14–21

a keg party. Then they went to a bar near campus, where pledges consumed massive quantities of alcohol.

15   Among the pledges were Donald Hunt, Jr., a 21-year-old freshman and Army veteran, and his roommate, Benjamin Wynne, a 20-year-old sophomore. Friends since high school, the two gamely drank the alcoholic concoctions offered to them and everyone else.

16   Before long, many in the group began vomiting into trash cans. (Donald Hunt would later allege in a lawsuit that these "vomiting stations" were set up for that very purpose, something the defendants adamantly deny.) About 9:30, incapacitated pledges were taken back to sleep it off at the frat house.

17   The 911 call came around midnight. Paramedics were stunned at what they found: more than a dozen young men sprawled on the floor, on chairs, on couches, reeking of alcohol. The paramedics burst into action, shaking the pledges and shouting, "Hey! Can you hear me?" Four couldn't be roused, and of those, one had no vital signs: Benjamin Wynne was in cardiac arrest.

18   Checking to see that nothing was blocking Wynne's airway, the paramedics began CPR. Within minutes they'd inserted an oxygen tube into his lungs, hooked up an I.V., attached a cardiac monitor and begun shocking him with defibrillation paddles, trying to restart his heart.

19   Still not responding, Wynne was rushed by ambulance to Baton Rouge General Hospital. Lab work revealed that his blood-alcohol content was an astonishing 0.588 percent, nearly six times the legal driving limit for adults—the equivalent of taking about 21 shots in an hour.

20   Meanwhile, three other fraternity pledges were undergoing similar revival efforts. One was Donald Hunt. He would suffer severe alcohol poisoning and nearly die.

21   After working furiously on Wynne, the hospital team admitted defeat. He was pronounced dead of acute alcohol poisoning.

22   One simple fact people tend to lose sight of is that alcohol is a poison—often pleasurable, but a toxin nonetheless. And for a person with little experience processing this toxin, it can come as something of a physical shock.

23   In general, a bottle of beer has about the same alcohol content as a glass of wine or shot of liquor. And the body can remove only the equivalent of less than one drink hourly from the bloodstream.

24   Many students are not just experimenting once or twice. In the Harvard study, half of binge drinkers were "frequent binge drinkers," meaning they had binged three or more times in the previous two weeks.

25   It also is assumed by some that bingeing is a "guy thing," an activity that, like cigar smoking and watching televised sports, belongs in the realm of male bonding. Statistics, however, show that the number of heavy-drinking young women is significant. Henry Wechsler's Harvard study found that a hefty 48 percent of college men were binge drinkers, and women were right behind them at 39 percent.

Extended example:
paragraphs 26–32   26   Howard Somers had always been afraid of heights. Perhaps his fear was some sort of an omen. On an August day in 1997 he helped his 18-year-old daughter, Mindy, move into her dorm at Virginia Tech. As they unloaded her things in the eighth-floor room, Somers noted with unease the position of the window. It opened inward like an oven door, its lip about level with her bed. He mentioned it, but Mindy dismissed his concern with a smile.

27   "I have gone through more guilt than you can imagine," Somers says now quietly. "Things I wish I had said or done. But I never thought this would happen. Who would?"

Illustration   **473**

28   Mindy Somers knew the dangers of alcohol and tried to stay aware of her limits. She'd planned not to overdo it that Friday night, since her mother was coming in that weekend to celebrate Mindy's 19th birthday on Sunday. But it was Halloween, the campus was alive with activity, and Mindy decided to stop in at several off-campus parties.

29   When she returned to her room at 3 A.M., she was wiped out enough to fall into bed fully clothed. Mindy's bed was pushed lengthwise against the long, low window. Her roommate and two other girls, who were on the floor, all slept too soundly to notice that sometime after 4 A.M. Mindy's bed was empty.

30   When the paperboy found her facedown on the grass at 6:45 A.M., he at first thought it was a Halloween prank. Police and EMTs swarmed to the scene in minutes. Somers was pronounced dead of massive chest and abdominal injuries. She had a blood-alcohol content of 0.21 percent, equal to her having drunk about five beers in one hour.

31   Police surmised that Mindy had tried to get out of bed during the night but, disoriented, had slipped out the window, falling 75 feet to her death. "It was a strange, tragic accident," Virginia Tech Police Chief Michael Jones says.

32   A terrible irony was that the week prior to Mindy's death had been Virginia Tech's annual Alcohol Awareness Week.

33   While binge drinking isn't always lethal, it does have other, wide-ranging effects. Academics is one realm where it takes a heavy toll.

34   During my trip to Wisconsin most students told me they didn't plan on attending classes the following day. "Nah, I almost never go to class on Friday. It's no big deal," answered Greg, a sophomore. According to a survey of university administrators, 38 percent of academic problems are alcohol-related, as are 29 percent of dropouts.

35   Perhaps because alcohol increases aggression and impairs judgment, it is also related to 25 percent of violent crimes and roughly 60 percent of vandalism on campus. According to one survey, 79 percent of students who had experienced unwanted sexual intercourse in the previous year said that they were under the influence of alcohol or other drugs at the time. "Some people believe that alcohol can provide an excuse for inappropriate behavior, including sexual aggression," says Jeanette Norris, a University of Washington researcher. Later on, those people can claim, "It wasn't me—it was the booze."

36   Faced with the many potential dangers, college campuses are scrambling for ways to reduce binge drinking. Many offer seminars on alcohol during freshman orientation. Over 50 schools provide alcohol-free living environments. At the University of Michigan's main campus in Ann Arbor, for instance, nearly 30 percent of undergrads living in university housing now choose to live in alcohol-free rooms. Nationwide several fraternities have announced that by the year 2000 their chapter houses will be alcohol-free.

37   After the University of Rhode Island topped the *Princeton Review* party list two yeas in a row, administrators banned alcohol at all student events on campus; this year URI didn't even crack the top ten. Some campuses respond even more severely, unleashing campus raids and encouraging police busts.

38   Researchers debate, however, if such "zero-tolerance" policies are helpful or if they might actually result in more secret, off-campus drinking. Other academics wonder if dropping the drinking age to 18 would take away the illicit thrill of alcohol and lower the number of kids drinking wildly. Others feel this would just create more drinking-related fatalities.

39   Whatever it takes, changing student behavior won't be easy. "What you've got here are people who think they are having fun," Harvard's Henry Wechsler

explains. "You can't change their behavior by preaching at them or by telling them they'll get hurt."

Conclusion: paragraphs 40–41;
returns to opening example

40   Around 2 A.M. at UW–Madison a hundred kids congregate at a downtown intersection in a nightly ritual. One girl is trying to pull her roommate up off the ground. "I'm not that drunk," the one on the ground insists. "I just can't stand up."

41   Two fights break out. A police car cruises by and the crowd thins, some heading to after-hours parties. Then maybe at 3 or 4 A.M. they'll go home to get some sleep, so they will be rested for when they start to drink again. Tomorrow night.

DISCUSSION QUESTIONS

1. Discuss the effectiveness of Rubin Erdely's title.
2. What does Rubin Erdely accomplish in paragraphs 6–7 and in paragraphs 9–13, 22–25, and 33–38?
3. How do you account for the slang expressions found in this essay: "Chug! Chug! Chug!" in paragraph 2 and "wasted" in paragraph 3?
4. Comment on the effectiveness of the two-word sentence fragment that ends the essay.

TOWARD KEY INSIGHTS

Why would "many college students today see not just drinking but being *drunk* as their primary way of socializing"?

What can be done to counter this mind-set?

SUGGESTION FOR WRITING

Write an essay illustrating some type of benefit available on campus—perhaps academic counseling, the campus ministry, or some ethnic or racial organization. Develop your essay with several short examples or one extended one.

MARTIN GOTTFRIED

Rambos of the Road

Martin Gottfried is a native of New York City and a writer on theatrical matters. Born in 1933, he earned an A.B. degree at Columbia University and then, after attending law school, served two years in the military intelligence branch of the U.S. Army. Following his discharge in 1959, he spent four years as a music and movie critic and since 1963 has worked as a drama critic.

Illustration   **475**

He has authored several books on the theater as well as magazine articles on a variety of topics. In our selection, Gottfried examines the driving behavior of all too many motorists.

1   The car pulled up and its driver glared at us with such sullen intensity, such hatred, that I was truly afraid for our lives. Except for the Mohawk haircut he didn't have, he looked like Robert De Niro in "Taxi Driver," the sort of young man who, delirious for notoriety, might kill a president.

2   He was glaring because we had passed him and for that affront he pursued us to the next stoplight so as to express his indignation and affirm his masculinity. I was with two women and, believe it, was afraid for all three of us. It was nearly midnight and we were in a small, sleeping town with no other cars on the road.

3   When the light turned green, I raced ahead, knowing it was foolish and that I was not in a movie. He didn't merely follow, he chased, and with his headlights turned off. No matter what sudden turn I took, he followed. My passengers were silent. I knew they were alarmed, and I prayed that I wouldn't be called upon to protect them. In that cheerful frame of mind, I turned off my own lights so I couldn't be followed. It was lunacy. I was responding to a crazy *as* a crazy.

4   "I'll just drive to the police station," I finally said, and as if those were the magic words, he disappeared.

5   ***Elbowing Fenders:*** It seems to me that there has recently been an epidemic of auto macho—a competition perceived and expressed in driving. People fight it out over parking spaces. They bully into line at the gas pump. A toll booth becomes a signal for elbowing fenders. And beetle-eyed drivers hunch over their steering wheels, squeezing the rims, glowering, preparing the excuse of not having seen you as they muscle you off the road. Approaching a highway on an entrance ramp recently, I was strong-armed by a trailer truck so immense that its driver all but blew me away by blasting his horn. The behemoth was just inches from my hopelessly mismatched coupe when I fled for the safety of the shoulder.

6   And this is happening on city streets, too. A New York taxi driver told me that "intimidation is the name of the game. Drive as if you're deaf and blind. You don't hear the other guy's horn and you sure as hell don't see him."

7   The odd thing is that long before I was even able to drive, it seemed to me that people were at their finest and most civilized when in their cars. They seemed so orderly and considerate, so reasonable, staying in the right-hand lane unless passing, signaling all intentions. In those days you really eased into highway traffic, and the long, neat rows of cars seemed mobile testimony to the sanity of most people. Perhaps memory fails, perhaps there were always testy drivers, perhaps—but everyone didn't give you the finger.

8   A most amazing example of driver rage occurred recently at the Manhattan end of the Lincoln Tunnel. We were four cars abreast, stopped at a traffic light. And there was no moving even when the light had changed. A bus had stopped in the cross traffic, blocking our paths: it was normal-for-New-York-City gridlock. Perhaps impatient, perhaps late for important appointments, three of us nonetheless accepted what, after all, we could not alter. One, however, would not. He would not be helpless. He would go where he was going even if he couldn't get there. A Wall Street type in suit and tie, he got out of his car and strode toward the bus, rapping smartly on its doors. When they opened, he exchanged words with the driver. The doors folded shut. He then

stepped in front of the bus, took hold of one of its large windshield wipers and broke it.

9   The bus doors reopened and the driver appeared, apparently giving the fellow a good piece of his mind. If so, the lecture was wasted, for the man started his car and proceeded to drive directly *into the bus*. He rammed it. Even though the point at which he struck the bus, the folding doors, was its most vulnerable point, ramming the side of a bus with your car has to rank very high on a futility index. My first thought was that it had to be a rental car.

10   *Lane Merger:* To tell the truth, I could not believe my eyes. The bus driver opened his doors as much as they could be opened and he stepped directly onto the hood of the attacking car, jumping up and down with both his feet. He then retreated into the bus, closing the doors behind him. Obviously a man of action, the car driver backed up and rammed the bus again. How this exercise in absurdity would have been resolved none of us will ever know for at that point the traffic unclogged and the bus moved on. And the rest of us, we passives of the world, proceeded, our cars crossing a field of battle as if nothing untoward had happened.

11   It is tempting to blame such belligerent, uncivil and even neurotic behavior on the nuts of the world, but in our cars we all become a little crazy. How many of us speed up when a driver signals his intention of pulling in front of us? Are we resentful and anxious to pass him? How many of us try to squeeze in, or race along the shoulder at a lane merger? We may not jump on hoods, but driving the gantlet, we seethe, cursing not so silently in the safety of our steel bodies on wheels—fortresses for cowards.

12   What is it within us that gives birth to such antisocial behavior and why, all of a sudden, have so many drivers gone around the bend? My friend Joel Katz, a Manhattan psychiatrist, calls it, "a Rambo pattern. People are running around thinking the American way is to take the law into your own hands when anyone does anything wrong. And what constitutes 'wrong'? Anything that cramps your style."

13   It seems to me that it is a new America we see on the road now. It has the mentality of a hoodlum and the backbone of a coward. The car is its weapon and hiding place, and it is still a symbol even in this. Road Rambos no longer bespeak a self-reliant, civil people tooling around in family cruisers. In fact, there aren't families in these machines that charge headlong with their brights on in broad daylight, demanding we get out of their way. Bullies are loners, and they have perverted our liberty of the open road into drivers' license. They represent an America that derides the values of decency and good manners, then roam the highways riding shotgun and shrieking freedom. By allowing this to happen, the rest of us approve.

DISCUSSION QUESTIONS

1. Identify the thesis statement of this essay.
2. What paragraphs make up the introduction? Besides starting the essay, what function do they perform?
3. Why are several examples a better choice for this essay than one extended example?
4. In what order does Gottfried arrange his examples?
5. What does Gottfried accomplish in paragraphs 11–12?
6. What function, other than ending the essay, is served by the final paragraph?

Illustration   **477**

TOWARD KEY INSIGHTS
....

Do you agree with Gottfried's claim that the "new America we see on the road now . . . has the mentality of a hoodlum and the backbone of a coward"? Why or why not?

Where else have you encountered macho behavior? At athletic events? At activities that generate long lines? At political demonstrations?

What conclusions can you draw about those who engage in such behavior?

SUGGESTION FOR WRITING
....

Write an illustration essay exploring the behavior, good or bad, that you have experienced on campus, in the workplace, or while engaged in some activity such as shopping. Use several examples, arrange them in an appropriate order, and try to account for the behavior.

MATEA GOLD AND DAVID FERRELL

Going for Broke

Matea Gold, a native of Northampton, Massachusetts, earned a B. A. degree from UCLA and then joined David Ferrell as a staff writer for the Los Angeles Times. *Gold earned Sacramento Press Club awards in 1994 and 1995, while Ferrell was a 1996 finalist for the Investigative Reporters and Editors Award, which recognizes outstanding investigative work. The information in this article is drawn from a seven-month nationwide investigation of legalized gambling. Its case studies offer a sobering view of the consequences of gambling addiction.*

1   Rex Coile's life is a narrow box, so dark and confining he wonders how he got trapped inside, whether he'll ever get out.

2   He never goes to the movies, never sees concerts, never lies on a sunny beach, never travels on vacation, never spends Christmas with his family. Instead, Rex shares floor space in cheap motels with other compulsive gamblers, comforting himself with delusional dreams of jackpots that will magically wipe

away three decades of wreckage. He has lost his marriage, his home, his Cadillac, his clothes, his diamond ring. Not least of all, in the card clubs of Southern California, he has lost his pride.

3   Rex no longer feels sorry for himself, not after a 29-year losing streak that has left him scrounging for table scraps to feed his habit. Still, he agonizes over what he has become at 54 and what he might have been.

4   Articulate, intellectual, he talks about existential philosophy, the writings of Camus and Sartre. He was once an editor at Random House. His mind is so jampacked with tidbits about movies, television, baseball and history that card room regulars call him "Rex Trivia," a name he cherishes for the remnant of self-respect it gives him. "There's a lot of Rexes around these card rooms," he says in a whisper of resignation and sadness.

5   And their numbers are soaring as gambling explodes across America, from the mega-resorts of Las Vegas to the gaming parlors of Indian reservations, from the riverboats along the Mississippi to the corner mini-marts selling lottery tickets. With nearly every state in the union now sanctioning some form of legalized gambling to raise revenues, evidence is mounting that society is paying a steep price, one that some researchers say must be confronted, if not reversed.

6   Never before have bettors blown so much money—a whopping $50.9 billion last year—five times the amount lost in 1980. That's more than the public spent on movies, theme parks, recorded music and sporting events combined. A substantial share of those gambling losses—an estimated 30% to 40%—pours from the pockets and purses of chronic losers hooked on the adrenaline rush of risking their money, intoxicated by the fast action of gambling's incandescent world.

7   Studies place the total number of compulsive gamblers at about 4.4 million, about equal to the nation's ranks of hard-core drug addicts. Another 11 million, known as problem gamblers, teeter on the verge. Since 1990, the number of Gamblers Anonymous groups nationwide has doubled from about 600 to more than 1,200.

8   Compulsive gambling has been linked to child abuse, domestic violence, embezzlement, bogus insurance claims, bankruptcies, welfare fraud and a host of other social and criminal ills. The advent of Internet gambling could lure new legions into wagering beyond their means.

9   Every once in a while, a case is so egregious it makes headlines: A 10-day-old baby girl in South Carolina dies after being left for nearly seven hours in a hot car while her mother plays video poker. A suburban Chicago woman is so desperate for a bankroll to gamble that she allegedly suffocates her 7-week-old daughter 11 days after obtaining a $200,000 life-insurance policy on the baby.

10   But these tragedies that flash before the public eye are just lightning strokes of a roiling night storm. Far more often, compulsive gambling bends lives more subtly, less sensationally, over the course of years.

11   Gwen, one of the unseen masses trying to keep her head above water, sits on an easy chair in the living room of her worn Jefferson Park bungalow, watching the movie "Titanic" on an old TV. Her hair is uncombed and there are bags under her eyes. She puffs on a cigarette and shakes her foot nervously. On the screen, the great ship begins to founder.

12   "That's me," she says, tears rolling down her checks. "I'm sinking."

13   Gwen has just come off a three-day bender at the Hollywood Park Casino in Inglewood. She blew a paycheck, emptied out her new checking account, gambled right through her work shift. Driving home from the casino, she contemplated

Illustration   **479**

veering off the road, ending it all. "I just don't want to be here," she mumbles, watching Titanic's Rose and Jack struggling to hold on to a piece of driftwood in the freezing sea. "I just feel like I'm living a hopeless life. So hopeless."

14   She's written bad checks and maxed out her credit cards. One bank closed her checking account after she put too many fake deposit slips in the ATM to withdraw cash. She lies. She tells her boss she needs a salary advance because her son is in the hospital. Late on the rent, she parks a block from the house to duck the landlord. For the last eight years, this has been her life, one so empty of joy and options that the card clubs have become her only hope of filling the hole.

15   She thinks back to that night a few years ago when, desperate to recoup her gambling losses, she pilfered several thousand dollars from the safe of a restaurant where she was working. She just needed something to get herself started, she told herself. She'd pay it back with the winnings. She blew it all in one weekend.

16   Overwhelmed by guilt, she came clean with her manager. She was booked, fingerprinted and briefly thrown behind bars. "It was the worst experience of my life," she says.

17   Gwen now makes monthly $75 restitution payments to the restaurant as part of her court-ordered probation.

18   "I have hurt so many people with my gambling," says Gwen. "I have lost best friends. After all the pain I've caused everybody, the pain I caused myself, I still have the urge to gamble. I never know what I'm going to do. I'm so afraid. I'm really afraid."

19   Science has begun to uncover clues to compulsive gambling—genetic predispositions that involve chemical receptors in the brain, the same pleasure pathways implicated in drug and alcohol addiction. But no amount of knowledge, no amount of enlightenment, makes the illness any less confounding, any less destructive. What the gamblers cannot understand about themselves is also well beyond the comprehension of family members, who struggle for normality in a world of deceit and madness.

20   Money starts vanishing: $500 here, $200 there, $800 a couple of weeks later. Where is it? The answers come back vague, nonsensical. It's in the desk at work. A friend borrowed it. It got spent on family dinners, car repairs, loans to in-laws. Exasperated spouses play the sleuth, combing through pockets, wallets, purses, searching the car. Sometimes the incriminating evidence turns up—a racing form, lottery scratchers, a map to an Indian casino. Once the secret is uncovered, spouses usually fight the problem alone, bleeding inside, because the stories are too humiliating to share.

21   "Anybody who is living with a compulsive gambler is totally overwhelmed," says Tom Tucker, president of the California Council on Problem Gambling. "They're steeped in anger, resentment, depression, confusion. None of their personal efforts will ever stop a person from their [sic] addiction. And they don't really see any hope because compulsive gambling in general is such an under-recognized illness."

22   One Los Angeles woman, whose husband's gambling was tearing at her sanity, says she slept with her fists so tightly clenched that her nails sliced into her palms. She had fantasies of death—first her own, thinking he'd feel sorry for her and stop gambling. Later, she harbored thoughts of turning her rage on her husband. She imagined getting a gun, hiding in the closet and blasting him out of her life.

23   "The hurt was so bad I think I would have pulled the trigger," she says. "There were times the pain was so much I thought being in jail, or being in the electric chair, would be less than this."

24   Five years in Gam-Anon, the 12-step support group for family and friends of compulsive gamblers, has only begun to heal her. "I don't think I'm even halfway there," she says.

25   Too often, families of gambling addicts endure more than warped finances and wrecked psyches. They have come to fear for their physical safety.

26   Trena, a 42-year-old Whittier homemaker, is among them. Several months ago, after years of agony, she filed for divorce. Her husband, a manager in an industrial plant, was making decent money and took pride in his job. He had two good children and a nice home, an airy bungalow with hardwood floors and a white-brick fireplace. Inside him, though, was a fearsome need to fulfill some glossy vision.

27   Lottery keno became the rhythmic pulse of his life. For five years, Trena says, she awoke in an empty bed every weekend. Her husband would be gone by 5:30 or 6, joining other keno regulars at the neighborhood doughnut shop, watching the numbers flash on an overhead monitor. He'd shuffle home hours later, refusing to divulge his losses.

28   Trena did what tens of thousands of spouses do: She struggled desperately to pay the bills. She hid money in Cheerios boxes, books, couch cushions, under the doormat. She drew up household budgets—hundreds of them. They became her obsession. She drafted a new one almost every day, never able to get one to work.

29   Absurd dramas were played out. On paydays, when her husband's check was directly deposited into their account, they would race each other to the bank. Trena would go to one branch, he'd head to another. She would sit at the drive-up window, jamming her withdrawal slip in the pneumatic tube the moment the bank opened. If she got the money, they could pay the utilities and keep the phone connected. If not, he'd be off to the races, the casinos or the doughnut shop.

30   Like a caged animal, she threw things—smashed a clock against the wall, broke the portable TV in the bedroom. She yelled, clawed and sometimes just sank down and cried. Trena had no money for herself, for the important personal things. She got nothing for her mom on Mother's Day.

31   Increasingly reclusive, she stopped returning calls. Chit-chatting with friends seemed a frivolous distraction when dealing with foreclosure notices, filing for bankruptcy or, worse, fending off her husband's angry demands for cash.

32   He would burst into the house shouting, "Give me my money!" Pacing, following her, tipping over plants, rifling through drawers, dumping them out to try to find it. "Don't you touch my money!"

33   Joining Gam-Anon, where Trena receives emotional support from the spouses of other gamblers, has helped her deal with her decade-long ordeal. She says she is not bitter and understands that compulsive gambling is an illness.

34   While her husband now lives with his parents, she remains in their home of 19 years, a place filled with memories as wistful as they are painful.

35   With drug or alcohol abusers, there is the hope of sobering up, an accomplishment in itself, no matter what problems may have accompanied their addictions. Compulsive gamblers often see no way to purge their urges when suffocating debts suggest only one answer: a hot streak. "They have nowhere to turn—they feel cornered," says Dr. Richard J. Rosenthal, a Beverly Hills psychiatrist who founded the California Council on Problem Gambling. "Very

Illustration 481

often they are motivated by their shame into more and more desperate attempts to avoid being found out."

36   David Phillips, a UC San Diego sociology professor, studied death records from 1982 to 1988—before legalized gambling exploded across America—and found that people in Las Vegas, Atlantic City and other gambling meccas showed significantly higher suicide rates than people in non-gambling cities.

37   Rex Trivia is not about to kill himself, but like most compulsive gamblers, he occasionally thinks about it. Looking at him, it's hard to imagine he once had a promising future as a smart young New York book editor. His pale eyes are expressionless, his hair yellowish and brittle. In his fifties, his health is failing: emphysema, three lung collapses, a bad aorta, rotting teeth.

38   His plunge has been so dizzying that at one point he agreed to aid another desperate gambler in a run of bank robberies—nine in all, throughout Los Angeles and Orange counties. When the FBI busted him in 1980, he had $50,000 in cash in a dresser drawer and $100,000 in traveler's checks in his refrigerator's vegetable crisper. Rex, who ended up doing a short stint in prison, hasn't seen that kind of money since.

39   At 11 P.M. on a Tuesday night, with a bankroll of $55—all he has—he is at a poker table in Gardena. With quick, nervous hands he stacks and unstacks his $1 chips. The stack dwindles. Down $30, he talks about leaving, getting some sleep. Midnight comes and goes. Rex starts winning. Three aces. Four threes. Chips pile up—$60, $70. "A shame to go when the cards are falling my way." He checks the time: "I'll go at 2. Win, lose or draw."

40   Fate, kismet, luck—the cards keep falling. At 2 A.M., Rex is up $97. He stands, leaves his chips on the table and goes out for a smoke. In the darkness at the edge of the parking lot, he loiters with other regulars, debating with himself whether to grab a bus and quit.

41   "I should go back in there and cash in and get out of here," he says. "That's what I should do."

42   A long pause. Crushing out his cigarette, Rex turns and heads back inside. He has made his decision.

43   "A few more hands."

DISCUSSION QUESTIONS

1. Discuss the irony of the essay's title.
2. Why do you think Gold and Ferrell repeat "never" five times in paragraph 2?
3. Identify the essay's thesis statement.
4. By referring to specific paragraphs, point out the various illustrations that the writers use in this essay.
5. Why do you think that Gold and Ferrell cite quotations at various points?
6. What do the writers accomplish by ending the selection with a continuation of the first example?

TOWARD KEY INSIGHTS

What factors account for the explosive growth of legalized gambling?
What benefits, if any, have resulted from this growth?
How should we address the problem of compulsive gambling?

Write an essay illustrating addiction to television viewing or smoking. Choose an appropriate number of examples and develop them with specific details.

ELLEN GOODMAN

The Company Man

Ellen Goodman (born 1941) is a native of Massachusetts and a 1963 graduate of Radcliffe College. A journalist since graduation, she has worked as a researcher and reporter for Newsweek *magazine as well as a writer for several major newspapers and a commentator for national radio and TV shows. She has also written articles for* MS., McCall's, *and the* Village Voice. *Book-length publications include* Turning Points *(1979),* Value Judgments *(1993), and several collections of newspaper columns. Her latest book, which she co-authored with Patricia O'Brien, is entitled* I Know Just What You Mean: The Power of Friendship in Women's Lives *(2000). She has received numerous writing awards including a 1980 Pulitzer Prize for distinguished commentary. Our selection, originally a newspaper article, depicts a workaholic whose total dedication to his job killed him.*

1   He worked himself to death, finally and precisely, at 3:00 A.M. Sunday morning.

2   The obituary didn't say that, of course. It said that he died of a coronary thrombosis—I think that was it—but everyone among his friends and acquaintances knew it instantly. He was a perfect Type A, a workaholic, a classic, they said to each other and shook their heads—and thought for five or ten minutes about the way they lived.

3   This man who worked himself to death finally and precisely at 3:00 A.M. Sunday morning—on his day off—was fifty-one years old and a vice-president. He was, however, one of six vice-presidents, and one of three who might conceivably—if the president died or retired soon enough—have moved to the top spot. Phil knew that.

4   He worked six days a week, five of them until eight or nine at night, during a time when his own company had begun the four-day week for everyone but the executives. He worked like the Important People. He had no outside "extracurricular interests," unless, of course, you think about a monthly golf game that way. To Phil, it was work. He always ate egg salad sandwiches at his desk. He was, of course, overweight, by 20 to 25 pounds. He thought it was okay, though, because he didn't smoke.

5   On Saturdays, Phil wore a sports jacket to the office instead of a suit, because it was the weekend.

Illustration   **483**

6   He had a lot of people working for him, maybe sixty, and most of them liked him most of the time. Three of them will be seriously considered for his job. The obituary didn't mention that.

7   But it did list his "survivors" quite accurately. He is survived by his wife, Helen, forty-eight years old, a good woman of no particular marketable skills, who worked in an office before marrying and mothering. She had, according to her daughter, given up trying to compete with his work years ago, when the children were small. A company friend said, "I know how much you will miss him." And she answered, "I already have."

8   "Missing him all these years," she must have given up part of herself which had cared too much for the man. She would be "well taken care of."

9   His "dearly beloved" eldest of the "dearly beloved" children is a hardworking executive in a manufacturing firm down South. In the day and a half before the funeral, he went around the neighborhood researching his father, asking the neighbors what he was like. They were embarrassed.

10   His second child is a girl, who is twenty-four and newly married. She lives near her mother and they are close, but whenever she was alone with her father, in a car driving somewhere, they had nothing to say to each other.

11   The youngest is twenty, a boy, a high-school graduate who has spent the last couple of years, like a lot of his friends, doing enough odd jobs to stay in grass and food. He was the one who tried to grab at his father, and tried to mean enough to him to keep the man at home. He was his father's favorite. Over the last two years, Phil stayed up nights worrying about the boy.

12   The boy once said, "My father and I only board here."

13   At the funeral, the sixty-year-old company president told the forty-eight-year-old widow that the fifty-one-year-old deceased had meant much to the company and would be missed and would be hard to replace. The widow didn't look him in the eye. She was afraid he would read her bitterness and, after all, she would need him to straighten out the finances—the stock options and all that.

14   Phil was overweight and nervous and worked too hard. If he wasn't at the office, he was worried about it. Phil was a Type A, a heart-attack natural. You could have picked him out in a minute from a lineup.

15   So when he finally worked himself to death, at precisely 3:00 A.M. Sunday morning, no one was really surprised.

16   By 5:00 P.M. the afternoon of the funeral, the company president had begun, discreetly of course, with care and taste, to make inquiries about his replacement. One of three men. He asked around: "Who's been working the hardest?"

DISCUSSION QUESTIONS

1. Goodman says that Phil was "a perfect Type A" (paragraph 2). After reflecting on her essay, explain the characteristics of this type.
2. Why do you think Goodman doesn't supply Phil's last name or the name of the company he works for?
3. What idea is Goodman trying to present?
4. Unlike the essay by Rubin Erdely, Goodman's uses one longer illustration rather than several shorter ones. Why?
5. What is the significance of Phil's oldest son going "around the neighborhood

researching his father, asking the neighbors what he was like" (paragraph 9)? Why were they embarrassed?

6. How do you account for Goodman's relatively short paragraphs?

TOWARD KEY INSIGHTS

What social values would cause individuals to work themselves to death?

In that regard, what is the significance of the company president asking "Who's been working the hardest?"

Are these values basically good, or should we make some changes in our attitudes toward work and success? If so, what kinds of changes?

SUGGESTION FOR WRITING

Using one extended example, write an essay that illustrates the lifestyle of a laid-back employee or friend. Your paper need not, of course, feature a death.

CLASSIFICATION

Reading Strategies

1. Identify your purpose for reading the essay and the writer's purpose for the classification. This will determine how carefully you will need to read the selection.
2. Do not lose the big picture. Identify what is being classified—types of cars, kinds of dates—and why it is being classified.
3. Notice each of the major categories and the distinctive characteristics of each category. When this material is important to you, it can be very useful to make a table that identifies each major classification and identifies the distinctive features of each category. When carefully organized, such a table can be very helpful.

Reading Critically

1. Determine if there is reasonable evidence for the classification system or if the system is arbitrary.
2. Try to come up with an alternative classification system.
3. Check to see if the categories of the classification are clear or overlap.
4. Determine whether the defining features are distinct enough to clearly apply the system.
5. Try applying the system. Does it work?

Reading As a Writer

1. Identify how the essay establishes the characteristics of the classification system.
2. Often the transition sentences in a classification essay are awkward. Examine the transition sentences and evaluate the effectiveness of the transitions.

MARION WINIK

What Are Friends For?

Marion Winik (born 1958) is a graduate of Brown University and of Brooklyn College, where she earned a master of fine arts degree in creative writing. Since graduation, she has pursued a career in education, writing, and marketing. Her writings include poems, short stories, essays, and books, and the shorter pieces have appeared in a variety of major newspapers and popular magazines. Her book, The Lunch-Box Chronicles: Notes from the Parenting Underground *(1998), discusses her experiences in raising her sons after her husband's death. In this selection, Winik takes a humorous look at the different categories of friends and the benefits derived from each one.*

1   I was thinking about how everybody can't be everything to each other, but some people can be something to each other, thank God, from the ones whose shoulder you cry on to the ones whose half-slips you borrow to the nameless ones you chat with in the grocery line.

Introduction: indicates value of friends

2   Buddies, for example, are the workhorses of the friendship world, the people out there on the front lines, defending you from loneliness and boredom. They call you up, they listen to your complaints, they celebrate your successes and curse your misfortunes, and you do the same for them in return. They hold out through innumerable crises before concluding that the person you're dating is no good, and even then understand if you ignore their good counsel. They accompany you to a movie with subtitles or to see the diving pig at Aquarena Springs. They feed your cat when you are out of town and pick you up from the airport when you get back. They come over to help you decide what to wear on a date. Even if it is with that creep.

Body: paragraphs 2–14

First category

3   What about family members? Most of them are people you just got stuck with, and though you love them, you may not have very much in common. But there is that rare exception, the Relative Friend. It is your cousin, your brother, maybe even your aunt. The two of you share the same views of the other family members. Meg never should have divorced Martin. He was the best thing that ever happened to her. You can confirm each other's memories of things that happened a long time ago. Don't you remember when Uncle Hank and Daddy had that awful fight in the middle of Thanksgiving dinner? Grandma always hated Grandpa's stamp collection; she probably left the window open during the hurricane on purpose.

Second category: paragraphs 3–4

4   While so many family relationships are tinged with guilt and obligation, a relationship with a Relative Friend is relatively worry-free. You don't even have to hide your vices from this delightful person. When you slip out Aunt Joan's back door for a cigarette, she is already there.

5   Then there is that special guy at work. Like all the other people at the job site, at first he's just part of the scenery. But gradually he starts to stand out from the crowd. Your friendship is cemented by jokes about co-workers and thoughtful favors around the office. Did you see Ryan's hair? Want half my bagel? Soon you know the names of his turtles, what he did last Friday night, exactly which

Third category: paragraphs 5–6

model CD player he wants for his birthday. His handwriting is as familiar to you as your own.

6   Though you invite each other to parties, you somehow don't quite fit into each other's outside lives. For this reason, the friendship may not survive a job change. Company gossip, once an infallible source of entertainment, soon awkwardly accentuates the distance between you. But wait. Like School Friends, Work Friends share certain memories which acquire a nostalgic glow after about a decade.

Fourth category: paragraphs 7–9

7   A Faraway Friend is someone you grew up with or went to school with or lived in the same town as until one of you moved away. Without a Faraway Friend, you would never get any mail addressed in handwriting. A Faraway Friend calls late at night, invites you to her wedding, always says she is coming to visit but rarely shows up. An actual visit from a Faraway Friend is a cause for celebration and binges of all kinds. Cigarettes, Chips Ahoy, bottles of tequila.

8   Faraway Friends go through phases of intense communication, then may be out of touch for many months. Either way, the connection is always there. A conversation with your Faraway Friend always helps to put your life in perspective: when you feel you've hit a dead end, come to a confusing fork in the road, or gotten lost in some crackerbox subdivision of your life, the advice of the Faraway Friend—who has the big picture, who is so well acquainted with the route that brought you to this place—is indispensable.

9   Another useful function of the Faraway Friend is to help you remember things from a long time ago, like the name of your seventh-grade history teacher, what was in that really good stir-fry, or exactly what happened that night on the boat with the guys from Florida.

Fifth category

10   Ah, the Former Friend. A sad thing. At best a wistful memory, at worst a dangerous enemy who is in possession of many of your deepest secrets. But what was it that drove you apart? A misunderstanding, a betrayed confidence, an unrepaid loan, an ill-conceived flirtation. A poor choice of spouse can do in a friendship just like that. Going into business together can be a serious mistake. Time, money, distance, cult religions: all noted friendship killers. . . .

Sixth category: paragraphs 11–12

11   And lest we forget, there are the Friends You Love to Hate. They call at inopportune times. They say stupid things. They butt in, they boss you around, they embarrass you in public. They invite themselves over. They take advantage. You've done the best you can, but they need professional help. On top of all this, they love you to death and are convinced they're your best friend on the planet.

12   So why do you continue to be involved with these people? Why do you tolerate them? On the contrary, the real question is, What would you do without them? Without Friends You Love to Hate, there would be nothing to talk about with your other friends. Their problems and their irritating stunts provide a reliable source of conversation for everyone they know. What's more, Friends You Love to Hate make you feel good about yourself, since you are obviously in so much better shape than they are. No matter what these people do, you will never get rid of them. As much as they need you, you need them too.

Seventh category

13   At the other end of the spectrum are Hero Friends. These people are better than the rest of us, that's all there is to it. Their career is something you wanted to be when you grew up—painter, forest ranger, tireless doer of good. They have beautiful homes filled with special handmade things presented to them by villagers in the remote areas they have visited in their extensive travels. Yet they are modest. They never gossip. They are always helping others, especially those who

have suffered a death in the family or an illness. You would think people like this would just make you sick, but somehow they don't.

14   A New Friend is a tonic unlike any other. Say you meet her at a party. In your bowling league. At a Japanese conversation class, perhaps. Wherever, whenever, there's that spark of recognition. The first time you talk, you can't believe how much you have in common. Suddenly, your life story is interesting again, your insights fresh, your opinion valued. Your various short-comings are as yet completely invisible.

Eighth category

Conclusion: memorable observation meshes stylistically with rest of essay

15   It's almost like falling in love.

DISCUSSION QUESTIONS

1. Comment on the effectiveness of Winik's title.
2. Characterize the level of diction that Winik uses in her essay.
3. What elements of Winik's essay interest you the most? What elements interest you the least?

TOWARD KEY INSIGHTS

What traits characterize the various types of friend that you have? In what ways are these friendships mutually beneficial?

SUGGESTION FOR WRITING

Write an essay classifying the various types of people that you consider undesirable. Choose an appropriate number of categories and support them with appropriate specific details.

SCOTT RUSSELL SANDERS

The Men We Carry in Our Minds

Scott Russell Sanders was born (1945) in Memphis, Tennessee. After earning a B.A. degree from Brown University in 1967 and a Ph.D. from Cambridge University in 1971, he joined the English faculty at Indiana University, where he is a full professor. Sanders is the author of numerous books of fiction and nonfiction. These books span a wide range of genres, including science fiction, historical novels, children's stories, folk tales, biographies, and personal essays. He has contributed to several essay anthologies, and his articles have appeared in literary journals and popular magazines. He has won several awards for his writing. In this essay, Sanders, in light of what he knows about the lives of working men, examines the view that power is rooted in gender.

1   The first men, besides my father, I remember seeing were black convicts and white guards, in the cottonfield across the road from our farm on the outskirts of Memphis. I must have been three or four. The prisoners wore dingy gray-and-black zebra suits, heavy as canvas, sodden with sweat. Hatless, stooped, they chopped weeds in the fierce heat, row after row, breathing the acrid dust of boll-weevil poison. The overseers wore dazzling white shirts and broad shadowy hats. The oiled barrels of their shotguns flashed in the sunlight. Their faces in memory are utterly blank. Of course those men, white and black, have become for me an emblem of racial hatred. But they have also come to stand for the twin poles of my early vision of manhood—the brute toiling animal and the boss.

2   When I was a boy, the men I knew labored with their bodies. They were marginal farmers, just scraping by, or welders, steel workers, carpenters; they swept floors, dug ditches, mined coal, or drove trucks, their forearms ropy with muscle; they trained horses, stoked furnaces, built tires, stood on assembly lines wrestling parts onto cars and refrigerators. They got up before light, worked all day long whatever the weather, and when they came home at night they looked as though somebody had been whipping them. In the evenings and on weekends they worked on their own places, tilling gardens that were lumpy with clay, fixing broken-down cars, hammering on houses that were always too drafty, too leaky, too small.

3   The bodies of the men I knew were twisted and maimed in ways visible and invisible. The nails of their hands were black and split, the hands tattooed with scars. Some had lost fingers. Heavy lifting had given many of them finicky backs and guts weak from hernias. Racing against conveyor belts had given them ulcers. Their ankles and knees ached from years of standing on concrete. Anyone who had worked for long around machines was hard of hearing. They squinted, and the skin of their faces was creased like the leather of old work gloves. There were times, studying them, when I dreaded growing up. Most of them coughed, from dust or cigarettes, and most of them drank cheap wine or whiskey, so their eyes looked bloodshot and bruised. The fathers of my friends always seemed older than the mothers. Men wore out sooner. Only women lived into old age.

4   As a boy I also knew another sort of men, who did not sweat and break down like mules. They were soldiers, and so far as I could tell they scarcely worked at all. During my early school years we lived on a military base, an arsenal in Ohio, and every day I saw GIs in the guardshacks, on the stoops of barracks, at the wheels of olive drab Chevrolets. The chief fact of their lives was boredom. Long after I left the Arsenal I came to recognize the sour smell the soldiers gave off as that of souls in limbo. They were all waiting—for wars, for transfers, for leaves, for promotions, for the end of their hitch—like so many braves waiting for the hunt to begin. Unlike the warriors of older tribes, however, they would have no say about when the battle would start or how it would be waged. Their waiting was broken only when they practiced for war. They fired guns at targets, drove tanks across the churned-up fields of the military reservation, set off bombs in the wrecks of old fighter planes. I knew this was all play. But I also felt certain that when the hour for killing arrived, they would kill. When the real shooting started, many of them would die. This was what soldiers were *for*, just as a hammer was for driving nails.

5   Warriors and toilers: those seemed, in my boyhood vision, to be the chief destinies for men. They weren't the only destinies, as I learned from having a

few male teachers, from reading books, and from watching television. But the men on television—the politicians, the astronauts, the generals, the savvy lawyers, the philosophical doctors, the bosses who gave orders to both soldiers and laborers—seemed as remote and unreal to me as the figures in tapestries. I could no more imagine growing up to become one of these cool, potent creatures than I could imagine becoming a prince.

6   A nearer and more hopeful example was that of my father, who had escaped from a red-dirt farm to a tire factory, and from the assembly line to the front office. Eventually he dressed in a white shirt and tie. He carried himself as if he had been born to work with his mind. But his body, remembering the earlier years of slogging work, began to give out on him in his fifties, and it quit on him entirely before he turned sixty-five. Even such a partial escape from man's fate as he had accomplished did not seem possible for most of the boys I knew. They joined the Army, stood in line for jobs in the smoky plants, helped build highways. They were bound to work as their fathers had worked, killing themselves or preparing to kill others.

7   A scholarship enabled me not only to attend college, a rare enough feat in my circle, but even to study in a university meant for the children of the rich. Here I met for the first time young men who had assumed from birth that they would lead lives of comfort and power. And for the first time I met women who told me that men were guilty of having kept all the joys and privileges of the earth for themselves. I was baffled. What privileges? What joys? I thought about the maimed, dismal lives of most of the men back home. What had they stolen from their wives and daughters? The right to go five days a week, twelve months a year, for thirty or forty years to a steel mill or a coal mine? The right to drop bombs and die in war? The right to feel every leak in the roof, every gap in the fence, every cough in the engine, as a wound they must mend? The right to feel, when the layoff comes or the plant shuts down, not only afraid but ashamed?

8   I was slow to understand the deep grievances of women. This was because, as a boy, I had envied them. Before college, the only people I had ever known who were interested in art or music or literature, the only ones who read books, the only ones who ever seemed to enjoy a sense of ease and grace were the mothers and daughters. Like the menfolk, they fretted about money, they scrimped and made-do. But, when the pay stopped coming in, they were not the ones who had failed. Nor did they have to go to war, and that seemed to me a blessed fact. By comparison with the narrow, ironclad days of fathers, there was an expansiveness, I thought, in the days of mothers. They went to see neighbors, to shop in town, to run errands at school, at the library, at church. No doubt, had I looked harder at their lives, I would have envied them less. It was not my fate to become a woman, so it was easier for me to see the graces. Few of them held jobs outside the home, and those who did filled thankless roles as clerks and waitresses. I didn't see, then, what a prison a house could be, since houses seemed to me brighter, handsomer places than any factory. I did not realize—because such things were never spoken of—how often women suffered from men's bullying. I did learn about the wretchedness of abandoned wives, single mothers, widows; but I also learned about the wretchedness of lone men. Even then I could see how exhausting it was for a mother to cater all day to the needs of young children. But if I had been asked, as a boy, to choose between tending a baby and tending a machine, I think I would have chosen the baby. (Having now tended both, I know I would choose the baby.)

9   So I was baffled when the women at college accused me and my sex of having cornered the world's pleasures. I think something like my bafflement has been felt by other boys (and by girls as well) who grew up in dirt-poor farm country, in mining country, in black ghettos, in Hispanic barrios, in the shadows of factories, in Third World nations—any place where the fate of men is as grim and bleak as the fate of women. Toilers and warriors. I realize now how ancient these identities are, how deep the tug they exert on men, the undertow of a thousand generations. The miseries I saw, as a boy, in the lives of nearly all men I continue to see in the lives of many—the body-breaking toil, the tedium, the call to be tough, the humiliating powerlessness, the battle for a living and for territory.

10   When the women I met at college thought about the joys and privileges of men, they did not carry in their minds the sort of men I had known in my childhood. They thought of their fathers, who were bankers, physicians, architects, stockbrokers, the big wheels of the big cities. These fathers rode the train to work or drove cars that cost more than any of my childhood houses. They were attended from morning to night by female helpers, wives and nurses and secretaries. They were never laid off, never short of cash at month's end, never lined up for welfare. These fathers made decisions that mattered. They ran the world.

11   The daughters of such men wanted to share in this power, this glory. So did I. They yearned for a say over their future, for jobs worthy of their abilities, for the right to live at peace, unmolested, whole. Yes, I thought, yes yes. The difference between me and these daughters was that they saw me, because of my sex, as destined from birth to become like their fathers, and therefore as an enemy to their desires. But I knew better. I wasn't an enemy, in fact or in feeling. I was an ally. If I had known, then, how to tell them so, would they have believed me? Would they now?

DISCUSSION QUESTIONS

1. Why is the essay titled "The Men *We* Carry in *Our Minds*" rather than "The Men *I* Carry in *My Mind*"?
2. Other than starting the essay, what does paragraph 1 accomplish?
3. What primary categories of men does Sanders discuss? What principle of classification does he use?
4. Sanders uses a number of comparisons, such as "zebra suits, heavy as canvas" in paragraph 1, to enhance his writing. Point out other comparisons and comment on their effectiveness.
5. The last sentence of paragraph 10 and the second, sixth, and eighth sentences of paragraph 11 are short statements. What do you think Sanders accomplishes with these statements?
6. Judging by what Sanders writes in the essay, how do you think he would answer the questions he poses in the final two sentences of paragraph 11?

TOWARD KEY INSIGHTS

To what extent do you believe that the views expressed in the essay by the college women and Sanders reflect the views of today's college women and men?

How do you account for any changes you might note?

Write an essay classifying the different grade school or high school teachers that you carry in your mind. Develop your categories with specific, informative details.

BERNICE MCCARTHY

A Tale of Four Learners

Bernice McCarthy, Ph.D., earned her doctorate in education and learning theory from Northwestern University. She founded About Learning, Inc., a consulting firm on educational theory and research. She has published a number of articles and presented workshops at major institutions. In this essay, she classifies learners based on THE 4MAT System® she created.

1   A young man at a midwestern middle school said of his social studies teacher, "She doesn't label us, and she helps us do all kinds of things." That student expressed very simply my evolving understanding of style since I created the 4MAT System in 1979. The way one perceives reality and reacts to it forms a pattern over time. This pattern comes to dominate the way one integrates ideas, skills, and information about people and the way one adapts knowledge and forms meaning.

2   But to learn successfully, a student also needs expertise in other learning styles; together these styles from a natural cycle of learning. That middle school teacher apparently honored the unique style that each student brought to her classroom, while helping each one do some stretching and master all the ways of learning.

3   Following are true stories about four types of learners. They illustrate how students with different learning styles experience school and why we must create opportunities for diverse learning experiences for every child.

4   Linda was in 6th grade when she hit the wall in math. She had loved school up until then. Her teachers and classmates agreed that her poetry was quite good, and her poems often appeared in local publications. But math was a problem. She couldn't connect it to anything—she simply could not see the patterns. Her teachers were not pleased with her and she longed to please them.

5   Linda went on to college, and when she was a junior, a new professor arrived on campus. The day before Linda's statistics class began, she met him in the hallway. He said, "Oh, you're Linda; I've been reading your poetry. You are going to do very well in statistics."

6   She looked at him in amazement. "How can you say that? I have such difficulty in all my math classes."

7   He smiled and answered, "I can tell from your poetry that you understand symmetry. Statistics is about symmetry. As a matter of fact, statistics is the poetry of math." Linda went on to earn an A in that class. Her professor had connected statistics to her life and showed her the patterns (McCarthy 1996).

8   Linda is a Type 1 learner—the highly imaginative student who favors feeling and reflecting. These learners

9   ■ are at home with their feelings, people-oriented, outstanding observers of people, great listeners and nurturers, and committed to making the world a better place.

10   ■ prefer to learn by talking about experiences; listening and watching quietly, then responding to others and discussing ideas; asking questions; brainstorming; and examining relationships. They work well in groups or teams but also enjoy reading quietly.

11   ■ experience difficulty with long verbal explanations, with giving oral presentations, and with memorizing large chunks of abstract information. They dislike confusion or conflict, environments where mistakes are openly criticized, or where they cannot discuss their perceptions.

12   ■ have a cognitive style that puts perception before judgment, subjective knowledge before objective facts, and reflection before action. They prefer to make decisions based on feeling, are visual/auditory/kinesthetic, and experiential before conceptual.

13   As a Type 1 learner, Linda needed to connect math to her real life, to know why it was useful as a way of thinking and a way of formulating problems and solutions. She also needed her teachers to believe in her and to spend time with and nurture her.

14   Marcus was in 1st grade, and he loved school. Everything he longed for was present there—the teacher's loving interest, the thrill of deciphering the symbols that meant things, the things he could touch and feel, the addition problems that the teacher wrote on the chalkboard. He could always see the answers. His excitement was like that of the basketball player who knows that if he can just get his hands on the ball, he can sink it. Each question became an exciting foray into even more questions. And as his reading improved rapidly, he could not get enough of books. He welcomed the words and ideas of each new writer. He felt confident; he knew he belonged (McCarthy 1996).

15   Marcus is a Type 2 learner—the analytic student who favors reflecting and thinking. These learners

16   ■ have a knowledge-oriented style; are outstanding at conceptualizing material; analyze and classify their experiences and organize ideas; are highly organized and at home with details and data; are good at step-by-step tasks; are fascinated with structure; believe in their ability to understand; and are committed to making the world more lucid.

17   ■ prefer to learn through lectures and objective explanations, by working independently and systematically, and by reading and exchanging ideas.

18   ■ experience difficulty in noisy, high-activity environments, ambiguous situations, and working in groups. They also have trouble with open-ended assignments, as well as with presentations, role-playing, and nonsequential instructions. They have difficulty talking about feelings as well.

19   ■ have a cognitive style that is objective thinking, reflection before action, impersonal, auditory/visual/kinesthetic, conceptual over experiential. They tend to make judgments first, then support them with their perceptions.

20   As a Type 2 learner, Marcus found school an absolute joy. Testing, so frightening to Linda, was a tonic for him, a chance to prove he could do it. Because he was naturally verbal and school is mostly a verbal challenge, he was—and continues to be—successful.

21   When Jimmy was in 2nd grade he did not like to read, and that made school difficult. He did enjoy having others read to him, and his younger brother, a 1st grader, read him stories every night. Jimmy did excel in math and art. He loved to work alone on projects and never wanted help. When he was asked to illustrate a story or build something to depict a math concept, he approached the task excitedly. He was happiest when he could solve a problem by creating a three-dimensional solution.

22   Unfortunately, Jimmy had a rigid teacher whose timing was always different from his own. Jimmy either finished too fast or took too long when he got really interested in a project. Once his teacher said in exasperation, "I didn't say you had to do your best work, Jimmy, just get it done!" When Jimmy's family bought a new VCR, they read the directions aloud to figure out how it worked. Jimmy stepped up and simply made it work. His reading problem continued into 3rd grade when he caught up with the others, but he never let it get him down—he was simply too busy doing other kinds of things (McCarthy 1996).

23   Jimmy is a Type 3 learner—the common-sense learner who favors thinking and doing. These learners

24   ■   are great problem solvers and are drawn to how things work. They are at home with tasks and deadlines, are productive and committed to making the world work better, and they believe in their ability to get the job done. They are also active and need opportunities to move around.

25   ■   prefer to learn through active problem solving; step-by-step procedures; touching, manipulating, and constructing; demonstrations; experimentation and tinkering; and competition.

26   ■   experience difficulty when reading is the primary means of learning and whenever they cannot physically test what they are told. They have trouble with verbal complexity, paradoxes or unclear choices, subtle relationships, and open-ended academic tasks. They also have difficulty expressing feelings.

27   ■   have a cognitive style that features objective thinking and facts over ideas, action before reflection, and judgment before perception. Their style is impersonal and kinesthetic/auditory/visual.

28   As a Type 3 learner, Jimmy needed to work things out in his own way, to create unique solutions to problems, and, most of all, to show what he learned by doing something concrete with it. His verbal skills did not kick in until well into the 3rd grade. Although this is not unusual with highly spatial learners, teachers treated it as an aberration. School was simply too regimented and too verbal for Jimmy. What saved him was his focus on his own learning.

29   When Leah was a high school freshman, she liked her new friends and some of her teachers. But she had a fierce need to learn, and school was, not nearly exciting enough for her. She found so much of it deadening—memorizing endless facts that were totally irrelevant to her life. Leah had a wonderful spontaneity, and when it took hold of her, she focused so intensely that

time became meaningless. Her teachers came to regard this spontaneity as a liability that was taking her away from the things she needed to know.

30   At first Leah persevered. Instead of preparing a juvenile justice report based on her social studies text, she asked to be allowed to go to juvenile court and see for herself, and then present her findings in a skit. Her teachers seldom agreed to her proposals, and after a while Leah stopped trying. She had natural leadership talent, which she expressed through her extra-curricular activities—the one part of school she came to love. She graduated, but has believed ever since then that real learning does not happen in school (McCarthy 1996).

31   Leah is a Type 4 learner—the dynamic learner who favors creating and acting. These learners

32   ■ are proud of their subjectivity, at home with ambiguity and change, and great risk takers and entrepreneurs. They act to extend and enrich their experiences and to challenge the boundaries of their worlds for the sake of growth and renewal, and they believe in their ability to influence what happens. They initiate learning by looking for unique aspects of the information to learn and they sustain learning through trial and error.

34   ■ prefer to learn by self-discovery, talking, convincing others, looking for creative solutions to problems, and engaging in free flights of ideas. They also like to work independently and tackle open-ended academic tasks with lots of options, paradox, or subtle relationships. Their interpersonal skills are good.

35   ■ experience difficulty with rigid routines when they are not allowed to question. They also have trouble with visual complexity, methodical tasks, time management, and absolutes.

36   ■ have a cognitive style that is perception first with slight attention to judgment, subjective, relational, action-oriented, kinesthetic/auditory/visual, and experiential over conceptual.

37   Leah found learning for school's sake incomprehensible. As in Jimmy's case, doing was crucial to her approach. She preferred interviewing over reading, going to court to see for herself, exploring instead of hearing how others see things.

38   In any classroom, Linda, Marcus, Jimmy, Leah, and their many shades and varieties sit before the teacher—challenging and waiting to be challenged. The frustrating question is: why are some learners honored in our schools and others ignored, discouraged, or even frowned upon? Why did Marcus fare so well, while Linda, Jimmy, and Leah struggled to be accepted?

39   In my definition of learning, the learner makes meaning by moving through a natural cycle—a movement from feeling to reflecting to thinking and, finally, to acting. This cycle results from the interplay of two separate dimensions—perceiving and processing (Kolb 1984).

40   In perceiving, we take in what happens to us by (1) feeling, as we grasp our experience, and then by (2) thinking, as we begin to separate ourselves from the experience and name and classify it. The resulting concepts become our way of interpreting our world (Kegan 1982).

41   We also process experiences in two ways: by (1) reflecting on them, and then by (2) acting on those reflections. We also try things; we tinker.

42   The places in this cycle that we find most comfortable—where we function with natural ease and grace—are our learning preferences or styles, the "spins" we put on learning.

43   Unfortunately, schools tend to honor only one aspect of perceiving—thinking. This is very tough on kids whose approach to learning is predominately feeling. Linda and Leah, like many other Type 1 and 4 learners—both male and female—are naturals on the feeling end of experience. Jimmy and Marcus, the Type 2 and 3 learners, favor the thinking end.

44   As with feeling and thinking, reflecting and acting need to be in balance. But our schools favor reflecting. Marcus excelled at that, while both Jimmy and Leah needed to act. The lack of hands-on learning created difficulties for both of them.

45   Even as I define styles in my work, I caution that we must be wary of labels. Over time, and with experience, practice, and encouragement, students become comfortable with learning styles that aren't naturally their own. Successful learners, in fact, develop multiple styles.

46   The 4MAT framework is designed to help students gain expertise in every learning style. We design lesson units as cycles built around core concepts, each of which incorporates experiencing (Type 1), conceptualizing (Type 2), applying (Type 3), and creating (Type 4). The styles answer the questions:

47
- Why do I need to know this? (the personal meaning of Type 1).

- What exactly is this content or skill? (the conceptual understanding of Type 2).

- How will I use this in my life (the real-life skills of Type 3).

- If I do use this, what possibilities will it create? (the unique adaptations of Type 4).

48   Had the teachers of Linda, Marcus, Jimmy, and Leah used the entire cycle of learning styles, including those areas in which each student needed to stretch, all four students would have acquired expertise in all facets of the cycle. They would have made personal connections to the learning, examined expert knowledge, used what they were learning to solve problems, and come up with new ways to apply the learning—both personally and in the world at large. (As it happened, the students learned to do these things on their own.)

49   In addressing the various learning styles, the 4MAT System also incorporates elements of brain research—in particular, the different ways that the right and left hemispheres of the cerebral cortex process information (Benson 1985, McCarthy 1981 and 1987, Sylwester 1995, Wittrock 1985). I call these contrasting mental operations the Left and Right Modes.

50   The Left Mode is analytical and knows those things we can describe with precision. It examines cause and effect, breaks things down into parts and categorizes them, seeks and uses language and symbols, abstracts experience for comprehension, generates theory, and creates models. It is sequential and works in time.

51   The Right Mode knows more than it can tell, filling in gaps and imagining. It is intuitive. It senses feelings; forms images and mental combinations; and seeks and uses patterns, relationships, and connections. It manipulates form, distance, and space.

52   Excellence and higher-order thinking demand that we honor both sides of the brain, teaching interactively with hands-on, real-life, messy problem solving. Learners speak in words, signs, symbols, movement, and through music. The more voices students master, the more new learning they will do. Unfortunately, however, teachers persist in lecturing and using logical, sequential problem solving most of the time.

53   In assessing student performance, traditional methods work fairly well for Type 2 learners, who like to prove themselves, and Type 3 learners, who do well on tests in general. Traditional testing doesn't work as well for Types 1 and 4, however. Type 1 learners have difficulty in formal testing situations, especially when tests are timed and call for precise answers. Type 4 learners have trouble doing things by the book and with absolutes and rigid routines when they are not allowed to ask questions.

54   Further, students change roles as they move through the learning cycle. Tests that require students to recall facts obviously do not reflect the subtlety of these changes.

55   We need assessment tools that help us understand the whole person. We must assess the students' ability to picture the concept, to experiment with the idea, to combine skills in order to solve complex problems, to edit and refine their work, and to adapt and integrate learning. We need to know how students are connecting information to their own experiences, how they are blending expert knowledge with their own, and how creative they are. We also need some way of measuring how students reflect on material, conceptualize, and represent what they have learned through various kinds of performances.

56   Successful learning is a continuous, cyclical, lifelong process of differentiating and integrating these personal modes of adaptation. Teachers do not need to label learners according to their style; they need to help them work for balance and wholeness. Leah needs to learn the ways of Marcus; Jimmy needs Linda's ways. And all learners need encouragement to grow.

57   Learning is both reflective and active, verbal and nonverbal, concrete and abstract, head and heart. The teacher must use many instructional methods that are personally meaningful to each student. The more students can travel the cycle, the better they can move to higher-order thinking.

58   As a final note, what became of the students I described earlier? Linda directs the management division of a major human resources consulting firm. Marcus, a former professor of statistics at a prestigious university, is now president of a research firm. Jimmy will be a senior in high school this fall. He scored 100 percent on the Illinois State Math Achievement Test and achieved cum laude in the International Latin Exam. He also had his art portfolio favorably reviewed by the Art Institute of Chicago. And Leah? Leah is a pseudonym for the author of this article.

■ *References*

Benson, D. F. "Language in the Left Hemisphere." *The Dual Brain: Hemispheric Specialization in Humans.* Ed. D. F. Benson and E. Zaidel. New York: Guilford, 1985.

Kegan, R. *The Evolving Self: Problems and Process in Human Development.* Cambridge, MA: Harvard UP, 1982.

Kolb, D. A. *Experiential Learning: Experience as the Source of Learning and Development.* Englewood Cliffs, NJ: Prentice-Hall, 1984.

McCarthy, B. *The 4MAT System: Teaching to Learning Styles with Right/Left Mode Techniques.* Barrington, IL: Excel, Inc., 1981, 1987.

McCarthy, B. *About Learning.* Barrington, IL: Excel, Inc., 1996.

Sylvester, R. *A Celebration of Neurons: An Educator's Guide to the Human Brain.* Alexandria, VA: ASCD, 1995.

Wittrock, M. C. "Education and Recent Neuropsychological and Cognitive Research."
  The Dual Brain: Hemispheric Specialization in Humans. Ed. D. F. Benson and E.
  Zaidel. New York: Guilford, 1985.

DISCUSSION QUESTIONS

1. The author starts with an example of praise for a teacher who did not "label"
   her students but then goes on to classify learning styles. Is this a contradiction?
2. With each type of learning style, the author follows the same pattern. What is
   the pattern that she uses and is it effective?
3. In paragraphs 4, 22, and 30, the author identifies the problems three out of the
   four sample students had in school. Why does she do this? Is it effective?
4. After discussing the four learning styles, the author discusses in paragraphs 38–48
   what she identifies as the learning cycle. What is the connection between this
   learning cycle and how is this important in relation to the classification system?
5. It could be easy to imagine someone who had qualities of more than one
   learning style. Is this a problem for the writer's classification of learning styles?
6. In the conclusion the author informs us of the successes of her four example
   students. How is this conclusion important to the essay?

TOWARD KEY INSIGHTS

1. Try to match yourself to the four learning styles. Does one learning style seem
   most like you? What does this say about the classification system?
2. What learning styles seem to dominate in most of your classes? What effects
   does this seem to have on the learning success of students? Do people who
   have different learning styles have difficulty adjusting to the dominant learning
   style of educational institutions?

SUGGESTION FOR WRITING

*Write an essay classifying teaching styles, including the different kinds of activities involved
in the classroom and the different kinds of assessment.*

RON GERACI

Which Stooge Are You?

Ron Geraci became a Three Stooges *fan while watching
TV reruns of their movies as a youngster in southern New
Jersey. Former features editor of* Men's Health, *he has
written numerous articles on men's physical and emotional
health for that magazine. In our selection, Geraci contends
that each of the Stooges represents a different universal personality type and that recognizing our own particular type can help us avoid its pitfalls.*

1   Men spend millions of dollars on psychotherapy trying to figure out why they're unhappy, why their kids don't respect them, why women treat them like idiots. Perhaps shrinks help some men, but for many others, it's money that would have been better spent on popcorn and videotapes. To solve many of life's problems, all you really need to do is watch the *Three Stooges*.

2   We're all variations of Moe, Larry, or Curly, and our lives are often short subjects filled with cosmic slapstick. When Moe (your boss) hits Curly (your buddy) with a corporate board and then blindsides you when you try to make it all nice, you're living a Stooge moment. Here you'll find the personality type each Stooge represents. Once you determine which Stooge you are, you'll better understand the problems you bring on yourself—and how you can be a generally happier, more successful knucklehead.

3   Everyone knows more than one Moe. These men are the insufferable know-it-alls who become driving instructors, gym teachers, and divorce attorneys. The coach who had you do pushups in front of the team? He was a Moe. So was that boss who made you carry his golf bag.

4   In short, Moes are hot-tempered men who intimidate people with verbal slaps and managerial eye pokes, according to Stuart Fischoff, Ph.D., a psychologist at California State University. "Moe has a paternalistic personality, which is pretty common among men," Fischoff says. "He treats everyone like a child and bullies people to keep them off balance." Being a temperamental loudmouth also helps Moe scare off critics who might expose his little secret: He's no smarter than the saps he terrorizes. Moe himself proved that point. Although he served up most of the nose gnashings and belly bonks in 190 shorts, he always ended up back in the mud with Larry and Curly.

5   Even if you've never actually threatened to tear somebody's tonsils out, there are a few other clues that can tag you as a Moe. First, naturally, Moes are explosive hot-heads who storm through life constantly infuriated by other people. "These men suffer from classic low frustration tolerance," says Allen Elkin, Ph.D., a psychologist in New York. "This not only makes them difficult to work with, but it also gives them high blood pressure, high cholesterol, and a much greater risk of heart attack." In fact, Moes often end up seeking counseling to control their anger, usually after it costs them a job, a marriage, or a couple of good pals. "I tell them to just get away from infuriating situations quickly," says Elkin. "Remember, you don't *have* to poke Curly in the eye because he destroyed the plumbing."

6   Second, in the likely event that a Moe manages to foul things up himself, he'll find a way to blame his mistakes on other people, says Fischoff. In *Healthy, Wealthy, and Dumb* (1938), for example, Moe breaks a $5,000 vase with a 2-by-4 and screams at Larry, "Why didn't you bring me a softer board?!"

7   Your habits on the job are the most telling signs. If you're a Moe, you're probably the hardest-driving wise guy at work. "High-strung, bossy men with Moe personalities tend to live at their jobs," says Elkin. To help stop overloading themselves with work they can't possibly finish (a common Moe peccadillo), workaholic Moes should make a list of projects they *won't* do each day—and then make sure they keep their hands off those folders.

8   Moe Howard (1897–1975) had a classic Moe personality. Even offscreen, he was the fiery, short-fused leader of the trio who made all the decisions. Of course, this put a lot of worries on Moe's shoulders. "My father was an anxiety-ridden, nervous man," says Paul Howard, Moe's son. "He didn't have much

patience. He always worried about his kid brother Curly, and if Larry flubbed a line, my father could become upset and criticize him almost like a director." Larry probably shaped up fast; Moe could always put some English into the next eye gouge.

9   Now, in fairness to all men with bowl cuts and bad attitudes, there are some big advantages to having a Moe personality. "If I could choose my Stooge, I'd sure as hell be a Moe," says Fischoff. Because they're usually so domineering and assertive, Moes are often able to bark their way into leadership positions quickly. (Kennedy and Nixon were Moes; Carter is a Larry.) If you crammed all the *Fortune*-100 CEOs into one Bennigan's, you'd have Moe Central with a wet bar.

10   Another Moe perk: Women flock to you like geeks to a *Star Trek* premier. Moe is an aggressive, tenacious SOB, and women are genetically programmed to find those traits sexually attractive, says Barbara Keesling, Ph.D., a Southern California sex therapist. That's because prehistoric Moes used their superior eye-poking abilities to scare off those wise-guy tigers. It's why that Moe who gave you noogies in high school went through skirts faster than J. Edgar Hoover—and why he's probably divorced now.

11   "Moes are control freaks," says Keesling. "That can be sexually exciting at first, but women get tired of it very quickly. I know—I've dated examples of all three Stooges. I'm thankful they didn't all try to sleep in my bed at once."

12   Larry is the passive, agreeable fellow who scrapes through life by taking his licks and collecting his paycheck. "Generally, things happen *to* a Larry; he doesn't make them happen," says Alan Entin, Ph.D., a psychologist with the American Psychological Association. Larry is the ubiquitous "nice guy" who commutes to his mediocre job, congenially tries to cover Curly's ass, and spends his day trying to avoid getting whacked in the nose by Moe.

13   That's right: John Q. Taxpayer is a Larry.

14   A subtle testosterone shift, though, can make all the difference in what kind of life this lovable sap leads. Give the classic Larry a little more testicularity, and you have a good-natured man who isn't a biological doormat. He'll kick a wino off your lawn but won't fink on your free cable. That makes him a perfect coworker, neighbor, and pal.

15   But subtract a little gonad power, and a Larry can be an indecisive wimp whose greatest ambition in life is to watch *Everybody Loves Raymond*. These pitiful, wishy-washy slobs constantly get clobbered for being—as Larry put it—"a victim of soicumstance," and that typically makes them passive-aggressive, says Fischoff.

16   "A Larry doesn't have the nerve to be assertive, so he protests by not doing something," Fischoff says: not securing the ladder on the triple-bunk bed, or not mentioning that the coffee is actually rat poison. Consequently, Larrys are rarely promoted. If a Larry actually does work up the courage to ask for a raise, the Moe he works for will usually give a meaningless title upgrade—or say, "Get outta here before I murder ya."

17   To determine if you're an overly passive Larry, answer these three questions.

18   *What's new?* If you're a classic Larry, nothing is new. Your answer will be the latest yarn about the office Curly who once photocopied his own butt. "Larrys live vicariously through Moes and Curlys," says Fischoff. "They don't really have a strong identity of their own."

19   *Still dream about writing a screenplay?* "Larrys don't have a life plan," says Fischoff. They bumble from one opportunity to the next while awaiting their "break"; a Moe plots his life like a war and a Curly flatly avoids challenges.

20   *Do you weasel out of big projects?* Larrys become good at deflecting responsibility. This lets them avoid the risk of failure (and success) without looking like a bum. In *Idiots Deluxe* (1945), as Curly is being attacked by a giant bear, Moe screams, "Go out there and help him!" "The bear don't need no help!" Larry yells back.

21   The chief bonus in being a Larry, of course, is that almost everyone thinks you're a swell chum. The dames eventually warm up to you, too, although it might take a few decades. Women reeling from years of turbulent relationships with Moes and Curlys often settle down with a Larry, says Keesling, because he's a stable, predictable, okeydokey guy who won't mind heading to the 7-Eleven for tampons. That makes him husband material. "I'd date Moe and Curly, but I'd marry Larry," confided several women we asked.

22   Like most Larrys, Larry Fine (1902–1975) spent his career following Moe and his free time ducking him. "Larry and Moe weren't friends," says Lyla Budnick, Larry's sister. "Their dealings were all business." Like any good Larry, he found passive-aggressive ways to make Moe fume. "My father would be at an airport hours early," says Joan Maurer, Moe's daughter, "but Larry would show up 5 minutes before the plane took off. This made my dad very upset." For Larry, making Moe sweat in a crowded airport terminal was probably a tiny payback for the daily humiliations.

23   In *The Sweet Pie and Pie* (1941), Curly tries to throw a pie at the usual gang of rich idiots but gets nailed with a pastry each time he cocks his arm. Finally he bashes himself with the pie to deprive others of the satisfaction. This illustrates Curly's strategy for life. "These men laugh at themselves so other people can't ridicule them first," says Elkin. "It comes across as funny, but this kind of defense mechanism really stems from a large reservoir of anger and resentment."

24   Curly had what's called an oral personality, and a particularly self-destructive one. Boisterous, attention-seeking men, especially those who are secretly ashamed of something, like a beer gut or a bald head, often feel that they must perform in order to be liked, says Keesling. "These guys always come in for counseling, because they experience mood swings and addiction problems. It's what killed Curly and his modern-day version, Chris Farley."

25   Men with Curly personalities are almost always fat, says Fischoff, because they live to binge. They overdose on food, booze, gambling, drugs, or sex—and sometimes on all five in one badly soiled hotel bed. Curly, a consummate binger, even outlined his plans for a utopian life in *Healthy, Wealthy, and Dumb:* "Oh boy! Pie à la mode with beer chasers three times a day!"

26   On the job, Curlys pride themselves on providing comedic relief. "A Curly senses he's no leader, so he garners attention by being a fool," says Fischoff. This nets him no respect, but it does defuse criticism. Who can fire a guy when he's down on the carpet running in circles?

27   Just like his two nitwit cohorts, Curly Howard's offscreen personality was pretty similar to that of the Stooge he portrayed. He drank heavily, overate, and smoked several cigars a day. "He would always be out carousing and drinking, and playing the spoons in nightclubs," remembers Paul Howard, his nephew.

28   "I've heard stories that my father sometimes had to pay for the damage Curly caused while drinking," says Joan Maurer, Moe's daughter. If woo-wooing was enough to get Curly belted onscreen, can you imagine what Moe dished out over a real-life antic like this?

29   Curly's lifestyle apparently made him foggy at work, too. When he barked at women or said "nyuk-nyuk-nyuk!" it was often because he had forgotten his lines. After having a series of obvious mini-strokes (he could barely grumble out his woos in 1945's *If a Body Meets a Body*), Curly had a career-ending stroke in 1946 and died in 1952 at age 48.

30   He had a hoot along the way, of course. Everybody loves a clown, so Curlys get plenty of party invites—and nightcaps with attractive women. "If each of the Stooges were to flirt with a woman, Curly would probably take her home, because his humor radiates confidence," Keesling says. (And what woman could resist an opener like "Hiya, Toots"?) But a Curly's neuroses usually shine through within a few dates, which explains why Curlys tend to have few long-term sex partners, says Keesling.

31   Curly Howard was married four times. "With the exception of his fourth marriage, his best relationship was with his dogs," says Paul Howard. Curly expressed his marital outlook pretty clearly in 1941's *An Ache in Every Stake,* as he shaved a lathered block of ice with a razor: "Are you married or happy?"

DISCUSSION QUESTIONS

1. What is Geraci's purpose in writing this essay, and where is it stated?
2. Demonstrate your understanding of coherence by pointing out how paragraphs 3–6 are linked to one another. Refer to the essay when answering.
3. What audience do you think Geraci is trying to reach? Explain your answer.
4. Characterize the level of diction used in this essay. Refer to appropriate passages to support your answer.
5. Do you feel that you are a rather pure version of a Moe, Larry, or Curly, somewhat of a mixture, or that you bear little resemblance to any of them?

TOWARD KEY INSIGHTS

How do you cope with the various personality types that you encounter at school? In your social life? On the job?

Do you think it is an oversimplification to assert that "To solve many of life's problems, all you really need to do is watch the *Three Stooges*" (paragraph 1)? Why or why not?

SUGGESTION FOR WRITING

Write an essay classifying three distinctive personality types. Develop your paper with relevant, specific details and write with a specific audience in mind.

COMPARISON

Reading Strategies

1. Identify your purpose for reading the comparison and the author's purpose for the comparison. Determine how carefully you need to read the comparison.
2. Identify the items that are being compared.

3. Identify the pattern of organization (point by point or block) that is used in the comparison.
4. Read carefully to establish the points of similarities and differences. When the information might be necessary for future purposes, it can be helpful to create a table that matches similarities and differences.

Reading Critically

1. Test to see if there are any biases guiding the comparison. Does the writer show any preference or prejudice?
2. Determine if the accounts of similarities and differences are accurate or whether they are exaggerated.
3. Test to see if there are other similarities or differences that can be established. Are the items more alike or more different than the author tries to suggest?

Reading As a Writer

1. Examine how the author organized the essay. Was the organization effective in guiding the reader through the essay? Note what organizational pattern was most effective.
2. Notice the sentences that the writer uses for transitions. Jot down any useful techniques.
3. Observe how much detail was used to substantiate the comparison.

| Title sets up differences |

BRUCE CATTON

Grant and Lee: A Study in Contrasts

Bruce Catton (1899–1978) was a nationally recognized expert on the Civil War. Born in Petoskey, Michigan, he attended Oberlin College, then worked as a reporter for several large newspapers. Between 1942 and 1948, he held several positions in the U.S. government and then became an editor of American Heritage *magazine. His first book on the Civil War,* Mr. Lincoln's Army, *appeared in 1951 and was followed by* Glory Road *(1952) and* A Stillness at Appomattox *(1953). This last book won the Pulitzer Prize and the National Book Award and established Catton's reputation as a Civil War historian. In the years that followed, Catton continued to write books on the Civil War. In 1972 he published the autobiographical* Waiting for the Morning Train *and in 1974* Michigan: A Bicentennial History. *In our selection, Catton points out differences as well as similarities in the two foremost adversaries of the Civil War.*

| Introduction: paragraphs 1–3; background; significance of following contrasts |

1   When Ulysses S. Grant and Robert E. Lee met in the parlor of a modest house at Appomattox Court House, Virginia, on April 9, 1865, to work out the

terms for the surrender of Lee's Army of Northern Virginia, a great chapter in American life came to a close, and a great new chapter began.

2　　These men were bringing the Civil War to its virtual finish. To be sure, other armies had yet to surrender, and for a few days the fugitive Confederate government would struggle desperately and vainly, trying to find some way to go on living now that its chief support was gone. But in effect it was all over when Grant and Lee signed the papers. And the little room where they wrote out the terms was the scene of one of the poignant, dramatic contrasts in American history.

3　　They were two strong men these oddly different generals, and they represented the strengths of two conflicting currents that, through them, had come into final collision.

4　　Back of Robert E. Lee was the notion that the old aristocratic concept might somehow survive and be dominant in American life.

> Body: paragraph 4 to first part, paragraph 16; alternating pattern throughout

5　　Lee was tidewater Virginia, and in his background were family, culture, and tradition . . . the age of chivalry transplanted to a New World which was making its own legends and its own myths. He embodied a way of life that had come down through the age of knighthood and the English country squire. America was a land that was beginning all over again, dedicated to nothing much more complicated than the rather hazy belief that all men had equal rights and should have an equal chance in the world. In such a land Lee stood for the feeling that it was somehow of advantage to human society to have a pronounced inequality in the social structure. There should be a leisure class, backed by ownership of land; in turn, society itself should be keyed to the land as the chief source of wealth and influence. It would bring forth (according to this ideal) a class of men with a strong sense of obligation to the community; men who lived not to gain advantage for themselves, but to meet the solemn obligations which had been laid on them by the very fact that they were privileged. From them the country would get its leadership; to them it could look for the higher values—of thought, of conduct, or personal deportment—to give it strength and virtue.

> First difference paragraphs 4–6: Lee's background, character

6　　Lee embodied the noblest elements of this aristocratic ideal. Through him, the landed nobility justified itself. For four years, the Southern states had fought a desperate war to uphold the ideals for which Lee stood. In the end, it almost seemed as if the Confederacy fought for Lee; as if he himself was the Confederacy . . . the best thing that the way of life for which the Confederacy stood could ever have to offer. He had passed into legend before Appomattox. Thousands of tired, underfed, poorly clothed Confederate soldiers, long since past the simple enthusiasm of the early days of the struggle, somehow considered Lee the symbol of everything for which they had been willing to die. But they could not quite put this feeling into words. If the Lost Cause, sanctified by so much heroism and so many deaths, had a living justification, its justification was General Lee.

7　　Grant, the son of a tanner on the Western frontier, was everything Lee was not. He had come up the hard way and embodied nothing in particular except the eternal toughness and sinewy fiber of the men who grew up beyond the mountains. He was one of a body of men who owed reverence and obeisance to no one, who were self-reliant to a fault, who cared hardly anything for the past but who had a sharp eye for the future.

> Paragraphs 7–9: Grant's background, character

8　　These frontier men were the precise opposites of the tidewater aristocrats. Back of them, in the great surge that had taken people over the Alleghenies and into the opening Western country, there was a deep, implicit dissatisfaction with a past that had settled into grooves. They stood for democracy not from any reasoned conclusion about the proper ordering of human society, but simply because they had grown up in the middle of democracy and knew how it worked. Their society might have privileges, but they would be privileges each man had won for himself. Forms and patterns meant nothing. No man was born to anything, except perhaps to a chance to show how far he could rise. Life was competition.

9   Yet along with this feeling had come a deep sense of belonging to a national community. The Westerner who developed a farm, opened a shop, or set up in business as a trader could hope to prosper only as his own community prospered—and his community ran from the Atlantic to the Pacific and from Canada down to Mexico. If the land was settled, with towns and highways and accessible markets, he could better himself. He saw his fate in terms of the nation's own destiny. As its horizons expanded, so did his. He had, in other words, an acute dollars-and-cents stake in the continued growth and development of his country.

Second difference: Lee's loyalty

10   And that, perhaps, is where the contrast between Grant and Lee becomes most striking. The Virginia aristocrat, inevitably, saw himself in relation to his own region. He lived in a static society which could endure almost anything except change. Instinctively, first loyalty would go to the locality in which that society existed. He would fight to the limit of endurance to defend it, because in defending it he was defending everything that gave his own life its deepest meaning.

Grant's loyalty

11   The Westerner, on the other hand, would fight with an equal tenacity for the broader concept of society. He fought so because everything he lived by was tied to growth, expansion, and a constantly widening horizon. What he lived by would survive or fall with the nation itself. He could not possibly stand by unmoved in the face of an attempt to destroy the Union. He would combat it with everything he had, because he could only see it as an effort to cut the ground out from under his feet.

Summary of significant differences

12   So Grant and Lee were in complete contrast, representing two diametrically opposed elements in American life. Grant was the modern man emerging; beyond him, ready to come on the stage, was the great age of steel and machinery, of crowded cities and a restless burgeoning vitality. Lee might have ridden down from the old age of chivalry, lance in hand, silken banner fluttering over his head. Each man was the perfect champion of his cause, drawing both his strengths and his weaknesses from the people he led.

Transition paragraph signals switch to similarities

13   Yet it was not all contrast, after all. Different as they were—in background, in personality, in underlying aspiration—these two great soldiers had much in common. Under everything else, they were marvelous fighters. Furthermore, their fighting qualities were really very much alike.

First similarity

14   Each man had, to begin with, the great virtue of utter tenacity and fidelity. Grant fought his way down the Mississippi Valley in spite of acute personal discouragement and profound military handicaps. Lee hung on in the trenches at Petersburg after hope itself had died. In each man there was an indomitable quality . . . the born fighter's refusal to give up as long as he can still remain on his feet and lift his two fists.

Second similarity

15   Daring and resourcefulness they had, too; the ability to think faster and move faster than the enemy. These were the qualities which gave Lee the dazzling campaigns of Second Manassas and Chancellorsville and won Vicksburg for Grant.

Third similarity: notes order of climax

16   Lastly, and perhaps greatest of all, there was the ability, at the end, to turn quickly from war to peace once the fighting was over. Out of the way these two men behaved at Appomattox came the possibility of a peace of reconciliation. It was a possibility not wholly realized, in the years to come, but which did, in

the end, help the two sections to become one nation again . . . after a war whose bitterness might have seemed to make such a reunion wholly impossible. No part of either man's life became him more than the part he played in this brief meeting in the McLean house at Appomattox. Their behavior there put all succeeding generations of Americans in their debt. Two great Americans, Grant and Lee—very different, yet under everything very much alike. Their encounter at Appomattox was one of the great moments of American history.

Conclusion: significance of the meeting

Discussion Questions

1. Where is Catton's thesis statement?
2. Summarize the way of life that Lee stood for, and then do the same for Grant.
3. Why do the differences between Grant and Lee receive more extended treatment than the similarities? Why are the similarities discussed last?
4. How would you characterize Catton's attitude toward the two men? Refer to specific parts of the essay when answering.

Toward Key Insights

To what extent does modern society reflect the values embodied by Grant and Lee?

How would you characterize the upper class in the United States today? Does it consist of leisured individuals who own extensive property, as Lee did, or does it have other characteristics? Are its values the same as Lee's? If not, how are they different?

If Grant was typical of the "self-reliant" non-aristocrat, how is his contemporary counterpart similar to and different from him?

Suggestion for Writing

Write an essay comparing two past or present political or military figures—perhaps Abraham Lincoln and Jefferson Davis or Dwight Eisenhower and Erwin Rommel. Try for a balanced treatment and select an appropriate organization.

Nancy Masterson Sakamoto

Conversational Ballgames

Nancy Masterson Sakamoto graduated Phi Beta Kappa from UCLA with a degree in English. Married to a Japanese artist and Buddhist priest, she lived in Japan for twenty-four years before moving with her husband and two sons to Honolulu in

1982. While in Japan, she was visiting professor at the University of Osaka. She gave in-service training to Japanese junior and senior high school English teachers and talks on intercultural topics, both in English and in Japanese, to various business, educational, and women's groups. In addition to her book, Polite Fictions: Why Japanese and Americans Seem Rude to Each Other, *still used as a textbook in Japanese universities, she coauthored a research project report sponsored by the Japanese Ministry of Education and wrote various articles for Japanese English-teaching publications. In Hawaii, she has been a speaker and seminar leader for many educational, business, and professional organizations. Her current position is professor of American Studies, Shitennoji Gakuen University (Hawaii branch). In this essay, she discusses the different conversational styles of Americans and Japanese, just one example of the many differences that distinguish different cultures.*

1   After I was married and had lived in Japan for a while, my Japanese gradually improved to the point where I could take part in simple conversations with my husband and his friends and family. And I began to notice that often, when I joined in, the others would look startled, and the conversational topic would come to a halt. After this happened several times, it became clear to me that I was doing something wrong. But for a long time, I didn't know what it was.

2   Finally, after listening carefully to many Japanese conversations, I discovered what my problem was. Even though I was speaking Japanese, I was handling the conversation in a western way.

3   Japanese-style conversations develop quite differently from western-style conversations. And the difference isn't only in the languages. I realized that just as I kept trying to hold western-style conversations even when I was speaking Japanese, so my English students kept trying to hold Japanese-style conversations even when they were speaking English. We were unconsciously playing entirely different conversational ballgames.

4   A western-style conversation between two people is like a game of tennis. If I introduce a topic, a conversational ball, I expect you to hit it back. If you agree with me, I don't expect you simply to agree and do nothing more. I expect you to add something—a reason for agreeing, another example, or an elaboration to carry the idea further. But I don't expect you always to agree. I am just as happy if you question me, or challenge me, or completely disagree with me. Whether you agree or disagree, your response will return the ball to me.

5   And then it is my turn again. I don't serve a new ball from my original starting line. I hit your ball back again from where it has bounced. I carry your idea further, or answer your questions or objections, or challenge or question you. And so the ball goes back and forth, with each of us doing our best to give it a new twist, an original spin, or a powerful smash.

6   And the more vigorous the action, the more interesting and exciting the game. Of course, if one of us gets angry, it spoils the conversation, just as it spoils a tennis game. But getting excited is not at all the same as getting angry. After all, we are not trying to hit each other. We are trying to hit the ball. So long as we attack only each other's opinions, and do not attack each other personally, we don't expect anyone to get hurt. A good conversation is supposed to be interesting and exciting.

7   If there are more than two people in the conversation, then it is like doubles in tennis, or like volleyball. There's no waiting in line. Whoever is nearest

and quickest hits the ball, and if you step back, someone else will hit it. No one stops the game to give you a turn. You're responsible for taking your own turn.

8   But whether it's two players or a group, everyone does his best to keep the ball going, and no one person has the ball for very long.

9   A Japanese-style conversation, however, is not at all like tennis or volleyball. It's like bowling. You wait for your turn. And you always know your place in line. It depends on such things as whether you are older or younger, a close friend or a relative stranger to the previous speaker, in a senior or junior position, and so on.

10   When your turn comes, you step up to the starting line with your bowling ball, and carefully bowl it. Everyone else stands back and watches politely, murmuring encouragement. Everyone waits until the ball has reached the end of the alley, and watches to see if it knocks down all the pins, or only some of them, or none of them. There is a pause, while everyone registers your score.

11   Then, after everyone is sure that you have completely finished your turn, the next person in line steps up to the same starting line, with a different ball. He doesn't return your ball, and he does not begin from where your ball stopped. There is no back and forth at all. All the balls run parallel. And there is always a suitable pause between turns. There is no rush, no excitement, no scramble for the ball.

12   No wonder everyone looked startled when I took part in Japanese conversations. I paid no attention to whose turn it was, and kept snatching the ball halfway down the alley and throwing it back to the bowler. Of course the conversation died. I was playing the wrong game.

13   This explains why it is almost impossible to get a western-style conversation or discussion going with English students in Japan. I used to think that the problem was their lack of English language ability. But I finally came to realize that the biggest problem is that they, too, are playing the wrong game.

14   Whenever I serve a volleyball, everyone just stands back and watches it fall, with occasional murmurs of encouragement. No one hits it back. Everyone waits until I call on someone to take a turn. And when that person speaks, he doesn't hit my ball back. He serves a new ball. Again, everyone just watches it fall.

15   So I call on someone else. This person does not refer to what the previous speaker has said. He also serves a new ball. Nobody seems to have paid any attention to what anyone else has said. Everyone begins again from the same starting line, and all the balls run parallel. There is never any back and forth. Everyone is trying to bowl with a volleyball.

16   And if I try a simpler conversation, with only two of us, then the other person tries to bowl with my tennis ball. No wonder foreign English teachers in Japan get discouraged.

17   Now that you know about the difference in the conversational ballgames, you may think that all your troubles are over. But if you have been trained all your life to play one game, it is no simple matter to switch to another, even if you know the rules. Knowing the rules is not at all the same thing as playing the game.

18   Even now, during a conversation in Japanese I will notice a startled reaction, and belatedly realize that once again I have rudely interrupted by instinctively trying to hit back the other person's bowling ball. It is no easier for me to "just listen" during a conversation, than it is for my Japanese students to "just relax" when speaking with foreigners. Now I can truly sympathize with how hard they must find it to try to carry on a Western-style conversation.

19   If I have not yet learned to do conversational bowling in Japanese, at least I have figured out one thing that puzzled me for a long time. After his first trip to America, my husband complained that Americans asked him so many questions and made him talk so much at the dinner table that he never had a chance to eat. When I asked him why he couldn't talk and eat at the same time, he said that Japanese do not customarily think that dinner, especially on fairly formal occasions, is a suitable time for extended conversation.

20   Since westerners think that conversation is an indispensable part of dining, and indeed would consider it impolite not to converse with one's dinner partner, I found this Japanese custom rather strange. Still, I could accept it as a cultural difference even though I didn't really understand it. But when my husband added, in explanation, that Japanese consider it extremely rude to talk with one's mouth full, I got confused. Talking with one's mouth full is certainly not an American custom. We think it very rude, too. Yet we still manage to talk a lot and eat at the same time. How do we do it?

21   For a long time, I couldn't explain it, and it bothered me. But after I discovered the conversational ballgames, I finally found the answer. Of course! In a western-style conversation, you hit the ball, and while someone else is hitting it back, you take a bite, chew, and swallow. Then you hit the ball again, and then eat some more. The more people there are in the conversation, the more chances you have to eat. But even with only two of you talking, you still have plenty of chances to eat.

22   Maybe that's why polite conversation at the dinner table has never been a traditional part of Japanese etiquette. Your turn to talk would last so long without interruption that you'd never get a chance to eat.

Discussion Questions

1. Sakamoto notes in paragraph 1 that she "had lived in Japan for a while" and in paragraph 2 that she has listened "carefully to many Japanese conversations." Why does she note these facts at the outset of her essay?
2. What purpose is served by the first two sentences of paragraph 3?
3. Why do you think Sakamoto uses various games—tennis, volleyball, bowling—to help explain the differences between American and Japanese conversational styles?
4. Point out specific supporting details that help make this comparison successful.
5. For what audience is Sakamoto writing? Refer to the essay when answering.
6. Sakamoto ends paragraph 17 with the assertion that "Knowing the rules is not at all the same thing as playing the game." Explain what she means.

Toward Key Insights

In what ways other than conversational style might cultures exhibit pronounced differences?

What problems might these differences create, and how can we best deal with them?

Suggestion for Writing

Write a paper that discusses a problem that arose between you and someone else because of a difference in outlook or lifestyle and explain how you resolved the matter. Use either the block or alternating method of organization.

MARIFLO STEPHENS

Barbie Doesn't Live Here Anymore

Mariflo Stephens lives in Charlottesville, Virginia, where she writes essays and fiction. Her work appears in a number of major periodicals such as The Washington Post *and the* Virginia Quarterly Review. *This essay, from her memoir in progress,* Last One Home: Life After Oprah, *compares the place of the common Barbie doll in her and her daughter's lives to demonstrate the differences between two generations of women.*

1   I've always known there was something wrong with Barbie. She looks nice enough. And she has her own Corvette, her own band, and her own dream house. Still, I just didn't want my daughter playing with her. But how can we snub Barbie? Little girls all over Charlottesville, all over Virginia, and, yes, all over the world, seem to be spending hour after hour with her.

2   I considered relying on my own experience. When, in 1962, I was presented with my first Barbie doll, I did what all the other little girls did with their Barbies: I took her clothes off. Wow! I could hardly wait to have a pair of my very own.

3   Then I put her clothes back on. It was hard. There was a snap the size of a pinhead and Barbie hardly cooperated. I pulled the tight dress up her legs, over her hips; and it stopped right there. Had a liquid Barbie been poured into this to harden? She was stiff as stone but still smelled like new rubber. I had to put her head between my teeth to get her dress past that chest. I was exhausted. But was it ever fun, I told myself.

4   Now where were those high heels and that pair of long white gloves? I found one glove. Later my friend Jane came over to play. She took the dress off, too. We waited for something to happen. Then we went out to climb some trees. Four hours later, we told our mothers we'd had a great time playing Barbie. (This was lobbying. Jane's mother looked quizzical and noted the leaves in our hair.)

5   I was twelve in 1962, so I didn't have too many good years left for Barbie. Soon I would *be* Barbie. I was blond, wasn't I? And I would be an American teenager with no time left for playing. My time would be devoted to the serious business of dressing and dating and talking on the telephone.

6   In the months to come, I made the best of it. I spent my entire piggybank savings on Barbie clothes—sequined evening gowns, fake-fur wraps, and high heels. The outfits had themes like Barbie Goes to the Prom and Barbie Steps Out printed in a fast-moving script with exclamation marks at the end. There wasn't much to do, however, but dress and undress Barbie, and I found I had to spend most of my time looking for a lost pink high heel the size of my little fingernail.

7   Buying the clothes was the exciting part. Since I liked horses, I picked out Barbie's rodeo skirt set with white high-heeled boots and fringe. These weren't Barbie's clothes, they were mine. If I could've worn Barbie's lavender loungewear with its pink feather boa to my seventh-grade classroom, I would have. If, that is, I could find it. Much was located under the sofa cushions, but far too late, I'm afraid.

8   Barbie retired early. I waited for my body to fill out, Barbie-style. My legs didn't grow to those proportions and neither did anything else. I got the idea that every time a teenage boy looked at me he saw only what was missing—what Barbie had that I didn't.

9   Even the blond hair didn't live up to expectations. Mine was fuzzy and its shape varied from day to day. Barbie's seemed to stay in a permanent coiffure. Evening gowns weren't even in style.

10   And not very many blondes can manage a nose that turns up that way.

11   Worst of all, Barbie doesn't do anything but lose her clothes.
          I had wasted a lot of money, not to mention rich fantasy time, on a false goddess.

12   When my daughter, Jane, was born, I told myself there would be no false goddesses. I didn't name her after a goddess, I named her after the girl I'd climbed trees with.

13   When relatives started to inquire about birthday gifts, I didn't say "No Barbies, please," though I wanted to. I said instead that books were very nice gifts. I mentioned there wasn't much to do with a Barbie doll except comb her hair and I was sure we'd lose those little combs.

14   Jane turned seven. She had five Barbie dolls. I didn't see her playing with them much, although every few days I would find a pink high heel somewhere. I would spot the dolls around the house—their legs splayed crazily and scarves tied around their bodies for clothes.

15   One day Jane said: "Barbies don't do anything. They don't even bend their legs when you sit them down. Their legs stick straight out." I knew she was on to something. Then we cleaned up her room. I found most of the clothes and even some of the high heels. I was pretty proud of myself. But behind me I heard Jane saying: "Let's get rid of the Barbies."

16   "Huh?"

17   "They're dumb and prissy. They clutter up everything. Let's sell them."

18   "What do you mean by 'dumb and prissy'?"

19   "They look like this," she said and raised to tiptoe and smiled maniacally. "They've got globs of blue makeup over their eyes and they can't do anything. You can't even bend their legs to sit them on a model horse."

20   I seized the moment. "What else is wrong with the Barbies?"

21   "They don't have toes. Their shoes fall off. They're always on tiptoe."

22   "That would be tiring," I said, sympathetically.

23   "They never get tired. They don't do anything."

24   "What else is wrong?"

25   "They don't wear socks or pants. Just dresses or fish-net stockings or they go barefoot. All the commercials compliment their hair, but once their hair is tangled, it never goes back."

26   "Anything else wrong?" I asked—and here she won my heart if ever there was a contest for it.

27   "They're all the same age. There are no Barbie babies and no old people."

28   "Sounds like Barbie lives in a dull world," I said.

29   "No, not dull. Dumb and prissy. Let's sell them."

30   "How much should we charge for each one?"

31   "A penny," she said disgustedly, then immediately saw her error. "No, no. A dollar."

32   "Oh," I said, seeing my own error. Just because I considered Barbie small change didn't mean everyone else did. Six Barbies went out the back door to a secondhand shop and, in a matter of minutes, six dollars came in the front door.

33   Maybe Barbie's business suit with its one-inch briefcase inspired Jane's market wisdom.

34   After all, the new Barbies are still in stores, housed in pink boxes with bold script that seems to shout: Barbie Goes to the Office! My old dolls, with their narrow eyes and puckered lips, are upstairs like other mad women of the attic, whispering: "Who stole my feather boa?"

DISCUSSION QUESTIONS

1. This essay compares the different reactions of mother and daughter to Barbie dolls. What are the differences in their responses? What is the real point of this comparison?
2. How does this writer organize her comparison? What is the effect of this strategy?
3. Crucial to this essay is the dialogue between mother and daughter. What does the dialogue accomplish in the essay?
4. Reread the last paragraph. What point is the author trying to make in the conclusion? Is the conclusion effective?
5. How is the image of the feather boa used in the essay? What is the meaning of the feather boa for the author? What clues in the text demonstrate this meaning?

TOWARD KEY INSIGHTS

What role do Barbies have in the developing attitudes of girls, and is that role positive or negative?

More generally, what kinds of impacts do toys have on the developing attitudes of children?

SUGGESTION FOR WRITING

Compare how a toy such as video games, or how people play with a toy, has changed over a specific period of time.

Select someone of either sex whom you know well and write an essay comparing how you and the other person, as adolescents, handled such matters as peer pressure, self-image, dating, and relationships with family members. Develop the essay with relevant supporting material.

Richard Rodriguez

Private Language, Public Language

Richard Rodriguez (born 1944) is a native of San Francisco who is of Mexican ancestry. After learning English in the elementary grades, he went on to earn a baccalaureate degree in English at Stanford University (1967) and graduate degrees at Columbia University (1969) and the University of California at Berkeley (1975). Rejecting job offers from several major universities, he spent the next six years writing Hunger of Memory: The Education of Richard Rodriguez *(1982), a book that traces his educational odyssey.* Days of Obligation *was published in 1992, and* Brown: The Last Discovery of America *was published in 2003. His articles have appeared in a variety of scholarly magazines. In the following essay, Rodriguez explores his contrasting childhood perceptions concerning English and his native Spanish.*

1   I remember to start with that day in Sacramento—a California now nearly thirty years past—when I first entered a classroom, able to understand some fifty stray English words.

2   The third of four children, I had been preceded to a neighborhood Roman Catholic school by an older brother and sister. But neither of them had revealed very much about their classroom experiences. Each afternoon they returned, as they left in the morning, always together, speaking in Spanish as they climbed the five steps of the porch. And their mysterious books, wrapped in shopping-bag paper, remained on the table next to the door, closed firmly behind them.

3   An accident of geography sent me to a school where all my classmates were white, many the children of doctors and lawyers and business executives. All my classmates certainly must have been uneasy on that first day of school—as most children are uneasy—to find themselves apart from their families in the first institution of their lives. But I was astonished.

4   The nun said, in a friendly but oddly impersonal voice, "Boys and girls, this is Richard Rodriguez." (I heard her sound out: *Rich-heard Road-ree-guess.*) It was the first time I had heard anyone name me in English. "Richard," the nun repeated more slowly, writing my name down in her black leather book. Quickly I turned to see my mother's face dissolve in a watery blur behind the pebbled glass door.

5   Many years later there is something called bilingual education—a scheme proposed in the late 1960s by Hispanic-American social activists, later endorsed by a congressional vote. It is a program that seeks to permit non-English-speaking children, many from lower-class homes, to use their family language as the language of school. (Such is the goal its supporters announce.) I hear them and am forced to say no: It is not possible for a child—any child—ever to use his family's language in school. Not to understand this is to misunderstand the public uses of schooling and to trivialize the nature of intimate life—a family's "language."

6   Memory teaches me what I know of these matters; the boy reminds the adult. I was a bilingual child, a certain kind—socially disadvantaged—the son of working-class parents, both Mexican immigrants.

7   In the early years of my boyhood, my parents coped very well in America. My father had steady work. My mother managed at home. They were nobody's victims. Optimism and ambition led them to a house (our home) many blocks from the Mexican south side of town. We lived among *gringos* and only a block from the biggest, whitest houses. It never occurred to my parents that they couldn't live wherever they chose. Nor was the Sacramento of the fifties bent on teaching them a contrary lesson. My mother and father were more annoyed than intimidated by those two or three neighbors who tried initially to make us unwelcome. ("Keep your brats away from my sidewalk!") But despite all they achieved, perhaps because they had so much to achieve, any deep feeling of ease, the confidence of "belonging" in public was withheld from them both. They regarded the people at work, the faces in crowds, as very distant from us. They were the others, *los gringos*. That term was interchangeable in their speech with another, even more telling, *los americanos*.

8   I grew up in a house where the only regular guests were my relations. For one day, enormous families of relatives would visit and there would be so many people that the noise and the bodies would spill out to the backyard and front porch. Then, for weeks, no one came by. (It was usually a salesman who rang the doorbell.) Our house stood apart. A gaudy yellow in a row of white bungalows. We were the people with the noisy dog. The people who raised pigeons and chickens. We were the foreigners on the block. A few neighbors smiled and waved. We waved back. But no one in the family knew the names of the old couple who lived next door; until I was seven years old, I did not know the names of the kids who lived across the street.

9   In public, my father and mother spoke a hesitant, accented, not always grammatical English. And they would have to strain—their bodies tense—to catch the sense of what was rapidly said by *los gringos*. At home they spoke Spanish. The language of their Mexican past sounded in counterpoint to the English of public society. The words would come quickly, with ease. Conveyed through those sounds was the pleasing, soothing, consoling reminder of being at home.

10   During those years when I was first conscious of hearing, my mother and father addressed me only in Spanish; in Spanish I learned to reply. By contrast, English (*inglés*), rarely heard in the house, was the language I came to associate with *gringos*. I learned my first words of English overhearing my parents speak to strangers. At five years of age, I knew just enough English for my mother to trust me on errands to stores one block away. No more.

11   I was a listening child, careful to hear the very different sounds of Spanish and English. Wide-eyed with hearing, I'd listen to sounds more than words. First, there were English (*gringo*) sounds. So many words were still unknown that when the butcher or the lady at the drugstore said something to me, exotic polysyllabic sounds would bloom in the midst of their sentences. Often the speech of people in public seemed to me very loud, booming with confidence. The man behind the counter would literally ask, "What can I do for you?" But by being so firm and so clear, the sound of his voice said that he was a *gringo;* he belonged in public society.

12   I would also hear then the high nasal notes of middle-class American speech. The air stirred with sound. Sometimes, even now, when I have been traveling abroad for several weeks, I will hear what I heard as a boy. In hotel lobbies or airports, in Turkey or Brazil, some Americans will pass, and suddenly I will hear it again—the high sound of American voices. For a few seconds I will hear it with pleasure, for it is now the sound of *my* society—a reminder of home.

But inevitably—already on the flight headed for home—the sound fades with repetition. I will be unable to hear it anymore.

13   When I was a boy, things were different. The accent of *los gringos* was never pleasing nor was it hard to hear. Crowds at Safeway or at bus stops would be noisy with sound. And I would be forced to edge away from the chirping chatter above me.

14   I was unable to hear my own sounds, but I knew very well that I spoke English poorly. My words would not stretch far enough to form complete thoughts. And the words I did speak I didn't know well enough to make into distinct sounds. (Listeners would usually lower their heads, better to hear what I was trying to say.) But it was one thing for *me* to speak English with difficulty. It was more troubling for me to hear my parents speak in public: their high-whining vowels and guttural consonants; their sentences that got stuck with "eh" and "ah" sounds; the confused syntax; the hesitant rhythm of sounds so different from the way *gringos* spoke. I'd notice, moreover, that my parents' voices were softer than those of *gringos* we'd meet.

15   I am tempted now to say that none of this mattered. In adulthood I am embarrassed by childhood fears. And, in a way, it didn't matter very much that my parents could not speak English with ease. Their linguistic difficulties had no serious consequences. My mother and father made themselves understood at the county hospital clinic and at government offices. And yet, in another way, it mattered very much—it was unsettling to hear my parents struggle with English. Hearing them, I'd grow nervous, my clutching trust in their protection and power weakened.

16   There were many times like the night at a brightly lit gasoline station (a blaring white memory) when I stood uneasily, hearing my father. He was talking to a teenaged attendant. I do not recall what they were saying, but I cannot forget the sounds my father made as he spoke. At one point his words slid together to form one word—sounds as confused as the threads of blue and green oil in the puddle next to my shoes. His voice rushed through what he had left to say. And, toward the end, reached falsetto notes, appealing to his listener's understanding. I looked away to the lights of passing automobiles. I tried not to hear anymore. But I heard only too well the calm, easy tones in the attendant's reply. Shortly afterward, walking toward home with my father, I shivered when he put his hand on my shoulder. The very first chance that I got, I evaded his grasp and ran on ahead into the dark, skipping with feigned boyish exuberance.

17   But then there was Spanish. *Español:* my family's language. *Español:* the language that seemed to me a private language. I'd hear strangers on the radio and in the Mexican Catholic church across town speaking in Spanish, but I couldn't really believe that Spanish was a public language, like English. Spanish speakers, rather, seemed related to me, for I sensed that we shared—through our language—the experience of feeling apart from *los gringos*. It was thus a ghetto Spanish that I heard and I spoke. Like those whose lives are bound by a barrio, I was reminded by Spanish of my separateness from *los otros, los gringos* in power. But more intensely than for most barrio children—because I did not live in a barrio—Spanish seemed to me the language of home. (Most days it was only at home that I'd hear it.) It became the language of joyful return.

18   A family member would say something to me and I would feel myself specially recognized. My parents would say something to me and I would feel embraced by the sounds of their words. Those sounds said: *I am speaking with ease in Spanish. I am addressing you in words I never use with* los gringos. *I recognize you as someone special, close, like no one outside. You belong with us. In the family.*

19   *(Ricardo.)*

20   At the age of five, six, well past the time when most other children no longer easily notice the difference between sounds uttered at home and words spoken in public, I had a different experience. I lived in a world magically compounded of sounds. I remained a child longer than most; I lingered too long, poised at the edge of language—often frightened by the sounds of *los gringos,* delighted by the sounds of Spanish at home. I shared with my family a language that was startlingly different from that used in the great city around us.

21   For me there were none of the gradations between public and private society so normal to a maturing child. Outside the house was public society; inside the house was private. Just opening or closing the screen door behind me was an important experience. I'd rarely leave home all alone or without reluctance. Walking down the sidewalk, under the canopy of tall trees, I'd warily notice the—suddenly—silent neighborhood kids who stood warily watching me. Nervously, I'd arrive at the grocery store to hear there the sounds of the *gringo*—foreign to me—reminding me that in this world so big, I was a foreigner. But then I'd return. Walking back toward our house, climbing the steps from the sidewalk, when the front door was open in summer, I'd hear voices beyond the screen door talking in Spanish. For a second or two, I'd stay, linger there, listening. Smiling, I'd hear my mother call out, saying in Spanish (words): "Is that you, Richard?" All the while her sounds would assure me: *You are home now; come closer; inside. With us.*

22   "*Sí,*" I'd reply.

23   Once more inside the house I would resume (assume) my place in the family. The sounds would dim, grow harder to hear. Once more at home, I would grow less aware of that fact. It required, however, no more than the blurt of the doorbell to alert me to listen to sounds all over again. The house would turn instantly still while my mother went to the door. I'd hear her hard English sounds. I'd wait to hear her voice return to soft-sounding Spanish, which assured me, as surely as did the clicking tongue of the lock on the door, that the stranger was gone.

24   Plainly, it is not healthy to hear such sounds so often. It is not healthy to distinguish public words from private words so easily. I remained cloistered by sounds, timid and shy in public, too dependent on voices at home. And yet it needs to be emphasized: I was an extremely happy child at home. I remember many nights when my father would come back from work, and I'd hear him call out to my mother in Spanish, sounding relieved. In Spanish, he'd sound light and free notes he never could manage in English. Some nights I'd jump up just at hearing his voice. With *mis hermanos* I would come running into the room where he was with my mother. Our laughing (so deep was the pleasure!) became screaming. Like others who know the pain of public alienation, we transformed the knowledge of our public separateness and made it consoling—the reminder of intimacy. Excited, we joined our voices in a celebration of sounds. *We are speaking now the way we never speak out in public. We are alone—together,* voices sounded, surrounded to tell me. Some nights, no one seemed willing to loosen the hold sounds had on us. At dinner, we invented new words. (Ours sounded Spanish, but made sense only to us.) We pieced together new words by taking, say, an English verb and giving it Spanish endings. My mother's instructions at bedtime would be lacquered with mock-urgent tones. Or a word like *sí* would become, in several notes, able to convey added measures of feeling. Tongues explored the edges of words, especially the fat vowels. And we happily sounded that military drum roll, the twirling roar of the Spanish *r* Family

language: my family's sounds. The voices of my parents and sisters and brother. Their voices insisting: *You belong here. We are family members. Related. Special to one another. Listen!* Voices singing and sighing, rising, straining, then surging, teeming with pleasure that burst syllables into fragments of laughter. At times it seemed there was steady quiet only when, from another room, the rustling whispers of my parents faded and I moved closer to sleep.

DISCUSSION QUESTIONS

1. What does Rodriguez accomplish in his first four paragraphs? What connection do you see between these paragraphs and later parts of the essay?
2. What is Rodriguez's main point? Where is it stated?
3. Discuss the significance of paragraphs 7–9.
4. Why did his parents' difficulties with English cause Rodriguez such concern?
5. In paragraph 16 Rodriguez tells us that he "looked away to the lights of passing automobiles" and that he "ran on ahead into the dark. . . ." Explain these actions.
6. Rodriguez does not begin to develop his discussion of Spanish—the private language—until paragraph 17. Why do you think this discussion didn't occur earlier in the essay?
7. Explain why the concluding paragraph is effective.

TOWARD KEY INSIGHTS

In what ways other than those noted by Rodriguez do children and their families create or inhabit private worlds that are separate from their public worlds?

What are some of the benefits and problems that result from this dichotomy?

How important is language to a person's identity and social world?

SUGGESTION FOR WRITING

Write a comparison essay discussing some noteworthy difference between you, or some group you belong to, and the larger public. The difference may be one of race, ethnic background, religion, or lifestyle. Demonstrate clearly how the difference affects your relationship with that public.

MARJORIE WATERS

Coming Home

Marjorie Waters was born and educated in upstate New York. A freelance writer who works in Boston, she has authored numerous articles in popular and literary magazines, as well as one longer work, The Victory Garden Kids' Book *(1988).*
In the essay that follows, Ms. Waters draws an analogy between a house that has weathered a severe winter and an individual who has weathered a period of severe grief.

1   After the cruelest of winters, the house still stood. It was pale, washed clean by elements gone wild, and here and there a shutter dangled from a broken hinge. But the structure was sound; the corners had held. I walked around it slowly, studying every detail: the fine edge where window frame met clapboard, the slice of shadow across the roofline, the old wooden railing around the porch. When I climbed the stairs toward the door, I heard the floorboards groan beneath my weight as they had always done. Hello yourself, old friend, I said.

2   Inside, I made those rooms my own again, drew the curtains back, threw open the window, pulled the covers from the furniture, slapped all the upholstery with my hands. I could feel fresh air move in through open windows, replacing a season's worth of staleness with a smell of moist earth, a hint of flowers. After all the months of darkness light poured again into the house, fell in familiar angled patterns across furniture, walls, and floors. Where light beams passed through moving air, even the dust seemed alive; I watched it swirl, dance, resettle.

3   I made myself at home, kicked off my shoes so I could feel the floors beneath my feet again. I tilted my head, read the titles on the spines of all my books, I played old songs I hadn't heard in months, felt the summer music move through me as if my muscles were the strings. It carried me from room to room while I swept away the mustiness of winter, shook the rugs, cleaned cobwebs out of corners, hung laundered linens on the line to whip dry in the outdoor air. I pulled closed boxes out of closets and unwrapped all my things, slowly, one by one. I held and turned them in my hands before I put them out again on shelves, in cupboards and drawers. And when I had each room all full of me again, I showered and washed away the last of winter's claims in hot lather and steam.

4   Night fell and brought a chill to the air outside. I built a fire in the stove, drank tea that smelled of oranges and spice. I warmed my fingers round the cup and thought of how my house would look to passers-by, drowsy and content, with soft rectangles of light on the ground below the windows, a breath of smoke from the chimney. She's come back, they would say as they walked through the dark night. She's home again.

5   For me, the end of grief was a homecoming like this one, a returning to myself made sweeter by the long separation. I remember well the months that had followed that most unexpected death, when I felt cut loose, caught in my own cold storm, far away from all that made me feel at home. I wondered if I would ever again belong to any time or place. People spoke to me of sadness and loss, as if they were burdens to carry in my hands. I nodded in agreement, afraid to tell them that I felt no burdens, only weightlessness. I thought the world had pulled itself away from me, that I would drift, beyond reach, forever.

6   But winter ends, and grief does pass. As I had reclaimed my house and made it my own again, so I slowly reclaimed my life. I resumed my small daily rituals: a cup of coffee with a friend, long walks at sunset. I felt like myself again, and when I laughed, it was my own laugh I heard, rich and full. I had feared that, in my absence, the space that I had left behind would close over from disuse, but I returned to find that my house still stood, even after the cruelest of winters.

DISCUSSION QUESTIONS

1. Consider the essay as a whole and then point out the significance of this sentence in paragraph 1: "But the structure was sound; the corners had held."

2. Waters does not introduce her analogy at the start of the essay. Suggest why. Where are we first aware of her analogy?

3. Why do you think Waters, in paragraph 5, doesn't identify the person who died?

4. Reread the "As . . . so . . ." sentence in paragraph 6. What can you learn from its structure that can help you write your own analogy?

5. Does this analogy further explain the familiar by presenting information on the unfamiliar, or does it explain the unfamiliar by likening it to the familiar?

6. What does Waters accomplish by beginning and ending her essay with " . . . the cruelest of winters"?

Toward Key Insights

What does it mean to say we leave or return to ourselves?

How and under what conditions do we have such experiences?

What is it like to return to oneself, and what allows us to do so?

Suggestion for Writing

Write an analogy that helps explain a time of great joy in your life. Feel free either to reveal or conceal the actual joy. Announce your analogy at the point that seems most effective.

CAUSE AND EFFECT

Reading Strategies

1. Identify the main event that is trying to be explain or the event whose effects are being studied.

2. Determine whether the writer is identifying a chain of causes that yield a result or is considering multiple causes for the same event.

3. Be careful. In more sophisticated academic writing, authors often look at several causes that they try to show are not the real explanation. Only after ruling out some key explanations do they offer the explanation that they think is most plausible.

4. It can be helpful to make a diagram showing the connection between the causes and the effects.

Reading Critically

1. Evaluate the evidence the writer gives for the relationship between cause and effect. How does he or she prove that the cause(s) have the effect(s) in question?

2. Try to determine if there could be other causes or effects that the writer hasn't mentioned.

3. Writers often confuse "correlation" for causation. Just because something happens before or around another event doesn't mean that it is the cause of

the event. Just because George W. Bush was President when the terrorists attacked the World Trade Centers does not mean that his presidency was in any way a cause of the attack. Does the writer confuse correlation and causation?

Reading As a Writer

1. Note how the writer organizes the causes and effects to keep them clear and distinct.
2. Observe what devices the writer uses to demonstrate the connection between the causes and the effects.
3. Examine how the writer pulls his or her ideas together in the conclusion.

RICHARD TOMKINS

Old Father Time Becomes a Terror

Richard Tomkins is consumer industries editor of the Financial Times, *where he has been a member of the editorial staff since 1983. He is currently based at the company's London headquarters, where he leads a team of journalists covering the consumer goods sector and writes about consumer trends. Previously, he was the* FT*'s marketing correspondent and, from 1993 to 1999, he was a correspondent in the newspaper's New York bureau, where he covered the consumer goods sector. Earlier positions in London included writing about the transport sector and corporate news. Tomkins was born in Walsall, England, in 1952. His formal education ended at the age of seventeen. Before becoming a journalist, he was a casual laborer, a factory worker, a truck driver, a restaurant cashier, a civil servant, and an assistant private secretary to a government minister. He left government service in 1978 to hitchhike around the world, and on returning to the U.K. in 1979, joined a local newspaper as a trainee reporter. He joined the* FT *as a subeditor four years later. In this selection, Tomkins discusses the time squeeze that many people are experiencing and offers a way to combat the problem.*

1   It's barely 6:30 A.M. and already your stress levels are rising. You're late for a breakfast meeting. Your cell-phone is ringing and your pager is beeping. You have 35 messages in your e-mail, 10 calls on your Voicemail and one question on your mind.

2   Why was it never like this for Dick Van Dyke?

3   Somehow, life seemed much simpler in the 1960s. In *The Dick Van Dyke Show*, the classic American sitcom of the era, Rob Petrie's job as a television

> Introduction: paragraphs 1–8; compares the leisurely 1960s (paragraphs 1–5) with the time-stressed present

scriptwriter was strictly nine-to-five. It was light when he left for work and light when he got home. There was no teleconferencing during his journey from the Westchester suburbs to the TV studio in Manhattan.

4   At work, deadlines loomed, but there was plenty of time for banter around the office typewriter. There was no Internet, no Voicemail, no fax machine, no CNN. The nearest Petrie came to information overload was listening to a stream of wisecracks from his colleague Buddy Sorrell about Mel, the bald producer.

5   Meanwhile, at home, Rob's wife Laura—Mary Tyler Moore—led a life of leisure. After packing little Richie off to school, she had little to do but gossip with Millie, the next-door neighbour, and prepare the evening meal. When Rob came home, the family sat down to dinner: then it was television, and off to bed.

6   Today, this kind of life seems almost unimaginable. The demands on our time seem to grow ever heavier. Technology has made work portable, allowing it to merge with our personal lives. The nine-to-five job is extinct: in the U.S. people now talk about the 24-7 job, meaning one that requires your commitment 24 hours a day, seven days a week.

7   Home life has changed, too. Laura and Millie no longer have time for a gossip: they are vice-presidents at a bank. Richie's after-school hours are spent at karate classes and Chinese lessons. The only person at home any more is Buddy, who went freelance six months ago after being de-layered by Mel.

8   New phrases have entered the language to express the sense that we are losing control of our lives. "Time famine" describes the mismatch between things to do and hours to do them in, and "multi-tasking" the attempt to reconcile the two. If multi-tasking works, we achieve "time deepening," making better use of the time available: but usually it proves inadequate, resulting in "hurry sickness" and an increasingly desperate search for "life balance" as the sufferer moves closer to break-down.

9   It was not supposed to be this way. Technology, we thought, would make our lives easier. Machines were expected to do our work for us, leaving us with ever-increasing quantities of time to fritter away on idleness and pleasure.

Body: paragraphs 10–31

10   But instead of liberating us, technology has enslaved us. Innovations are occurring at a bewildering rate: as many now arrive in a year as once arrived in a millennium. And as each invention arrives, it eats further into our time.

First cause and specific effects of time stress, paragraphs 10–14: technological innovations

11   The motor car, for example, promised unimaginable levels of personal mobility. But now, traffic in cities moves more slowly than it did in the days of the horse-drawn carriage, and we waste our lives immobilized by congestion.

12   The aircraft promised new horizons, too. The trouble is, it delivered them. Its very existence created a demand for time-consuming journeys that we would never previously have dreamed of undertaking—the transatlantic shopping expedition, for example, or the trip to a convention on the other side of the world.

13   In most cases, technology has not saved time, but enabled us to do more things. In the home, washing machines promised to free women from the drudgery of the laundry. In reality, they encouraged us to change our clothes daily instead of weekly, creating seven times as much washing and ironing. Similarly, the weekly bath has been replaced by the daily shower, multiplying the hours spent on personal grooming.

14   Meanwhile, technology has not only allowed work to spread into our leisure time—the laptop-on-the-beach syndrome—but added the new burden of dealing with faxes, e-mails and Voicemails. It has also provided us with the opportunity to spend hours fixing software glitches on our personal computers or filling our heads with useless information from the Internet.

15   Technology apart, the Internet points the way to a second reason why we feel so time-pressed: the information explosion.

Second cause and specific effects, paragraphs 15–18: the information explosion

16   A couple of centuries ago, nearly all the world's accumulated learning could be contained in the heads of a few philosophers. Today, those heads could not hope to accommodate more than a tiny fraction of the information generated in a single day.

17   News, facts and opinions pour in from every corner of the world. The television set offers 150 channels. There are millions of Internet sites. Magazines, books and CD-Roms proliferate.

18   "In the whole world of scholarship, there were only a handful of scientific journals in the 18th century, and the publication of a book was an event," says Edward Wilson, honorary curator in entymology at Harvard University's museum of comparative zoology. "Now, I find myself subscribing to 60 or 70 journals or magazines just to keep me up with what amounts to a minute proportion of the expanding frontiers of scholarship."

19   There is another reason for our increased stress levels, too: rising prosperity. As ever-larger quantities of goods and services are produced, they have to be consumed. Driven on by advertising, we do our best to oblige: we buy more, travel more and play more, but we struggle to keep up. So we suffer from what Wilson calls discontent with super abundance—the confusion of endless choice.

Third cause and specific effects: rising prosperity

20   Of course, not everyone is overstressed. "It's a convenient shorthand to say we're all time-starved, but we have to remember that it only applies to, say, half the population," says Michael Willmott, director of the Future Foundation, a London research company.

Distribution of time stress, paragraphs 20–26

21   "You've got people retiring early, you've got the unemployed, you've got other people maybe only peripherally involved in the economy who don't have this situation at all. If you're unemployed, your problem is that you've got too much time, not too little."

22   Paul Edwards, chairman of the London-based Henley Centre forecasting group, points out that the feeling of pressures can also be exaggerated, or self-imposed. "Everyone talks about it so much that about 50 percent of unemployed or retired people will tell you they never have enough time to get things done," he says. "It's almost got to the point where there's stress envy. If you're not stressed, you're not succeeding. Everyone wants to have a little bit of this stress to show they're an important person."

23   There is another aspect to all of this too. Hour-by-hour logs kept by thousands of volunteers over the decades have shown that, in the U.K., working hours have risen only slightly in the last 10 years, and in the U.S., they have actually fallen—even for those in professional and executive jobs, where the perceptions of stress are highest.

24   In the U.S., John Robinson, professor of sociology at the University of Maryland, and Geoffrey Godbey, professor of leisure studies at Penn State University, both time-use experts, found that, since the mid-1960s, the average

American had gained five hours a week in free time—that is, time left after working, sleeping, commuting, caring for children and doing the chores.

25   The gains, however, were unevenly distributed. The people who benefited the most were singles and empty-nesters. Those who gained the least—less than an hour—were working couples with pre-school children, perhaps reflecting the trend for parents to spend more time nurturing their offspring.

26   There is, of course, a gender issue here, too. Advances in household appliances may have encouraged women to take paying jobs: but as we have already noted, technology did not end household chores. As a result, we see appalling inequalities in the distribution of free time between the sexes. According to the Henley Centre, working fathers in the U.K. average 48 hours of free time a week. Working mothers get 14.

First general effect of time stress, paragraphs 27–28: maximizing pleasure in minimum time

27   Inequalities apart, the perception of the time famine is widespread, and has provoked a variety of reactions. One is an attempt to gain the largest possible amount of satisfaction from the smallest possible investment of time. People today want fast food, sound bytes and instant gratification. And they become upset when time is wasted.

28   "People talk about quality time. They want perfect moments," says the Henley Centre's Edwards. "If you take your kids to a movie and McDonald's and it's not perfect, you've wasted an afternoon, and it's a sense that you've lost something precious. If you lose some money you can earn some more, but if you waste time you can never get it back."

Second general effect: buying time

29   People are also trying to buy time. Anything that helps streamline our lives is a growth market. One example is what Americans call concierge services—domestic help, child care, gardening and decorating. And on-line retailers are seeing big increases in sales—though not, as yet, profits.

Third general effect: re-evaluating jobs, long work hours

30   A third reaction to time famine has been the growth of the work-life debate. You hear more about people taking early retirement or giving up high pressure jobs in favour of occupations with shorter working hours. And bodies such as Britain's National Work-Life Forum have sprung up, urging employers to end the long-hours culture among managers—"presenteeism"—and to adopt family-friendly working policies.

31   The trouble with all these reactions is that liberating time—whether by making better use of it, buying it from others or reducing the amount spent at work—is futile if the hours gained are immediately diverted to other purposes.

Conclusion: paragraphs 32–36; sources of time stress; author's solution to the problem

32   As Godbey points out, the stress we feel arises not from a shortage of time, but from the surfeit of things we try to cram into it. "It's the kid in the candy store," he says. "There's just so many good things to do. The array of choices is stunning. Our free time is increasing, but not as fast as our sense of the necessary."

33   A more successful remedy may lie in understanding the problem rather than evading it.

34   Before the industrial revolution, people lived in small communities with limited communications. Within the confines of their village, they could reasonably expect to know everything that was to be known, see everything that was to be seen, and do everything that was to be done.

35   Today, being curious by nature, we are still trying to do the same. But the global village is a world of limitless possibilities, and we can never achieve our aim.

36   It is not more time we need: it is fewer desires. We need to switch off the cell-phone and leave the children to play by themselves. We need to buy less, read less and travel less. We need to set boundaries for ourselves, or be doomed to mounting despair.

DISCUSSION QUESTIONS

1. Identify the thesis statement of this essay and suggest why it is located at this spot.
2. The following sentence appears in paragraph 4: "There is no Internet, no Voicemail, no fax machine, no CNN." What does the structure of this sentence accomplish?
3. Reread paragraph 14 and then suggest Tomkins's intention in using the word "opportunity."
4. Explain the meaning of "the confusion of endless choice" at the end of paragraph 19. Then suggest examples that illustrate this idea.
5. Why do you think Tomkins calls attention to groups that are unstressed (paragraph 21) and to studies showing the time gains for average Americans?

TOWARD KEY INSIGHTS

Regarding the essay's final sentence, what type of boundaries do you think time-stressed individuals should set?

How can people establish these boundaries without sacrificing quality of life?

SUGGESTION FOR WRITING

Write an essay discussing the causes and/or effects of some type of stress other than time stress. Possibilities might include academic or financial stress or the stress associated with personal relationships. Develop your paper with appropriate examples.

ANNE ROIPHE

Why Marriages Fail

A native of New York City, Anne Roiphe was born in 1935 and earned a B.A. degree from Sarah Lawrence College in 1957. In a writing career spanning more than three decades, she has produced nearly a dozen works of fiction and non-fiction centering on such matters as alienation, divorce, religious tradition, children's emotional health, and the conflicts arising from the demands of family and the desire for independence. Her many periodical articles reflect these as well as similar concerns. In this essay Roiphe examines the forces leading to marital breakup.

1   These days so many marriages end in divorce that our most sacred vows no longer ring with truth. "Happily ever after" and "Till death do us part" are expressions that seem on the way to becoming obsolete. Why has it become so hard for couples to stay together? What goes wrong? What has happened to us that close to one-half of all marriages are destined for the divorce courts? How could we have created a society in which 42 percent of our children will grow up in single-parent homes? If statistics could only measure loneliness, regret, pain, loss of self-confidence and fear of the future, the numbers would be beyond quantifying.

2   Even though each broken marriage is unique, we can still find the common perils, the common causes for marital despair. Each marriage has crisis points and each marriage tests endurance, the capacity for both intimacy and change. Outside pressures such as job loss, illness, infertility, trouble with a child, care of aging parents and all the other plagues of life hit marriage the way hurricanes blast our shores. Some marriages survive these storms and others don't. Marriages fail, however, not simply because of the outside weather but because the inner climate becomes too hot or too cold, too turbulent or too stupefying.

3   When we look at how we choose our partners and what expectations exist at the tender beginnings of romance, some of the reasons for disaster become quite clear. We all select with unconscious accuracy a mate who will recreate with us the emotional patterns of our first homes. Dr. Carl A. Whitaker, a marital therapist and emeritus professor of psychiatry at the University of Wisconsin, explains, "From early childhood on, each of us carried models for marriage, femininity, masculinity, motherhood, fatherhood and all the other family roles." Each of us falls in love with a mate who has qualities of our parents, who will help us rediscover both the psychological happiness and miseries of our past lives. We may think we have found a man unlike Dad, but then he turns to drink or drugs, or loses his job over and over again or sits silently in front of the TV just the way Dad did. A man may choose a woman who doesn't like kids just like his mother or who gambles away the family savings just like his mother. Or he may choose a slender wife who seems unlike his obese mother but then turns out to have other addictions that destroy their mutual happiness.

4   A man and a woman bring to their marriage bed a blended concoction of conscious and unconscious memories of their parents' lives together. The human

way is to compulsively repeat and recreate the patterns of the past. Sigmund Freud so well described the unhappy design that many of us get trapped in: the unmet needs of childhood, the angry feelings left over from frustrations of long ago, the limits of trust and the recurrence of old fears. Once an individual senses this entrapment, there may follow a yearning to escape, and the result could be a broken, splintered marriage.

5   Of course people can overcome the habits and attitudes that developed in childhood. We all have hidden strengths and amazing capacities for growth and creative change. Change, however, requires work—observing your part in a rotten pattern, bringing difficulties out into the open—and work runs counter to the basic myth of marriage: "When I wed this person all my problems will be over. I will have achieved success and I will become the center of life for this other person and this person will be my center, and we will mean everything to each other forever." This myth, which every marriage relies on, is soon exposed. The coming of children, the pulls and tugs of their demands on affection and time, place a considerable strain on that basic myth of meaning everything to each other, of merging together and solving all of life's problems.

6   Concern and tension about money take each partner away from the other. Obligations to demanding parents or still-depended-upon parents create further strain. Couples today must also deal with all the cultural changes brought on in recent years by the women's movement and the sexual revolution. The altering of roles and the shifting of responsibilities have been extremely trying for many marriages.

7   These and other realities of life erode the visions of marital bliss the way sandstorms eat at rock and the ocean nibbles away at the dunes. Those euphoric, grand feelings that accompany romantic love are really self-delusions, self-hypnotic dreams that enable us to forge a relationship. Real life, failure at work, disappointments, exhaustion, bad smells, bad colds and hard times all puncture the dream and leave us stranded with our mate, with our childhood patterns pushing us this way and that, with our unfulfilled expectations.

8   The struggle to survive in marriage requires adaptability, flexibility, genuine love and kindness and an imagination strong enough to feel what the other is feeling. Many marriages fall apart because either partner cannot imagine what the other wants or cannot communicate what he or she needs or feels. Anger builds until it erupts into a volcanic burst that buries the marriage in ash.

9   It is not hard to see, therefore, how essential communication is for a good marriage. A man and a woman must be able to tell each other how they feel and why they feel the way they do; otherwise they will impose on each other roles and actions that lead to further unhappiness. In some cases, the communication patterns of childhood—of not talking, of talking too much, of not listening, of distrust and anger, of withdrawal—spill into the marriage and prevent a healthy exchange of thoughts and feelings. The answer is to set up new patterns of communication and intimacy.

10   At the same time, however, we must see each other as individuals. "To achieve a balance between separateness and closeness is one of the major psychological tasks of all human beings at every stage of life," says Dr. Stuart Bartle, a psychiatrist at the New York University Medical Center.

11   If we sense from our mate a need for too much intimacy, we tend to push him or her away, fearing that we may lose our identities in the merging of marriage. One partner may suffocate the other partner in a childlike dependency.

12   A good marriage means growing as a couple but also growing as individuals. This isn't easy. Richard gives up his interest in carpentry because his wife,

Helen, is jealous of the time he spends away from her. Karen quits her choir group because her husband dislikes the friends she makes there. Each pair clings to each other and are angry with each other as life closes in on them. This kind of marital balance is easily thrown as one or the other pulls away and divorce follows.

13   Sometimes people pretend that a new partner will solve the old problems. Most often extramarital sex destroys a marriage because it allows an artificial split between the good and the bad—the good is projected on the new partner and the bad is dumped on the head of the old. Dishonesty, hiding and cheating create walls between men and women. Infidelity is just a symptom of trouble. It is a symbolic complaint, a weapon of revenge, as well as an unraveler of closeness. Infidelity is often that proverbial last straw that sinks the camel to the ground.

14   All right—marriage has always been difficult. Why then are we seeing so many divorces at this time? Yes, our modern social fabric is thin, and yes the permissiveness of society has created unrealistic expectations and thrown the family into chaos. But divorce is so common because people today are unwilling to exercise the self-discipline that marriage requires. They expect easy joy, like the entertainment on TV, the thrill of a good party.

15   Marriage takes some kind of sacrifice, not dreadful self-sacrifice of the soul, but some level of compromise. Some of one's fantasies, some of one's legitimate desires have to be given up for the value of the marriage itself. "While all marital partners feel shackled at times it is they who really choose to make the marital ties into confining chains or supporting bonds," says Dr. Whitaker. Marriage requires sexual, financial and emotional discipline. A man and a woman cannot follow every impulse, cannot allow themselves to stop growing or changing.

16   Divorce is not an evil act. Sometimes it provides salvation for people who have grown hopelessly apart or were frozen in patterns of pain or mutual unhappiness. Divorce can be, despite its initial devastation, like the first cut of the surgeon's knife, a step toward new health and a good life. On the other hand, if the partners can stay past the breaking up of the romantic myths into the development of real love and intimacy, they have achieved a work as amazing as the greatest cathedrals of the world. Marriages that do not fail but improve, that persist despite imperfections, are not only rare these days but offer a wondrous shelter in which the face of our mutual humanity can safely show itself.

DISCUSSION QUESTIONS

1. State in your own words what Roiphe means when she remarks at the end of paragraph 1, "If statistics could only measure loneliness, regret, pain, loss of self-confidence and fear of the future, the numbers would be beyond quantifying."
2. In which paragraphs does Roiphe cite expert opinion? Why do you think she includes it?
3. What is accomplished by using the short sentence "This isn't easy" in paragraph 12?
4. What additional reasons can you cite for marriage failure?

TOWARD KEY INSIGHTS

Which of the causes of marital breakdown do you consider most important? Why? What are the most essential things that couples can do to help lower the divorce rate?

SUGGESTION FOR WRITING

Write an essay explaining why certain individuals do well (or poorly) at forming friendships. Develop your causes with relevant specific details.

BRENT STAPLES

Black Men and Public Space

Brent Staples is a journalist whose academic background in psychology and upbringing in the poor and largely black industrial town of Chester, Pennsylvania, have uniquely equipped him to address black problems and concerns. After earning A.B. and M.A. degrees, Staples worked as a college instructor and employee of a management firm while completing his Ph.D. at the University of Chicago in 1982. In 1983, he became a reporter for the Chicago Sun-Times *and three years later accepted a position with the* New York Times, *where he now serves on that paper's editorial board. His most recent book* Parallel Time: Growing Up in Black and White *(2000)* won the prestigious Anisfield Wolff Book Award. His earlier book, *An American Love Story* (1999), explores the subject of interracial marriage. In our selection, Staples examines the fear and hostility that blacks in public places sometimes arouse.*

1   My first victim was a woman—white, well dressed, probably in her early twenties. I came upon her late one evening on a deserted street in Hyde Park, a relatively affluent neighborhood in an otherwise mean, impoverished section of Chicago. As I swung onto the avenue behind her, there seemed to be a discreet, uninflammatory distance between us. Not so. She cast back a worried glance. To her, the youngish black man—a broad six feet two inches with a beard and billowing hair, both hands shoved into the pockets of a bulky military jacket—seemed menacingly close. After a few more quick glimpses, she picked up her pace and was soon running in earnest. Within seconds she disappeared into a cross street.

2   That was more than a decade ago. I was twenty-two years old, a graduate student newly arrived at the University of Chicago. It was in the echo of that terrified woman's footfalls that I first began to know the unwieldy inheritance I'd come into—the ability to alter public space in ugly ways. It was clear that she thought herself the quarry of a mugger, a rapist, or worse. Suffering a bout of insomnia, however, I was stalking sleep, not defenseless wayfarers. As a softy who is scarcely able to take a knife to a raw chicken—let alone hold one to a person's throat—I was surprised, embarrassed, and dismayed all at once. Her flight made me feel like an accomplice in tyranny. It also made it clear that I was indistinguishable from the muggers who occasionally seeped into the area from the surrounding ghetto. That first encounter, and those that followed, signified

that a vast, unnerving gulf lay between nighttime pedestrians—particularly women—and me. And I soon gathered that being perceived as dangerous is a hazard in itself. I only needed to turn a corner into a dicey situation, or crowd some frightened, armed person in a foyer somewhere, or make an errant move after being pulled over by a policeman. Where fear and weapons meet—and they often do in urban America—there is always the possibility of death.

3   In that first year, my first away from my hometown, I was to become thoroughly familiar with the language of fear. At dark, shadowy intersections, I could cross in front of a car stopped at a traffic light and elicit the *thunk, thunk, thunk, thunk* of the driver—black, white, male, or female—hammering down the door locks. On less traveled streets after dark, I grew accustomed to but never comfortable with people crossing to the other side of the street rather than pass me. Then there were the standard unpleasantries with policemen, doormen, bouncers, cabdrivers, and others whose business it is to screen out troublesome individuals *before* there is any nastiness.

4   I moved to New York nearly two years ago and I have remained an avid night walker. In central Manhattan, the near-constant crowd cover minimizes tense one-on-one street encounters. Elsewhere—in SoHo, for example, where sidewalks are narrow and tightly spaced buildings shut out the sky—things can get very taut indeed.

5   After dark, on the warrenlike streets of Brooklyn where I live, I often see women who fear the worst from me. They seem to have set their faces on neutral, and with their purse straps strung across their chests bandolier-style, they forge ahead as though bracing themselves against being tackled. I understand, of course, that the danger they perceive is not a hallucination. Women are particularly vulnerable to street violence, and young black males are drastically overrepresented among the perpetrators of that violence. Yet these truths are no solace against the kind of alienation that comes of being ever the suspect, a fearsome entity with whom pedestrians avoid making eye contact.

6   It is not altogether clear to me how I reached the ripe old age of twenty-two without being conscious of the lethality nighttime pedestrians attributed to me. Perhaps it was because in Chester, Pennsylvania, the small, angry industrial town where I came of age in the 1960s, I was scarcely noticeable against a backdrop of gang warfare, street knifings, and murders. I grew up one of the good boys, had perhaps a half-dozen fistfights. In retrospect, my shyness of combat has clear sources.

7   As a boy, I saw countless tough guys locked away; I have since buried several, too. They were babies, really—a teenage cousin, a brother of twenty-two, a childhood friend in his mid-twenties—all gone down in episodes of bravado played out in the streets. I came to doubt the virtues of intimidation early on. I chose, perhaps unconsciously, to remain a shadow—timid, but a survivor.

8   The fearsomeness mistakenly attributed to me in public places often has a perilous flavor. The most frightening of these confusions occurred in the late 1970's and early 1980's, when I worked as a journalist in Chicago. One day, rushing into the office of a magazine I was writing for with a deadline story in hand, I was mistaken for a burglar. The office manager called security and, with an ad hoc posse, pursued me through the labyrinthine halls, nearly to my editor's door. I had no way of proving who I was. I could only move briskly toward the company of someone who knew me.

9   Another time I was on assignment for a local paper and killing time before an interview. I entered a jewelry store on the city's affluent Near North Side. The proprietor excused herself and returned with an enormous red Doberman

pinscher straining at the end of a leash. She stood, the dog extended toward me, silent to my questions, her eyes bulging nearly out of her head. I took a cursory look around, nodded, and bade her good night.

10   Relatively speaking, however, I never fared as badly as another black male journalist. He went to nearby Waukegan, Illinois, a couple of summers ago to work on a story about a murderer who was born there. Mistaking the reporter for the killer, police officers hauled him from his car at gunpoint and but for his press credentials would probably have tried to book him. Such episodes are not uncommon. Black men trade tales like this all the time.

11   Over the years, I learned to smother the rage I felt at so often being taken for a criminal. Not to do so would surely have led to madness. I now take precautions to make myself less threatening. I move about with care, particularly late in the evening. I give a wide berth to nervous people on subway platforms during the wee hours, particularly when I have exchanged business clothes for jeans. If I happen to be entering a building behind some people who appear skittish, I may walk by, letting them clear the lobby before I return, so as not to seem to be following them. I have been calm and extremely congenial on those rare occasions when I've been pulled over by the police.

12   And on late-evening constitutionals I employ what has proved to be an excellent tension-reducing measure: I whistle melodies from Beethoven and Vivaldi and the more popular classical composers. Even steely New Yorkers hunching toward nighttime destinations seem to relax, and occasionally they even join in the tune. Virtually everybody seems to sense that a mugger wouldn't be warbling bright, sunny selections from Vivaldi's *Four Seasons*. It is my equivalent of the cowbell that hikers wear when they know they are in bear country.

DISCUSSION QUESTIONS

1. Discuss the effectiveness of Staple's opening paragraph.
2. Identify the thesis statement of the essay.
3. Consider the essay as a whole and then point out the significance of the first sentence in paragraph 2.
4. What does Staples accomplish by mentioning at several points in the essay his distaste for violence?
5. Which patterns of causal analysis, discussed on pages 141–142, do you find in this essay?
6. Trace Staples's changing responses to the fear and hostility that he encounters.

TOWARD KEY INSIGHTS

What could and should be done to alleviate some of the racial tension and stereotyping that led to the experiences described in this essay?

SUGGESTION FOR WRITING

Write a cause-and-effect essay exploring your reactions to some actual or perceived threat to you. Possibilities might include engine trouble on a plane flight; a snowstorm that traps you in your car; or recurring head, chest, or stomach pains that send you to your doctor. Include your reactions both at the time and afterward.

DIANA BLETTER

Refuse to Live in Fear

Diane Bletter was born (1957) in New York. After graduating from Cornell University with a degree in comparative literature, she worked as a freelance writer. Her articles have appeared in many well-known periodicals, including Newsday. *She was nominated for a national Jewish book award for her book* The Invisible Thread: A Portrait of Jewish Women. *In this selection, based on her experience of living as an American in Israel, she examines the impact terrorism can have on everyday life.*

1   For most of my life, I thought a shoe box was just a shoe box. Until the afternoon I discovered that it could also be considered a lethal weapon.

2   This is what happened: I had just gone shopping for shoes—one of my favorite pastimes—in the small Mediterranean town of Nahariyya in northern Israel, where I've lived for the last five years. I sat down on a bench to change into my new purchase. I was so busy admiring my feet that I left the shoe box (with my old shoes) on the bench. Fifteen minutes later, I suddenly remembered it and turned back. When I approached the street, I saw crowds of people, barricades and at least five policemen.

3   "What happened?" I asked.

4   "Everyone's been evacuated. Someone reported a suspicious object on a bench down the street."

5   "Oh, no!" I shouted. "My shoes!"

6   Had I arrived even a few seconds later, a special bomb squad—complete with robot—would have imploded my shoe box to deactivate what could have been a bomb hidden inside. The policeman shook his finger at me. "This is the Middle East!" he said angrily. "You can't be careless like that!"

Reality Bites, Hard

7   Moving to Israel from America's tranquil suburbia has taught me about living with the threat of terrorism, something we Americans—after the bomb at Atlanta's Olympic Games and the explosion of TWA Flight 800—are finally being forced to think about on our own turf. The brutal fact of a terrorist attack is that it shatters the innocent peace of our days, the happy logic of our lives. It inalterably changes the way we live.

8   I can no longer daydream as I walk down a street—now I know that, to stay alive, I have to remain aware of who and what surrounds me. As my fiance always tells me, "Your eyes are your best friends!" and I use them to keep track of emergency exits, the closest windows, the nearest heavy object that could be used in self-defense.

9   I used to be a reflexive litter-grabber—in my hometown, I never hesitated to pick up a coffee cup from the sidewalk and toss it in a nearby garbage can. In Israel, I've learned not to touch litter and to stay away from garbage cans—on several occasions, bombs have been placed in them. If I see a knapsack, shopping bag or—yes—a shoe box left unattended, I now do three things: One, ask passersby if they forgot the package; two, get away from it as fast as I can; and three, report it to the police.

Necessary Inconveniences

10   Living in a country where terrorism is always a possibility means that at every entrance to a public place, guards search every bag. I forgot this the first

time I walked into Nahariyya's lone department store; a guard stopped me to look through my pocketbook. "How could I have shoplifted?" I asked. "I haven't set foot in the store." Then I remembered that in America, people worry about what someone might sneak *out* of a store; in Israel, people worry what weapons or bombs someone might sneak *in* to a store.

11   The first few days after a terrorist attack seem very quiet. Since all of Israel is only the size of New Jersey, everybody usually knows someone who was hurt or killed. The nation slips into mourning: People avoid going out, attending parties, sitting in cafés.

12   Gradually, though, daily life returns to normal. Israelis (and now, Americans) have to prove again and again to potential terrorists that we're not giving in to our fears. If we voluntarily restrict our movements and our lives, terrorists have vanquished us.

13   During the latest hostilities in Lebanon (whose border is about seven miles from Nahariyya), Samia Zina, my dear friend—and a Muslim Arab—dreamed about me, one of those vivid dreams that seems prophetic when you wake. She dreamed that the fighting had forced her to flee her home, and that I'd hidden her and her children in my house (and I certainly would have, had the nightmare been a reality). The next day, Samia popped by to tell me her dream and give me the two stuffed chickens she'd been moved to cook for me.

14   "Thank you," I said, astonished by the food and the dream. "But I know you would have hidden me, too."

15   Terrorists attempt to divide people by fear, but in our community they've brought so-called enemies together: Even Arabs and Jews watch out for each other in public places, knowing that terrorists target everyone. By resisting the temptation to become paranoid and isolated, by sticking up for one another, we remain undefeated.

DISCUSSION QUESTIONS

1. Diana Bletter starts her essay be describing her own mistake in leaving a shoe box unattended. Why does she start in this fashion? What does it demonstrate?
2. Identify some of the effects of terrorism mentioned in the article.
3. After September 11, her comments about the Olympic Games and Flight 800 may seem dated. Is the article dated? Why or why not?
4. At first glance, her concluding three paragraphs seem inconsistent with the rest of the essay. What role does this ending have in relation to the rest of the article?

TOWARD KEY INSIGHTS

The article explains how a major event such as a terrorist attack can change our perceptions of simple everyday activities. Consider how other events, an accident or a theft or the death of a loved one, can change our perceptions. What happens over time?

SUGGESTIONS FOR WRITING

Everyone has experienced some kind of threat or loss. Write an essay on how that kind of experience can change a person's relationship to the world.

DEFINITION

Reading Strategies

1. Clearly identify the term being defined.
2. Mark as you read the characteristics that are part of the defining characteristic of the concept. It can help to make a list of these defining characteristics.
3. Note specifically what the term being defined is *not* supposed to mean.
4. Observe any analogies, similes, or metaphors, noting specifically what the concept is suppose to be like.
5. Try to see if you can apply the concept.

Reading Critically

1. Check to see if the definition matches your intuition.
2. Determine if the definition is too narrow. If a person defines literature as works of fiction, the definition could leave out poetry.
3. Determine by applying the definition if it is too broad. If a person defines literature as works of writing, the definition would include phone books—a clearly unintended consequence of the definition.
4. Test if there are other available or possible definitions.

Reading As a Writer

1. Notice how the writer uses the introduction to explain the importance of the concept and the definition.
2. Identify the key strategies the writer uses to construct a definition—stating the defining characteristics, providing examples, indicating that to which the term does not apply.
3. Observe how the writer limits the definition so that it is not overapplied.
4. If the writer employs analogy, simile, or metaphor, determine how the device works in the context of the definition.

LAURENCE SHAMES

The Sweet Smell of Success Isn't All That Sweet

Laurence Shames (born 1951) is a native of Newark, New Jersey, and a graduate of New York University. After completing his education, he began a career as a nonfiction writer contributing to a variety of popular magazines and to the New York Times. *Shames's book-length publicactions include two nonfiction works,*

The Big Time: The Harvard Business School's Most Successful Class and How It Shaped America (1986) and The Hunger for More (1991), which focuses on the search for values in a world of greed. He also co-authored Peter Barton's memoir Not Fade Away *(2003). He has also authored several fictional works, with an emphasis on detective fiction.* The Naked Detective *appeared in 2000. Shames's concern for values is apparent in this selection, which attacks contemporary attitudes about success.*

1   John Milton was a failure. In writing "Paradise Lost," his stated aim was to "justify the ways of God to men." Inevitably, he fell short of accomplishing that and only wrote a monumental poem. Beethoven, whose music was conceived to transcend Fate, was a failure, as was Socrates, whose ambition was to make people happy by making them reasonable and just. The inescapable conclusion seems to be that the surest, noblest way to fail is to set one's own standards titanically high.

Introduction: paragraphs 1–4: captures attention by ironically attacking high success standards, defending low standards

2   The flip-side of that proposition also seems true, and it provides the safe but dreary logic by which most of us live: The surest way to succeed is to keep one's strivings low—or at least to direct them along already charted paths. Don't set yourself the probably thankless task of making the legal system better; just shoot at becoming a partner in the firm. Don't agonize over questions about where your talents and proclivities might most fulfillingly lead you; just do a heads-up job of determining where the educational or business opportunities seem most secure.

3   After all, if "success" itself—rather than the substance of the achievements that make for success—is the criterion by which we measure ourselves and from which we derive our self-esteem, why make things more difficult by reaching for the stars?

4   What is this contemporary version of success really all about?

Body paragraphs 5–12

5   According to certain beer commercials, it consists in moving up to a premium brand that costs a dime or so more per bottle. Credit-card companies would have you believe success inheres in owning their particular piece of plastic.

Development by examples and brief definitions

6   If these examples sound petty, they are. But take those petty privileges, weave them into a fabric that passes for a value system and what you've got is a national mood that has vast motivating power that can shape at least the near future of the entire country.

Development by effect

7   Under the flag of success, modern-style, liberal arts colleges are withering while business schools are burgeoning—and yet even business schools are having an increasingly hard time finding faculty members, because teaching isn't considered "successful" enough. Amid a broad consensus that there is a glut of lawyers and an epidemic of strangling litigation, record numbers of young people continue to flock to law school because, for the individual practitioner, a law degree is still considered a safe ticket.

Development by comparison, examples, and causes

8   The most sobering thought of all is that today's M.B.A.'s and lawyers are tomorrow's M.B.A.'s and lawyers: Having invested so much time and money in their training, only a tiny percentage of them will ever opt out of their early chosen fields. Decisions made in accordance with today's hothouse notions of ambition are locking people into careers that will define and also limit their activities and yearnings for virtually the rest of their lives.

Development by effects

9   Many, by external standards, will be "successes." They will own homes, eat in better restaurants, dress well and, in some instances, perform socially useful work. Yet there is a deadening and dangerous flaw in their philosophy: It has little room, little sympathy and less respect for the noble failure, for the person who ventures past the limits, who aims gloriously high and falls unashamedly short.

Development by effects and argument

10   That sort of ambition doesn't have much place in a world where success is proved by worldly reward rather than by accomplishment itself. That sort of ambition is increasingly thought of as the domain of irredeemable eccentrics,

Development by effects

of people who haven't quite caught on—and there is great social pressure not to be one of them.

Development by effects

11   The result is that fewer people are drawn to the cutting edge of noncommercial scientific research. Fewer are taking on the sublime, unwinnable challenges of the arts. Fewer are asking questions that matter—the ones that can't be answered. Fewer are putting themselves on the line, making as much of their minds and talents as they might.

Development by effect, causes, and comparison

12   The irony is that today's success-chasers seem obsessed with the idea of *not settling*. They take advanced degrees in business because they won't settle for just a so-so job. They compete for slots at law firms and investment houses because they won't settle for any but the fastest track. They seem to regard it as axiomatic that "success" and "settling" are opposites.

Conclusion: argues against contemporary notions of success

13   Yet in doggedly pursuing the rather brittle species of success now in fashion, they are restricting themselves to a chokingly narrow swath of turf along the entire range of human possibilities. Does it ever occur to them that, frequently, success is what people settle for when they can't think of something noble enough to be worth failing at?

DISCUSSION QUESTIONS

1. Shames notes in paragraph 3 that "'success' itself—rather than the substance of the achievements that make for success—" seems to be the touchstone by which we measure our worth. What do you think he means? Why is the distinction positioned at this point?
2. Why do you think Shames ends his essay with a rhetorical question, that is, one for which no answer is expected?
3. To what extent do you agree with Shames's idea of success? Discuss.

TOWARD KEY INSIGHTS

What evidence do you find that not all people are consumed by the desire for money?

What qualities do you consider crucial to living a "good" life? To happiness?

SUGGESTION FOR WRITING

Write a definition essay explaining how the popular view of responsibility, greed, marriage, single life, friendship, or some other concept needs redefining. Use whatever writing strategies advance your purpose.

MARC ZWELLING

The Blended Economy

Marc Zwelling graduated with a B.S. degree in journalism from Northwestern University in 1968. After graduating, he worked for Canadian Press, the Toronto Telegram, *and as public relations official for the United*

Steelworkers of America. He is currently president of Vector Research and Development, Inc., and conducts opinion surveys and completes feasibility studies. He has facilitated numerous workshops and written extensively about future trends. In our selection, he examines the changing nature of the business marketplace.

1　　The traditional way to innovate is to carve a specialized niche. Some building contractors specialize in renovating nineteenth-century homes. Lawyers practice trade law, criminal law, family law, labor law, immigration, copyright, or libel. Doctors can be ear-nose-throat specialists, gerontologists, or pediatricians. Specialization is efficient; specialists do their jobs faster because they know them better than non-specialists. And a niche is usually more profitable than the mass market from which someone sliced it. The trouble with a niche is that when competitors recognize it's profitable they rush in.

2　　Blending is the opposite of specialization. Instead of burrowing deeper into a field or product to specialize, blending creates a new market category. The secret in the technique is to unite different, not similar, ideas, products, or services. Minivans and sport-utility vehicles, for example, grew from blending cars and trucks, creating whole new categories of consumer vehicles.

3　　Companies can continually generate new ideas by blending. Most new products today are simply extrapolations of successful products, such as a faster microprocessor, a cheaper airline ticket, a smaller camera, and so on. These innovations eventually run out of possibilities. Blending different ideas instead produces limitless new directions for innovative products.

4　　A food company searching for a new product for kids might think of blending different items from a list of opposites like "frozen or unfrozen," "milk or cola," "peanut butter or peanuts," "salad or soup." Perhaps kids who love peanuts would savor them in a soup. And perhaps a cola could be frozen so it would stay cold longer, requiring no ice. The ideas may prove impractical, nonsensical, or just plain awful, but the point is to generate more ideas because they can lead to practical products.

5　　Blending also operates within social and economic trends. For instance, barriers are falling between work and leisure, devastating some retail clothing chains and department stores as employees don the same outfits at home and the office.

6　　In the job market, there is vast potential to create opportunities by combining apparently unrelated occupations. Consider the number of specialists you must work with to buy or sell a house: There is a real estate agent, the loan officer, the building inspector, an insurance agent, and the mover. One specialist hands you off to another. The blending opportunity here is for, perhaps, a "home transitions" professional who can manage all these different steps.

6　　Some employees may have over-specialized. Specialization narrows a worker's opportunities in a slowly growing economy and causes bottlenecks in a booming economy. Blending avoids these problems.

7　　*The New York Times* recently reported unprecedented growth in the new profession of legal nurse consultant. From none a decade ago, there are more than 4,000 in America today. Blending the skills of nurses and lawyers, legal nurse consultants help lawyers in medical-related lawsuits. Blending professions is not the same as stacking one university degree on another. The legal nurse consultant is still a nurse, not a lawyer. Nurses learn enough law in training institutes to become legal nurse consultants.

8　　Another example of a blended career opportunity might be an ergonomic architect—a designer and engineer with special training in child development to make safer houses for families with small children.

9   Try mixing and matching completely dissimilar occupations, such as carpenter, receptionist, software writer, investment adviser, security guard, dentist, chemical engineer, lifeguard, teacher, embalmer, chef, hairstylist, pharmacist, actor.

10   A list like this may yield few blended jobs in the literal sense, but it triggers thinking about ways to add value to products and services and differentiate businesses in super-competitive markets. For instance, a funeral home could offer caskets carved by its own carpenters. A supermarket could build customer loyalty if its meat cutters demonstrate cooking techniques. A chef with pharmaceutical training or a pharmacist with cooking skills could help customers create healthier meals using herbs and other natural supplements.

11   Career blending is most likely to develop among entrepreneurs, as attempts to blend work in traditional settings have historically met with resistance: Unions protest that management wants to make one employee do two jobs for one worker's pay. Management says unions obstruct change and efficiency.

12   Indeed, most fields resist merging and consolidating because of tradition. But since nobody can predict what the market will bear, the greater the number of innovations you can generate in products, services, and careers, the greater your chance of success.

DISCUSSION QUESTIONS

1. In the first two paragraphs, the author contrasts blending with specialization. What might be his reason for such an approach?
2. What techniques does the writer use to define blends? How effective are those approaches?
3. What examples of blends were most effective, which least effective, and why?

TOWARD KEY INSIGHTS

Often we are trapped in our thinking by established categories. How can blending help break us out of those established categories?

SUGGESTION FOR WRITING

Create a blend of your own, perhaps even creating a new word for the blend just as brunch is a blend of breakfast and lunch. Write a short paper defining your blend.

STEPHEN L. CARTER

The Insufficiency of Honesty

Stephen L. Carter (born 1954) earned a B.A. degree from Stanford University in 1976 and a law degree from Yale

University in 1979. Between 1979 and 1982, he worked as a law clerk, first for the U.S. Court of Appeals, District of Columbia circuit, and then for Justice Thurgood Marshall of the U.S. Supreme Court. Since 1982, he has served on the faculty of the Yale Law school. Carter's recent books include The Emperor of Ocean Park *(2002),* God's Name in Vain *(2000),* Civility: Manners, Morals, and the Etiquette of Democracy *(1999), and* The Dissent of the Governed *(1998). Earlier books critique affirmative action policies, attack current political and legal attitudes toward religion, and examine the nature of integrity. In the following selection, Carter examines integrity by distinguishing it from honesty.*

1   A couple of years ago I began a university commencement address by telling the audience that I was going to talk about integrity. The crowd broke into applause. Applause! Just because they had heard the word "integrity": that's how starved for it they were. They had no idea how I was using the word, or what I was going to say about integrity, or, indeed, whether I was for it or against it. But they knew they liked the idea of talking about it.

2   Very well, let us consider this word "integrity." Integrity is like the weather: everybody talks about it but nobody knows what to do about it. Integrity is that stuff that we always want more of. Some say that we need to return to the good old days when we had a lot more of it. Others say that we as a nation have never really had enough of it. Hardly anybody stops to explain exactly what we mean by it, or how we know it is a good thing, or why everybody needs to have the same amount of it. Indeed, the only trouble with integrity is that everybody who uses the word seems to mean something slightly different.

3   For instance, when I refer to integrity, do I mean simply "honesty"? The answer is no; although honesty is a virtue of importance, it is a different virtue from integrity. Let us, for simplicity, think of honesty as not lying; and let us further accept Sissela Bok's definition of a lie: "any intentionally deceptive message which is *stated.*" Plainly, one cannot have integrity without being honest (although, as we shall see, the matter gets complicated), but one can certainly be honest and yet have little integrity.

4   When I refer to integrity, I have something very specific in mind. Integrity, as I will use the term, requires three steps: discerning what is right and what is wrong; acting on what you have discerned, even at personal cost; and saying openly that you are acting on your understanding of right and wrong. The first criterion captures the idea that integrity requires a degree of moral reflectiveness. The second brings in the ideal of a person of integrity as steadfast, a quality that includes keeping one's commitments. The third reminds us that a person of integrity can be trusted.

5   The first point to understand about the difference between honesty and integrity is that a person may be entirely honest without ever engaging in the hard work of discernment that integrity requires: she may tell us quite truthfully what she believes without ever taking the time to figure out whether what she believes is good and right and true. The problem may be as simple as someone's foolishly saying something that hurts a friend's feelings; a few moments of thought would have revealed the likelihood of the hurt and the lack of necessity for the comment. Or the problem may be more complex, as when a man who was raised from birth in a society that preaches racism states his belief in one race's inferiority as a fact, without ever really considering that perhaps this deeply held view is wrong. Certainly the racist is being honest—he is telling us what he actually thinks—but his honesty does not add up to integrity.

Telling Everything You Know

6   A wonderful epigram sometimes attributed to the filmmaker Sam Goldwyn goes like this: "The most important thing in acting is honesty; once you learn to fake that, you're in." The point is that honesty can be something one *seems* to have. Without integrity, what passes for honesty often is nothing of the kind; it is fake honesty—or it is honest but irrelevant and perhaps even immoral.

7   Consider an example. A man who has been married for fifty years confesses to his wife on his deathbed that he was unfaithful thirty-five years earlier. The dishonesty was killing his spirit, he says. Now he has cleared his conscience and is able to die in peace.

8   The husband has been honest—sort of. He has certainly unburdened himself. And he has probably made his wife (soon to be his widow) quite miserable in the process, because even if she forgives him, she will not be able to remember him with quite the vivid image of love and loyalty that she had hoped for. Arranging his own emotional affairs to ease his transition to death, he has shifted to his wife the burden of confusion and pain, perhaps for the rest of her life. Moreover, he has attempted his honesty at the one time in his life when it carries no risk; acting in accordance with what you think is right and risking no loss in the process is a rather thin and unadmirable form of honesty.

9   Besides, even though the husband has been honest in a sense, he has now twice been unfaithful to his wife: once thirty-five years ago, when he had his affair, and again when, nearing death, he decided that his own peace of mind was more important than hers. In trying to be honest he has violated his marriage vow by acting toward his wife not with love but with naked and perhaps even cruel self-interest.

10   As my mother used to say, you don't have to tell people everything you know. Lying and nondisclosure, as the law often recognizes, are not the same thing. Sometimes it is actually illegal to tell what you know, as, for example, in the disclosure of certain financial information by market insiders. Or it may be unethical, as when a lawyer reveals a confidence entrusted to her by a client. It may be simple bad manners, as in the case of a gratuitous comment to a colleague on his or her attire. And it may be subject to religious punishment, as when a Roman Catholic priest breaks the seal of the confessional—an offense that carries automatic excommunication.

11   In all the cases just mentioned, the problem with telling everything you know is that somebody else is harmed. Harm may not be the intention, but it is certainly the effect. Honesty is most laudable when we risk harm to ourselves; it becomes a good deal less so if we instead risk harm to others when there is no gain to anyone other than ourselves. Integrity may counsel keeping our secrets in order to spare the feelings of others. Sometimes, as in the example of the wayward husband, the reason we want to tell what we know is precisely to shift our pain onto somebody else—a course of action dictated less by integrity than by self-interest. Fortunately, integrity and self-interest often coincide, as when a politician of integrity is rewarded with our votes. But often they do not, and it is at those moments that our integrity is truly tested.

Error

12   Another reason that honesty alone is no substitute for integrity is that if forthrightness is not preceded by discernment, it may result in the expression of an incorrect moral judgment. In other words, I may be honest about what I believe, but if I have never tested my beliefs, I may be wrong. And here I mean "wrong" in a particular sense: the proposition in question is wrong if I would change my mind about it after hard moral reflection.

13   Consider this example. Having been taught all his life that women are not as smart as men, a manager gives the women on his staff less-challenging assignments than he gives the men. He does this, he believes, for their own benefit: he does not want them to fail, and he believes that they will if he gives them tougher assignments. Moreover, when one of the women on his staff does poor work, he does not berate her as harshly as he would a man, because he expects nothing more. And he claims to be acting with integrity because he is acting according to his own deepest beliefs.

14   The manager fails the most basic test of integrity. The question is not whether his actions are consistent with what he most deeply believes but whether he has done the hard work of discerning whether what he most deeply believes is right. The manager has not taken this harder step.

15   Moreover, even within the universe that the manager has constructed for himself, he is not acting with integrity. Although he is obviously wrong to think that the women on his staff are not as good as the men, even were he right, that would not justify applying different standards to their work. By so doing he betrays both his obligation to the institution that employs him and his duty as a manager to evaluate his employees.

16   The problem that the manager faces is an enormous one in our practical politics, where having the dialogue that makes democracy work can seem impossible because of our tendency to cling to our views even when we have not examined them. As Jean Bethke Elshtain has said, borrowing from John Courtney Murray, our politics are so fractured and contentious that we often cannot even reach *disagreement*. Our refusal to look closely at our own most cherished principles is surely a large part of the reason. Socrates thought the unexamined life not worth living. But the unhappy truth is that few of us actually have the time for constant reflection on our views—on public or private morality. Examine them we must, however, or we will never know whether we might be wrong.

17   None of this should be taken to mean that integrity as I have described it presupposes a single correct truth. If, for example, your integrity-guided search tells you that affirmative action is wrong, and my integrity-guided search tells me that affirmative action is right, we need not conclude that one of us lacks integrity. As it happens, I believe—both as a Christian and as a secular citizen who struggles toward moral understanding—that we *can* find true and sound answers to our moral questions. But I do not pretend to have found very many of them, nor is an exposition of them my purpose here.

18   It is the case not that there aren't any right answers but that, given human fallibility, we need to be careful in assuming that we have found them. However, today's political talk about how it is wrong for the government to impose one person's morality on somebody else is just mindless chatter. *Every* law imposes one person's morality on somebody else, because law has only two functions: to tell people to do what they would rather not or to forbid them to do what they would.

19   And if the surveys can be believed, there is far more moral agreement in America than we sometimes allow ourselves to think. One of the reasons that character education for young people makes so much sense to so many people is precisely that there seems to be a core set of moral understandings—we might call them the American Core—that most of us accept. Some of the virtues in this American Core are, one hopes, relatively noncontroversial. About 500 American communities have signed on to Michael Josephson's program to emphasize the "six pillars" of good character: trustworthiness, respect, responsibility, caring, fairness, and citizenship. These virtues might lead to a similarly noncontroversial set of political values: having an honest regard for ourselves

and others, protecting freedom of thought and religious belief, and refusing to steal or murder.

Honesty and Competing Responsibilities

20   A further problem with too great an exaltation of honesty is that it may allow us to escape responsibilities that morality bids us bear. If honesty is substituted for integrity, one might think that if I say I am not planning to fulfill a duty, I need not fulfill it. But it would be a peculiar morality indeed that granted us the right to avoid our moral responsibilities simply by stating our intention to ignore them. Integrity does not permit such an easy escape.

21   Consider an example. Before engaging in sex with a woman, her lover tells her that if she gets pregnant, it is her problem, not his. She says that she understands. In due course she does wind up pregnant. If we believe, as I hope we do, that the man would ordinarily have a moral responsibility toward both the child he will have helped to bring into the world and the child's mother, then his honest statement of what he intends does not spare him that responsibility.

22   This vision of responsibility assumes that not all moral obligations stem from consent or from a stated intention. The linking of obligations to promises is a rather modern and perhaps uniquely Western way of looking at life, and perhaps a luxury that only the well-to-do can afford. As Fred and Shulamit Korn (a philosopher and an anthropologist) have pointed out, "If one looks at ethnographic accounts of other societies, one finds that, while obligations everywhere play a crucial role in social life, promising is not preeminent among the sources of obligation and is not even mentioned by most anthropologists." The Korns have made a study of Tonga, where promises are virtually unknown but the social order is remarkably stable. If life without any promises seems extreme, we Americans sometimes go too far the other way, parsing not only our contracts but even our marriage vows in order to discover the absolute minimum obligation that we have to others as a result of our promises.

23   That some societies in the world have worked out evidently functional structures of obligation without the need for promise or consent does not tell us what *we* should do. But it serves as a reminder of the basic proposition that our existence in civil society creates a set of mutual responsibilities that philosophers used to capture in the fiction of the social contract. Nowadays, here in America, people seem to spend their time thinking of even cleverer ways to avoid their obligations, instead of doing what integrity commands and fulfilling them. And all too often honesty is their excuse.

DISCUSSION QUESTIONS

1. Discuss the effectiveness of Carter's title.
2. Identify the thesis statement of this essay.
3. What writing strategies does Carter use to develop his essay? Refer to specific parts of the essay when answering.
4. In paragraph 8, Carter notes that the husband's deathbed confession "carries no risk." Explain what he means.
5. Point out the linking devices that Carter uses to connect paragraphs.
6. Identify what paragraphs constitute Carter's conclusion and explain why it is effective.
7. Discuss examples of situations you have known when people displayed honesty without integrity and also situations when people displayed honesty with integrity.

TOWARD KEY INSIGHTS

> To what extent do you believe that our moral obligations extend beyond our promises and stated intentions?
>
> Do Americans typically try to fulfill their "absolute minimum obligation?" What evidence can you cite to support your answer?

SUGGESTION FOR WRITING

Write an essay defining loyalty. Use appropriate examples and whatever writing strategies will further your purpose.

NANCY GIBBS

When Is It Rape?

A native New Yorker, Nancy Gibbs holds a degree in history from Yale University, from which she graduated with highest honors, and another in politics and philosophy from Oxford University. In 1985 she joined Time *magazine, where she is now a senior editor who writes major stories on national affairs and domestic policy issues. These stories have covered such topics as the right to die, violence in America, welfare reform, the separation of church and state, and the O.J. Simpson case. Several of Gibbs's stories have received awards for excellence. A 1996 book,* Mad Genius, *details the pursuit and capture of the Unabomber. In our selection, Gibbs explores the many dimensions of the term* rape.

1   Be careful of strangers and hurry home, says a mother to her daughter, knowing that the world is a frightful place but not wishing to swaddle a child in fear. Girls grow up scarred by caution and enter adulthood eager to shake free of their parents' worst nightmares. They still know to be wary of strangers. What they don't know is whether they have more to fear from their friends.

2   Most women who get raped are raped by people they already know—like the boy in biology class, or the guy in the office down the hall, or their friend's brother. The familiarity is enough to make them let down their guard, sometimes even enough to make them wonder afterward whether they were "really raped." What people think of as "real rape"—the assault by a monstrous stranger lurking in the shadows—accounts for only 1 out of 5 attacks.

3   So the phrase "acquaintance rape" was coined to describe the rest, all the cases of forced sex between people who already knew each other, however casually. But that was too clinical for headline writers, and so the popular term is the narrower "date rape," which suggests an ugly ending to a raucous night on the town.

4   These are not idle distinctions. Behind the search for labels is the central mythology about rape: that rapists are always strangers, and victims are women who ask for it. The mythology is hard to dispel because the crime is so rarely exposed. The experts guess—that's all they can do under the circumstances—that while 1 in 4 women will be raped in her lifetime, less than 10% will report the assault, and less than 5% of the rapists will go to jail.

5   When a story of the crime lodges in the headlines, the myths have a way of cluttering the search for the truth. The tale of Good Friday in Palm Beach landed in the news because it involved a Kennedy, but it may end up as a watershed case, because all the mysteries and passions surrounding date rape are here to be dissected. William Kennedy Smith met a woman at a bar, invited her back home late at night and apparently had sex with her on the lawn. She says it was rape, and the police believed her story enough to charge him with the crime. Perhaps it was the bruises on her leg; or the instincts of the investigators who found her, panicked and shaking, curled up in the fetal position on a couch; or the lie-detector tests she passed.

6   On the other side, Smith has adamantly protested that he is a man falsely accused. His friends and family testify to his gentle nature and moral fiber and insist that he could not possibly have committed such a crime. Maybe the truth will come out in court[1] —but regardless of its finale, the case has shoved the debate over date rape into the minds of average men and women. Plant the topic in a conversation, and chances are it will ripen into a bitter argument or a jittery sequence of pale jokes.

7   Women charge that date rape is the hidden crime; men complain it is hard to prevent a crime they can't define. Women say it isn't taken seriously; men say it is a concept invented by women who like to tease but not take the consequences. Women say the date-rape debate is the first time the nation has talked frankly about sex; men say it is women's unconscious reaction to the excesses of the sexual revolution. Meanwhile, men and women argue among themselves about the "gray area" that surrounds the whole murky arena of sexual relations, and there is no consensus in sight.

8   In court, on campus, in conversation, the issue turns on the elasticity of the word *rape,* one of the few words in the language with the power to summon a shared image of a horrible crime.

9   At one extreme are those who argue that for the word to retain its impact, it must be strictly defined as forced sexual intercourse: a gang of thugs jumping a jogger in Central Park, a psychopath preying on old women in a housing complex, a man with an ice pick in a side street. To stretch the definition of the word risks stripping away its power. In this view, if it happened on a date, it wasn't rape. A romantic encounter is a context in which sex *could* occur, and so what omniscient judge will decide whether there was genuine mutual consent?

10   Others are willing to concede that date rape sometimes occurs, that sometimes a man goes too far on a date without a woman's consent. But this infraction, they say, is not as ghastly a crime as street rape, and it should not be taken as seriously. The *New York Post,* alarmed by the Willy Smith case, wrote in a recent editorial, "If the sexual encounter, *forced or not,* has been preceded by a series of consensual activities—drinking, a trip to the man's home, a walk on a deserted beach at 3 in the morning—the charge that's leveled

---

[1]Smith, nephew of Senator Edward Kennedy, was acquitted by a jury.

against the alleged offender should, it seems to us, be different than the one filed against, say, the youths who raped and beat the jogger."

11   This attitude sparks rage among women who carry scars received at the hands of men they knew. It makes no difference if the victim shared a drink or a moonlit walk or even a passionate kiss, they protest, if the encounter ended with her being thrown to the ground and forcibly violated. Date rape is not about a misunderstanding, they say. It is not a communications problem. It is not about a woman's having regrets in the morning for a decision she made the night before. It is not about a "decision" at all. Rape is rape, and any form of forced sex—even between neighbors, co-workers, classmates and casual friends—is a crime.

12   A more extreme form of that view comes from activists who see rape as a metaphor, its definition swelling to cover any kind of oppression of women. Rape, seen in this light, can occur not only on a date but also in a marriage, not only by violent assault but also by psychological pressure. A Swarthmore College training pamphlet once explained that acquaintance rape "spans a spectrum of incidents and behaviors, ranging from crimes legally defined as rape to verbal harassment and inappropriate innuendo."

13   No wonder, then, that the battles become so heated. When innuendo qualifies as rape, the definitions have become so slippery that the entire subject sinks into a political swamp. The only way to capture the hard reality is to tell the story.

14   A 32-year-old woman was on business in Tampa last year for the Florida supreme court. Stranded at the courthouse, she accepted a lift from a lawyer involved in her project. As they chatted on the ride home, she recalls, "he was saying all the right things, so I started to trust him." She agreed to have dinner, and afterward, at her hotel door, he convinced her to let him come in to talk. "I went through the whole thing about being old-fashioned," she says. "I was a virgin until I was 21. So I told him talk was all we were going to do."

15   But as they sat on the couch, she found herself falling asleep. "By now, I'm comfortable with him, and I put my head on his shoulder. He's not tried anything all evening, after all." Which is when the rape came. "I woke up to find him on top of me, forcing himself on me. I didn't scream or run. All I could think about was my business contacts and what if they saw me run out of my room screaming rape."

16   "I thought it was my fault. I felt so filthy, I washed myself over and over in hot water. Did he rape me?, I kept asking myself. I didn't consent. But who's gonna believe me? I had a man in my hotel room after midnight." More than a year later, she still can't tell the story without a visible struggle to maintain her composure. Police referred the case to the state attorney's office in Tampa, but without more evidence it decided not to prosecute. Although her attacker has admitted that he heard her say no, maintains the woman, "he says he didn't know that I meant no. He didn't feel he'd raped me, and he even wanted to see me again."

17   Her story is typical in many ways. The victim herself may not be sure right away that she has been raped, that she had said no and been physically forced into having sex anyway. And the rapist commonly hears but does not heed the protest. "A date rapist will follow through no matter what the woman wants because his agenda is to get laid," says Claire Walsh, a Florida-based consultant on sexual assaults. "First comes the dinner, then a dance, then a drink, then the coercion begins." Gentle persuasion gives way to physical intimidation,

with alcohol as the ubiquitous lubricant. "When that fails, force is used," she says. "Real men don't take no for an answer."

18   The Palm Beach case serves to remind women that if they go ahead and press charges, they can expect to go on trial along with their attacker, if not in a courtroom then in the court of public opinion. The *New York Times* caused an uproar on its own staff not only for publishing the victim's name but also for laying out in detail her background, her high school grades, her driving record, along with an unattributed quote from a school official about her "little wild streak." A freshman at Carleton College in Minnesota, who says she was repeatedly raped for four hours by a fellow student, claims that she was asked at an administrative hearing if she performed oral sex on dates. In 1989 a man charged with raping at knife-point a woman he knew was acquitted in Florida because his victim had been wearing lace shorts and no underwear.

19   From a purely legal point of view, if she wants to put her attacker in jail, the survivor had better be beaten as well as raped, since bruises become a badge of credibility. She had better have reported the crime right away, before taking the hours-long shower that she craves, before burning her clothes, before curling up with the blinds down. And she would do well to be a woman of shining character. Otherwise the strict constructionist definitions of rape will prevail in court. "Juries don't have a great deal of sympathy for the victim if she's a willing participant up to the nonconsensual sexual intercourse," says Norman Kinne, a prosecutor in Dallas. "They feel that many times the victim has placed herself in the situation." Absent eyewitnesses or broken bones, a case comes down to her word against his, and the mythology of rape rarely lends her the benefit of the doubt.

20   She should also hope for an all-male jury, preferably composed of fathers with daughters. Prosecutors have found that women tend to be harsh judges of one another—perhaps because to find a defendant guilty is to entertain two grim realities: that anyone might be a rapist, and that every woman could find herself a victim. It may be easier to believe, the experts muse, that at some level the victim asked for it. "But just because a woman makes a bad judgment, does that give the guy a moral right to rape her?" asks Dean Kilpatrick, director of the Crime Victim Research and Treatment Center at the Medical University of South Carolina. "The bottom line is, Why does a woman's having a drink give a man the right to rape her?"

21   [In 1991,] the Supreme Court waded into the debate with a 7-to-2 ruling that protects victims from being harassed on the witness stand with questions about their sexual history. The Justices, in their first decision on "rape-shield laws," said an accused rapist could not present evidence about a previous sexual relationship with the victim unless he notified the court ahead of time. In her decision, Justice Sandra Day O'Connor wrote that "rape victims deserve heightened protection against surprise, harassment and unnecessary invasions of privacy."

22   That was welcome news to prosecutors who understand the reluctance of victims to come forward. But there are other impediments to justice as well. An internal investigation of the Oakland police department found that officers ignored a quarter of all reports of sexual assaults or attempts, though 90% actually warranted investigation. Departments are getting better at educating officers in handling rape cases, but the courts remain behind. A New York City task force on women in the courts charged that judges and lawyers were routinely less inclined to believe a woman's testimony than a man's.

23   The present debate over degrees of rape is nothing new: All through history, rapes have been divided between those that mattered and those that did not. For the first few thousand years, the only rape that was punished was the defiling of a virgin, and that was viewed as a property crime. A girl's virtue was a marketable asset, and so a rapist was often ordered to pay the victim's father the equivalent of her price on the marriage market. In early Babylonian and Hebrew societies, a married woman who was raped suffered the same fate as an adulteress—death by stoning or drowning. Under William the Conqueror, the penalty for raping a virgin was castration and loss of both eyes—unless the violated woman agreed to marry her attacker, as she was often pressured to do. "Stealing an heiress" became a perfectly conventional means of taking—literally—a wife.

24   It may be easier to prove a rape case now, but not much. Until the 1960s it was virtually impossible without an eyewitness; judges were often required to instruct jurors that "rape is a charge easily made and hard to defend against; so examine the testimony of this witness with caution." But sometimes a rape was taken very seriously, particularly if it involved a black man attacking a white woman—a crime for which black men were often executed or lynched.

25   Susan Estrich, author of *Real Rape*, considers herself a lucky victim. This is not just because she survived an attack 17 years ago by a stranger with an ice pick, one day before her graduation from Wellesley. It's because police, and her friends, believed her. "The first thing the Boston police asked was whether it was a black guy," recalls Estrich, now a University of Southern California law professor. When she said yes and gave the details of the attack, their reaction was, "So, you were really raped." It was an instructive lesson, she says, in understanding how racism and sexism are factored into perceptions of the crime.

26   A new twist in society's perception came in 1975, when Susan Brownmiller published her book *Against Our Will: Men, Women and Rape*. In it she attacked the concept that rape was a sex crime, arguing instead that it was a crime of violence and power over women. Throughout history, she wrote, rape has played a critical function. "It is nothing more or less than a conscious process of intimidation, by which *all men* keep *all women* in a state of fear."

27   Out of this contention was born a set of arguments that have become politically correct wisdom on campus and in academic circles. This view holds that rape is a symbol of women's vulnerability to male institutions and attitudes. "It's sociopolitical," insists Gina Rayfield, a New Jersey psychologist. "In our culture men hold the power, politically, economically. They're socialized not to see women as equals."

28   This line of reasoning has led some women, especially radicalized victims, to justify flinging around the term *rape* as a political weapon, referring to everything from violent sexual assaults to inappropriate innuendos. Ginny, a college senior who was really raped when she was 16, suggests that false accusations of rape can serve a useful purpose. "Penetration is not the only form of violation," she explains. In her view, rape is a subjective term, one that women must use to draw attention to other, nonviolent, even nonsexual forms of oppression. "If a woman did falsely accuse a man of rape, she may have had reasons to," Ginny says, "Maybe she wasn't raped, but he clearly violated her in some way."

29   Catherine Comins, assistant dean of student life at Vassar, also sees some value in this loose use of "rape." She says angry victims of various forms of sexual intimidation cry rape to regain their sense of power. "To use the word carefully would be to be careful for the sake of the violator, and the survivors don't

care a hoot about him." Comins argues that men who are unjustly accused can sometimes gain from the experience. "They have a lot of pain, but it is not a pain that I would necessarily have spared them. I think it ideally initiates a process of self-exploration. 'How do I see women?' 'If I didn't violate her, could I have?' 'Do I have the potential to do to her what they say I did?' Those are good questions."

30   Taken to extremes, there is an ugly element of vengeance at work here. Rape is an abuse of power. But so are false accusations of rape, and to suggest that men whose reputations are destroyed might benefit because it will make them more sensitive is an attitude that is sure to backfire on women who are seeking justice for all victims. On campuses where the issue is most inflamed, male students are outraged that their names can be scrawled on a bathroom-wall list of rapists and they have no chance to tell their side of the story.

31   "Rape is what you read about in the *New York Post* about 17 little boys raping a jogger in Central Park," says a male freshman at a liberal-arts college, who learned that he had been branded a rapist after a one-night stand with a friend. He acknowledges that they were both very drunk when she started kissing him at a party and ended up back in his room. Even through his haze, he had some qualms about sleeping with her: "I'm fighting against my hormonal instincts, and my moral instincts are saying, 'This is my friend and if I were sober, I wouldn't be doing this,'" but he went ahead anyway. "When you're drunk, and there are all sorts of ambiguity, and the woman says 'Please, please' and then she says no some-time later, even in the middle of the act, there still may very well be some kind of violation, but it's not the same thing. It's not rape. If you don't hear her say no, if she doesn't say it, if she's playing around with you—oh, I could get squashed for saying it—there is an element of say no, mean yes."

32   The morning after their encounter, he recalls, both students woke up hung over and eager to put the memory behind them. Only months later did he learn that she had told a friend that he had torn her clothing and raped her. At this point in the story, the accused man starts using the language of rape. "I felt violated," he says. "I felt like she was taking advantage of me when she was very drunk. I never heard her say 'No!,' 'Stop!,' anything." He is angry and hurt at the charges, worried that they will get around, shatter his reputation and force him to leave the small campus.

33   So here, of course, is the heart of the debate. If rape is sex without consent, how exactly should consent be defined and communicated, when and by whom? Those who view rape through a political lens tend to place all responsibility on men to make sure that their partners are consenting at every point of a sexual encounter. At the extreme, sexual relations come to resemble major surgery, requiring a signed consent form. Clinical psychologist Mary P. Koss of the University of Arizona in Tucson, who is a leading scholar on the issue, puts it rather bluntly: "It's the man's penis that is doing the raping, and ultimately he's responsible for where he puts it."

34   Historically, of course, this has never been the case, and there are some who argue that it shouldn't be—that women too must take responsibility for their be-havior, and that the whole realm of intimate encounters defies regulation from on high. Anthropologist Lionel Tiger has little patience for trendy sexual politics that make no reference to biology. Since the dawn of time, he argues, men and women have always gone to bed with different goals. In the effort to keep one's genes in the gene pool, "it is to the male advantage to fertilize as many females as possible, as quickly as possible and as efficiently as possible." For the female,

however, who looks at the large investment she will have to make in the offspring, the opposite is true. Her concern is to "select" who "will provide the best
setup for their offspring." So, in general, "the pressure is on the male to be aggressive and on the female to be coy."

35   No one defends the use of physical force, but when the coercion involved
is purely psychological, it becomes hard to assign blame after the fact. Journalist Stephanie Gutmann is an ardent foe of what she calls the date-rape dog-
matists. "How can you make sex completely politically correct and completely
safe?" she asks. "What a horribly bland, unerotic thing that would be! Sex is,
by nature, a risky endeavor, emotionally. And desire is a violent emotion.
These people in the date-rape movement have erected so many rules and regulations that I don't know how people can have erotic or desire-driven sex."

36   Nonsense, retorts Cornell professor Andrea Parrot, co-author of
Acquaintance Rape: The Hidden Crime. Seduction should not be about lies, manipulation, game playing or coercion of any kind, she says. "Too bad that people think that the only way you can have passion and excitement and sex is if
there are miscommunications, and one person is forced to do something he or
she doesn't want to do." The very pleasures of sexual encounters should lie in
the fact of mutual comfort and consent: "You can hang from the ceiling, you
can use fruit, you can go crazy and have really wonderful sensual erotic sex, if
both parties are consenting."

37   It would be easy to accuse feminists of being too quick to classify sex as
rape, but feminists are to be found on all sides of the debate, and many protest
the idea that all the onus is on the man. It demeans women to suggest that they
are so vulnerable to coercion or emotional manipulation that they must always
be escorted by the strong arm of the law. "You can't solve society's ills by making everything a crime," says Albuquerque attorney Nancy Hollander. "That
comes out of the sense of overprotection of women, and in the long run that is
going to be harmful to us."

38   What is lost in the ideological debate over date rape is the fact that men
and women, especially when they are young, and drunk, and aroused, are not
very good at communicating. "In many cases," says Estrich, "the man thought it
was sex, and the woman thought it was rape, and they are both telling the
truth." The man may envision a celluloid seduction, in which he is being commanding, she is being coy. A woman may experience the same event as a de-
grading violation of her will. That some men do not believe a woman's protests
is scarcely surprising in a society so drenched with messages that women have
rape fantasies and a desire to be overpowered.

39   By the time they reach college, men and women are loaded with cultural
baggage, drawn from movies, television, music videos and "bodice ripper" romance novels. Over the years they have watched Rhett sweep Scarlett up the
stairs in *Gone With the Wind;* or Errol Flynn, who was charged twice with statutory
rape, overpower a protesting heroine who then melts in his arms; or Stanley rape
his sister-in-law Blanche du Bois while his wife is in the hospital giving birth to a
child in *A Streetcar Named Desire.* Higher up the cultural food chain, young people can read of date rape in Homer or Jane Austen, watch it in *Don Giovanni* or
Rigoletto.

40   The messages come early and often, and nothing in the feminist revolution
has been able to counter them. A recent survey of sixth- to ninth-graders in
Rhode Island found that a fourth of the boys and a sixth of the girls said it was
acceptable for a man to force a woman to kiss him or have sex if he has spent

money on her. A third of the children said it would not be wrong for a man to rape a woman who had had previous sexual experiences.

41   Certainly cases like Palm Beach, movies like *The Accused* and novels like Avery Corman's *Prized Possessions* may force young people to re-examine assumptions they have inherited. The use of new terms, like *acquaintance rape* and *date rape,* while controversial, has given men and women the vocabulary they need to express their experiences with both force and precision. This dialogue would be useful if it helps strip away some of the dogmas, old and new, surrounding the issue. Those who hope to raise society's sensitivity to the problem of date rape would do well to concede that it is not precisely the same sort of crime as street rape, that there may be very murky issues of intent and degree involved.

42   On the other hand, those who downplay the problem should come to realize that date rape is a crime of uniquely intimate cruelty. While the body is violated, the spirit is maimed. How long will it take, once the wounds have healed, before it is possible to share a walk on a beach, a drive home from work, or an evening's conversation without always listening for a quiet alarm to start ringing deep in the back of the memory of a terrible crime?

DISCUSSION QUESTIONS

1. What answer, if any, does Gibbs provide to the question posed in her title? Refer to specific parts of the essay when answering.
2. Identify the three brief definitions that Gibbs uses in the first three paragraphs. Consider the essay as a whole and then suggest why she uses them at the beginning of the essay.
3. What writing strategies does Gibbs use to develop the essay? Where does she use them?
4. Where does Gibbs define by negation?
5. What function does paragraph 13 serve in the essay?
6. Why do you think Gibbs uses direct quotations at so many places in the essay?

TOWARD KEY INSIGHTS

Reflect on the case of the male freshman discussed in paragraphs 31–32. Do you think that he was guilty of rape? Why or why not?

Do you agree with the idea of placing "all responsibility on men to make sure that their partners are consenting at every point of a sexual encounter" (paragraph 33)?

Should date rape be considered the same kind of crime as rape by a stranger, or should it be considered a lesser offense? Explain your answer.

Do you agree with the notion that rape is a means by which all men keep all women in a state of fear? Defend your answer.

SUGGESTION FOR WRITING

Write an essay that defines the many dimensions of sexism or racism. Use whatever strategies are appropriate for your purpose.

ARGUMENT

Reading Strategies

1. Identify the background of the author if possible. Does the author bring any expertise or experience that helps make the argument more credible?
2. Read the introduction and conclusion to gain a sense of the thesis and main points of the argument.
3. Read the argument quickly to gain an overall sense of the major points of the essay and an understanding of the organizational pattern.
4. Look for the organizational pattern of the essay and keep an eye out for transition sentences. Often an author argues by first presenting the viewpoint of several other authors, then pointing out limitations of those views, then presenting his or her own position and offering support, and finally admitting possible limitations and problems with the author's position (possibly answering these objections). This pattern often confuses readers.
5. Read carefully to identify the major claims of the argument, the reasons for the author's position, and any evidence presented for any of the claims. It can be very helpful to outline an argument, making a special note of the major reasons and evidence for the claim. Note the author's approach. Is the argument mostly deductive or inductive? Does the author try to show the negative consequences of opposing views? Does the author base the argument on authority?

Reading Critically

1. Check to see if the author demonstrates any overt bias.
2. Test to determine if the reasons given really support the author's thesis.
3. Test to see if the evidence is adequate. Does the evidence support the claims? Is the source of the evidence trustworthy and unbiased? Is the evidence extensive or scanty? Could contrary evidence be offered?
4. Check the essay for informal fallacies.
5. Try to offer objections to the author's claims. Write objections in the margins or on a separate piece of paper.
6. See if you can formulate alternative conclusions to those proposed by the author.
7. Try to formulate reasons and concerns that the author may have neglected.
8. Read essays that present other viewpoints and compare.

Reading As a Writer

1. Note the organizational pattern of the argument. Identify how you might use the pattern in your arguments.
2. Examine how the writer connects the reasons with the major thesis.
3. Identify how the evidence is presented and connected as support.
4. Notice any effective word choice that helps cement the emotional argument.
5. Evaluate how the author establishes tone and ethos.
6. Examine how the author answers possible objections.

VIRGINIA POSTREL

Yes, Don't Impede Medical Progress

Virginia Postrel graduated with a degree in English from Princeton University. She was the editor of Reason Magazine *from 1988 to 2000 and received the Free Press Association's Mencken Award for Commentary based on her editorials. More recently she has been writing the economic scene column for the* New York Times *business section. In this selection, she argues that we should not get in the way of scientific progress.*

1   To many biologists, the recently announced creation of a cloned human embryo was no big deal. True, researchers at Advanced Cell Technology (ACT) replaced the nucleus of a human egg with the genetic material of another person. And they got that cloned cell to start replicating. But their results were modest. It took seventy-one eggs to produce a single success, and in the best case, the embryo grew to only six cells before dying. That's not a revolution. It's an incremental step in understanding how early-stage cells develop.

2   And it's far from the one hundred or so cells in a blastocyst, the hollow ball from which stem cells can be isolated. Scientists hope to coax embryonic stem cells into becoming specialized tissues such as nerve, muscle, or pancreatic islet cells. Therapeutic cloning, or nucleus transplantation, could make such treatments more effective.

3   In theory, it would work like this: Suppose I need new heart tissue or some insulin-secreting islet cells to counteract diabetes. You could take the nucleus from one of my cells, stick it in an egg cell from which the nucleus had been removed, let that develop into stem cells, and then trigger the stem cells to form the specific tissue needed. The new "cloned" tissue would be genetically mine and would not face rejection problems. It would function in my body as if it had grown there naturally, so I wouldn't face a lifetime of immunosuppressant drugs.

4   But all of that is a long way off. ACT and others in the field are still doing very basic research, not developing clinical therapies. Indeed, because of the difficulty of obtaining eggs, therapeutic cloning may ultimately prove impractical for clinical treatments. It could be more important as a technique for understanding cell development or studying the mutations that lead to cancer. We simply don't know right now. Science is about exploring the unknown and cannot offer guarantees.

5   Politics, however, feeds on fear, uncertainty, and doubt, and the word "cloning" arouses those emotions. While its scientific importance remains to be seen, ACT's announcement has rekindled the campaign to criminalize nucleus transplantation and any therapies derived from that process. Under a bill passed by the House and endorsed by the president, scientists who transfer a human nucleus into an egg cell would be subject to ten-year federal prison sentences and $1 million fines. So would anyone who imports therapies developed through such research in countries where it is legal, such as Britain. The bill represents an unprecedented attempt to criminalize basic biomedical research.

6   The legislation's backers consider the fear of cloning their best hope for stopping medical research that might lead to gene-level therapies. Opponents make three basic arguments for banning therapeutic cloning.

Explains first opposing argument paragraphs 6–8

7   The first is that a fertilized egg is a person, entitled to full human rights. Taking stem cells out of a blastocyst is, in this view, no different from cutting the heart out of a baby. Hence, we hear fears of "embryo farming" for "spare parts."

8   This view treats microscopic cells with no past or present consciousness, no organs or tissues, as people. A vocal minority of Americans, of course, do find compelling the argument that a fertilized egg is someone who deserves protection from harm. That view animates the anti-abortion movement and exercises considerable influence in Republican politics.

9   But most Americans don't believe we should sacrifice the lives and well-being of actual people to save cells. Human identity must rest on something more compelling than the right string of proteins in a petri dish, detectable only with high-tech equipment. We will never get a moral consensus that a single cell, or a clump of one hundred cells, is a human being. That definition defies moral sense, rational argument, and several major religious traditions.

Refutes first opposition by value

10   So cloning opponents add a second argument. If we allow therapeutic cloning, they say, some unscrupulous person will pretend to be doing cellular research but instead implant a cloned embryo in a woman's womb and produce a baby. At the current stage of knowledge, using cloning to conceive a child would indeed be dangerous and unethical, with a high risk of serious birth defects. Anyone who cloned a baby today would rightly face, at the very least, the potential of an enormous malpractice judgment. There are good arguments for establishing a temporary moratorium on reproductive cloning.

Explains second opposition

11   But the small possibility of reproductive cloning does not justify making nucleus transfer a crime. Almost any science might conceivably be turned to evil purposes. This particular misuse is neither especially likely—cell biology labs are not set up to deliver fertility treatments—nor, in the long run, especially threatening.

Refutes second opposition by fact, paragraphs 11–13

12   Contrary to a lot of scary rhetoric, a healthy cloned infant would not be a moral nightmare, merely the not-quite-identical twin of an older person. (The fetal environment and egg cytoplasm create some genetic variations.) Certainly, some parents might have such a baby for bad reasons, to gratify their egos or to "replace" a child who died. But parents have been having children for bad reasons since time immemorial.

13   Just as likely, cloned babies would be the cherished children of couples who could not have biological offspring any other way. These children might bear an uncanny resemblance to their biological parents, but that, too, is not unprecedented. Like the "test tube babies" born of in vitro fertilization, cloned children need not be identifiable, much less freaks or outcasts.

14   Why worry so much about a few babies? Because, say opponents, even a single cloned infant puts us on the road to genetic dystopia, a combination of Brave New World and Nazi Germany. A cloned child's genetic makeup is too well known, goes the argument, and therefore transforms random reproduction into "manufacturing" that robs the child of his autonomy. This is where the attack broadens from nucleus transfer to human genetic engineering more generally. An anti-therapeutic cloning petition, circulated by the unlikely duo of conservative publisher William Kristol and archtechnophobe Jeremy Rifkin, concludes, "We are mindful of the tragic history of social eugenics movements in the first half of the twentieth century, and are united in our opposition to any use of biotechnology for a commercial eugenics movement in the twenty-first century."

Explains third opposition

<table>
<tr><td>Refutes third opposition by values</td><td>15</td><td>But the "eugenics" they attack has nothing to do with state-sponsored mass murder or forced sterilization. To the contrary, they are the ones who want the state to dictate the most private aspects of family life. They are the ones who want central authorities, rather than the choices of families and individuals, to determine our genetic future. They are the ones who demand that the government control the means of reproduction. They are the ones who measure the worth of human beings by the circumstances of their conception and the purity of their genetic makeup. They are the ones who say "natural" genes are the mark of true humanity.</td></tr>
</table>

16   Winners in the genetic lottery themselves, blessed with good health and unusual intelligence, they seek to deny future parents the chance to give their children an equally promising genetic start. In a despicable moral equivalency, they equate loving parents with Nazis.

Ethical argument   17   Biomedicine does have the potential to alter the human experience. Indeed, it already has. Life expectancy has doubled worldwide in the past century. Childbirth is no longer a peril to mother and infant. Childhood is no longer a time for early death. The pervasive sense of mortality that down through the ages shaped art, religion, and culture has waned.

Conclusion   18   Our lives are different from our ancestors' in fundamental ways. We rarely remark on the change, however, because it occurred incrementally. That's how culture evolves and how science works. We should let the process continue.

DISCUSSION QUESTIONS

1. What is the thesis statement that the author is trying to support? Why does she place it where she does?
2. How does the author connect her argument to the broader issues of scientific progress? What is her implicit argument? How effective is this argument?
3. The author dedicates a significant amount of the article to answering the objections of critics. Why is this strategy important? What are the main arguments she answers? What argumentative strategies does she employ to answer those critics?
4. The author uses the word fear through out the essay. How does she use this word and what place does it have in her overall argument?
5. In her conclusion, Postrel does not address her main topic of cloning at all. What might be the reason for this strategy? What effect does this have? Is this argument tactic legitimate?

TOWARD KEY INSIGHTS

Often scientific progress is met with fear. Should scientific progress be unregulated or should society create legal and moral limits on scientific studies? What should be the basis of such limits?

If therapeutic cloning could save large numbers of lives, would it be worth the risks?

SUGGESTION FOR WRITING

Write a paper responding in more depth to one of the arguments Postrel answers.

CHARLES KRAUTHAMMER

Crossing Lines

Dr. Charles Krauthammer majored in political science and economics at McGill University, studied at Oxford University, and received his medical degree from Harvard. He practiced medicine and became chief resident in psychiatry at Massachussetts General Hospital. In 1978 he served as the director of psychiatric research for the Carter Administration. Since then he has written articles and commentary for The New Republic *and* The Washington Post, *with his syndicated columns appearing in more than 100 newspapers. He won the 1987 Pulitzer Prize for distinguished commentary. In this essay he argues against cloning research.*

Problem

1   You were once a single cell. Every one of the 100 trillion cells in your body today is a direct descendent of that zygote, the primordial cell formed by the union of mother's egg and father's sperm. Each one is genetically identical (allowing for copying errors and environmental damage along the way) to that cell. Therefore, if we scraped a cell from, say, the inner lining of your cheek, its DNA would be the same DNA that, years ago in the original zygote, contained the entire plan for creating you and every part of you.

2   Here is the mystery: Why can the zygote, as it multiplies, produce every different kind of cell in the body—kidney, liver, brain, skin—while the skin cell is destined, however many times it multiplies, to remain skin forever? As the embryo matures, cells become specialized and lose their flexibility and plasticity. Once an adult cell has specialized—differentiated, in scientific lingo—it is stuck forever in that specialty. Skin is skin; kidney is kidney.

3   Understanding that mystery holds the keys to the kingdom. The Holy Grail of modern biology is regenerative medicine. If we can figure out how to make a specialized adult cell dedifferentiate—unspecialize, i.e., revert way back to the embryonic stage, perhaps even to the original zygotic stage—and then grow it like an embryo under controlled circumstances, we could reproduce for you every kind of tissue or organ you might need. We could create a storehouse of repair parts for your body. And, if we let that dedifferentiated cell develop completely in a woman's uterus, we will have created a copy of you, your clone.

4   That is the promise and the menace of cloning. It has already been done in sheep, mice, goats, pigs, cows, and now cats and rabbits (though cloning rabbits seems an exercise in biological redundancy). There is no reason in principle why it cannot be done in humans. The question is: Should it be done?

5   Notice that the cloning question is really two questions: (1) May we grow that dedifferentiated cell all the way into a cloned baby, a copy of you? That is called reproductive cloning. And (2) may we grow that dedifferentiated cell just into the embryonic stage and then mine it for parts, such as stem cells? That is called research cloning.

6   Reproductive cloning is universally abhorred. In July 2001 the House of Representatives, a fairly good representative of the American people, took up the issue and not a single member defended reproductive cloning. Research cloning, however, is the hard one. Some members were prepared to permit the cloning of the human embryo in order to study and use its component parts, with the proviso that the embryo be destroyed before it grows into a fetus or child. They were a minority, however. Their amendment banning baby-making but permitting research cloning was defeated by 76 votes. On July 31, 2001, a bill outlawing all cloning passed the House decisively.

7   Within weeks, perhaps days, the Senate will vote on essentially the same alternatives. On this vote will hinge the course of the genetic revolution at whose threshold we now stand.

The Promise

8   This is how research cloning works. You take a donor egg from a woman, remove its nucleus, and inject the nucleus of, say, a skin cell from another person. It has been shown in animals that by the right manipulation you can trick the egg and the injected nucleus into dedifferentiating—that means giving up all the specialization of the skin cell and returning to its original state as a primordial cell that could become anything in the body.

9   In other words, this cell becomes totipotent. It becomes the equivalent of the fertilized egg in normal procreation, except that instead of having chromosomes from two people, it has chromosomes from one. This cell then behaves precisely like an embryo. It divides. It develops. At four to seven days, it forms a "blastocyst" consisting of about 100 to 200 cells.

10   The main objective of cloning researchers would be to disassemble this blastocyst: pull the stem cells out, grow them in the laboratory, and then try to tease them into becoming specific kinds of cells, say, kidney or heart or brain and so on.

11   There would be two purposes for doing this: study or cure. You could take a cell from a person with a baffling disease, like Lou Gehrig's, clone it into a blastocyst, pull the stem cells out, and then study them in order to try to understand the biology of the illness. Or you could begin with a cell from a person with Parkinson's or a spinal cord injury, clone it, and tease out the stem cells to develop tissue that you would reinject into the original donor to, in theory, cure the Parkinson's or spinal cord injury. The advantage of using a cloned cell rather than an ordinary stem cell is that, presumably, there would be no tissue rejection. It's your own DNA. The body would recognize it. You'd have a perfect match.

12   The conquest of rejection is one of the principal rationales for research cloning. But there is reason to doubt this claim on scientific grounds. There is some empirical evidence in mice that cloned tissue may be rejected anyway (possibly because a clone contains a small amount of foreign—mitochondrial—DNA derived from the egg into which it was originally injected). Moreover, enormous advances are being made elsewhere in combating tissue rejection. The science of immune rejection is much more mature than the science of cloning. By the time we figure out how to do safe and reliable research cloning, the rejection problem may well be solved. And finally, there are less problematic alternatives—such as adult stem cells—that offer a promising alternative to cloning because they present no problem of tissue rejection and raise none of cloning's moral conundrums.

13   These scientific considerations raise serious questions about the efficacy of, and thus the need for, research cloning. But there is a stronger case to be made. Even if the scientific objections are swept aside, even if research cloning is as doable and promising as its advocates contend, there are other reasons to pause.

14   The most obvious is this: Research cloning is an open door to reproductive cloning. Banning the production of cloned babies while permitting the production of cloned embryos makes no sense. If you have factories all around the country producing embryos for research and commerce, it is inevitable that someone will implant one in a woman (or perhaps in some artificial medium in the farther future) and produce a human clone. What then? A law banning reproductive cloning but permitting research cloning would then make it a crime not to destroy that fetus—an obvious moral absurdity.

15   This is an irrefutable point and the reason that many in Congress will vote for the total ban on cloning. Philosophically, however, it is a showstopper. It lets us off too early and too easy. It keeps us from facing the deeper question: Is there anything about research cloning that in and of itself makes it morally problematic?

Objection I: Intrinsic Worth

16   For some people, life begins at conception. And not just life—if life is understood to mean a biologically functioning organism, even a single cell is obviously alive—but personhood. If the first zygotic cell is owed all the legal and moral respect due a person, then there is nothing to talk about. Ensoulment starts with Day One and Cell One, and the idea of taking that cell or its successor cells apart to serve someone else's needs is abhorrent.

17   This is an argument of great moral force but little intellectual interest. Not because it may not be right. But because it is unprovable. It rests on metaphysics. Either you believe it or you don't. The discussion ends there.

18   I happen not to share this view. I do not believe personhood begins at conception. I do not believe a single cell has the moral or legal standing of a child. This is not to say that I do not stand in awe of the developing embryo, a creation of majestic beauty and mystery. But I stand in equal awe of the Grand Canyon, the spider's web, and quantum mechanics. Awe commands wonder, humility, appreciation. It does not command inviolability. I am quite prepared to shatter an atom, take down a spider's web, or dam a canyon for electricity. (Though we'd have to be very short on electricity before I'd dam the Grand.)

19   I do not believe the embryo is entitled to inviolability. But is it entitled to nothing? There is a great distance between inviolability, on the one hand, and mere "thingness," on the other. Many advocates of research cloning see nothing but thingness. That view justifies the most ruthless exploitation of the embryo. That view is dangerous.

20   Why? Three possible reasons. First, the Brave New World Factor: Research cloning gives man too much power for evil. Second, the Slippery Slope: The habit of embryonic violation is in and of itself dangerous. Violate the blastocyst today and every day, and the practice will inure you to violating the fetus or even the infant tomorrow. Third, Manufacture: The very act of creating embryos for the sole purpose of exploiting and then destroying them will ultimately predispose us to a ruthless utilitarianism about human life itself.

Objection II: The Brave New World Factor

21   The physicists at Los Alamos did not hesitate to penetrate, manipulate, and split uranium atoms on the grounds that uranium atoms possess intrinsic worth that entitled them to inviolability. Yet after the war, many fought to curtail atomic power. They feared the consequences of delivering such unfathomable power—and potential evil—into the hands of fallible human beings. Analogously, one could believe that the cloned blastocyst has little more intrinsic worth than the uranium atom and still be deeply troubled by the manipulation of the blastocyst because of the fearsome power it confers upon humankind.

22   The issue is leverage. Our knowledge of how to manipulate human genetics (or atomic nuclei) is still primitive. We could never construct ex nihilo[1] a human embryo. It is an unfolding organism of unimaginable complexity that took nature three billion years to produce. It might take us less time to build it from scratch, but not much less. By that time, we as a species might have acquired enough wisdom to use it wisely. Instead, the human race in its infancy has stumbled upon a genie infinitely too complicated to create or even fully understand, but understandable enough to command and perhaps even control. And given our demonstrated unwisdom with our other great discovery—atomic power: As we speak, the very worst of humanity is on the threshold of acquiring the most powerful weapons in history—this is a fear and a consideration to be taken very seriously.

23   For example. Female human eggs seriously limit the mass production of cloned embryos. Extracting eggs from women is difficult, expensive, and potentially dangerous. The search is on, therefore, for a good alternative. Scientists have begun injecting human nuclei into the egg cells of animals. In 1996 Massachusetts scientists injected a human nucleus with a cow egg. Chinese scientists have fused a human fibroblast with a rabbit egg and have grown the resulting embryo to the blastocyst stage. We have no idea what grotesque results might come from such interspecies clonal experiments.

24   In October 2000 the first primate containing genes from another species was born (a monkey with a jellyfish gene). In 1995 researchers in Texas produced headless mice. In 1997 researchers in Britain produced headless tadpoles. In theory, headlessness might be useful for organ transplantation. One can envision, in a world in which embryos are routinely manufactured, the production of headless clones—subhuman creatures with usable human organs but no head, no brain, no consciousness to identify them with the human family.

25   The heart of the problem is this: Nature, through endless evolution, has produced cells with totipotent power. We are about to harness that power for crude human purposes. That should give us pause. Just around the corner lies the logical by-product of such power: human-animal hybrids, partly developed human bodies for use as parts, and other horrors imagined—Huxley's Deltas and Epsilons—and as yet unimagined. This is the Brave New World Factor. Its grounds for objecting to this research are not about the beginnings of life, but about the ends; not the origin of these cells, but their destiny, not where we took these magnificent cells from, but where they are taking us.

Objection III: The Slippery Slope

26   The other prudential argument is that once you start tearing apart blastocysts, you get used to tearing apart blastocysts. And whereas now you'd only be doing that at the seven-day stage, when most people would look at this tiny

[1]ex nihilo means "from nothing."—Editors

clump of cells on the head of a pin and say it is not inviolable, it is inevitable that some scientist will soon say: Give me just a few more weeks to work with it and I could do wonders.

27   That will require quite a technological leap because the blastocyst will not develop as a human organism unless implanted in the uterus. That means that to go beyond that seven-day stage you'd have to implant this human embryo either in an animal uterus or in some fully artificial womb.

28   Both possibilities may be remote, but they are real. And then we'll have a scientist saying: Give me just a few more months with this embryo, and I'll have actual kidney cells, brain cells, pancreatic cells that I can transplant back into the donor of the clone and cure him. Scientists at Advanced Cell Technology in Massachusetts have already gone past that stage in animals. They have taken cloned cow embryos past the blastocyst stage, taken tissue from the more developed cow fetus, and reimplanted it back into the donor animal.

29   The scientists' plea to do the same in humans will be hard to ignore. Why grow the clone just to the blastocyst stage, destroy it, pull out the inner cell mass, grow stem cells out of that, propagate them in the laboratory, and then try chemically or otherwise to tweak them into becoming kidney cells or brain cells or islet cells? This is Rube Goldberg. Why not just allow that beautiful embryonic machine, created by nature and far more sophisticated than our crude techniques, to develop unmolested? Why not let the blastocyst grow into a fetus that possesses the kinds of differentiated tissue that we could then use for curing the donor?

30   Scientifically, this would make sense. Morally, we will have crossed the line between tearing apart a mere clump of cells and tearing apart a recognizable human fetus. And at that point, it would be an even smaller step to begin carving up seven- and eight-month-old fetuses with more perfectly formed organs to alleviate even more pain and suffering among the living. We will, slowly and by increments, have gone from stem cells to embryo farms to factories with fetuses in various stages of development and humanness, hanging (metaphorically) on meat hooks waiting to be cut open to be used by the already born.

31   We would all be revolted if a living infant or developed fetus were carved up for parts. Should we build a fence around that possibility by prohibiting any research on even the very earliest embryonic clump of cells? Is the only way to avoid the slide never to mount the slippery slope at all? On this question, I am personally agnostic. If I were utterly convinced that we would never cross the seven-day line, then I would have no objection on these grounds to such research on the inner cell mass of a blastocyst. The question is: Can we be sure? This is not a question of principle; it is a question of prudence. It is almost a question of psychological probability. No one yet knows the answer.

Objection IV: Manufacture

32   Note that while, up to now, I have been considering arguments against research cloning, they are all equally applicable to embryonic research done on a normal—i.e., noncloned—embryo. If the question is tearing up the blastocyst, there is no intrinsic moral difference between a two-parented embryo derived from a sperm and an egg and a single-parented embryo derived from a cloned cell. Thus the various arguments against this research—the intrinsic worth of the embryo, the prudential consideration that we might create monsters, or the prudential consideration that we might become monsters in exploiting post-embryonic forms of human life (fetuses or even children)—are identical to the arguments for and against stem-cell research.

33   These arguments are serious—serious enough to banish the insouciance of the scientists who consider anyone questioning their work to be a Luddite—yet,

in my view, insufficient to justify a legal ban on stem-cell research (as with stem cells from discarded embryos in fertility clinics). I happen not to believe that either personhood or ensoulment occurs at conception. I think we need to be apprehensive about what evil might arise from the power of stem-cell research, but that apprehension alone, while justifying vigilance and regulation, does not justify a ban on the practice. And I believe that given the good that might flow from stem-cell research, we should first test the power of law and custom to enforce the seven-day blastocyst line for embryonic exploitation before assuming that such a line could never hold.

34   This is why I support stem-cell research (using leftover embryos from fertility clinics) and might support research cloning were it not for one other aspect that is unique to it. In research cloning, the embryo is created with the explicit intention of its eventual destruction. That is a given because not to destroy the embryo would be to produce a cloned child. If you are not permitted to grow the embryo into a child, you are obliged at some point to destroy it.

35   Deliberately creating embryos for eventual and certain destruction means the launching of an entire industry of embryo manufacture. It means the routinization, the commercialization, the commodification of the human embryo. The bill that would legalize research cloning essentially sanctions, licenses, and protects the establishment of a most ghoulish enterprise: the creation of nascent human life for the sole purpose of its exploitation and destruction.

36   How is this morally different from simply using discarded embryos from in vitro fertilization (IVF) clinics? Some have suggested that it is not, that to oppose research cloning is to oppose IVF and any stem-cell research that comes out of IVF. The claim is made that because in IVF there is a high probability of destruction of the embryo, it is morally equivalent to research cloning. But this is plainly not so. In research cloning there is not a high probability of destruction; there is 100 percent probability. Because every cloned embryo must be destroyed, it is nothing more than a means to someone else's end.

37   In IVF, the probability of destruction may be high, but it need not necessarily be. You could have a clinic that produces only a small number of embryos, and we know of many cases of multiple births resulting from multiple embryo implantation. In principle, one could have IVF using only a single embryo and thus involving no deliberate embryo destruction at all. In principle, that is impossible in research cloning.

38   Furthermore, a cloned embryo is created to be destroyed and used by others. An IVF embryo is created to develop into a child. One cannot disregard intent in determining morality. Embryos are created in IVF to serve reproduction. Embryos are created in research cloning to serve, well, research. If certain IVF embryos were designated as "helper embryos" that would simply aid an anointed embryo in turning into a child, then we would have an analogy to cloning. But, in fact, we don't know which embryo is anointed in IVF. They are all created to have a chance of survival. And they are all equally considered an end.

39   Critics counter that this ends-and-means argument is really obfuscation, that both procedures make an instrument of the embryo. In cloning, the creation and destruction of the embryo is a means to understanding or curing disease. In IVF, the creation of the embryo is a means of satisfying a couple's need for a child. They are both just means to ends.

40   But it makes no sense to call an embryo a means to the creation of a child. The creation of a child is the destiny of an embryo. To speak of an embryo as a

means to creating a child empties the word "means" of content. The embryo in IVF is a stage in the development of a child; it is no more a means than a teenager is a means to the adult he or she later becomes. In contrast, an embryo in research cloning is pure means. Laboratory pure.

41   And that is where we must draw the line. During the great debate on stem-cell research, a rather broad consensus was reached (among those not committed to "intrinsic worth" rendering all embryos inviolable) that stem-cell research could be morally justified because the embryos destroyed for their possibly curative stem cells were derived from fertility clinics and thus were going to be discarded anyway. It was understood that human embryos should not be created solely for the purpose of being dismembered and then destroyed for the benefit of others. Indeed, when Senator Bill Frist made his impassioned presentation on the floor of the Senate supporting stem-cell research, he included among his conditions a total ban on creating human embryos just to be stem-cell farms.

42   Where cloning for research takes us decisively beyond stem-cell research is in sanctioning the manufacture of the human embryo. You can try to regulate embryonic research to prohibit the creation of Brave New World monsters; you can build fences on the slippery slope, regulating how many days you may grow an embryo for research; but once you countenance the very creation of human embryos for no other purpose than for their parts, you have crossed a moral frontier.

43   Research cloning is the ultimate in conferring thingness upon the human embryo. It is the ultimate in desensitization. And as such, it threatens whatever other fences and safeguards we might erect around embryonic research. The problem, one could almost say, is not what cloning does to the embryo, but what it does to us. Except that, once cloning has changed us, it will inevitably enable further assaults on human dignity. Creating a human embryo just so it can be used and then destroyed undermines the very foundation of the moral prudence that informs the entire enterprise of genetic research: the idea that, while a human embryo may not be a person, it is not nothing. Because if it is nothing, then everything is permitted. And if everything is permitted, then there are no fences, no safeguards, no bottom.

DISCUSSION QUESTIONS

1. What are the main points of Krauthammer's argument against cloning research?
2. Krauthammer directly indicates the reasons why individuals might want cloning research. What is the effect of this discussion on Krauthammer's argument?
3. Krauthammer rejects the argument based on intrinsic worth. Why does he reject this argument? What effect does this have on his overall argument?
4. What is the overall tone of Krauthammer's argument? What impact does that have on the relative effectiveness of the essay?
5. Krauthammer raises a number of horrifying possibilities in his essay, including humans without heads, living infants being carved up into parts, and human genes being mixed with animal genes. Does such speculation help or hurt his arguments?
6. Krauthammer directly refers to "the slippery slope," something that you have learned is a logical fallacy. Are his slippery slope arguments legitimate? Do they help or hurt his overall argument?

TOWARD KEY INSIGHTS

Krauthammer directly indicates that humans lack the wisdom to handle the complex power of nature. Should scientific and technological development that holds powerful implications beyond our wisdom be restricted?

Based on both essays of human cloning, should research in cloning be allowed for therapeutic or reproductive purposes?

SUGGESTION FOR WRITING

Read both articles and write an essay to argue either for or against research into possible therapeutic cloning.

ALAN EHRENHALT

The Misguided Zeal of the Privacy Lobby

Alan Ehrenhalt was born in 1947 in Chicago. He received an A.B. from Brandeis University and an M.S. from Columbia University. He was a reporter for Congressional Quarterly *and serves as executive editor of* Governing *magazine. He has written numerous articles, editorials, and books including* The Lost City: Discovering the Forgotten Virtues of Community in the Chicago of the 1950's. *In this essay, he makes the provocative argument that there have been exaggerated and even harmful demands for privacy that overcome reasonable proposals such as the one for national identity cards.*

1   My Social Security number is 349-40-7931. I don't mind telling you that largely because I'm confident you have no interest in knowing it. You won't even write it down. Of course, you could be a secret enemy of mine, eager to use any available information to discredit me in some way. But I'm not too worried about that, either. I have my share of secrets, just like anybody else, but at the moment I can't think of a single one that's vulnerable to exposure simply upon presentation of an I.D. number.

2   But I will tell you one secret belief I have that I'm usually careful not to blurt out in polite company. It's this: I think privacy is the single most overrated issue in the entire lexicon of public policy—state, local, federal or anyplace else. Of all the dangers that this society faces as it starts the new millennium, one of the most remote is the risk that America will become an Orwellian police state, watching everything citizens do and taking down every word they say. And yet people all over the country lose a lot of sleep every night worrying about it.

3   I have great admiration for George Orwell, as a writer and thinker, and as a lifelong leftist who had the courage to expose communism for the hypocritical

sham it was. But in one important way, Orwell did posterity a disservice. He depicted the surveillance methods of totalitarian society so vividly and so convincingly that an entire generation of otherwise reasonable Americans has convinced itself that Big Brother is watching them even when the truth is that Big Brother has far more important ways to spend his time.

4   "They could plug in your wire whenever they wanted to," Orwell wrote a few pages into his novel, *1984*. "You had to live—did live, from habit that became instinct—in the assumption that every sound you made was overheard, and, except in darkness, every movement scrutinized."

5   I'm not a simpleton. I know there are governments in this century that have operated that way. The Stasi collected tons of data on the daily habits of ordinary East Germans and filed them away for later use. The KGB knew who the Soviet dissidents were almost from the moment they opened their mouths. I am also aware that even in a free society, horrible miscarriages of justice take place. Waco was indefensible. The police in a one-party dictatorship couldn't have acted any more irresponsibly.

6   But mature citizens in a civilized country are required to make distinctions between aberration and routine. Those of us who lay awake at night in America in 1999 worrying about the government's desire to snoop on them are mostly either (1) paranoid or (2) guilty of something. If there is a legitimate threat to our personal privacy these days, it comes from corporate capitalism, from the companies that make their living on the sale of information for commercial use. It doesn't come from the county commission, the legislature, or the U.S. Department of Health and Human Services.

7   But merely to say such a thing is to risk provoking shock and even ridicule among most members of the educated elite in this country. In the past generation, the idea that our precious privacy is under siege has transcended ideological differences, from the Cato institute on the right, which says "the history of government programs indicates privacy rights are violated routinely whenever expediency dictates," to Justice William O. Douglas on the left, who wrote near the end of his life that "we are rapidly entering the age of no privacy, where everyone is open to surveillance at all times, where there are no secrets from the government." Ask to see the evidence for these propositions, and you won't get much. But you will be branded as a naif, or a proto-Fascist, or both.

8   That is why I am so impressed with the courage of Amitai Etzioni, who dares to challenge the conventional wisdom in his new book, *The Limits of Privacy*. Etzioni is a reasonable man. He doesn't claim that our personal liberty is unimportant, or deny that the government possesses the technological capacity to invade it. He merely argues that we have gone overboard in our privacy obsession in recent years, and we need to tilt the balance back a few steps in the direction of common sense and provision for the common good.

9   And he offers convincing detail on why this is so. For reasons of privacy, for example, we fail to require HIV testing for mothers and infants, even though the information gained by such testing would save many of the infants' lives. We refuse to give law enforcement officials the tools to decipher encrypted computer messages, even though encryption makes systematic criminality easier to practice with each passing year. And on and on through a whole range of current public policy questions.

10   But of all the issues Etzioni takes up, none illustrates his point better than the controversy surrounding creation of a uniform identification process for American citizens.

11   The costs of not having such a system are hard to dispute. As Etzioni re-counts, there are more than 30,000 fugitives from the federal criminal justice system running free on false identification. Each year, several thousand convicted sex offenders seek work in the child-care business alone. The use of fake identities by crooked taxpayers costs honest ones an amount estimated to be as much as $5 billion a year. Another $5 billion is thought to be owed by deadbeat parents fleeing their child-support responsibilities. At the end of 1997, the Secret Service reported that it had arrested nearly 10,000 people during the year for various financial crimes involving false or stolen identities, and placed the cost of that fraud to banks and legitimate credit-holders at $745 million.

12   There's no way such figures can be exact. Quite likely some of them have been inflated a little bit in the process of reporting. But if they are even roughly accurate, they make it quite clear that identity crime is a genuine problem in this country.

13   And it's a problem that could be solved relatively easily, by creating a card or other universal identifier proving that the person in search of a job or transferring money is in fact who he or she claims to be. We already use Social Security cards and numbers as a de facto identifier for many public purposes. It's just that they're easy to cheat on. How dangerous could it be to create a new version that liars would have to respect?

14   Not very dangerous at all, is the correct answer. But it's an answer that a privacy-obsessed American polity is stubbornly unwilling to consider. In 1993, when the Clinton administration included establishment of a medical "security card" as part of its national health care proposal, it soon discovered it had made a major tactical error. Anything that sounded remotely like a national I.D. card set the privacy lobby going full blast.

15   Of course, it doesn't take much to do that. Pick up any ordinary newspaper these days, and there's a good chance that somewhere within its pages you will find a warning that an identification system is merely the opening move in Big Brother's bid for absolute power. "Don't we remember the Nazi experience in Europe?" the editor of *Privacy Journal* asked in the *New York Times* a couple of years ago. "Don't we realize the dangers of allowing government to establish identity and legitimacy?"

16   Just last campaign season, a Nevada gubernatorial candidate offered up identity cards as a sign that America was "rushing headlong into becoming a socialist totalitarian society." Privacy zealots left and right are fond of repeating the warning of former California Senator Alan Cranston: ID cards are "a primary tool of totalitarian governments."

17   Well, yes, they are. So are whips, but they are not a cause of torture. So is tear gas. That doesn't make tear gas an emblem of totalitarianism. A little common sense would be useful here. If America starts to go down the road to Fascism, it won't be because people are carrying identification in their wallet. As Etzioni says, "Cards do not transform democratic societies into totalitarian ones."

18   In America in the 1990s, the obsession with privacy is more than just a simple overreaction to George Orwell or to horror stories about something that happened in Moscow or Beijing. It is a reflection of the hyperindividualism to which the political system has succumbed in the past generation or so, and the ways that prevents us from becoming civic grown-ups in a democratic society.

19   One trait that marks just about all of us during childhood and adolescence is an unremitting anxiety about what other people think of us. When we get older, if we are lucky, we begin to realize that, in fact, other people aren't thinking about us at all most of the time. Other people are worried about themselves.

The rest of the world isn't watching us with a pair of binoculars. The sensible thing to do is figure out what we want to do and then go on and do it.

20   Of course, some people never figure this out, even in middle age. They go through life searching desperately for clues about the impressions they are creating—at home, at work, even among strangers on the street. They are convinced their friends and acquaintances are judging the most minute details of their lives, and making mental notes about their performance for use later.

21   It's not a very pleasant way to live, and it doesn't bear much resemblance to reality. As individuals, most of us manage to figure that out somewhere between adolescence and middle age. If we learned a similar lesson in our capacity as citizens, we would all be better off.

DISCUSSION QUESTIONS

1. What seems to be the purpose of Ehrenhalt's essay? Is it essential for him to make a very strong argument?
2. What are Ehrenhalt's major arguments in favor of national identity cards?
3. What purpose does it serve for Ehrenhalt to indicate his social security number at the beginning of the article and then later indicate that we do use social security cards and numbers as forms of public identification?
4. In response to the argument that ID cards are the tools of totalitarian governments, Ehrenhalt answers that whips and tear gas are also tools of such governments. What is the point of his response? Is it an appropriate argumentative strategy?
5. What point does the author make in the concluding three paragraphs? How effective is this conclusion?

TOWARD KEY INSIGHTS

Often we must make decisions weighing conflicting values. How important is privacy as a value compared to other values such as the protection of life and health?

Currently the government and companies have extensive amounts of information about us. There is also a scattered system of identification including driver's licenses and social security numbers. Would a national identification card actually decrease our liberty?

SUGGESTIONS FOR WRITING

Write a paper arguing whether we as Americans are excessively concerned about privacy.

Write a paper on whether or not we should require HIV testing for mothers and infants.

BARBARA DORITY

Halt and Show Your Papers!

Barbara Dority serves as the executive director of the Washington Coalition Against Censorship. She is the president of the Humanists of Washington and edits the Secular

Humanist Press. *Her columns on civil liberties appear regularly in* The Humanist Magazine. *In this selection, she argues against the use of national identity cards.*

1   The idea of a national identity (ID) card seems simple enough. Take the photographic and alphanumerical information on our birth certificates, Social Security cards, driver's licenses, and voter registration card; add a bar code, magnetic strip, fingerprint, microchip, or other biometric identifier; and display all that information (and more) on a neat plastic card no larger than a credit card. Our lives would be simplified. We'd always know for sure who we are and who everyone else really is.

2   But beneath this smooth surface lurks a complex terrain of issues and perhaps the greatest threat to personal freedom Americans have ever confronted.

3   The concept of a national ID card has been debated in the United States for over three decades. In the past, the opposition has been strong and bipartisan and has always prevailed. Extension of the Social Security number to the status of an ID card was rejected in 1971 by the Social Security Administration. In 1976, the Federal Advisory Committee on False Identification rejected the idea of a national identifier. The Carter and Reagan administrations both went on record as opposed to a national ID system.

4   In 1996, uniform national driver's license standards—which some considered tantamount to a national ID card—were enacted into law. However, their implementation was delayed, and a permanent repeal of the proposal was contained in the FY2000 Transportation Appropriations Act signed by President Clinton. In October 1999, House Majority Leader Dick Armey's website featured an article entitled "Good Riddance to the National ID Card." Armey's accompanying statement included these words:

5   This is a classic victory of freedom over "Big Brother." Because we acted quickly, no American will have to carry a National ID Card. A national driver's license with "biometric identifiers" or social security numbers is more suited to a police state than to a free country. It took three years of hard work, but we finally laid this disturbing idea to rest.

6   Not.

7   As a result of the September 11, 2001, terrorist attacks, the debate has been renewed and elevated to a higher and much more dangerous level. Just look at this sampling of headlines from recent newspaper articles around the country:

- "Support Grows for National ID Card Proposal" (*San José Mercury News,* October 16).
- "National ID Card System Failing to Attract Supporters" (*Los Angeles Times,* October 24).
- "U.S. Security Advisor: National ID Card Not Feasible" (*NewsFactor Network,* November 8).
- "National ID Card Gaining Support" (*Washington Post,* December 17).

8   Members of Congress, security experts, and high-tech executives have rushed to endorse the idea of some new form of identification system as a critical weapon in the "fight against terrorism." Unfortunately, little of this discussion has been open to the public (no surprise there), so it has been difficult to determine where the concept currently stands in the minds of the nation's decision makers.

9   George W. Bush, thankfully, has publicly stated his opposition, saying that national ID cards are unnecessary to improve security. Richard Clarke, Bush's chief of cyberspace security, agrees and does "not think it's a very smart idea." Fierce opposition comes from a wide range of privacy advocates, the American Civil Liberties Union, and even conservative organizations like the CATO Institute, Eagle Forum, and the John Birch Society.

10   And yet, as Roger Gay headlines his article in the November 29, 2001, conservative *Toogood Reports,* perhaps "It's Too Late to Stop a National I.D. Card." Marty Abrams, an information technology specialist at the law firm Hunton and Williams and a former senior credit bureau executive, summarizes the current state of the U.S. psyche well: "We're willing to accept this immense flow of data to law enforcement and their proxies to make sure we feel safe and secure. . . . The equilibrium point has shifted as a result of September 11."

11   Most disturbingly, recent Pew Research Center and Harris polls show strong support for a national ID card by those polled: 70 percent and 68 percent, respectively. This preference is undoubtedly hinged on the assumption that such a system would largely prevent terrorists and other "evil-doers" from entering the county—an assumption that is, at best, extremely dubious.

12   Other ID card supporters include the Department of Defense (which already has such a system in place), Oracle CEO Larry Ellison (who has offered to provide the ID software for free and would be glad to offer his company's services to maintain the system and its massive databases—for a fee, of course), the American Association of Motor Vehicle Administrators (which sees this as an opportunity for a national driver's license system), the Air Transportation Association, the Justice Department, lawmakers in U.S.–Mexico border states, and all those in charge of immigration committees in Congress. To my absolute horror, even Bill of Rights champion Alan Dershowitz has recently endorsed the concept, claiming it would reduce racial profiling!

13   The single best overview I've found of the basic questions about national ID cards and concepts involved in their debate is contained on the objective "Frequently Asked Questions" (FAQ) page of the Privacy International website at www.privacy.org/pi/activities/idcard/idcard_faq.html. Its points are summarized below.

14   1. Who uses ID cards now? About a hundred countries currently utilize official, compulsory, national IDs for various purposes. These include Belgium, France, Germany, Greece, and Spain. Among the developed countries that don't have such a card are Australia, Canada, Ireland, New Zealand, Sweden, and the United States. Most countries that don't have a national universal card do have a health or social security card or other documents of identity.

15   2. What are the primary purposes of ID cards? Race, politics, and religion are often at the heart of older ID systems. Card systems have been instituted to control the threat of insurgents or political extremists, to facilitate religious discrimination, to enforce quota systems, and to allow for social engineering. The FAQ notes: "At the heart of such plans is a parallel increase in police powers. Even in democratic nations, police retain the right to demand ID on pain of detention."

16   3. What is the cost of an ID card system? The expense of implementing such a system has been at the forefront of both political and public opposition in a number of countries, including Australia, the Philippines, and the United Kingdom. Cost estimates to create and issue national ID cards in the United States are around $3 billion.

17   4. Can ID cards assist law enforcement? The usefulness of ID cards to law enforcement has been marginal. Little evidence has been advanced to demonstrate that they would either reduce the incidence of crime or enhance the success of prosecution. Police authorities in the Netherlands and the United Kingdom have stated their reluctance to administer a compulsory card that might erode relations with the public. Furthermore, forgeries would be inevitable. Obviously, the more an ID card is used, the greater the value placed on it and, consequently, the higher its value to criminal elements.

18   5. Can ID cards help to control illegal immigration? The impact of such cards on controlling illegal immigration has been patchy. The use of a card for purposes of checking resident status depends on the police and other officials being given very broad powers to check identity—either a vastly increased level of constant checking of the entire population or a discriminatory checking procedure that would undoubtedly target minorities (numerous examples are included in the FAQ).

19   6. Which countries have rejected proposals for ID cards? The most celebrated campaign against a national ID card occurred just over a decade ago in Australia. In response to proposed legislation, tens of thousands of people took to the streets in opposition, and the government became dangerously split over the issue. The proposal caused such hostility that it was withdrawn in 1987. A similar proposal was presented in New Zealand a few years later and, under the leadership of the Auckland Council for Civil Liberties, an opposition campaign was formed and the proposal was abandoned.

20   In summary, the benefits of a national ID card are highly questionable, while the risks threaten the very heart of a free, democratic society. The national ACLU provides one of the most succinct summaries of the rights issues by boiling down the debate to five major reasons why a national ID card will keep us neither safe nor free:

21   Reason 1: A national ID card system won't solve the problem: it won't prevent terrorism. It wouldn't have thwarted any of the September 11 hijackers, for example, many of whom reportedly had identification documents on them and were in the country legally. Terrorists and criminals will continue to be able to obtain—by legal and illegal means—the documents needed to get a government ID, such as a birth certificate.

22   Reason 2: An ID card system will lead to a slippery slope of surveillance and monitoring of citizens. While such a system cannot protect us from terrorism it would create a system of internal passports that would significantly diminish the freedom and privacy of law-abiding citizens. Once put in place, it is exceedingly unlikely that such a system would be restricted to its original purpose. For example, the original Social Security Act contained strict prohibitions against using Social Security cards for unrelated purposes, but those strictures have been routinely ignored and steadily abandoned over the past fifty years. A national ID system would threaten the privacy that Americans have always enjoyed and gradually increase the control that government and business wields over everyday citizens.

23   Reason 3: A national ID card system would require the establishment of a database of all people in the United States. What happens then when an ID card is stolen? What proof may be used to decide who gets a card? The records of every individual would require continuous updating; would likely contain many errors,

any one of which could render someone unemployable and possibly much worse until they get their "file" straightened out. And once created, the use of such a database would almost certainly expand. Law enforcement and other government agencies would soon ask to link into it, while employers, landlords, credit agencies, mortgage brokers, telemarketers, private investigators, civil litigants, and a long list of other parties would begin seeking access, further eroding the privacy that people have always expected in their personal lives. We already see this happening with a proposed airline security database of passenger profiles that would be designed to rate the security risk posed by each passenger.

24   Reason 4: ID cards would function as "internal passports" that monitor citizens' movements. Americans have long had a visceral aversion to building a society in which the authorities could act like totalitarian sentries and demand "your papers please!" That everyday intrusiveness would be conjoined with the full power of modern computer and database technology. For example, if a police officer or security guard scans your ID card with a pocket barcode reader, would a permanent record be created of that check, including the time and your location? The end result could be a nation where citizens' movements inside their own country are monitored and recorded.

25   Reason 5: ID cards would foster new forms of discrimination and harassment. Rather than eliminating discrimination, as some have claimed, a national identity card would foster new forms of discrimination and harassment of anyone perceived as looking or sounding "foreign." That is exactly what happened after Congress passed the Employer Sanctions provision of the Immigration Reform and Control Act of 1985; it resulted in widespread discrimination against foreign-looking U.S. workers, especially Asians and Hispanics. A 1990 General Accounting Office study found almost 20 percent of employers engaged in such discriminatory practices. A national ID card would have the same effect on a massive scale, with Latinos, Asians, Arabs, and other minorities becoming subject to ceaseless status and identity checks from police, banks, merchants, and others. Failure to carry a national ID card would likely come to be viewed as a reason for search, detention, or arrest of minorities. The stigma and humiliation of constantly having to prove that they are U.S. citizens or legal immigrants would weigh heavily on such groups.

26   New York attorney Duncan Frissell writes in the *Sierra Times:* Most critics of a national ID card mention Hitler, police stops, and personal privacy to argue against the proposal. Those are certainly good reasons to oppose a national ID card, but they miss the idea's worst features. A national ID card is not really about identity. It is about authorization. A modern national ID system will:

27   ■ Require Americans to obtain federal government authorization to travel, work, rent or buy housing, obtain medical care, use financial services, and make many purchases.

28   ■ This federal authorization could be denied for many reasons, including database errors, a suspicious transaction profile, being a deadbeat parent, failure to pay taxes or fines, and any other social control measures Congress wishes to hang on the system.

29   ■ The system will almost certainly create an outlaw class—as large as 10 to 20% of the population—cut off from "normal" life in America. This class will include political refuseniks, as well as those whose behavior has caused the system's software to deny their transactions. This outlaw class will sustain the underground economy for the use of future terrorists (and ordinary criminals).

30   These effects are easy to predict because they've already happened on a smaller scale.

31   Robert Ellis Smith, a lawyer and privacy specialist, says the push for a national ID card is based on the false belief that there can be a simple, high-tech solution to an immensely complex problem. "One way to predict the effectiveness of a national ID number or document is to look at environments where the true identity of all residents is known: prisons, the military, many workplaces, many college campuses," he writes in a new paper about national ID cards. "And yet these places are far from crime free."

32   Ari Schwartz, a policy analyst for the Center for Democracy and Technology, supports a national ID program that is done in a way to allow individuals to control the information held about them. But he is still concerned about the unintended consequences of a central database. "There are some measures that we should definitely be moving forward on today, and then there are some other ideas that we need to have a longer-term discussion about," he said. "This is definitely one of those longer-term ideas."

33   A similar message is offered by Peter Neumann and Lauren Weinstein, moderaters[*sic*] of the RISKS Forum (www.risks.org) and the PRIVACY Forum (www.privacyforum.org), respectively, and co-founders of People For Internet Responsibility:

34   We have noted here before that technological solutions entail risks that should be identified and understood in advance of deployment to the greatest extent possible, regardless of any panic of the moment. The purported (yet unproven) benefits of a national ID card system notwithstanding, these risks deserve to be discussed and understood in detail before any decisions regarding its adoption in any form should be made.

35   The specter of a national ID card has been cropping up in my nightmares for years. On top of the current horrifying attack on the Bill of Rights under the guise of "fighting terrorism," the potential imposition of this ultimate "Big Brother" tactic in my America leaves me in virtual despair.

36   But according to the Attorney General of the United States John Ashcroft, by writing such articles as "Invading the Bill of Rights" (*The Humanist,* November/December 2001) and this one, I'm "scaring peace-loving people with phantoms of lost liberty" and "aiding the terrorists." When I first heard this accusation, I was outraged. Upon reflection, however, I've decided I don't mind. In John Ashcroft's America, where everything is literally turned on its head, being called un-American has become the mark of a citizen who truly loves and defends the principles of the United States. (Not to mention that the company is most gratifying.)

DISCUSSION QUESTIONS

1. What is the overall structure of the argument?
2. What are Dority's major objections to identity cards?
3. What does Dority do to demonstrate that national identity cards is a real issue? Why is this an important step in her argument?
4. Like many writers, Dority does not generate all her reasons herself but rather brings in ideas from other sources. Does the inclusion of material from the Web and ACLU weaken or strengthen the argument? How might it have been more effectively handled?
5. In paragraphs 31, 32, and 33 what is Dority's argumentative strategy? Is it effective?
6. What is the possible purpose for the conclusion? Is it effective?

TOWARDS KEY INSIGHTS

In our computerized age, the government and businesses have access to extensive
   amounts of information about citizens. To what extent does a national identity
   card pose a threat to civil liberties?
How much liberty is worth surrendering for greater security?

SUGGESTIONS FOR WRITING

Take a stance and write an essay in support of or opposed to national identity cards.
Colleges often use identification numbers and identification cards to keep track of students.
   Write an essay about whether such a system infringes on students.

MARTIN LUTHER KING, JR.

I Have a Dream

*Martin Luther King, Jr. (1929–1968) has earned lasting
fame for his part in the civil rights struggles of the 1950s
and 1960s. Born in Atlanta, Georgia, he was ordained a
Baptist minister in his father's church in 1947. A year
later, he graduated from Morehouse College, then went on
to take a Bachelor of Divinity degree at Crozier Theological Seminary (1951) and a
Ph.D. in philosophy at Boston University (1954), after which he accepted a pastorate in
Montgomery, Alabama. King's involvement with civil rights grew when he organized
and led a boycott that succeeded in desegregating Montgomery's bus system. In 1957, he
founded and became the first president of the Southern Christian Leadership Conference
and assumed a leading role in the civil rights movement. King advocated a policy of
nonviolent protest based on the beliefs of Thoreau and Gandhi and never veered from it
despite many acts of violence directed at him. The success of King's crusade helped bring
about the passage of the Civil Rights Act of 1964 and the Voting Rights Act of 1965
and won him the Nobel Peace Prize in 1964. King was assassinated on April 4, 1968,
in Memphis. Since then, his birthday, January 15, has been made a national holiday.
The speech "I Have a Dream" was delivered August 28, 1963, at the Lincoln Memor-
ial in Washington, D.C., before a crowd of 200,000 people who had gathered to com-
memorate the centennial of the Emancipation Proclamation and to demonstrate for
pending civil rights legislation. It stands as one of the most eloquent pleas ever made for
racial justice.*

1   I am happy to join with you today in what will go down in history as the
   greatest demonstration for freedom in the history of our nation.

2   Five score years ago, a great American, in whose symbolic shadow we stand
   today, signed the Emancipation Proclamation. This momentous decree came as
   a great beacon light of hope to millions of Negro slaves who had been seared

in the flames of withering injustice. It came as a joyous daybreak to end the long night of their captivity.

3   But one hundred years later, the Negro still is not free; one hundred years later, the life of the Negro is still sadly crippled by the manacles of segregation and the chains of discrimination; one hundred years later, the Negro lives on a lonely island of poverty in the midst of a vast ocean of material prosperity; one hundred years later, the Negro is still languishing in the corners of American society and finds himself in exile in his own land.

4   So we've come here today to dramatize a shameful condition. In a sense we've come to our nation's capital to cash a check. When the architects of our republic wrote the magnificent words of the Constitution and the Declaration of Independence, they were signing a promissory note to which every American was to fall heir. This note was the promise that all men, yes, black men as well as white men, would be guaranteed the unalienable rights of life, liberty, and the pursuit of happiness.

5   It is obvious today that America has defaulted on this promissory note in so far as her citizens of color are concerned. Instead of honoring this sacred obligation, America has given the Negro people a bad check; a check which has come back marked "insufficient funds." But we refuse to believe that the bank of justice is bankrupt. We refuse to believe that there are insufficient funds in the great vaults of opportunity of this nation. And so we've come to cash this check, a check that will give us upon demand the riches of freedom and the security of justice.

6   We have also come to this hallowed spot to remind America of the fierce urgency of now. This is no time to engage in the luxury of cooling off or to take the tranquilizing drug of gradualism. Now is the time to make real the promises of democracy; now is the time to rise from the dark and desolate valley of segregation to the sunlit path of racial justice; now is the time to lift our nation from the quicksands of racial injustice to the solid rock of brotherhood; now is the time to make justice a reality for all of God's children. It would be fatal for the nation to overlook the urgency of the moment. This sweltering summer of the Negro's legitimate discontent will not pass until there is an invigorating autumn of freedom and equality.

7   Nineteen sixty-three is not an end, but a beginning. And those who hope that the Negro needed to blow off steam and will now be content will have a rude awakening if the nation returns to business as usual. There will be neither rest nor tranquility in America until the Negro is granted his citizenship rights. The whirlwinds of revolt will continue to shake the foundations of our nation until the bright day of justice emerges.

8   But there is something that I must say to my people, who stand on the worn threshold which leads into the palace of justice. In the process of gaining our rightful place, we must not be guilty of wrongful deeds. Let us not seek to satisfy our thirst for freedom by drinking from the cup of bitterness and hatred. We must forever conduct our struggle on the high plain of dignity and discipline. We must not allow our creative protests to degenerate into physical violence. Again and again we must rise to the majestic heights of meeting physical force with soul force. The marvelous new militancy, which has engulfed the Negro community, must not lead us to a distrust of all white people. For many of our white brothers, as evidenced by their presence here today, have come to realize that their destiny is tied up with our destiny. And they have come to realize that their freedom is inextricably bound to our freedom. We cannot walk

alone. And as we walk, we must make the pledge that we shall always march ahead. We cannot turn back.

9   There are those who are asking the devotees of Civil Rights, "When will you be satisfied?" We can never be satisfied as long as the Negro is the victim of the unspeakable horrors of police brutality; we can never be satisfied as long as our bodies, heavy with the fatigue of travel, cannot gain lodging in the motels of the highways and the hotels of the cities; we cannot be satisfied as long as the Negro's basic mobility is from a smaller ghetto to a larger one; we can never be satisfied as long as our children are stripped of their selfhood and robbed of their dignity by signs stating "For White Only"; we cannot be satisfied as long as the Negro in Mississippi cannot vote and a Negro in New York believes he has nothing for which to vote. No! No, we are not satisfied, and we will not be satisfied until "justice rolls down like waters and righteousness like a mighty stream."

10   I am not unmindful that some of you have come here out of great trials and tribulations. Some of you have come fresh from narrow jail cells. Some of you have come from areas where your quest for freedom left you battered by the storms of persecution and staggered by the winds of police brutality. You have been the veterans of creative suffering. Continue to work with the faith that unearned suffering is redemptive. Go back to Mississippi. Go back to Alabama. Go back to South Carolina. Go back to Georgia. Go back to Louisiana. Go back to the slums and ghettos of our Northern cities, knowing that somehow this situation can and will be changed. Let us not wallow in the valley of despair.

11   I say to you today, my friends, that even though we face the difficulties of today and tomorrow, I still have a dream. It is a dream deeply rooted in the American dream. I have a dream that one day this nation will rise up and live out the true meaning of its creed, "We hold these truths to be self-evident, that all men are created equal." I have a dream that one day on the red hills of Georgia, sons of former slaves and the sons of former slave owners will be able to sit down together at the table of brotherhood. I have a dream that one day even the state of Mississippi, a state sweltering with the heat of injustice, sweltering with the heat of oppression, will be transformed into an oasis of freedom and justice. I have a dream that my four little children will one day live in a nation where they will not be judged by the color of their skin, but by the content of their character.

12   I HAVE A DREAM TODAY!

13   I have a dream that one day down in Alabama—with its vicious racists, with its Governor having his lips dripping with the words of interposition and nullification—one day right there in Alabama, little black boys and black girls will be able to join hands with little white boys and white girls as sisters and brothers.

14   I HAVE A DREAM TODAY!

15   I have a dream that one day every valley shall be exalted, every hill and mountain shall be made low. The rough places will be plain and the crooked places will be made straight, "and the glory of the Lord shall be revealed, and all flesh shall see it together."

16   This is our hope. This is the faith that I go back to the South with. With this faith we will be able to hew out of the mountain of despair, a stone of hope. With this faith we will be able to transform the jangling discords of our nation into a beautiful symphony of brotherhood. With this faith we will be able to work together, to pray together, to struggle together, to go to jail together, to

stand up for freedom together, knowing that we will be free one day. And this will be the day. This will be the day when all of God's children will be able to sing with new meaning, "My country 'tis of thee, sweet land of liberty, of thee I sing. Land where my fathers died, land of the pilgrim's pride, from every mountain side, let freedom ring." And if America is to be a great nation, this must become true.

17   So let freedom ring from the prodigious hilltops of New Hampshire; let freedom ring from the mighty mountains of New York; let freedom ring from the heightening Alleghenies of Pennsylvania; let freedom ring from the snow-capped Rockies of Colorado; let freedom ring from the curvaceous slopes of California. But not only that. Let freedom ring from Stone Mountain of Georgia; let freedom ring from Lookout Mountain of Tennessee; let freedom ring from every hill and mole hill of Mississippi. "From every mountainside, let freedom ring."

18   And when this happens, and when we allow freedom to ring, when we let it ring from every village and every hamlet, from every state and every city, we will be able to speed up that day when all of God's children, black men and white men, Jews and Gentiles, Protestants and Catholics, will be able to join hands and sing in the words of the old Negro spiritual: "Free at last. Free at last. Thank God Almighty, we are free at last."

DISCUSSION QUESTIONS

1. Why do you think King begins with a reference to Lincoln?
2. Does this speech have a stated or an implied proposition? What is the proposition?
3. What does King hope to accomplish by the speech? How does he go about achieving his aim(s)?
4. What is the audience for the speech?
5. How does King organize his speech? How does this organization advance his purpose?
6. Which type(s) of argumentative appeal does King use? Cite appropriate parts of the speech.
7. What kinds of stylistic devices does King use? Where do they occur? How do they increase the effectiveness of the speech?

TOWARD KEY INSIGHTS

To what extent do people of all races relate to King's message today? Explain your answer.

SUGGESTION FOR WRITING

Write an essay calling for some major social or political change. For example, you might recommend that the country enact national health insurance, institute a peacetime draft, ban smoking in all public places, amend the Constitution to ban or legalize abortions, establish federally funded day-care centers for working parents, or offer all workers a thirty-day leave of absence without pay.

WILLIAM RASPBERRY

A Journalist's View of Black Economics[1]

William Raspberry (born 1935) grew up in Okolona, Mississippi, and received his education at Indiana Central College, where he earned a Bachelor of Science degree in 1958. In college, he worked as a reporter for the Indianapolis Recorder *and following graduation continued with that publication until he entered the army. In 1962, after his military service, he began working for the* Washington Post, *an association that continues to the present. Raspberry now authors a nationally syndicated column dealing with current issues, such as criminal justice and minority concerns. In this selection Raspberry argues that black Americans should spend less time blaming their problems on racial injustice and more time creating businesses and programs to help solve these problems.*

1   I am intensely interested in the subject of the economics of black America. However, I am neither a businessman, an economist, nor a social scientist. I'm a "newspaper guy."

2   That's not an apology. I like being a newspaper guy, and I like to think I'm a pretty good one. I point it out simply to warn you up front that what you will hear from me is neither economic analysis nor nuts-and-bolt business proposals. I like to think about things in general and my proposal is that we ought to approach this subject in this fashion.

3   ***Myths About Race.*** One of the things I would like us to think about is a myth: a myth that has crippled black America, sent us off on unpromising directions, and left us ill-equipped to deal with either political or economic reality.

4   That myth is that race is of overriding importance, that it is a determinant not just of opportunity but also of potential, a reliable basis for explaining political and economic realities, a reasonable way of talking about geopolitics, and the overwhelming basis on which to deal with the relationships between us.

5   When I refer to race-based explanations of the plight of black America as myth, I do not mean to suggest that all such explanations are false. My reference is to the definition of myth as a "traditional account of unknown authorship, ostensibly with a historical basis, but serving usually to explain some observed phenomenon."

6   The historical basis of our preoccupation with race is easy enough to see. America did not invent slavery. Slavery as an institution predates the Bible. But American slavery was peculiarly race-based. Since slavery is the basis for the very presence of black people in America, small wonder that race has assumed such importance in our mythology.

[1]William Raspberry, "A Journalist's View of Black Economics," © 1990, Washington Post Writers Group. Reprinted with permission.

7   But slavery was more than just involuntary, unpaid servitude. Unlike other populations, to whom enslavement seemed a reasonable way of dealing with conquered enemies, America was never happy with the concept of one group of human beings holding another group of human beings in bondage. I suppose it was taken as a sin against God. But rather than forgo the economic benefits of slavery, American slaveholders resolved the dilemma by defining blacks not as fellow human beings but more like beasts of burden. There is nothing ungodly about a man requiring unremunerated work of an animal. Didn't God give man dominion over the animals?

8   Now it may have been that Africans were a special kind of animal: capable of thought, and human language, and even worship. But as long as whites could persuade themselves that blacks were not fully human, they could justify slavery.

9   Thus was born and reinforced the myth of inherent white superiority, which later became the basis for racial separation, for Jim Crow laws, for unequal opportunity and all sorts of evil. Nor is it just among whites that the myth survives. . . .

10   The myth that blacks cannot prevail in intellectual competition, that Chinese youngsters cannot play basketball, that Jews are specially vulnerable to guilt trips—these are negative myths whose acceptance has led to failure because they feed the assumption that failure is inevitable.

11   Objective reality is the arena in which we all must perform. But the success or failure of our performance is profoundly influenced by the attitudes—the myths—we bring to that reality.

12   Two things flow from the racism-is-all myth that we have used to account for our difficulties. The first is that it puts the solution to our difficulties outside our control. If our problems are caused by racism, and their solutions dependent on ending racism, our fate is in the hands of people who, by definition, don't love us.

13   *A Skewed Definition of Civil Rights.* The second outcome of the myth is our inclination to think of our problems in terms of a failure of racial justice. "Civil rights," which once referred to those things whose fair distribution was a governmental responsibility, now refers to any discrepancy. Income gaps, education gaps, test-score gaps, infant-mortality gaps, life-expectancy gaps, employment gaps, business-participation gaps—all now are talked about as "civil rights" issues.

14   The problems indicated by all these gaps are real. But describing them as "civil rights" problems steers us away from possible solutions. The civil rights designation evokes a sort of central justice bank, managed by the government, whose charge is to ladle out equal portions of everything to everybody. It prompts us to think about our problems in terms of inadequate or unfair distribution. It encourages the fallacy that to attack racism as the source of our problems is the same as attacking our problems. As a result, we expend precious resources—time, energy, imagination, political capital—searching (always successfully) for evidence of racism, while our problems grow worse.

15   Maybe I can make my point clearer by reference to two other minorities. The first group consists of poor whites. There are in America not just individuals but whole pockets of white people whose situation is hardly worse than our own.

16   And yet these poor whites have their civil rights. They can vote, live where their money permits them to live, eat where their appetites and their pocketbooks dictate, work at jobs for which their skills qualify them. And yet they are in

desperate straits. It doesn't seem to occur to us that the full grant and enforcement of our civil rights would leave black Americans in about the same situation that poor white people are now in. That isn't good enough for me.

17   There is another minority whose situations may be more instructive. I refer to recently arrived Asian-Americans. What is the difference between them and us? Certainly it isn't that they have managed to avoid the effects of racism. Neither the newly arrived Southeast Asians nor the earlier arriving Japanese-Americans, Chinese-Americans, and Korean-Americans are loved by white people. But these groups have spent little of their time and energy proving that white people don't love them.

18   *Opportunity Knocks: Who Answers?* The difference between them and us is our operating myths. Our myth is that racism accounts for our shortcomings. Theirs is that their own efforts can make the difference, no matter what white people think.

19   They have looked at America as children with their noses pressed to the window of a candy store: if only I could get in there, boy, could I have a good time. And when they get in there, they work and study and save and create businesses and job opportunities for their people.

20   But we, born inside the candy store, have adopted a myth that leads us to focus only on the maldistribution of the candy. Our myth leads us into becoming a race of consumers, when victories accrue to the producers.

21   Interestingly enough, this is a fairly recent phenomenon. There was a time when we, like the more recent arrivals in this country, sought only the opportunity to be productive, and we grasped that opportunity under circumstances far worse—in law, at least—than those that obtain now.

22   Free blacks and former slaves, though denied many of the rights that we take for granted today, were entrepreneurial spirits. They were artisans and inventors, shopkeepers and industrialists, financiers and bankers. The first female millionaire in America was Madame C. J. Walker. At least two companies founded at the turn of the century are now on the *Black Enterprise* list of the 100 top black firms in the country.

23   Black real estate operatives transformed white Harlem into a haven for blacks. The early 1900s saw the founding of a number of all-black towns: Mound Bayou, Mississippi; Boley, Oklahoma; Nicodemus, Kansas; and others.

24   Boley at one time boasted a bank, twenty-five grocery stores, five hotels, seven restaurants, a waterworks, an electricity plant, four cotton gins, three drug stores, a bottling plant, a laundry, two newspapers, two colleges, a high school, a grade school, four department stores, a jewelry store, two hardware stores, two ice cream parlors, a telephone exchange, five churches, two insurance agencies, two livery stables, an undertaker, a lumber yard, two photography studios, and an ice plant [from J. DeSane, *Analogies and Black History: A Programmed Approach*]. Not bad for an all-black town of 4,000.

25   As Robert L. Woodson observed in his book, *On the Road to Economic Freedom,* "The Harlem and Boley experiences, which matched aggressive black entrepreneurial activity with the self-assertion drive of the black masses, was multiplied nationwide to the point that, in 1913, fifty years after Emancipation, black America had accumulated a personal wealth of $700 million.

26   "As special Emancipation Day festivals and parades were held that year in cities and towns across the country, blacks could take pride in owning 550,000 homes, 40,000 businesses, 40,000 churches, and 937,000 farms. The literacy

rate among blacks climbed to a phenomenal 70 percent—up from 5 percent in 1863."

27   ***Over-learning the Civil Rights Lesson.*** What has happened since then? A lot of things, including a good deal of success that we don't talk much about. But among the things that have happened are two that have created problems for us. First is the overemphasis on integration, as opposed to desegregation and increased opportunity. Hundreds of thriving restaurants, hotels, service outlets, and entertainment centers have gone out of business because we preferred integration to supporting our own painstakingly established institutions. Indeed, aside from black churches and black colleges, little remains to show for that entrepreneurial spurt of the early decades of this century.

28   The other thing that has happened is that we over-learned the lessons of the civil rights movement. That movement, brilliantly conceived and courageously executed, marked a proud moment in our history. The upshot was that black Americans, for the first time in our sojourn here, enjoy the full panoply of our civil rights.

29   Unfortunately, that period also taught us to see in civil rights terms things that might more properly be addressed in terms of enterprise and exertion rather than in terms of equitable distribution. Even when we speak of business now, our focus is on distribution: on set-asides and affirmative action.

30   ***Entrepreneurs and Self-Help.*** Our 1960s success in making demands on government has led us to the mistaken assumption that government can give us what we need for the next major push toward equality. It has produced in us what Charles Tate of the Booker T. Washington Foundation recently described as a virtual antipathy toward capitalism.

31   Even middle-class blacks seldom talk to their children about going into business. Instead our emphasis is on a fair distribution of jobs in business created and run by others. We ought to have a fair share of those jobs. But the emphasis, I submit, ought to be finding ways to get more of us into business and thereby creating for ourselves the jobs we need.

32   That is especially true with regard to the so-called black underclass who tend to reside in areas abandoned by white businesses.

33   In addition to figuring out ways of getting our unemployed to jobs that already exist, we need to look for ways to encourage blacks in those abandoned neighborhoods to create enterprises of their own. What I have in mind are not merely the shops and Mom & Pop stores that we still patronize (but whose owners are far likelier to be Vietnamese or Koreans than blacks), but also an entrepreneurial approach to our social problems.

34   I am not suggesting that government has no role in attacking these problems. It has a major role. What I am suggesting is that we need to explore ways of creating government-backed programs that instead of merely making our problems more bearable go in the direction of solving those problems. We are forever talking about the lack of day care as an impediment to work for welfare families. But why aren't we lobbying for legislation that would relax some of the anti-entrepreneurial rules and permit some of the money now spent on public welfare to be used to establish child-care centers run by the neighbors of those who need the care? Why aren't we looking for ways to use the funds

that are already being expended to create small jitney services to transport job-seekers to distant jobs?

35   ***Success Is the Goal.*** I said at the beginning that I am not a theoretician, but I do have one little theory that may have some relevance to our subject. It is this: When people believe that their problems can be solved, they tend to get busy solving them—partly because it is the natural thing to do and partly because they would like to have the credit. When people believe that their problems are beyond solution, they tend to position themselves so as to avoid blame for their nonsolution.

36   Now none of the black leadership will tell you that they think the problems we face are beyond solution. To do so would be to forfeit their leadership positions. But their behavior, if my theory is correct, suggests their pessimism.

37   Let me offer an example of what I am talking about. Take the woeful inadequacy of education in the predominantly black central cities. Does the black leadership see the ascendancy of black teachers and school administrators and the rise of black politicians to positions of local leadership as assets to be used in improving those dreadful schools? Rarely. What you are more likely to hear are charges of white abandonment, white resistance to integration, white conspiracies to isolate black children even when the schools are officially desegregated. In short, white people are responsible for the problem.

38   But if the youngsters manage to survive those awful school systems and make their way to historically black colleges—that is, if the children begin to show signs that they are going to make it—these same leaders sing a different song. Give our black colleges a fair share of public resources, they say, and we who know and love our children will educate them.

39   The difference, I submit, is that they believe many of our high school students won't succeed, and they conspire to avoid the blame for their failure. But they believe that most of our college youngsters will make it, and they want to be in position to claim credit for their success.

40   I suspect something like that is happening in terms of our economic well-being. Many of us are succeeding, in an astonishing range of fields, and the leadership does not hesitate to point out—with perfect justification—that our success is attributable to the glorious civil rights movement: that black exertion and courage made our success possible.

41   But many of us aren't succeeding. Teenage pregnancy, dope trafficking, lawlessness, and lack of ambition make us doubt that they ever will succeed. But do our leaders suggest that the reasons have to do with the inadequacy of the civil rights movement, or with any lack of exertion and courage on the part of the leadership? No. When we see failure among our people, and have reason to believe that the failure is permanent, our recourse is to our mainstay myth: Racism is the culprit. Mistakenly, we credit black pride for our successes and blame prejudice for our shortfalls.

42   I leave it to others to suggest the specifics by which we will move to increase the economic success of black America. I will tell you only that I believe it can be done—not only because it is being done by an encouraging number of us, but also because it has been done by earlier generations who struggled under circumstances of discrimination, deprivation, and hostility far worse than anything we now face.

43   My simple suggestion is that we stop using the plight of the black under-class as a scourge for beating up on white racists and examine both the black community and the American system for clues to how we can transform ourselves from consumers to producers.

44   I used to play a little game in which I would concede to members of the black leadership the validity of the racism explanation. "Let's say you're exactly right, that racism is the overriding reason for our situation, and that an all-out attack on racism is our most pressing priority," I'd tell them.

45   "Now let us suppose that we eventually win the fight against racism and put ourselves in the position now occupied by poor whites. What would you urge that we do next?"

46   "Pool our resources? Establish and support black businesses? Insist that our children take advantage of the opportunities that a society free of racism would offer? What should be our next step?"

47   "Well, just for the hell of it, why don't we pretend that the racist dragon has been slain already—and take that next step right now?"

DISCUSSION QUESTIONS

1. Explain why Raspberry identifies himself as a "newspaper guy" in paragraph 1.
2. Why do you think Raspberry offers a precise definition of "myth" in paragraph 5?
3. Reread paragraphs 13 and 14 and point out specifically how Raspberry's views differ from those of Martin Luther King, Jr., in "I Have a Dream" (pages 569–572).
4. Discuss the effectiveness of the analogy Raspberry uses in paragraphs 19–20.
5. Cite three places in the essay where Raspberry states an idea and uses specific examples to clarify its meaning.
6. What writing strategy does Raspberry use to develop paragraphs 21–29?
7. Paragraphs 44–47 function as Raspberry's conclusion. Indicate why you think the conclusion is or is not effective.
8. Raspberry's and King's arguments were both delivered as speeches, King's in 1963 and Raspberry's in 1989. Which argument seems more effective? Does your answer stem from the content, effectiveness of presentation, or both?

TOWARD KEY INSIGHTS

Raspberry makes an "entrepreneurial approach" seem like a relatively simple solution to widespread black poverty and related problems. What difficulties might such an approach face?

Is Raspberry right in suggesting that black Americans need to spend less time blaming racial injustice for their problems and more time creating businesses and enterprises? Why or why not?

SUGGESTION FOR WRITING

Develop an argument that proposes how a minority group can best enhance its economic prosperity. Use whatever types of evidence seem appropriate.

DANIEL JAMES

Close the Borders to All Newcomers

Daniel James's opposition to immigration is expressed most fully in Illegal Immigration: An Unfolding Crisis *(1991). In our essay James presents his reasons why the United States should impose a moratorium on all immigration.*

1   Strip the rhetoric from the evolving immigration debate and the bottom line becomes crystal clear: We may desire more and more immigrants, but can we afford so many of them? In his recently published memoirs, *Around the Cragged Hill*, George F. Kennan, perhaps our most eminent statesman, goes to the heart of the matter:

2   "We are already, for better or for worse, very much a polyglot country; and nothing of that is now to be changed. What I have in mind here are sheer numbers. There *is* such a thing as overcrowding. It has its psychic effects as well as its physical ones. There *are* limits to what the environment can stand."

3   The sheer numbers are indeed mind-boggling:

- 10.5 million immigrants, including those arriving illegally, entered the U.S. in the 1980s. That topped the previous record of 8.8 million who came here from 1901 to 1910.

- 15 to 18 million more newcomers, both legal and illegal, are projected to reach America in the 1990s, assuming our present immigration policy remains unchanged. Already, the number arriving in this decade is greater than for the same period in the previous decade. And there were nearly 1.2 million immigrants in 1992, 20 percent more than in 1991.

- 30 million immigrants—perhaps as many as 36 million—are expected to arrive in the first two decades of the next century, according to demographic projections and extrapolation of 1991–92 Census Bureau data.

4   The last two projections indicate that between 45 million and 54 million people—almost equal to the population of Great Britain—will be entering the U.S. in little more than a generation.

5   Add the 20 million immigrants who arrived from 1965 to 1990, and the grand total who will have entered the U.S. in just over a half-century (1965–2020) will be 65 million to 74 million.

6   There is no precedent for these numbers anywhere in the world. They constitute the biggest wave of immigration ever to a single country. Called the "fourth wave" of immigration to the U.S., it is really a tidal wave.

7   Yet the numbers are conservative. Unforeseeable trends in countries that generate immigrants could swell the tidal wave even higher than projected. It is likely, for example, that the demise of Cuba's communist dictatorship would send a flood of refugees to Miami comparable to the 125,000 *Marielitos* who inundated it in 1980.

8   Mexico is an even bigger concern. In the 1980s, it sent the U.S. nearly 4 million immigrants, more than the total for all of Asia. Two great "push" factors will drive ever more of them northward: high population growth—Mexico's present 90 million inhabitants will become 110 million by 2000—and unemployment/underemployment levels of 40 to 50 percent.

9   The North American Free Trade Agreement . . . may generate a temporary upsurge in illegal border crossings. It [will] draw more Mexicans to the relatively affluent north and make entering the U.S. affordable. Meanwhile, an expected rise in imports of cheaper U.S. corn [will] bankrupt Mexico's peasant class, the *campesinos,* and drive them to seek work stateside. Only years from now [will] NAFTA create enough jobs to keep Mexicans at home.

10   The cost to U.S. taxpayers of accepting endless numbers of immigrants is intolerable. We learn from a study, "The Costs of Immigration," by economist Donald Huddle, that the net 1992 public assistance cost of the 19.3 million immigrants who have settled here since 1970 was $42.5 billion, after subtracting $20.2 billion they paid in taxes.

11   Huddle examined costs in 22 categories of federal, state and local assistance available to immigrants, including a package of 10 county welfare and health services. The largest net costs for immigrants in 1992 were $16 billion for education (primary, secondary and bilingual), $10.6 billion for health and welfare services and $8.5 billion for Medicaid.

12   Criminal justice and corrections costs for immigrants were found by Huddle to total more than $2 billion in 1992. The social price was greater: A disproportionately large number of illegals were in prison for committing felonies. In California, they made up 11 percent of all inmates.

13   Huddle also found that immigrants in 1992 displaced—probably forever— 2.07 million American workers. This should answer the oft-debated question: Do immigrants take jobs away from Americans?

14   It is true that American workers frequently turn down tasks that immigrants willingly perform, such as picking fruit and vegetables under inhumane conditions or making garments in urban sweatshops. But that hardly explains the virtual elimination of blacks from jobs in entire industries. In Los Angeles, unionized blacks have been displaced by nonunion Hispanics in janitorial services, and in Washington, D.C., by Latino immigrants in hotels and restaurants.

15   The puzzling question is: Why does the U.S. continue to import competition for American workers at a time of high unemployment? The Labor Department reports that 8.5 million Americans, about 6.7 percent of our work force, are unemployed. Our two principal minorities suffer most from joblessness—12.6 percent of blacks and 9.7 percent of Latinos—and they are the most vulnerable to displacement.

16   Immigration costs will rise further in this decade, Huddle forecasts. He projects that from 1993 to 2002, 11.1 million legal and illegal immigrants will be added to the 19.3 million post-1970 immigrants already here, for a total of 30.4 million. Their net cost to taxpayers during the next decade would come to $668.5 billion. . . .

17   Impossible to quantify, but perhaps more devastating in the long run, is the cost of excessive immigration to the environment. As more and more people are added to our population—already excessive at 260 million—the greater the environmental degradation will be. The immigrants will contribute to increasing energy use, toxic waste, smog and urban crowding, all of which affect our mental and emotional health as well as the ecosystem.

18   Our population is increasing by 3 million a year, a rate faster than that of any other advanced country. California provides an example of what can happen to a nearly ideal environment when it is overwhelmed by too many people. Since 1980, its population has zoomed from 23.7 million to more than 31 million, an increase of almost one-third. As a consequence, Los Angeles and its

once pristine bay are all but hopelessly polluted, and San Diego and Orange counties are fast becoming sad miniatures of Los Angeles.

19   Equally alarming is the impetus that uncontrolled immigration provides to separatism and its obverse, multiculturalism. Those living in areas where there are many other immigrants, such as Los Angeles and Texas's Rio Grande Valley, see no need to learn English and so live in virtual isolation from the general population. As long as these barrios are constantly replenished with newcomers from Mexico—virtually a stone's throw away—their inhabitants will feel less and less need or desire to assimilate. This process encourages a kind of natural separatism that could lead to political separatism.

20   Richard Estrada, a journalist and scholar, sees an ominous parallel with Quebec: "If Francophone Quebec can bring the Canadian confederation to the brink of disintegration even though France lies an ocean away, should there not at least arise a certain reflectiveness about our Southwest, which lies contiguous to an overpopulated Third World nation?"

21   A growing number of Americans of all classes and ethnic groups share these concerns about immigration and favor reducing it. For at least two decades, a majority of Americans have expressed in various polls their desire to stop or reduce immigration. In January 1992, a Gallup Poll found that 64 percent of registered voters would vote for a presidential candidate who favored tougher laws on immigration. In December, the Latino National Political Survey discovered that Hispanics overwhelmingly believed there is too much immigration.

22   Even politicians who previously shunned immigration as a taboo subject are . . . clamoring to curb illegal immigration. We can hope that they soon will understand that the main problem, as the public generally has perceived, is legal immigration.

23   Serious though illegal immigration is, *legal* immigration poses a much graver problem. We receive more than three times as many legal immigrants, including refugees, as illegal ones. Their numbers are projected to grow exponentially, because under the 1990 Immigration Act they are permitted to bring in an endless procession of family members. In 1992, for example, family-related immigrants totaled 594,000, or 49 percent of the 1.2 million immigrants who entered the U.S. that year.

24   Legal immigrants account for almost three-quarters of the total costs calculated by the Huddle study. Thus, of the $668.5 billion projected net cost to taxpayers for all immigrants from 1993 to 2002, legal immigrants would account for $482 billion. Illegal aliens would cost $186.4 billion.

25   The most effective way to curb illegal immigration is to declare a moratorium on *all* immigration. Why? If the U.S. clamps down on illegals but permits legal immigration to continue uncontrolled, that tells the world we are not serious about solving either problem, for it is easier to reduce or halt the legal flow than to hunt down those who arrive undercover. To do so would require a mere stroke of the pen and wouldn't cost taxpayers extra—Congress could just reform the Immigration Act of 1990, which is directly responsible for the 40 percent increase in immigration. That would send the unequivocal message to anyone who plans to enter the U.S. that we cannot afford to receive them—at least for the time being.

26   The message would ring loud and clear to would-be illegal immigrants that we mean business. It must be backed up, however, by a whole range of law enforcement measures that are now on the books but are ignored or not used effectively. In addition, to smoke out illegals and also eliminate the racket in fraudulent documents, Congress should approve a universal ID. . . .

27   The ID cards would identify those who are legally in the U.S. and entitled to work and receive benefits. Local and state authorities should be directed to share information on illegals with the Immigration and Naturalization Service to aid in apprehending them; at present, authorities deny such information to the INS, in effect protecting illegals.

28   Instead of sending the National Guard to patrol the border as advocated by some lawmakers, it would be more effective to give the Border Patrol sufficient personnel to do its job. At least 2,000 new agents should be added to the current force of about 4,000, as well as equipment such as better night sensors and new vehicles. . . .

29   A vital component of any program to curb immigration must be the cooperation of the Mexican government. The White House should take advantage of our cordial relations with Mexico and our growing economic clout to request that our southern neighbor cease its traditional (though unwritten) policy of regarding the U.S. as a safety valve.

30   A U.S. moratorium on immigration would yield highly positive gains by allowing the 20 million immigrants now within our borders time to assimilate into the mainstream. It would remove the pressure of new millions crowding into inner-city barrios and encourage existing inhabitants to break out of them. This would mitigate the danger of separatism, counter multiculturalist trends, defuse interethnic tensions and reduce crime and violence.

31   If this prescription sounds like a pipe dream, let us recall that restrictive legislation in 1924 cut immigration to a trickle, allowing enough time for the masses of immigrants the U.S. had then to overcome the obstacles to assimilation. That literally saved America. For when the Japanese struck at Pearl Harbor in 1941 and the U.S. was confronted by their military might plus that of Germany, which already had conquered Europe and had just invaded the Soviet Union, our nation stood united against them. Sadly, one doubts whether today's America, torn by an identity crisis spawned by divisive forces, would be capable of meeting a similar threat.

32   The United States is headed for a crisis of incalculable magnitude if mass immigration continues unchecked. The argument of those who favor an open border is that immigrants have always contributed to our society, and so they have. But we no longer can afford the world's "huddled masses" when our own are so often homeless and jobless. If we permit immigration to continue uncontrolled, it will explode in a full-blown crisis that will extend beyond the vociferous separatism/multiculturalism debate to engulf us in a violent civil conflict.

33   America is under siege. It is threatened from without by international terrorism and from within by centrifugal forces that already have revealed their capacity for destruction in bloody riots from Los Angeles to Miami, from Washington to Manhattan.

DISCUSSION QUESTIONS

1. What is James's proposition and where is it located? How do you account for this location? Is the proposition one of fact, policy, action, or value?

2. Why do you think James identifies George F. Kennan as "perhaps our most eminent statesman" in paragraph 1?

3. Point out the different kinds of evidence that James uses to develop his argument. Refer to specific parts of the essay when answering.

4. What types of appeal does James use?

5. Cite two places in the essay where James concedes points to the opposing side.

6. Comment on the effectiveness of the following short sentence in paragraph 31: "That literally saved America."

7. James's views on immigration differ markedly from those of Stephen Moore, which are set forth in the following essay. Read Moore's essay and then evaluate the differing attitudes of the authors.

TOWARD KEY INSIGHTS

Do you believe that "the United States is headed for a crisis of incalculable magnitude" (paragraph 32) if we don't stop immigration? What are the reasons for your position?

SUGGESTION FOR WRITING

Write an essay arguing that children of illegal immigrants should or should not receive public assistance benefits. Develop your topic with appropriate evidence.

STEPHEN MOORE

Give Us Your Best, Your Brightest

Stephen Moore directs fiscal policy at the Cato Institute, a Libertarian think tank. Born (1960) in Chicago, he earned an undergraduate degree at the University of Chicago and a graduate degree in economics at George Mason University. He is the author of Still an Open Door: Immigration Policy and the American Economy *(1994) and* Welfare for the Well-Off *(1997). He contributes regularly to a variety of newspapers and magazines. In this selection, Moore argues for liberalized but carefully targeted immigration.*

1   For many Americans, the word "immigration" immediately conjures up an image of poor Mexicans scrambling across the border near San Diego to find minimum-wage work and perhaps collect government benefits. Recent public opinion polls confirm that the attitude of the American public toward immigration is highly unfavorable. Central Americans are perceived as welfare abusers who stubbornly refuse to learn English, Haitians are seen as AIDS carriers, Russian Jews are considered to be mafiosi, and Asians are seen as international terrorists. The media reinforce these stereotypes by battering the public with negative depictions of immigrants.

2   The conception of immigrants as tired, poor, huddled masses seems permanently sketched into the mind of the public, just as the words are sketched irrevocably at the feet of the Statue of Liberty. But the Emma Lazarus poem simply does not describe the hundreds of thousands of people who are building new lives here in the 1990s. It would be more appropriate if the words at the base of the statue read: "Give us your best, your brightest, your most energetic and talented." Why? Because in large part those are the people who come to the United States each year.

3   Before we start slamming shut the golden door, it might be worthwhile to find out who the newcomers are and how they truly affect our lives.

4   Anyone who believes that immigrants are a drain on the U.S. economy has never visited the Silicon Valley in California. Here and in other corridors of high-tech entrepreneurship, immigrants are literally the lifeblood of many of the nation's most prosperous industries. In virtually every field in which the United States asserted global leadership in the 1980s—industries such as computer design and software, pharmaceuticals, bioengineering, electronics, superconductivity, robotics and aerospace engineering—one finds immigrants. In many ways these high-growth industries are the modern version of the American melting pot in action.

5   Consider Intel Corp., ... one of the most prolific and fast-expanding companies in the United States, employing tens of thousands of American workers. It is constantly developing exciting, cutting-edge technologies that will define the computer industry in the 21st century.

6   And it is doing all of this largely with the talents of America's newest immigrants. Three members of Intel's top management, including Chief Executive Officer Andrew S. Grove, from Hungary, are immigrants. Some of its most successful and revolutionary computer technologies were pioneered by immigrants, such as the 8080 microprocessor (an expanded-power computer chip), invented by a Japanese, and polysilicon FET gates (the basic unit of memory storage on modern computer chips), invented by an Italian. Dick Ward, manager of employee information systems at Intel, says: "Our whole business is predicated on inventing the next generation of computer technologies. The engine that drives that quest is brainpower. And here at Intel, much of that brainpower comes from immigrants."

7   Or consider Du Pont-Merck Pharmaceutical Co., an $800 million-a-year health care products company based in Wilmington, Del., which reports that immigrants are responsible for many of its most promising new product innovations. For example, losartan, an antihypertensive drug, was developed by a team of scientists that included two Chinese and a Lithuanian. Joseph Mollica, Chief Executive Officer of Du Pont-Merck, says that bringing together such diverse talent "lets you look at problems and opportunities from a slightly different point of view."

8   Intel and Du Pont-Merck are not alone in relying on immigrants. Robert Kelley Jr., president of SO/CAL/TEN, an association of nearly 200 high-tech California companies, insists: "Without the influx of Asians in the 1980s, we would not have had the entrepreneurial explosion we've seen in California." David N.K. Wang, vice president for worldwide business operations at Applied Materials Inc., a computer-technology company in California, adds that because of immigration, "Silicon Valley is one of the most international business centers in the world."

9   Take away the immigrants, and you take away the talent base that makes such centers operate. Indeed, it is frightening to think what would happen to

America's global competitiveness if the immigrants stopped coming. Even scarier is the more realistic prospect that U.S. policymakers will enact laws to prevent them from coming.

10   Research has begun to quantify the contributions of immigrants to American industry. The highly respected National Research Council reported in 1988 that "a large fraction of the technological output of the United States [is] dependent upon foreign talent and that such dependency is growing." Noting that well over half of all scientists graduating with doctorate degrees from American universities and one in three engineers working in the United States are immigrants, the report states emphatically: "It is clear . . . that these foreign-born engineers enrich our culture and make substantial contributions to the U.S. economic well-being and competitiveness."

11   The United States' competitive edge over the Japanese, Germans, Koreans and much of Europe is linked closely to its continued ability to attract and retain highly talented workers from other countries. A 1990 study by the National Science Foundation says, "Very significant, positive aspects arise from the presence of foreign-born engineers in our society."

12   For example, superconductivity, a technology that is expected to spawn hundreds of vital new commercial applications in the next century, was discovered by a physicist at the University of Houston, Paul C.W. Chu. He was born in China and came to the U.S. in 1972. His brilliance and inventiveness have made him a top contender for a Nobel Prize.

13   Of course, if Chu does win a Nobel, he will join a long list of winners who were immigrants to America. In the 20th century, between 20 percent and 50 percent of the Nobel Prize winners, depending on the discipline involved, have been immigrants to the United States. Today there are more Russian Nobel Prize winners living in the U.S. than there are living in Russia.

14   Public opinion polls consistently reveal that a major worry is that immigrants take jobs from American workers. The fear is understandable but misplaced. Immigrants don't just take jobs, they create jobs. One way is by starting new businesses. Today, America's immigrants, even those who come with relatively low skill levels, are highly entrepreneurial.

15   Take Koreans, for example. According to sociologists Alendro Portes and Ruben Rumbaut, "In Los Angeles, the propensity for self-employment is three times greater for Koreans than among the population as a whole. Grocery stores, restaurants, gas stations, liquor stores and real estate offices are typical Korean businesses." Cubans also are prodigious creators of new businesses. The number of Cuban-owned businesses in Miami has expanded from 919 in 1967 to 8,000 in 1976 to 28,000 in 1990. On Jefferson Boulevard in Dallas, more than 800 businesses operate, three-quarters of them owned by first and second generation Hispanic immigrants. Just 10 years ago, before the influx of Mexicans and other Central Americans, the neighborhood was in decay, with many vacant storefronts displaying "for sale" signs in the windows. Today it is a thriving ethnic neighborhood.

16   To be sure, few immigrant-owned businesses mature into an Intel. In fact, many fail completely. Like most new businesses in America, most immigrant establishments are small and only marginally profitable. The average immigrant business employs two to four workers and records roughly $200,000 in annual sales. However, such small businesses . . . are a significant source of jobs.

17   It should not be too surprising that immigrants are far more likely than average U.S. citizens to take business risks. After all, uprooting oneself, traveling to a foreign culture and making it requires more than the usual amount of

courage, ambition, resourcefulness and even bravado. Indeed, this is part of the self-selection process that makes immigrants so particularly desirable. Immigrants are not just people—they are a very special group of people. By coming, they impart productive energies on the rest of us.

18   This is not just romanticism. It is well-grounded in fact. Countless studies have documented that immigrants to the United States tend to be more skilled, more highly educated and wealthier than the average citizen of their native countries.

19   Thomas Sowell, an economist and senior fellow at the Hoover Institution in Stanford, Calif., reports in his seminal study on immigration, "Ethnic America," that black immigrants from the West Indies have far higher skill levels than their countrymen at home. He also finds that the income levels of West Indies immigrants are higher than those of West Indies natives, American blacks and native-born white Americans.

20   Surprisingly, even illegal immigrants are not the poverty-stricken and least skilled from their native countries. Surveys of undocumented immigrants from Mexico to the United States show that only about 5 percent were unemployed in Mexico, whereas the average unemployment rate there was about three times that level, and that a relatively high percentage of them worked in white-collar jobs in Mexico. In addition, surveys have found that illiteracy among undocumented Mexicans in the U.S. is about 10 percent, whereas illiteracy in Mexico is about 22 percent.

21   Perhaps the greatest asset of immigrants is their children, who tend to be remarkably successful in the U.S. Recently, the city of Boston reported that an incredible 13 of the 17 valedictorians in its public high schools were foreign-born—from China, Vietnam, Portugal, El Salvador, France, Italy, Jamaica and the former Czechoslovakia. Many could not speak a word of English when they arrived. Public high schools in Washington, Chicago and Los Angeles also report remarkably disproportionate numbers of immigrant children at the top of the class. Similarly, Westinghouse reports that over the past 12 years, about one-third of its prestigious National Science Talent Search winners have been Asians. Out of this group might emerge America's next Albert Einstein, who himself was an immigrant.

22   So one hidden cost of restricting immigration is the loss of immigrants' talented and motivated children.

23   In the past century, America has admitted roughly 50 million immigrants. This has been one of the largest migrations in the history of the world. Despite this infusion of people—no, because of it—the United States became by the middle of the 20th century the wealthiest nation in the world. Real wages in America have grown more than eightfold over this period. The U.S. economy employed less than 40 million people in 1900; today it employs nearly 120 million people. The U.S. job machine had not the slightest problem expanding and absorbing the 8 million legal immigrants who came to this country in the 1980s. Eighteen million jobs were created.

24   But what about those frightening headlines? "Immigration Bankrupting Nation." "Immigrants Displacing U.S. Workers." "Foreigners Lured to U.S. by Welfare."

25   Here are the facts. The 1990 census reveals that roughly 6 percent of native-born Americans are on public assistance, versus 7 percent of the foreign-born, with less than 5 percent of illegal immigrants collecting welfare. Not much reason for alarm. Because immigrants tend to come to the United States when they are young and working, over their lifetimes they each pay about $20,000 more in taxes than they use in services, according to economist Julian

Simon of the University of Maryland. With 1 million immigrants per year, the nation gains about $20 billion more than cost. Rather than fiscal burdens, immigrants are huge bargains. . . .

26   We are now witnessing in America what might be described as the return of the nativists. They are selling fear and bigotry. But if any of their allegations against immigrants are accurate, then America could not have emerged as the economic superpower it is today.

27   In fact, most Americans do accept that immigration in the past has contributed greatly to the nation's economic growth. But they are not so sanguine in their assessment of present and future immigrants. It is strangely inconsistent that Americans believe that so long-standing and crucial a benefit is now a source of cultural and economic demise.

28   Shortly before his death, Winston Churchill wrote, "The empires of the future are the empires of the mind." America is confronted with one of the most awesome opportunities in world history to build those empires by attracting highly skilled, highly educated and entrepreneurial people from all over the globe. The Andrew Groves and the Paul Chus of the world do not want to go to Japan, Israel, Germany, France or Canada. Almost universally they want to come to the United States. We can be selective. By expanding immigration but orienting our admission policies toward gaining the best and the brightest, America would enjoy a significant comparative advantage over its geopolitical rivals.

29   By pursuing a liberal and strategic policy on immigration, America can ensure that the 21st century, like the 20th, will be the American century.

DISCUSSION QUESTIONS

1. Why do you think Moore cites popular stereotypes of immigrants in paragraph 1?
2. What is Moore's proposition and where is it located? How do you account for this location? Is the proposition one of fact, policy, action, or value?
3. Point out the different types of evidence that Moore uses to develop his argument. Refer to specific parts of the essay when answering.
4. What type of appeal does Moore use?
5. Cite two places in the essay where Moore refutes errors in the opposing opinion.
6. Explain what you think Moore means by the phrase "the return of the nativists" in paragraph 26.
7. Who makes the more convincing case for his position, James (pages 579–582) or Moore? Does your answer stem primarily from the essay's content, the manner of presentation, or both?

TOWARD KEY INSIGHTS

To what extent do you agree that "a liberal and strategic policy on immigration" will be instrumental in making the twenty-first century "the American century" (paragraph 29)? What reasons underlie your thinking?

SUGGESTION FOR WRITING

Write an essay favoring or opposing a liberal policy on admission to your college or university. Develop your essay with appropriate types of evidence.

MIXING THE WRITING STRATEGIES

Reading Strategies

1. When skimming, identify the main point the author is attempting to make.
2. To orient your reading, note in the margins the strategy the reader is using.
3. Focus on how the points fit together to develop the author's thesis.

Reading Critically

1. Test whether the claims throughout the text really support the thesis.
2. Evaluate the claims based on the critical reading strategy appropriate to the technique being used.
3. Judge whether the writer's strategies are appropriate to the point he or she is making.

Reading As a Writer

1. Identify how the writer effectively changes from strategy to strategy.
2. Look to determine how the writer connects each strategy to the main thesis.
3. Read the conclusion carefully to determine how the writer pulls a complex essay back together to make his or her main point.

As we noted on page 199, most essays mix various writing strategies for assorted purposes. This section features three examples. Margin notations on the Zimmerman essay point out the interplay of several strategies, and the discussion questions following the other essays direct your attention to the strategies these writers use as well as other relevant aspects of the essays.

SUSAN ZIMMERMAN

Blur: Cheetahs. Ranchers. Hope.

Susan Zimmerman is a native of St. Louis, Missouri, and a graduate of the University of Texas in Austin, where she received a bachelor of business administration degree in international business. She has also completed several years of journalism study at St. Louis's Washington University. A freelance writer, she contributes regularly to science, travel, and natural history magazines on various topics. In our selection Zimmerman examines the joint efforts of environmentalists and African ranchers to preserve the local cheetah population—an unlikely alliance offering a possible model for collaborations elsewhere.

1   Midnight, the Frey ranch, central Namibia—The subcutaneous IV hangs on the back of the kitchen door next to a flyswatter, while test tubes, a centrifuge, and a stethoscope mingle with pots and pans on the counter and the stove. The full moon has long since set and cold desert air chases away any lingering odors of a gulped-down chicken dinner. A four-person crew is bent intently over their two patients, laid out on hastily arranged tables in the middle of the dimly lit kitchen. Their sense of urgency is reflected in their conversation: "Where's the centrifuge? . . . Did anyone bring a stethoscope? . . . Don't label the vials till I draw the blood, it's bad luck!" Veterinary technician Sandy Hurlbut is drawing blood from the thigh of one patient while one of the volunteers takes the temperature. Principal investigator Laurie Marker-Kraus is working on the other, checking the teeth. It could almost pass for a war-time emergency medical station, except for the patients: two adult cheetahs.

Introduction: paragraphs 1-3; illustrates how cheetahs are being helped: Description

Illustration in narrative form: paragraphs 1-2; examination, tag-and-release of cheetahs

2   The people doing the work are part of Marker-Kraus's organization, the Cheetah Conservation Fund (CCF), the last bastion of hope for the world's last large population of cheetahs. And the work itself is an essential part of this effort, determining the health of the cats and providing vital information on their habits and behavior. The cats' faces are covered with a towel to avoid visual stimulation as they are poked and prodded for measurements, skin analysis, blood tests, and ear tagging. Up close, these exquisite animals seem frail and vulnerable stretched out on the table. Each one's long, slender, spotted body is designed with one exclusive purpose: speed. Its flexible spine, oversized liver, enlarged heart, wide nostrils, and increased lung capacity make for the fastest land mammal on Earth. The two black "tear marks" that run down its face guard against glare and help it focus on its prey while racing at 110 kilometers per hour.

Description

3   The urge to reach out and touch this extraordinary creature steals into my heart. My hand caresses its warm, heaving body, rubs its short, coarse fur, and then I listen to its racing heartbeat through a stethoscope. This simple sound brings to life for me the plight of this beleaguered species struggling to survive.

Description

An Earthwatch Primer on How to Save Cheetahs

4   **1. Identify the problem.** Cheetah numbers overall are anemic—12,500 remain in the world compared to 100,000 at the turn of the century. Ten years ago, there were 25,000, a drop of 50 percent in 10 years. Found mostly in sub-Saharan Africa with a few hundred in Iran, Namibia's 2,500 cats represent the species' largest wild population. But Namibia also represents its greatest threat. Nearly 7,000 cheetahs were removed from Namibia's farmlands from 1980–1991, according to the Convention of International Trade in Endangered Species (CITES, 1992). Ranchers considered them a threat to their livestock and knew this predator was itself easy prey because of its nonaggressive nature. By law, ranchers were allowed to remove cheetahs only if they posed a threat to livestock or to humans. But during this period, ranchers live trapped over 90 percent in large steel cages at their so-called "playtrees" (socializing areas for cheetahs) and then shot them.

Body: paragraphs 4–29

Step in process

Comparison

Cause and effects

Definition

5   To make matters worse, because of their declining populations and some peculiarities of cheetah reproduction, their gene pool is drastically constricted. Marker-Kraus's blood sampling has revealed that whole populations are 10 to 100 times more closely related than human racial groups. One fatal disease could wipe an entire colony. At the same time, scientists are eager to preserve the Namibian cheetah in particular, because it is one of the last populations in

Causes and effects

Comparison

Definition

Continuation of initial narrative: paragraph 6 to second sentence, paragraph 7

Comparison

Comparison

Cause and effect, comparison

Step in process

Comparison

Description

Comparison

Africa free of FIV, the feline version of AIDS, and may offer important clues in AIDS research. The Cheetah Conservation Fund's ambitious goal, then, is to save habitat, rebuild the cheetah's gene pool, and broker a truce with Namibia's ranchers.

6   After 45 minutes of intensive examination, the cheetahs start regaining consciousness. When the towels are removed, they begin slowly blinking their eyes and drowsily scanning the ceiling and the strangers who have abducted them. As one cat begins growling, someone gasps, "Uh-oh, this one wants to wake up." The methodical pace shifts into high gear as three people swiftly lift the 39-kilogram cheetah and race for the recovery cage outside. A wild cheetah pouncing about a kitchen is not desirable.

7   Early the next morning the cheetahs are released. Bewildered from their alien abduction, the cats hesitate a few seconds when the cage door is lifted, then explode into a classic cheetah sprint, leaving a puff of dust. Acceleration is the cheetahs' specialty. They can't keep up the pace for long, but from a standstill to 110 kph, they are faster than any sports car ever made. They can turn on a dime as well. And that's enough. They have a higher kill rate than any other cat, catching 53 percent of the animals they chase, mostly warthogs, small antelope, and the young of large antelope. For CCF director Laurie Marker-Kraus and her colleagues, this morning's release is cause for celebration. It marks yet another successful tag-and-release for the cheetah and the CCF crew. Marker-Kraus's political savvy and her multipronged, cross-disciplinary approach of conservation, research, and education is earning her the ranchers' respect and cooperation to this end: CCF has examined over 200 cheetahs that would once have been simply shot in the ranchers' traps and discarded as trash.

8   *2. Identify the key players.* If one could see the cheetah's future in its huge crystal-ball-like eyes, it would be as a living symbol of conservation. But for this cat to survive, the ranchers must see their future in the cheetah's eyes. Eby Frey, a third-generation Namibian rancher and the son of South African missionaries, has this vision. Clad in a green fatigue jacket, sunglasses, and bush hat, he reflects the changing attitudes of his colleagues. "In the past," he says, "nobody talked about cheetahs, nobody cared about them. They were here and that's it. People shot them and caught them just like they wanted to. I myself had some cheetahs in pens here."

9   Harry Schneider-Waterberg, another third-generation Namibian rancher who lives next to Elands Joy, the farm where CCF is based, echoes those sentiments. "Everybody knew catching cheetahs was easy, and if we took them out we wouldn't have a problem. There was nobody there that really stopped it." Then, five years ago, he and Frey met Marker-Kraus.

10   Today Frey is a professional game guide, out of necessity, having sold off his cattle due to the drought, while Schneider-Waterberg now makes his land available for CCF research and radio-collaring.

11   Frey is an unconventional character—part Dr. Dolittle, James Herriot, and game guide. A sign cautions arriving vehicles to his farm: "Slowly—Disabled Animals." One of his two dogs, Xavier, was crippled in a fight with a baboon. Besides the current residents, which include an orphaned meerkat and a warthog, he used to have a wildebeest, and hartebeests occasionally galloped through the kitchen. His homestead is well-furnished, complete with guest facilities for his game-hunting clients.

12   Without Frey's help, CCF's midnight mission might not have been as triumphant. He drove an hour to a neighboring farm to help CCF retrieve the

cheetahs, volunteered his kitchen for tabletop medicine, assisted in the entire operation, provided beds and a barn for his overnight guests, and then offered his land for the cheetahs' release. Ranchers like Frey are the CCF's greatest asset. As a Namibian farmer, he is not an outsider and can go where CCF cannot. "I talk to other farmers about problems with cheetahs," says Frey. As he drives his truck to assist with one last rescue, a CCF car stuck in the sand, Frey says of the successful release, "it feels good to see a cheetah in the open here."

13   **3. Add one passionate scientist.** When a farmer calls in a cheetah capture, it is CCF's job to retrieve the animal from a field trap, gather biological information, and then relocate or release it. Normally the work is done in the field and not in a farmer's kitchen. Until last night, there had not been a call in a month—proof that farmers are learning to co-exist with cheetahs rather than to shoot first and ask questions later. "This is what it's all about," says Marker-Kraus at Elands Joy. Long, brown, wavy hair and large frame glasses eclipse a small face and disguise the tenacity it takes to do her job. Strands of gray are the only hint of the stress on this 42-year-old wildlife specialist, who has dedicated the past five years to establishing and solidifying CCF's place in Namibia's political and cultural landscape.

14   Marker-Kraus has made a life-long commitment to protect the cheetah's last stronghold. Her passion for cheetahs began over 20 years ago at a wildlife park in Oregon. "I wanted to know what was so special about this animal that people have raised it for 5,000 years, yet its numbers have continued to decline." In 1991, after several years as director of the Center for New Opportunities for Animal Health Sciences at the U.S. National Zoo, Marker-Kraus became so frustrated by her inability to save the cheetah from afar that she moved to Namibia. Having now achieved residency status, her ultimate goal is to create a reserve for cheetahs in Namibia. She juggles her own self-inflicted demands as administrator, spokesperson, educator, researcher, and fundraiser, wearing whatever hat the situation warrants. "People were seeing the cheetah before through ranchers' eyes," says Marker-Kraus. "Now they are seeing through the eyes of people that love the cheetah."

15   Marker-Kraus's crusade for the cheetahs zeroed in on the ranchers. Opting for a rancher-friendly approach, CCF conducted a three-year survey to first understand the rancher's plight—predation and management problems. "We spent the first couple of years," she says, "going door to door through the ranching community and meeting 240 ranchers. We just put out a book of the findings. This has made us link together with the ranchers in our project."

16   **4. Form an alliance.** When neighbor rancher Hans Diekmann arrives in his pickup at Elands Joy, we can see that linking clearly. Marker-Kraus invites him into her house, where the two kneel on the kitchen floor papered with telemetry maps. "These are three males, this is a leopard and we just got a brown hyena," she notes as she points out some of CCF's 25 radio-collared cheetahs. The leopard and hyena come from helping out a visiting German student with his research project.

17   CCF's approach is that once ranchers understand how cheetahs live, there is a better chance for the cats' survival. By radio-collaring cheetahs, CCF has shown ranchers that cat movements through their land do not mean problems. With home ranges equivalent to 10 farms averaging 6,000 hectares each, cheetahs are just passersby on any given ranch. Indiscriminate killing is a poor solution, since the cat's territory will simply be taken over by another. "Our problem is trying to find ways cheetahs can live with humans," says Marker-Kraus.

Step in process

Description

Narrative

Step in process

Effect and cause, comparison

18   Livestock losses to predators are definitely an economic factor. The Namibian Department of Veterinary Services estimates that wild predators kill 10 to 15 percent of domestic cattle and 30 to 40 percent of small stock (goats and sheep). But, according to the 1991 CCF survey, cheetahs are responsible for only a third of cattle and a fifth of small livestock predation. Hyenas, jackals, and leopards do the bulk of the damage. The survey noted that ranchers' attitudes toward cheetahs did not reflect cheetahs' small role in predation. CCF's efforts have painstakingly peeled away myths about the cheetah as the arch enemy of livestock. "Cheetahs have been the scapecat so to speak. They are daytime hunters so they are seen more regularly," says Marker-Kraus. "We found that very few cheetahs are livestock-catching animals," she says. "A predator would much rather have its own game." Cheetahs need the inducement to chase brought on by their prey's "flee" reaction. Though domestic livestock does not act like wild game, all predators are opportunistic. Marker-Kraus explains that if a calf or lamb happens to be at the right place at the right time, a cheetah will go after it.

19   CCF continues to wage a campaign to show locals there is enough room for everyone to make a living off the land—both cheetah and rancher. "We want ranchers to make a good living and in the process the cheetah will live," Marker-Kraus says. With CCF's help, Namibian ranchers are changing old habits.

Classification of measures, effects that followed

20   Simple measures, such as breeding cows within a few days of one another to ensure a short calving season, have helped cut losses from predators. Another successful strategy is protecting the herd with guard donkeys, which, like zebras, aggressively chase cheetahs. One rancher told CCF that in the eight years he had been using donkeys, he had lost only one calf to predators. Before donkeys, he had lost 32 calves in one year. Where cheetah did prey on sheep and goats, CCF has provided free Turkish Anatolian shepherds as guard dogs, and losses in many flocks have since been eliminated. Ranchers are now on a waiting list for these canines, reflecting CCF's progress.

Comparison

Illustration

21   "He belongs to the sheep. He thinks he is a sheep," comments Badie Badenhorst, one of the 28 sheep ranchers with a guard dog. "He is always with them. We have no trouble with any predators." When just two months old, his dog Danie was put out with the sheep to imprint on the flock. He has since had little contact with humans and will faithfully protect his flock to the death, warding off hyenas, jackals, baboons, and the occasional cheetah.

Effect

22   After five years, CCF's efforts are paying off. Though ranchers have not packed away their cheetah traps, when they have trapped a cat now, they are more likely to pick up the phone and call CCF rather than kill it. More and more ranchers are becoming participants helping CCF in its fieldwork.

Step in process

Cause and effect

23   **5. Find a way to make ideals pay off.** One of the brightest hopes for cheetahs is actually the result of adversity. With the growing pains following the country's recent emancipation from South Africa and the stress of a long series of droughts, many ranchers have had to reduce their livestock and reevaluate their livelihoods. Some of them are choosing to test the newest concept of land use in Namibia, called land conservancies.

Definition

Effect

24   Conservancies, consisting of adjoining ranches that pool resources to manage livestock and wildlife for maximum sustainability, offer ranchers a way to improve profits through ecotourism and ranching. Schneider-Waterberg and the CCF are partners in such a conservancy, pooling Elands Joy's 7,300 hectares and Schneider-Waterberg's 50,000-plus hectares along with six other farms to create the 130,000-hectare Waterberg Conservancy.

25   "You can use your land without eradicating the predators," says Schneider-Waterberg, "whether consumptive, as in trophy hunting, or nonconsumptive, as in ecotourism." Though the Conservancy's goals do not exactly mirror CCF's, trophy hunting allows ranchers to make some money out of wildlife, so they have a vested interest in preserving the cheetah. "I very much believe in the concept 'if it pays, it stays' in conservation," says this rancher-turned-conservationist. "You want to look at the whole picture, what to preserve, what to cull. That is where research comes in and why I work with CCF, in order to know something more about what is happening on my land."

	Effect

26   During a CCF team's tag-and-release of a brown hyena on Schneider-Waterberg's ranch, he accompanies the crew. "Harry and I were dreaming on the drive," says Marker-Kraus as she gets out of his pickup truck. Schneider-Waterberg's plans are big. He sees his farm changing: "The goats will go; the sheep will go; over time the cattle will be reduced if not altogether removed. I have even started a seeding program for waterfowl," says this land baron, whose ranch is big even by Namibian standards. What will be left is basically wildlife and his dream of making a living out of it, a radical change in a country whose beef products are 87 percent of the country's agricultural income.

27   Since 90 percent of cheetahs are found on the 2,500 commercial ranches covering almost half of the country, alliances like the Waterberg Conservancy will play an increasingly important role in wildlife and habitat conservation. More cheetahs are found on commercial ranches than even in national parks, where competition from lions, hyenas, and other predators that eat their cubs and steal their kills keeps cheetah populations in check. "This is the first place for the cheetah and the most important piece of land, because ranchers will allow them to live here," says Marker-Kraus about the Waterberg Conservancy.

28   *6. Prime the next generation.* The idea of conservancies is exciting, and clearly winning over ranchers is critical in conserving cheetahs, but Marker-Kraus knows that if you really want to preserve cheetahs in the long run, you have to win over the ranchers' children. So the CCF team goes into local schools with its "cheetah-in-a-box"—props of skins and pictures. Wearing a spotted cheetah belt, Marker-Kraus and her crew of volunteers enthusiastically explain to rooms full of Namibian schoolchildren that their cheetah is in trouble. So far, the CCF's programs have already reached some 35,000 students.

	Step in process

	Causes and effects

29   Marker-Kraus tells the story of one 12-year-old boy who had attended a CCF school assembly program. When a cheetah was caught outside his father's sheep pen, the boy explained to his father that cheetahs are endangered and told him not to kill it and to call CCF. Thanks to that boy, the cheetah was saved. In gratitude, CCF honored the boy and also gave the parents a livestock-guarding dog.

	Illustration
	Effect

30   "A lot of people say the cheetah is doomed to genetic extinction," says Marker-Kraus. "It is not. It has survived 10,000 years with its genetic problems. It is doomed to humans." This oldest of all the big cats survived the mass extinction that occurred around the Pleistocene Epoch. Having survived the ravages of nature, the cheetah is now poised on the brink of extinction due to human interference. Here in Namibia, CCF is brokering a peace that everyone can live with. After years of animosity and thousands of casualties, this cease-fire holds real promise for the hunted and hunter to co-exist. The cheetah and rancher have more in common than either realizes—they are both dependent on an unforgiving environment and ultimately bonded to one another.

	Argument

	Conclusion: expresses hope for survival of cheetahs

DISCUSSION QUESTIONS

1. Discuss the effectiveness of Zimmerman's title.
2. Why, in paragraph 1, do you think Zimmerman holds back the identity of the patients until the last three words of the paragraph?
3. Discuss Zimmerman's writing style.
4. What other endangered animals have drawn your attention? What efforts are being made to save them?

TOWARD KEY INSIGHTS

What do you think motivates someone like Marker-Kraus to devote a lifetime to protecting an endangered animal like the cheetah?

Would you devote your life to a similar cause? Why or why not?

SUGGESTION FOR WRITING

Write an essay that explains your own or someone else's efforts to pursue a worthwhile cause. Develop your paper with an appropriate mixture of writing strategies.

DEBORAH A. SULLIVAN

Social Bodies: Tightening the Bonds of Beauty

Deborah A. Sullivan teaches sociology at Arizona State University. She is the coauthor of Labor Pains: Modern Midwives and Home Birth, *in addition to a number of articles. The selection here is taken from the first chapter of her book* Cosmetic Surgery: The Cutting Edge of Commercial Medicine in America. *In this section she examines the reasons for and changing meanings of tattooing.*

1   Every culture has some customs that prescribe deliberately changing a body's natural appearance (Brain 1979). The methods, however, are diverse and particular to a culture at a specific period of time. Paints, for example, are used to decorate bodies in many cultures, but the pigments, patterns, permanency, and purpose of each culture's body customs vary widely. Only a nine-teenth-century Bedouin woman could appreciate the eroticism of painting the whites of a man's eyes blue. While she would have regarded her own culture's customs as highly "civilized," she probably would have thought the full body de-signs of Aboriginal Australians, American Indians, and Africans savage. Like

eighteenth-century European explorers, she might have considered the tattooing and tooth-blackening in the Pacific region bizarre, and found the deeply carved black spirals and curves on Maori faces frightening and repulsive. It is no more likely that she could have discerned the beauty intended by the African and South American tribes who create elaborate patterns of raised scars, insert large lip plates and ear and nose plugs, and file teeth to sharp points. Nor is it likely that she could have appreciated the charm of Chinese women's bound "lotus" feet, Padaung women's elongated necks, or Western women's constricted waists during the Victorian era and augmented breasts in recent decades. Instead, in the implausible circumstance that a nineteenth-century Bedouin woman was exposed to such body customs, she probably would have regarded them as barbaric mutilations, much as contemporary Americans' view of female circumcision, which she might have considered normal.

2   The diversity of body customs has led anthropologists (e.g., Douglas 1970; Strathern 1996) to conclude that a body is both a physical and a symbolic artifact, forged by nature and by culture at a particular moment in history. Social institutions, ideology, values, beliefs, and technology transform a physical body into a social body. The resulting social body bears the imprint of the more powerful elements of its cultural context. Bodies, therefore, provide important clues to the mechanics of society.

3   There are many well-documented examples of the cultural construction of a social body. Although some body customs may be merely decorative, many, if not most, have social significance. Cultures in which female circumcision is common are strongly patriarchal and pronatalist. Women in these traditional cultures are believed to be weak and incapable of controlling their sexual urges. They are allowed little contact with men outside their families and are expected to hide their bodies from public view. Their social roles are circumscribed to child care and domestic functions. They receive little education and are economically dependent on men and politically powerless. They are socialized by their mothers to believe that removal of external female genitalia is a religious obligation that promotes purity, cleanliness, and fertility and that unexcised women are unattractive and beastly. Their identities as desirable women depend on the submission of their physical bodies to the dictates of social norms. The custom embodies their inferior status.

4   As female circumcision illustrates, the body can be a site for the expression of power in a culture. It also is used to communicate group membership, individual status, and social identity, along with associated beliefs and values. The body is often ritually modified in connection with major life transitions. In the Australian Aboriginal culture, for example, one or two front teeth are removed at puberty. Some time later boys are painted white, secluded, and circumcised to symbolize their passage into the world of men. At the end of the ceremony, they are painted red to celebrate their reentry into society as young men with all the corresponding rights and expectations of their new status. In some tribes young men undergo a subincision ceremony in which their urethra is split open before they marry and assume full adult male rights. Rites of passage between life stages in many other cultures are marked by ritualized patterns of scarification, piercing, and tattooing. These same techniques are used to proclaim more permanent kinds of social status, such as gender and social class, as are head molding and other body modifications.

5   Using the body to communicate power, group membership, individual status, and social identity is not limited to exotic non-Western societies. It is ubiquitous in modern societies as well. American sailors, prisoners, bikers, and

other gang members have tattooed their bodies throughout most of the twentieth century. Clinton Sanders (1989) argues that they use this particular body custom, considered vulgar by most middle-class, middle-aged Americans, to proclaim their resistance to conventional social norms of appearance and behavior. Their preference for death symbols, predatory animals, insulting and salacious images further enhances their rebellious statement.

6   After the mid-1960s the shock value of tattoos made them popular among some younger artistic individuals looking for attention and innovative, creative modes of expression. By the 1980s they were de rigueur among heavy metal and rap performers seeking a following among adolescents and young adults based on flaunting the conventional values and beliefs of their parents and other authority figures. Punks, freaks, Goths, skinheads, stoners, tweakers, and other disaffected young adults who identified with the counterculture heroes of their generation went to shops with names like Hierarchy, Crawling Squid, and Pigments of Imagination to record their sense of alienation on their bodies.

7   The meaning of tattoos changed in the 1990s. They became a badge of youth. Professional athletes, middle-class college students, blue-collar workers, and even some suburban housewives marked their bodies with tribal patterns, Kanji lettering, and sexy butterflies and flowers. As the shock value of tattoos declined, the most alienated subgroups added other forms of body modifications to advertise their contempt for middle-class conventions. They pierced their ears, noses, eyebrows, lips, tongues, nipples, navels, and genitalia with safety pins, barbells, studs, and various rings. These cultural pioneers established Internet news groups to share information about techniques, complications, public reaction, and erotic effects. Pop singers and other media celebrities adopted less extreme versions of this new body custom to advertise their hip identity. High school girls turned nose studs and navel rings into a fashion statement, undermining their deviance value. Those seeking a body symbol of resistance capable of generating strong public revulsion experimented with more extreme forms of self-stigmatization, such as scalp implants and scarification, to proclaim their marginalized status.

8   Tattooing and piercing at the end of the twentieth century appear to have much in common with previous fashion fads that visually differentiated each young generation over the course of the twentieth century, although some cultural observers (e.g., Polhemus and Randall 1996) find deeper meaning in these trends. They suggest the practices express a yearning for continuity, community, and commitment in a fragmented postmodern culture where ritual is rare and anomie prevails. Tattooing and piercing offer more permanent ways of recording life transitions and one's place in society.

9   All body customs, whether temporary, like tweezing eyebrows and clipping nose hair, or more permanent, like tattoos and cosmetic surgery, are forms of self-creation. They are an effort to achieve a desired identity and connection with a reference group—marginal, hip, or mainstream. The process of reincarnation is universal.

10   Kim Hewitt (1997) additionally argues that body customs, particularly painful ones, can be used as part of a self-chosen health ritual. She theorizes that the physiological effects of pain can stimulate at least a temporary reprieve from numbing feelings of alienation (118). The acute awareness of feeling alive induced by pain has the potential to replace psychological fragmentation with holistic integration and a euphoric feeling of self-mastery. She claims that young women who starve and cut their bodies, like the punks and other marginalized subgroups who customize their bodies in extreme ways, are not only rebelling against societal constrictions, they also are trying to reclaim control of their bodies and establish individuality and autonomy. Other body customs,

including female bodybuilding (Heywood 1998) and cosmetic surgery (Davis 1995), have been similarly interpreted as methods of psychological healing and cultural empowerment.

11   Those with a more Foucauldian perspective, such as Susan Bordo (1993, 1997), argue that such "disciplinary" body customs are outward manifestations of internalized cultural oppression. The discipline comes from an awareness of prevailing values, beliefs, norms and voluntary self-surveillance. Consequently, the sense of power experienced by disciplining one's own body, whether to resist prevailing cultural dictates with tattoos and piercings or successfully conform to them with diets and cosmetic surgery, is merely a personal achievement that lacks political effect to change the culture. Instead, as Rosemary Gillespie (1996) points out, customs such as cosmetic surgery perpetuate wider social inequalities.

12   This debate raises perennial philosophical questions about the nature of social control and the extent of free will. It also raises contemporary concerns that interpreting personal behavior as victimization deprives individuals of agency and castes them as gullible cultural dupes. My own perspective is similar to that of Bordo. Respect for the right of competent adults to make decisions about their own bodies should not blind us to the impact of the larger cultural and social context in which personal choices occur. My aim is to bring the structural aspects of this context, aspects that construct cosmetic surgery, into sharper focus. This larger cultural and social context influences individual body choices, gives them social meaning, and makes some, like cosmetic surgery, common enough to be considered body customs.

Works Cited

Brain, Robert. The Decorated Body. London: Hutchinson, 1979.

Bardo, Susan. *Unbearable Weight: Feminism, Western Culture, and the Body*. Berkeley: U of California Press, 1993.

Bordo, Susan. "Braveheart, Babe, and the Body: Contemporary Images of the Body." In *Twilight Zone: The Hidden Life of Cultural Images from Plato to O.J.*, ed. Susan Bordo. Berkeley: U of California Press, 1997.

Davis, Kathy. *Reshaping the Female Body: The Dilemma of Cosmetic Surgery*. New York: Routledge, 1995.

Douglas, Mary. *Natural Symbols: Explorations in Cosmology*. New York: Pantheon, 1970.

Gillespie, Rosemary. 1996. "Women, the Body, and Brand Extension in Medicine: Cosmetic Surgery and the Paradox of Choice." *Women and Health* 24: 69–85.

Hewitt, Kim. *Mutilating the Body: Identity in Blood and Ink*. Bowling Green, Ohio: Bowling Green State U Popular Press, 1997.

Heywood, Leslie. 1998. *Bodymakers: A Cultural Anatomy of Women's Body Building*. New Brunswick, NJ: Rutgers U Press.

Polhemus, Ted, and Housk Randall. *The Customized Body*. New York: Serpent's Tale, 1996.

Sanders, Clinton. *Customizing the Body: The Art and Culture of Tatooing*. Philadelphia: Temple UP, 1989.

Strathern, Andrew. 1996. *Body Thoughts*. Ann Arbor: Michigan Press.

DISCUSSION QUESTIONS

1. Identify the author's thesis statement. Explain as fully as possible what the author means by the thesis statement.
2. What are the advantages of the author's using many examples of body modification? How does that help make her point?
3. In the introduction, the author starts by describing the possible reaction of a nineteenth-century Bedouin woman to a variety of body modifications. What are the effects of this approach?
4. Why does the author discuss the changing meaning of tattooing?
5. This selection not only illustrates the author's thesis but does so by specifying possible causes for body modification. Identify the causes the author discusses. Do those that apply to modern tattooing seem correct to you?
6. This section from a chapter of a book draws on a variety of sources and is extensively documented. What effect does this have on the essay?
7. In the conclusion of this selection, the author raises a number of broader questions. What role do these questions play given that this selection is part of the first chapter of a book? Are they effective here where they are serving as a conclusion?

TOWARD KEY INSIGHTS

Tattooing, piercing, and scarification are increasingly common practices. What reasons do you see for these practices?

Are those who participate in such practices "cultural dupes" who blindly follow cultural expectations or free individuals who make personal choices?

SUGGESTION FOR WRITING

Write a paper that illustrates a cultural practice that you think is significant, such as the crucial role of music in the life of many college students and teens.

DEBORAH TANNEN

Gender Gap in Cyberspace[1]

Deborah Tannen (born 1945) earned a B.S. degree from the State University of New York in 1966 and a Ph.D. from the University of California in 1979. She is now a member of

---

[1]Deborah Tannen, "Gender Gap in Cyberspace." From *Newsweek,* April 16, 1994. Newsweek, Inc. All rights reserved. Reprinted by permission.

the linguistics department of Georgetown University. Tannen has authored a number of books on speaking and writing as well as numerous shorter pieces that have appeared in the New York Times, Newsweek, People, *and the* Harvard Business Review. *In this selection, Tannen investigates the causes and effects of the differing male and female attitudes toward e-mail.*

1   I was a computer pioneer, but I'm still something of a novice. That paradox is telling.

2   I was the second person on my block to get a computer. The first was my colleague Ralph. It was 1980. Ralph got a Radio Shack TRS-80, I got a used Apple II+. He helped me get started and went on to become a maven, reading computer magazines, hungering for the new technology he read about, and buying and mastering it as quickly as he could afford. I hung on to old equipment far too long because I dislike giving up what I'm used to, fear making the wrong decision about what to buy, and resent the time it takes to install and learn a new system.

3   My first Apple came with videogames; I gave them away. Playing games on the computer didn't interest me. If I had free time I'd spend it talking on the telephone to friends.

4   Ralph got hooked. His wife was often annoyed by the hours he spent at his computer and the money he spent upgrading it. My marriage had no such strains—until I discovered E-mail. Then I got hooked. E-mail draws me the same way the phone does: it's a souped-up conversation.

5   E-mail deepened my friendship with Ralph. Though his office was next to mine, we rarely had extended conversations because he is shy. Face to face he mumbled so, I could barely tell he was speaking. But when we both got on E-mail, I started receiving long, self-revealing messages: we poured our hearts out to each other. A friend discovered that E-mail opened up that kind of communication with her father. He would never talk much on the phone (as her mother would), but they have become close since they both got online.

6   Why, I wondered, would some men find it easier to open up on E-mail? It's a combination of the technology (which they enjoy) and the obliqueness of the written word, just as many men will reveal feelings in dribs and drabs while riding in the car or doing something, which they'd never talk about sitting face to face. It's too intense, too bearing-down on them, and once you start you have to keep going. With a computer in between, it's safer.

7   It was on E-mail, in fact, that I described to Ralph how boys in groups often struggle to get the upper hand whereas girls tend to maintain an appearance of cooperation. And he pointed out that this explained why boys are more likely to be captivated by computers than girls are. Boys are typically motivated by a social structure that says if you don't dominate you will be dominated. Computers, by their nature, balk; you type a perfectly appropriate command and it refuses to do what it should. Many boys and men are incited by this defiance: "I'm going to whip this into line and teach it who's boss! I'll get it to do what I say!" (and if they work hard enough, they always can). Girls and women are more likely to respond, "This thing won't cooperate. Get it away from me!"

8   Although no one wants to think of herself as "typical"—how much nicer to be *sui generis*—my relationship to my computer is—gulp—fairly typical for a woman. Most women (with plenty of exceptions) aren't excited by tinkering with the technology, grappling with the challenge of eliminating bugs or getting the biggest and best computer. These dynamics appeal to many men's interest

in making sure they're on the top side of the inevitable who's-up-who's-down struggle that life is for them. E-mail appeals to my view of life as a contest for connections to others. When I see that I have fifteen messages, I feel loved.

9   I once posted a technical question on a computer network for linguists and was flooded with long dispositions, some pages long. I was staggered by the generosity and the expertise, but wondered where these guys found the time—and why all the answers I got were from men.

10   Like coed classrooms and meetings, discussions on E-mail networks tend to be dominated by male voices, unless they're specifically women-only, like single-sex schools. Online, women don't have to worry about getting the floor (you just send a message when you feel like it), but, according to linguists Susan Herring and Laurel Sutton, who have studied this, they have the usual problems of having their messages ignored or attacked. The anonymity of public networks frees a small number of men to send long, vituperative, sarcastic messages that many other men either can tolerate or actually enjoy, but that turn most women off.

11   The anonymity of networks leads to another sad part of the E-mail story: there are men who deluge women with questions about their appearance and invitations to sex. On college campuses, as soon as women students log on, they are bombarded by references to sex, like going to work and finding pornographic posters adorning the walls.

12   Most women want one thing from a computer—to work. This is significant counterevidence to the claim that men want to focus on information while women are interested in rapport. That claim I found was most often true in casual conversation, in which there is no particular information to be conveyed. But with computers, it is often women who are more focused on information, because they don't respond to the challenge of getting equipment to submit.

13   Once I had learned the basics, my interest in computers waned. I use it to write books (though I never mastered having it do bibliographies or tables of contents) and write checks (but not balance my checkbook). Much as I'd like to use it to do more, I begrudge the time it would take to learn.

14   Ralph's computer expertise costs him a lot of time. Chivalry requires that he rescue novices in need, and he is called upon by damsel novices far more often than knaves. More men would rather study the instruction booklet than ask directions, as it were, from another person. "When I do help men," Ralph wrote (on E-mail, of course), "they want to be more involved. I once installed a hard drive for a guy, and he wanted to be there with me, wielding the screwdriver and giving his own advice where he could." Women, he finds, usually are not interested in what he's doing; they just want him to get the computer to the point where they can do what they want.

15   Which pretty much explains how I managed to be a pioneer without becoming an expert.

DISCUSSION QUESTIONS

1. Does Tannen deal with causes, effects, or both? Refer to the essay when answering.
2. Characterize the level of diction in this essay.
3. Why do you think Tannen cites the two linguists in paragraph 10?
4. Point out the connecting devices that link the paragraphs in this essay.

5. What additional strategies does Tannen use?
6. Does your experience in cyberspace bear out Tannen's assertion about a gender gap? Discuss, citing specific examples.

Toward Key Insights

How do you account for the differences that Tannen describes? Do you believe that they are inborn or stem mainly from cultural patterns?
What steps might be taken to lessen these differences?

Suggestion for Writing

Write an essay exploring how gender affects dating done through the Internet. Support your essay with relevant, specific details.

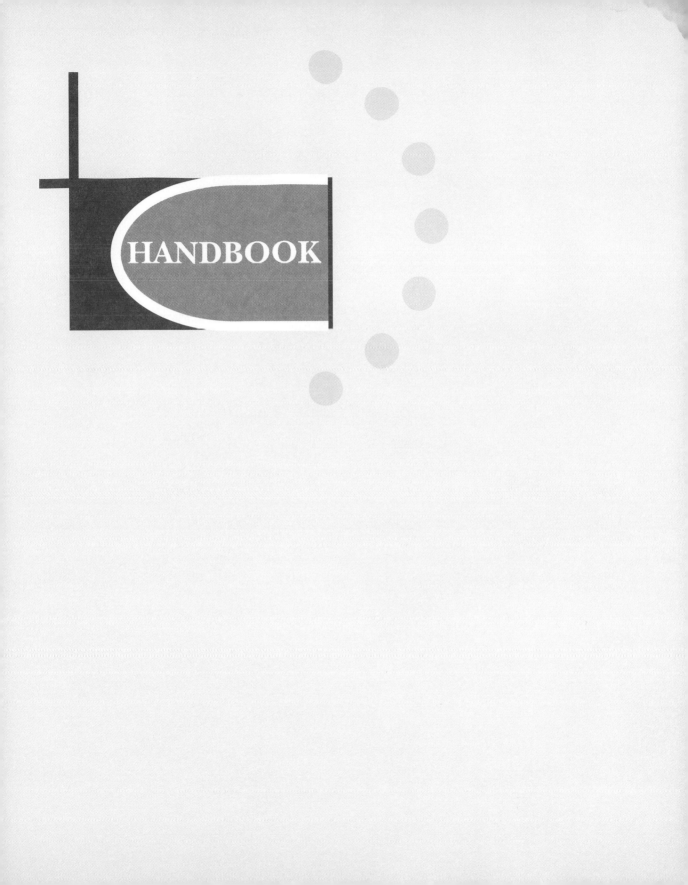

HANDBOOK

HANDBOOK

SENTENCE ELEMENTS

Learning the parts of English sentences won't in itself improve your writing, but it will equip you to handle errors at the sentence level. Before you can identify and correct unwarranted shifts from past to present time, for example, you need to know about verbs and their tenses. Similarly, recognizing and correcting pronoun case errors require a knowledge of what pronouns are and how they are used. In this section we first cover subjects and predicates, then complements, appositives, and the parts of speech, and finally phrases and clauses.

Subjects and Predicates

The subject of a sentence tells who or what it is about. A *simple subject* consists of a noun (that is, a naming word) or a noun substitute. A *complete subject* consists of a simple subject plus any words that limit or describe it.

The predicate tells something about the subject and completes the thought of the sentence. A *simple predicate* consists of one or more verbs (words that show action or existence); a *complete predicate* includes any associated words also. In the following examples the simple subjects are underlined once and the simple predicates twice. The subjects and predicates are separated with slash marks.

William/laughed.

Mary/has moved.

Sarah/painted the kitchen.

The student over there in the corner/is majoring in art.

sent

Complex subjects can be very long; it is helpful to be able to pick the simple subject out of a complex subject.

The <u>storms</u> in March, which dropped a record rain fall in a one week time, <u>resulted</u> in fierce floods.

A sentence can have a compound subject (two or more separate subjects), a compound predicate (two or more separate predicates), or both.

The <u>elephants</u> and their <u>trainer</u>/<u>bowed</u> to the audience and <u>left</u> the ring.

Sentences that ask questions don't follow the usual simple subject–simple predicate order. Instead, the word order may be changed slightly.

When questions use forms of the verb *be* (*is, am, are*), the verb appears before the subject while the rest of the predicate still follows the subject.

> *Is*/<u>Angela</u>/ *an experienced mountain climber?*

When the sentences include auxiliary, or helping, verbs, the auxiliary is moved in front of subject while the rest of the predicate remains in the same place.

> *Has*/<u>a package</u>/ *arrived yet for me?*

Sometimes a question word such as *when, why, who,* and *where* appears in front of the sentence with the helping verb.

> *When will*/<u>we</u>/ *be allowed to park on campus?*

Sometimes certain types of phrases and clauses can fall between the subject and the predicate. These should not be confused with the subject. They are usually easy to detect since they can be moved elsewhere in the sentence. The subject is underlined.

<u>My dog</u>/, *since he has gotten old,* simply lies around the house.

<u>My dog</u>/ simply lies around the house *since he has gotten old.*

Sometimes a phrase that is not part of the subject can introduce the sentence. This phrase can also usually be moved.

After we have repaired the rock wall,/<u>we</u>/will begin to plant the new flowers.

<u>We</u>/will begin to plant the new flowers *after we have repaired the rock wall.*

Usage Considerations   Because subjects are such important sentence elements, think carefully about each one you write so that your sentences won't be vague or misleading. Read the example below:

Our government has failed to enact a national value-added tax.

This statement can be expressed more precisely:

Congress has failed to enact a national value-added tax.

The *President* has vetoed the proposed national value-added tax.

Paying close attention to subjects lets you present your ideas more accurately and clearly.

◁EXERCISE *Place a slash mark between the complete subject and the complete predicate; then underline the simple subject once and the verb(s) twice. If a subject comes between an auxiliary verb and the main verb, set it off with two slash marks. If a phrase that is not the subject comes between the subject and the predicate, set it off with two slash marks.*

1. Boston is one of my favorite cities.
2. My brother built a barn for his horses.
3. The cup of coffee on the counter is mine.
4. Do you know how to design a Web page?
5. The driver of the pickup truck backed into my car and then sped away.
6. The psychology final, though it was very long, was not very hard.
7. Bulimia and anorexia are disorders that affect too many young women.
8. If you plan to make a purchase using the Internet, you should make sure that the site is secure.
9. Where can visitors to the campus park their cars?
10. The advice that we scorned in our youth may seem like wisdom in our old age.   ◀

Complements

A complement is a word or word group that forms part of the predicate and helps complete the meaning of the sentence. Anything that comes after the verb is usually a complement. There are many kinds of complement, including phrases and clauses that will be reviewed later in this chapter.

- I think *that Copland was the quintessential American composer.*
- Robert hesitated *to trap the ground hog behind his house.*
- We were late *because our car would not start.*

Four common complements of traditional grammar are direct objects, indirect objects, subject complements, and object complements.

A *direct object* names whatever receives, or results from, the action of a verb.

The millwright repaired the *lathe.* (Direct object receives action of verb *repaired.*)

Hilary painted a *picture.* (Direct object results from action of verb *painted.*)

They took *coffee* and *sandwiches* to the picnic. (Direct objects receive action of verb *took.*)

An *indirect object* identifies someone or something that receives whatever is named by the direct object.

Doris lent *me* her calculator. (Indirect object *me* receives *calculator,* the direct object.)

Will and Al bought their *boat* new sails. (Indirect object *boat* receives *sails,* the direct object.)

An indirect object can be converted to a prepositional phrase that begins with *to* or *for* and follows the direct object.

Doris lent her calculator *to me.*

Will and Al bought new sails *for their boat.*

A *subject complement* follows a linking verb—one that indicates existence rather than action. It renames or describes the subject.

Desmond is a *carpenter*. (Complement *carpenter* renames subject *Desmond*.)

The lights are too *bright* for Percy. (Complement *bright* describes subject *lights*.)

An *object complement* follows a direct object and renames or describes it.

The council named Donna *treasurer*. (Object complement *treasurer* renames direct object *Donna*.)

The audience thought the play *silly*. (Object complement *silly* describes direct object *play*.)

If a word is an object complement, you can form a short test sentence using *is*.

Donna is *treasurer*.

The play is *silly*.

Usage Considerations   Like subjects, direct objects can be revised for greater precision, as these examples show:

John sent *a gift*.

John sent *a giant coloring book as a birthday gift*.

Often, you can carry the revision one step further by adding an indirect object, subject complement, or other complement to the sentence.

John sent his *niece* a giant coloring book as a birthday gift. (Indirect object added.)

Appositives

An appositive is a noun or word group serving as a noun that follows another noun or noun substitute and expands its meaning. Appositives may be restrictive or nonrestrictive. Restrictive appositives distinguish whatever they modify from other items in the same class. They are written without commas.

My sister *Heidi* is a professional golfer. (Appositive *Heidi* distinguishes her from other sisters.)

I have just read a book by the novelist *Henry James*. (Appositive *Henry James* distinguishes him from other novelists.)

Nonrestrictive appositives provide more information about whatever they modify. This sort of appositive is set off by a pair of commas except at the end of a sentence; then it is preceded by a single comma.

Anatoly Karpov, *the Russian chess player*, was interviewed on TV. (Appositive names *Karpov's* occupation.)

Todd plans to major in paleontology, *the study of fossils*. (Appositive defines *paleontology*.)

Usage Considerations   When a brief definition is necessary, appositives can help you improve your sentences.

John Cage wrote hundreds of pieces for prepared piano.

John Cage, *a twentieth-century avant-garde composer*, wrote hundreds of pieces for prepared pianos, *instruments with odds and ends stuck between their strings to provide unusual effects.*

Don't, however, clutter your writing with appositives that provide unneeded information; the overload will impede and irritate your reader.

EXERCISE   *Identify each italicized item as a direct object (DO), an indirect object (IO), a subject complement (SC), an object complement (OC), or an appositive (AP).*

1. Will and Allison purchased new furniture for their *apartment*.
2. The critics considered the movie *a masterpiece*.
3. The milk tasted *rancid*.
4. Robert Heinlein, a science fiction *writer*, thought that writers should tell an interesting story.
5. Jasmine completed her research *paper* two weeks ahead of the due date.
6. John sent his wife *candy* and *flowers* for Valentine's Day.
7. Some find bad manners *unacceptable*.
8. My roommate, a terrible *procrastinator*, finally relaxed after he turned in his paper.
9. Mr. Hanley offered *me* a job.
10. Darrel is a fine young *man*. ◄

Parts of Speech

Traditional English grammar classifies words into eight parts of speech: *nouns, pronouns, verbs, adjectives, adverbs, prepositions, conjunctions,* and *interjections.* This section discusses these categories as well as verbals, phrases, and clauses, which also serve as parts of speech.

It is important to recognize that words that may look like one part of speech can function as another part of speech. For example, the verb *swim* can function as a noun. *Swimming* is good for your health. To identify a word as a part of speech is to identify how it functions in a sentence.

Traditional grammar defined nouns as words that name persons, places, things, conditions, ideas, or qualities. Most nouns can take a plural (book, books), possessive (Andy, Andy's), or article (bench, the bench).

Proper Nouns

Some nouns, called *proper nouns,* identify one-of-a-kind items like the following and are commonly capitalized.

France	New Years
Pacific Ocean	North Dakota
Pulitzer Prize	World Series
Spirit of St. Louis	Wyandotte Corporation
Declaration of Independence	Miami-Dade Junior College

Common Nouns

Common nouns name general classes or categories of items. Some common nouns are *abstract* and name a condition, idea, or quality that we can't experience with our five senses. *Abstract nouns* often cannot accept the plural; we cannot usually say we have *envys. Concrete nouns* identify something that we can experience with one or more of our senses and usually have plural forms.

Abstract Nouns	**Concrete Nouns**
arrogance	man
fear	bicycle
liberalism	desk
sickness	cartoon
understanding	smoke

Count and Non-Count Nouns

Most nouns identify things we can count and such nouns usually can take the plural form: *three bananas, a book, two children.* Some nouns, including many abstract nouns, cannot accept a plural: *coffee, water, bread.*

Usage Considerations   Good writing demands precise, potent nouns. If you carefully select your nouns, you can sharpen your message. Ill-chosen nouns, on the other hand, suggest poor thinking. Note how the vague word *freedom* robs the following sentence of any specific meaning:

Our *freedom* needs to be protected.

What did the writer have in mind? Here are a few possibilities:

Our *right to own guns* needs to be protected.

Our *private behavior* needs to be protected.

Our *national sovereignty* needs to be protected.

Even when meaning does not present problems, sentences can be sharpened by careful attention to nouns. Note the greater precision of the second sentence below:

Our *dog* has a savage bite.

Our *pit bull* has a savage bite.

⟨EXERCISE⟩ *Identify the nouns in the following sentences. Indicate if they are proper nouns (PN) or common nouns (CN), count nouns (count) non-count nouns (non-count), or collective nouns (coll). Clearly a noun can belong to more than one category.*

1. Josh downloaded the new song by Rufus Wainwright from the Internet.
2. Americans want to be secure from terrorist attacks without surrendering their fundamental liberties.
3. Students quickly develop an addiction to coffee as they try to survive night-long cram sessions.
4. Our football team had an excellent season even if we didn't make it to a bowl game.
5. Math, especially algebra, is a subject that gives many students a fair amount of difficulty.
6. The water in the Gulf of Mexico can be uncomfortably warm by August.
7. Whether you agree or disagree with the views of the organization, the National Rifle Association has played an important role in the debate over how we should understand the Second Amendment.
8. Our understanding of the human genetic code has exploded in the last decade.
9. As everyone knows, Bill Clinton came from a town called *Hope*.
10. Human cloning is a very disturbing possibility for many citizens. ◄◼

Pronouns

Pronouns are a special class of words that can fit the place of nouns in a sentence and sometimes can be seen as taking the place of a noun in a sentence. Pronouns can help you avoid the awkward repetition of nouns.

Personal Pronouns   Personal pronouns refer to identifiable persons or things. Personal pronouns have different cases. The subjective case is used when the pronoun serves as the subject of the sentence or clause. *I helped Steve.* The objective case is used when the pronoun is the object of a verb or preposition. *Steve helped* **me**. *We spoke about* **him**. The possessive case shows possession or ownership. *That is* **my** *briefcase. My, your, our, and their* always precede nouns, as in *their car. Mine, hers, ours, yours, and theirs* do not precede nouns, as in *That book is mine. His* and *its* may or may not precede nouns.

	Subjective	**Objective**	**Possessive**
Singular			
First person	I	me	my, mine
Second person	you	you	your, yours
Third person	he, she, it	him, her, it	his, her, hers, its
Plural			
First person	we	us	our, ours
Second person	you	you	your, yours
Third person	they	them	their, theirs

Relative Pronouns   A relative pronoun relates a dependent clause—a word group that has a subject and a predicate but cannot function as an independent sentence—to a noun or pronoun, called an antecedent, in the main part of the sentence.

The relative pronouns include the following:

| who | whose | what | whoever | whichever |
| whom | which | that | whomever | whatever |

Who in its various forms refers to people, *which* to things, and *that* to either people or things.

Mary Beth Cartwright, *who* was arrested last week for fraud, was Evansville's "Model Citizen" two years ago. (The antecedent of *who* is *Mary Beth Cartwright.*)

He took the electric razor, *which* needed a new cutting head, to the repair shop. (The antecedent of *which* is *electric razor.*)

David Bullock is someone *whom* we should definitely hire. (The antecedent of *whom* is *someone.*)

Montreal is a city *that* I've always wanted to visit. (The antecedent of *that* is *city.*)

Which typically introduces nonrestrictive clauses, that is, clauses that provide more information about whatever they modify (see page 674).

The palace, *which* was in bad condition a century ago, is finally going to be restored. (Clause adds information about palace.)

That is typically used in other situations, especially to introduce restrictive clauses: those that distinguish the things they modify from others in the same class (see page 675).

The used car *that* I bought last week at Honest Bill's has already broken down twice. (Clause distinguishes writer's used car from others.)

Page 656 explains the use of *who* and *whom.*

Interrogative Pronouns   Interrogative pronouns introduce questions. All of the relative pronouns except *that* also function as interrogative pronouns.

who	which	whoever	whichever
whom	what	whomever	whatever
whose			

What is the matter?

Who asked you?

Whatever do you mean?

When *what, which* and *whose* are followed by nouns, they act as adjectives, not pronouns.

Which movie should we see?

Demonstrative Pronouns   As their name suggests, demonstrative pronouns point things out. There are four such pronouns.

pro

this	these
that	those

This and its plural *these* identify recent or nearby things.

This is the play to see.

These are the times that try men's souls.

That and its plural *those* identify less recent or more distant things.

That is Mary's house across the road.

Those were very good peaches you had for sale last week.

Reflexive and Intensive Pronouns A reflexive pronoun is used when the pronoun refers back to a noun in the same clause. An intensive pronoun lends emphasis to a noun or pronoun. The two sets of pronouns are identical.

myself	herself	ourselves
yourself	itself	yourselves
himself	oneself	themselves

My father cut *himself* while shaving. (reflexive pronoun)

The President *himself* has asked me to undertake this mission. (intensive pronoun)

Don't substitute a reflexive pronoun for a personal pronoun.

Faulty	*Jill* and *myself* are going to a movie.
Revision	*Jill* and *I* are going to a movie.
Faulty	*Give the tickets to John and myself.*
Revision	*Give the tickets to John and me.*

Sometimes you'll hear people say things like "He made it *hisself,*" "They're only fooling *theirself,*" or "They bought *theirselves* sodas." Such forms are nonstandard. Say "himself" and "themselves" instead.

Indefinite Pronouns These pronouns refer to unidentified persons, places, or things. One group of indefinite pronouns consistently acts as pronouns.

anybody	everything	one
anyone	nobody	somebody
anything	no one	someone
everybody	nothing	something
everyone		

A second group may function as either pronouns or adjectives.

all	any	most	few	much
another	each	either	many	neither

Here are some examples:

> *Everyone* is welcome. (indefinite pronoun)
>
> *Many* are called, but *few* are chosen. (indefinite pronouns)
>
> *Many* men but only a *few* women attend the Air Force Academy. (adjectives)

Pages 648–650 discuss indefinite pronouns as antecedents.

Reciprocal Pronouns   The two reciprocal pronouns show an interchange of action between two or more parties. *Each other* is used when two parties interact, *one another* when three or more do.

> Pam and Patty accidentally gave *each other* the same thing for Christmas. (two persons)
>
> The members of the football team joyfully embraced *one another* after their victory. (more than two persons)

Usage Considerations   Many students handle pronouns carelessly, damaging the clarity of their writing. Problems include letting the same pronoun stand for different nouns or using a pronoun where detailed, vivid language would be more effective. The following passage illustrates poor pronoun usage:

> My brother loves fly fishing. He thinks *it* is the only way to spend a summer weekend. In fact, whenever he's off work, he'll do *it*.

Rewritten as follows, the passage has been notably improved:

> My brother loves fly fishing. He thinks that *wading a stream and casting leisurely for trout* is the only way to spend a summer weekend. In fact, whenever he's off work, he *can be found up to his hips in water, offering his hand-tied flies to the waiting rainbows.*

EXERCISE   *Identify each pronoun in the following sentences and indicate its type (personal, relative, interrogative, demonstrative, reflexive, intensive, indefinite, reciprocal). If it is a personal pronoun, indicate if it is in the subjective (S), objective (O), or possessive (P) case.*

1. Anyone who wants to be successful needs to be able to use the Internet.
2. John helped himself to my copy of *The Canterbury Tales.*
3. Which fraternity did he say he was considering joining?
4. The black Subaru that is parked at the back of the lot is mine.
5. This is the kind of day that I really enjoy.
6. The president himself will teach one of the classes in political science.
7. We will all be more likely to succeed as writers if we help each other by offering our honest responses to drafts.
8. We greatly appreciate the kindness that you have shown our daughter.
9. Despite his bad back, Brian offered to help us move.
10. The prospect for manned space flights to Mars and Venus, which looked so promising in the 70s, became increasingly less likely until today they seem only a remote possibility.

Verbs

A verb indicates action or existence. Main verbs fall into two classes: *action verbs* and *linking verbs.* A very different type of verb is the *auxiliary* (or *helping*) verb, which adds specific kinds of meaning to the main verb.

Action Verbs As its name suggests, an action verb expresses action. Some action verbs are transitive, others intransitive. A *transitive* verb has a direct object that receives or results from the action and rounds out the meaning of the sentence.

> The photographer *took* the picture.

Without the direct object, this sentence would not express a complete thought. In contrast, an *intransitive* verb requires no direct object to complete the meaning of the sentence.

> Lee Ann *gasped* loudly.
>
> Little Tommy Tucker *sings* for his supper.

Many action verbs can play both transitive and intransitive roles, depending on the sentences they are used in.

> Kari *rode* her bicycle into town. (transitive verb)
>
> Karl *rode* in the front seat of the car. (intransitive verb)

Linking Verbs A linking verb shows existence or a state of affairs such as taste rather than action. Linking verbs are often followed by subject complements that reflect back on the subject of the sentence.

> Ms. Davis *is* our new director. (Complement *director* renames subject *Ms. Davis.*)
>
> The soup *was* lukewarm. (Complement *lukewarm* describes subject *soup.*)

The most common linking verbs are forms of the verb *to be (is, are, am, was, were, be, being, been.)* Likewise, verbs such as *seem, become, appear, remain, feel, look, smell, sound,* and *taste* function as linking verbs when they do not indicate actual physical action. In such cases, they are followed by adjectives (see pages 623–625). Here is an example:

> Harry looked *angry.*

When such verbs do indicate physical action, they function as action verbs and are followed by adverbs (see pages 626–627).

> Harry looked *angrily* at the referee.

Linking verbs can also be followed by adverb phrases of place or time.

> Your dinner is *on the table* (adverb phrase of place).
>
> The meeting will be *at 8:00* A.M. (adverb phrase of time).

vbs

Auxiliary Verbs   Auxiliary (helping) verbs accompany action or linking verbs and provide information about time, possibility, or obligation, or establish the passive. *Have, be,* and *do* can function as both auxiliary and main verbs.

The auxiliary verbs *have (has, had)* and *be (is, are, was, were)* can provide information about time.

> Carol has repaired your computer.

> Carol is reformatting your hard drive.

The auxiliary verb *do* is inserted to form the negative or a question when there is no other auxiliary.

> Ellen *did* not resign.

> *Did* Ellen resign?

Auxiliary verbs called modals show time, obligation, possibility, or ability: shall, should, will, would, can, could, may, might.

With questions, the auxiliary verb is often moved to the front.

> *Will* Ellen *resign?*

 Identify each verb or auxiliary in the following sentences and indicate whether it is a main verb (MV) or auxiliary (AUX).

1. An explosion rocked the apartment building and scattered debris in all directions.
2. We should be considering ways that we can improve the quality of our lives.
3. Americans have been buying CD players at a tremendous rate.
4. Did you ask Jennifer if she has her digital camera in her backpack?
5. With genetic screening we can identify individuals who are at higher risk for many serious diseases.
6. An espresso doesn't always taste good but it is always an eye-opener.
7. Beethoven's string quartets have stood the test of time as masterpieces that are rivaled only by Bartok's works in the genre.
8. It is almost impossible today to tune an engine yourself without the sophisticated computer equipment found in auto shops.
9. Advertisements can be an art form when they are created with imagination and aesthetic vision.
10. If yesterday's wildest dreams are today's reality, will today's wildest dreams be tomorrow's reality?

Usage Considerations   Energetic writing requires precise verbs. Don't take verbs for granted; revise them as necessary to strengthen a sentence. Note the improved precision of the second example.

> I *gave* the maître d' a ten-dollar bill.

> I *slipped* the maître d' a ten-dollar bill.

Tense   Verbs change in form to show distinctions in time. Every main verb has two basic tenses: present and past.

The *present tense* shows present condition and general or habitual action, indicates permanent truths, tells about past events in the historical present, and sometimes denotes action at some definite future time.

Verbs in the present tense must agree with their subjects. If the subject of a verb is a singular noun or pronoun (*he, she, it*), add *s* or *es* (if the word ends with an *s* or *ch* sound, as in *talks* or *teaches*). If the subject is plural or a second-person pronoun (*you*), the verb takes no ending (*talk, teach*).

Helen *looks* beautiful in her new gown. (present condition)

John *works* on the eighteenth floor. (general action)

I *brush* my teeth each morning. (habitual action)

The earth *rotates* on its axis. (permanent truth)

On November 11, 1918, the guns *fall* silent, and World War I *comes* to an end. (historical present)

Monday, I *begin* my new job. (future action)

The past tense shows that a condition existed or an action was completed in the past. This verb tense leaves the time indefinite, but surrounding words may specify it. Most verbs are regular and form the past tense by adding *-ed: talk, talked.* Some verbs are irregular and form the past by changing the vowel: *stand, stood.* A very few verbs do not change forms at all in creating the past: *set, set.*

Paul *was* angry with his noisy neighbors. (past condition, time indefinite)

Sandy *received* a long letter yesterday. (past action, time specified by *yesterday*)

Past Participle   In addition to the basic tenses, there is a *past participle* form of the main verb that is used to form the perfect form of the verb phrase and the passive voice. For most verbs, the past participle form is identical with the past tense in form.

Present	**Past**	**Past Participle**
talk	talk**ed**	talk**ed**
stand	sto**o**d	sto**o**d
set	set	set

Some verbs have different past forms and past participles. This can often lead to errors where less experienced writers often use the regular past (*He has* **swam** *this river before*) when the past participle form is required (*he has* **swum** *this river before*). Below is a table of many but not all of the irregular verbs for your reference.

Present Infinitive	**Past**	**Past Participle**	**Present Infinitive**	**Past**	**Past Participle**
arise	arose	arisen	blow	blew	blown
be	was, were	been	break	broke	broken
become	became	become	choose	chose	chosen
bite	bit	bitten	come	came	come

vbs

Present Infinitive	Past	Past Participle	Present Infinitive	Past	Past Participle
do	did	done	grow	grew	grown
draw	drew	drawn	hide	hid	hidden
drink	drank	drunk	know	knew	known
drive	drove	driven	ride	rode	riden
eat	ate	eaten	see	saw	seen
fall	fell	fallen	shake	shook	shaken
fly	flew	flown	slay	slew	slain
freeze	froze	frozen	speak	spoke	spoken
get	got	gotten	spring	sprang	sprung
give	gave	given	write	wrote	written

Time and Verb Forms

In addition to the tenses in English, many other forms of the verb express time.

Future Time   *Future time* is frequently indicated by the auxiliary modals *shall* or *will* with the present tense form of the verb.

> You *will feel* better after a good night's sleep. (future condition)

> I *shall attend* the concert next week. (future action)

Perfect Verb Forms   The perfect form of a verb is formed by a form of the auxiliary verb *have* and the past participle of the verb.

The *present perfect* tense is formed with *has* or *have* and the past participle of the main verb. It shows that a past condition or action, or its effect, continues until the present time.

> The players *have been* irritable since they lost the homecoming game. (Condition continues until present.)

> Juanita *has driven* a United Parcel Service truck for five years. (Action continues until present.)

> William *has repaired* the snow blower. (Effect of action continues until present although the action itself was completed in the past.)

The *past perfect* tense combines *had* and the past participle of the main verb. It refers to a past condition or action that was completed before another past condition or action.

> He *had been* in the army two years when the war ended. (Past perfect condition occurred first.)

> Vivian moved into the house that she *had built* the summer before. (Past perfect action occurred first.)

The *future perfect* tense is formed from the verbs *shall have* or *will have* plus the past participle of the main verb. It shows that a condition or an action will have been completed at some time in the future. Surrounding words specify time.

Our sales manager *will have been* with the company ten years next July. (Condition will end.)

By the end of this year, I *shall have written* the great American novel. (Action will be completed.)

Progressive Verb Forms Each verb form, including the basic tenses, has a *progressive form* that indicates action in progress. The progressive is always indicated by some form of the verb *to be* followed by a present participle (or progressive), a verb that ends in *-ing.*

Present progressive	I am running.
Past progressive	I was running.
Future progressive	I will be running.
Present perfect progressive	I have been running.
Past perfect progressive	I had been running.
Future perfect progressive	I will have been running.

Pages 658–660 discuss unwarranted shifts in tense and their correction.

An easy way to identify the form of the verb phrase is to use the following formula.

(modal) + (have + en/ed) + (be + ing) + main verb
             Perfect   *Progressive*

Simply read the first available tense. If the modal is *will* then that designates future time. Then if *have, has, or had* is present, the verb phrase is *perfect.* If a form of *be* is present and the main verb ends with *ing,* then the verb phrase is progressive.

will	*have*	*been*	*living*
Future	Perfect	Progressive	

Usage While most students use regular tenses and the progressive accurately, many less experienced writers do not always use the perfect verb form where appropriate. This is acceptable in informal writing; it is not acceptable for most formal writing.

Not acceptable Jim *studied* accounting for the last three years. (This suggests that the action is over and done with.)

Acceptable Jim *has studied* accounting for the last three years. (The present perfect verb form shows that the action comes right up to the present and may not be finished yet.)

Voice Transitive verbs have two voices: active and passive. A verb is in the *active voice* when the subject carries out the action named by the verb.

Barry *planned* a picnic. (Subject *Barry* performs action.)

A verb is in the *passive voice* when the subject receives the action. The performer may be identified in an accompanying phrase or go unmentioned.

vbs

A picnic *was planned* by Barry. (The phrase *by Barry* identifies the performer.)

The picnic *was canceled*. (The performer goes unmentioned.)

A passive construction always uses a form of *to be* and the past participle of an action verb. Like other constructions, the passive may show past, present, or future time.

Amy *is paid* handsomely for her investment advice. (present tense)

I *was warned* by a sound truck that a tornado was nearby. (past tense)

I *will be sent* to Ghana soon by the Peace Corps. (future tense)

I *have been awarded* a sizable research grant. (present perfect tense)

The city *had been shelled* heavily before the infantry moved in. (past perfect tense)

By the end of this month, the site for our second factory *will have been chosen*. (future perfect tense)

To convert a sentence from the passive to the active voice, make the performer the subject, the original subject the direct object, and drop the form of *to be*.

The treaty *was signed* by the general. (passive)

The general *signed* the treaty. (active)

Technical and scientific writing commonly uses the passive voice to explain processes since its flat, impersonal tone adds an air of scientific objectivity and authority. Other kinds of writing, however, avoid the passive voice except when it is desirable to conceal the one performing the action or when the action is more significant than the actor. See pages 238–240 for more information on usage.

 EXERCISE   *Identify each verb group in the following sentences, indicate its form (present, past, future, present perfect, past perfect, future perfect, and any of the progressive forms), and note any use of the passive voice.*

1. Devon broke his leg when he was thrown from his horse.
2. Deidra has managed our money for the last several years.
3. The Chicago Symphony is performing Mahler's *Resurrection Symphony*.
4. We will have completed the repairs on your computer by next Friday.
5. John finally bought the used BMW convertible that he had coveted for the past year.
6. Computers will be placed in every classroom as soon as the funds are available.
7. Maria has been acting in Shakespeare plays every summer since she first moved to Michigan.
8. At last the ceiling in the McCracken Building has been repaired.
9. The faculty had been consulted before the new attendance policy was implemented.
10. The future will bring many surprising changes. ◼

Mood   The mood of a verb shows whether the writer regards a statement as a

1. fact
2. command or request
3. wish, possibility, condition contrary to fact, or the like.

English has three moods: the indicative, imperative, and subjunctive.

A sentence in the *indicative mood* states a real or supposed fact or asks a question.

> Nancy *graduates* from high school tomorrow.

> We *lived* in Oakmont when Rachel was born.

> He *had been* a sailor during the war.

> *Has* Joe *asked* anyone to the prom yet?

Most verbs are used in the indicative mood.

A sentence in the *imperative mood* delivers a command or makes a request.

> *Leave* the room immediately! (command)

> Please *turn* the CD player down. (request)

The subject of a sentence in the imperative mood is always *you*. Although ordinarily unstated, the subject sometimes appears in the sentence.

> *You* leave the room immediately!

The *subjunctive mood* is used

1. in *if, as if,* and *as though* clauses to express a wish, a possibility, or an action or a condition contrary to fact
2. in *that* clauses expressing orders, demands, requests, resolutions, proposals, or motions
3. with modal auxiliaries to express wishes, probability, possibility, permission, requirements, recommendations, suggestions, and conditions contrary to fact.

To express a present or future wish, possibility, condition or action in an *if, as if,* or *as though* clause, use *were* with any personal pronoun or noun serving as the subject of the clause.

> If only Stan *were* less gullible! (present wish contrary to fact)

> Even if Kay *were* to explain, Mary wouldn't believe her. (future possibility)

> Arthur is behaving as if he *were* a millionaire (present condition contrary to fact)

To express a wish, possibility, or condition contrary to past facts, use *had been* or *had* plus the past participle of an action verb.

> If the engine *had been lubricated,* the bearing wouldn't have burned out. (past condition contrary to fact)

> Alice looked as if she *had lost* her best friend. (condition expressed in clause occurs before action of verb *looked*)

vbs

When writing *that* clauses expressing orders, demands, requests, resolutions, proposals, or motions, use *be* or the present plural form of an action verb.

I move that they *be* rewarded for their bravery.

The group proposed that Margaret *go* to the scene of the accident and *inspect* it personally.

In other *that* clauses, use the appropriate indicative form of the verb.

I know that they *were* rewarded for their bravery.

The group believed that Margaret *had gone* to the scene of the accident and *inspected* it personally.

The modal auxiliaries include the helping verbs *can, could, may, might, must, shall, will, would, should,* and *ought to.* The examples below illustrate the meanings they can express.

1. Wishes *(could, would)*

   I wish I *could* shimmy like my sister Kate.
   The Republicans wish the Democrats *would* go away and vice versa.

2. Probability *(should)*

   Because I've studied diligently, I *should* do better on my next chemistry test.

3. Possibility *(may, might, can, could)*

   Low inflation *could* cause our stock market to soar.
   I *might* stay up to watch the eclipse of the moon tonight.

4. Permission *(can, may)*

   The public *can* use these tennis courts every afternoon.
   You *may* leave as soon as you've finished filing these folders.

5. Requirements *(must)*

   The landlord has raised our rent again; we *must* find another apartment.

6. Recommendations, suggestions *(should, ought to)*

   Randy *should* see a doctor about his chest pains.
   All of us *ought to* exercise regularly.

7. Conditions contrary to fact *(could)*

   If only I *could* live my life over!

EXERCISE *For each of the following sentences, identify the mood as indicative (IND), imperative (IMP), or subjunctive (SUB):*

1. See your doctor before starting a strenuous exercise program.
2. The tired runner staggered across the finish line.
3. These new cell phones should prove very popular.
4. Let me know what you think of this novel.
5. Hang gliding is a great sport for anyone unafraid of heights.
6. If you practiced more, you could become an outstanding pianist.
7. The latest unemployment figures should help calm inflation fears.

8. Stop talking right now or leave the class.
9. This movie could have been shortened by fifteen minutes without harming the story.
10. Who wants to play Scrabble this evening? ◄

Adjectives

An adjective *modifies* a noun or pronoun by describing it, limiting it, or otherwise making its meaning more exact.

> The *brass* candlestick stood next to the *fragile* vase. (*Brass* modifies *candlestick,* and *fragile* modifies *vase.*)

> The cat is *long-haired* and *sleek.* (*Long-haired* and *sleek* modify *cat.*)

There are three general categories of adjectives: limiting, descriptive, and proper.

Limiting Adjectives   A limiting adjective identifies or points out the noun or pronoun it modifies. It may indicate number or quantity. Several categories of pronouns can serve as limiting adjectives, as can numbers and nouns.

> *Whose* briefcase is on the table? (interrogative adjective)

> The couple *whose* car was stolen called the police. (relative adjective)

> *This* restaurant has the best reputation for gourmet food. (demonstrative adjective)

> *Some* people have no social tact at all. (indefinite adjective)

> Sally swerved *her* car suddenly to avoid an oncoming truck. (possessive adjective)

> *Three* people entered the lecture hall late. (number as adjective)

> The *schoolgirl* look is fashionable this year. (noun as adjective)

Descriptive Adjectives   A descriptive adjective names a quality, characteristic, or condition of a noun or pronoun. Two or more of these adjectives, members of the largest category of adjectives, may modify the same noun or pronoun.

> The *yellow* submarine belongs to the Beatles.

> He applied *clear* lacquer to the tabletop.

> The *slim, sophisticated* model glided onto the runway.

> The child was *active, happy,* and *polite.*

Proper Adjectives   A proper adjective is derived from a proper noun and is always capitalized.

> Harwell is a *Shakespearean* actor.

Articles as Adjectives   Articles appear immediately before nouns and can therefore be considered adjectives. There are three articles in English: *a, an,*

adj

and *the. The* points to a specific item; *a* and *an* do not. *A* precedes words beginning with consonant sounds; *an* precedes words with vowel sounds, making pronunciation easier.

> *The* right word at *the* right moment can save a friendship. (Definite articles suggest there is one right word and one right moment.)

> *A* right word can save a friendship. (Indefinite article suggests there are several right words.)

> I think I'd like *an* apple with my lunch. (No particular apple is specified.)

Sometimes the definite article refers to a class of items.

> *The* tiger is fast becoming an endangered species.

Context shows whether such a sentence refers to particular items or entire classes.

Comparison with Adjectives   Adjectives can be used to show comparison. When two things are compared, shorter adjectives usually add *-er* and longer adjectives add *more*. When three or more things are compared, shorter adjectives usually add *-est* and longer ones add *most*.

> John is *taller* than Pete. (short adjective comparing two things)

> Sandra seems *more cheerful* than Jill today. (long adjective comparing two things)

> John is the *tallest* of the three brothers. (short adjective comparing three things)

> Sandra is the *most cheerful* girl in the class. (longer adjective comparing more than three things)

Some adjectives, like the examples below, have irregular forms for comparisons.

> good—better—best

> bad—worse—worst

Don't use the *-est* form of the shorter adjective to compare just two things.

> *Faulty* This is the *smallest* of the two castles.

Instead, use the *-er* form.

> *Revision* This is the *smaller* of the two castles.

Position of Adjectives   Most adjectives come immediately before the words they modify. In a few set expressions (for example, heir *apparent*), the adjective immediately follows the word it modifies. Similarly, adjective pairs sometimes appear in a follow-up position for added emphasis (The rapids, *swift* and *dangerous,* soon capsized the raft). Sometimes adjectives also serve as subject complements and follow their subjects (The puppy was *friendly*).

Usage Considerations   Some students overuse adjectives, especially in descriptions, but most underuse them. Review your sentences carefully to see where adding or cutting adjectives can increase the impact of your writing.

My Buick is the talk of my friends.

My *old, dilapidated, rusty, fenderless 1970* Buick is the talk of my friends.

My *rusty, fenderless 1970* Buick is the talk of my friends.

The first sentence lacks adjectives that show why the car is discussed. The second sentence overcorrects this fault by including two adjectives that repeat the information provided by the others. The final sentence strikes the proper balance.

Determiners   There is a category of words that are sometimes classified with adjectives that limit the noun or pronoun but do not name a quality or characteristic of the noun or pronoun.

Three sailboats raced around the island.

While we know how many sailboats are involved, there is no descriptive content added to the concept of sailboats.

There are many different kinds of determiners.

Determiners	**Name**
a, an	Indefinite article
the	Definite article
this, that, these, those	Demonstrative
one, two, three, four, five	Cardinal number
first, second, third, fourth	Ordinal number
my, our, your, his, her, hers, its, their	Possessive pronoun
some, any, no, every, another, enough, either, neither, all, both, each, less, other, many, more, most, few, several	Indefinite pronoun
Tom's, Mary's	Possessive noun

With the indefinite article a/an, *A* precedes words beginning with consonant sounds; *an* precedes words with a vowel sound to make pronunciation easier.

EXERCISE   *Identify the adjectives and determiners in the following sentences.*

1. The climbers seemed very tiny as they rappelled down the sheer cliff.
2. Janine's paper offered an insightful and well-supported argument.
3. Fresh grapefruit juice can be a tart but tasty breakfast beverage.
4. In some Medieval cathedrals there were statues representing the seven deadly sins.
5. Many expeditions to climb Mt. Everest were defeated more by the inhospitable environment than by the actual challenges of the climb.

6. A good educational environment can be made better by smaller classes.
7. After the chilly air conditioning in the restaurant, Christy was grateful to step out into the warm, damp summer air.
8. Cody's sleek new convertible looked ready to fly around tight corners.
9. The black Focus seemed to pulse with the loud, heavy beat of the rock music.
10. Many Canadian writers are better known than most American critics would like to admit. ◄

Adverbs

An adverb modifies a verb, an adjective, another adverb, or a whole sentence. Adverbs generally answer questions such as "How?" "When?" "Where?" "How often?" and "To what extent?"

> The floodwaters receded *very* slowly. (Adverb modifies adverb and answers the question "How?")

> My sister will visit me *tomorrow.* (Adverb modifies verb and answers the question "When?")

> The coach walked *away* from the bench. (Adverb modifies verb and answers the question "Where?")

> The tire is *too* worn to be safe. (Adverb modifies adjective and answers the question "To what extent?")

> The teller is *frequently* late for work. (Adverb modifies adjective and answers the question "How often?")

> *Unfortunately,* the game was canceled because of rain. (The adverb modifies the whole sentence but does not answer any question.)

Formation of Adverbs   Most adverbs are formed by adding *-ly* to adjectives.

> The wind is *restless.* (*Restless* is an adjective modifying *wind.*)

> He walked *restlessly* around the room. (*Restlessly* is an adverb modifying *walked.*)

> Many common adverbs, however *(almost, never, quite, soon, then, there,* and *too),* lack *-ly* endings.

> I *soon* realized that pleasing my boss was impossible.

> This movie is *too* gruesome for my taste.

Furthermore, some words such as *better, early, late, hard, little, near, only, straight,* and *wrong* do double duty as either adjectives or adverbs.

> We must have taken a *wrong* turn. (*Wrong* is an adjective modifying the noun *turn.*)

> Where did I go *wrong?* (*Wrong* is an adverb modifying the verb *go.*)

Comparison with Adverbs   Like adjectives, adverbs can show comparison. When two things are compared, adverbs add *more*. When three or more things are compared, *most* is used.

> Harold works *more* efficiently than Don. (adverb comparing two people)

> Of all the people in the shop, Harold works the *most* efficiently. (adverb comparing more than two people)

Some adverbs, like some adjectives, use irregular forms for comparisons.

> well—better—best

> much—more—most

Position of Adverbs   Adverbs are more movable than any other part of speech. Usually, adverbs that modify adjectives and other adverbs appear next to them to avoid confusion.

> Her *especially* fine tact makes her a welcome guest at any party. (Adverb *especially* modifies adjective *fine*.)

> The novel was *very* badly written. (Adverb *very* modifies adverb *badly*.)

Adverbs that modify verbs, however, can often be shifted around in their sentences without causing changes in meaning.

> *Quickly*, he slipped through the doorway.

> He slipped *quickly* through the doorway.

> He slipped through the doorway *quickly*.

Usage Considerations   You can often sharpen the meaning of a sentence by adding a well-chosen adverb.

> The student squirmed in his chair.

> The student squirmed *anxiously* in his chair.

Including the adverb *anxiously* in the second sentence shows the mental state of the student.

Be careful, however, not to overuse adverbs because they can bog down your writing.

> EXERCISE   *Identify the adverbs in the following sentences:*

1. Three friends slowly but steadily hiked up the mountain trail.
2. Everyone agreed that it was too hot to mow the lawn.
3. While the screenplay was exceptionally well written, the movie itself was poorly directed and badly miscast.
4. The violins entered too early but no one but the conductor really noticed.
5. We should meet tomorrow to plan our camping trip.
6. Some people are strangely attracted to unusually dangerous activities.
7. The two planes came nearer to each other than anyone would like.

8. Few people compete more fiercely than Phillip.
9. Gradually but persistently erosion will wear away a mountain.
10. Ms. Draco patiently explained to the class how they could approach the assignment more imaginatively. ◄

Prepositions

A preposition links its object—a noun or noun substitute—to some other word in the sentence and shows a relationship between them. The relationship is often one of location, time, means, or reason or purpose. The word group containing the preposition and its object makes up a prepositional phrase.

The new insulation *in* the attic keeps my house much warmer now. (Preposition *in* links object *attic* to *insulation* and shows location.)

We have postponed the meeting *until* tomorrow. (Preposition *until* links object *tomorrow* to *postponed* and shows time.)

The tourists traveled *by* automobile. (Preposition *by* links object *automobile* to *traveled* and shows means.)

Warren swims *for* exercise. (Preposition *for* links object *exercise* to *swims* and shows reason or purpose.)

The following list includes the most common prepositions, some of which consist of two or more words:

above	before	except	on
about	behind	for	onto
across	below	from	out of
after	beside	in	over
against	between	instead of	since
along with	by	into	through
among	by reason of	like	to
around	contrary to	near	toward
at	down	next to	under
because of	during	of	with
			without

Many of these combine to form additional prepositions: *except for, in front of, by way of, on top of,* and the like.

Some words that are usually used as prepositions such as *up, on,* and *in* can also function as a different part of speech called a *verb particle.* Here are two examples.

The instructor let Jeff make *up* the test.

The officer turned *in* his best friend.

The verb particle is closely associated with the verb and is a part of its meaning. If a word is a verb particle, it can usually be moved after the noun.

The instructor let Jeff make the test *up.*

The officer turned his best friend *in.*

Usage Considerations   It is easy to use a small group of prepositions over and over in your writing. This habit often results in imprecise or misleading sentences. To avoid this problem, think carefully about your choice of prepositions as you revise. Read the following example:

He walked *by* the railroad tracks on his way home.

Note that two interpretations are possible.

He walked *along* the railroad tracks on his way home.

He walked *past* the railroad tracks on his way home.

Clearly you would use the preposition that conveys your intended meaning.

EXERCISE   *Identify the prepositions (P) and their objects (O) in the following sentences:*

 1. Angela searched her house for a book of poems by Rilke.
 2. Dave and Silvia traveled across America on a motorcycle.
 3. Because of the hurricane, the causeway from the Florida Keys was closed.
 4. Contrary to everyone's expectation, Barry decided to go into advertising instead of theater.
 5. Before her first class, Carrie likes to swim twenty-five laps in the school's pool.
 6. The two boys hid for several hours in the woods behind their house.
 7. In his paper on cloning, James cut through the confusion about the topic and clearly presented the arguments for each side of the issue.
 8. Almost out of gas, Janine's car raced across the finish line in first place.
 9. A good listener sometimes needs to hear the message behind the words.
10. I always hated it when trapeze artists flew through the air without a net beneath them.

Conjunctions

Conjunctions serve as connectors, linking parts of sentences or whole sentences. These connectors fall into three groups: coordinating conjunctions, subordinating conjunctions, and conjunctive adverbs.

Coordinating Conjunctions   Coordinating conjunctions connect terms of equal grammatical importance: words, word groups, and simple sentences. These conjunctions can occur singly (*and, but, or, nor, for, yet, so*) or in pairs called correlative conjunctions (*either—or, neither—nor, both—and,* and *not only—but also*). The elements that follow correlative conjunctions must be parallel, that is, have the same grammatical form.

Tom *and* his cousin are opening a video arcade. (Coordinating conjunction connects nouns.)

Shall I serve the tea in the living room *or* on the veranda? (Coordinating conjunction connects phrases.)

I am going to Europe this summer, *but* Marjorie is staying home. (Coordinating conjunction connects simple sentences.)

Amy *not only* teaches English *but also* writes novels. (Correlative conjunctions connect parallel predicates.)

You can study nursing *either* at Ferris State University *or* at DeWitt College. (Correlative conjunctions connect parallel phrases.)

Friendship is *both* pleasure *and* pain. (Correlative conjunctions connect parallel nouns.)

Subordinating Conjunctions   Like relative pronouns, subordinating conjunctions introduce subordinate clauses, relating them to independent clauses, which can stand alone as complete sentences. Examples of subordinating conjunctions include *because, as if, even though, since, so that, whereas,* and *whenever* (see page 000 for a more comprehensive list).

I enjoyed the TV program *because* it was so well acted. (Conjunction connects *it was so well acted* to rest of sentence.)

Whenever you're ready, we can begin dinner. (Conjunction connects *you're ready* to rest of sentence.)

Conjunctive Adverbs   These connectors resemble both conjunctions and adverbs. Like conjunctions, they serve as linking devices between elements of equal rank. Like adverbs, they function as modifiers, showing such things as similarity, contrast, result or effect, addition, emphasis, time, and example.

The job will require you to travel a great deal; *however,* the salary is excellent.

Sean cares nothing for clothes; *in fact,* all of his socks have holes in their toes. The following list groups the most common conjunctive adverbs according to function:

Similarity: likewise, similarly

Contrast: however, nevertheless, on the contrary, on the other hand, otherwise

Result or effect: accordingly, as a result, consequently, hence, therefore, thus

Addition: also, furthermore, in addition, in the first place, moreover

Emphasis or clarity: in fact, in other words, indeed, that is

Time: afterward, later, meanwhile, subsequently

Example: for example, for instance, to illustrate

Conjunctive adverbs should not be confused with coordinating conjunctions. Unlike conjunctions and more like adverbs, conjunctive adverbs can move, often to create a specific emphasis.

The job will require you to travel a great deal; the salary, *however,* is excellent.

The job will require you to travel a great deal; *however,* the salary is excellent.

Sean cares nothing for clothes; all of his socks, *in fact,* have holes in their toes.

Sean cares nothing for clothes; *in fact,* all of his socks have holes in them.

Because conjunctive adverbs can move, the second independent clause must be treated as a complete sentence and either be joined to the previous independent clause with a semicolon or be separated by a period.

Usage Considerations You can add variety and precision to your writing by varying the conjunctions you use. If you consistently rely on the conjunction *because,* try substituting *as* or *since.* Likewise, you may periodically replace *if* with *provided that.* The right conjunction shows the realtionship among ideas.

When you have choppy sentences, try combining them by using a conjunction.

> You can buy smoked salmon at Sally's Seafoods. You can buy it at Daane's Thriftland as well.

> You can buy smoked salmon *either* at Sally's Seafoods *or* at Daane's Thriftland.

The revision is much smoother than the original sentence pair.

Interjections

An interjection is an exclamatory word used to gain attention or to express strong feeling. It has no grammatical connection to the rest of the sentence. An interjection is followed by an exclamation point or a comma.

> *Hey!* Watch how you're driving! (strong interjection)

> *Oh,* is the party over already? (mild interjection)

EXERCISE *Identify the coordinating conjunctions (CC), subordinating conjunctions (SC), conjunctive adverbs (CA), and interjections (I) in the following sentences:*

1. There is evidence that the polar ice caps are receding; however, scientists do not yet know the probable impact of this event.
2. Neither term limits nor campaign reform will take money out of politics.
3. Since there has been an increase in the alligator population, some lawmakers think the ban on alligator hide products should be lifted.
4. Rats! My computer ate my report.
5. Most companies work hard to secure their Internet sites, but hackers can usually find their way around these safeguards.
6. Extensive resources have been committed to the war on drugs; nevertheless, illegal narcotics continue to flow into this country.
7. After Barbara got the promotion, she took all her co-workers out to celebrate.
8. Basketball and racquetball are both excellent aerobic activities.
9. You can either enjoy a brisk game of tennis or relax in the hot tub.
10. Most people like to snack while they watch television.

Phrases and Clauses

Phrases

A phrase is a group of words that lacks a subject and a predicate and serves as a single part of speech. This section discusses four basic kinds of phrase: *prepositional, phr*

participial, gerund, and *infinitive.* The last three are based on participles, gerunds, and infinitives, verb forms known as verbals. A fifth type of phrase, the verb phrase, consists of sets of two or more verbs (*has fixed, had been sick, will have been selected,* and the like).

Prepositional Phrases   A prepositional phrase consists of a preposition, one or more objects, and any associated words. These phrases serve as adjectives or adverbs.

> The picture *over the mantel* was my mother's. (prepositional phrase as adjective)

> He bought ice skates *for himself.* (prepositional phrase as adverb modifying verb)

> The toddler was afraid *of the dog.* (prepositional phrase as adverb modifying adjective)

> Our visitors arrived late *in the day.* (prepositional phrase as adverb modifying another adverb)

Frequently, prepositional phrases occur in series. Sometimes they form chains in which each phrase modifies the object of the preceding phrase. At other times some or all of the phrases may modify the verb or verb phrase.

> John works *in a clothing store / on Main Street / during the summer.*

Here the first and third phrases serve as adverbs modifying the verb *works* and answering the questions "Where?" and "When?" while the second phrase serves as an adjective modifying *store* and answering the question "Where?"

On occasion, especially in questions, a preposition may be separated from its object, making the phrase difficult to find.

> Dr. Perry is the person *whom* I've been looking *for.*

> *What* are you shouting *about*?

Participial Phrases   A participial phrase consists of a participle plus associated words. Participles are verb forms that, when used in participial phrases, function as adjectives or adverbs. A present participle ends in *-ing* and indicates an action currently being carried out. A past participle ends in *-ed, -en, -e, -n, -d,* or *-t* and indicates some past action.

> The chef *preparing dinner* trained in France. (present participial phrase as adjective)

> The background, *sketched in lightly,* accented the features of the woman in the painting. (past participial phrase as adjective)

> She left *whistling a jolly melody.* (present participial phrase as adverb)

A perfect participial phrase consists of *having* or *having been* plus a past participle and any associated words. Like a past participial phrase, it indicates a past action.

Having alerted the townspeople about the tornado, the sound truck returned to the city garage. (perfect participial phrase)

Having been alerted to the tornado, the townspeople sought shelter in their basements. (perfect participial phrase)

Some participial phrases that modify persons or things distinguish them from others in the same class. These phrases are written without commas. Other phrases provide more information about the persons or things they modify and are set off with commas. For a further discussion of these usages, see pages 674–675.

The man *fixing my car* is a master mechanic. (Phrase distinguishes man fixing car from others.)

Mr. Welsh, *fatigued by the tennis game,* rested in the shade. (Phrase provides more information about Mr. Welsh.)

Gerund Phrases   A gerund phrase consists of a gerund and the words associated with it. Like present participles, gerunds are verb forms that end in *-ing*. Unlike participles, though, they function as nouns rather than as adjectives or adverbs.

Kathryn's hobby is *collecting stamps.* (gerund phrase as subject complement)

Kathryn's hobby, *collecting stamps,* has made her many friends. (gerund phrase as appositive)

He devoted every spare moment to *overhauling the car.* (gerund phrase as object of preposition.)

Infinitive Phrases   An infinitive phrase consists of the present principal part of a verb preceded by *to* (*to fix, to eat*), together with any accompanying words. These phrases serve as adjectives, adverbs, and nouns.

This looks like a good place *to plant the shrub.* (infinitive phrase as adjective)

Lenore worked *to earn money for college.* (infinitive phrase as adverb)

My goal is *to have my own business some day.* (infinitive phrase as noun)

Gerunds can often be substituted for infinitives and vice versa.

To repair this fender will cost two hundred dollars. (infinitive phrase as subject)

Repairing this fender will cost two hundred dollars. (gerund phrase as subject)

At times the *to* in an infinitive is omitted following verbs such as *make, dare, let,* and *help.*

Kristin didn't dare *(to) move* a muscle.

The psychiatrist helped me *(to) overcome* my fear of flying.

Verbals Not in Phrases   Participles, gerunds, and infinitives can function as nouns, adjectives, or adverbs, even when they are not parts of phrases.

phr

That *sunbathing* woman is a well-known model. (participle as adjective)

Dancing is fine exercise. (gerund)

The children want *to play.* (infinitive as noun)

If you're looking for a job, Sally is the person *to see.* (infinitive as adjective)

I'm prepared *to resign.* (infinitive as adverb)

Usage Considerations   Phrases can often clarify or develop the information in a sentence or combine choppy sentences.

Original	My brother is fishing.
Revision	My brother is fishing *for trout just below Barnes Dam on Sidewinder Creek.* (prepositional phrases added)
Original	The boat barely made shore.
Revision	The boat, *listing heavily and leaking badly,* barely made shore. (participial phrases added)

To avoid ponderous sentences, don't, however, weigh them down with phrases, as in the following example:

My brother is fishing for trout just below Barnes Dam on Sidewinder Creek *near Perry Pass in the mountains of Central Colorado.*

Testing a Phrase's Function

To determine whether a phrase is functioning as noun, adjective, or adverb, try a substitution test; if a common noun (something, someone, or it), adjective or adjective phrase, or adverb fits, that demonstrates the function of the phrase.

Walking at a brisk pace is excellent exercise. (participial phrase)

Something is excellent exercise. (noun phrase)

I am prepared *to finish the job.* (infinitive phrase)

I am prepared *completely.* (adverb phrase)

He was a man *of unusual craftiness.* (prepositional phrase)

He was a *crafty* man. (adjective phrase)

 Identify the italicized phrases as prepositional, participial, gerund, or infinitive and indicate whether each is used as a noun, an adjective, or an adverb.

1. Sleeping in late can be one of the great pleasures of a holiday.
2. The students waited *for ten minutes* before they left.
3. Racing around the corner, Tim crashed into another student and sent her sprawling.
4. The employees were afraid that there was a plan *to lay off a third of the workforce.*

5. The grass *in the backyard* had grown so long that it was impossible to cut with a lawnmower.
6. The company has decided *to go forward* with the direct marketing campaign.
7. Our guest speaker has written a book about *kayaking around New Zealand.*
8. Most high school students cannot wait *to graduate.*
9. David broke his leg *skiing in Colorado.*
10. We cheered as Joan, *panting with exhaustion,* crossed the finish line. ◀

Clauses

A clause is a word group that includes a subject and a predicate. An *independent clause,* sometimes called a main clause, expresses a complete thought and can function as a simple sentence. A *subordinate clause,* or dependent clause, cannot stand by itself. Subordinate clauses may serve as nouns, adjectives, or adverbs.

Noun Clauses   A noun clause can serve in any of the ways that ordinary nouns can.

What the neighbor told John proved to be incorrect. (noun clause as subject)

The woman asked *when the bus left for Spokane.* (noun clause as direct object)

I'll give a reward to *whoever returns my billfold.* (noun clause as object of preposition *to*)

Noun clauses normally begin with one of the following words:

Relative Pronouns		Interrogative Pronouns
who	whoever	when
whom	whomever	why
whose	that	where
what	whatever	how
which	whichever	whether

The complementizer *that* is sometimes omitted from the beginning of a clause that acts as a direct object.

Dr. Kant thinks *(that) he knows everything.*

If a clause is serving as a noun, you can replace it with the word *something* or *someone,* and the sentence will still make sense.

Dr. Kant thinks *something.*

If the clause is serving as an adjective or an adverb, making the substitution turns the sentence into nonsense.

The person *who wins the lottery* will receive two million dollars.

The person *someone* will receive two million dollars.

Adjective Clauses   Like ordinary adjectives, adjective clauses, often called *relative clauses,* modify nouns and noun substitutes.

cl

Give me one reason *why you feel the way you do.* (Adjective clause modifies noun.)

I'll hire anyone *that Dr. Stone recommends.* (Adjective clause modifies pronoun.)

Generally, adjective clauses begin with one of the following words:

Relative Pronouns	Relative Adverbs
who	when
whom	where
whose	why
what	after
which	before
that	

Sometimes the word that introduces the clause can be omitted.

The chair *(that) we ordered last month* has just arrived. (pronoun *that* omitted but understood)

The man *(whom) we were talking to* is a movie producer. (pronoun *whom* omitted but understood)

Sometimes, too, a preposition comes ahead of the introductory pronoun.

The grace *with which Nelson danced* made the onlookers envious.

An adjective clause may be restrictive and distinguish whatever it modifies from others in the same class, or it may be nonrestrictive and provide more information about whatever it modifies.

Flora wiped up the cereal *that the baby had spilled.* (restrictive clause)

Harriet Thomas, *who was born in Alaska,* now lives in Hawaii. (nonrestrictive clause)

As these examples show, restrictive clauses are not set off with commas, but nonrestrictive clauses are. See pages 674–675 for further information.

Adverb Clauses   These clauses modify verbs, adjectives, adverbs, and sentences, answering the same questions that ordinary adverbs do.

You may go *whenever you wish.* (Adverb clause modifies verb.)

Sandra looked paler *than I had ever seen her look.* (Adverb clause modifies adjective.)

Darryl shouted loudly *so that the rescue party could hear him.* (Adverb clause modifies adverb.)

Unless everyone cooperates, this plan will never succeed. (Adverb clause modifies whole sentence.)

The word or word group that introduces an adverb clause is always a subordinating conjunction. Here are the most common of these conjunctions, grouped according to the questions they answer.

When? after, as, as soon as, before, since, until, when, whenever, while

Where? where, wherever

How? as if, as though

Why? as, because, now that, since, so that

Under what conditions? although, if, once, provided that, though, unless

To what extent? than

Occasionally in an adverb clause, the omission of one or more words won't hurt its meaning. Such a construction is called an *elliptical clause.*

While (he was) making a sandwich, Garth hummed softly. (*he was* omitted but understood)

Unlike noun and adjective clauses, adverb clauses can often be moved about in their sentences.

Garth hummed softly *while (he was) making a sandwich.*

Usage Considerations   Like phrases, clauses can help develop sentences as well as smooth out choppiness.

Original	The old grandfather clock ticked loudly through the night.
Revision	The old grandfather clock *that my great-aunt gave me before she died* ticked loudly through the night. (Clause adds information.)
Original	The chemistry professor insisted on lab safety. He had been hurt in a lab explosion the previous year.
Revision	The chemistry professor, *who had been hurt in a lab explosion the previous year,* insisted on lab safety. (Clause adds smoothness.)

To avoid clumsiness, avoid overloaded sentences like the one below:

The old grandfather clock that my great-aunt gave me before she died *and that I took with me to England when my company transferred me there for two years* ticked loudly through the night.

EXERCISE   *Identify the italicized clauses as noun, adjective, or adverb.*

1. Brad pulled a muscle in his back *while he was lifting weights.*
2. The astronauts *who landed on the moon* should still be household names.
3. Some astronomers suggested *that Pluto should not be considered a planet.*
4. Jody Singleton was touched by the cards *her students sent her.*
5. *Although coffee shops would seem like the quintessential small business,* some companies have turned America's coffee habit into multimillion dollar chains.
6. *Whoever decorated this house* has an excellent eye.
7. Andrea was pleased to find out that her new employer used the kind of accounting software *on which she had been trained.*

8. The Concorde, *which offers supersonic trips across the Atlantic,* has been much less popular than was originally expected.

9. *While she was waiting at the check-in counter of the airport,* Jasmine was able to read two chapters in her history text.

10. Many companies like to go *where the labor costs and taxes are lowest.* ◀

Coordination and Subordination

Coordination and subordination are ways to rank ideas in sentences. Coordination makes ideas equal; subordination makes them unequal. To understand coordination and subordination, you need to know about four kinds of sentences: simple, compound, complex, and compound–complex.

Simple Sentences   A simple sentence has one subject and one predicate. Some simple sentences consist merely of a single noun and a single verb.

> Millicent shouted.

Others include elements such as compound subjects, compound verbs, direct objects, indirect objects, and subject complements.

> Jim and Sue have bought a car. *(compound subject, direct object)*

> Lucretia Borgia smiled and mixed her guests a cocktail. *(compound verb, indirect object, direct object)*

> Autumn is a sad season. *(subject, complement)*

Compound Sentences   A compound sentence contains two or more, independent clauses, each holding the same (coordinate) rank. As a result, the idea in the first clause receives the same emphasis as the idea in the second.

In some cases, a comma and a coordinating conjunction *(and, but, or, nor, for, yet, so)* link successive clauses.

> Name the baby Huey, *or* I'll cut you out of my will.

> The audience was young, friendly, and responsive, *so* it cheered for each speaker.

In others, a semicolon and a conjunctive adverb *(for example, however, in fact, likewise, meanwhile, instead,* and the like) furnish the connection.

> Tod wants to see the play; *in fact,* he's talked about it for weeks.

> Today, many young women do not rush into marriage and motherhood; *instead,* they spend several years establishing careers.

Finally, a writer may omit any connecting word and separate the clauses with a semicolon.

> The sky grew pitch black; the wind died; an ominous quiet hung over the whole city.

> Be sure to read this Hemingway novel; it suggests how to cope gracefully with pressure.

As the preceding sentences show, compound sentences allow writers to express simple relationships among simple ideas. However, such sentences have one important limitation: It is impossible to highlight one particular idea. To do this, we need complex sentences.

Complex Sentences   A complex sentence has one independent clause and one or more dependent clauses. Relegating an idea to a dependent clause shows that the writer wishes it to receive less emphasis than the idea in the main clause. In the following examples the dependent clauses are italicized.

Because the young, friendly audience was responsive, it cheered for each speaker.

After the dance was over, Arthur collapsed on the sofa.

Once they had reached the lakeshore, the campers found a level spot *where they could pitch their tent.*

Unlike compound sentences, complex ones allow writers to vary the emphasis of ideas.

While I watered the grass, I discussed stock options with Liz.

I watered the grass *while I discussed stock options with Liz.*

The first sentence emphasizes the talk with Liz, the second watering the lawn.

Compound–Complex Sentences   This type of sentence features two or more independent clauses and one or more dependent clauses. Here are two examples with the dependent clauses italicized:

Ms. Harris works as an investment manager, and Mr. Williams, *who lives next door to her,* owns a jewelry store.

If you are to communicate properly, your thoughts must be clear and correct; thoughts are wasted *when language is muddled.*

EXERCISE   *Label the independent and dependent clauses in the sentences below. Then identify each sentence as simple, compound, complex, or compound–complex.*

1. A career in broadcasting requires good verbal skills, an extensive wardrobe, and a pleasant smile.
2. Because its bag was too full, the vacuum cleaner backfired, leaving the room dirtier than it had been.
3. Leave your boots in the back hall, please.
4. When Tom arrived home, his roommate asked him where he had really gone; six hours seemed too long a time to spend in the library.
5. My orange tree blossomed last week; however, the grapefruit trees have withered, probably because of the freeze last month.
6. Kites make good gifts for children; even if a child already has a kite, a second one will come in handy if the first one becomes tangled in a tree.

7. It's risky to confide in a co-worker because one can never be sure that the confidence will be kept.

8. I know why he moved here: He likes having the only dental practice in this part of the state.

9. The pencil and the stapler are on the table next to the window in Mr. Brigg's office.

10. Don't add bleach to your load of colored shirts; the colors will fade and the fibers weaken.

EDITING TO CORRECT SENTENCE ERRORS

frag

Accepted usage improves the smoothness of your prose, makes your writing easier to understand, and demonstrates that you are a careful communicator. These assets, in turn, increase the likelihood that the reader will accept your ideas.

When you've finished revising the first draft of a piece of writing, edit it with a critic's eye to ensure that you eliminate errors. Circle sentences or parts of them that are faulty or suspect. Then check your circled items against this section of the Handbook, which deals with the most common errors in college writing.

Revising Sentence Fragments

A sentence fragment is a group of words that fails to qualify as a sentence but is capitalized and punctuated as if it were a sentence. To be a sentence, a word group must (1) have a subject and a verb and (2) make sense by itself. The first of the following examples has a subject and a verb; the second does not. Neither makes sense by itself.

If you want to remain.

His answer to the question.

Methods of Revision Eliminating a sentence fragment is not hard. Careful reading often shows that the fragment goes with the sentence that comes just before or just after it. And sometimes two successive fragments can be joined. Note how we've corrected the fragments (italicized) in the following pairs:

Faulty	*Having been warned about the storm.* We decided to stay home.
Revision	Having been warned about the storm, we decided to stay home.
Faulty	*After eating.* The dog took a nap.
Revision	After eating, the dog took a nap.
Faulty	Sally went to work. *Although she felt sick.*
Revision	Sally went to work although she felt sick.
Faulty	Dave bought a new suit. *Over at Bentley's.*

Revision	Dave bought a new suit over at Bentley's.
Faulty	*That bronze clock on the mantel. Once belonged to my grandmother.*
Revision	That bronze clock on the mantel once belonged to my grand-mother.

frag

Joining a fragment to a sentence or to another fragment works only if the problem is simply one of mispunctuation. If the fragment stems from an improperly developed thought, revise the thought into correct sentence form.

Punctuating Your Corrections   When you join a fragment to the following sentence, you need not place a comma between the two unless the fragment has six or more words or if omitting a comma might cause a misreading. When joining a fragment to the preceding sentence, omit a comma unless there is a distinct pause between the two items. The preceding examples illustrate these points.

Intentional Fragments   Fragments are commonly used in conversation and the writing that reproduces it. Professional writers also use fragments to gain special emphasis or create special effects. Pages 231–232 discuss these applications.

CONNECTED DISCOURSE EXERCISE

Identify and correct the sentence fragments in the following letter:

Dear Phone Company:

Recently I received a phone bill for over $500. While I do use the phone fairly extensively. Most of the calls I make are local ones. In this case, many of the calls on my bill were to other countries. Including a phone call to New Delhi, India. I can hardly be held responsible for these calls. Especially since I don't know anyone who lives overseas. Since the only long-distance call I made was to Kalamazoo, Michigan. I have deducted the charges for all the other long-distance calls from my bill and am sending you the balance. In order to prevent this type of error from happening again. Would you please have a representative determine why these charges appeared on my bill?

Sincerely,

Desperate

 EXERCISE   *Ten main clauses paired with fragments are shown below. In each case identify the sentence (S) and the fragment (F) and then eliminate the fragment.*

1. I would like you to meet Janine Lee. One of my good friends from high school.
2. Jason and Steve bought several posters. To spruce up their dorm room walls.
3. In order to get tickets to the concert. We had to stand in line for hours.

4. After we finish studying for our math test. We plan to go out for pizza.

5. The road to Cedar Lake will be closed for months. Because the flood has washed away the bridge over the Rouge River.

6. Carol bought the new computer. That she had wanted for months.

7. If the debate team lives up to its potential. We are sure to win the state finals.

8. There are several ways for companies to save on energy costs. One of them energy recycling.

9. Kristen first searched the library for information for her report. And then turned to the Internet for additional material.

10. Pleased by the amount of the painting he had already completed. John allowed himself a two-hour break to watch the football game.

Revising Run-On Sentences and Comma Splices

A run-on, or fused, sentence occurs when one sentence runs into another without anything to mark their junction. A comma splice occurs when only a comma marks the junction. These errors lead your readers to think that you are hasty or careless. Here are several examples:

Run-on sentence	Laura failed to set her alarm she was late for work.
Comma splice	Violets are blooming now, my lawn is covered with them.
Run-on sentence	Rick refused to attend the movie he said he hated horror shows.
Comma splice	Perry watched the road carefully, he still missed his turn.
Run-on sentence	Janet worked on her term paper her friend studied for a calculus test.
Comma splice	Janet worked on her term paper, her friend studied for a calculus test.

Testing for Errors   To check out a possible comma splice or fused sentence, read what precedes and follows the comma or suspected junction and see whether the two parts can stand alone as sentences. If *both parts* can stand alone, there is an error. Otherwise, there is not.

Darryl is a real troublemaker, someday he'll find himself in serious difficulty.

Examination of the parts preceding and following the comma shows that each is a complete sentence:

Darryl is a real troublemaker.

Someday he'll find himself in serious difficulty.

The writer has therefore committed a comma splice that needs correction.

Methods of Revision   You can correct run-on sentences and comma splices in several ways.

1. Create two separate sentences.

   Revision   Violets are blooming now. My lawn is covered with them.

   Revision   Rick refused to attend the movie. He said he hated horror shows.

2. Join the sentences with a semicolon.

   Revision   Violets are blooming now; my yard is covered with them.

   Revision   Rick refused to attend the movie; he said he hated horror shows.

3. Join the sentences with a comma and a coordinating conjunction *(and, but, or, nor, for, yet, so)*.

   Revision   Laura failed to set her alarm, *so* she was late for work.

   Revision   Perry watched the road carefully, *but* he still missed his turn.

4. Join the sentences with a semicolon and a conjunctive adverb (see pages 630–631).

   Revision   Laura failed to set her alarm; *consequently,* she was late for work.

   Revision   Violets are blooming now; *in fact,* my yard is covered with them.

5. Introduce one of the sentences with a subordinating conjunction (see pages 630, 636–637).

   Revision   *Because* Laura failed to set her alarm, she was late for work.

   Revision   Janet worked on her term paper *while* her friend studied for a calculus test.

As our examples show, you can often correct an error in several ways.

CONNECTED DISCOURSE EXERCISE

Identify and correct the comma splices and run-on sentences in the following letter:

Dear Desperate:

We are sorry to hear that you are having difficulty paying your bill, it is, however, your responsibility. Unfortunately we have no way to prevent you from making overseas calls, you have to curb your own tendency to reach out and touch your friends. Following your instructions, we are sending a technician to remove your phone. Please be home this Friday morning he will arrive then. Even though we will remove your phone, you are still responsible for the unpaid portion of your bill, it is your financial obligation. We would dislike referring this matter to a collection agency, it could ruin your credit rating.

Sincerely,

Your friendly phone representative

EXERCISE *Indicate whether each item is correct (C), is a run-on sentence (RO), or contains a comma splice (CS) and then correct the faulty items.*

1. Our company's Internet-based sales are up twenty percent; however, our store sales are down thirty percent.
2. Our computer assistants have only had three weeks of training, you cannot expect them to know the answer to every technical question.
3. Ellen worked very hard on her report she really earned her A.
4. The research on the effect of T.V. violence on children remains inconclusive, but still most of us would think that excessive exposure to images of violence would be harmful.
5. Alternative forms of punishment such as home incarceration have proven very effective, nevertheless prison is still the standard punishment for most nonviolent crimes.
6. The photographer accidentally exposed his film to the light as a result all our wedding pictures were ruined.
7. Jason got a terrific tan, he spent the winter break in Florida.
8. While tuberculosis is a terrible disease, it is rare and usually can be treated with antibiotics.
9. Many doctors' offices want to decrease costs they increasingly use physician assistants.
10. We have carefully reviewed your proposal for flexible work hours, we think it would improve employee satisfaction.

Creating Subject–Verb Agreement

A verb should agree in number with its subject. Singular verbs should have singular subjects, and plural verbs should have plural subjects.

Correct   My *boss is* a grouch. (singular subject and verb)

Correct   The *apartments have* two bedrooms. (plural subject and verb)

Ordinarily, matching subjects and verbs causes no problems. The following special situations, however, can create difficulties.

Subject and Verb Separated by a Word Group   Sometimes a word group that includes one or more nouns comes between the subject and the verb. When this happens, match the verb with its subject, not a noun in the word group.

Correct	Our *basket* of sandwiches *is* missing.
Correct	Several *books* required for my paper *are* not in the library.
Correct	*Mr. Schmidt,* along with his daughters, *runs* a furniture store.
Correct	The old *bus,* crammed with passengers, *was* unable to reach the top of the hill.

Two Singular Subjects   Most singular subjects joined by *and* take a plural verb.

Correct	The *couch* and *chair were* upholstered in blue velvet.

Sentences like the one above almost never cause problems. With subjects like *restoring cars* and *racing motorcycles,* however, singular verbs are often mistakenly used.

Faulty	*Restoring cars* and *racing motorcycles consumes* most of Frank's time.
Revision	*Restoring cars* and *racing motorcycles consume* most of Frank's time.

When *each* or *every* precedes the subjects, use a *singular* verb in place of a plural.

Correct	Every *book* and *magazine was* badly water-stained.

Singular subjects joined by *or, either—or,* or *neither—nor* also take singular verbs.

Correct	A *pear* or an *apple is* a good afternoon snack.
Correct	Neither *rain* nor *snow slows* our letter carrier.

Finally, use a singular verb when two singular subjects joined by *and* name the same person, place, or thing.

Correct	My *cousin* and business *partner* is retiring next month.

Cousin and *partner* refer to the same person.

One Singular and One Plural Subject   When one singular subject and one plural subject are joined by *or, either—or,* or *neither—nor,* match the verb with the closer of the two.

Correct	Neither *John* nor his *parents were* at home.
Correct	Neither his *parents* nor *John was* at home.

As these examples show, the sentences are usually smoother when the plural subject follows the singular.

Collective Nouns As Subjects   Collective nouns (*assembly, class, committee, family, herd, majority, tribe,* and the like) are singular in form but stand for groups

sv agr

or collections of people or things. Ordinarily, collective nouns are considered to be singular and therefore take singular verbs.

Correct   The *class* is writing a test.

Correct   The *herd was* clustered around the water hole.

Sometimes, though, a collective noun refers to the separate individuals making up the grouping, and then it requires a plural verb.

Correct   The *jury are* in dispute about the verdict.

Sentences in Which the Verb Comes Ahead of the Subject   Sentences that begin with words such as *here, there, how, what*, and *where* fall into this category. With such sentences, the verb must agree with the subject that follows it.

Correct   Here *is* my *house.*

Correct   Where *are* my *shoes?*

Correct   There *is* just one *way to* solve this problem.

Correct   There *go* my *chances* for a promotion.

CONNECTED DISCOURSE EXERCISE

Identify and correct the subject–verb agreement errors in the following letter:

Regional Accounts Manager:

One of your area phone representatives have seriously misread a letter I submitted with my bill. I refused to pay for long-distance overseas calls since neither I nor my roommate know anyone who lives overseas. Instead of deducting the calls from my bill, she sent someone to remove my phone. Now my phone, along with many of my valuable possessions, have been removed. Unfortunately the technician, whom I allowed into my apartment only after carefully checking his credentials, were a thief. He locked me in a closet and cleared out the apartment. I have called the police, but I also expect the phone company to reimburse me for my losses. There is only two choices. Either the stolen items or a check covering the loss need to be sent to me immediately. Otherwise I am afraid I will be forced to sue. A jury are sure to rule in my favor. In addition, I expect to find that those overseas calls has been deducted from my bill.

Sincerely,

Desperately Desperate

EXERCISE   *Choose the correct verb form from the pair in parentheses.*

1. The library, along with many of the books, (*was, were*) severely damaged by the storm.
2. Congress (*retains, retain*) the right to control the country's purse strings.
3. A house with two baths and four bedrooms (*is, are*) for sale in my neighborhood.
4. What (*does, do*) these new printers cost?
5. A van or three cars (*is, are*) needed to drive the wrestling team to the meet.
6. Each of these suggestions (*has, have*) a lot of merit.
7. John Finch and his assistant (*plans, plan*) to review the contract with you next Friday.
8. There (*is, are*) a few advantages to carefully planning your work schedule.
9. Every piece of clothing and bedding (*has, have*) to be washed in scalding water.
10. Each of our employees (*knows, know*) the answer to the most common questions about our product.

Achieving Pronoun–Antecedent Agreement

The antecedent of a pronoun is the noun or pronoun to which it refers. Just as subjects should agree with their verbs, pronouns should agree with their antecedents: singular antecedents require singular pronouns, and plural antecedents require plural pronouns. Ordinarily, you will have no trouble matching antecedents and pronouns. The situations below, however, can cause problems.

Indefinite Pronouns As Antecedents   Indefinite pronouns include words like *each, either, neither, any, everybody, somebody,* and *nobody.* Whenever an indefinite pronoun is used as an antecedent, the pronoun that refers to it should be singular.

> *Faulty*   *Neither* of the actors had learned *their* lines.
>
> *Revision*   *Neither* of the actors had learned *his* lines.

As the revised example shows, this rule applies even when the pronoun is followed by a plural noun.

When the gender of the antecedent is unknown, you may follow it with *his or her,* or if this results in awkwardness, rewrite the sentence in the plural.

> *Correct*   *Anyone* who has studied *his or her* assignments properly should do well on the test.
>
> *Correct*   *Those* who have studied *their* assignments properly should do well on the test.

Occasionally, a ridiculous result occurs when a singular pronoun refers to an indefinite pronoun that is obviously plural in meaning. When this happens, rewrite the sentence to eliminate the problem.

Faulty	*Everybody* complained that the graduation ceremony had lasted too long, but I didn't believe *him*.
Revision	Everybody complained that the graduation ceremony had lasted too long, but I didn't agree.

Two Singular Antecedents   Two or more antecedents joined by *and* ordinarily call for a plural pronoun.

pa agr

Correct	Her briefcase and umbrella were missing from *their* usual place on the hall table.

When *each* or *every* precedes the antecedent, use a singular pronoun.

Incorrect	Every college and university must do *their* best to provide adequate student counseling.
Correct	Every college and university must do *its* best to provide adequate student counseling.

Singular antecedents joined by *or, either–or,* or *neither–nor* call for singular pronouns.

Correct	Neither Carol nor Irene had paid *her* rent for the month.

Applying this rule can sometimes yield an awkward or foolish sentence. When this happens, rewrite the sentence to avoid the problem.

Faulty	Neither James nor Sally has finished *his or her* term project.
Revision	James and Sally have not finished *their* term projects.

Singular antecedents joined by *and* that refer to the same person, place, or thing use a singular pronoun.

Correct	My *cousin* and business *partner* is retiring to *his* condo in Florida next month.

Singular and Plural Antecedents   If one singular and one plural antecedent are joined by *or, either—or,* or *neither—nor,* the pronoun agrees with the closer one.

Correct	Either Terrence James or the Parkinsons will let us use *his* lawn mower.
Correct	Either the Parkinsons or Terrence James will let us use *his* lawn mower.

Sentences of this sort are generally smoother when the plural subject follows the singular.

Collective Nouns As Antecedents   When a collective noun is considered a single unit, the pronoun that refers to it should be singular.

Correct	The *troop* of scouts made *its* way slowly through the woods.

When the collective noun refers to the separate individuals in the group, use a plural pronoun.

Correct   The *staff* lost *their* jobs when the factory closed.

CONNECTED DISCOURSE EXERCISE

Identify and correct the pronoun–antecedent agreement errors in the following letter:

Dear Desperately Desperate:

We were sorry to hear about the theft from your apartment. Apparently a gang of con artists recently had their base of operations in your city. It posed as repair technicians and presented false credentials to anyone expecting their phone to be repaired. Someone also must have intercepted your mail and written their own response since we have no record of any previous letter from you. Clearly neither the representative you mentioned nor the phony phone technician could have held their position with our company. Every one of our technicians must provide us with their fingerprints and take periodic lie detector tests. Further, none of our representatives will answer correspondence since it is not a part of their job description. For these reasons, we do not believe we are responsible for your losses. However, a review of our records shows that you owe $500; we have included a copy of the bill in case you have misplaced the original.

Sincerely,

Accounts Manager

 EXERCISE   *Choose the right pronoun from the pair in parentheses.*

1. Company rules require every memo and letter to receive (*its, their*) correct authorization number.
2. Neither the Grangers nor Tom Cauldwell knew (*his, their*) lines by opening night.
3. After weeks of deliberation, the jury finally reached (*its, their*) decision.
4. Maria and Tim completed (*his or her, their*) project by the deadline.
5. Either Roderick or Shannon will present (*his or her, their*) personalized invitation to our special sale.
6. Either Sally or the Randalls will lend us (*her, their*) punch bowl for our party.
7. The class rushed into the computer room and took (*his or her, their*) seats.
8. Everybody has been assigned (*his or her, their*) own log-on name and password.
9. Every one of the women in our police force has proved that (*she, they*) can handle the duties of an officer.

10. Either Richard or Frank will be able to offer you (*his, their*) help in planning the science fiction film festival. ◄

Using Effective Pronoun Reference

Any pronoun except an indefinite pronoun should refer to just one noun or noun substitute—its antecedent. Reference problems result when the pronoun has two or more antecedents, a hidden antecedent, or no antecedent. These errors can cause mixups in meaning as well as ridiculous sentences.

pr ref

More Than One Antecedent The following sentences lack clarity because their pronouns have two possible antecedents rather than just one:

Faulty   Take the screens off the windows and wash *them*.

Faulty   Harry told Will that *he* was putting on weight.

The reader can't tell whether the screens or the windows should be washed or who is putting on weight.

Sometimes we see a sentence like this one:

Faulty   If the boys don't eat all the Popsicles, put *them* in the freezer.

In this case, we know it's the Popsicles that should be stored, but the use of *them* creates an amusing sentence.

Correct these faults by replacing the pronoun with a noun or by rephrasing the sentence.

Revision   Wash the windows after you have taken off the screens.

Revision   Take off the screens so that you can wash the windows.

Revision   Harry told Will, "I am (you are) putting on weight."

Revision   Put any uneaten Popsicles in the freezer.

Hidden Antecedent An antecedent is hidden if it takes the form of an adjective rather than a noun.

Faulty   The movie theater is closed today, so we can't see *one*.

Faulty   As I passed the tiger's cage, it lunged at me.

To correct this fault, replace the pronoun with the noun used as an adjective or switch the positions of the pronoun and the noun and make any needed changes in their forms.

Revision   The theater is closed today, so we can't see a movie.

Revision   As I passed its cage, the tiger lunged at me.

No Antecedent A no-antecedent sentence lacks any noun to which the pronoun can refer. Sentences of this sort occur frequently in everyday conversation but should be avoided in formal writing. The examples below illustrate this error:

Faulty   The lecture was boring, but *they* took notes anyway.

Faulty   On the news program, *it* told about a new crisis in the Persian Gulf.

To set matters right, substitute a suitable noun for the pronoun or reword the sentence.

Revision   The lecture was boring, but the students took notes anyway.

Revision   The news program told about a new crisis in the Persian Gulf.

Sometimes *this, that, it,* or *which* will refer to a whole idea rather than a single noun. This usage is acceptable provided the writer's meaning is obvious, as in this example:

Correct   The instructor spoke very softly, *which* meant we had difficulty hearing him.

Problems occur, however, when the reader can't figure out which of two or more ideas the pronoun refers to.

Faulty   Ginny called Sally two hours after the agreed-upon time and postponed their shopping trip one day. *This* irritated Sally very much.

What caused Sally to be irritated—the late call, the postponement of the trip, or both? Again, rewording or adding a clarifying word will correct the problem.

Revision   Ginny called Sally two hours after the agreed-upon time and postponed their shopping trip one day. *This tardiness* irritated Sally very much.

Revision   Ginny called Sally two hours after the agreed-upon time and postponed their shopping trip one day. Ginny's *change of plans* irritated Sally very much.

The first of these examples illustrates the addition of a clarifying word; the second illustrates rewriting.

CONNECTED DISCOURSE EXERCISE

Identify and correct any faulty pronoun references in the following memorandum:

To: Director of Food Services, Groan University

From: Vice-President of College Services

Date: February 19, 20__ __

Subject: Student Complaints about Cafeteria

Complaints about food quality and cafeteria hours are common but easily resolved. They can be extended by simply installing vending machines. It might not make for a nutritious meal, but it certainly will undercut some of the dissatisfaction. Of course, no matter how good the food, they will complain. Still, you can partially defuse those complaints by having students list their major concerns and then meeting them. Of course, you can always increase student satisfaction by purchasing a soft ice cream machine and offering it for dessert.

shft

EXERCISE   *Indicate whether each sentence is correct (C) or contains a faulty pronoun reference (F) and then correct the faulty sentences.*

1. When Al accidentally slammed down on his car's accelerator instead of the brake, it roared forward into the intersection.
2. They have informed me that we have seen a 15 percent increase in sales this month.
3. When the supervisor walked by the water cooler, they stopped talking.
4. I like trout fishing because it is very relaxing.
5. Since I knew that our employees found their chairs uncomfortable, I replaced them with new ones.
6. In the report, it suggested that we needed to be more attentive to employee suggestions.
7. Because the batting cap hurt his head, Fred removed it.
8. Frank told his best friend that his wife wanted to spend more time with him.
9. At Electronic City, they sell many brands of computers.
10. Janine asked Caroline if she could rewrite her paper for her English class. ◀

Managing Shifts in Person

Pronouns can be in the first person, second person, or third person. *First-person* pronouns identify people who are talking or writing about themselves, *second-person* pronouns identify people being addressed directly, and *third-person* pronouns identify persons or things that are being written or spoken about. The following table sorts pronouns according to person:

First Person	Second Person	Third Person
I	you	he
me	your	she
my	yours	it
mine	yourself	his
we	yourselves	her
us		hers
our		its
ours		one
ourselves		they
		their
		theirs
		indefinite pronouns

shft

All nouns are in the third person. As you revise, be alert for unwarranted shifts from one person to another.

> *Faulty*   I liked *my* British vacation better than *my* vacation in France and Italy because *you* didn't have language problems.
>
> *Revision*   I liked *my* British vacation better than *my* vacation in France and Italy because *I* didn't have language problems.
>
> *Faulty*   Holidays are important to *everyone.* They boost *your* spirits and provide a break from *our* daily routine.
>
> *Revision*   Holidays are important to *everyone.* They boost *one's* spirits and provide a break from *one's* daily routine.
>
> *Faulty*   The taller the *golfer,* the more club speed *you* will have with a normally paced swing.
>
> *Revision*   The taller the *golfer,* the more club speed *he* or *she* will have with a normally paced swing.

As these examples show, the shift can occur within a single sentence or when the writer moves from one sentence to another.

Some shifts in person, however, are warranted. Read the following correct sentence:

> *Correct*   *I* want *you* to deliver these flowers to Ms. Willoughby by three o'clock. *She* needs them for a party.

Here the speaker identifies himself or herself (*I*) while speaking directly to a listener *(you)* about someone else *(she).* In this case, shifts are needed to get the message across.

CONNECTED DISCOURSE EXERCISE

Identify and correct the unwarranted shifts in person in the following paragraph:

Good health is clearly important to you. But it is one's responsibility to ensure our own good health. You can start with simple exercises. We would like to provide you with a low-impact aerobics videotape for only $9. We guarantee that the more out of shape the customer, the quicker you will notice the benefits. The way our bodies feel affects the quality of one's lives. Let our tape help you to a better life.

 Indicate whether the sentence is correct (C) or contains an unwarranted shift in person (S). Correct faulty sentences.

1. After the teacher collected our essays, she told the students that she would return the graded papers on Wednesday.

2. For someone to be successful in today's marketplace, you need to have adequate technical skills.

3. If you each will bring the results of your assigned research to the next meeting, we will be ready to begin working on our collaborative report.

4. Because our tickets were in the nosebleed section of the stadium, many of the fans felt they would have been better off watching the football game on TV.

5. If you want theater tickets, I will be glad to purchase them on my way home from work.

6. Anyone who would like to purchase the discounted Caribbean cruise tickets should place your order by May 15.

7. We enjoy living in the Grand Rapids area very much; you have access to theater, sporting events, and fine dining.

8. On major holidays, most Americans travel long distances, often at great inconvenience, to visit our relatives.

9. If you would like to learn to kayak, novices can usually get free lessons from the people who sell kayaks.

10. In our attempt to determine whether there has been an increase in tornado activity over the last twenty years, the researchers collected data on storm sightings and damage reports. ◄◼

Using the Right Pronoun Case

Case means the changes in form that a personal pronoun (see page 611) undergoes to show its function in a sentence. English has three cases: the *subjective*, the *nonsubjective* (objective), and the *possessive*. The following chart shows the different forms:

Subjective Form	Nonsubjective Form	Possessive Form
I	me	my, mine
he	him	his
she	her	her, hers
we	us	our, ours
you	you	your, yours
they	them	their, theirs
who	whom	whose

The subjective case is used for subjects and subject complements, the nonsubjective for direct objects, indirect objects, and objects of prepositions. The possessive case shows ownership and is also used with gerunds.

The following pointers will help you select the proper pronoun as you revise.

We and Us Preceding Nouns   Nouns that serve as subjects take the pronoun *we*. Other nouns take the pronoun *us*.

Correct   *We* tourists will fly home tomorrow. (*We* accompanies the subject.)

Correct   The guide showed *us* tourists through the cathedral. (*Us* accompanies a nonsubject.)

case

If you can't decide which pronoun is right, mentally omit the noun and read the sentence to yourself, first with one pronoun and then with the other. Your ear will indicate the correct form.

My mother made (*we, us*) children vanilla pudding for dessert.

Omitting *children* shows immediately that *us* is the right choice.

> *Correct*   My mother made *us* children vanilla pudding for dessert.

case

Pronouns Paired with Nouns   When such a combination serves as the subject of a sentence or accompanies the subject, use the subject form of the pronoun. When the combination plays a nonsubject role, use the nonsubject form of the pronoun.

> *Correct*   Arlene and *I* plan to join the Peace Corps. (*I* is part of the compound subject.)
>
> *Correct*   Two people, Mary and *I*, will represent our school at the meeting. (*I* is part of a compound element accompanying the subject.)
>
> *Correct*   The superintendent told Kevin and *him* that they would be promoted soon. (*Him* is part of a compound nonsubject.)
>
> *Correct*   The project was difficult for Jeffrey and *him* to complete. (*Him* is part of a compound nonsubject.)

Again, mentally omitting the noun from the combination will tell you which pronoun is correct.

Who and Whom in Dependent Clauses   Use *who* for the subjects of dependent clauses; otherwise use *whom*.

> *Correct*   The Mallarys prefer friends *who are interested in the theater*. (*Who* is the subject of the clause.)
>
> *Correct*   Barton is a man *whom very few people like*. (*Whom* is not the subject of the clause.)

A simple test will help you decide between *who* and *whom*. First, mentally isolate the dependent clause. Next, block out the pronoun in question and then insert *he* (or *she*) and *him* (or *her*) at the appropriate spot in the remaining part of the clause. If *he* (or *she*) sounds better, *who* is right. If *him* (or *her*) sounds better, *whom* is right. Let's use this test on the sentence below:

> The woman *who(m) Scott is dating* works as a mechanical engineer. Scott is dating (*she, her*).

Clearly *her* is correct; therefore, *whom* is the proper form.

> *Correct*   The woman *whom Scott is dating* works as a mechanical engineer.

Pronouns As Subject Complements   In formal writing, pronouns that serve as subject complements (see page 608) always take the subject form.

    Correct   It is *I*.

    Correct   It was *she* who bought the old Parker mansion.

This rule, however, is often ignored in informal writing.

    It's *her*.

    That's *him* standing over by the door.

case

Comparisons Using *than* or *as . . . as*   Comparisons of this kind often make no direct statement about the second item of comparison. When the second naming word is a pronoun, you may have trouble choosing the right one.

    Harriet is less outgoing than (*they, them*).

    My parents' divorce saddened my sister as much as (*I, me*).

Not to worry. Expand the sentence by mentally supplying the missing material. Then try the sentence with each pronoun and see which sounds right.

    Harriet is less outgoing than (*they, them*) are.

    My parents' divorce saddened my sister as much as it did (*I, me*).

Obviously *they* is the right choice for the first sentence, and *me* is the right choice for the second one.

    Correct   Harriet is less outgoing than *they* are.

    Correct   My parents' divorce saddened my sister as much as it did *me*.

Pronouns Preceding Gerunds   Use the possessive form of a pronoun that precedes a gerund (see page 633).

    I dislike *their* leaving without saying goodbye.

    Ted can't understand *her* quitting such a good job.

This usage emphasizes the action named by the gerund instead of the person or persons performing it. Thus, in the above sentences, the possessive form of the pronoun signals that it's the *leaving* the writer dislikes and the *quitting* that Ted can't understand. The persons involved are secondary.

When the pronoun precedes a participle (see pages 631–633), it should be in the nonsubject case. The emphasis is then on the actor rather than the action.

    Jennifer caught *them* listening to records instead of studying.

In this example, Jennifer caught the listeners, not the listening.

If you have trouble deciding between the nonsubject and possessive forms of a pronoun, ask yourself whether you want to emphasize the action or the actor; then proceed accordingly.

time

Identify and correct the pronoun case errors in the following paragraph:

Between my brother and I, we are always able to pull at least five good-sized trout a day from the creek behind our house. Us rural trout fishermen just seem to have the knack. Of course, those city fishermen whom insist on employing artificial flies won't appreciate our methods even if they can't do as well as us. We just let our bait, usually a juicy worm, float downstream to the waiting trout. Of course, my brother won't let the fishing interfere with him sleeping. In fact, it was him that developed the idea of looping the line around his toe so that he would wake up when a trout took the bait. Others have told my brother and I that this method is dangerous, but neither of us has lost a toe yet. Of course, the people who we invite to dinner don't complain about our methods, and they seem to enjoy the fish.

EXERCISE *Choose the right form of the pronoun for each of the following sentences. For the purpose of this exercise, assume that there would have been the appropriate pronoun antecedent in the sentence preceding the one that is shown.*

1. No one is as pleased as (*I, me*) by John's recent promotion to assistant vice-president.
2. There is no excuse for (*him, his*) yelling at us in public.
3. The newspaper's editor praised Marge and (*I, me*) for our co-authored article on women in the military.
4. Randy has a better grasp of European history than (*I, me*).
5. Megan is one student (*who, whom*) I believe really understands the importance of writing well.
6. (*We, Us*) Americans pride ourselves on our individuality.
7. The conductor decided that Marie and (*I, me*) should sing a duet at the next recital.
8. Rilke is the poet (*who, whom*) I like best.
9. The judge told (*we, us*) contestants that we would be called when it was our turn.
10. The manager of the movie theater gave Tom and (*I, me*) four free passes.

Creating Consistency in Showing Time

Inconsistencies occur when a writer shifts from the past tense to the present or vice versa without a corresponding shift in the time of the events being described. The following paragraph contains an uncalled-for shift from the present tense to the past:

As *The Most Dangerous Game* opens, Sanger Rainsford, a famous hunter and author, and his old friend Whitney are standing on the deck of a yacht and discussing a mysterious island as the ship passes near it. Then, after everyone else has gone to bed, Rainsford manages to fall overboard. He swims to the island and ends up at a chateau owned by General Zaroff, a refugee from the Communist takeover in Russia. Zaroff, bored with hunting animals, has turned to hunting humans on his desert island. Inevitably, Rainsford is turned out into the jungle to be hunted down. There were [shift to past tense] actually four hunts over a three-day period, and at the end of the last one, Rainsford jumped into the sea, swam across a cove to the chateau, and killed Zaroff in the general's own bedroom. Afterward he sleeps [shift back to present tense] and decides "he had never slept in a better bed."

The sentence with the unwarranted shift in tense should read as follows:

There are actually four hunts over a three-day period, and at the end of the last one, Rainsford jumps into the sea, swims across a cove to the chateau, and kills Zaroff in the general's own bedroom.

The time shift in the quotation part of the final sentence is justified because the sleeping has occurred before Rainsford's thoughts about it.

A second kind of inconsistency results when a writer fails to distinguish the immediate past from the less immediate past. The following sentence illustrates this error:

Faulty   Mary *answered* all thirty test questions when the class ended.

This sentence indicates that Mary completed all thirty test questions during the final instant of the class, an impossibility. When you detect this type of error in your writing, determine which action occurred first and then correct the error by adding *had* to the verb. In this case, the first verb needs correcting:

Revision   Mary *had answered* all thirty test questions when the class ended.

Besides adding *had*, you may sometimes need to alter the verb form.

Faulty   Before he turned twenty, John *wrote* two novels.

Revision   Before he turned twenty, John *had written* two novels.

CONNECTED DISCOURSE EXERCISE

Identify and correct any inconsistencies in showing time in the following passage:

There is no better time to go swimming than at night. The summer after I had graduated from high school, I worked for a landscaping company. After a sweaty day mowing lawns and digging up gardens, all of us who worked there would jump into the back of Dick's old pickup and rattle out to Woods Lake. It is just dark as we arrive. The moon is beautiful, reflected in that black mirror set in a frame of hills. We stumble down a small, sandy hill to the beach, where we strip off our dusty jeans and sweaty shirts before plunging into the cool reflection of stars.

 EXERCISE *Indicate whether each sentence is correct (C) or contains an unwarranted shift (S) in tense. Then correct the faulty sentences.*

1. A thin wisp of smoke drifts from under the hood, and then the engine burst into flames.
2. After Kyra finishes checking the computers for viruses, she will load the new software.
3. Jason took on many projects but finishes few of them.
4. After I finished preparing dinner, I went for a long walk.
5. As Charlie laid pieces of the model on the table, his wife picks them up.
6. As soon as the snow falls, we break out our cross-country skis.
7. David is building his own house but found it harder work than he anticipated.
8. While Robert applies the adhesive, David carefully positioned the floor tiles.
9. Tonya stood in line for the movie tickets while Doug searches for a parking space.
10. Although it started to rain heavily, Debbie continues to mow the lawn.

Using Adjectives and Adverbs Effectively

Inexperienced writers often use adjectives when they should use adverbs and also confuse the comparative and superlative forms of these parts of speech when making comparisons.

Misusing Adjectives for Adverbs   Although most adjectives can be misused as adverbs, the following seven, listed with the corresponding adverbs, cause the most difficulty.

Adjectives	Adverbs
awful	awfully
bad	badly
considerable	considerably
good	well
most	almost
real	really
sure	surely

The following sentences show typical errors:

Faulty   Bryan did *good* in his first golf lesson. (*good* mistakenly used to modify verb *did*)

Faulty   *Most* every graduate from our auto service program receives several job offers. (*Most* mistakenly used to modify adjective *every*)

Faulty   The speech was delivered *real* well. (*real* mistakenly used to modify adverb *well*)

Because adverbs modify verbs, adjectives, and other adverbs (see page 626), and adjectives modify nouns and noun substitutes (see page 623), the above sentences clearly require adverbs.

Revision   Bryan did *well* in his first golf lesson.

Revision   *Almost* every graduate from our auto service program receives several job offers.

Revision   The speech was delivered *really* well.

*mis /
adj/adv*

In one notable case, an adverb is commonly misused as an adjective.

Faulty   I feel *badly* about providing the wrong phone number. (*Badly* is mistakenly used as a subject complement.)

Revision   I feel *bad* about providing the wrong phone number.

If you can't decide whether a sentence requires an adjective or an adverb, determine the part of speech of the word being modified and proceed accordingly.

Confusing the Comparative and Superlative Forms in Comparisons   The comparative form of adjectives and adverbs is used to compare two things, the superlative form to compare three or more things. Adjectives with fewer than three syllables generally add *-er* to make the comparative form and *-est* to make the superlative form (tall, tall*er*, tall*est*). Adjectives with three or more syllables generally add *more* to make the comparative and *most* to make the superlative (enchanting, *more* enchanting, *most* enchanting), as do most adverbs of two or more syllables (loudly, *more* loudly, *most* loudly).

When making comparisons, beginning writers sometimes mistakenly use double comparatives or double superlatives.

Faulty   Harry is *more taller* than James. (double comparative)

Faulty   The Chrysler Building has the *most splendidest* lobby I've ever seen. (double superlative)

The correct versions read as follows:

Revision   Harry is *taller* than James.

Revision   The Chrysler Building has the *most splendid* lobby I've ever seen.

In addition, writers may erroneously use the superlative form, rather than the comparative form, to compare two things.

Faulty   Barry is the *richest* of the two brothers.

Faulty   Jeremy is the *most talented* of those two singers.

Here are the sentences correctly written:

> *Revision*   Barry is the *richer* of the two brothers.

> *Revision*   Jeremy is the *more talented* of those two singers.

Reserve the superlative form for comparing three or more items.

> *Correct*   Barry is the *richest* of the three brothers.

> *Correct*   Jeremy is the *most talented* of those four singers.

mis
adj/adv

CONNECTED DISCOURSE EXERCISE

Identify and correct the adjective–adverb errors in the following paragraph:

This year our football team is outstanding. Spike Jones, our quarterback, has been playing real good this past season. Stan Blunder, the most talented of our two ends, hasn't dropped a pass all season. The team can most always count on Stan to catch the crucial first-down pass. Of course, the team wouldn't be where it is today without John Schoolyard's good coaching. He has made this team much more better than it was even a year ago. Only the kicking team has done bad this season. Of course, with this most wonderfulest offense, the defensive players haven't gotten much practice. The good news is, then, that we can sure expect to watch some terrific college football for years to come.

EXERCISE   *For each of the following sentences, choose the proper word from the pair in parentheses:*

1. The milk in the refrigerator tastes (*bad, badly*).
2. Old science fiction movies can be (*real, really*) funny to watch because of the clumsy special effects and stilted dialogue.
3. Steve did (*good, well*) on his history project.
4. The Vandorns have the (*prettiest, most prettiest*) house in the development.
5. Dana is the (*quieter, quietest*) of our three children.
6. Terry hurt his knees (*bad, badly*) playing football.
7. The Mustang is the (*less, least*) expensive of the two sports cars you are considering.
8. (*Most, Almost*) all of our employees make use of the day care facility we provide on the premises.
9. It is (*real, really*) important to read the entire manual.
10. The Powermax is the (*stronger, strongest*) of the three kinds of garage door openers we sell.

Placing Modifiers Correctly

A misplaced modifier is a word or word group that is improperly separated from the word it modifies. When separation of this type occurs, the sentence often sounds awkward, ridiculous, or confusing.

Usually, you can correct this error by moving the modifier next to the word it is intended to modify. Occasionally, you'll also need to alter some of the phrasing.

mm

Faulty	There is a bicycle in the basement *with chrome fenders.* (The basement appears to have chrome fenders.)
Faulty	David received a phone call from his uncle *that infuriated him.* (The uncle appears to have infuriated David.)
Revision	There is a bicycle *with chrome fenders* in the basement.
Revision	David received an *infuriating* phone call from his uncle. (Note the change in wording.)

In shifting the modifier, don't inadvertently create another faulty sentence.

Faulty	Fritz bought a magazine with an article about Michael Jackson *at the corner newsstand.* (The article appears to tell about Jackson's visit to the corner newsstand.)
Faulty	Fritz bought a magazine *at the corner newsstand* with an article about Michael Jackson. (The corner newsstand appears to have an article about Jackson.)
Revision	*At the corner newsstand,* Fritz bought a magazine with an article about Michael Jackson.

As you revise, watch also for *squinting modifiers*—that is, modifiers positioned so that the reader doesn't know whether they are supposed to modify what comes ahead of them or what follows them.

Faulty	The man who was rowing the boat *frantically* waved toward the onlookers on the beach.

Is the man rowing frantically or waving frantically? Correct this kind of error by repositioning the modifier so that the ambiguity disappears.

Revision	The man who was *frantically* rowing the boat waved toward the onlookers on the beach.
Revision	The man who was rowing the boat waved *frantically* toward the onlookers on the beach.

> EXERCISE
>
> *Indicate whether each sentence is correct (C) or contains a misplaced modifier (MM). Correct faulty sentences.*

1. Jason handed his report to his teacher neatly tucked into a binder.
2. The girl driving past the school wildly waved at her friends.
3. The dancers practiced Swan Lake for a month before the performance.
4. I tossed the rainbow trout to my brother still hooked firmly in the mouth.
5. Most companies do not like placing managers in charge of employees who are inexperienced.
6. There is a computer in our classroom that beeps loudly at the most unexpected times.
7. You can learn about recent volcanic eruptions at your local library.
8. Steve devoured greasy barbecued spareribs wearing a new suit.
9. The instructor reminded students on the last day of classes to turn in their twenty-page paper.
10. Stacey found beautiful and inexpensive macramé wall hangings for her dorm room in the Bahamas. ◄

dm

Revising Dangling Modifiers

A dangling modifier is a phrase or clause that lacks clear connection to the word or words it is intended to modify. As a result, sentences are inaccurate, often comical. Typically, the modifier leads off the sentence, although it can also come at the end.

Sometimes the error occurs because the sentence fails to specify who or what is modified. At other times, the separation is too great between the modifier and what it modifies.

Faulty	*Walking in the meadow,* wildflowers surrounded us. (The wildflowers appear to be walking in the meadow.)
Faulty	Dinner was served *after saying grace.* (The dinner appears to have said grace.)
Faulty	*Fatigued by the violent exercise,* the cool shower was very relaxing. (The cool shower appears to have been fatigued.)

The first of these sentences is faulty because the modifier is positioned too far away from *us.* The other two are faulty because they do not identify who said grace or found the shower relaxing.

You can correct dangling modifiers in two basic ways. First, leave the modifier unchanged and rewrite the main part of the sentence so that it begins with the term actually modified. Second, rewrite the modifier so that it has its own subject and verb, thereby eliminating the inaccuracy.

Revision	*Walking in the meadow,* we were surrounded by wildflowers. (The main part of the sentence has been rewritten.)
Revision	*As we walked in the meadow,* wildflowers surrounded us. (The modifier has been rewritten.)
Revision	*Dinner was served after we had said grace.* (The modifier has been rewritten.)

Revision	*Fatigued by the violent exercise,* Ted found the cool shower very relaxing. (The main part of the sentence has been rewritten.)
Revision	*Because Ted was fatigued by the violent exercise,* the cool shower was very relaxing. (The modifier has been rewritten.)

Ordinarily, either part of the sentence can be rewritten, but sometimes only one part can.

EXERCISE   *Indicate whether each sentence is correct (C) or contains a dangling modifier (DM). Correct faulty sentences.*

1. After listening to a tape of Orson Welles' radio broadcast of *The War of the Worlds,* I understood why many who tuned into the middle of the broadcast panicked.
2. The baseball game will start after singing *The Star-Spangled Banner.*
3. Looking at the night sky, a million stars seemed to smile down on us.
4. Driving with his emergency brake on, Matt wore down the brake pads.
5. Having scored 100 percent on the pre-test, the teacher placed two students in the next level math class.
6. Picasso was known to leave customers waiting for several days, painting furiously.
7. John cataloged his CD collection, listing each CD in a database.
8. Sitting on the back porch, a black bear shuffled across the lawn to raid our garbage cans.
9. Please send an e-mail to the project head listing your concerns.
10. Rushing over the banks, Main Street was soon under three feet of water.

Maintaining Parallelism

Nonparallelism results when equivalent ideas follow different grammatical forms. One common kind of nonparallelism occurs with words or word groups in pairs or in a series.

Faulty	Althea enjoys *jogging, to bike,* and *to swim.*
Faulty	The superintendent praised the workers *for their productivity* and *because they had an excellent safety record.*
Faulty	The banner was *old, faded,* and *it had a rip.*

Note how rewriting the sentences in parallel form improves their smoothness.

Revision	Althea enjoys *jogging, biking,* and *swimming.*
Revision	The superintendent praised the workers for *their productivity* and *their excellent safety record.*
Revision	The banner was *old, faded,* and *ripped.*

Nonparallelism also occurs when correlative conjunctions *(either—or, neither—nor, both—and,* and *not only—but also)* are followed by unlike elements.

Faulty   That sound *either* <u>was a thunderclap</u> *or* <u>an explosion</u>.

Faulty   The basement was *not only* <u>poorly lighted</u> *but also* <u>it had a foul smell</u>.

comp

Ordinarily, repositioning one of the correlative conjunctions will solve the problem. Sometimes, however, one of the grammatical elements must be rewritten.

Revision   That sound was *either* <u>a thunderclap</u> *or* <u>an explosion</u>. *(Either* has been repositioned.)

Revision   The basement was *not only* <u>poorly lighted</u> *but also* <u>foul smelling</u>. (The element following *but also* has been rewritten.)

 EXERCISE   *Indicate whether each sentence is correct (C) or nonparallel (NP). Correct faulty sentences.*

1. The cause of the fire either was faulty wiring or an overloaded outlet.
2. After graduation, Marci will be moving to Chicago and work for a large public relations firm.
3. For spring break, Steve and his friends plan to visit either New Orleans or Orlando.
4. A good candidate for social work enjoys talking with people, helps solve problems, and seeing projects through to their conclusion.
5. This course will involve reading a number of short stories, and you will need to turn in weekly journal responses.
6. Although he was an excellent auto mechanic, Andy could neither repair air conditioning units nor car stereos.
7. Canton chicken balls are sweet, tangy, and satisfying.
8. In my spare time, I enjoy reading, canoeing, and to play the piano.
9. As stage manger, Susan had to design, construct, and maintain the set for the school play.
10. As a reference librarian, Colin is responsible for instructing students in how to perform database searches, helping researchers find the material they need, maintaining the reference section, and he also manages the patent collection.

Revising Faulty Comparisons

A faulty comparison results if you (1) mention one of the items being compared but not the other, (2) omit words needed to clarify the relationship, or (3) compare different sorts of items. Advertisers often offend in the first way.

Faulty   Irish tape has better adhesion.

With what other tape is Irish tape being compared? Scotch tape? All other transparent tape? Mentioning the second term of a comparison eliminates reader guesswork.

Revision   Irish tape has better adhesion than any other transparent tape.

Two clarifying words, *other* and *else,* are frequently omitted from comparisons, creating illogical sentences.

Faulty   Sergeant McNabb is more conscientious than any officer in his precinct.

Faulty   Stretch French is taller than anyone on his basketball team.

comp

The first sentence is illogical because McNabb is one of the officers in his precinct and therefore cannot be more conscientious than any officer in the precinct. Similarly, because French is a member of his basketball team, he can't be taller than anyone on his team. Adding *other* to the first sentence and *else* to the second corrects matters.

Revision   Sergeant McNabb is more conscientious than any *other* officer in his precinct.

Revision   Stretch French is taller than anyone *else* on his basketball team.

Comparing unlike items is perhaps the most common kind of comparison error. Here are two examples:

Faulty   The cities in California are larger than North Dakota.

Faulty   The cover of this book is much more durable than the other book.

The first sentence compares the cities of California with a state, while the second compares the cover of a book with a whole book. Correction consists of rewriting each sentence so that it compares like items.

Revision   The cities in California are larger than *those in* North Dakota.

Revision   The cover of this book is much more durable than *that of* the other book.

CONNECTED DISCOURSE EXERCISE

Identify and correct the misplaced modifiers, dangling modifiers, nonparallelism, and faulty comparisons in the following memorandum:

TO: All Residence Hall Advisors in Knuckles Hall

FROM: John Knells, Residency Hall Director

DATE: March 13, 20___ ___

SUBJECT: Noise in Residence Hall

Recently I received a report from a student that deeply disturbed me. Apparently, after quiet hours students still have visitors in their rooms, are playing their stereos loudly, and are even staging boxing matches in the halls.

comp

The student who wrote me desperately tries to study. However, he is often forced to leave his room disturbed by the noise. He was not the only one to complain. You should know that we have had more complaints about Knuckles Hall than any dorm on campus. Since discussing this problem with you at the last staff meeting, things haven't seemed to get any better. The rules are not only poorly enforced but also they are completely ignored. Your job performance is worse than the students. If you don't improve immediately, I will be forced to dismiss you.

EXERCISE *Indicate whether each sentence is correct (C) or contains a faulty comparison (FC). Correct the faulty comparison.*

1. *Death of a Salesman* is performed more often than any American play.
2. The power of today's laptop computers is much greater than the large defense department mainframes of the 1950s.
3. This quarter's earning report shows significantly greater net profits.
4. The Sunday brunch at the 1913 room is much more elegant than the Eatery.
5. Of the two quarterbacks, Allen has a stronger throwing arm than Tom.
6. In contrast to your car, I usually get 40 miles to the gallon.
7. The winters in North Dakota are much worse than Maine.
8. Our new ice cream shop offers many more flavors.
9. The paint on the front of the house is much lighter than the back.
10. Professor Hinkley has published many more articles than the other members of his department.

EDITING TO CORRECT FAULTY PUNCTUATION AND MECHANICS

Punctuation marks indicate relationships among different sentence elements. As a result, these marks help clarify the meaning of written material. Similarly, a knowledge of mechanics—capitalization, abbreviations, numbers, and italics—helps you avoid distracting inconsistencies.

This part of the Handbook covers the fundamentals of punctuation and mechanics. Review it carefully when you edit your final draft.

Apostrophes

Apostrophes (') show possession, mark contractions, and indicate plurals that are singled out for special attention.

Possession   Possessive apostrophes usually show ownership *(Mary's cat)*. Sometimes, though, they identify the works of creative people *(Hemingway's novels)* or indicate an extent of time or distance *(one hour's time, one mile's distance)*.

Possessive apostrophes are used with nouns and with pronouns like *someone, no one, everybody, each other,* and *one another.* The possessive form is easily recognized because it can be converted to a prepositional phrase beginning with *of.*

The collar of the dog

The whistle of the wind

The intention of the corporation

The birthday of Scott

To show possession with pronouns like those above, singular nouns, and plural nouns that do not end in an *s,* add an apostrophe followed by an *s.*

Someone's car is blocking our drive. (possessive of pronoun *someone*)

The *manager's* reorganization plan will take effect next week. (possessive of singular noun *manager*)

The *women's* lounge is being redecorated. (possessive of plural noun *women*)

Sentences that make comparisons sometimes include two possessives, the second coming at the very end. In such cases, be sure to use an apostrophe with the second possessive.

Birmingham's football team is much better than *Central's.*

With singular nouns that end in *s,* the possessive is sometimes formed by merely adding an apostrophe at the end *(James' helmet).* The preferred usage, however, is *'s (James's helmet)* unless the addition of the *s* would make it awkward to pronounce the word.

Moses's followers entered the Promised Land. (awkward pronunciation of *Moses's)*

Moses' followers entered the Promised Land. (nonawkward pronunciation of *Moses')*

Plural nouns ending in *s* form the possessive by adding only an apostrophe at the end.

All the *ladies'* coats are on sale today. (possessive of plural noun *ladies)*

The *workers'* lockers were moved. (possessive of plural noun *workers)*

To show joint ownership by two or more persons, use the possessive form for the last-named person only. To show individual ownership, use the possessive form for each person's name.

Ronald and *Joan's* boat badly needed overhauling. (joint ownership)

Laura's and *Alice's* term projects are almost completed. (individual ownership)

Hyphenated nouns form the possessive by adding *'s* to the last word.

My *mother-in-law's* house is next to mine.

Never use an apostrophe with the possessive pronouns *his, hers, whose, its, ours, yours, theirs.*

This desk is *his;* the other one is *hers.* (no apostrophes needed)

Contractions Contractions of words or numbers omit one or more letters or numerals. An apostrophe shows exactly where the omission occurs.

Wasn't that a disappointing concert? (contraction of *was not)*

Around here, people still talk about the blizzard of *'79.* (contraction of *1979)*

Don't confuse the contraction *it's,* meaning *it is* or *it has,* with the possessive pronoun *its,* which should never have an apostrophe. If you're puzzled by an *its* that you've written, try this test. Expand the *its* to *it is* or *it has* and see whether the sentence still makes sense. If it does, the *its* is a contraction and needs the apostrophe. If the result is nonsense, the *its* is a possessive pronoun and does not get an apostrophe. Here are some examples:

> *Its* awfully muggy today.

> *Its* been an exciting trip.

> Every dog has *its* day.

The first example makes sense when the *its* is expanded to *it is*.

> *It is* awfully muggy today.

The second makes sense when the *its* is expanded to *it has*.

> *It has* been an exciting trip.

Both of these sentences therefore require apostrophes.

> *It's* awfully muggy today.

> *It's* been an exciting trip.

The last sentence, however, turns into nonsense when the *its* is expanded.

> Every dog has *it is* day.

> Every dog has *it has* day.

In this case, the *its* is a possessive pronoun and requires no apostrophe.

> Every dog has *its* day.

Plurals   To improve clarity, the plurals of letters, numbers, symbols, and words being singled out for special attention are written with apostrophes.

> Mind your *p's* and *q's*. (plurals of letters)

> Your *5's* and *6's* are hard to tell apart. (plurals of numbers)

> The formula was sprinkled with Π*'s* and σ*'s*. (plurals of symbols)

> Don't use so many *however's* and *therefore's* in your writing. (plurals of words)

Apostrophes can be used, though they are not needed, to form the plurals of abbreviations.

> How many *CD's* (or *CDs*) do you own? (plurals of abbreviation for *compact discs*)

When no danger of confusion exists, an *s* alone will suffice.

> During the late *1960s*, many university students demanded changes in academic life.

Supply, delete, or relocate apostrophes as necessary in the following memorandum:

TO: The Records Office Staff

FROM: The Assistant Registrar

DATE: January 27, 20__ __

SUBJECT: Faulty Student Transcripts

Recently, we have had too many student complaints' about handwritten transcripts. Apparently its hard to tell the B's and D's apart. One staff members' handwriting is totally illegible. This staffs carelessness is unacceptable. Someone's even gone so far as to write grade change's in pencil, which allows students to make changes. This can't continue. In a short time, John and Mary's student assistants will be typing the past transcripts into our new computer system. Once grades are entered, the computers ability to generate grade reports will solve this problem. Until that time, lets make an effort to produce clear and professional-looking transcripts.

comma

 EXERCISE   *Supply apostrophes where necessary to correct the following sentences:*

1. This years winter promises to be significantly more severe than last years.
2. Everyones office will be furnished with the newest ergonomic chairs and work spaces.
3. Were attempting to determine how our students needs can best be met.
4. When you are writing numbers quickly by hand, its important to keep your 7s and 1s very distinct.
5. Somebodys purse was left in Dean Smiths office.
6. Once everybodys research has been presented, well be better able to reach a decision.
7. Cindys computer program was much more efficient than her peers programs.
8. There are two Rs and two Ss in the word "embarrassment."
9. Lets determine what caused the schools mainframe computer to fail before we panic.
10. Every city has its own charms that are available for the informed visitors delight.
    ◄

Commas

Since commas (,) occur more frequently than any other mark of punctuation, it's vital that you learn to use them correctly. When you do, your sentence structure is clearer, and your reader grasps your meaning without having to reread.

Commas separate or set off independent clauses, items in a series, coordinate adjectives, introductory elements, places and dates, nonrestrictive expressions, and parenthetical expressions.

Independent Clauses   When you link two independent clauses with a coordinating conjunction (*and, but, or, nor, for, yet,* or *so*), put a comma in front of the conjunction.

Arthur is majoring in engineering, *but* he has decided to work for a clothing store following graduation.

The water looked inviting, *so* Darlene decided to go for a swim.

Don't confuse a sentence that has a compound predicate (see page 605) with a sentence that consists of two independent clauses.

Tom watered the garden and mowed the lawn. (single sentence with compound predicate)

Tom watered the garden, *and* Betty mowed the lawn. (sentence with two independent clauses)

Here's a simple test. Read what follows the comma. Unless that part can stand alone as a sentence, don't use a comma.

comma

Items in a Series   A series consists of three or more words, phrases, or clauses following on one another's heels. Whenever you write a series, separate its items with commas.

Sarah, Paul, and *Mary* are earning *A*'s in advanced algebra. (words in a series)

Nancy strode *across the parking lot, through the revolving door,* and *into the elevator.* (phrases in a series)

The stockholders' report said *that the company had enjoyed record profits during the last year, that it had expanded its work force by 20 percent,* and *that it would soon start marketing several new products.* (clauses in a series)

Coordinate Adjectives   Use commas to separate coordinate adjectives—those that modify the same noun or noun substitute and can be reversed without altering the meaning of the sentence.

Andrea proved to be an efficient, cooperative employee.

Andrea proved to be a cooperative, efficient employee.

When reversing the word order wrecks the meaning of the sentence, the adjectives are not coordinate and should be written without a comma.

Many new brands of videocassette recorders have come on the market lately.

Reversing the adjectives *many* and *new* would turn this sentence into nonsense. Therefore, no comma should be used.

Introductory Elements   Use commas to separate introductory elements—words, phrases, and clauses—from the rest of the sentence. When an introductory element is short and the sentence will not be misread, you can omit the comma.

Correct	After bathing, Jack felt refreshed.
Correct	Soon I will be changing jobs.
Correct	Soon, I will be changing jobs.
Correct	When Sarah smiles her ears wiggle.
Correct	When Sarah smiles, her ears wiggle.

The first example needs a comma; otherwise, the reader might become temporarily confused.

After bathing Jack . . .

Always use commas after introductory elements of six or more words.

| *Correct* | Whenever I hear the opening measure of Beethoven's *Fifth Symphony,* I get goose bumps. |

Places and Dates   Places include mailing addresses and geographical locations. The following sentences show where commas are used:

Sherry Delaney lives at 651 Daniel Street, Memphis, Tennessee 38118.

I will go to Calais, France, next week.

Morristown, Oklahoma, is my birthplace.

Note that commas appear after the street designation and the names of cities, countries, and states, except when the name of the state is followed by a zip code.
Dates are punctuated as shown in the following example:

On Sunday, June 9, 1991, Elaine received a degree in environmental science.

Here, commas follow the day of the week, the day of the month, and the year.

With dates that include only the month and the year, commas are optional.

| *Correct* | In July 1989 James played chess for the first time. |
| *Correct* | In July, 1989, James played chess for the first time. |

Nonrestrictive Expressions   A nonrestrictive expression supplies added information about whatever it modifies. This information, however, is *nonessential* and does not affect the basic meaning of the sentence. The two sentences below include nonrestrictive expressions:

Senator Conwell, *the senior senator from this state,* faces a tough campaign for re-election.

My dog, *frightened by the thunder,* hid under my bed while the storm raged.

If we delete the phrase *the senior senator from this state* from the first sentence, we still know that Senator Conwell faces a tough re-election battle. Likewise, if we delete *frightened by the thunder* from the second sentence, we still know that the dog hid during the storm.

comma

Restrictive expressions, which are written *without commas*, distinguish whatever they modify from other persons, places, or things in the same category. Unlike nonrestrictive expressions, they are almost always *essential* sentence elements. Omitting a restrictive expression alters the meaning of the sentence, and the result is often nonsense.

Any person *caught stealing from this store* will be prosecuted.

Dropping the italicized part of this sentence leaves us with the absurd statement that any person, not just those caught stealing, faces prosecution.

Parenthetical Expressions   A parenthetical expression is a word or a word group that links one sentence to another or adds information or emphasis to the sentence in which it appears. Parenthetical expressions include the following:

Clarifying phrases

Names and titles of people being addressed directly

Abbreviations of degree titles

Echo questions

"Not" phrases

Adjectives that come after, rather than before, the words they modify

The examples that follow show the uses of commas:

All of Joe's spare time seems to center around reading. Kevin, *on the other hand*, enjoys a variety of activities. (phrase linking two sentences)

Myra Hobbes, *our representative in Seattle*, is being transferred to Spokane next month. (clarifying phrase)

I think, *Jill*, that you'd make a wonderful teacher. (name of person addressed directly)

Tell me, *Captain*, when the cruise ship is scheduled to sail. (title of person addressed directly)

Harley Kendall, *Ph.D.*, will be this year's commencement speaker. (degree title following name)

Alvin realizes, *doesn't he*, that he stands almost no chance of being accepted at West Point? (echo question)

Mathematics, *not home economics*, was Tammy's favorite high school subject. ("not" phrase)

The road, *muddy and rutted*, proved impassable. (adjectives following word they modify)

Punctuating Conjunctive Adverbs   Writers often mistakenly punctuate conjunctive adverbs with commas and create, as a result, a comma splice.

Floridians do not have the heating bills of their Northern neighbors, however, they do have extensive air-conditioning bills.

comma

Conjunctive adverbs actually do not join sentences and can actually be moved, revealing the underlying comma splice.

Floridians do not have the heating bills of their Northern neighbors, they do, however, have extensive air-conditioning bills.

To fix such comma splices, join the sentences with a semi-colon or punctuate with a period and start a new sentence.

Floridians do not have the heating bills of their Northern neighbors; however, they do have extensive air-conditioning bills.

Floridians do not have the heating bills of their Northern neighbors. However, they do have extensive air-conditioning bills.

CONNECTED DISCOURSE EXERCISE

Add or delete commas as necessary in the following letter:

Dear Loy Norrix Knight:

While we know you will be busy this summer we hope you will take time to join us for the twenty-five-year reunion of the graduating class of 1977. The reunion will include a cocktail hour a buffet dinner and a dance. For your entertainment we are going to bring in a professional band and a band starring some of your good, old high school chums. John Mcleary who is now a well-known professional nightclub performer will serve as the emcee. Do you remember him hosting our senior-year assemblies?

Yes many of your former, hardworking teachers will be at the reunion. You can thank them for the difference they made in your life or you can tell them what you've thought of them all these years. This reunion will also be your opportunity to catch up on the lives of your former friends find out what that old flame now looks like and brag a little about your own successes. And if you are really lucky you might even be able to sneak a dance with your high school prom partner.

We hope you will make plans, to join us here at the Kalamazoo Hilton on July 28, 2002, at 7 P.M. Wear your best 1970s-style clothes. Remember revisiting the past can be fun.

Sincerely,

The Reunion Committee

EXERCISE   *Supply commas as necessary to correct the following sentences:*

1. Let us know Ms. Granger when you would like to enjoy your free stay at Rolling Hills Resort.

2. The landscapers killed the existing grass rototilled the ground added new topsoil and sprayed the prepared ground with hydroseed.

3. If you are interested in making a tax-deductible donation to the Stratford Festival please write Carla Darma treasurer at 165 University Avenue Suite 700 Toronto Ontario Canada M5H 3B8.

4. The day was unusually beautiful so Mr. Collins decided to hold his class on the Romantic poets outside.

5. Standing in the long winding line for hours on a hot muggy New York summer day Tom was able to get discount tickets to one of the most popular musicals.

6. Mr. Carlin was hired by our New York office on March 25 1997 and was supposed to report to work in our Nome Alaska office three months after his hiring date.

7. Before eating raccoons carefully wash their paws.

8. Despite the many kinds of electronic entertainment available today many people continue to prefer to read a good book.

9. Your fireplace which is cracked in several places will need to be repaired before you can use it.

10. When it is performed well *Waiting for Godot* considered by many to be a masterpiece of existential theater is actually quite humorous.

Semicolons

The main use of the semicolon (;) is to separate independent clauses, which may or may not be connected with a conjunctive adverb (see pages 630–631). Other uses include separating

two or more series of items

items containing commas in a single series

independent clauses that contain commas and are connected with a coordinating conjunction.

Independent Clauses   The examples that follow show the use of semicolons to separate independent clauses.

The fabric in this dress is terrible; its designer must have been asleep at the swatch. (no conjunctive adverb)

Steve refused to write a term paper; *therefore,* he failed the course. (conjunctive adverb *therefore* joining independent clauses)

Conjunctive adverbs can occur within, rather than between, independent clauses. When they do, set them off with commas.

Marsha felt very confident. Jane, *on the other hand,* was nervous and uncertain. (conjunctive adverb within independent clause)

To determine whether a pair of commas or a semicolon and comma are required, read what comes before and after the conjunctive adverb. Unless both sets of words can stand alone as sentences, use commas.

Two or More Series of Items   With sentences that have two or more series of items, writers often separate the series with semicolons in order to lessen the chances of misreading.

> My duties as secretary include typing letters, memos, and purchase orders; sorting, opening, and delivering mail; and making plane and hotel reservations for traveling executives.

The semicolons provide greater clarity than commas would.

Comma-Containing Items within a Series   When commas accompany one or more of the items in a series, it's often better to separate the items with semicolons instead of commas.

> The meal included veal, which was cooked to perfection; asparagus, my favorite vegetable; and brown rice, prepared with a touch of curry.

Once again, semicolons provide greater clarity than additional commas.

Independent Clauses with Commas and a Coordinating Conjunction
Ordinarily, a comma is used to separate independent clauses joined by a coordinating conjunction. When one or more of the clauses have commas, however, a semicolon provides clearer separation.

> The long black limousine pulled up to the curb; and Jerry, shaking with excitement, watched the President alight from it.

The semicolon makes it easier to see the two main clauses.

CONNECTED DISCOURSE EXERCISE

Add and delete semicolons as appropriate in the following letter. You may have to substitute semicolons for commas.

Dear Student:

Our college, as you are well aware, has been going through a number of changes, and these developments, both in the registration system and the curriculum, will continue next year. In the end these improvements will only benefit you; but we know that many of you have been anxious about the exact nature of the changes. To answer your questions, we have arranged an open forum with Linda Peters, president of the college, Drake Stevens, the registrar, and Jerry Mash, vice-president of academic affairs. The meeting will be held in Johnston Hall; 2 P.M.; March 23. Please come with your questions, this is your opportunity to put your fears to rest.

Sincerely,
John X. Pelle
Dean of Students

EXERCISE *Supply semicolons wherever they are necessary or desirable in the following sentences. You may have to substitute semicolons for commas. If a sentence is correct, write C.*

1. When he visits the main office, Mr. Harmon would like to meet with the vice-president of marketing, Carol Chaffe, the personnel director, Carl Hart, and the vice-president of finance, Mary Angelo.

2. Donald Nathanson, a clinical psychologist, has written an insightful book on shame, and other psychologists, who at first were very critical of his work, have begun to use his ideas in their practice.

3. E-mail is a crucial part of most businesses; in fact, some companies have replaced all memos with electronic communication.

4. This year a number of new musicals have opened on Broadway, it promises to be an exciting theater season.

5. The reading for the course was eclectic, including *The Invisible Man,* a science fiction novel, *Shane,* a western, and *Antigone,* a classic Greek play.

6. Computers can crash at any time, therefore, it is important to back up your data frequently.

7. Sales have decreased significantly this past year, we are likely to see an equivalent drop in our profits.

8. The landscaper planted carpet juniper, canby pachistima, and English ivy for ground cover, rhododendron, pyracantha, and pieris for shrubs, and a blue spruce, a Japanese black pine, and a maple for trees.

9. Chess, a game played by millions, can sharpen your mind, and now there are computer programs, most very inexpensive, that can help you learn the game.

10. We will offer sales training this summer in Lansing, Michigan, Ames, Iowa, and Minneapolis, Minnesota.

Periods, Question Marks, and Exclamation Points

Since periods, question marks, and exclamation points signal the ends of sentences, they are sometimes called *end marks*. In addition, periods and question marks function in several other ways.

Periods Periods (.) end sentences that state facts or opinions, give instructions, make requests that are not in the form of questions, and ask indirect questions—those that have been rephrased in the form of a statement.

Linda works as a hotel manager. (Sentence states fact.)

Dean Harris is a competent administrator. (Sentence states opinion.)

Clean off your lab bench before you leave. (Sentence gives instruction.)

Please move away from the door. (Sentence makes request.)

I wonder whether Ruthie will be at the theater tonight. (Sentence asks indirect question.)

Periods also follow common abbreviations as well as a person's initials.

Mr.	Sr.	P.M.
Mrs.	B.C.	lb.
Jr.	A.D.	St.
Dr.	A.M.	Corp.

Mark J. Valentini, Ph.D., has consented to head the new commission on traffic safety.

Writers today often omit periods after abbreviations for the names of organizations or government agencies, as the following examples show:

ABC	FBI	IRS
ACLU	FHA	NAM
AFL-CIO	GM	USAF

An up-to-date college dictionary will indicate whether a certain abbreviation should be written without periods.

Periods also precede decimal fractions and separate numerals standing for dollars and cents.

0.81 percent	$5.29
3.79 percent	$0.88

Question Marks   A question mark (?) ends a whole or a partial sentence that asks a direct question (one that repeats the exact words of the person who asked it).

Do you know how to operate this movie projector? (whole sentence asking a direct question)

Has Cinderella scrubbed the floor? Swept the hearth? Washed the dishes? (sentence and sentence parts asking direct questions)

Dr. Baker—wasn't she your boss once?—has just received a promotion to sales manager. (interrupting element asking a direct question)

The minister inquired, "Do you take this woman to be your lawful wedded wife?" (quotation asking a direct question)

A question mark may be used to indicate uncertainty.

Jane Seymour (1509?–1537), third wife of Henry VIII, was a lady in waiting to his first two wives.

Exclamation Points   Exclamation points (!) are used to express strong emotion or especially forceful commands.

Darcy! I never expected to see you again!

Sam! Turn that radio down immediately!

Help! Save me!

Use exclamation points sparingly; otherwise, they will quickly lose their force.

Add, change, or remove end marks as necessary. You may want to do some slight rewording.

It was horrifying, the mob of screaming fans grabbed Jack Slitherhips as he left the concert hall. Soon all I could see were his arms reaching for help. But it never came. Why do fans act this way. I am left wondering whether they love or hate their idols? They tore the clothes off Slitherhips, they tore out patches of his hair, someone even snatched his false teeth. Is this any way to treat a fading rock star. Jack is now in the hospital in a complete body cast; when I finally got to see him, he mumbled that he was giving up show business, he plans to settle down on a small farm. Who can blame him?

EXERCISE *Supply periods, question marks, or exclamation points wherever they are necessary. You may have to change existing punctuation marks. If a sentence is correct, write C.*

1. Be sure to proofread your paper before you submit it for a grade.
2. Sigmund Freud—isn't he now generally dismissed by many psychologists— really established the concept of the unconscious.
3. The sales tax in our state was raised to 65 percent.
4. Great we will have to buy another candle.
5. Carla used to study until 2 A.M. every night.
6. When you shopped for a new computer, did you consider what programs you wanted to run, set a budget for yourself, check the reliability of the different brands.
7. The engineer wanted to know how much stress would be placed on the beams.
8. Has Dr Stevens read the research on the most recent anti-clotting medication.
9. Run for your life, the tiger has escaped from the zoo.
10. Be sure to check your e-mail as soon as you start work.

Colons, Dashes, Parentheses, and Brackets

Colons, dashes, parentheses, and brackets separate and enclose, thereby clarifying relationships among the various parts of a sentence.

Colon   Colons (:) introduce explanations and anticipated lists following words that could stand alone as a complete sentence.

His aim in life is grandiose: to corner the market in wheat. (explanation)

Three students have been selected to attend the conference: Lucille Perkins, Dan Blakely, and Frank Napolis. (list)

Three factors can cause financial problems for farmers: (1) high interest rates, (2) falling land values, and (3) a strong dollar, which makes it difficult to sell crops abroad. (numbered list)

The first of the following sentences is incorrect because the words preceding the colon can't stand alone as a sentence:

Faulty   The tools needed for this job include: a hacksaw, a file, and a drill.

Revision   The tools needed for this job include a hacksaw, a file, and a drill.

Colons also frequently introduce formal quotations that extend beyond a single sentence.

The speaker stepped to the lectern and said: "I am here to ask for your assistance. Today several African nations face a food crisis because drought has ruined their harvests. Unless we provide help quickly, thousands of people will die of starvation."

In such situations, the material preceding the quotation need not be a complete sentence.

Colons also separate hours from minutes (8:20 A.M.), salutations of business letters from the body of the letters (Dear Ms. Stanley:), titles of publications from subtitles (*The Careful Writer: A Guide to English Usage*), numbers indicating ratios (a 3:2:2 ratio), and chapter from verse in biblical references (Luke 6:20–49).

Dashes   Like colons, dashes (—) set off appositives, lists, and explanations but are used in less formal writing. A dash emphasizes the material it sets off.

Only one candidate showed up at the political rally—Jerry Manders. (appositive)

The closet held only three garments—an out-at-the-elbows sports coat, a pair of blue jeans, and a tattered shirt. (list)

I know what little Billy's problem is—a soiled diaper. (explanation)

Dashes set off material that interrupts the flow of thought within a sentence.

Her new car—didn't she get it just three months ago?— has broken down twice.

Similarly, dashes are used to mark an interrupted segment of dialogue.

"I'd like to live in England when I retire."

"In England? But what will your wife—?"

"My wife likes the idea and can hardly wait for us to make the move."

Dashes set off parenthetical elements containing commas, and a dash can set off comments that follow a list.

The comedian—short, fat, and squeaky-voiced—soon had everyone roaring with laughter. (parenthetical element with commas)

A brag, a blow, a tank of air—that's what Senator Conwell is. (comment following a list)

Type a dash as two unspaced hyphens and leave no space between it and the words on either side of it.

Parentheses   Parentheses () are used to enclose numbers or letters that designate the items in a formal list and to set off incidental material within sentences. Except in the kind of list shown in the first example below, a comma does not usually precede a parenthesis.

Each paper should contain (1) an introduction, (2) several paragraphs developing the thesis statement, and (3) a conclusion.

Some occupations (computer programming, for example) may be overcrowded in ten years.

If the material in parentheses appears within a sentence, don't use a capital letter or period, even if the material is itself a complete sentence.

The growth of genetic engineering (one cannot foresee its consequences) worries some people today.

If the material in parentheses is written as a separate sentence, however, then punctuate it as you would a separate sentence.

Paula's angry outburst surprised everyone. (She had seemed such a placid person.)

If the material in parentheses comes at the end of a sentence, put the final punctuation after the closing parenthesis.

This company was founded by Willard Manley (1876–1951).

In contrast to dashes, parentheses de-emphasize the material they enclose.

Brackets   In quoted material, brackets [] enclose words or phrases that have been added to make the message clearer. They are also used with the word *sic* (Latin for "thus") to point out errors in quoted material.

"This particular company [Zorn Enterprises, Inc.] pioneered in the safe disposal of toxic wastes," the report noted. (The bracketed name is added to the original.)

"[John Chafin's] expertise in science has made him a popular figure on the lecture circuit," his friend stated. (The bracketed name replaces *his* in the original.)

"The principle [sic] cause of lung cancer is cigarette smoking," the article declared. (the word *principal* is misspelled "principle" in the original.)

To call attention to an error, follow it immediately with the bracketed *sic*. The reader will then know that the blame rests with the original writer, not with you.

() []

CONNECTED DISCOURSE EXERCISE

Supply any necessary or appropriate colons, dashes, parentheses, and brackets in the following letter:

Wayout Auto Company

We at Oldfield Sales a subsidiary of Jip, Inc., have had a serious problem with the cars we ordered from your company for leasing to our customers who will probably never return to us again. Two major parts fell off while the cars were sitting in the customers' driveways the exhaust system and the transmission. If this had happened while they were driving thank goodness it didn't, our customers could have been killed. Just imagine what that especially once it got into the newspapers would have done to our business. We must hold you to your claim that "while our cars are the cheepest sic on the market, we garuntee sic every car we sell." We expect immediate reimbursement for all the cars we purchased from you plus one million dollars to cover the damage to our reputation. A menace, a rip-off, a bad business deal, that's what your cars are. If you don't issue a formal recall for all your vehicles by 530 P.M., Friday, July 23, we will be forced to forward this matter to the federal government.

> Sincerely,
> Ken Swindelle
> Service Manager

 EXERCISE *Supply colons, dashes, parentheses, and brackets wherever they are necessary.*

1. Many former Presidents Millard Fillmore, for example have been largely forgotten by most Americans.
2. Our international sales have outperformed domestic sales by an 83 ratio.
3. The newspaper headline read, "Piece sic deal broken."
4. Among our social ills, one condition seems to be the source of many other problems poverty.
5. The new library better considered an information center will have over fifty computers with full Internet capability.
6. Our city area offers many advantages to businesses a skilled workforce, a well-developed infrastructure, and low taxes.
7. His Friedrich Nietzsche's *Thus Spoke Zarathustra* should be very familiar to anyone interested in the history of ideas.
8. In early June every elementary school student's thoughts turn to one thing summer vacation.
9. Mozart, Miles Davis, The Talking Heads his tastes certainly are eclectic.
10. The activities at the Pine Tree Resort include horseback riding, kayaking, swimming, water skiing, and much more. ◄

Quotation Marks

Quotation marks (" ") set off direct quotations, titles of short written or broadcast works, subdivisions of books, and expressions singled out for special attention.

Direct Quotations   A direct quotation repeats a speaker's or writer's exact words.

> "Tell me about the movie," said Debbie. "If you liked it, I may go myself."

> The placement director said, "The recruiter for Procter and Gamble will be on campus next Thursday to interview students for marketing jobs." (spoken comment)

> "The U.S. trade deficit is expected to reach record levels this year," the *Wall Street Journal* noted. (written comment)

> Jackie said the party was "a total flop."

As these sentences show, a comma or period that follows a direct quotation goes inside the quotation marks. When a quotation is a sentence fragment, the comma preceding it is omitted.

When an expression like "he said" interrupts a quoted sentence, use commas to set off the expression. When the expression comes between two complete quoted sentences, use a period after the expression and capitalize the first word of the second sentence.

> "Hop in," said Jim. "Let me give you a ride to school."

> "Thank you," replied Kelly, opening the car door and sliding into the front seat.

> "I can't remember," said Jim, "when we've had a worse winter."

Titles of Short Works and Subdivisions of Books   These short works include magazine articles, essays, short stories, chapters of books, one-act plays, short poems, songs, and television and radio episodes.

> The article was titled "The Real Conservatism." (article)

> Last night I read John Cheever's "The Enormous Radio," "Torch Song," and "The Swimmer." (short stories)

> Many John Denver fans consider "Take Me Home, Country Roads" to be his greatest piece of music. (song)

> The unsuccessful TV show *Pursued* ended its brief run with a segment titled "Checkmate." (TV episode)

Here, as with direct quotations, a comma or period that follows a title goes inside the quotation marks.

Expressions Singled Out for Special Attention   Writers who wish to call the reader's attention to a word or symbol sometimes put it within quotation marks.

The algebraic formula included a "π," a "Θ," and a "Δ."

"Bonnets" and "lifts" are British terms for car hoods and elevators.

More frequently, however, these expressions are printed in italics (page 696).

Again, any commas and periods that follow expressions set off by quotation marks go inside the marks.

Quotation Marks within Quotation Marks   When a direct quotation or the title of a shorter work appears within a direct quotation, use single quotation marks (').

> "I heard the boss telling the foreman, 'Everyone will receive a Christmas bonus,'" John said.

> The instructor told the class, "For tomorrow, read Ernest Hemingway's 'The Killers.'"

Note that the period goes inside of both the single and double quotation marks.

Positioning of Semicolons, Colons, and Question Marks   Position semicolons and colons that come at the end of quoted material after, not before, the quotation marks.

> Marcia calls Francine "that greasy grind"; however, I think Marcia is simply jealous of Francine's abilities.

> There are two reasons why I like "Babylon Revisited": the characters are interesting and the writing is excellent.

When a question mark accompanies a quotation, put it outside the quotation marks if the whole sentence rather than the quotation asks the question.

> Why did Cedric suddenly shout, "This party is a big bore"?

Put the question mark inside the quotation marks if the quotation, but not the whole sentence, asks a question or if the quotation asks one question and the whole sentence asks another.

> Marie asked, "What college is your brother planning to attend?" (The quoted material, not the whole sentence, asks the question.)

> Whatever possessed him to ask, "What is the most shameful thing you ever did?" (The whole sentence and the quoted material ask separate questions.)

CONNECTED DISCOURSE EXERCISE

Use quotation marks correctly in the following paragraph:

Mr. Silver recently lectured our class on Stephen Crane's The Bride Comes to Yellow Sky. One thing we shouldn't forget, Mr. Silver insisted, is that the town is deliberately named Yellow Sky. What is the significance of Crane's choice of the words Yellow Sky? Mr. Silver pointed out a number of possible associations, including cowardice, the setting sun, the open expanse of the West, freedom, the sand in the concluding passage. The story, Mr. Silver stated, is drenched in color words. For example, he pointed out, in the first three paragraphs alone Crane mentions vast flats of green grass, brick-colored hands, new black clothes, and a dress of blue cashmere.

EXERCISE *Supply properly positioned quotation marks wherever they are necessary.*

1. Some linguists think that the quintessential American ok may have come from the African waka.
2. My favorite piece of jazz music is St. James Infirmary.
3. What did Yeats mean by the line in his famous poem The Second Coming, Things fall apart, the center cannot hold?
4. Carl Thomas described the performance as extremely intense.
5. I managed to read Faulkner's short story The Bear, Jennifer sighed, but I don't really know what I want to say about it in my paper for English.
6. Why do so many student writers consistently confuse effect with affect?
7. In response to the Great Depression, Franklin Roosevelt declared The only thing we have to fear is fear itself; however, many families who had lost their homes and couldn't even earn enough for food really did have something to fear.
8. Yiddish words like mishugana and kibitz have come to be used outside the Jewish community.
9. In his closing argument, the defense attorney asked the jury, How would any one of us act if accused of a crime we knew we didn't commit?
10. Henry Ford supposedly called history bunk.

Hyphens

Hyphens (-) are used to join compound adjectives and nouns, compound numbers and word-number combinations, and certain prefixes and suffixes to the words with which they appear. In addition, hyphens help prevent misreadings and awkward combinations of letters or syllables and are used to split words between two lines.

Compound Adjectives   Hyphens are often used to join separate words that function as single adjectives and come before nouns. Typical examples follow:

Howard is a very *self-contained* person.

The *greenish-yellow* cloud of chlorine gas drifted toward the village.

Betty's *devil-may-care* attitude will land her in trouble someday.

When the first word of the compound is an adverb ending in *-ly* or when the compound adjective follows the noun it modifies, no hyphen is used.

The *badly* burned crash victim was rushed to the hospital.

The color of the chlorine gas was *greenish yellow.*

When two or more compound adjectives modify the same last term, the sentence will flow more smoothly if that term appears just once, after the last item in the series. The hyphens accompanying the earlier terms in the series are kept, however.

Many seventeenth-, eighteenth-, and nineteenth-century costumes are on display in this museum.

Compound Nouns　　Hyphenated nouns include such expressions as the following:

secretary-treasurer	good-for-nothing
sister-in-law	man-about-town

Here is a sentence with hyphenated nouns:

Denton is *editor-in-chief* of the largest newspaper in this state.

Compound Numbers and Word–Number Combinations　　Hyphens are used to separate two-word numbers from twenty-one to ninety-nine and fractions that have been written out.

Marcy has worked *twenty-one* years for this company.

One-fourth of my income goes for rent.

Similarly, hyphens are used to separate numerals from units of measurement that follow them.

This chemical is shipped in *50-gallon* drums.

Prefixes and Suffixes　　A prefix is a word or set of letters that precedes a word and alters its meaning. A suffix is similar but comes at the end of the word. Although most prefixes are not hyphenated, the prefixes *self-* and *all-* do get hyphens, as does the suffix *-elect*. Also the prefix *ex-* is hyphenated when it accompanies a noun.

This stove has a *self-cleaning* oven.

Let Claire Voyant, the *all-knowing* soothsayer, read your future in her crystal ball.

Ethel is the *chairperson-elect* of the club.

Several *ex-teachers* work in this department.

A prefix used before a capitalized term is always hyphenated.

The *ex-FBI* agent gave an interesting talk on the operations of that agency.

Preventing Misreadings and Awkward Combinations of Letters and Syllables Hyphens help prevent misreadings of certain words and also break up awkward combinations of letters and syllables between certain prefixes and suffixes and their core words.

The doctor *re-treated* the wound with a new antibiotic. (The hyphen prevents the misreading *retreated*.)

The company plans to *de-emphasize* sales of agricultural chemicals. (The hyphen prevents the awkward repetition of the letter *e* in *deemphasize*.)

Between Syllables Whenever you have to split a word between two lines, place a hyphen at the end of the first line to show the division. The word is always broken, and the hyphen inserted, between syllables. (Any good dictionary shows the syllable divisions of each word it includes.) Never divide a one-syllable word or leave two letters to be placed on the second line, even if those two letters constitute a syllable.

cap

EXERCISE *Supply hyphens wherever they are necessary. If the sentence is correct, write C.*

1. The piece of music ended with bird like sounds made by the entire woodwind section.
2. In this brokerage firm we follow sound investment strategies rather than chase after will o' the wisp schemes.
3. It can be sobering for the president elect to learn the full requirements of the job.
4. The union negotiators were forced to retreat from their initial demands.
5. One fifth of the shipment of fresh tomatoes turned out to be spoiled.
6. The classical radio station can be received by anyone within a 100 mile radius of its broadcasting tower.
7. In this class, we will study nineteenth and twentieth century American authors.
8. Emerson thought that it was important for people to be self reliant.
9. Once the power came back on, I had to recreate the file.
10. The Gundersons have been married for thirty five years.

Capitalization

Capitalize the first word in any sentence, the pronoun *I*, proper nouns and adjectives, titles used with names, and the significant words in literary and artistic titles.

Proper Nouns A proper noun names one particular person, group of persons, place, or thing. Such nouns include the following:

Persons
Organizations
Racial, political, and religious groups

Countries, states, cities, and streets
Companies and buildings
Geographical locations and features
Days, months, and holidays
Trademarks
Languages
Ships and aircraft
Abbreviations for academic degrees
Sacred writings and pronouns standing for God and Jesus
Titles used in place of names

The sentences below show the capitalization of proper nouns:

Sigmund works for the *National Psychoanalytical Institute,* an organization that has done much to advance the science of psychiatry.

How much does this roll of *Saran Wrap* cost?

Gwen Greene moved to *Paris, France,* when her father became the consul there.

On *Friday, December* 10, 1993, *Michael Jordan* visited our city.

Larry has a master of arts degree, and his sister has a *Ph.D.*

My father works for the *Ford Motor Company,* but I work for *Daimler Chrysler.*

Do not capitalize words like *institute, college, company,* or *avenue* unless they form part of a proper name. Likewise, do not capitalize the names of courses unless they start a sentence, are accompanied by a course number, or designate a language.

I have a 95 average in *Economics* 112 but only a 73 average in sociology.

Harry plans to take intermediate *German* in his junior year.

Do you plan to attend *Drew College* or some other college?

Proper Adjectives   Adjectives created from proper nouns are called proper adjectives. Like the nouns themselves, they should be capitalized.

Lolita Martinez, our class valedictorian, is of *Mexican* ancestry. (*Mexican* is derived from the proper noun *Mexico.*)

Abbreviations   As a general rule, capitalize abbreviations only if the words they stand for are capitalized.

Milton DeWitt works for the *IRS.* (*IRS* is capitalized because *Internal Revenue Service* would be.)

The flask holds 1,500 *ml* of liquid. (The abbreviation *ml* is not capitalized because *milliliters* would not be.)

cap

A few abbreviations are capitalized even though all or some of the words they stand for aren't. Examples include TV (television) and VCR (videocassette recorder). Others are shown on page 680.

Personal Titles Capitalize a personal title if it precedes a name or is used in place of a name. Otherwise, do not capitalize.

The division is under the command of *General* Arnold Schafer.

Tell me, *Doctor,* do I need an operation?

The *dean* of our engineering division is Dr. Alma Haskins.

Many writers capitalize titles of high rank when they are used in place of names.

The *President* will sign this bill tomorrow.

The *president* will sign this bill tomorrow.

Either usage is acceptable.

cap

Titles of Literary and Artistic Works When citing the titles of publications, pieces of writing, movies, television programs, paintings, sculptures, and the like, capitalize the first and last words and all other words except *a, an, the,* coordinating conjunctions, and one-syllable prepositions.

Last week I played *Gone with the Wind* on my VCR and read Christopher Isherwood's *Goodbye to Berlin.* (the preposition *with,* the article *the,* and the preposition *to* are not capitalized.)

John is reading a book called *The Movies of Abbott and Costello.* (The preposition *of* and the coordinating conjunction *and* are not capitalized. *The* is capitalized because it is the first word of the title.)

Although I'm no TV addict, I used to watch every episode of *Murder, She Wrote.* (All of the words in the title are capitalized.)

Note that the titles of literary and artistic works are italicized.

 EXERCISE *Identify any word or abbreviation that should be capitalized in the following sentences:*

1. Every friday at 1:00 P.M. the computer support team meets to review the problems that occurred during the previous week.
2. Any student of mexican history will soon see how radically different that history has been from american history.
3. Though many consider it a liberal organization, the aclu has actually protected the right to free speech of many extremely conservative groups.
4. Many students in the rotc choose to take history 321: american military history to satisfy their humanities requirement.
5. A student has a right to be proud upon earning an a.a.s. or a b.s. degree.

6. All requests for sabbatical leave must be submitted to dean Styron by october 1.

7. Though many consider latin a dead language, others continue to study it since so many great classical works were written in that language.

8. Your request for a leave of absence cannot be approved by professor Murphy.

9. Students of roman literature should be familiar with ovid's *metamorphoses*.

10. During World War II, dr. Johnson served on the u.s. submarine eel. ◀

Abbreviations

Items that are abbreviated include certain personal titles, names of organizations and agencies, Latin terms, and specific and technical terms.

Personal Titles   Abbreviate *Mister, Doctor,* and similar titles when they come just ahead of a name, and *Junior, Senior,* and degree titles when they follow names.

Will *Mr.* Harry Babbitt please come to the front desk?

Arthur Compton, *Sr.,* is a well-known historian; his son, Arthur Compton, *Jr.,* is a television producer.

This article on marital discord was written by Irma Quarles, *Ph.D.*

Names of Organizations and Agencies   Many organizations and agencies are known primarily by their initials rather than their full names. Several examples follow:

AAA	FBI	NBC
CARE	FHA	NATO
CIA	IBM	UNESCO

Latin Terms   Certain Latin terms are always abbreviated; others are abbreviated when used with dates or times.

e.g. (*exempli gratia:* for example)

i.e. (*id est:* that is)

etc. (*et cetera:* and [the] others)

vs. or v. (*versus:* against)

A.D. (*anno Domini:* in the year of our Lord)

A.M. or a.m. (*ante meridiem:* before noon)

P.M. or p.m. (*post meridiem:* after noon)

The play starts at 8 P.M.

Many writers (*e.g.,* Dylan Thomas and Truman Capote) have had serious problems with alcohol.

For consistency with A.D., the term "before Christ" is abbreviated as B.C.

ab

Scientific and Technical Terms   For brevity's sake, scientists and technicians abbreviate terms of measurement that repeatedly occur. Terms that the reader would not know are written out the first time they are used, and they are accompanied by their abbreviation in parentheses. Unfamiliar organizations and agencies that are mentioned repeatedly are handled in like manner.

The viscosity of the fluid measured 15 centistokes (cs) at room temperature. Common practice calls for writing such abbreviations without periods unless they duplicate the spelling of some word.

Standard dictionaries list common abbreviations. When you don't recognize one, look it up. Use abbreviations sparingly in essays. If you're unsure about what is appropriate, don't abbreviate.

> EXERCISE   *Supply abbreviations wherever they are necessary or are customarily used.*

1. Despite extensive competition, International Business Machines continues to be a major player in the computer industry.
2. We are pleased that Mister Jones has decided to join our firm.
3. Dissolve 1 gram of NaCl in 20 milliliters of water.
4. The freezing point of water at sea level is 32° Fahrenheit (0° Celsius).
5. Since its start, the National Broadcasting Company has been strongly committed to its news programming.
6. Doctor Baxter has been doing extensive research on nanotechnology, supported by a National Science Foundation grant.
7. Carl Thorton, Junior, will offer a workshop on how to save for retirement.
8. Many composers who are now seen as giants of classical music (*exempli gratia*, Mozart and Beethoven) died paupers.
9. After Friday's performance of Shakespeare's *Midsummer Night's Dream,* Carol Brice, Doctor of Philosophy, will discuss the use of nature imagery in the play.
10. Crimes that cross state boundaries are often investigated by the Federal Bureau of Investigation.   ◄

mm

Numbers

Some instructors ask their students to use figures for numbers larger than ninety-nine and to spell out smaller numbers.

Boise is *100* miles from here.

Boise is *ninety-nine* miles from here.

Other instructors prefer that students switch to figures beginning with the number ten.

My son will be *nine* years old on his next birthday.

My son will be *10* years old on his next birthday.

With either practice, the following exceptions apply.

Numbers in a Series   Write all numbers in a series the same way regardless of their size.

Gatsby has *64* suits, *110* shirts, and *214* ties.

In just one hour the emergency room personnel handled *two* stabbings, *five* shootings, and *sixteen* fractures.

We have *150* salespeople, *51* engineers, and *7* laboratory technicians.

Dates   Use figures for dates that include the year.

February *14, 1985* or 14 February 1935 (not February 14th, 1985)

When the date includes the day but not the year, you may use figures or spell out the number.

June 9

June ninth

the ninth of June

num

Page Numbers and Addresses   Use figures for page numbers and street numbers in addresses.

Check the graph on page *415*.

I live at *111* Cornelia Street, and my office is at *620* Fifth Avenue.

Numbers Beginning Sentences   Spell out any number that begins a sentence. If this requires three or more words, rephrase the sentence so that the number comes after the opening and numerals can be used.

The year *1989* was a good year for this wine.

Sixty thousand fans jammed the stadium.

An army of *265,000* troops assaulted the city. (If this number began the sentence, five words—an excessive number—would be needed to write it out.)

Decimals, Percentages, Times   Use figures for decimals and percentages as well as for expressions of time that are accompanied by A.M. or P.M.

The shaft has a *0.37*-inch diameter.

Last year the value of my house jumped *25* percent.

The plane leaves here at *9:50* A.M. and reaches New Orleans at *2:30* P.M.

One Number Following Another   When a number-containing term that denotes a unit of weight or measurement comes immediately after another number, spell out the first number, if smaller than 100, and use numerals for the second one. If the first number is larger than 100, use numerals for it and spell out the second one.

We ordered *six 30*-gallon drums of solvent for the project.

The supplier shipped us *600 thirty*-gallon drums by mistake.

> **EXERCISE** *Identify any miswriting of numbers in the following sentences and rewrite these numbers correctly:*

1. The supermarket ordered five hundred five-pound bags of sugar.
2. The Whitney Museum of American Art is at Nine Hundred and Forty-Five Madison Avenue, New York City.
3. The holes that the automated system drilled in the brackets were off by two hundredths of an inch.
4. The first memo warning the company of the problem was dated May fifteenth, 1993.
5. There will be a meeting at three-thirty P.M., May fifth, to discuss our new marketing plan.
6. Our local library has 658 CDs, 132 videocassettes, and sixty-three computer programs.
7. 8,000 people usually subscribe to our symphony orchestra series.
8. There are a number of serious editing errors on page thirty-nine of the report.
9. Over the last year, sales have increased by twenty-three percent.
10. We found that only 3 computers needed to be upgraded.

Italics

Italics are used for the titles of longer publications, the names of vehicles and vessels, foreign words and phrases, and expressions singled out for special attention. Use underlining to represent italics when hand writing or typing papers.

Titles of Longer Publications and Artistic Works   These items may include the following:

books	record albums	long musical works and poems
magazines	paintings	plays
newspapers	movies	sculptures

As noted on page 685, quotation marks are used for the titles of articles, short stories, short poems, one-act plays, and other brief pieces of writing.

Last night I finished F. Scott Fitzgerald's *The Great Gatsby* and read two articles in *The New Yorker*. (book, magazine)

Michelangelo's *David* is surely one of the world's greatest sculptures. (sculpture)

The *Detroit Free Press* had praise for the revival of Tennessee Williams's play *The Glass Menagerie*. (newspaper, play)

Stephen Vincent Benét's poem *John Brown's Body* won a Pulitzer Prize in 1929. (book-length poem)

Do not use italics when naming the Bible and its parts or other religious works such as the Torah and Koran.

Joanna's favorite book of the Bible is the Book of Ecclesiastes, part of the Old Testament.

Names of Vehicles and Vessels   Names of particular airplanes, ships, trains, and spacecraft are italicized.

The plane in which Charles Lindbergh flew over the Atlantic Ocean was named *The Spirit of St. Louis.*

Foreign Expressions   Use italics to identify foreign words and phrases that have not yet made their way into the English language.

The writer has a terribly pessimistic *weltanschauung.* (philosophy of life)

This season, long skirts are the *dernier cri.* (the latest thing)

When such expressions become completely assimilated, the italics are dropped. Most dictionaries use an asterisk (*), a dagger (†), or other symbol to identify expressions that need italicizing.

Expressions Singled Out for Special Attention   These include words, letters, numerals, and symbols.

The Greek letter *pi* is written Π.

I can't tell whether this letter is meant to be an *a* or an *o* or this number a *7* or a *9.*

In England, the word *lorry* means truck.

As noted on pages 685–686, quotation marks sometimes replace italics for this purpose.

CONNECTED DISCOURSE EXERCISE

Use hyphens, capitalization, abbreviations, numbers, and italics properly in the following passage:

Because I can speak Russian fluently, I was recruited by the central intelligence while still at Boston college. I suspected that it was professor Hogsbottom, a Political Science teacher, who had suggested that they consider me. After all, he had been a General during World War II and still had connections with the intelligence community. It turned out that my brother in law was responsible; he was an ex FBI agent. Soon I was an

ital

american spy located, of all places, in England. Who would suspect that we had to spy on the english? For 3 years I posed as a british aristocrat who was a general bon vivant and man about town. I went by the alias of Mister Henry Higgins, Junior. Everyone, of course, wanted to know if I had seen My Fair Lady. Personally I thought the whole thing was a monty python type of joke until I found a position in the british secret service. Who could have believed the british kept so many secrets from their american allies? For twenty one years I spied on the british without anyone suspecting that I was an all american boy. I did find out recently, however, that because of my fluent russian they had suspected me of being a russian spy and had been feeding me false information all along. ◄■

EXERCISE   *Supply italics wherever they are necessary.*

1. The British often use the word lift to refer to an elevator.
2. Arthur Miller's Death of a Salesman is considered by many critics to be the great American tragedy.
3. Linguists consider b to be voiced and p to be unvoiced.
4. Given the quality of the movie version, it takes a considerable amount of courage to produce a stage version of the musical West Side Story.
5. The delight many people take in the discomfort of characters in situation comedies suggests that all of us may be subject to some schadenfreude.
6. The USS Enterprise was the first nuclear aircraft carrier.
7. I have always fantasized about taking a ride on the Orient Express, which figured so prominently in a mystery by Agatha Christie.
8. There are few artistic statements against war that are stronger than Picasso's Guernica.
9. There has been a very conscious effort to make Scientific American available to a larger segment of the reading public.
10. It is a shame that so few students read Dostoevsky's Crime and Punishment as part of their education. ◄■

SPELLING

"Why the big deal about accurate spelling?"
"Does it really make that much difference if I have an *i* and an *e* turned around or if I omit a letter when spelling a word?"

Students frequently question the importance of proper spelling. Perhaps the answer is suggested by the following sentence, taken from a student essay:

I spent over seven hours *studing* one day last week.

The omission of a *y* in *studing* changes the person from one who is studious to one who is a dreamer. Not only does inaccurate spelling smack of carelessness, but also it sometimes drastically alters meaning.

Although there is no sure-fire way of becoming a good speller, you can minimize the difficulties by learning basic spelling rules, applying helpful spelling tips, and memorizing the proper spelling of troublesome words.

Spelling Rules

The following four rules should ease spelling pains.

Rule 1   If a word has the double vowels* *ie* or *ei* and the combination has a long *e* sound (as in *me*), use *ie* except after *c*. If the combination has an *a* sound, use *ei*.

ie (as long *e*)	*ei* after *c*	*ei* (as long *a*)
relieve	deceive	freight
belief	receive	neighbor
grieve	receipt	reign
piece	perceive	weigh

The main exceptions to this rule include *either, financier, leisure, neither, seize, species,* and *weird.*

Rule 2   If a one-syllable word (example: *sin*) ends in a single consonant preceded by a single vowel, double the consonant before adding a suffix (see page 688) that starts with a vowel. Apply the same rule with a word of two or more syllables (example: *admit*) if the final syllable is accented and ends with a single consonant preceded by a vowel.

---

*The vowels are *a, e, i, o,* and *u.* The consonants are the remaining letters of the alphabet.

"Dear Mom. Wud you belive I lost my job at the offise today? I gess sumwun thair doesnt like me."

From Recess Time, The Best Cartoons from The Kappan, edited by Kristin Herzog, 1983.

Words with Single Syllables	Words with Two or More Syllables
rig—rigged	admit—admittance
sin—sinned	control—controller
stop—stopping	equip—equipped

If the accent does not fall on the last syllable, do not double the final consonant.

audit—audited	chatter—chattered
counsel—counselor	simmer—simmering

Rule 3   If a word ends in *y* preceded by a single consonant, change the *y* to an *i* unless you are adding the suffix *-ing*.

y changed to *i*	*y* retained
beauty—beautiful	copy—copying
fury—furious	defy—defying
easy—easily	dry—drying
vary—various	vary—varying

Rule 4   If a word ends in a silent *e*, the *e* is usually dropped when a suffix starting with a vowel is added.

blue—bluish	fame—famous
dense—density	grieve—grievous

In a few cases, the *e* is retained to avoid pronunciation difficulties or confusion with other words.

dye—dyeing (not dying)   singe—singeing (not singing)
shoe—shoeing (not shoing)

The *e* is also retained when it is preceded by a soft *c* sound (pronounced like the letter *s*) or a soft *g* sound (pronounced like the letter *j*) and the suffix being added starts with an *a* or an *o*.

peace—peaceable   courage—courageous
change—changeable   manage—manageable

Helpful Spelling Tips

Here are some tips that can further improve your spelling:

1. Examine each problem word carefully, especially prefixes (*au*dience, *au*dible), suffixes (superintend*ent*, descend*ant*), and double consonants (sate*ll*ite, roo*mm*ate, and co*ll*apsible).

2. Sound out each syllable carefully, noting its pronunciation. Words like *height, governor,* and *candidate* are often misspelled because of improper pronunciation.

3. Make a list of your problem words and review them periodically. Concentrate on each syllable and any unusual features (ar*c*tic, ambig*uous*).

4. Use any crutches that will help: there is *gain* in *bargain;* to *breakfast* is to *break a fast;* a disease causes *dis-ease.*

5. When you copy anything from the blackboard or a textbook, copy it carefully. Writing a word correctly helps you to spell it correctly the next time.

6. Buy a good collegiate dictionary and look up the words you don't know how to spell. (See pages 244–246 for more information on dictionaries.)

7. If you have a word processor that has a spell checker, use it. But a word of caution: Don't rely exclusively on this tool. Your spell checker may not distinguish between *to* and *too, their* and *there,* and similar sound-alike words. The ultimate spell checker is you.

sp

List of Troublesome Words

Students frequently misspell the words in the following list. Study these words carefully until the correct spelling becomes automatic. Then have a friend read them to you while you write them down. Tag the ones you misspell and whenever you revise a paper, check especially for these words.

abandoned	allotted	barbiturate	commit
abbreviate	allowed	beautiful	commitment
absence	all right	beggar	committed
absorb	already	believe	committee
absorption	although	beneficial	committing
absurd	altogether	benefit	comparatively
academy	always	benefited	competent
accelerate	amateur	biscuit	competition
accept	ambiguous	boundary	concede
access	among	bourgeois	conceive
accessible	analysis (analyses)	breathe	condemn
accident	analyze	Britain	condescend
accidentally	anonymous	bulletin	confident
accommodate	anxiety	bureau	congratulations
accomplish	apartment	bureaucracy	connoisseur
accumulate	apparent	business	conqueror
accustom	appearance	cafeteria	conscience
achieve	appreciate	calendar	conscientious
achievement	appropriate	camouflage	conscious
acknowledge	architecture	campaign	consistency
acknowledgment	arctic	candidate	consistent
acquaintance	argue	carburetor	conspicuous
acquire	arguing	carriage	contemptible
acquit	argument	carrying	continuous
acquitted	arithmetic	casual	controversy
address	ascent	category	convenience
advice	assassin	causal	convenient
advise	assent	ceiling	coolly
aerial	assistance	cellar	cooperate
aggravate	assistant	cemetery	corollary
aggravated	athlete	changeable	corps
aggression	athletics	changing	corpse
aggressive	attempt	characteristic	correlate
aging	attendance	chauffeur	counterfeit
alcohol	average	chief	courteous
allege	bachelor	colloquial	criticism
alleviate	balance	colonel	criticize
alley(s)	balloon	column	cruelty
allot	barbarous	commission	curiosity

sp

curriculum	environment	hygiene	mattress
dealt	equal	hypocrisy	meant
deceit	equip	hysterical	medicine
deceive	equipment	illiterate	medieval
decent	equipped	illogical	mediocre
decision	equivalent	illusion	melancholy
defendant	especially	immediate	miniature
defense	exaggerate	implement	minute
definite	exceed	impromptu	miscellaneous
definitely	excellent	inadequate	mischievous
dependent	except	incident	misspell
descendant	excerpt	incidentally	modifies
descent	excess	independent	modify
describe	excitement	indict	modifying
description	exercise	indispensable	moral
desert	existence	individual	morale
desirable	experience	inevitable	mortgage
despair	extraordinary	infinitely	mosquitoes
desperate	extremely	ingenious	muscle
dessert	fallacy	ingenuous	mysterious
develop	familiar	innocent	necessary
development	fascinate	intelligent	neither
difference	fascist	interest	nevertheless
dilemma	February	interfere	niece
disappear	fiery	irresistible	noticeable
disastrous	finally	irresponsible	obedience
discernible	financier	jeopardy	occasion
disciple	foreign	judgment	occasionally
discipline	foreword	judicial	occur
discussion	forfeit	knowledge	occurred
disease	forward	knowledgeable	occurrence
dissatisfied	friend	laboratory	occurring
dissipate	fulfill	legitimate	official
dominant	gaiety	leisure	omission
drunkenness	gases	library	omit
echoes	gauge or gage	license	omitted
ecstasy	genius	lightning	omitting
efficiency	genuine	loneliness	opinion
efficient	government	loose	opponent
eighth	grammar	lose	opportunity
eligible	guarantee	magnificent	optimistic
eliminate	guard	maintain	original
embarrass	handkerchief	maintenance	outrageous
emphasis	harass	maneuver	pamphlet
employee	height	manual	parallel
engineer	heroes	marriage	paralysis
enthusiastic	hindrance	mathematics	parliament

particularly
pastime
patent
peaceable
perceive
perfectible
perform
permanent
permissible
perseverance
persuade
physical
physician
picnic
picnicked
playwright
pleasant
pleasurable
politician
possess
possession
possible
potatoes
practice
precede
precedent
precious
predominant
preference
preferred
prejudice
preparation
privilege
probably
procedure
proceed
professor
prominent
pronounce
pronunciation
propaganda
propagate
propeller
prophecy
prophesy
prostate
prostrate

protein
psychiatry
psychology
pursue
pursuit
quantity
questionnaire
quiet
quite
quiz
quizzes
realize
receipt
receive
recipe
recognizable
recommend
refer
reference
referring
reign
relevant
relieve
religious
remembrance
reminisce
reminiscence
reminiscent
rendezvous
repellent
repentance
repetition
representative
resemblance
resistance
restaurant
rhetoric
rhyme
rhythm
roommate
sacrifice
sacrilege
sacrilegious
safety
salary
sandwich
scarcely

scene
scenic
schedule
science
secretary
seize
sensible
separate
sergeant
severely
siege
similar
simultaneous
sincerely
skeptical
skiing
skillful
skis
society
sophomore
source
specifically
specimen
sponsor
spontaneous
statistics
steely
strategy
studying
subtle
subtlety
subtly
succeed
success
successful
succinct
suffrage
superintendent
supersede
suppose
suppress
surprise
syllable
symmetry
sympathize
synonym
synonymous

tangible
tariff
technical
technique
temperament
temperature
temporary
tenant
tendency
thorough
thought
through
traffic
trafficking
tragedy
tranquillity or
  tranquility
transcendent
transcendental
transfer
transferred
transferring
translate
tries
truly
twelfth
tyrannical
tyranny
unanimous
unconscious
undoubtedly
unmistakable
unnecessary
until
unwieldy
urban
urbane
usage
useful
using
usual
usually
vacancy
vacillate
vacuum
valuable
vegetable

sp

vengeance	warring	wholly	wreak
victorious	weather	wield	wreck
village	Wednesday	wintry	writing
villain	weird	wiry	written
waive	whether	worshiped or	yield
warrant	whole	worshipped	

sp

GLOSSARY OF WORD USAGE

The English language has many words and expressions that confuse writers and thereby lessen the precision and effectiveness of their writing. These troublesome items include the following:

Word pairs that sound alike or almost alike but are spelled differently and have different meanings

Word pairs that do not sound alike but still are often confused

Words or phrases that are unacceptable in formal writing

The following glossary identifies the most common of these troublemakers. Familiarize yourself with its contents. Then consult it as you revise your writing if you have even the slightest doubt about the proper use of a word, phrase, or expression.

a, an   Use *a* with words beginning with a consonant sound (even if the first written letter is a vowel); use *an* with words beginning with a vowel or a vowel sound.

> *a* brush, *a* student, *a* wheel, *a* risky situation, *a* once-in-a-lifetime opportunity
>
> *an* architect, *an* apple, *an* unworthy participant, *an* interesting proposal, *an* honest politician

accept, except   *Accept* is a verb meaning "to receive" or "to approve." *Except* is used as a verb or a preposition. As a verb, *except* means "to take out, exclude, or omit." As a preposition, it means "excluding," "other than," or "but not."

> She *accepted* the bouquet of flowers.
>
> Linda *excepted* Sally from the list of guests. (verb)
>
> All of Linda's friends *except* Sally came to the party. (preposition)

access, excess   *Access* is a noun meaning "means or right to enter, approach, or use." In the computer field it is a verb meaning "gain entrance to." *Excess* is an adjective meaning "too much; more than needed; lack of moderation."

> I have *access* to a summer cottage this weekend.
>
> The code permits users to *access* the computer.
>
> The airline booked an *excess* number of passengers on that flight.

adapt, adopt   To *adapt* is "to adjust," often by modification. To *adopt* is "to take as one's own."

> He *adapted* to the higher elevations of the Rocky Mountains.
>
> She *adopted* the new doctrine expounded by the prophet.

adverse, averse   *Adverse* is an adjective meaning "unfavorable." *Averse* is an adjective meaning "disinclined" or "feeling distaste for."

Adverse circumstances caused the ceremony to be postponed.

Martha was *averse* to naming all the guilty children.

advice, advise   *Advice* is a noun meaning "a recommendation about how to deal with a situation or problem." *Advise* is a verb meaning "to recommend or warn."

The young man followed his sister's *advice*.

Mr. Smith *advised* John to buy 10,000 shares of the stock.

affect, effect   Although both words may function as nouns and verbs, usually *affect* is a verb and *effect* is a noun. The verb *affect* means "to influence, cause a change in, or arouse the emotions of." The noun *affect* is a technical term in psychology and refers to feeling. The noun *effect* means "result or outcome." The verb *effect* means "to bring about or achieve."

His speech *affected* me greatly. (verb)

The *effect* of the announcement was felt immediately. (noun)

The doctor was soon able to *effect* a cure. (verb)

aggravate   *Aggravate* is a verb meaning "to intensify or make worse" an existing situation. The use of *aggravate* to mean "annoy" or "anger" is colloquial.

| *Colloquial* | Susan's behavior at the dance really *aggravated* me. |
| *Standard* | Marcy's interference only *aggravated* the conflict between Bill and Nadine. |

ain't   This nonstandard term for *isn't, aren't, hasn't,* or *haven't* is unacceptable in college writing.

all ready, already   *All ready* means "completely prepared" or "everyone is ready." *Already* means "previously, even now, even then."

The scouts are *all ready* for the camp out.

When we arrived we found he had *already* gone.

The report is *already* a week overdue.

all right, alright   *Alright* is a nonstandard spelling of *all right* and is not acceptable in college writing.

all together, altogether   *All together* means "all in one place" or "in unison." *Altogether* is an adverb meaning "completely, entirely."

The family was *all together* at the wedding.

All together, men, push!

Mr. Doe is *altogether* at fault for writing the letter.

allusion, delusion, illusion   An *allusion* is an indirect reference. A *delusion* is a mistaken belief, often part of a psychological condition. An *illusion* is a deceptive appearance presented to the sight or created by the imagination.

In his sermon, the minister made many *allusions* to the New Testament.

He suffers from the *delusion* that he is a millionaire.

They wore makeup to give the *illusion* of beauty.

a lot, alot   *Alot* is an erroneous spelling of the two words *a lot*. The phrase *a lot* is usually colloquial; in formal writing replace it with "many."

already   See *all ready, already*.

alright   See *all right, alright*.

alternately, alternatively   *Alternately* means "occurring by turns, one after the other." *Alternatively* means "providing a choice between two items."

The U.S. flag has seven red and six white stripes, arranged *alternately*.

Highway 44 offers the most direct route to Junction City. *Alternatively*,

Highway 88 is much more scenic.

altogether   See *all together, altogether*.

among, between   Use *between* when referring to two things and *among* when referring to more than two.

He divided the candy *between* Allan and Stephanie.

He divided the candy *among* the five children.

amoral, immoral   *Amoral* means "neither moral nor immoral; morally neutral." *Immoral* means "contrary to the moral code."

The movie, which takes no clear position on the behavior it depicts, seems curiously *amoral*.

Murder is an *immoral* act.

amount, number   *Amount* refers to total quantities, things in bulk, or weight. *Number* refers to countable things. Never use *amount* when referring to people.

Cassandra inherited a large *amount* of money.

Cassandra now has a large *number* of friends.

an, a   See *a, an*.

and/or   Although often used in commercial and legal documents, this combination should be avoided in other writing.

angry, mad   *Mad* means "insane," although it is often used colloquially to mean "annoyed" or "angry." To be precise, use *mad* only to mean insane.

Colloquial	I was *mad* at Debbie.
Standard	I was *angry* with Debbie.

any, any other   Do not use *any* when you mean *any other*. Using *any* in the following example would mean that Theresa is more qualified than herself:

Theresa is more qualified than *any other* candidate.

usage

anyone, any one   *Anyone* means "any person." *Any one* means "any single person or thing."

I can whip *anyone* in this room.

I saw three movies last week but didn't like *any one* of them.

appraise, apprise   *Appraise* means "to determine the value of something." *Apprise* means "to notify" or "to tell."

The jeweler *appraised* the gold brooch at $1,500.

Having been *apprised* of the situation, the family priest was able to reconcile the parents and the children.

apt, liable, likely   Both *apt* and *liable* express a tendency or inclination. *Liable* suggests something unpleasant or likely to result in legal action. It should be used only when the event may have unpleasant consequences.

We are *liable* to miss the train.

My lawyer said that I was *liable* for the damage my car had caused.

If the probable consequences are not unpleasant, *apt* is the better word.

I am *apt* to buy books if we go to the shopping center.

Likely merely implies strong probability.

Sandra is *likely* to pass this course without difficulty.

around   *Around* is colloquial use for "approximately" or "about."

Colloquial	She arrived *around* 10:00 P.M.
	The blouse cost *around* $15.
Standard	She arrived at *approximately* 10:00 P.M.
	The blouse cost *about* $15.

as   *As* is frequently used as a weak substitute for *because, since, when,* and *while.*

| *Weak* | She ran out of the house *as* it was on fire. |
| *Better* | She ran out of the house *because* it was on fire. |

As should not be used in place of *whether* or *that.*

Nonstandard	I don't know *as* I like her.
Standard	I don't know *that* I like her.
	I don't know *whether* I like her.

as, like   *As* may be used as a conjunction that introduces an adverb clause, but *like* should not be used this way.

| *Unacceptable* | *Like* my father always said, "You can fool some of the people all of the time." |
| *Standard* | *As* my father always said, "You can fool some of the people all of the time." |

Like may, however, be used as a preposition.

usage

In times *like* this, it's hard not to despair.

Any woman *like* Sally can expect a successful career in business.

assure, ensure, insure   To *assure* is "to make safe from risk, to guarantee" or "to convince." *Ensure* and *insure* can be variant spellings meaning "to make certain." *Insure*, however, is now generally associated with the business of insurance.

The counselor tried to *assure* the students that they had made a wise choice.

The captain *assured* them that they would be rescued.

The father, wanting to *ensure* his son's college education, applied for a federally *insured* loan.

averse   See *adverse, averse.*

awful, awfully   In everyday speech, *awful* is used to describe things disagreeable or objectionable: "an *awful* movie," "an *awful* character." *Awfully* is used colloquially as an intensifier: "*awfully* nice," "*awfully* bad." Unless they are used to mean "solemnly impressive," however, both words should be avoided in formal writing.

The *awful* majesty of the cathedral silenced the chattering tourists.

awhile, a while   *A while,* consisting of the noun *while* and the article *a,* means "a period of time." *Awhile* is an adverb meaning "for a short time."

Dinner will be served in *a while.*

Sit *awhile* and tell me the latest gossip.

bad, badly   *Bad* is an adjective. *Badly* is an adverb. *Badly* is colloquial when used to mean "very much."

Unacceptable	She feels *badly* about her mistake.
	Tom behaved *bad* at the circus.
Colloquial	I want a new car *badly.*
Standard	She feels *bad* about her mistake. (adjective as subject complement)
	Tom behaved *badly* at the circus. (adverb)
	I want a new car *very much.*

being as, being that   When used as substitutes for *because* or *since,* these expressions are nonstandard.

Nonstandard	*Being that* I was the first in line, I was able to purchase choice tickets.
Standard	*Because* I was first in line, I was able to purchase choice tickets.

beside, besides   Both words are prepositions, but they have different meanings. *Beside* means "at the side of," and *besides* means "in addition to."

Sheila and Bill sat *beside* the trailer to eat their lunch.

Besides Harvey, Seymour is coming to dinner.

between   See *among, between.*

usage

breath, breathe   *Breath* is a noun and *breathe* is its verb counterpart.

> Nicole stepped outside the stuffy cabin for a *breath* of fresh air.

> The cabin was so stuffy that Nicole could hardly *breathe.*

broke   *Broke,* when used to mean "without money," is colloquial.

> *Colloquial*   Because Shelley was *broke,* she had to miss the movie.

> *Standard*   Because Shelley *had no money,* she had to miss the movie.

can, may   *Can* refers both to permission and to the ability to do something, while *may* refers to permission only.

> I think I *can* pass the exam on Friday. (ability)

> My mother says I *can* go to the movies. (permission)

> *May* I take the test next Monday? (permission)

When used to denote permission, *can* lends a less formal air to writing than does *may.*

cannot, can not   The use of *cannot* is preferred unless the writer wishes to italicize the *not* for emphasis.

> You *cannot* expect a raise this year.

> No, you can *not* expect a raise this year.

can't hardly   This nonstandard form for *cannot, can't,* or *can hardly* is unacceptable in college writing.

can't help but   In college writing, this colloquial phrase should be revised to the simpler *I can't help* or *I cannot help.*

> *Colloquial*   I *can't help but* wish that I were going to the concert.

> *Standard*   I *can't help* wishing that I were going to the concert.

capital, capitol   *Capital* means "a city that serves as a seat of government." *Capitol* means "a building in which a state legislature meets" or "the building in which Congress meets."

> Dover is the *capital* of Delaware.

> The *capitol* in Dover is popular with visitors.

Capital can also refer to wealth or assets, to an offense punishable by death, or to something excellent or first-rate.

> My *capital* consists entirely of stocks and bonds.

> Murder is a *capital* crime in this state.

> That's a *capital* suggestion!

censor, censure   To *censor* is "to judge"—literature, movies, letters, and the like—and to decide what material is unfit to be read or seen. To *censure* is "to judge harshly" or "find fault with."

> The warden *censored* all the prisoners' mail.

> The judge *censured* Clyde's criminal behavior.

childish, childlike   Both of these terms mean "like a child." *Childish,* however, has a negative connotation.

He is fifty-two years old, but he behaves in a *childish* manner.

Jon's face has a *childlike* quality that everyone likes immediately.

cite, sight, site   *Cite* means "to mention or quote as an example," *sight* means "to see" or "a view," and *site* means "a location."

Cheryl *cited* Abraham Lincoln's Emancipation Proclamation in her talk.

He was able to *sight* the enemy destroyers through the periscope.

The building *site* is a woody area south of town.

climactic, climatic   *Climactic* is an adjective that means "of, being, or relating to a climax." *Climatic* is an adjective meaning "of or relating to a climate."

Riding the roller coaster was the *climactic* event of Alice's day.

The *climatic* features of Arizona are desirable to many people.

complement, compliment   Both words can act as nouns or verbs. As a noun, *complement* means "something that completes or makes up the whole." As a verb, it means "to complete or perfect." As a noun, *compliment* means "a flattering or praising remark." As a verb, it means "to flatter or praise."

A *complement* of navy personnel boarded the foreign freighter. (noun)

This fruit will *complement* the meal nicely. (verb)

Scott paid Sara Jane a lovely *compliment* at the time of her graduation. (noun)

Mother *complimented* me for cleaning my room. (verb)

conscience, conscious   *Conscience* refers to the sense of moral right or wrong. *Conscious* refers to the awareness of one's feelings or thoughts.

Edgar's *conscience* forced him to return the money.

Basil was not *conscious* of his angry feelings.

Do not confuse *conscious* with *aware;* although these words are similar in meaning, one is *conscious* of feelings or actions but *aware* of events.

usage

contemptible, contemptuous   *Contemptible* means "deserving of contempt." *Contemptuous* means "displaying contempt."

Peter's drunkenness is *contemptible.*

Mary is *contemptuous* of Peter's drunkenness.

continual, continuous   *Continual* means "frequently or regularly repeated." *Continuous* means "uninterrupted."

The telephone's *continual* ringing made the morning a nightmare.

His wound caused him *continuous* pain for a week.

could have, could of   *Could of* is an unacceptable substitute for *could have* because a preposition cannot substitute for a verb.

| Nonstandard | I *could of* gone with my parents to Portugal. |
| Standard | I *could have* gone with my parents to Portugal. |

council, counsel   A *council* is a group of people that governs or advises. *Counsel* can be used as both a noun and a verb. The noun means "advice," and the verb means "to advise."

The city *council* meets on the second Tuesday of every month.

The lawyer's *counsel* was sound. (noun)

The psychologist *counsels* many abused children. (verb)

couple   *Couple* denotes two things and should not be used to refer to more than that number.

criteria, criterion   *Criterion* is always singular, *criteria* always plural.

The primary *criterion* for performing this job is manual dexterity.

Manual dexterity is but one of many *criteria* on which you will be judged.

cute   *Cute*, an overused colloquialism, should be avoided; it has too many connotations to be used precisely in writing.

data   *Data* is the plural of *datum*. Although *data* is sometimes used with a singular verb, this use is considered incorrect.

| Standard | These *data* are incorrect. |
| Unacceptable | This *data* is incorrect. |

definite, very definite   Since *definite* means "precise" or "unmistakable," *very definite* is repetitive. One really cannot be more definite than *definite*.

delusion   See *allusion, delusion, illusion*.

desert, deserts, dessert   *Desert* is land that is arid. With the accent on the last syllable, it is a verb meaning "to abandon." *Deserts* means "that which is deserved." *Dessert* is food served after dinner.

The Sonoran *desert* is full of plant life.

You'll get your just *deserts* if you *desert* me now.

They had cheesecake for *dessert* every Thursday night.

device, devise   *Device* is a noun meaning "a mechanical contrivance, gadget, or tool." *Devise* is a verb meaning "to plan or invent."

This new *device* gives us better gas mileage.

We must *devise* a new approach to our problem.

different from, different than   *Different from* is preferred over *different than*.

His ideas on marriage were *different from* those of his wife.

Different than is accepted, however, when a clause follows and the *from* construction would be wordy.

| Acceptable | Susan looks *different than* she did last summer. |
| Wordy | Susan looks *different from* the way she looked last summer. |

discreet, discrete   To be *discreet* means to be "prudent, tactful, or careful of one's actions." *Discrete* means "distinct or separate."

> Jack was always *discreet* when he talked to his grandparents.

> When two atoms of hydrogen combine with one atom of oxygen, they are no longer *discrete* entities.

disinterested, uninterested   A person who is *disinterested* is impartial or unbiased. A person who is *uninterested* is indifferent or not interested.

> We need a *disinterested* judge to settle the dispute.

> Joe is completely *uninterested* in sports.

don't   This contraction for *do not* should never be used with singular subjects such as *he, she,* or *it.* Instead, use *doesn't*, the contraction for *does not*, with singular subjects.

Nonstandard	*Don't* he know how to spell? She *don't* think of anyone except herself. That mistake *don't* help your image.
Standard	*Doesn't* he know how to spell? She *doesn't* think of anyone except herself. That mistake *doesn't* help your image.

due to   *Due to* has always been acceptable following a linking verb.

> Her success was *due to* hard work.

Purists, however, object to *due to* when it is used in other situations, especially in introductory phrases.

> *Due to* the many requests we have had, not everyone who wishes tickets will receive them.

In such cases, you may wish to recast the sentence.

> *Because* we have had so many requests, not everyone who wishes tickets will receive them.

effect   See *affect, effect.*

e.g.   This abbreviation, from the Latin *exempli gratia*, means "for example." Avoid using it except in comments in parentheses and in footnotes, and always follow it with a comma.

elicit, illicit   *Elicit* is a verb that means "to draw forth." *Illicit* is an adjective meaning "not permitted."

> A good professor can always *elicit* responses from students.

> He was engaged in many types of *illicit* activities.

emigrate, immigrate   When people *emigrate*, they move out of a country. When people *immigrate*, they move into a country.

> The family *emigrated* from Poland.

> Many Russians *immigrated* to America.

eminent, imminent   *Eminent* means "prominent," whereas *imminent* means "about to happen."

usage

Niels Bohr was an *eminent* physicist.

Our instruments show that an earthquake is *imminent*.

ensure   See *assure, ensure, insure.*

enthused, enthusiastic   *Enthused* is a colloquial word and should not be used in place of *enthusiastic.*

Colloquial	John was *enthused* about the prospects for jobs in his hometown.
Standard	John was *enthusiastic* about the prospects for jobs in his hometown.

especially, specially   The term *especially* means "particularly, notably." *Specially* means "for a specific purpose."

He is an *especially* talented pianist.

He was *specially* chosen to represent his group.

et al.   This expression, from the Latin *et alia*, means "and others," referring to people. Ordinarily, the abbreviation should be used only in footnotes and bibliographic entries.

etc.   This abbreviation, from the Latin *et cetera*, means "and other things" and is used in reference to objects rather than people. It should be avoided except in comments in parentheses or in footnotes. It should never be preceded by *and*.

everyone, every one   *Everyone* means "every person." *Every one* means "every particular person or thing."

Everyone who wants to go to the ball game should let me know today.

If you carefully check *every one* of your paragraphs, you can improve your writing.

except   See *accept, except.*

excess   See *access, excess.*

explicit, implicit   *Explicit* means "clearly expressed" or "straightforward." *Implicit* means "implied" or "understood without direct statement."

You must state your needs *explicitly* if you want them fulfilled.

When I took on the project, I made an *implicit* commitment to see it through.

extant, extent   *Extant* is an adjective meaning "still existing." *Extent* is a noun meaning "scope, size, range, limit."

The dodo bird is no longer *extant*.

From Nevada to Colorado is the *extent* of my travels.

farther, further   The traditional distinction is that *farther* refers to physical distance and *further* to distance in time. Only *further* should be used to mean "additional" or "additionally."

In the race for the Muscular Dystrophy Association, Janet ran *farther* than Cindy.

If you think *further* on the matter, I am certain we can reach an agreement.

Let me make one *further* point.

usage

fewer, less   *Fewer* refers to countable items. *Less* refers to quantity or degree.

     Mrs. Smith has *fewer* dogs than cats.

     There is *less* money in Joan's checking account than in Stanley's.

     Jack was *less* ambitious in his later years.

Never use *less* to refer to people.

     Nonstandard   *Less* people were there than I expected.

     Standard   *Fewer* people were there than I expected.

flaunt, flout   To *flaunt* is "to display in a showy way." To *flout* is "to express contempt" or "to show scorn."

     Jay *flaunted* his handsome physique before all his friends.

     Jerrold *flouted* the convention of dressing for dinner by arriving in tennis shoes.

formally, formerly   *Formally* means "according to established forms, conventions, and rules; ceremoniously." *Formerly* means "in the past."

     The ambassador *formally* greeted his dinner guests.

     Formerly, smallpox was one of our most serious diseases.

funny   *Funny* refers to something that is amusing. In college writing it should not be used to mean "odd" or "unusual."

     Colloquial   I felt *funny* visiting my old fourth-grade classroom.

     Standard   I felt *odd* visiting my old fourth-grade classroom.

further   See *farther, further.*

get   *Get,* in any of its many colloquial senses, should not be used in writing.

     Colloquial   Her way of looking at a man really *gets* me.
                        I'll *get* him if it's the last thing I do.

     Standard   Beth will *get* at least a *B* in this course.

good and   Replace this colloquial phrase with *very.*

     Colloquial   She is *good and* tired of the cafeteria food.

     Standard   She is *very* tired of the cafeteria food.

good, well   Do not mistakenly use *good* as an adverb when an adjective is required.

     Unacceptable   John did *good* on his first test.

     Standard   John is making *good* progress on his report.
                       John is a *good* student.

Well can be used as an adjective meaning "in good health." Otherwise it should always be used as an adverb.

     Last week I had a bad cold, but now I am *well.* (adjective)

     John did *well* on his first test. (adverb)

got, gotten   Both are acceptable past-participle forms of the verb *to get.*

usage

had ought, hadn't ought   Both are incorrect in formal writing. The correct forms are *ought* and *ought not*.

I *ought* to start studying.

You *ought not* to cut class again.

hanged, hung   People may be *hanged*. Objects may be *hung*.

The prisoner was *hanged* at noon.

Mavis *hung* the picture in the dining room.

hisself, theirself, theirselves   These are nonstandard forms of *himself* and *themselves*.

hopefully   *Hopefully* means "in a hopeful manner." In informal speaking, it is used to mean "it is hoped" or "I hope," but this usage is not correct in formal writing. (Compare this with *carefully*, which means "in a careful manner"; no one uses *carefully* to mean "it is cared.")

Colloquial	*Hopefully*, it will not rain during the class picnic.
Standard	Sally walked *hopefully* into the boss's office to ask for a raise.

hung   See *hanged, hung*.

i.e.   This abbreviation, meaning "that is," comes from the Latin *id est*. Avoid using it except in comments in parentheses or footnotes, and always follow it with a comma.

if, whether   *If* is used to introduce adverb clauses, where it means "assuming that."

If I finish my report on time, I'll attend the concert with you.

If and *whether* are often used interchangeably to introduce noun clauses that follow verbs such as *ask, say, doubt, know,* and *wonder*. In formal writing, however, *whether* is preferred.

Less Desirable	I don't know *if* we'll be able to see the North Star tonight.
More Desirable	I don't know *whether* we'll be able to see the North Star tonight.

usage

illicit   See *elicit, illicit*.

illusion   See *allusion, delusion, illusion*.

immigrate   See *emigrate, immigrate*.

imminent   See *eminent, imminent*.

immoral   See *amoral, immoral*.

impact   Although *impact* is sometimes used in colloquial speech as a verb meaning "affect," this use is unacceptable in college writing.

Colloquial	This new law will greatly *impact* political campaigning.
Standard	This new law will greatly *affect* political campaigning.

implicit   See *explicit, implicit*.

imply, infer   To *imply* is "to indicate indirectly or give implication." To *infer* is "to conclude from facts, evidence, or indirect suggestions."

Jack *implied* that he wanted a divorce when he told his wife that all marriages come to an end.

Doris *inferred* that Jack wanted a divorce when he told her all marriages come to an end.

As these examples indicate, speakers and writers imply; listeners and readers infer.

incidence, incidents   *Incidents* are separate, countable experiences. *Incidence* refers to the rate at which something occurs.

Two *incidents* during childhood led to her reclusiveness.

The *incidence* of cancer in Japan is less than that in the United States.

incredible, incredulous   *Incredible* means "fantastic, unbelievable." *Incredulous* means "skeptical, disbelieving."

That she could run so fast seemed *incredible*.

Why is Bill wearing that *incredulous* look?

infer   See *imply, infer.*

ingenious, ingenuous   *Ingenious* means "clever and inventive." *Ingenuous* means "unsophisticated and innocent."

Sue presented an *ingenious* solution to our problem.

Mary's *ingenuous* comments amused everyone in the room.

in regards to   This is an incorrect use of *in regard to.*

insure   See *assure, ensure, insure.*

inter-, intra-   *Inter-* means "between or among." *Intra-* means "within."

From Chicago to Milwaukee is an *interstate* drive of approximately ninety miles.

From San Francisco to Los Angeles is an *intrastate* drive of about 400 miles.

in terms of   Avoid this vague, overused expression.

Vague	*In terms of* the price he is asking, I would not recommend purchasing Tom's car.
Preferred	*Because* of the price he is asking, I would not recommend purchasing Tom's car.

usage

irregardless   This nonstandard form of *regardless* includes the repetitive elements of *ir* and *less,* both of which mean "without."

is when, is where   *Is when* properly refers only to time.

April *is when* our lilac bush blooms.

Is where properly refers only to place.

Athens *is where* I met him.

The following sentences are *faulty* because of poorly phrased predicates which indicate that muckraking is a place and an abscess is a time:

Muckraking *is where* someone investigates corporate or governmental abuses of power.

An abscess *is when* some spot in body tissue fills with pus.

These sentences should be rephrased to eliminate the faulty assertion.

Muckraking is the investigation of corporate or governmental abuses of power.

An abscess occurs when some spot in body tissue fills with pus.

its, it's, its'   *Its* is a possessive pronoun. *It's* is a contraction of *it is* or *it has*.

The gold chair was ruined, for someone had torn *its* seat.

It's all I have to offer. (It is all I have to offer.)

It's been a difficult day. (It has been a difficult day.)

There is no correct use for *its'*.

kind of, sort of   In college writing, these are unacceptable substitutes for *somewhat, rather,* or *slightly.*

Colloquial	She is *sort of* angry.
	I am *kind of* glad she went away.
Standard	She is *somewhat* angry.
	I am *rather* glad she went away.

When *kind* and *sort* refer to a type, use them with singular nouns and verbs. With their plural forms, *kinds* and *sorts,* use plural nouns and verbs.

Unacceptable	These *kind* of exams are difficult.
Standard	This *kind* of exam is difficult.
	These *kinds* of exams are difficult.

In such constructions, be certain that *kind of* or *sort of* is essential to your meaning. Otherwise, these phrases are unnecessary.

later, latter   *Later* refers to time; *latter* points out the second of two items. If more than two items are listed, use *last* to refer to the final one.

He arrived at the party *later* than he was expected.

Although Professors Stein and Patterson both lectured during the course, only the *latter* graded the final exam.

Of my three cats, Sheba, Tiger, and Spot, only the *last* still needs the vaccination.

lay, lie   *Lie* means "to recline" or "to remain in a particular position." It never takes a direct object. *Lay* means "to place" and always takes a direct object. These verbs are often confused, in part because the past tense of *lie* is *lay.* (The past tense of *lay* is *laid.*)

If I *lie* here a minute, I shall feel better.

Lay the book on the table, please.

As I *lay* asleep, a robber entered my apartment and stole my stereo.

He *laid* a hand on her shoulder.

leave, let   *Leave* means "to depart," and *let* means "to allow." Never use *leave* when *let* is meant.

usage

Nonstandard	*Leave* him figure it out alone.
Standard	*Let* him figure it out alone.

lend, loan   Traditionally, *loan* has been classed as a noun and *lend* as a verb. Today, the use of *loan* as a verb is so commonplace that it is accepted as colloquial English.

Standard	I have applied for a *loan* so that I can buy a car. (noun) Please *lend* me your class notes. (verb)
Colloquial	Please *loan* me your class notes. (verb)

less   See *fewer, less.*

let   See *leave, let.*

liable   See *apt, liable, likely.*

lie   See *lay, lie.*

like   See *as, like.*

likely   See *apt, liable, likely.*

literally   The word *literally* means "restricted to the exact, stated meaning." In formal writing, use *literally* only to designate factual statements.

Colloquial	It was 65°, but I was *literally* freezing.
Standard	Our dog was *literally* foaming at the mouth. It was 65°, but I was *very* cold.

loan   See *lend, loan.*

loose, loosen, lose   *Loose* can be used as both a verb and an adjective. As a verb, it means "untie or unfasten"; as an adjective, it means "unattached, unrestrained, not confined." *Loosen* is a verb meaning "undo or ease." *Lose* can be used only as a verb meaning "mislay, fail to win, unable to maintain."

He *loosed* the restraints on the tiger. (verb)

One should wear *loose* clothing when bowling. (adjective)

When will Mrs. Brady *loosen* her control over young Tom? (verb)

You would *lose* your nose if it were not attached to your face. (verb)

lots, lots of   *Lots* and *lots of* colloquially mean "many, much, a large amount, or a great amount." Avoid these expressions in college writing

Colloquial	I've spent *lots of* money in my life.
Standard	I have spent *much* money in my life.

mad   See *angry, mad.*

many, much   *Many* is used when referring to countable items; *much* is used when referring to an indefinite amount or to abstract concepts.

There are *many* students in the biology class.

How did Betty learn so *much* in so little time?

usage

may   See *can, may.*

may be, **maybe**   *May be* is always used as a verb phrase. *Maybe* is an adverb meaning "perhaps."

> I *may be* chairman of the board by next June.

> *Maybe* we will see Jim at home.

medium, media   *Medium* is the singular form of this word; *media* is the plural.

> Television is the *medium* I use most to get the news.

> The *media* have given extensive coverage to the brain transplant story.

much   See *many, much.*

myself   *Myself* is an intensive and a reflexive pronoun; it cannot substitute for a personal pronoun such as *I* or *me.*

> *Unacceptable*   Four other students and *myself* founded the club.

> *Standard*   Four other students and *I* founded the club.

nice   *Nice* is an adjective suggesting delicacy, precision, subtlety, accuracy, the ability to discriminate, or the need for great care.

> These two seemingly identical proposals actually have several *nice* differences.

> This author's short stories have a *nice* touch.

Nice as a term of approval meaning "pleasing, enjoyable, attractive" is too generalized for use in college writing.

not hardly   This is a nonstandard variation of *hardly* and is inappropriate in college writing.

number   See *amount, number.*

of between, **of from**, **off of**   Eliminate the unnecessary *of* from these colloquial phrases.

> *Colloquial*   There was a crowd *of between* three and four thousand people at the contest.
> Get *off of* my property!

> *Standard*   The crowd at the contest numbered *between* three and four thousand people.
> Get *off* my property!

on account of   When used to begin an adverb clause (see pages 636–637), this is a nonstandard substitute for *because.*

> *Nonstandard*   The team was unable to practice *on account of* everyone was still upset over Tuesday's loss.

> *Standard*   The team was unable to practice *because* everyone was still upset over Tuesday's loss.

When *on account of* precedes a single word or a phrase, it is considered colloquial.

> *Colloquial*   The game was called *on account of* rain.

over, **more than**   *Over* should not be substituted for *more than;* if *more than* fits the phrase, use it.

> Nonstandard   My brother likes ice cream *over* cake.
>
> Standard   My brother likes ice cream *more than* cake.

passed, **past**   *Passed* is a verb designating activity that has taken place. *Past* is a noun or an adjective designating a former time.

The parade *passed* the reviewing stand at 10:30 A.M.

In the *past*, few people were concerned about the environmental effects of pesticides.

This *past* summer, I visited France.

patience, **patients**   *Patience* means "the ability to wait or endure without complaining." *Patients* are "people being treated by health-care professionals."

Thad's *patience* was exhausted by the slow service in the restaurant.

Following the tornado, doctors in the emergency room treated over sixty *patients*.

persecute, **prosecute**   *Persecute* means "to harass persistently because of race, religion, or belief." *Prosecute* means "to bring legal suit against."

Ethnic groups are often *persecuted*.

The company will *prosecute* anyone caught stealing.

personal, **personnel**   *Personal* is an adjective meaning "private, individual." *Personnel* are the people working in an organization.

Religious preference is a *personal* matter that you do not have to reveal during a job interview.

The *personnel* of the sanitation department will not be involved in the city workers' strike.

plenty   When used as an adverb, *plenty* should be replaced by *very*.

> Colloquial   That geology exam was *plenty* hard.
>
> Standard   That geology exam was *very* hard.

precede, **proceed**   *Precede* means "to go before or ahead of." *Proceed* means "to go on" or "to go forward."

The ritual of sharpening his pencils always *preceded* doing his homework.

The guide then said, "If you will *proceed*, I will show you the paintings by da Vinci."

predominant, **predominate**   *Predominant* is an adjective meaning "chief, main, most frequent." *Predominate* is a verb meaning "to have authority over others."

The *predominant* European influence on South American culture was Spanish.

In America, the will of the people should *predominate*.

presently   *Presently* means "soon" rather than "at the present time." *Currently* is correct for the second meaning.

I will be there *presently.*

Currently, I am otherwise engaged.

principal, principle   *Principal,* which means "chief," "most important," or "the amount of money on which interest is computed," is used as both a noun and an adjective. *Principle* is used only as a noun and means "truths, beliefs, or rules generally dealing with moral conduct."

The *principal* suspect in the case was arrested last Friday by the police.

The *principal* of Lewiston High School is Alison Cooperstein.

At this interest rate, your *principal* will double in ten years.

His *principles* are unconventional.

proceed   See *precede, proceed.*

prosecute   See *persecute, prosecute.*

quiet, quite   *Quiet* is an adjective meaning "silent, motionless, calm." *Quite* is an adverb meaning "entirely" or "to a considerable extent or degree."

The class grew *quiet* when the teacher walked in.

He is *quite* wrong.

The movie was *quite* good.

raise, rise   *Raise* is a transitive verb and therefore requires a direct object. *Rise,* its intransitive counterpart, takes no direct object.

We plan to *raise* horses on our new farm.

The temperature is expected to *rise* to 75°F tomorrow.

Raise can also be a noun meaning "an increase in pay."

Tammy received a 25 percent *raise* last week.

real, really   *Real* is an adjective; *really* is an adverb.

She had *real* plants decorating the bedroom.

When used as an adverb, *real* is a colloquialism and should be replaced with *really.*

Colloquial	We had a *real* good time at the party.
Standard	We had a *really* good time at the party.

reason is because, reason is that   The *reason is because* is colloquial and unacceptable in formal writing; the *reason is that* is the correct usage.

Colloquial	The *reason is because* I love her.
Standard	The *reason is that* I love her.

respectfully, respectively   *Respectfully* means "with respect." *Respectively* indicates that the items in one series are related to those in a second series in the order given.

Joseph should treat his parents *respectfully.*

Tom, Anna, and Susan were assigned *Bleak House, Great Expectations,* and *Dombey and Son, respectively,* for their reports.

usage

rise   See *raise, rise.*

sensual, **sensuous**   *Sensual* refers to bodily or sexual sensations. *Sensuous* refers to impressions experienced through the five senses.

> Singles bars offered *sensual* pleasures without emotional commitments.

> The Tivoli Garden provides many *sensuous* delights for visitors.

set, **sit**   Generally, *set* means "to place" and takes a direct object. *Sit* means "to be seated" and does not take a direct object.

> Alice *set* her glass on the mantel.

> May I *sit* in this chair?

When it refers to the sun, however, *set* is used without a direct object.

> As the sun *set*, we turned homeward.

shall, **will**   *Shall* is used in first-person (see page 653) questions and in specialized forms of writing such as military orders and laws. Otherwise, *will* is generally used.

> *Shall* we go to the movies tonight?

> The company *shall* fall into formation at precisely twelve noon.

> No family home *shall* be assessed at more than 50 percent of its actual value.

should have, **should of**   *Should of* is an unacceptable substitute for *should have* because a preposition cannot substitute for a verb.

> | *Nonstandard* | I *should of* gone to the lake. |
> | *Standard* | I *should have* gone to the lake. |

[sic]   This Latin word, always enclosed in brackets, follows quoted errors in grammar, spelling, or information. Inclusion of [sic] indicates that the error appeared in the original, which is being quoted exactly.

sight   See *cite, sight, site.*

sit   See *set, sit.*

site   See *cite, sight, site.*

so   *So* is an acceptable coordinating conjunction but tends to add an informal effect to writing and should therefore be used sparingly. For example, "Tom said he was divorcing me, so I began to cry" would be more effective if restated as follows: "When Tom said he was divorcing me, I began to cry." Do not use *so* as a substitute for *extremely* or *very* except with adverb clauses beginning with *that.*

> | *Colloquial* | You are *so* careless in what you say. |
> | | The discussion was *so* informative that I took many notes. |
> | *Standard* | You are *very* careless in what you say. |
> | | The discussion was *extremely* informative. |

some   *Some* is colloquial and unacceptable in writing when used as an intensifier (We had *some* time of it!) or an adverb (He'll probably pout *some* after you leave).

sometime, **some time**, **sometimes**   *Sometime* means "at a future unspecified time," *some time* means "a span of time," and *sometimes* means "occasionally."

We should get together *sometime* and play bridge.

The weather has been hot for *some time*.

Sometimes I go to dinner with Ethel.

sort of   See *kind of, sort of*.

specially   See *especially, specially*.

stationary, **stationery**   *Stationary* means "not moving" or "fixed." *Stationery* means "paper for writing letters."

The circular part in the center must remain *stationary*, or the machine will not function.

Sue always writes on scented *stationery*.

such, such . . . that   The use of *such* when it means "very" or "extremely" is unacceptable unless it is followed by a *that* clause completing the thought.

Colloquial	They were *such* good cookies.
Standard	They were *such* good cookies *that* I asked Steve for his recipe.

suppose to, **supposed to**   *Suppose to* is the nonstandard form of *supposed to*. In speech, it is difficult to hear the final *d* on *supposed*, and one may say *suppose to* without being detected; however, the correct written form is always *supposed to*.

sure, **surely**   *Sure* is colloquial for the adverb *surely*.

Colloquial	You *sure* know how to make good coffee, Mrs. Olsen.
Standard	You *surely* know how to make good coffee, Mrs. Olsen.

Although *surely* is correct, it may sound too formal and insincere. Therefore, *certainly* is often a better word to use.

take and, **try and**   Avoid these expressions. Simply eliminate them from the sentence or substitute *try to* for *try and*.

Unacceptable	If you *take and* cover the tomato plants, they probably won't freeze.
	I think you should *try and* settle your differences.
Standard	If you cover the tomato plants, they probably won't freeze.
	I think you should *try to* settle your differences.

than, **then**   *Than* is used to make comparisons; *then* means "at that time, in that case," or "after that."

Jill is taller *than* her brother.

First we will eat, and *then* we will discuss business.

that, **which**   These two words have the same meaning. *That* may refer both to things and groups of people; *which*, only to things. When referring to things, *that* is generally used with clauses that distinguish the things they modify from others in the same class (restrictive clauses). *Which* is generally used with clauses that add information about the things they modify (nonrestrictive clauses). Note that clauses starting with *which*, unlike those starting with *that*, are generally preceded by a comma.

usage

Any book *that* she likes is certain to be trashy. (restrictive clause)

The Winthrop Building, *which* cost two million dollars to construct, could not now be duplicated for ten times that much. (nonrestrictive clause)

See pages 674–675 of the Handbook for a more comprehensive explanation of restrictive and nonrestrictive expressions.

their, **there**, **they're**   These three separate words are often confused because they sound alike. *Their* is the possessive form of *they*. *There* is an expletive that appears at the beginning of a sentence and introduces the real subject, or it is an adverb meaning "in or at that place, at that point." *They're* is a contraction of *they are*.

It is *their* basketball.

There are many reasons why I cannot come.

Put the sofa down *there*.

They're going to be here soon.

theirself, **theirselves**   See *hisself, theirself, theirselves*.

then   See *than, then*.

there   See *their, there, they're*.

thorough, **through**   *Thorough* means "careful, complete, exact, painstaking." *Through* means "in one side and out the other, from end to end, from start to finish, over the whole extent of, finished."

Brenda has done a *thorough* job.

Let's run *through* the plan again.

thusly   *Thusly* is a nonstandard form of *thus*.

to, **too**, **two**   *To* is a preposition meaning "as far as, toward, until, onto." *Too* is an adverb meaning "excessively" or "also." *Two* is a number.

I'm going *to* the store.

Are you going *too*?

This car is *too* expensive for me.

There are *two* characters in the play.

toward, **towards**   Both forms are correct. *Toward* generally is used in the United States and *towards* in England.

try and   See *take and, try and*.

two   See *to, too, two*.

uninterested   See *disinterested, uninterested*.

unique   *Unique* means "without an equal" or "extremely unusual" and thus should not be modified by an adverb such as *very*.

use to, **used to**   *Use to* is the nonstandard form of *used to*. In speech it is difficult to hear the *d* on *used*, and one may say *use to* without being detected; however, the correct written form is always *used to*.

usage

used to could This phrase is nonstandard for *used to be able to.*

Nonstandard	I *used to could* run ten miles.
Standard	I *used to be able to* run ten miles.

very definite See *definite, very definite.*

wander, wonder *Wander* is a verb meaning "to move about without a plan or set destination." *Wonder* is a noun meaning "something causing surprise, admiration, or awe" or a verb meaning "to be curious about."

Some people like to *wander* through shopping malls for recreation.

That child is a *wonder* at mathematics.

I *wonder* whether I have received an *A* on that test.

way, ways *Ways* may be used to refer to two or more means or methods but not to time or distance.

Unacceptable	Timbuktu is a long *ways* from the United States.
Standard	There are two *ways* of thinking about that issue. Timbuktu is a long *way* from the United States.

well See *good, well.*

were, where *Were* is the past form of the verb *to be. Where* is an adverb or a pronoun meaning "in, at, to, from a particular place or situation" or "which or what place."

I'm sorry that you *were* ill yesterday.

Mr. Morris will show you *where* to register.

where . . . at, to, from *At, to,* and *from* are unnecessary after *where.*

Wordy	*Where* are you taking the car *to*? *Where* does she live *at*? *Where* did you get the book *from*?
Standard	*Where* are you taking the car? *Where* does she live? *Where* did you get the book?

whether See *if, whether.*

which See *that, which.*

who, whom In formal writing, *who* should be used only as a subject in clauses and sentences and *whom* only as an object.

Unacceptable	*Who* are you taking to dinner on Friday? I know *who* the boss will promote. John is the candidate *whom* I think will be elected.
Standard	*Whom* are you taking to dinner on Friday? I know *whom* the boss will promote. John is the candidate *who* I think will be elected.

See page 656 of the Handbook for a fuller discussion of *who* and *whom.*

usage

who's, whose   *Who's* is a contraction of *who is* or *who has*, and *whose* is the possessive form of *who*.

Who's coming to see us tonight?

I would like to know *who's* been dumping trash in my yard.

Whose book is that?

will   See *shall, will.*

wise   Do not randomly add *wise* to the ends of nouns. Such word coinings are ineffective.

Ineffective	Personality *wise,* Sheila is ideal for the job.
Standard	Sheila has an *ideal personality* for the job.

wonder   See *wander, wonder.*

would have, would of   *Would of* is an unacceptable substitute for *would have*. A preposition cannot substitute for a verb.

Nonstandard	I *would of* enjoyed seeing the Picasso exhibit.
Standard	I *would have* enjoyed seeing the Picasso exhibit.

would have been, had been   When *would* occurs in the main part of a sentence, use *had been* (not *would have been*) in an "if" clause.

Nonstandard	If the engine *would have been* lubricated, the bearing *would not have* burned out.
Standard	If the engine *had been* lubricated, the bearing *would not have* burned out.

your, you're   *Your* is a possessive form of *you; you're* is a contraction of *you are*.

Where is *your* history book?

Tell me when *you're* ready to leave.

usage

CREDITS
●●●●●●●●●●●●●●●●●●●●●●●●●●●●●●●●●●●●●●

R. T. Allen, "The Porcupine," from *Children, Wives, and Other Wildlife* by Robert Thomas Allen Copyright © 1970 by Robert Thomas Allen (New York: Doubleday, 1970).

Bonnie Angelo, "Those Good Ole Boys," *Time,* Sept. 27, 1976, p. 47.

Maya Angelou, "Mamma's Encounter," from *I Know Why the Caged Bird Sings.* Copyright © 1969 by Maya Angelou. Used by permission of Random House, Inc.

"Antigen," *Encyclopaedia Britannica,* 1974, I, 417.

Carl Becker, *Freedom and Responsibility in the American Way of Life* (New York: Vintage-Knopf, 1945).

Bruno Bettelheim, "Joey: A 'Mechanical Boy,' " *Scientific American,* March 1959, p. 122.

Ray Allen Billington, "The Frontier Disappears," *The American Story,* ed. Earl Schenck Miers (Great Neck, NY: Channel, 1956).

Diana Bletter, "Refuse to Live in Fear," from *Mademoiselle,* Nov. 1996. Reprinted by permission of Condé Nast Publications, Inc.

"The Brink of a Disaster," *America,* March 31, 1979, p. 247.

Claude Brown, *Manchild in the Promised Land* (New York: Macmillan, 1965), p. 304.

James L. Buckley, "Three Cheers for the Snail Darter," *National Review,* Sept. 14, 1979, pp. 1144–45.

Gladys Hasty Carroll, *Sing Out the Glory* (Boston: Little Brown, and Co., 1958).

Rachel Carson, *Silent Spring* (Boston: Houghton Mifflin, 1962).

Stephen L. Carter, "The Insufficiency of Honesty." Copyright © 1996. Reprinted by author's permission.

Bruce Catton, "Grant and Lee: A Study in Contrasts," from *The American Story,* ed. Earl Schenck Miers. Reprinted by permission of U.S. Capital Historical Society.

Shari Caudron, "Can Generation X Be Trained?" pp. 20–4 from *Training and Development Magazine,* v. 51 (March 1997). Reprinted by permission.

Lorna Dee Cervantes, "Cannery Town in August" is from *Emplumada* by Lorna Dee Cervantes, © 1981. Reprinted by permission of the University of Pittsburgh Press.

John Ciardi, "What Is Happiness?" in *Manner of Speaking* (New Brunswick, NJ: Rutgers University Press, 1972).

Robert Claiborne, "Future Schlock," *The Nation,* Jan. 25, 1971, p. 117.

Cecil Clutton and John Stanford, *The Vintage Motor-car* (New York: Charles Scribner's Sons, 1955), p. 135.

Joseph Conrad, *Lord Jim* (New York: Holt, Rinehart and Winston, 1957), p. 13.

"Controlling Phobias Through Behavior Modification." *USA Today,* August 1978.

Countee Cullen, "Yet Do I Marvel" Copyrights held by the Amistad Research Center, Tulane University, New Orleans, Louisiana. Administered by JJKR Associates, New York, NY.

Kelly Davis, "Health and High Voltage: 765 KV Lines," *Sierra,* July-Aug. 1978.

Vine Deloria, Jr. "Custer Died for Your Sins," *Playboy,* Aug. 1969.

Lester del Ray, *The Mysterious Shy* (New York: Chilton Book Company, 1964).

Magda Denes, *In Necessity and Sorrow: Life and Death in an Abortion Hospital* (New York: Basic Books, 1976), p. xiv.

Robert Dick-Read, *Sanamu: Adventures in Search of African Art* (New York: E. P. Dutton, 1964), pp. 228–29.

Joan Didion, "On Self-Respect," in *Slouching Toward Bethlehem* (New York: Farrar, Straus and Giroux, 1968), pp. 143–44.

Michael Dorris, excerpt from *A Yellow Raft in Blue Water*, (New York: Henry Holt and Co., Inc.), 1987.

Barbara Dority, "Halt and Show Your Papers!," from *The Humanist*, v.62 no. 2 (Mar.-Apr. 2002), pp. 10–13. Reprinted by permission.

Ian Dunbar, "Fast Track to Perfection." *Dog Fancy*, April 1999, reprinted by permission of the author.

Leo Durocher, *Nice Guys Finish Last* (New York: Simon & Schuster, 1975), p. 54.

Wayne Dyer, *What Do You Really Want for Your Children?* (New York: William Morrow, Inc., 1985).

Alan Ehrenhalt, "The Misguided Zeal of the Privacy Lobby," from *Governing*, v.12 no. 8 (May 1999), pp. 7–8. Reprinted by permission.

Loren Eiseley, *The Unexpected Universe* (New York: Harcourt Brace Jovanovich, 1969) p. 88.

Loren Eiseley, "The Judgment of the Birds," in *The Immense Journey* (New York: Random House, 1956), pp. 174–75.

Marian Engle, review of *The Goddess and Other Women*, by Joyce Carol Oates, *New York Times Book Review*, Nov. 24, 1974, p. 7.

Sabrina Rubin Erdely, "Binge Drinking, A Campus Killer." Reprinted from the Nov. 1998 *Reader's Digest*, with permission from the author.

Howard Ensign Evans, *Life on a Little-Known Planet* (New York: E.P. Dutton, 1968), pp. 107–8.

Henry Fairlie, "A Victim Fights Back," *The Washington Post*, April 30, 1978.

David Finkelstein, "When the Snow Thaws," *The New Yorker*, Sept. 10, 1979, p. 127.

"Formlessness" from *Roget's International Thesaurus*, 5th edition by Peter Mark Roget, Copyright © 1992 by HarperCollins Publishers, Inc. Reprinted by permission of HarperCollins Publishers, Inc.

Adam Frank, excerpts from "Winds of Change," in *Discover*, June 1994, pp. 100–4.

Bruce Jay Friedman, "Eating Alone in Restaurants," from *The Lonely Guy's Book of Life*, 1978. Reprinted by permission of McGraw-Hill.

Otto Friedrich, "There are 00 Trees in Russia," *Harper's Magazine*, Oct. 1964.

Ron Geraci, "Which Stooge Are You?" From *Men's Health* Magazine, Sept. 1999. Reprinted by permission of *Men's Health* Magazine. Copyright © 1999 Rodale Press, Inc. All rights reserved.

Nancy Gibbs, "When Is It Rape?" Copyright © 1991 Time Inc. Reprinted by permission.

Matea Gold and David Ferrell, "Going for Broke," Excerpt from the Dec. 13, 1998, *Los Angeles Times*. Copyright, 1998, *Los Angeles Times*, Reprinted with permission.

Ellen Goodman, "The Company Man." Reprinted with the permission of Simon & Schuster from *Close to Home* by Ellen Goodman. Copyright © 1979 by The Washington Post Company.

Martin Gottfried, "Rambos of the Road," *Newsweek*, Sept. 8, 1986. Reprinted by permission of the author.

Dan Greenburg, "Sound and Fury." Reprinted by permission of the author. All rights reserved.

Amy Gross, "The Appeal of the Androgynous Man." *Mademoiselle*. Copyright © 1976 by The Condé Nast Publications, Inc. Reprinted by permission of Amy Gross.

L. D. Hamilton, "Antibodies and Antigens," *The New Book of Knowledge*, 1967, I, 317.

Albert L. Harlow, Jr. "Software Breakthrough Advances Robotic Painting," from *AM* Magazine. Reprinted by permission.

S. T. Hayakawa, *Language in Thought and Action*, 3rd ed. (New York: Harcourt Brace Jovanovich, 1972), p. 50.

Lesley Hazleton, "Assembly Line Adventure." Reprinted with the permission of The Free Press, a division of Simon & Schuster, Inc., from *Driving to Detroit: An Automotive Odyssey* by Lesley Hazleton, Copyright © 1998 by Lesley Hazleton.

John Hersey, *Hiroshima* (New York: Modern Library, 1946), p. 4.

Nancy K. Hill, "Scalling the Heights: The Teacher as Mountaineer," *The Chronicle of Higher Education,* June 16, 1980, p. 48.

Thomas Henry Huxley, "A Liberal Education and Where to Find It," *Macmillan's Magazine,* March 17, 1868.

Dina Ingber, "Computer Addicts," *Science Digest,* July 1981.

Washington Irving, "The Spectre Bridegroom," in *Selected Writings of Washington Irving,* ed. Saxe Commins (New York: Modern Library, 1945), p. 53.

Bruce Jackson, "Who Goes to Prison: Caste and Careerism in Crime," *Atlantic Monthly,* Jan. 1966, p. 52.

Daniel James, "Close the Borders to All Newcomers." Reprinted with permission from *Insight.* Copyright 1997 News World Communications, Inc. All rights reserved.

Robert Jastrow, *Until the Sun Dies* (New York: Norton, 1977).

Ellen Herbert Jordan, "My Affair with the One-Armed Bandit," *Modern Maturity,* July-Aug. 1995: 37, 864.

Vernon E. Jordan, Jr., "The New Negativism," *Newsweek*, Aug. 14, 1978, p. 13. Copyright © 1978, Newsweek, Inc.

Doris Kearns, "Who Was Lyndon Baines Johnson?" from *Lyndon Johnson and the American Dream* (New York: Harper & Row, 1976).

Helen Keller, "Three Days to See," *Atlantic Monthly,* Jan. 1933, p. 35.

John F. Kennedy, "Inaugural Address," Washington, D. C., Jan. 20, 1961.

Martin Luther King, Jr., "I Have a Dream." Reprinted by arrangement with the heirs to the Estate of Martin Luther King, Jr., c/o Writers House, Inc., as agent for the proprietor. Copyright 1963 by Martin Luther King, Jr., copyright renewed 1991 by Coretta Scott King.

Martin Luther King, Jr., "Pilgrimage to Nonviolence," in *Stride Toward Freedom* (New York: Harper & Row, 1958), p. 84.

Marilyn Kluger, "A Time of Plenty," *Gourmet,* Nov. 1976, p. 22.

Edward I. Koch, "Death and Justice." Reprinted by permission of *The New Republic,* copyright © 1985. The New Republic, Inc.

Charles Krauthammer, "Crossing Lines," from *The New Republic,* v. 226 no. 16 (April 29, 2002), p. 20. Reprinted by permission.

Kenneth Labich, "The Scandal of Killer Trucks," *Fortune,* March 30, 1987.

John Lovesey, "A Myth is as Good as a Mile," *Sports Illustrated,* Nov. 9, 1964.

Marilyn Machlowitz, "Workaholism: What's Wrong with Being Married to Your Work?" *Working Woman,* May 1978, p. 51.

Malcolm X, *The Autobiography of Malcolm X* (New York: Baliantine Books, 1964), p. 171.

Marshall Mandell, "Are You Allergic to Your House?" *Prevention,* Sept. 1979, p. 101.

Marya Mannes, "Wasteland," in *More in Anger* (Philadelphia: J. B. Lippincott, 1958). p. 40.

Bernice McCarthy, "A Tale of Four Learners," from *Educational Leadership*, v. 54, March 1997, pp. 46–51.

Margaret Mead, "New Superstitions for Old," from *A Way of Seeing* by Margaret Mead and Rhoda Metraux. Copyright © 1966 by Margaret Mead and Rhoda Metraux.

L. David Mech, "Where Can the Wolves Survive?" *National Geographic,* Oct. 1977, p. 536.

H. L. Mencken, "The Libido for the Ugly," Copyright 1927 by Alfred A. Knopf, Inc., and renewed 1955 by H. L. Mencken. Reprinted from *A Mencken Chrestomathy,* edited and annotated by H. L. Mencken, by permission of the publisher.

Thomas H. Middleton, "The Magic Power of Words," *Saturday Review,* Dec. 11, 1976, p. 90.

SUBJECT INDEX

EDITING SYMBOLS

Symbol	Problem	Page	Symbol	Problem	Page
ab	improper abbreviation	692–93	*nsu*	nonstandard usage	
agr pa	faulty agreement of pronoun and antecedent	648–50	¶	new paragraph needed	
agr sv	faulty agreement of subject and verb	645–48	*no* ¶	new paragraph not needed	
ᵛ *or apos*	missing or misused apostrophe	669–72	⊙	period needed	679–80
awk	awkward phrasing		‖ *or para*	nonparallelism	665–66
bib	faulty bibliographic form	381–96	? *or ques*	missing or misused question mark	680
cap	capital letter needed	689–92	" / " *or quot*	missing or misused quotation marks	685–87
case	wrong case	655–58	*ref*	unclear reference of pronoun to antecedent	651–53
cl	cliché	261	*ro*	run-on sentence	643–45
⌒ *or com*	missing or misused comma	672–77	; *or sem*	missing or misused semicolon	677–79
cs	comma splice	643–45	*sp*	spelling error	698–704
comp	faulty comparison	666–68	*shift p*	shift in person	653–55
dm	dangling modifier	664–65	*shift t*	shift in tense	658–60
⊙ *or ellip*	missing or misused ellipsis	352–53	*sq*	squinting modifier	663
frag	sentence fragment	641–43	*t or tense*	wrong tense	616–17
ital	missing or misused italics	695–97	*trans*	poor transition	
lc	lowercase (small) letter needed	689–92	*vb*	wrong verb form	
‖ *or lev*	wrong level of usage	247–52	*wdy*	wordiness	260
log	faulty logic		*ww*	wrong word	
mm	misplaced modifier	663–64	♪	delete (omit)	
num	use numerals	693–95	∧	material omitted	
			⊙	meaning unclear or word illegible	